Professional School Counseling

THIRD EDITION

Professional School Counseling

Best Practices for Working in the Schools

THIRD EDITION

Rosemary A. Thompson

Routledge
Taylor & Francis Group
New York   London

Routledge
Taylor & Francis Group
711 Third Avenue
New York, NY 10017

Routledge
Taylor & Francis Group
27 Church Road
Hove, East Sussex BN3 2FA

© 2012 by Taylor & Francis Group, LLC
Routledge is an imprint of Taylor & Francis Group, an Informa business

Printed in the United States of America on acid-free paper
Version Date: 20111130

International Standard Book Number: 978-0-415-99849-9 (Paperback)

Library of Congress Cataloging-in-Publication Data

Thompson, Rosemary, 1950-
  Professional school counseling : best practices for working in the schools / Rosemary A. Thompson. -- 3rd ed.
      p. cm.
  Rev. ed. of: School counseling, 2002.
  Summary: "Today's children and adolescents are constantly facing new and unique challenges, and school counselors must respond to this by expanding their role and function within the school. This practical and highly useful guidebook will address these issues, as well as the necessary steps school counselors need to take in order to adapt and effectively deal with them"-- Provided by publisher.
  Includes bibliographical references and index.
  ISBN 978-0-415-99849-9 (pbk.)
  1. Educational counseling--United States. I. Thompson, Rosemary, 1950- School counseling. II. Title.

LB1027.5.T46 2011
371.4'22--dc23   2011023051

Visit the Taylor & Francis Web site at
http://www.taylorandfrancis.com

and the Routledge Web site at
http://www.routledgementalhealth.com

Contents

List of Figures

List of Tables

Preface

This is the third edition of *Professional School Counseling: Best Practices for Working in the Schools*, and today the profession has emerged with National Standards for School Counseling Programs and a national mission to close the achievement gap between minority students and students of poverty. Chapter 1 traces the history of guidance and counseling from the Industrial Age to the Information Age, highlighting pivotal people in the counseling field such as Frank Parsons, Clifford Beers, Jesse Davis, and Norman Gysbers. It shows the shift from a services-driven counseling model to a data-driven, standards-based counseling program that emphasizes the role of leadership, advocacy, collaboration and teaming, managing resources, the use of data for responsible decision making, and the use of technology with the goal of demonstrating how students are different as a result of what school counselors do. To help answer this question, the American School Counselor Association (ASCA, 2003, 2005a, b) created the ASCA National Model®, a framework for comprehensive, data-driven school counseling programs.

Chapter 2 outlines comprehensive guidance and counseling programs (CGCP), a developmental approach to professional school counseling, and describes the benefits of a CGCP. The components of a CGCP are discussed, including beliefs and philosophy, mission, goals, school counseling standards and competencies, guidance and counseling curriculum, individual student planning, responsive services, system support, school counselor–administrator agreements, advisory councils and focus groups, use of school improvement data and student monitoring of results based on data, action plans, use of systematic timelines and calendars, systematic reporting of counseling outcomes and results, and school counselor performance standards. The chapter concludes with developmental tasks for children and adolescents in the domains of thinking, feeling, and relating.

Chapter 3 outlines the evolution of professional school counselor accountability and the need to be standards based. It is important that comprehensive guidance and counseling programs be conceptualized as results-based systems, not just a system of isolated services. The chapter addresses different kinds of data that can be collected, including data on achievement, demographics, process, perception, and results, along with formative assessment, program evaluation, summative assessment, and longitudinal data. Finally, three data-based models or outcome models are presented in this chapter: the Poynton & Carey (2006) *IDEAS* model; Dahir and Stone's (2003a) *MEASURE-ing Student Success;* and Brott's (2005, 2006, 2008) *Get a Grip!*

Chapter 4 portrays a profile of adolescent health and well-being and outlines 11 risk factors: poverty; family structure; achievement gaps; diversity, immigration, and English-language learners; dropouts and lack of higher education attainment; teen unintended pregnancy; adolescent drug and alcohol abuse; mental illness and emotional disorders; school violence, bullying, and relational aggression; child maltreatment; and depression and child and adolescent suicide. It also reveals risk and protective factors for some of these risk factors. Developmental assets are included, as well as information on the success of wraparound, parallel, or full-service schools. Such approaches have demonstrated academic gains, improvement in school attendance, reduction in high-risk behaviors, increased parent involvement, lower incidence of child abuse and neglect, and lower rates of violence in the participating schools and communities and are provided as an alternative to prevention and intervention initiatives.

As a follow-up to Chapter 4, Chapter 5 addresses the newest research regarding implementing best practices or evidence-based practices in prevention and intervention initiatives. It provides primary prevention and intervention practices for high-risk behavior among youth today. For example, best practices for youth violence prevention are provided for grades K–12, as well as currently recognized evidence-based programs recognized by the Substance Abuse and Mental Health Services Administration. Professional school counselors are always looking for programs or interventions that work, and this chapter provides an array of initiatives that can be implemented in response to a needs assessment of a particular school.

Consulting with teachers, parents, administrators, and the greater community is critical for professional school counselors. Chapter 6 presents Epstein's Framework of Six Types of Parent or Guardian Involvement, including sample practices, challenges, redefinitions, and expected results in six areas: parenting, communicating, volunteering, learning at home, decision making, and collaboration with community. It also highlights the enduring work of the National Network of Partnership Schools. The chapter addresses the value of implementing a teacher advisor system to advocate for all students. It further discusses the benefit of student-led parent-teacher conferences, which put the onus of responsibility for work performance and articulation of strengths and weaknesses on the student.

Chapter 7 addresses the negative outcomes of dropping out of school; describes the influence of race, ethnicity, and income groups; and provides a brief overview of career theories. The role of the professional school counselor as career counselor specialist is illuminated. The 109th Congress passed new career/technical legislation—the Carl D. Perkins Career and Technical Education Improvement Act of 2006, known as Perkins IV. The legislation was aimed at helping today's students gain the academic and technical skills and knowledge necessary for high-demand, high-wage jobs while maintaining a strong academic focus that promotes instruction and accountability consistent with the No Child Left Behind (NCLB) Act, which also is outlined in this chapter. The States' Career Clusters Initiative (SCCI) 16-cluster format used by the U.S. Department of Education and the U.S. Department of Labor/Employment and Training Administration is explained in this chapter as a national initiative. Finally, the chapter presents the notion of being adaptable and flexible as a portfolio worker.

Chapter 8 is new to this edition of the book and focuses on students who are disenfranchised from traditional school programs and the special programs that have been developed to deal with these students who may fall between the cracks. It addresses the changing demographics of schools and empirically demonstrated efforts to close the achievement gap between minorities and children of poverty. Numerous model enrichment or intervention programs are outlined in detail, including Advanced Placement, America's Choice, AVID, the Coalition of Essential Schools, Dual Enrollment, EQUITY 2000, First Things First, GEAR UP, the GE Foundation College Bound, High Schools That Work, the International Baccalaureate, Middle College and Early College High Schools, Smaller Learning Environments, Talent Development, Tech Prep/2+2 Articulation, the Urban Systemic Initiative, and Project GRAD.

Chapter 9 is another new addition to this book, exploring the dynamics of children with disabilities and the struggle for a free and appropriate education. It discusses the foundations of the Individuals with Disabilities Education Act (IDEA, 2004), along with definitions of different categories. This is a critical component for the professional school counselor in understanding the children-with-disabilities process. The chapter contains a primer of common terms, definitions, and acronyms in special education as a resource for professional school counselors in their role as advocate for children with disabilities and their families.

Chapter 10 is a third new chapter. Because diversity—from English speakers of other languages (ESOL) to sexually minority youth—is an increasingly important issue for professional school counselors and schools, counselors must be able to advocate, coordinate, and collaborate on services for students and their families or guardians. Essential knowledge and communication skills, verbal and nonverbal nuances in cultural behaviors, counselor attributes that build rapport, and the need for cultural competence are discussed. Sexual minority and risk/protective factors and their specific needs are also addressed, along with terminology to help educate those who must confront such issues.

Chapter 11 discusses mental health issues for children and adolescents. The burden of suffering experienced by children with mental health needs and their families has reached crisis proportions in this country. Growing numbers of children are suffering needlessly because their emotional, behavioral, and developmental needs are not being met by those very institutions, systems, and agencies that were explicitly created to take care of them. "It is time that we as a Nation took seriously the task of preventing mental health problems and treating mental illnesses in youth" (U.S. Public Health Service, 2000, p. 1). A shortened version of the *DSM-IV* is provided as a reference for the professional school counselor.

Chapter 12 addresses the various counseling groups that are applicable to schools: primary prevention and structured groups, problem-solving groups, and psychoeducational groups that focus on enhancing social, emotional, and cognitive deficits. Within the psychoeducational life skills group, 41 social, 78 emotional, and 51 cognitive skills are presented. In addition, the chapter describes Student Success Skills as a means to reinforce the professional school counselor's role as an integral catalyst in the national school reform initiatives.

Chapter 13 provides a theoretical perspective for crisis intervention and crisis management. It addresses psychological disequilibrium and the importance of meeting the emotional needs of survivors—students, faculty, and parents. The need for systematic school-based procedures and interventions is addressed, as is the need for crisis management. The roles and responsibilities of the crisis response team in restoring equilibrium are explained, along with specific action plans for administrators, lead school counselors, and staff members. Debriefing strategies are presented, differentiating among major school-wide crises, community crises, small group crises, or individual crises. Topics discussed include crisis management briefings, posttraumatic loss debriefing, critical incident stress management, the Adaptive Family Debriefing Model, psychological first aid, and the Family Safety Watch, as well as specific coping responses for professional school counselors such as "Review, Respond, Remind" for debriefs after a traumatic or critical-incident school event.

Chapter 14 is also new to this edition of the book, because ethical and legal issues are becoming important, especially when considering issues of the Family Education Rights and Privacy Act (FERPA), the Protection of Pupil Rights (PPRA), and the Health Insurance Portability and Accountability Act (HIPAA). This pragmatic chapter provides ethical scenarios and answers regarding ASCA principles of ethical behavior, a summary of steps or stages of practice-based ethical decision-making models, and legal terms professional school counselors should be familiar with as they provide guidance and services.

Chapter 15, "Professional Development and Renewal," is probably the last chapter professional school counselors will read because by nature of their calling they tend to be "type-E" personalities—"everything to everybody." But this is not healthy, nor is it wise. This chapter covers what professional school counselors are most reluctant to read about: issues of self-care and time management, such as managing the paper chase, stress management, using support staff effectively, holding effective meetings, avoiding and managing interruptions, delegating effectively, and recognizing the symptoms of "compassion fatigue," the liability of caring too much. All these nuances come into play when trying to be a professional school counselor and to do the job well.

Acknowledgments

Many professional school counselors, directly or indirectly, have contributed to or influenced the development of this book. I offer special thanks for their ideas, encouragement, and support. The school counselors of Chesapeake Public Schools in Chesapeake, Virginia, have been significant professional influences; I offer special thanks for their encouragement and support. Appreciation also is extended to the graduate students at Old Dominion University in Norfolk, Virginia, and at Regent University in Virginia Beach, Virginia; all have provided fresh perspectives and invaluable knowledge from the diversity of their personal and professional experiences.

I am most grateful to the late pioneer Dr. Joseph Hollis, former publisher of *Accelerated Development,* who launched my writing career. His guidance, support, and suggestions through the years have been invaluable. I also wish to thank Dr. Nina W. Brown, professor and eminent scholar of counseling at Old Dominion University, who is a prolific writer and has been both a mentor and a friend. Through the years, she has shared her resourceful ideas and valued perspectives on the dynamic influence of counseling and psychotherapy.

I would like to extend my appreciation as well to Dr. Rosemarie Scottie Hughes, professor and dean emeritus of the School of Psychology and Counseling at Regent University, who recognized in 2003 my professional commitment to "transform school counseling" as she asked me to teach potential professional school counselors in the ASCA model while embracing Council for Accreditation of Counseling and Related Educational Programs (CACREP) standards to nurture her vision and mission for professional school counseling at Regent University. Her insight, vision, and leadership led Regent to be recognized as the first online CACREP-accredited PhD program in counseling education and supervision and online MA program in clinical mental health counseling, which I helped to develop and currently coordinate. Her vision and commitment to the field of psychology and counseling profession is unprecedented.

I would be remiss if I did not mention the support of the most exceptional staff at Routledge/Taylor & Francis, most notably senior editor Dana Bliss and senior editorial assistant Chris Tominich, who conscientiously provided integrity, intense scrutiny, and quality management of this publication. Also Robert Sims, who is the most meticulous production editor I have encountered in the past twenty years, and Rebecca L. Edwards, senior project manager, who was critical and vital to overseeing this project to fruition with her intense scrutiny. Their collective compassion and dedication to accountability and proper citations for publications are to be commended in this era of the Internet, personal blogs, social networks, and Wikipedia, the free encyclopedia that anyone can edit and believe as the truth.

Finally, I am most indebted to my husband Charles and our two children, Jessica and Ryan, all of whom are in the fields of either architecture or engineering. As an author and counselor educator, I represent the only known alien in our home. None of us can understand each other's books or can hold a meaningful conversation about them. It has provided a unique contribution to our family system because we never talk about work and sometimes that's a good thing! However, opening a conversation with "How do you feel about that?" does provide a venue for processing important information.

PART ONE

Background, Fundamentals, and Models

History of School Counseling From Guidance Worker to Professional School Counselor and a Standards-Based Program Model

1

> The professional school counselor is a certified/licensed educator trained in school counseling with unique qualifications and skills to address all students' academic, personal/social and career development needs. Professional school counselors implement a comprehensive school counseling program that promotes and enhances student achievement. Professional school counselors serve a vital role in maximizing student achievement. Incorporating leadership, advocacy and collaboration, professional school counselors promote equity and access to opportunities and rigorous educational experiences for all students. Professional school counselors support a safe learning environment and work to safeguard the human rights of all members of the school community. Collaborating with other stakeholders to promote student achievement, professional school counselors address the needs of all students through prevention and intervention programs that are a part of a comprehensive school counseling program.
>
> American School Counselor Association (2004b)

Professional school counseling as a recognized specialty evolved as the result of educational, political, social, and economic trends that have emerged between the extraordinary demands of the Industrial Age and the exponential explosion of the Information Age. The early emphasis of guidance in schools centered on a narrow concept of selected services, rendered either by a few specialists or assumed as ancillary services by teachers, for a small population of problem students with school adjustment problems. This remains a threatening undercurrent in many professional school counseling programs across the nation, especially in programs that have failed to integrate the American School Counselor Association (ASCA, 2005a) National Model or to acknowledge the need to reflect the changing demographics and the growing diversity of today's students in schools.

The first guidance programs of the late 1800s were closely connected to vocational education and classes to promote character or moral development; teach socially appropriate behaviors, such as proper etiquette and appropriate hygiene; and assist with vocational planning to match the student's traits and personality characteristics to the requirements of a specific job. Fundamentally, professional school counseling evolved from social and humanitarian concerns toward improving the well-being of individuals adversely affected by the Industrial Revolution (Aubrey, 1983), the initiation of social welfare reform, and

3

the growing influx of immigrants to the United States (Goodyear, 1984). Early proponents of professional school counseling identified themselves with social reform and educational initiatives to meet the specific needs of this particular population. An emphasis was placed on teaching children and adolescents self-awareness and understanding of others, along with the current career demands to fit individual traits to job compatibility in a more predictable economy. Specific information and classroom lessons at this juncture focused predominately on moral and character development, as well as interpersonal and intrapersonal skill development (Nugent & Jones, 2005).

The role and function of professional school counseling has evolved from such titles as "guidance worker" and "vocational guidance counselor" to "guidance teacher" and "guidance counselor." School counselors have emerged as professionals primarily in response to societal needs and demands that have impacted their role, the new demands of the Information Age in an era of educational reform, and a commitment to a more distinct professional identity (Beesley, 2004; Burnham & Jackson, 2000; Gysbers & Henderson, 2001). Dahir (2004) aptly stated that "the history of school counseling has depicted a profession in search of an identity" (p. 345). Today, however, the profession has emerged with clear role statements, as well as an articulated foundation, a delivery system, and a true identity based on national standards, role statements, and a clearly defined accountability model to promote school improvement planning and to close the achievement gap between marginalized subgroups within the school setting such as children of poverty, children who are minorities, and children who are immigrants.

THE HISTORICAL EVOLUTION OF PROFESSIONAL SCHOOL COUNSELING

Frank Parsons is often considered the "father of guidance," particularly regarding vocational or career features of school counseling programs (Baker, 2000; Gladding, 2004; Herr, 2001). Parsons was a Boston educator whose interest was on personal growth and vocational development from a trait and factor perspective or talent-matching approach—that is, looking at aptitude, interests, and personal abilities and knowledge of jobs and the labor market and matching all these variables for clients. In 1908, shortly before he died, Parsons founded the Boston Vocational Bureau, which was a major impetus for the promotion of the value of vocational guidance into the mainstream of public education, thought, and action. This was followed by his posthumous book *Choosing a Vocation* (1909), which provided a vocational/career model to match a person's personal characteristics with an occupation as a way of maximizing one's educational future and the exposure to career opportunities within respective communities.

Parsons is credited with providing a foundation on which vocational or career counseling was initially based and integrated into school counseling programs (Kiselica & Robinson, 2001). As early as 1900, Parsons had identified two major deficits in the U.S. educational system that are still evident over a century later: (1) not enough opportunities for all students, particularly those from low socioeconomic status, and (2) an inability to meet the needs of those who lack basic mathematics and language skills (Parsons, 1909). Because of his efforts, "vocational counselors" were established in elementary and secondary schools in Boston, and the model spread to other major cities in the United States (Nugent & Jones, 2005).

Jesse B. Davis, an educator who was influenced by the progressive education movement, also had a significant influence on professional school counseling programs in the United States at this time. The progressive movement maintained that students should be respected for their own abilities, interests, ideas, individual differences, and cultural identity. Guidance activities were developed to assist youths in reaching their full potential. Davis was acknowledged as the first person to institute a systematic guidance program in public schools. In 1907, he recommended that English teachers teach guidance lessons such as improving self-esteem once a week in an effort to prevent interpersonal problems and to build character. The underlying assumption was that proper guidance would help cure the maladies of American society amid the burgeoning stress of the Industrial Age, which brought about the emergence of child labor laws and political initiatives for labor unions for abused workers.

School guidance then became preventive in nature, intended to help students deal more effectively with life stressors and life events during the most mechanistic, industrial lockstep period in our nation's history. Teachers often assumed the role of guidance counselor, along with a list of other ancillary duties they fulfilled with no relief from their regular teaching responsibilities. Gysbers (1990) defines this organizational structure as the beginning of the "services model" (p. 3). That is, guidance activities were organized around six major services:

1. Orientation
2. Assessment
3. Information
4. Counseling
5. Placement
6. Follow-up

Problems existed with this model from the beginning because it primarily focuses on the secondary school setting and does not outline a specific, uniform role and function across all school systems and because of the nature of the delivery model, giving teachers this added responsibility in addition to their primary instructional roles.

The services model was viewed as a mechanism by which schools could better prepare students for the world of work based on aptitude, interest, and ability (Gysbers, 2001). A primary role of public education during this time was to prepare students to go to work, and vocational counselors could assist in the sorting and selecting students into the appropriate work paths (Gysbers, 2001). This initiative still exists as a priority today, and some school systems have designated specific career and technical counselors who work primarily with students to identify their career clusters and develop their career pathways. These individuals are generally on the secondary level and work with regular professional school counselors, but their primary role is to insure that students get further training for industry certifications in career and technical fields in their local communities.

A third figure who significantly influenced the professional school counseling movement in the United States was Clifford W. Beers, a former Yale student who went from a privileged life to being hospitalized for mental illness (bipolar disorder). He witnessed the depraved, deplorable conditions of mental institutions (or sanitariums, as they were called then). He emerged as a significant crusader for mental health awareness, which also influenced professional school counseling programs.

In 1908, Beers wrote his autobiography, *A Mind That Found Itself,* exposing the inhumane conditions of mental health institutions. Beers (1908) hoped that:

> I should one day prick the civic conscience into a compassionate activity and thus bring into a neglected field earnest men and women who should act as champion for those afflicted thousands least able to fight for themselves. (p. xxxii)

He advocated for better mental health facilities and more humane care. Beers's work became the impetus for the mental health movement in the United States today. Advocacy groups such as the National Mental Health Association and the National Alliance for the Mentally Ill carry on his work, as do two organizations that carry his name: the Clifford W. Beers Guidance Clinic in New Haven, Connecticut, and the Clifford W. Beers Foundation in Stafford, England.

With advent of the World War I, group testing emerged in an effort to identify the personnel for specific job roles and responsibilities in the military. Psychometrics—that is, psychological testing—became popular. The Great Depression brought a need to develop counseling strategies to help individuals obtain gainful employment. World War II then solidified the need for psychological testing, as the U.S. government needed counselors and psychologists to help sort, select, and train specialists for the military as well as industry (Ohlsen, 1983). In an effort to garner a more scientific identity and greater legitimacy, the vocational guidance movement embraced testing to legitimize its role in the field of psychology.

Further following Davis's guidance and counseling initiatives, John Brewer (1932) proposed that *every* teacher be a counselor and that guidance be integrated throughout the school curriculum to prepare students for successful transition outside of the school environment and into the community. In 1932, he published the book *Education as Guidance* to promote his model.

A few years later, E. G. Williamson from the University of Minnesota formulated the first theory of counseling, modifying Frank Parsons's theory. Williamson's (1939) Minnesota Point-of-View Trait-Factor Counseling promoted the counselor's ability to teach, mentor, and influence clients. His model of vocational counseling was published in 1939 in his book *How to Counsel Students: A Manual of Techniques for Clinical Counselors*. Williamson (1939) wrote:

> The most hopeful method of preventing failure to choose a vocation is to base continuous individualized counseling upon an understanding of the student's aptitudes and the relating of these aptitudes to achievable goals. It must not be expected that a student will know intuitively how to choose an achievable goal. Rather, he must be given self-understanding by means of valid diagnoses through professional counseling. (p. 440)

Williamson's theory of vocational counseling was a scientific, problem-solving, empirical method that was individually tailored to each client to assure effective decision making, although such individual attention proved to be time consuming and inefficient. Essentially, his theory stated that clients had the traits of aptitude, interest, personality, and achievement which could form factors or "constellations" of individual characteristics. Williamson dominated the field of counseling into the 1970s and broadened the counseling field beyond occupational concerns, focusing on topics such as under- or overachievement, reading disabilities, gifted students, social adjustment, and personality problems.

SCHOOL COUNSELING IN THE 1950S AND 1960S

Confusion reigned in the early years of guidance and counseling regarding what constituted an adequate guidance and counseling program in the school and who should assume this responsibility for delivering these services to students and their families. But the field was growing. "If one decade in history had to be singled out for the most profound impact on professional school counselors," wrote Roger Aubrey (1983), "it would be the 1950s" (p. 7). The 1950s can be acknowledged for three major events that dramatically influenced and changed the direction of the history of school counseling:

1. New theories of counseling
2. The passage of the National Defense Education Act of 1958
3. The establishment of the American Personnel and Guidance Association, which became the American Counseling Association

New Theories of Counseling Emerge on the School Counseling Landscape

Carl Rogers introduced his nondirective, person-centered approach to counseling in the 1940s. His publication *Counseling and Psychotherapy* (1942) challenged Williamson's counselor-centered/counselor-directed approach. Rogers maintained that clients are responsible for their *own* growth, especially if they are heard and understood with unconditional positive regard, genuineness, empathy, and congruence.

Prior to Rogers, the counseling literature documented topics such as testing, cumulative records, orientation activities, character development, vocational awareness, and the goals and purposes of guidance.

But with the advent of Rogers and other theories—behavior therapy, rational emotive therapy, Gestalt therapy, reality therapy, cognitive behavioral therapy, Adlerian therapy, solution-focused therapy, narrative therapy, and family systems therapy—the term *guidance* began to disappear from the literature and was replaced with a greater emphasis on counseling. Rogers's nondirective, person-centered theory, as well as a considerable number of alternative systems such as dialectical behavior therapy, is still important today (Corsini, 2008).

Rogers made an effort to cross over into educational settings by abstracting a number of principles of learning. These principles are:

1. Human beings have a natural potential for learning.
2. Significant learning takes place with great rapidity when the subject matter is perceived by the student as having relevance for his or her own purposes, has a goal he or she wishes to achieve, and sees the material presented as relevant to that goal.
3. Learning that involves a change in self-organization in the perception of oneself is threatening and tends to be resisted.
4. Those learnings that are threatening to the self are more easily perceived and assimilated when external threats are at a minimum.
5. When the threat to the self is low, experience can be perceived in differentiated fashion and learning can proceed.
6. Much significant learning is acquired through doing.
7. Learning is facilitated when the student participates responsibly in the learning process.
8. Self-initiated learning that involves the whole person of the learner—feeling as well as intellect—is the most lasting and pervasive.
9. Independence, creativity, and self-reliance are all facilitated when self-criticism and self-evaluation are basic and evaluation by others is of secondary importance.
10. The most socially useful learning in the modern world is the learning of the *process of learning,* a continuing openness to experience and to incorporate into oneself the process of change (Rogers, 1969, p. 114).

Some idea of what Rogers learned about methods of facilitating learning can be obtained from his guidelines for facilitating learning:

1. It is very important for the facilitator to set the initial mood or climate of the group or class experience.
2. The facilitator helps to elicit and clarify the purposes of the individuals in the class as well as the more general purposes of the group (Rogers, 1969, p. 164).

At this juncture, the school counselor emerged as a "specialist in (1) understanding child and adolescent growth and development; (2) personality development and educational-vocational concerns and applicable information; and (3) guidance techniques, with emphasis on testing and the counseling interview" (Peters & Farwell, 1959, p. 23).

The National Defense Education Act of 1958 and the Elementary and Secondary Education Act of 1965

The role and function the school guidance counselor changed again in direct response to the *Sputnik* satellite launched in 1957 by the Union of Soviet Socialist Republics during the Cold War. This event led to the passage of the National Defense Education Act of 1958 and the Elementary and Secondary Education Act of 1965 (Beesley, 2004; Gysbers & Henderson, 2001; Wittmer, 2000a), which were intended to increase achievement in mathematics and science in U.S. schools. This federal legislation directed a large amount of funding to the training of school guidance counselors to steer students into advanced mathematics and science disciplines in order to help the United States compete globally (Baker, 2001; Wittmer, 2000a). These Acts provided a large impetus to the counseling profession, because federal funds were made available to encourage the increase of counselor preparation programs, and consequently the number of school counselors tripled between 1958 and 1967 (Baker, 2000; Wittmer 2000b). Full-time school counselors and a field of personnel known as "pupil personnel" emerged (Gysbers & Henderson, 2000, p. 8). Gysbers (1990) asserts that the model that dominated professional theory during this period was the "counselor-clinical-services" (p. 1) or the process-model approach, where the elements of guidance programs consisted of counseling, consulting, and coordinating services within the school.

The American Personnel and Guidance Association

The American Personnel and Guidance Association (APGA) evolved from the Council of Guidance and Personnel Association (CGPA), which merged with the National Vocational Guidance Association; the National Association of Guidance and Counselor Trainers; the Student Personnel Association for Teacher Education; and the American College Personnel Association in hopes of providing a larger professional voice "concerned with educational and vocational guidance and other personnel activities" (ACA, 2011). APGA changed its name in 1983 to the American Association of Counseling and Development, and then on July 1, 1992, the association changed its name once again to the American Counseling Association (ACA) to reflect the common bond among association members and to reinforce their unity of purpose and professional counselor identity. ACA develops ethical standards and professional counselor competencies for all counselors, and membership in ACA provides opportunities for professional development, liability insurance, professional publications, continuing education, career assistance, and legal advice. The American School Counselor Association is affiliated with ACA and also provides professional publications, books, podcasts by significant professional school counselors in the field, position statements, and legislative alerts and numerous other resources for professional school counselors.

CONFUSION REIGNS AND ROLES ARE THREATENED FOR SCHOOL COUNSELORS IN THE 1970S AND 1980S

The helter-skelter evolution of school counseling from trait factor perspectives through person-centered orientations, specialists in human development, and practicing as service providers (i.e., coordinating, consulting, and counseling activities) created havoc for the profession in terms of professional identity and accountability in the 1970s and 1980s. Was the profession to be defined as guidance teachers, guidance counselors, school counselors, or professional school counselors?

Beesley (2004) maintains that these decades were one of the darkest periods for the profession of school counseling. During an economic downturn, it was a period in which declining enrollments, staff reductions, and economic cutbacks, exemplified by Proposition 13 in California, caused many professional school counselors to find themselves at risk of having their jobs eliminated entirely. The rhetoric that was often heard was: "We need to cut staff—should it be the guidance counselor or the reading specialist?" Decisions had to be made about which positions and related services were need most based on the needs of students.

Professional school counseling programs that once thrived began to wane during the 1970s, due in part to an identity crisis and the lack of ability on the part of professional school counselors to appropriately articulate or demonstrate the positive effects of their work in the schools. They could not demonstrate the difference they made in the lives of students or with schoolwide initiatives in general (Baker,

2000, 2001; Beesley, 2004). Essentially, they were viewed as an ancillary or resource service that was expendable, especially during bleak economic times.

This occurred in conjunction with the humanistic movement in education, which was a backlash against the detrimental, unhealthy environment of many U.S. schools that mimicked the Industrial Revolution and had become a rigid, lockstep, impersonal process for both faculty and staff. Critics said that such schools were not fit places for human beings. "Many are not even decent places for children to be. They damage, they thwart, they stifle children's natural capacity to learn and grow healthily" (Gross & Gross, 1969, p. 110). Holt (1967) asserted that public education hindered, rather than facilitated, learning because it instilled anxiety, fear of failure, tension, and lack of motivation; he blamed an emphasis on punishing students for being wrong and the proclivity to use shame and embarrassment in front of others when lesser students did not excel. This created a growing population of students who were disenchanted with school and led to a growing population of students who underachieved or dropped out of school entirely. This continues to be a national problem today.

A call to action began to be heard on several themes regarding the appropriate roles of school counselors (Baker, 2000). One initiative was developing comprehensive developmental school counseling programs. During the late 1970s, the developmental approach to guidance was gaining strength, and the concept of elementary-school guidance gained momentum because of the realization that primary prevention was a better investment in time and energy than secondary intervention and crisis management, which often occurred on the middle school and high school levels (Baker, 2000). Additionally, the services approach emerged in professional school counselor programs (Gysbers, 1990, p. 2); school guidance counselors were encouraged to base guidance programs on clearly stated goals and objectives founded on a set of functions from primary prevention to diagnosis and therapy. These services were all provided with the goal of maintaining a focus on the personal development of the student (Baker, 2000; Gysbers, 1990; Gysbers, Bragg Stanley, Kosteck-Bunch, Magnuson, & Starr, 2008).

The developmental guidance movement of the 1980s sought to reorganize school counseling around a comprehensive guidance curriculum or a comprehensive school counseling program (Baker, 2000, 2001; Gysbers & Henderson, 2006; Gysbers et al., 2008). According to Galassi and Akos (2004), comprehensive school guidance and counseling programs:

(a) De-emphasized administrative and clerical tasks as well as crisis-centered modes of intervention; and
(b) Promoted guidance activities and structured group experiences designed to support students in developing the personal, social, educational, and career skills needed to function as responsible and productive citizens. (p. 3)

The Missouri comprehensive school counseling program still exists today, and the curriculum was revised in 2008 after nearly three decades of evolution as a comprehensive school counseling program (Gysbers et al., 2008).

Guidance and counseling in the schools now resembled the services approach, but this rapidly changed with a standards-based approach to counseling services (Gysbers, 1990, p. 2).

STANDARDS OF TRAINING, CERTIFICATIONS, AND A PROFESSIONAL HONOR SOCIETY

Perhaps the most notable and attainable accomplishment in the 1980s was the standardization of training and certification in counseling, recognizing it as a distinct profession with a true professional identity. In 1981, the Council for Accreditation of Counseling and Related Educational Programs (CACREP) was formed as an affiliate organization of ACA. CACREP is an independent agency recognized by the Council for Higher Education Accreditation to standardize counselor education programs for masters and doctoral programs in career counseling; college counseling; community counseling; counselor education and supervision; gerontological counseling; marital, couple, and family counseling; clinical mental health counseling; and school counseling and student affairs. CACREP counselor programs voluntarily submit a self-study that is reviewed against the CACREP standards by counselors and counselor educators in the field to ensure that students receive a quality educational experience. New standards were developed in 2009. "Accreditation entails assessing a program's quality and its continual enhancement through compliance with the CACREP standards. The accreditation process uses both self-assessment and peer assessment to determine how well professional standards are being met. Accredited status indicates to the public at large that a program has accepted and is fulfilling its commitment to educational quality" (CACREP, 2009, p. 2).

The National Board for Certified Counselors (NBCC) was initiated in 1982 to certify counselors on a national level, bestowing the credential of National Certified Counselor (NCC). The NBCC developed a standardized test around eight central subject areas in which professional counselors should be knowledgeable: human growth and development, social and cultural foundations, helping relationships, group counseling, career and lifestyle development, appraisal, research and program evaluation, and professional orientation and ethics. Today, more than 43,000 counselors have their NCC certification.

In conjunction with this growth in counselor identity, Chi Sigma Iota, an international academic and professional honor society, was formed in 1985 in an effort to promote scholarship, research, professionalism, leadership, and excellence in counseling and to recognize high attainment in the pursuit of academic and clinical excellence in the profession of counseling. It had more than 66,000 members as of November 2009. Membership in this international honor society requires a 3.5 cumulative grade point average in graduate studies, further reinforcing higher standards, scholarship, leadership, professional development, and a strong counselor identity.

A NEW VISION FOR PROFESSIONAL SCHOOL COUNSELING: 1990 TO THE PRESENT

Within the last two decades, as professional school counselors were assuming their roles and allowing more and more ancillary activities to be added to their already overburdened positions (e.g., high-stakes testing, crisis management, child study committee responsibilities, and interventions for youth risk prevention), researchers in the field were trying to solidify roles and responsibilities. As Norman Gysbers (1990) noted, "The present day emphasis lies in developmental, organized programming that replaces even the more recent view of school counselor as 'counselor-clinical-services' provider" (p. 167). He reinforced the perception that "the change from position to program as the basic organizer for guidance in the schools represents a major paradigm shift for school counselors" (p. 168).

Gysbers (1990) outlined four axioms upon which school counseling programs should prevail. First and foremost, guidance is a program. Second, school counseling programs are developmental and comprehensive. Third, school counseling programs are built on a team approach. And finally, school counseling programs mandate articulation; that is, effective linkages between developmental levels, K–12, should exist so that program continuity is assured. This comprehensive guidance program model was originally developed by Gysbers in the 1970s and was updated in 2008 with an extensive curriculum (Gysbers et al., 2008). This model views guidance as an organized developmental education K–12 counseling program model rather than an ancillary set of randomly organized student services.

Concurrently, Paisley and Borders (1995) recognized the emergence of a focus on developmentally appropriate programs to address the social, emotional, and cognitive issues students face and that should be the central focus of professional school counseling reform. They maintained that delivery of a comprehensive developmental school counseling program is frequently cited as the foundation for the role of the professional school counselor. School counselors of the 1990s were given the task of designing, developing, and delivering programs that were, according to Brown (1999), "designed to facilitate human growth and learning and at the same time fostering resiliency with preventive, proactive focus while providing a support system" (p. 38). Lapan, Gysbers, and Sun (1997) found that in schools with more fully implemented comprehensive guidance programs:

- students reported higher grades;
- students were more likely to indicate that their school was preparing them well for later life;
- students were more likely to report that career and college information was readily available to them; and
- students were more likely to report a positive school climate (defined primarily in terms of perceptions of safety, orderliness, and belonging).

Responding to the lack of clarity of the role and function of the professional school counselor and the relentless historical problems recognized by major contributors in the field, ASCA and its founding organization, the ACA, introduced the Elementary School Counseling Demonstration Act in 1993, which was eventually signed into law as the Elementary School Counseling Demonstration Act of 1995 (Paisley & Borders, 1995). This seminal legislation provided necessary funding for schools that proposed promising and innovative approaches to the expansion of school counseling programs. These programs, by definition, would encourage collaborative efforts between the school counselor, the school psychologist, and the school social workers as working teams to benefit students and their families. Additionally, this Act called for student–counselor ratios not to exceed 250:1 and for 85% of the school counselor's time to be spent providing direct services to students, with no more than 15% of their time devoted to administrative tasks (Baker, 2000).

Regretfully, this initiative did not come to fruition in many school districts because school psychologists and social workers were already overburdened with a growing population of children with disabilities and were often relegated to psychometric responsibilities and home visits to determine a student's eligibility for special education services. In addition, even though ASCA (1999) suggested that the ideal student–counselor ratio should be 250:1, Marino, Sams, and Guerra (1999) reported the actual nationwide ratio at 513:1. Such elevated student–counselor ratios ultimately reduce school counselor availability to counsel students and to implement evidence-based programs and practice (Borders & Drury, 1992b). Recently, the U.S. Department of Education released findings of student–counselor ratios as high as 814:1 in California (U.S. Department of Education, 2007).

Additional pieces of key legislation that influenced the school counselor's role were the School-to-Work Opportunities Act of 1994 and the Carl D. Perkins Vocational and Technical Education Act of 1998. The legislative goals of both were to focus attention on assisting and guiding students in their transition from school to work, such as offering a structured sequence of courses directly related to preparing individuals for paid employment in emerging career and technical occupations. The professional school counselor's involvement in this process was emphasized because he or she is viewed as a person who has a vast knowledge of vocational, career, and technical decision making and interpersonal skills development. This, combined with the professional school counselor's knowledge of child and adolescent growth and development, fosters a role for the professional school counselor as an instrumental conduit in delivering a comprehensive program to assist students in the school-to-work transition.

THE EDUCATION TRUST: THE NATIONAL CENTER FOR TRANSFORMING SCHOOL COUNSELING EMERGES

In 1996, the Education Trust, a Washington, D.C.–based not-for-profit organization, began a five-year national initiative for transforming professional school counseling (Martin, 2002). The National Center for Transforming School Counseling (NCTSC) initiative came about primarily because professional school counselors—an integral part of the school achievement team—were left out of the reform movement of the No Child Left Behind Act of 2001. With this new program, an understanding of achievement data reported by schools on an annual basis was paramount to make professional school counselors an integral part of school improvement initiatives.

Fundamentally, professional school counselors can no longer ignore the achievement gap between students from poverty, minorities, and immigrants and their mainstream counterparts (i.e., white, native-born students from nonpoverty households). The 2003 Transforming School Counseling Initiative (TSCI), supported in part by the Dewitt Wallace–Reader's Digest Fund, attempted to reconcile the differences between the school counseling theory being taught to preservice professional school counselors and the actual practice that is required of the professional school counselor to assist in closing the achievement gap among students, especially minority, immigrant, and low-income students (Baker, 2000; Martin, 2002). School statistics are meaningful, and analyzing particular schools can provide significant indicators for intervention and primary prevention programming initiatives. The emphasis of this reform movement was to provide professional school counselors with the knowledge and data that they need in order to close the achievement gap between underserved populations of students that are lagging behind academically (Dollarhide & Saginak, 2008).

Perhaps paramount, this national TSCI was created to ensure that ultimately "professional school counselors serve as leaders as well as effective team members working with teachers and administrators to make sure that each student succeeds" (Education Trust, quoted in Dollarhide & Saginak, 2008, p. 199). The main focus of the national Education Trust was promoting high academic achievement for all students, as well as enhancing career development opportunities for all students at all levels (Baker, 2000). This is critical if professional school counselors are to address the specific needs of their school and community and to level the academic playing field for all students, so they can achieve and become productive citizens. One size no longer fits all students when it pertains to the implementation of programs and services and enhancing the achievement outcomes of *all* students.

The fundamental principle of the TSCI is a belief that students can achieve at higher levels when there are high expectations for student achievement across all socioeconomic and ethnic dimensions (Education Trust, 2007). Fundamentally, the NCTSC initiative is based on the belief that students enter the school building every day with the ability and potential to achieve and that professional school counselors are in a unique position to advocate for all students to see their potential fulfilled. The second fundamental principle of the NCTSC is that all students need access to a high-quality, rigorous curriculum that will adequately prepare them for viable work and college/university matriculation (Education Trust, 2007). The mission for professional school counselors is to play a critical role in ensuring that all students have access to viable and challenging curricula and to cease the use of watered-down curricula because no one rises to low expectations.

In addition, the NCTSC initiative has outlined five skills at which professional school counselors must be effective:

1. Teaming and collaboration
2. Leadership
3. Assessment and the use of data to effect change
4. Advocacy and counseling
5. Coordination (Education Trust, 2007; Musheno & Talbert, 2002)

The NCTSC believes that proficiency in these five critical areas will prepare professional school counselors to become integral leaders of educational reform initiatives in their respective programs as well as advocates for students to increase their academic achievement, thereby enhancing their self-sufficiency and overall well-being (Musheno & Talbert, 2002).

The 2001 reauthorization of the Elementary and Secondary Act legislation known as the No Child Left Behind (NCLB) Act of 2001 became what many consider the most sweeping national educational reform in the nation's history (Phelps, 2002). It is not rhetoric driven, but rather results driven, with

TABLE 1.1 Expanding School Counselor Role and Function

THE SERVICE-DRIVEN MODEL OF TRADITIONAL SCHOOL COUNSELING PROGRAMS	DATA-DRIVEN AND STANDARDS-BASED MODEL TO TRANSFORM SCHOOL COUNSELING PROGRAMS
Counseling (e.g., individual and group)	Leadership
Consultation (e.g., parents, administration, teachers, and support staff)	Advocacy
Coordination of services (e.g., scheduling, testing, registration, and other clerical duties)	Teaming and collaboration
	Counseling and coordination
	Assessment and use of data
	Use of technology

Sources: From Education Trust, *The National Guidance and Counseling Reform Program,* Washington, DC, 1997; Education Trust, 2000; and Education Trust, *National Center for Transforming School Counseling at the Education Trust,* 2007, http://www2.edtrust.org/EdTrust/Transforming+School+Counseling/main. Reprinted with permission.

standards-based accreditation stipulations and annual yearly progress requirements. The fundamental purpose of NCLB was to narrow achievement gaps between and among minority groups or students of color and their white and Asian-American counterparts (U.S. Department of Education, 2002). The primary goals of NCLB addressed curriculum, achievement, school climate, affective development, and graduation rates from high school (Chandler, 2006; Stone & Dahir, 2006, 2007). "The No Child Left Behind Act is a clear imperative for achievement, shares the pressures of school accountability, and demonstrate advocacy for every student to experience academic success" (ASCA, p. 4). Table 1.1 shows the sharp contrast from the traditional role of professional school counselors to one that truly serves to transform school counseling programs. Professional school counselors emerge as an integral component of school improvement efforts. This, along with the ASCA standards, solidifies the professional school counselor's niche, answering the question, "How are student different by what professional school counselors do?"

THE AMERICAN SCHOOL COUNSELOR ASSOCIATION: A CONSENSUS ON ROLE AND FUNCTION

The American School Counselor Association, an arm of ACA, was established in 1952 and supports school counselors' efforts to help students focus on academic, personal/social and career development so they can achieve success in school and graduate to lead fulfilling lives as responsible members of society. ASCA provides professional development, publications and other resources, research and advocacy to more than 28,000 professional school counselors nationally and internationally. In 2001, ASCA initiated the development of the *ASCA National Model* for School Counseling Programs as a framework for designing, developing, implementing, and evaluating standards-based, data-driven school counseling programs. The *ASCA National Model,* released in 2003 and revised in 2005, outlined how school counselors could connect their work to student achievement data and demonstrates their results as connected to the academic mission of their schools. *The ASCA National Model* initiative assumed that enhancing and documenting school counselor outcome productivity (through better management and accountability practices) at each individual school level would be both necessary and sufficient to cause changes in resource allocation at the building and district levels (Hatch, 2002, 2008).

ASCA has had a pivotal and dynamic influence on the development of the profession as well as professional school counseling in general (Burnham & Jackson, 2000; Paisley & Borders, 1995). As is evident from its evolution, school counseling as a profession historically has lacked clarity of role and function, and school counselors have not always met the needs of all students for a variety of reasons, such as growing enrollment, diversity, and burgeoning caseloads (Bemak, 2000; Gysbers, 2001; Hatch, 2002; House & Hayes, 2002; Perusse, Goodnough, Donegan, & Jones, 2004; Perusse, Goodnough, & Noel, 2001). In response to the increase in standards-based models of education, education reform, the accountability movement, and the need to close achievement and opportunity gaps, ASCA revised school counselor roles and school counseling program components to better focus the school counselor on meeting the needs of all students in creating the *ASCA National Model* framework for school counseling programs (American School Counselor Association, 2005a; Chen-Hayes, 2007; Hatch, 2002, 2008; Perusse & Goodnough, 2004; Stone & Dahir, 2006).

ASCA engaged in several initiatives to improve both the effectiveness of professional school counselors and the status of school counselors within the educational community (Hatch & Bowers, 2002; Perusse, Goodnough, et al., 2004). For example, it established role and position statements for school counselors (ASCA, 2002), established recommended guidelines for student-to-counselor ratios (ASCA, 2003), developed the ASCA National Standards for School Counseling Programs (Campbell & Dahir, 1997; Dahir, 2001; Dahir, Sheldon, & Valiga, 1998), and revised the ASCA code of ethics (ASCA, 2004a).

ASCA's intent in creating the ASCA National Standards was to increase the legitimacy of the school counseling profession and to ensure academic, career, and personal/social success competencies delivered to all students. Baker (2000) maintained that the national standards would:

1. shift the focus from counselors to counseling programs;
2. create a framework for a national school counseling model;
3. establish school counseling as an integral part of the academic mission of schools;
4. promote equal access to school counseling services for all students;
5. emphasize the key components of developmental school counseling;
6. identify the knowledge and skills that all students should have access to as a part of a comprehensive school counseling program; and
7. provide for the systematic delivery of a school counseling program.

The role of the school counselor as a member of the academic team within schools and the school counselor's as advocate and leader in the role of enhancing academic achievement of all students are highlighted in ASCA's National Model (Baker, 2000; Campbell & Dahir, 1997).

The *ASCA National Model* instructed professional school counselors to include program management and accountability practices based on objective data because of a dearth of outcome research; few professional school counselors were engaging in collecting data and demonstrating results of their program effectiveness in delivering competencies to all students (ASCA, 2005a; Dimmitt, Carey, & Hatch, 2007; Poynton & Carey, 2006; Whiston & Sexton, 1998). Several models of data-based decision making for implementing the *ASCA National Model* were developed (Dimmitt et al., 2007; Poynton & Carey, 2006; Stone & Dahir, 2006). Their use required a shift in professional school counselors' beliefs and behavior about analyzing, collecting, utilizing, and reporting data and outcome results at the building, district, state, and national levels (Dimmitt et al., 2007).

The *ASCA National Model* (2005a) included key tenets of the Education Trust's Transforming School Counseling Initiative's founder, Patricia J. Martin (2002), who stated, "If the beliefs are all across the board, that will be reflected programmatically.... Beliefs determine behavior" (p. 27). Successful implementation of the *ASCA National Model* school counseling program components requires lessening the fear of using data to make meaningful prevention and intervention efforts. It requires that professional school counselors understand the importance of developing data skills and then use data in both program management and accountability, to drive decision making, set measurable goals and objectives, and evaluate program effectiveness. With data and accountability skills, professional school counselors can leverage results to garner the political clout necessary to improve student–counselor staffing ratios and redefine professional school counselor roles and activities, thereby decreasing noncounseling activities that distract professional school counselors' intended purpose (Dimmitt et al., 2007).

THE *ASCA NATIONAL MODEL*

School counseling programs are an integral part of a student's personal, social, academic, and career development. *The ASCA National Model: A Framework for School Counseling Programs* (ASCA, 2005a) emphasizes the importance of school counselors being at the forefront of delivering accountable school counseling programs that document how students are different as a result of the school counseling program, which is the fundamental question.

This is one of the most comprehensive and succinct articulations of the role and function of professional school counselors for the 21st century. The model clearly outlines inappropriate (noncounseling) activities and appropriate (school counseling) responsibilities. A clear role identity has evolved in the literature from *school counselor* to *professional school counselor*.

The role of the professional school counselor is to seek systemic change, to provide leadership, to advocate for students, and to collaborate with individuals inside and outside of the school to develop a counseling program that is comprehensive in design and is delivered systematically to all students. The National Model, shown in Figure 1.1, has four major components: foundation, delivery system, accountability, and management system (ASCA, 2005b).

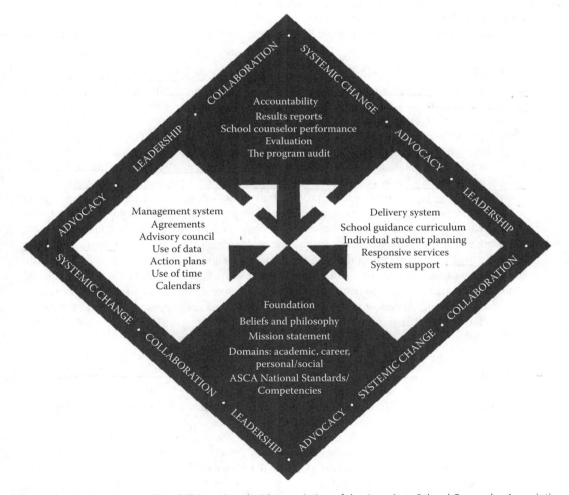

FIGURE 1.1   *ASCA National Model®*. Reprinted with permission of the American School Counselor Association.

The *foundation* describes the core beliefs, philosophies, and values that guide a comprehensive guidance and counseling program (CGCP). This includes the school's mission statement and program standards of academic, career, and personal social counseling that will be systematically evaluated.

The *delivery system* delineates the methods that school counselors use to provide services to students and their families, teachers, administrators, and the greater community. It consists of a comprehensive school counseling curriculum, individual student planning, and system supports. The most visible delivery method is responsive services, including social and emotional intervention, crisis intervention, crisis management, and crisis response.

Accountability procedures stress goals and the use of individual school data to determine whether school improvement goals and annual yearly progress have been reached. This puts professional school counselors in the forefront of school reform by making them an integral part of the school improvement team. Professional school counselors have access to all kinds of data, from school dropout rates to advance placement enrollment by race and ethnicity. Accountability is measured with results reports, school program audits, and school counselor performance evaluations.

Management systems are processes used to manage the school counseling program and make the program accountable. These include formal agreements with school administrators about appropriate professional school counseling responsibilities and annual goals. They provide for advisory councils, monthly and yearly calendars, and schedules to help school counselors manage their time most effectively and efficiently in collaboration with teachers, administrators, and support staff.

In addition, the National Model (ASCA, 2005b) clarifies the integral role of school counselors in the school improvement process. Inherent in these three theoretical frameworks are important manifests:

1. Professional school guidance and counseling have an established curriculum and a distinct content based on the three domains of academic achievement, career planning, and personal and social development. The curriculum reflects the same framework as the mathematics, English, and science initiatives with goals, expectations, and measurable outcomes—that is, helping students to develop core knowledge and self-sufficiency skills that will support lifelong learning and to become productive members of society.

2. Professional school guidance and counseling have an organizational structure to facilitate the design and implementation of a comprehensive program that addresses both program content and program process. Comprehensive professional school counseling programs use individual school data to target intervention and prevention strategies to meet the needs of *all* students and do not provide a series of isolated responsive services for small groups of students.

3. Comprehensive professional school counseling and guidance programs are goal driven and results oriented with a focus on meeting the needs of *all* students. Essentially, CGCPs seek to overcome obstacles with the goals of academic achievement, closing the achievement gap, and ultimately leading students to a successful and productive career or to postsecondary education. Fundamentally, students perform at higher levels and reach greater degrees of achievement when a CGCP is part of their daily school life (Gysbers & Henderson, 2006; Walsh, Barrett, & DePaul, 2007; Gysbers et al., 2008).

Integral components of a school's comprehensive guidance and counseling program include the following:

1. *Beliefs and Philosophy.* The philosophy is a set of principles that guides the development, implementation, and evaluation of the CGCP.

2. *Mission of Comprehensive Guidance and Counseling Programs.* The mission articulates the intentionality of the school counseling program. It represents the immediate and long-range impact (e.g., what is planned for every student five to ten years after graduation from high school).

3. *Goals.* Goals extend the mission and focus on the results that will be achieved by the time each student exits the school system. The foundational goals for the CGCP are designated in three

domains—academic, career, and personal/social development—providing the fundamental structure for the definition of the goals related to competencies.

4. *School Counseling Standards and Competencies.* Competencies are knowledge, attitudes, or skills that are observable and can be transferred from a learning situation to real life with measurable outcomes. Competencies are indicators that a student is making progress toward the goals of the CGCP. They are developed and organized into content areas across the curriculum.

5. *Guidance and Counseling Curriculum.* The guidance and counseling curriculum consists of structured developmental lessons designed to enable students to achieve competencies and are presented systematically and developmentally through pre-K–12 classroom and group activities and lessons. The purpose of the guidance and counseling curriculum is to provide all students with the knowledge, skills, and attitudes appropriate to their developmental level. The CGCP is organized to help students acquire, assimilate, develop, and demonstrate competencies within the three domains of academic achievement, career planning, and personal/social development.

6. *Individual Student Planning.* Professional school counselors coordinate ongoing systematic activities designed to the individual student in establishing personal goals and developing realistic future plans.

7. *Responsive Services.* The school counseling program's responsive services consist of activities to meet the immediate needs of students and their families, as well as faculty, administrators, and support staff. These needs or concerns may require counseling, consulting, crisis intervention, crisis management, referral, peer mediation, or information.

8. *System Support.* System support consists of management, prevention, and intervention activities that establish, maintain, and enhance the total school counseling program.

9. *School Counselor/Administrator Agreements.* Annual contracts or statements of responsibility between each professional school counselor and school administrator specify the program initiatives and results by grade level for which each counselor is accountable. These agreements are reviewed annually and negotiated with and approved by the designated administrator.

10. *Advisory Council and Focus Groups.* An advisory council or focus group is a group of people appointed to review the program audit, goals, mission, outcomes, and results. Their task is to report about the CGCP and make recommendations to the principal or superintendent. The advisory council or focus group has representatives of stakeholders that are affected by the school counseling program: students, parents/guardians, teachers, counselors, administrators, support staff, and community members.

11. *Use of School Improvement Data and Student Monitoring of Results Based on Data.* Analysis of data (e.g., achievement gains by race and ethnicity, poverty, attendance, dropout rates, minorities in advanced classes, students on free and reduced lunch, English language learners, and diversity) drives the program intervention and prevention initiative. Monitoring students' progress ensures that each student acquires the identified competencies in the academic, career, and social/personal development domains. Monitoring should be both systemic by district and specific to individual schools, assessing demographic data, achievement benchmarks, annual yearly progress, and achievement gaps between minority students, English-language learners, and those with intellectual disabilities.

12. *Action Plans (Guidance Curriculum and Closing the Achievement Gap).* For every competency taught or every prevention or intervention result anticipated by professional school counselors, there must be an accountability plan to demonstrate schoolwide desired competencies or results. Each plan contains:
    - Focus on competencies
    - Description of the activities
    - Data driving the decision to address the competencies
    - Timeline in which each activity is to be completed
    - Identification of who is responsible for delivery
    - Means of evaluating student success
    - Expected results for students

13. *Use of Systematic Timelines and Calendars.* An annual master calendar of programs and events should be systematically established to effectively plan and promote the school counseling program. This should be provided on the school website and the district website to maximize active knowledge and participation in the CGCP. The master calendar provides students and their families, teachers, administrators, and support staff with a knowledge base of all school counseling programs and activities.

14. *Systematic Reporting of Counseling Outcomes and Results.* Outcomes of school counseling programs and activities as well as other significant outcomes should be collected systematically and presented to important stakeholders such as administrators, faculty, support staff, parents, school boards, and the greater community.

15. *School Counselor Performance Standards.* Evaluation is an integral component of school counselor performance standards and is expected of professional school counselors implementing CGCPs. Performance standards serve two purposes: school counselor program evaluation and school counselor self-evaluation.

16. *Program Audit.* A program audit demonstrates evidence that the comprehensive school counseling program is aligned with local, state, and national models. The primary purpose for collecting and disseminating information is to provide guidelines for future initiatives, assess whether program goals are being accomplished, assure the needs within the CGCP are met, and improve future results for students.

A systematic program audit of a comprehensive developmental guidance and counseling program assesses the school counseling program within the framework of the *ASCA National Model*. Audits serve as a baseline and targeted outcomes for the school counseling program. Annual audits provide important feedback regarding program and student outcomes, identifying results, strengths, and weaknesses. Essentially, what gets measured gets done.

RECOGNIZED ASCA MODEL PROGRAM (RAMP)

School systems that are committed to delivering a comprehensive, data-driven school counseling program are encouraged to apply for the Recognized ASCA Model Program (RAMP) designation from the American School Counselor Association. The RAMP is organized with a philosophy statement, an advisory council, calendars, a small-group counseling curriculum, a classroom guidance curriculum, closing-the-achievement-gap initiatives, and programs to specifically answer the question of how students are different because of what professional school counselors do. The application process follows the guidelines below and is rated on a five-point scale from exemplary to poor. Only exemplary ratings are listed in the appendix.

Nonetheless, there continues to be a lack of consensus on the role of professional school counselors when one looks at Table 1.2 and the reform initiatives together, comparing noncounseling activities with appropriate counseling responsibilities. Currently, professional literature focuses on professional school counselor leadership in the schools to better meet the increasing complex academic, personal, and social needs of all students. The increasing call for this leadership has been propelled by school counselor reform initiatives to improve academic achievement for all students to close achievement gaps for minority and low-income students (Education Trust, 1997). Fundamentally, professional school counselors by virtue of their training and skills are strategically positioned to assume pivotal leadership roles to make a significant change in student achievement and school improvement planning.

Table 1.3 demonstrates the significant variables that have influenced the role of the professional school counselor. The service-driven traditional model of school counseling is completely outdated. The new *ASCA National Model*, data-driven and standard-based school counseling programs, and the legal

TABLE 1.2 Inappropriate and Appropriate Counseling Activities and Responsibilities

INAPPROPRIATE NONCOUNSELING ACTIVITIES	APPROPRIATE COUNSELING RESPONSIBILITIES
Registering and scheduling all new students	Designing individual student academic programs
Administering cognitive, aptitude, and achievement tests	Interpreting cognitive, aptitude, and achievement and career tests
Signing excuses for students who are tardy or absent	Counseling student with excessive tardiness, absenteeism, school phobia, or social anxiety
Performing disciplinary actions	Counseling students with disciplinary problems, violence, or relational aggression issues
Sending home students who are not appropriately dressed	Counseling students about appropriate school dress, appropriate social skills, and relationships skills
Teaching classes when teachers are absent	Collaborating with teachers to present classroom guidance curriculum lessons
Computing grade-point averages	Analyzing grade-point averages in relationship to achievement and potential academic and career goals
Maintaining student records	Interpreting student records regarding gaps in services, special education needs, or community resources
Supervising study halls	Providing teachers with suggestions for better study hall management
Clerical recordkeeping	Ensuring student records are maintained in accordance with state and federal regulations, such as FERPA, HIPAA, PPRA, and ADA
Assisting with duties in the principal's office	Assisting the principal in identifying and resolving student issues, needs, and problems
Working with one student at a time in a therapeutic, clinical mode	Collaborating with teachers to present proactive, preventive-based classroom guidance curriculum lessons

Source: Adapted from American School Counselor Association, *The ASCA National Model: A Framework for School Counseling Programs* (2nd ed.), Alexandria, VA, 2005b. Reprinted with permission.

TABLE 1.3 A Comparison of the Traditional Service Model of School Counseling Programs, the ASCA Model, the Data-Driven Standards-Based School Counseling Model, and No Child Left Behind

SERVICE-DRIVEN MODEL OF TRADITIONAL SCHOOL COUNSELING PROGRAMS	ASCA NATIONAL MODEL	DATA-DRIVEN AND STANDARDS-BASED SCHOOL COUNSELING TO TRANSFORM SCHOOL COUNSELING PROGRAM	NO CHILD LEFT BEHIND
Counseling	Beliefs and philosophy	Counseling	Curriculum
Consultation	Mission	Consultation	Achievement
Coordination	Guidance curriculum	Coordination of Services	School climate
	Individual student planning	Leadership	Affective development
	Responsive services	Advocacy	Graduation rates
	Systems support	Collaboration and teaming	Annual yearly progress
	Agreements	Managing resources	
	Advisory council	Use of data	
	Use of data	Use of technology	
	Action plans		
	Use of time		
	Use of calendars		
	Results reports		
	School counselor performance standards		
	Program audit		

implications of No Child Left behind focuses on accountability and closing the achievement gap between minority and poor children.

ASCA AND THE EDUCATION TRUST: A NATIONAL PARTNERSHIP TO CLOSE THE ACHIEVEMENT GAP

We are facing an unrecognized education crisis in this country. Our wide and sometimes growing achievement gap confirms that there is a two-tiered educational system. For the lucky few, their education is the best in the world, virtually ensuring those students have wonderful opportunities for further education, economic security professional rewards and personal freedom. For others, there is an underperforming system. Students come to school, but find little education. The vast majority of students left behind are disadvantaged or low income. Effectively, the education circumstances for these students are not unlike that of a de facto system of apartheid.

Rod Paige, former Secretary of Education (2003)

National initiatives have evolved that strongly urge professional school counselors to be more proficient and comfortable in expanding the role of traditional school counseling practice with the "three *C*'s": counseling, coordination of services, and consultation. The ASCA (2005a) model and the Education Trust (1997) initiatives have advocated that professional school counselors expand the roles and skills in collaboration and teaming, case management, leadership, advocacy, managing resources, assessment and use of data, and program design and evaluation and the use of technology to transform and propel school counseling into the 21st century with its changing student demographics and the demand for educational reform. This is very different than the traditional programs that many current school counselors embrace and represents a true paradigm shift by expanding school counselor focus. Table 1.4 poignantly illustrates this dynamic change in the role and function that professional school counselors must assume, i.e., from

TABLE 1.4 The Data-Driven and Standards-Based Model: A Definition of Terms

Leadership	Connecting the counseling program to the academic mission of schools and challenging the status quo. Forming relationships with students and adults in the school and community to ensure all students' academic success.
Advocacy	Advocating for the removal of systemic barriers that prevent all students from succeeding. Advocating for policies and practices that close gaps and promote academic success for all students.
Teaming and collaboration	Using group facilitation skills to work with educators, parents, community-based organizations, and other stakeholders to mobilize human, financial, and other resources needed to eliminate environmental and institutional barriers to college and career readiness for every pre-K–12 student.
Counseling and coordination	Using counseling skills to assist students in overcoming social, personal, and academic barriers. Brokering community resources to support students.
Assessment and use of data	Using data to create a sense of urgency to spur change. Using data to focus school counseling program actvities, establish measurable goals, and measure the results of initiatives designed to improve students' academic success. Using data in accountability for school counseling programs.
Use of Technology	Using technology as an effective advocacy tool. Includes using it to disaggregate data, present it, and share it.

Source: Education Trust. Transforming School Counseling (1997, 2000, 2004, 2005a, b, c, 2010). Washington, D.C. Author. Reprinted with permission.

counselor, coordinator, and consultant to leadership, advocacy, teaming and collaboration, counseling and coordination, assessment and use of data, and use of technology.

ROLE CONFLICT AND AMBIGUITY

Role conflict is the simultaneous occurrence of two or more sets of inconsistent, expected role behaviors for an individual's task or function. *Role ambiguity* is the lack of clear, consistent information regarding the duties and responsibilities of a role and how it can best be performed. Counselors have many names, from alphabet counselor to sophomore counselor, as well as such titles as director of guidance, college placement services coordinator, graduate opportunities counselor, student services counselor, student assistance counselor, vocational counselor, career and technical counselor, and resource counselor with students with special needs. The diversity of these titles indicates the varied roles counselors are expected to play. Chronic role conflict and ambiguity often result in a rather marked sense of futility and role confusion.

Role conflict also results when incompatible demands are placed on the counselor that are influenced by vague assumptions and differing expectations within the constraints of the school-as-institution. Concurrently, professional school counselors are expected to be involved in an unprecedented variety of guidance and counseling activities. Roles and functions include work on the academic curriculum; conducting placement and follow-up activities; intervention within, remediation of, and identification of students with special needs; consultation; high-stakes testing administration; group work; and a growing interface with business and industry. In addition, professional school counselors are expected to continue routine activities such as crisis counseling, teacher and parent consultation, assessment, scheduling, follow-up, and referrals to inside and outside agencies.

Yet today, many professional school counselors continue to function in a guidance mode and struggle to adapt to a 1970s service-delivery model to meet the growing mental health needs that evolved in the 1990s. Professional school counselors who maintain traditional models of guidance and counseling are essentially ineffective (Baker, 2000; Perry, 1995). Counseling, consultation, and coordination are three of the primary functions of a school counselor (Borders & Drury, 1992a; Paisley & Borders, 1995), but they require redefinition in light of the complex needs of contemporary youths in today's society. In response, ASCA has adopted a number of position statements on the role of school counselors in areas such as comprehensive school counseling programs, character education, child abuse/neglect prevention, dropout prevention, family and parenting education, gender equity, cross-/multicultural counseling, credentialing and licensure, gifted programs, and group counseling, as well as the ASCA (2005a) National Model.

Schools, parents, and politicians have called for increasing the number of counselors and conflict resolution programs, decreasing children's access to guns and violent content on television, putting a stop to bullying (including cyber bulling), and refocusing the nation on the problems of today's youths. In the wake of episodes of school violence, policy makers support more counselors in schools, more before- and after-school programs, more mentoring programs, more conflict resolution programs, a focus on character education, and school-based mental health programs.

Thus, once again, educational, political, and economic trends, as well as the critical needs of today's youths, are redefining the role and function of the professional school counselor. Many of the nation's problems can be addressed through prevention and early intervention initiatives. The demands of a multicultural society, increased diversity, and the need for an educated and caring citizenship affect the initiatives of schools and communities, as well as business and industry, in an effort to prevent the loss of human potential and provide for the total development of our nation's youth.

Fundamentally, public education has undergone a period of sweeping reform and transition (Darling-Hammond, 1996; Elmore, 1996; George & McEwin, 1999; Hargreaves & Fuller, 1992; ASCA 2005a; Education Trust, 2000), affecting the very core of the principles and values in which professional school counselors are trained and will practice in the future. The job description for professional school counselors must be redefined to align effectively with national and state educational objectives. There has been a call to redefine the professional school counselor's job responsibilities to include working with the larger community and ending professional isolation (Hobbs & Collison, 1995; Keys & Bemak, 1997; ASCA 2005a). However, this is difficult with growing student–counselor ratios that exceed the national norm. The need for service integration and coordination within the larger community is critical to addressing the complexity of the problems facing today's youths (Bemak, 2000; Keys, Bemak, Carpenter, & King-Sears, 1998). Educators are recognizing that they will be unable to continue to operate schools without the support and cooperation of the larger community (Dryfoos, 1994; Hobbs & Collison, 1995; Maag & Katsiyannis, 1996). Collaboration between schools and various agencies and organizations produces cohesive delivery systems (Skrtic & Sailor, 1996) as well as the ability to provide a full spectrum of services (Learner, 1995).

DEMAND EXCEEDS AVAILABILITY: UNDERSTANDING EMERGING DEMOGRAPHICS

According to the Children's Defense Fund (2010), "Every day in America:

- Every 10 seconds a high school student drops out of school.
- Every 35 seconds a child is born into poverty in America.
- Every 36 seconds a child is confirmed abused or neglected.
- Every 41 seconds a child is born without health coverage.
- Every minute a baby is born to a teenage mother.
- Every two minutes a baby is born at low birth weight.
- Every 18 minutes a baby dies before his or her first birthday." (p. 8)

It continues with more statistics:

- Every 10 seconds a high school student drops out of school.
- Only about half to two-thirds of children eligible for Head Start are enrolled.
- Only 14% of African American students, 17% of Latino students, and 42% of White 4th graders are reading at grade level.
- Only 11% of African American students, 15% of Latino students, and 41% of White 8th graders perform at grade level in math....
- Every year 13 million children live in poverty, which in turn costs our nation $500 billion in lost productivity higher crime, and poorer health.
- Almost 13 million children in America live in poverty—5.5 million in extreme poverty....
- An African American male born in 2001 has a 1 in 3 chance of going to prison in his lifetime; a Latino boy has a 1 in 6 chance.
- According to the most recent data, more than 3,000 children and teens died from gunfire in 2005, the first increase since 1994.
- Each year 800,000 children spend time in foster care.

Nationally, 99,395 professional school counselors worked in public schools in the 2002–2003 academic year. More than 48.5 million students were enrolled in public schools in 2003–2004, an increase of 5.1 million, or 12%, from 1993–1994. Approximately 6.0 million students or 14% of the total student population received special education services and had an individualized educational plan (IEP) in 2003–2004. English-language learners' services were provided for 3.8 million students or 11% of the total public school population, and 17.5 million or 36% were eligible for free or reduced-price meals (i.e., were living in poverty) (Hoffman, Sable, Naum, & Gray, 2005).

These statistics are often underestimated, especially on the secondary level, because students become sensitive to socioeconomic status among their peers and decline such pejorative services as free and reduced-price lunches. Further, a total of 2.7 million students were awarded a high school diploma in 2002–2003, while almost 47,000 received a certificate of completion or comparable credential because of their special education status or because they failed to complete high school high-stakes testing requirements. Almost 180,000 individuals age 19 or under passed the General Educational Development (GED) test (Hoffman et al., 2005).

These poignant demographics support the need to develop programs and services to close achievement gaps, to meet the needs of children with disabilities, and to assist a growing population of English-language learners in an environment that is increasingly punctuated with violence, abuse, relational aggression, cyber bullying, and gang activity. But this is increasingly difficult to achieve in light of the low counselor-to-student ratios.

The counselor-to-student ratio across the nation is approximately one counselor per 475 students, but as low as one counselor per 1,000 students in some urban areas. According to the American School Counselor Association (2005a) guidelines, schools should have one counselor per 250 students. These numbers make it clear that many students and their families across the nation have very limited access to guidance and counseling services at either the elementary or secondary school level. Figure 1.2 shows

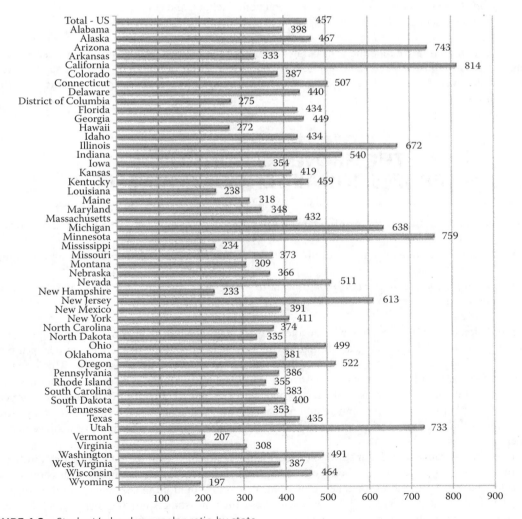

FIGURE 1.2   Student/school counselor ratio by state.

the wide discrepancies between student-to-counselor ratios across the nation. Demand from students and their families for counseling services far exceeds their availability. Students who often need information and assistance the most—minority-group members and the poor—are the least likely to receive the attention they so desperately need. Counselors are habitually assigned administrative tasks such as maintaining records and supervising students, which is an inadequate use of their special skills and talents.

The role of professional school counselors in the schools has undergone major changes in the last decade (Borders & Drury, 1992a; Peeks, 1993; Education Trust, 2000; ASCA 2005a). They need to move quickly to play a greater leadership role in helping schools and communities restructure support programs and services to create comprehensive multifaceted approaches that help *all* students succeed academically. The professional school counselor's role has encompassed such terms as *advocate, catalyst, broker,* and *facilitator of educational reform*, along with such skills as leadership, advocacy, collaboration and teaming, and the use of data and technology (Education Trust, 1997, 2000, 2007; ASCA 2005a). As agents of change, professional school counselors should assume a leadership role in:

- Creating readiness for systematic change
- Helping to develop mechanisms for mapping, analyzing, and redeploying relevant school resources
- Working to strengthen connections between home, school, and community resources (Taylor & Adelman, 2000; ASCA 2005a)

The country's future economic well-being depends on the improvement of professional school counseling programs. But the need for exceptional school counseling programs is even greater, as are the stakes for students who may see professional school counselors as keepers of the gates leading to all future opportunities.

THE GROWING PAINS OF THE PROFESSIONAL SCHOOL COUNSELOR

Within the context of the school, two fundamentally different counselor role orientations have evolved:

- the *guidance counselor* in an administrative role and resource role for facilitating programs and services, and
- the *professional school counselor* in a more therapeutic role and an integral part of school improvement efforts to close the achievement gaps and make all student succeed.

Professional school counselors who devote a larger percentage of their time to planning programs, grouping, making schedule changes, helping in college selection, and job placement are performing the sorting, allocating, and selecting function of the counselor as *guidance administrators*. This orientation embraces the National Defense Education Act of 1958 model for guidance and counseling in the schools. The therapeutic role, however, is more concerned with facilitating a relationship with a counselee to enhance his or her personal development and psychological competencies and ensuring that they provide interventions that prevent barriers to learning and by designing programs to improve achievement and academic success.

The administrative and therapeutic roles represent a major historical dichotomy that has influenced the present status of professional school counseling in the schools. In the past, many professional school counselors have had only a minimal sense of what their role should be in the school, so they turned to clerical and administrative duties (Wittmer, 1993). Absorbing this stance into their perceived professional repertoire has regrettably fostered a perception that professional school counselors are merely ancillary resources who are expendable in the school setting, rather than integral players in the overall school's mission for educational improvement and greater gains in achievement. When strained fiscal budgets occur, professional school counselors are often overloaded with larger time-consuming caseloads or are cut out of the school program altogether.

Currently, across the nation, a critical need exists to provide both early intervention services and services that reflect the changing needs of students and their families. From a primary prevention perspective, the role of the professional school counselor should be to assist individuals in gaining insight into their personal characteristics, in understanding their potentials, and in becoming educated to choose and plan constructive action for personal growth and development.

THE INFLUENCE OF SOCIAL CHANGE

Unfortunately, such views of school reform do not factor into their proposition that in many cases, because of deteriorating situations in homes, schools have become childrearing institutions, one of the few places in their lives where many children find predictability, safety support and food. Schools are one of the few places that allow children to escape violence in the home and in the community, the increasing lawlessness of gangs and cults, physical or psychological neglect in their home, a lack of family presence and support as the return home from school to empty apartments and houses, or to homes where chemical dependency robs parents of their ability to be responsible for the children. Many children are experiencing the multiple conditions of disintegrating families, the special tensions associated with rise of blended families, the growing pockets of child poverty and child malnutrition, and the growth in the number of single parents and grandparents raising children.

Herr (2002, p. 230)

In a period of rapid social change, single-parent families, dual-career households, chemical dependency, international unrest, shifting achievement profiles, greater occupational diversity, and changing population demographics, professional school counselors have come to represent a reservoir of stability and congruency of information. The school that was founded to merely educate must now accommodate and facilitate the psychological growth of both students and their families.

Future issues and trends that will inevitably influence school counseling are more numerous and complex. The following trends will have a significant impact on the services and needs of students and their families, administrators and teachers, and business and industry, both locally and globally:

- Increasing numbers of single-parent and low-income families in poverty
- Lack of supervision of children and a greater need for before- and after-school programs
- More students from minority and immigrant groups whose parents do not speak English
- Greater use of technology in the schools and workplace
- Higher expectations for student performance measured by standards of learning that all children must meet in order to be promoted or to graduate from high school
- More frequent career changes and the increase of portfolio workers
- Increasing violence in schools, families, and communities
- More program evaluation and accountability of programs and services to students and their families
- More brief counseling and solution-focused models in the school settings
- More structured psychoeducational life skills groups to enhance students' social, emotional, and cognitive skills in an effort to prevent violence and conflict and improve peer relationships
- More family counseling rather than consultation with parents from diverse family constellations and increasing need for home visits

- More family interventions to improve students' academic and behavioral problems
- More primary prevention and outreach rather than crisis intervention protocols
- Higher academic standards, with barrier tests to meet high school graduation requirements
- An increased focus on getting first-generation students into community colleges and universities
- More communication with parents from a variety of resources (e.g., home visits, voice mail, email, Internet websites, and social networking outlets)
- More early intervention with students at risk of failure at the preschool and primary school levels
- More emphasis on remediating social, emotional, and cognitive deficits in both children and adults
- More full-service or parallel schools that integrate community services within the school setting (such as health, mental health, and social agency services)
- Increased infusion of mental health services in schools and increasing recognition of students who are functioning outside the range of normal development
- Increased knowledge of community resources and partnerships with community agencies to provide services from child and family welfare, juvenile justice, social service, health care, and after-school supervision
- Increased emphasis on multicultural counseling techniques and on how culture affects student and family behavior, attitudes, feelings, and bonding with the school—for example, a professional school counselor taking a leadership role to reduce interethnic and interracial conflicts in the school and reaching out to immigrant families in their language of origin
- Increased resources, professional development, and opportunities for the current influx of a more diverse student populations (e.g., students from Africa, Central America, Asia, eastern Europe, and the Middle East)
- A redefinition of the professional school counselor role and function with respect to meeting the growing mental health needs of children and adolescents amid the concomitant problems that currently exist
- A greater demand for professional school counselors to maximize their skills with training and supervision in solution-focused counseling and providing psychoeducational groups for both students and families

To fulfill these emerging trends and issues, ASCA (2009) recently adopted the following statement on the role of the professional school counselor:

> Professional school counselors are certified/licensed educators with a minimum of a master's degree in school counseling making them uniquely qualified to address all students' academic, personal/social and career development needs by designing, implementing, evaluating and enhancing a comprehensive school counseling program that promotes and enhances student success. Professional school counselors are employed in elementary, middle/junior high and high schools; in district supervisory positions; and counselor education positions.
>
> Professional school counselors serve a vital role in maximizing student success (Lapan, Gysbers, & Kayson, 2007; Stone & Dahir, 2006). Through leadership, advocacy and collaboration, professional school counselors promote equity and access to rigorous educational experiences for all students. Professional school counselors support a safe learning environment and work to safeguard the human rights of all members of the school community (Sandhu, 2000), and address the needs of all students through culturally relevant prevention and intervention programs that are a part of a comprehensive school counseling program (Lee, 2001). The American School Counselor Association recommends a counselor-to-student ratio of 1:250.

Professional school counselors are responsible for developing comprehensive school counseling programs that promote and enhance student learning. By providing interventions within a comprehensive program, professional school counselors focus their skills, time, and energies on direct services to students, staff, and families. The ASCA model recommends that professional school counselors spend at least 70% of their time in direct services to students.

Above all, professional school counselors are student advocates who work cooperatively with other individuals and organizations within and outside the school to promote the development of children and families in their communities. Professional school counselors, as members of the educational team, consult and collaborate with teachers, administrators, families, and the greater community to assist students to be successful academically, vocationally, and personally. They work on behalf of students and their families to ensure that all school programs facilitate the educational process and offer the opportunity for school success for each student and prevent barriers to learning. Professional school counselors are an integral part of all school efforts, not an ancillary service, and strive to insure a safe and productive learning environment for all members of the school community. This comprehensive role is more inclusive to meet the needs of all children. It truly articulates the professional school counselor's role in three critical domains: career, academic, and personal/social development.

THE ROLE OF THE PROFESSIONAL ELEMENTARY SCHOOL COUNSELOR

The elementary school counselor is trained to meet the developmental needs of all students and to help them prosper as they confront critical issues in the process of growing, developing, and achieving. Elementary school counselors are specialists in child growth and development who have a strong background in the behavioral sciences and human relations. They possess knowledge of the elementary school program, including the curriculum, the learning process, the organization of school services, and community resources.

The elementary school counselor counsels students in the domains of primary prevention and intervention; consults with parents, teachers, and other helping professionals regarding student needs; coordinates school and community services; manages classroom guidance programs; conducts needs assessments and program evaluations; and participates in curriculum development. Program goals for elementary counselors could include but are not limited to:

- Helping children understand themselves and others
- Helping prevent self-defeating problems from developing
- Helping to identify children with special needs and finding appropriate school community services
- Providing crisis intervention and crisis management
- Collaborating with and coordinating efforts among parents, teachers, and school/community programs
- Individualizing programs and services, when applicable, based on child's strengths and weaknesses
- Assisting in providing career education awareness
- Coordinating special programs such as child safety, drug abuse prevention, and child abuse detection
- Enhancing social, emotional, and cognitive skills

THE ROLE OF THE PROFESSIONAL MIDDLE SCHOOL COUNSELOR

Middle school and/or junior high professional school counselors are confronted with early adolescence, a time when students are engaged in developmental exploration and experimentation to find out who they are, what they believe and value, and what they want to accomplish in life. The dependency of childhood is rapidly being replaced by concern for self and a need for enhanced interpersonal and intrapersonal skills. Often, teasing by peers is a problem because of advanced physical maturity or underdevelopment. Bullying by peers has also become a serious problem at this developmental level, especially with the advent of the Internet and social networking sites. Professional middle school counselors who are specialists in early adolescent growth and development address personal, emotional, social, educational, and vocational and career topics. Early adolescent issues include:

- Exploring options
- Coping with change
- Building relationships
- Formulating career and educational goals
- Dealing with peer pressure
- Being accepted by peers and adults
- Increasing self-understanding
- Adjusting to success and failure
- Developing problem-solving and decision-making skills
- Enhancing social, emotional, and cognitive skills

THE ROLE OF THE PROFESSIONAL HIGH SCHOOL COUNSELOR

The fundamental objective of the school counseling program at the secondary level is to assist students' transition into adulthood and appropriate career or educational paths. Students need counseling on personal, social, emotional, educational, and career issues that affect their lives. The secondary professional school counselor must develop and implement a comprehensive developmental counseling program that is life skills–based to assist students in developing interpersonal relationship skills, an awareness of personal strengths and weaknesses, independent living skills, problem-solving and decision-making skills, an appreciation of each person's uniqueness, and an acceptance and tolerance of individual differences. The developmental needs of all secondary or high school students include:

- Acquiring self-knowledge
- Developing specific career and educational goals
- Adjusting to changing social and economic conditions
- Planning a career and educational program to achieve goals
- Developing problem-solving and decision-making skills
- Coping with the outcome of decisions that are made
- Enhancing social, emotional, and cognitive skills

THE BENEFITS OF SCHOOL COUNSELING: OUTCOME RESEARCH

To further reinforce the value of the professional school counseling programs, numerous studies have documented outcome research to support the efficacy of professional school counseling programs. All counseling activities are coming under closer scrutiny, given the incessant stress on accountability (Sexton & Whiston, 1996). Inherently, outcome studies related to school counseling are consistent with other investigations of the influence of school counseling interventions and subsequent outcomes (Perry, 1993; Sexton, 1996).

It is important that role and function be articulated to all stakeholders: those who need to know what professional school counselors do (politicians, school board members) and those who need to know what our interventions have accomplished (parents, teachers, and administrators). Professional school counselors must be able to demonstrate how students are different because of their efforts.

A review of what has been empirically revealed about the counseling process and potential benefits also is important for the practicing professional school counselor. A compendium of empirical studies from the last three decades reveals information in three domains: the personal/social, academic/educational, and career development domains. As Perry (1993) aptly states, it is critical that school counselors be informed of outcome research and know which activities are supported by research and which are not. Borders and Drury (1992a) maintain that school counseling interventions have positive impacts on students. However, demonstrating what professional school counselors do with empirical studies (both quantitative and qualitative research) has been somewhat neglected in the last decade because legislative mandates such as the No Child Left Behind Act have dominated the educational landscape and program initiatives.

The Personal/Social Domain

- Longitudinal follow-ups of persons exposed to counseling and related guidance processes in high school can be distinguished on such criteria as higher income and contributions to society from follow-ups of their peers who did not participate in guidance and counseling (Campbell, 1965). Counselors who predominantly used individual counseling were more effective than those counselors who predominantly used classroom guidance activities (Wiggins & Wiggins, 1992). Group intervention using role-playing, expressive techniques (drawing), and peer discussion with adolescents from divorced families had a positive effect on adolescents' self-concept and locus of control (Omizo & Omizo, 1988b; Thompson, 1996, 2006).
- In follow-up studies of high school students at 2-, 5-, and 10-year intervals, differences were found between those who received extensive counseling and guidance services and those who received no special counseling efforts. The experimental students had better academic records after high school, made more realistic and more consistent vocational choices, made more progress in their employment, and were more satisfied with their lives (Prediger, Roth, & Noeth, 1973). Classroom guidance activities had a positive influence on academic achievement (Lee, 1993; Lavoritano & Segal, 1992).
- During periods of sociocultural transition, professional school counselors who are specially trained to provide personal counseling, resolve interpersonal conflicts, and coordinate classes designed to improve students' human relations skills and their understanding of different racial/ethnic groups can assist in reducing prejudice and conflict (Gordon, Brownell, & Brittell, 1972; Higgins, 1976; Katz & Zalk, 1978; Lewis & Lewis, 1970) and have positive impacts on students (Borders & Drury, 1992).
- The higher the degree of therapeutic conditions provided by the professional school counselor, the more likely it is that the counselee will achieve constructive change (Carkhuff & Berenson, 1976; Egan, 1982; Egan & Cowan, 1979; Herr, 1976; Lewis & Schaffner, 1970). Group counseling, mentoring, and behavior modification were found to be effective interventions with children who were having serious health problems (Cox, 1994; Katz, Rubinstein, Hubert, & Blew, 1988; Richburg & Cobia, 1994).
- It has been documented that students who have been helped by counselors to evaluate, break into components, and master their problems gain self-confidence (Bennett, 1975;

Herr, 1976). Study-skills classroom guidance programs designed to increase self-efficacy, awareness of metacognitive skills, and knowledge of learning styles resulted in dramatic increases in students' standardized achievement scores at the elementary level (Carns & Carns, 1991; Thompson, 1998). Single-session brief individual counseling using a problem-focused-with-task model, a problem-focused-without-task model, or a solution-focused-with-task model have been effective with secondary students (Littrell, Malia, & Vanderwood, 1995).

- Counseling activities can help children with self-concept development, peer relationships, improved adult–youth relationships, academic achievement, and career development (Thompson & Poppen, 1979). Integrating family systems approaches (e.g., structural-communications, strategic, and solution-focused models) to resolve school behavior problems have been demonstrated as effective (Morrison, Olivos, Dominguez, Gomez, & Lena, 1993).

- It has been recognized that group counseling sessions incorporating cognitive-behavioral techniques, modeling, role-playing, and positive reinforcement have been effective with children who display aggressive and hostile behaviors (Omizo, Hershberger, & Omizo, 1988; Thompson, 1999). Social skills training was found to be effective with children who were having behavioral problems (Verduyn, Lord, & Forrest, 1990; Thompson, 1999), with children who were learning disabled (Omizo & Omizo, 1988a), and with gifted students (Ciechalski & Schmidt, 1995).

- As a function of behavioral modification techniques, delinquent boys in a community-based home tend to improve dramatically in self-esteem and to move from external to internal locus of control as compared with a control group. Effective behavioral contracts have been shown to improve behavior (Thompson, 1999).

- Affective education provided by trained professional school counselors can improve racial understanding (Sue, 1978; Sue & Sue, 1977). Participation in primary prevention programs is helpful to students (Baker, Swisher, Nadenichek, & Popowicz, 1984; Sprinthall, 1981). D'Andrea & Daniels (1995) found that a multicultural group guidance project was effective in increasing social development with elementary students from diverse backgrounds.

- A rise in the self-esteem of students exposed to guidance and other counseling processes is related to a reduction in dropout rates, fewer school absences, and improvement in conduct and social adjustment (Bennett, 1975; Wiggins, 1977). Classroom guidance groups designed to promote wellness resulted in more knowledge about wellness and increased self-esteem (Omizo, Omizo, & D'Andrea, 1992). A developmental program designed to promote moral development among children with discipline problems showed a significant decrease in inappropriate behavior and more positive attitudes toward school (Brake & Gerler, 1994).

- Students exposed to the guidance and counseling process tend to organize their concepts about themselves in a more coherent way and to reconcile their differences between ideal and real self-concepts more effectively than persons without such experiences (Schunk, 1981; Washington, 1977; R. A. Thompson, 1987). In addition, Walsh-Bowers (1992) found that a creative drama prevention program for easing the transition from elementary to middle or junior high school strengthened peer relationships. Middle school students exposed to guidance and counseling initiatives designed to improve their interpersonal skills experience improved general behavior and interpersonal relationships (Hutchins & Cole, 1986).

- Minority students who are assisted in deciding on vocational objectives are typically found to have more positive self-concepts and higher ideal selves than those who do not have such objectives (Bennett, 1975; R. A. Thompson, 1985, 1987). Dunn and Veltman (1989) developed a summer program for minority adolescents that blended academics, career exploration, and career shadowing; this program significantly increased the overall career maturity of participants. Isaacs and Duffus (1995) created a "Scholars' Club," an organization designed to increase achievement and self-esteem of minority students. Members of the pilot study increased their grade point average by 52%, and 75% attended college immediately after high school.

- Individual counseling in combination with counselor-connected training programs designed to develop interpersonal, physical, emotional, and intellectual skills that are transferable to home, school, and community can reduce the recidivism rate of youthful offenders (Lewis & Boyle, 1976) and help at-risk youth (Thompson, 1998). Cognitive-behavioral stress management programs have had positive benefits for students who reported high levels of emotional arousal (Haines, 1994).
- Secondary students have been assisted through counseling to overcome debilitating behaviors such as anorexia, depressions, and substance abuse (Beck, Rush, Shaw, & Emery, 1979; Burns, 1981; Halmi, 1983; Johnston, Bachman, & O'Malley, 1982; Jones, 1980; Lazarus, 1981; Thompson, 1998).
- After peer counseling, counselees exhibited higher scores on communication skills, were better able to discuss plans for the future and school problems, and showed transference of peer mediation skills to conflicts with siblings at home. Students who were self-referred reported greater overall satisfaction than students who were referred by teachers or a counselor (Diver-Stamnes, 1991; Gentry & Benenson, 1992; Johnson, Johnson, Dudley, Ward, & Magnuson, 1995; Morey, Miller, Fulton, Rosen, & Daly, 1989; Morey, Miller, Rosen, & Fulton, 1993; Robinson, Morrow, Kigin, & Lindeman, 1991).
- Shechtman (2002) reviewed outcome research on group psychotherapy with children and found that in order to improve achievement, it is important to address the social, emotional, and academic needs of students. Zins, Weissberg, Wang, and Walberg (2004) made a strong empirical case linking social-emotional learning to improved behavioral and academic performance. Greenberg, Weissberg, O'Brien, Zins, Fredericks, Resnik, and Elias (2003), in a large review of school-based prevention programs, found school-based interventions built on coordinated social, emotional, and academic learning to be critically linked to positive social and academic outcomes. Other researchers also support a link between social-emotional learning and academic achievement particularly among students at risk for academic failure (Arbona, 2000; Daly, Duhon, & Witt, 2002; Kamps & Kay, 2001).
- Tobias and Myrick (1999) explored the impact of peer-led groups that focused on sixth-graders' self-concept, attitude toward school and others, attendance, and improving grades. They found that the students in the experimental group significantly increased their grades, attended school more regularly, and were less likely to be referred for disciplinary problems.

The Academic/Educational and Career Development Domains

- Either group or individual counseling extended for a reasonable amount of time helps students whose ability is adequate or better to improve their scholastic performance; greater results are likely if intervention focuses on the variables that predict underachievement rather than relying on more general approaches (Laport & Noth, 1976; Schmidt, 1976; R. A. Thompson, 1987). Nearpass (1990) found that using individual counseling and interventions that focus on improving school attendance were more effective than group counseling (including small group, larger group, and classroom interventions). Omizo, Omizo, and D'Andrea (1992) found that classroom guidance activities had more of an impact on achievement than on measures of self-esteem. Hadley (1988) and R. S. Lee (1993) also found that classroom guidance activities had a positive influence on academic achievement.
- Professional counselor teams that work closely with teachers, principals, and parents in dealing with emotional or social problems that are interfering with children's use of their intellectual potential are helpful in increasing general levels of student academic achievement (Bertoldi, 1975; Thompson, 1987). Group counseling was more effective than individual interventions

for secondary students (Prout & DeMartino, 1986; R. A. Thompson, 2000). Carns and Carns (1991) found that a study-skills guidance program resulted in dramatic increases in students' standardized achievement scores if it was designed to increase self-efficacy awareness of meta-cognitive skills and knowledge of learning styles. Fouad (1995) was successful in implementing a yearlong middle school intervention to infuse math and science career awareness into the eighth-grade curriculum.

- Interventions with upper-level high school students were more effective than interventions directed at lower-level students (R. A. Thompson, 1987; Nearpass, 1990). Academically gifted students who have difficulties with career decision making due to their "multipotentiality" benefited from career workshops that combined clarification of needs and values, goal setting, and individual career counseling (Hong, Whiston, & Milgram, 1993; Kerr & Ghrist-Priebe, 1988).

- Creative drama prevention programs have been effective in easing the transition from elementary to middle or junior high school (Walsh-Bowers, 1992).

- A collaborative language arts and career guidance unit focusing on learning to select and use references, organizing information, summarizing information, and using various sources of information have been effective on the secondary level in increasing vocational identity and positive feelings among students, teachers, and counselors (Lapan, Gysbers, Hughey, & Arni, 1993; Hughey, Lapan, & Gysbers, 1993).

- Guidance and counseling processes integrated with remedial instruction in mathematics and reading have been found to increase academic achievement significantly (Bertoldi, 1975; E. C. Thompson, 1987).

- Through group problem-solving methods, students can be helped to understand the relationship between educational and vocational development, to clarify goals, and to acquire skills in identifying and using relevant information for their decision making (Babcock & Kaufman, 1976; Martin & Stone, 1977; Stewart & Thoreson, 1968; Thompson, R. A., 1987, 1999).

- Students utilizing computer-based career guidance systems make larger gains than nonusers in such characteristics as degree of preparedness, knowledge and use of resources for career exploration, awareness of career options available to them, and cost–benefit risks associated with these options (Meyer, Strowig, & Hosford, 1970). Programs that teach parents skills for assisting their adolescent children's career development have been successful (Kush & Cochran, 1993; Palmer & Cochran, 1988).

- Short-term counseling (three sessions) with high school students has been found to facilitate the career maturity of these students with regard to such emphases as orientation to decision making, preparedness, and independence of choice (Flake, Roach, & Stenning, 1975; Thompson, 1999, 2000).

- Comprehensive programs involving self-awareness activities, job-seeking skills, peer interaction through group sessions, counseling, career materials displays, and testing information meetings cause observable, positive change among rural youths (Herr, 1976; Meyer et al., 1970; Wiggins, 1977).

- Students exposed to systematically planned career guidance classes dealing with topics such as values clarification, decision making, job satisfaction, sources of occupational information, work-power projections, and career planning make greater gains in self-knowledge and the relations of self-knowledge to occupations and engage in a greater number of career-planning activities than students who have not participated in such classes (Griggs, 1983; Krumboltz & Thoresen, 1964). Programs that emphasize career maturity enhancement, communication skills training, and deliberate psychological education programs have significant effects (Baker et al., 1984).

- Edmondson and White (1998) found that an intervention composed of tutoring plus counseling, compared to tutoring alone or no treatment, was an effective means for increasing the academic achievement of middle school students.

- Brigman and Goodman (2008) used classroom guidance and group counseling in their attempt to influence the academic achievement of 180 students. The students involved in the research scored between the 25th and 50th percentiles on the Florida Comprehensive Assessment Test (FCAT).
- Studies by Floyd (1996) and Keith and Lichtman (1994) support the efficacy of parental involvement as a means of improving academic achievement.
- Lapan, Gysbers, and Petroski (2001) found that students who attended schools with more fully implemented comprehensive school counseling programs reported that they earned higher *importance of school counselors* grades, had better relationships with their teachers, were getting a more relevant education, and had a more positive view of their school environment than students who did not have a comprehensive school counseling program.
- Thompson and O'Quinn (2001) reported that key ingredients in increasing the academic success of students are lower class size in kindergarten through third grade; experienced, fully prepared teachers; and the presence of supportive, ongoing, remedial services.
- Trusty (2004) and Trusty and Niles (2003) found that taking rigorous courses in high school has a strong effect on success in college.
- Webb, Brigman, and Campbell (2005) and Campbell and Brigman (2005) used the Student Success Skills (SSS) approach to improved the academic achievement and behavior of students in grades 5 and 6. The school counseling profession and the larger educational community are validating school counselor outcome data aimed at improving student learning began receiving increased amounts of attention. The SSS model also aligns directly with the ASCA (2005a) National Model with its focus on academic and social competence (Carey, 2004; Dahir, 2004; Myrick, 2003a; Paisley & Hayes, 2003; Sink & Stroh, 2003).

THE ASCA NATIONAL STANDARDS FOR SCHOOL COUNSELING PROGRAMS

Some critics have argued that counseling has been reluctant to identify "best practices" for delivering mental health and counseling services (Granello & Granello, 2007; Center for Mental Health in the Schools, 2006). Accountability in services and programs promotes growth and recognition for the profession. Today more than ever, it is critical for professional school counselors to demonstrate to the public and to public policy makers that their practices are effective and efficient, as well as ethical.

The National Standards for School Counseling Programs represents ASCA's (1999c, 2003b, 2004b, 2005) vision and commitment to bringing about necessary and positive changes in professional school counseling programs that will assist students in meeting the educational expectations and challenges of the next century. The standards provide an opportunity for professional school counselors, school administrators, faculty, parents, business, and the community to engage in conversations about expectations for students' academic success and the role of professional school counseling programs in enhancing student learning.

The ASCA National Standards for students do not substitute for, nor do they replace, a comprehensive developmental model. Standards define what students should know and be able to do as a result of participating in professional school counseling programs. A comprehensive developmental program model defines how services are delivered. In contrast, the national standards offer the framework for a consistent model for professional school counseling programs.

The ASCA standards provide the framework through which schools, school districts, and state professional school counseling programs can compare their already identified student competencies with the list of generic student competencies developed as part of the national standards. The list of student competencies under each standard is based on extensive research conducted with school counselors at all work-settings and can be used easily with only minor adaptations. The student competencies in the national standards describe the attitudes, skills, and knowledge that students need when they leave the K–12 educational system.

Widespread use of the national standards will provide more consistency in the description of professional school counseling programs and the services that need to be provided. They help to eliminate the confusion of trying to understand how school counseling programs benefit students. More solidarity, consistency, structure, and clarity in program standards will help to strengthen programs locally and nationally. They provide a benchmark for the elimination of significant gaps among students from different economic classes, genders, races, and ethnic groups. Consistency in expectations across all levels of education—elementary, middle, and high schools—has also been established. Standards provide the basis for assessing program quality. The evaluation process determines what students have learned as a result of participating in a national standards-based program. Measurable success demonstrates the effectiveness of professional school counseling programs and services.

The national standards outline the vision and goals for 21st-century professional school counseling programs. The nine ASCA National Standards shift the focus from the professional school counselor to the school counseling program. The standards create a framework for a national model for school counseling programs; establish school counseling as an integral component of the academic mission of the school; provide for equitable access to school counseling services for all students; identify the key components of a developmental school counseling program; identify the knowledge and skills that all students should acquire as a result of the K–12 school counseling program; and ensure that professional school counseling programs are comprehensive in design and delivered systematically for all students (Dahir, 1997, p. 11).

Furthermore, the ASCA National Standards emphasize the role school counselors can play in student achievement. The student competencies define the specific knowledge, attitudes, and skills that students should obtain or demonstrate as a result of participating in a school counseling program. School counselors, as education professionals, join with teachers and school administrators to improve student success in school. The professional school counselor nurtures student aspirations and orchestrates success for individual students and the total school improvement initiatives.

As a response to the National Educational Reform initiatives, ASCA (1999a) published the ASCA *National Standards for School Counseling Programs* as a benchmark for school counselors and school systems to further their own programs to meet the needs of all students in the new millennium. The standards list student competencies and articulate student outcomes. The ASCA National Standards focus on three broad areas: *academic development, career development,* and *personal/social development.* Implementing a comprehensive developmental school counseling program assists students in acquiring skills in these three domains.

The ASCA National Standards for academic development outline strategies, activities, skills, attitudes, and knowledge that will maximize each student's ability to learn. The focus is on integrating strategies to achieve success and developing an understanding of the relationship of course content, the world of work, and preparation for life.

The national standards for career development provide the foundation for a successful transition from school to work and from job to career across the life span. Career development employs strategies for achieving future career success and job satisfaction. Students are engaged in developing career goals as a result of participating in a comprehensive plan of career awareness, exploration, and preparation activities.

Finally, the national standards for personal/social development assist students in acquiring the skills, attitudes, and knowledge they need to understand and respect themselves and others; to acquire effective interpersonal skills; to assimilate social, emotional, and cognitive skills to improve the way they think, feel, and relate to peers and others; and to negotiate their way in the increasingly complex and diverse world of the new millennium.

A selection of the national standards follows (ASCA, 1999a). A complete version can be accessed at http://www.schoolcounselor.org.

Academic Development

The academic development domain includes the acquisition of skills in decision making, problem solving, goal setting, critical thinking, logical reasoning, and interpersonal communication and the application of these skills to academic achievement. An example of the standards is:

> *Standard A: Students will acquire the attitudes, knowledge, and skills that contribute to effective learning in school and across the lifespan*
>> **Student competencies: Improve academic self-concept.** Students will:
> * Articulate feelings of competence and confidence as learners;
> * Display a positive interest in learning;
> * Take pride in work and in achievement;
> * Accept mistakes as essential to the learning process; and
> * Identify attitudes and behaviors for successful learning.
>
>> **Student competencies: acquire skills for improving learning.** Students will:
> * Apply time management and task management skills;
> * Demonstrate how effort and persistence positively affect learning;
> * Use communication skills to know when and how to ask for help; and
> * Apply learning styles to positively influence school performance.

Career Development

Career development includes strategies and activities that support and enable students to develop a positive attitude toward work as well as the skills necessary to make a successful transition from school to work and from job to job across the life career span. The career development standards reflect the recommendations of the Organization for Economic Cooperation and Development (OECD, 2000) indicators.

> *Standard A: Students will acquire the skills to investigate the world of work in relation to knowledge of self and to make informed career decisions*
>> **Student competencies: develop career awareness.** Students will:
> * Develop skills to locate, evaluate, and interpret career information;
> * Learn about the variety of traditional and nontraditional occupations; and
> * Develop an awareness of personal abilities, skills, interests, and motivations.

Personal/Social Development

Standards in the personal/social area guide the professional school counseling program in implementing strategies and activities that support and maximize each student's personal growth and well-being and that enhance students' educational and career development.

> *Standard A: Students will acquire the knowledge, attitudes, and interpersonal skills to help them understand and respect self and others*
>> **Student competencies: acquire self-knowledge.** Students will:
> * Develop a positive attitude toward self as a unique and worthy person;
> * Identify personal values, attitudes, and beliefs;
> * Learn the goal-setting process;
> * Understand change as a part of growth;
> * Identify and express feelings;
> * Distinguish between appropriate and inappropriate behaviors;
> * Recognize personal boundaries, rights, and privacy needs;
> * Understand the need for self-control and how to practice it;

- Demonstrate cooperative behavior in groups;
- Identify personal strengths and assets;
- Identify and discuss changing personal and social roles; and
- Identify and recognize changing family roles.

Student competencies: acquire interpersonal skills. Students will:
- Recognize that everyone has rights and responsibilities, including family and friends;
- Respect alternative points of view;
- Recognize, accept, respect, and appreciate individual differences;
- Recognize, accept, and appreciate ethnic and cultural diversity,
- Recognize and respect differences in various family configurations;
- Use effective communication skills;
- Know that communication involves speaking, listening, and nonverbal behavior;
- Learn how to communicate effectively with family; and
- Learn how to make and keep friends.

The ASCA National Standards can guide state and local initiatives by grade level (see Tables 1.5 through 1.7). Standards represent broad guidelines for services. Curriculum represents the means to fulfill the various developmental issues socially, emotionally, and cognitively.

Professional school counselors also should enhance their role as human development specialists. Teachers and professional school counselors in partnerships could both become committed to effective counseling programs with a shared philosophy. Teachers, administrators, and support personnel need to assume more of the *guidance role* when nurturing children and adolescents. This involves providing therapeutic services that focus on life skills within a program development model that reflects consumer/community need.

Moreover, professional school counselors, teachers, administrators, parents, and important stakeholders must be integral partners in school improvement efforts and be significantly involved in all aspects of a comprehensive school counseling program. Educational and occupational planning, placement, and referral are three related areas that can become a shared responsibility of all members of the school staff. Professional school counselors need to acquire more skills in consulting to provide essential staff development experiences and to learn how to use the talents and resources of their colleagues. Inherently, professional school counselors, teachers, and administrators need to recognize that they are all members of the same team to improve student achievement and overall well-being. Ultimately, the goal is to enhance the academic, career, and personal/social competencies of all students.

THE IMPORTANCE OF COLLABORATING, TEAMING, AND ADVOCATING FOR PROGRAMS AND SERVICES

Professional school counselors must conduct an assessment of what models of school counseling are most likely to be effective given specific student needs, educational priorities, and availability of resources. Partnerships with service providers in the broader community are also helpful and productive (Dryfoos, 1994). Lavigne and colleagues (1998) report that the number of school-based mental health centers in the United States grew from 350 centers in 1992 to 607 centers in 1994 and 888 in 1996; 61% of these had full-time staff in school settings. In a transformed model of school counseling, the professional school counselor provides leadership within the school for an alliance with school-based mental health professionals and helps to establish school-based mechanisms to support a variety of collaborative efforts, such as those listed below.

School-family-community mental health teams bring together school-based personnel, family members, and representatives from service institutions (social services, health and mental health, juvenile justice, police) and helping institutions (churches, parks and recreation, libraries) for joint program planning (Keys & Bemak, 1997). The teams work to assure that school- and community-based programs are complementary and continuous.

TABLE 1.5 Elementary School Counseling Outcome Objectives

Academic Development

ES 1: The student will develop an orientation to the educational environment.

ES 2: The student will resolve problems that interfere with learning.

ES 3: The student will gain knowledge of his or her academic abilities, including strengths, educational needs, and interests.

ES 4: The student will gain knowledge of effective study skills.

ES 5: The student will pursue a planned and balanced program of studies consistent with abilities, interests, and educational needs.

Career Development

ES 6: The student will acquire knowledge of curricular alternatives available in the schools and the career goals to which they may lead.

ES 7: The student will become aware of and knowledgeable about the world of work.

ES 8: The student will develop positive work habits, skills, and attitudes.

ES 9: The student will understand that school experiences and learning help to develop skills and behaviors needed for life and work.

ES 10: The student will understand that workers in certain occupations require specific interests, abilities, personal characteristics, and training.

Personal/Social Development

ES 11: The student will develop increased self-understanding.

ES 12: The student will develop understanding of others and learn appropriate modes of interacting and communicating for the establishment of positive relationships.

ES 13: The student will acquire problem-solving, decision-making, coping, and mastery skills.

ES 14: The student will become increasingly self-directive and responsible for one's own behavior.

ES 15: The student will develop understanding of the need for positive attitudes toward school, learning, community, and society.

ES 16: The student will participate in small-group opportunities to enhance his or her social, emotional, and cognitive skills.

Note: ES = Elementary School

The team meets on a regular basis to identify school-family-community needs; specify mutual goals; develop a coordinated plan for services within the school and between the school and the broader community; initiate new programs; oversee communication about services and programs to students, school staff, families, and community agencies and institutions; and make recommendations for changes to school, agency, and governmental policies. This school-family-community mental health team supplants the more narrowly focused guidance advisory committee, the program planning body used by some professional school counselors (Wittmer, 1993). This new school-family-community team also works closely with the school improvement team to assure concurrence with broader school goals and higher academic standards articulated by national educational reform movements.

Program development groups are a second organizational mechanism that the professional school counselor takes responsibility for establishing and coordinating. The program development group, a subcommittee of the larger mental health team, meets to develop a plan or prepare a proposal for the larger team's consideration (Adelman & Taylor, 1993). The group is charged with developing a plan for community outreach, devising a strategy for identifying leaders in the community, and soliciting help from community groups to serve as mentors.

After completing this needs assessment process, the program development committee develops an intervention to assist families with the identified problem areas. Within this organizational model, the mental health team oversees all aspects of the program development group's work. Several program

TABLE 1.6 Middle School Counseling Outcome Objectives

Academic Development

MS 1: The student will gain an understanding of the educational environment and standards such as changing classes, grading, the honor roll system, rules and regulations, and specific programs such as enrichment, gifted, extracurricular, and counseling programs.

MS 2: The student will identify and examine problems that interfere with learning and development, in order to meet requirements of state-mandated standards of learning.

MS 3: The student will gain knowledge of academic and vocational abilities, needs, and interests.

MS 4: The student will gain knowledge about types of middle school courses, high school programs of studies, graduation requirements, and the general career directions to which these may lead.

MS 5: The student will gain knowledge of themselves and information from their records, such as grades, test scores, individual career plans, and interest inventories in developing a program of studies.

Career Development

MS 6: The student will become aware of careers, work attitudes, work values, educational/vocational job requirements, skill levels, lifestyles, career clusters, career ladders, and worker traits.

MS 7: The student will acquire information on curricular offerings, both academic and vocational, college vocational/technical/academic requirements, and postsecondary educational opportunities for further education and work.

MS 8: The student will acquire information about educational and vocational/training opportunities within and beyond school.

MS 9: The student will establish tentative career objectives.

MS 10: The student will begin and continue preparation for further education and employment.

Personal/Social Development

MS 11: The student will develop self-understanding by focusing on characteristics, emotions, attitudes, aptitudes, beliefs, interests, and behaviors.

MS 12: The student will develop understanding of positive relationships and acquiring effective interpersonal and communication skills.

MS 13: The student will continue learning decision-making/problem-solving processes and their application to problems of daily living.

MS 14: The student will gain coping behaviors and be provided with opportunities to learn coping skills for self-defeating behaviors that interfere with positive relationships.

MS 15: The student will gain an understanding of expected and accepted behaviors in school and the community.

MS 16: The student will participate in small-group opportunities to enhance their social, emotional, and cognitive skills.

Note: MS = Middle School

development groups may be operating, each focusing on different mental health needs of the student population (Adelman & Taylor, 1993).

Case management teams are a third mechanism in the transformed school counseling program's organizational structure. These school-based teams represent another subgroup of the larger school-family-community mental health team. Team members may include a school administrator, the professional school counselor, school social workers, the school psychologist, the school nurse or a representative from the local health department, the student's teacher or teachers, and representatives from the local department of mental health and other service agencies. The case management team is a multidisciplinary intervention for students with complex needs that cannot be addressed adequately by one person or service institution alone. Referrals come from school personnel, parents, or agencies. The team reviews each case with the referral source at a team meeting, develops an action plan of coordinated services, and monitors the plan's implementation (Hobbs & Collison, 1995).

TABLE 1.7   High School Counseling Outcome Objectives

Academic Development

HS 1: The student will gain understanding from interest inventories, achievement and aptitude tests, self-appraisal techniques, and personal data information to assess abilities, strengths, educational needs, and interests.

HS 2: The student will enhance effective study skills and test-taking strategies.

HS 3: The student will acquire continued knowledge of curricular alternatives available and the educational and vocational opportunities to which they may lead.

HS 4: The student will gain a comprehensive understanding of school-to-work opportunities and plan a corresponding program of studies.

HS 5: The student will plan a program of studies consistent with interest and measured ability, past achievement, and measured and expressed interests.

Career Development

HS 6: The student will be able to locate, evaluate, and interpret information about career and vocational opportunities.

HS 7: The student will acquire skills within the curriculum with increased attention on preparation and entry requirements for different occupational and career levels.

HS 8: The student will relate knowledge of self and assess abilities, occupational interests, and motivation to pursue careers consistent with student needs and aspirations.

HS 9: The student will establish career objectives based on annual reassessment of tentative career objectives in view of developmental changes, new knowledge, work experience, and developmental career objectives.

HS 10: The student will prepare for further education and employment by focusing on developing educational and job search plans that reflect continued learning directed toward preparation for and achieving career/vocational goals. Emphasis will also be placed on the steps required for entrance into training and postsecondary educational programs and financial aid for postsecondary education.

Personal/Social Development

HS 11: The student will develop an understanding of factors that result in a positive self-concept, such as identification of one's personal strengths and weaknesses, environmental influences, personal attributes, and self-management.

HS 12: The student will acquire skills for effective functioning in a social group, such as cooperation, communication, respect for others, and handling stress and conflict.

HS 13: The student will demonstrate acceptable personal behaviors in school tasks, accepting responsibility for one's decisions and the consequences of self-defeating behavior.

HS 14: The student will demonstrate an understanding of the importance of social, emotional, and cognitive skills and use such skills for conflict resolution, anger management, perspective taking, etc.

HS 15: The student will develop characteristics consistent with the norms of behavior and expectations of the school and community by demonstrating the principals of respect and service learning.

HS 16: The student will participate in small-group opportunities to enhance social, emotional, and cognitive skills.

Note: HS = High School

CONCLUSION

Programs and amenities spun from the school counseling process have been diverse and numerous. They demonstrate that support for and availability of professional school counseling programs, services, and processes do make a significant difference in the lives of children, youths, and adults. Fundamental techniques and processes have demonstrated universal utility in a wide arena of human problems and can be applied and modified to respond to changing populations and social conditions. These benefits are particularly critical in view of the growing concern over the maladies of today's youths.

APPENDIX: RAMP MODEL

Schools that are committed to delivering a comprehensive, data-driven school counseling program can apply for the Recognized ASCA Model Program (RAMP) designation from the American School Counselor Association if their program can successfully answer the question, "How are students different because of what school counselors do?" Schools are encouraged to apply for the RAMP designation if they can provide exemplary statements to the 11 items below.

1. Philosophy Statement

Include a copy of your school counseling program philosophy statement, which should reflect the needs of the school's constituents. If the philosophy statement is adapted from another source, please give the proper credit. The RAMP application signature page found at http://www.ascanationalmodel.org/files/sigpage.pdf and sent in with the application materials includes original signatures to verify that the philosophy statement was presented to and accepted by the school principal, all school counselors at the school, and advisory council representatives. Include a narrative of at least a half a page and no more than a page that explains how the statement of philosophy was developed. See pp. 28–29 of the *ASCA National Model* (2005a) for more information.

Exemplary statement of philosophy that includes an agreed-upon belief system about the ability of every student to achieve and includes ethical guidelines and standards. There is ample evidence that the statement of philosophy is school specific and has been presented to and accepted by the school's administration, counselors, and the advisory council based on the signature page.

2. Mission Statement

Include a copy of your school counseling mission statement *and* the school's mission statement. The school counseling mission statement must be tied to the school's mission statement. The RAMP application signature page, found at http://www.ascanationalmodel.org/files/sigpage.pdf and sent in with the application materials, includes original signatures to verify the mission statement was presented to and accepted by the school principal, all school counselors at the school, and advisory council representatives. Include a narrative of at least a half a page and no more than a page that explains how the mission statement was developed and why it includes the components it does. See pp. 30–31 of the *ASCA National Model* (2005a) for more information.

Exemplary mission statement clearly reflecting the school's needs, linking with the vision and mission statement, and reflecting students' growth and developmental needs in the areas of academic, career, and personal/social development. There is clear evidence, such as meeting minutes and the signature page, that the mission statement has been presented to and accepted by the school's administration, the counselors in the school, and the advisory council. The mission statement indicates the general content of the school counseling program and defines the school counselor's role in helping the school manifest its mission.

3. Competencies and Indicators

Use the template provided on pp. 108–113 of the *ASCA National Model* (2005a) to show the competencies and indicators the school counseling program is *currently* focusing on, or create one of your own.

In the narrative, provide an explanation as to how these competencies and indicators were selected and how they are reviewed and revised each year. The RAMP application signature page, found at http://www.ascanationalmodel.org/files/sigpage.pdf and sent in with the application materials, includes original signatures to verify that the competencies and indicators were presented to and accepted by the school principal, all school counselors at the school, and advisory council representatives. See pp. 32–37 of the *ASCA National Model* (2005a) for more information.

Developmentally appropriate and measurable competencies and indicators are identified for each applicable grade level and directly link to the counseling program's mission, goals, and the school's needs. Each competency and indicator selected clearly relates to the ASCA standards. All ASCA standards are thoroughly covered across grade levels. Complete explanation of how these competencies and indicators were chosen is provided. From the signature page, there is evidence the standards and competencies have been presented to and administration, counselors, and the advisory council.

4. Program Goals

Include your school counseling program goals for the current or previous academic year (use the goals that guided the "Closing the Gap" results report). In the narrative, include documentation, information, and data used to arrive at these goals and explain how and why these goals were selected. The RAMP application signature page, found at http://www.ascanationalmodel.org/files/sigpage.pdf and sent in with the application materials, includes original signatures to verify that the program goals were presented to and accepted by the school principal, all school counselors at the school, and advisory council representatives.

Exemplary program goals reflecting prioritized ASCA National Standards and the school's goals. There is clear and complete evidence showing how the goals were selected and that they are based upon school data and address academic, career, and personal/social development. The signature page indicates that the goals have been presented to and accepted by the school's administration, counselors, and the advisory council.

5. Management Agreement

Include a copy of a management agreement *for each counselor in the school*. Each management agreement must include the percentage of time allocated for each delivery system area and must closely align with the suggested use of time. You can use the sample agreements on pp. 122–124 of the *ASCA National Model* (2005a), or you can use one of your own. Provide a narrative of at least a half a page and no more than a page that includes a brief description of how duties are distributed among the counseling staff and how the decision to do this was made. See pp. 46–47 of the *ASCA National Model* (2005a) for more information.

Concise and thorough management agreement for each counselor at the school is included that reflects the scope of work of each counselor. The percentage of time spent in delivery highly correlates with the ideal/suggested use of time. The signature page indicates that each agreement is signed by the school counselor and the school's principal. Each agreement clearly reflects the school counseling program mission statement and goals.

6. Advisory Council

Attach a list of all your school counseling program advisory council members, along with their stakeholder positions (i.e., are they parents, faculty, community members, etc.). Also attach the agendas and minutes from *two* advisory council meetings. In the narrative, explain how the committee members were selected and explain how feedback from the committee guides the school counseling program. See pp. 47–48 of the *ASCA National Model* (2005a).

An exemplary school counseling advisory council exists with representatives from core stakeholder groups and clear evidence and documentation that the committee helps guide the school counseling program. The committee is solely focused on the school counseling program. Agendas and minutes from two meetings that reflect work related to the school counseling program mission and goals are included.

7. Calendars

Attach a copy of your school counseling master calendar for the *current* academic year. The calendar should include all school counseling activities and events for the year for the entire counseling program. Also include one detailed weekly calendar for each counselor in the school that is representative of the management agreement. In the narrative, provide a concise but thorough explanation of the items on the calendar, how they were selected, and how and why items are reviewed and revised as the school year progresses. See pp. 57–58 of the *ASCA National Model* (2005a) for more information.

Comprehensive master calendar and weekly calendars for each counselor in the school exist that strongly reflect prioritized ASCA National Standards and delivery system priorities as outlined in the management agreement and school counseling program goals. The calendars show the depth and breadth of the work of the counseling department. There is strong evidence the school counseling staff periodically reflects on the calendar, and there is clear evidence that the calendar highly correlates the percentage of time allocated in the management agreement.

8. Classroom Guidance Curriculum

Include three lesson plans for each counselor in the school. Each counselor's lesson plans should be part of a single topic/unit. In the narrative, provide a concise but thorough overview and explanation of the lessons and units and also include data and documentation as necessary. Include the number of students who participated in each lesson. See pp. 40–41 of the *ASCA National Model* (2005a) for more information.

Exemplary classroom guidance unit composed of at least three lessons for each counselor in the school is included. The units directly link to the ASCA National Standards and to ASCA or school competencies/indicators and school counseling program goals. The units are comprehensive enough to enable student to master the appropriate standards and competencies and indicators. Quality, clear and relevant process, perception and results data for the lessons are included.

9. Small-Group Curriculum

Attach all the lesson plans for a small-group (either appraisal, advisement, or responsive services) session that was conducted by a counselor at your school during the designated school year. The group must have met at least four times. In the narrative, provide a concise but thorough explanation of why and how this group was created and include data and documentation as necessary. Include how many times the group met and the number of students who participated in each group session. See p. 42 of the *ASCA National Model* (2005a) for more information.

Plans for an exemplary small group of at least four meetings are included. The group's purpose is directly tied to the ASCA National Standards or school competencies and indicators and school counseling program goals. The group is comprehensive in scope and enables student to master the appropriate standards and competencies/indicators. Quality, clear and relevant process, perception, and results data for the lessons are included.

Include a guidance curriculum results report for at least four different guidance curriculum activities from the current or previous school year. Use the template on p. 128 of the *ASCA National Model* (2005a) or include one of your own. In the narrative, provide a concise but thorough explanation of how the guidance curriculum activities were selected and include data and documentation as necessary. See p. 54 and pp. 59–61 of the *ASCA National Model* (2005a) for more information.

10. Closing the Gap Results Report

Include results from a closing-the-gap activity. In the narrative, provide a concise but thorough explanation of how this gap was identified and why it was important to address, and include data and documentation as necessary. See p. 54, pp. 59–61, and p. 129 of the *ASCA National Model* (2005a) for more information.

An exemplary "Closing the Gap" results report addressing a particular need in the school that reflects the school competencies/indicators. The report includes the target group, the type of services delivered and in what manner, and the start and end dates. Clear, concise, and relevant process, perception, and results data and implications from the data are included. Strong supplemental and supporting documentation is also included that provides a thorough explanation on how this gap was identified and why it was important to address.

11. Program Reflection

How does your comprehensive school counseling program use advocacy, leadership, systemic change, and collaboration to make a difference for students? See pp. 24–25 of the *ASCA National Model* (2005a) for more information. Responses should be at least 500 words and no more than 1,500.

An exemplary well-articulated and clearly organized response shows through the use of specific details and examples of how the school counseling program uses advocacy, leadership, systemic change, and collaboration to benefit students.

Comprehensive Guidance and Counseling Programs (CGCP)

2

A Developmental Approach for Professional School Counseling

Professional school counseling has evolved in response to national, economic, and education reform crises (e.g., the Cold War); societal needs (e.g., the need for capable, competent, prepared workers); national policy initiatives (e.g., literacy, mathematics, and achievement in science); economic trends (e.g., poverty and economic downturns); and school reform initiatives (e.g., *A Nation at Risk* [National Commission on Excellence in Education, 1983] and the No Child Left Behind Act of 2001). Professional school counseling has gone through three distinct phases (Gysbers & Henderson, 2001; Herr, 2001). From the turn of the century to the 1950s, the initial phase was essentially a "position" approach that concentrated on vocational and career information to prepare high school students for jobs and careers (Gysbers & Henderson, 2001). Today, with the evolution of the "portfolio" worker, career preparation is often tenuous at best as markets become more global and a career in the traditional sense of the word no longer exists.

During the second phase, from the 1960s to the 1980s, a "services" or pupil personnel model was implemented (Gysbers & Henderson, 2001; Herr, 2001; Sink, 2005a). During this phase of guidance and counseling programs, psychoeducational support and reactive services were provided to a growing population of students at risk for school failure (e.g., teens with unintended pregnancies, substance abusers, potential dropouts, and a growing population of children with disabilities and English-language learners), as well as those students experiencing personal or social difficulties (e.g., gang involvement, violence, relational aggression, suicide ideation).

In the late 1980s, a philosophical reorientation occurred to promote a comprehensive guidance and counseling program (CGCP) that is systematic, collaborative, developmental, and preventive in nature (Clark & Stone, 2000; Gysbers & Henderson, 2001, 2006; Gysbers, Bragg-Stanley, Kosteck-Bunch, Magnuson & Starr, 2008). Since the late 1990s, the CGCP has been the most widely used organizational framework for the profession, which has struggled with creating a clear identity. The CGCP is endorsed by the American School Counselor Association (ASCA, 1997, 1999e, 2004d, 2005b).

Since the late 1970s, comprehensive school counseling programs have primarily focused on a comprehensive developmental model that gained its impetus by focusing on various stages of human development theories (Borders & Drury, 1992a; Paisley & McMahon, 2001). Professional school counselors collectively will continue to be marginalized through their adherence to quasi-administrative duties and clerical responsibilities and will be perceived as ancillary services unless professional school counselors collectively embrace CGCP and the *ASCA* (2005a) *National Model* (Ripley, Erford, Dahir, & Eschbach, 2003; Gysbers et al., 2008). What has perpetuated throughout the profession is the traditional pupil personnel services model, which provided isolated services to a few groups of students and predominately crisis-centered approaches that did not meet the needs of all students (Bowers & Hatch, 2002). Table 2.1 outlines the differences between legitimate roles for professional school counselors and demonstrates how easy it is to allow ancillary activities to mutate professional school counselors' role and function.

One of the major problems of the professional school counseling movement and education in general has been the separation of personal growth from academic learning. In fact, enhancing personal

TABLE 2.1   Role Mutations and Responsibilities That Diminish the Professional School Counselor's Ability to Implement a Comprehensive School Counseling Program

DUTIES	COMMENTS AND SOLUTIONS
Coordinating and monitoring school assemblies	• This is an administrative function and is not viewed as a part of guidance program responsibilities.
Hall duty, cafeteria supervision, bus loading and unloading supervision, and restroom supervision	• These duties could be shared equally among all staff. • Teachers could be assigned to some of these duties as a regular part of their schedules. • Volunteers could assist with some of these tasks.
Chaperoning school functions and athletic event supervision	• These duties could be shared among the staff. • Booster club members could assist staff with some of the athletic events. • School staff could be paid extra to take on chaperoning duties.
Coordinating and administering the school testing program, including individual testing	• The overall coordination and administration of the school testing program are the responsibilities of the administration. • Retired teachers could be hired to handle this responsibility. • School personnel could collaborate to accomplish the coordination and administration of the school testing program. • Professional school counselors assist in *interpreting* test data for teachers, administrators, parents/guardians, and the community; however, they should not be responsible for coordinating and administering the school testing program. • Professional school counselors use test data when working with students to help them monitor and manage their academic, personal/social, and career development. • School psychologists and school psychological examiners are the professionals who are qualified to do individual testing.
Substitute teaching	• Professional school counselors are not substitute teachers. On an occasional basis, however, professional school counselors could conduct classroom guidance lessons.
Selling lunch tickets	• Office support staff or cafeteria staff should do this.
Collecting and mailing out progress reports and deficiency notices	• Sorting, stuffing, and mailing are clerical/secretarial functions. An individual could be hired on a temporary basis to handle sorting, stuffing, and mailing.
Conferences with students regarding progress reports	• Conferences with students regarding progress reports are school staff functions, which includes but should not be limited to professional school counselors.
Maintaining permanent records and handling transcripts	• This should be the responsibility of the school secretary.
Posting grades and test labels	• Part-time help could be hired if a full-time person is not available to handle these clerical functions.

TABLE 2.1   Role Mutations and Responsibilities That Diminish the professional School Counselor's Ability to Implement a Comprehensive School Counseling Program (continued)

DUTIES	COMMENTS AND SOLUTIONS
Monitoring attendance	• Accounting for daily attendance is not a guidance program's function. However, it is appropriate for professional school counselors to meet with students who have chronic attendance problems. • Computer software packages are available to monitor attendance in a very efficient and effective manner.
Calculating grade-point averages (GPAs), class ranks, or honor rolls	• Computer software packages are available to efficiently and effectively perform these tasks.
Developing and updating the student handbook	• This is an administrative function that the principal or assistant principal should perform.
Developing and updating course guides	• Department chairpersons (teaching staff) have the responsibility for developing course descriptions and course guides.
Completing the paperwork related to changing students' schedules	• The paperwork involved in changing schedules, balancing class loads, and processing student schedule cards is a clerical function. If full-time clerical assistance is not available, part-time clerical/secretarial help should be hired at key times during the school year. • A wide array of computer software is available to handle the scheduling process, including schedule changes, and can be purchased to facilitate the completion of these important activities.
Completing and managing Individual Education Plans (IEPs) and meeting other special education requirements	• Professional school counselors should not function as case managers for students with special needs. • Professional school counselors could be members of the team involved in the diagnostic aspects of the IEP. However, they should not be responsible for the development, implementation, and monitoring of the IEP or the Individualized Vocational Education Plan unless they are funded by special education or by vocational education funds.
Completing and managing 504 Plans	• As with IEPs, professional school counselors should not function as the case manager for 504 Plans, but should be a part of the team when it is warranted, especially when a student on the caseload of a professional school counselor is in need of a 504 Plan.
Developing the master schedule	• This is an administrative function. Administrators can seek input from professional school counselors, but it is their responsibility to plan and develop the master schedule.
Acting as the principal of the day	• The professional school counselor should not fill the role of acting principal. This sends the wrong message to students and jeopardizes trust and confidentiality. • Retired school administrators could be hired for this purpose. • This responsibility could be assigned to teachers who have administrative certification. • The superintendent or other central office administrators could be called upon to act as principal for the day.
Administering discipline	• Administering discipline and assessing consequences for student actions are administrative functions, not guidance functions. However, it is appropriate for professional school counselors to meet with students who have chronic discipline problems.
Managing schedule changes	• Students who desire or need to have their schedules revised are encouraged to first discuss the changes with the professional school counselor. The mechanics related to this process should be handled through administrative channels. • Much of the process is clerical in nature. It is the responsibility of the administration to see that class sizes are appropriate and that sufficient staff members are available to accommodate students' needs.

growth can have a significant influence on achievement. The developmental approach to professional school counseling considers the nature of human development, including the general stages and tasks that most individuals experience, as they mature from childhood to adulthood. Initially, Dinkmeyer and Caldwell (1970), in their landmark book *Developmental Counseling and Guidance: A Comprehensive School Approach,* outlined several abiding principles for this program initiative:

1. Developmental guidance and counseling should be an integral component of the overall educational process and tied in with the school's mission and philosophy.
2. Developmental guidance and counseling are for all students within the school.
3. Teachers must be a part of the program delivery system; therefore, teacher advisory programs should be encouraged.
4. Counseling programs function better when they are planned as a continuous set of services that help the student accomplish developmental tasks that lead to effective cognitive, emotional, and social development.
5. Programs consist of direct counseling, appraisal, and group counseling, as well as indirect services of consultation and coordination of programs and services.
6. Programs focus and encourage students' strengths, assets, and positive attributes. They center on positive self-concepts and acknowledge that one's self-concept is formed and re-formed through experience and education.

Myrick (2003a), Gysbers and Henderson (2006), Wittmer (2000b), and Gysbers et al. (2008) furthered this counseling perspective with an additional emphasis on the need for an organized, planned, and sequential guidance and counseling curriculum emphasizing a comprehensive developmental program. The state of Missouri took the lead in fervently demonstrating how students can benefit from participating in a comprehensive school counseling program with the Missouri Comprehensive Guidance Program (MCGP). The earlier comprehensive guidance program was revised to add an evaluative component that provided evidence that this transformed school counseling model worked to provide measurable results (Lapan, Gysbers, & Petroski, 2001).

It further recognizes that feelings, behaviors, and academics are closely linked together and that they are learned. The ultimate objective is to help students and their families learn more effectively and efficiently from a developmental perspective. Empowerment as a developmental catalyst can be the critical bridge between inaction and self-actualization. Developmental programs also represent a paradigm shift from the guidance and counseling initiatives of the last two decades.

Professional school counselors can exert more control over their scope of practice if they commit themselves to designing and implementing comprehensive guidance and counseling developmental school counseling programs. Utilizing school and community helping professionals enhances these efforts. Emphasizing developmental counseling programs permits counselors to be seen as contributing to the growth of *all* students, rather than merely attending to those in trouble. Developmental counseling programs facilitate activities and structured group experiences that focus on students' developmental needs. Yet, implementing developmental CGCPs can be a challenging process (Gysbers, Lapan, et al., 2000). Essentially, CGCP programs are a service-delivery model that reframes the traditional work of professional school counselors from a reactionary and crisis operational mode to a more proactive developmental focus (Paisley & Hubbard, 1994; Paisley & Peace, 1995; Wittmer, 2000; Gysbers et al., 2008). The benefits for a CGCP model for all those who interact with the schools are demonstrated in Table 2.2.

The CGCP initiative emerged as a viable alternative to a service orientation with the intention to be a competency-based programmatic approach (Johnson & Whitfield, 1991) that is also multisystemic, collaborative, and developmental with initiatives that are preventive and educational (Clark & Stone, 2000; Gysbers & Henderson, 2001, 2006; Thompson, 2002). This organizational framework has become the most widely used paradigm for the profession and is endorsed by the American School Counselor Association (ASCA 1997b, 1999c, 1999d, 2005a; Dahir, 2001; Wittmer, 2000a, 2000b).

The *ASCA* (2005a) *National Model* is the premier blueprint for the development and implementation of comprehensive school counseling programs. The model furthered ASCA's decade-long ambition to

TABLE 2.2   Benefits of a Comprehensive Guidance and Counseling Program (CGCP)

For students
- Focuses on academic, career, and social needs of *all* students
- Enhances students' academic achievement and performance as well to close the achievement gap
- Centers on students' identified needs (e.g., English-language learner students, students with disabilities, students from poverty)
- Seeks students' input via advisory boards, focus groups, or routine surveys
- Encourages more interaction among students
- Provides a developmental and preventative focus with strategic interventions (e.g., antibullying initiatives, substance abuse prevention, suicide prevention)
- Promotes knowledge and assistance in career exploration and development in a systematic manner
- Enhances life-coping skills in the social, emotional, and cognitive domains
- Develops decision-making, problem-solving, and conflict resolution skills
- Increases knowledge of self and others and promotes a tolerance for diversity
- Broadens knowledge of our changing work world and the notion of the portfolio worker in the 21st century
- Increases opportunities for professional school counselor–student interaction with systematically planned events
- Develops a system of long-range planning for students and meetings with students on an annual basis and during times of transition to elementary, middle, and high school

For parents/guardians/caregivers
- Enhances students' academic performance and assists in closing the achievement gap for minority and economically disadvantaged students
- Encourages the input of parents/guardians through advisory groups, surveys, and focus groups
- Encourages outreach to all parents/guardians in the community such as at places of worship
- Provides support for parents/guardians regarding each child's educational development and explains information that they can understand
- Increases opportunities for parent–professional school counselor interaction through advisory boards, focus groups, workshops, and seminars
- Provides parents/guardians with information about available resources (e.g., parenting, developmental needs of children and adolescents, and awareness behaviors that may be a barrier to their child's learning) in websites, streaming videos, email resources, and electronic newsletters
- Assures parents/guardians that all children will receive support from the counseling and guidance program using electronic media

For teachers
- Contributes to a team effort to enhance students' academic performance, close the achievement gap, and be an integral part of school improvement teams
- Provides relevant guidance and counseling curriculum ideas and partners in classroom guidance activities to ensure students' academic, social, and emotional well-being
- Encourages teachers' input via grade-level meetings, departmental meetings, surveys, advisory boards, and focus groups
- Establishes the professional school counselor as a resource/consultant and conduit to school and community resources
- Encourages positive, collaborative working relationships across the curriculum and in school extracurricular activities
- Defines the role of professional school counselors as educators and an integral part of school improvement efforts

continued

TABLE 2.2   Benefits of a Comprehensive Guidance and Counseling Program (CGCP) (continued)

For the community
- Encourages input from business, industry, labor, and other community partners such as the Chamber of Commerce
- Provides increased opportunities for collaboration between professional school counselors and business, industry, labor, and other community partners and routinely seeks their advice and input
- Enhances the role of the professional school counselor as a resource person to community programs and services
- Increases opportunities for business, industry, labor, and other community partners to actively participate in the total school program through such activities as career fairs, college fairs, and mentoring opportunities utilizing electronic media to make information readily available
- Enhances students' academic performance through experiences such as mentoring
- Supplies a future workforce that has decision-making skills, preemployment skills, and increased worker maturity and preparation
- Facilitates the development of students as active, responsible citizens with a tolerance for diversity

For school boards
- Enhances students' academic performance and focuses on closing the achievement gap for minority students and students who are academically disadvantaged
- Encourages greater school–community interaction with open forums and focused groups
- Meets the guidance standards found in the National School Improvement Program
- Provides a rationale for including a CGCP in a school system
- Provides program information to district patrons electronically and in paper form
- Provides a basis for determining funding allocations based on individual school needs
- Provides ongoing data relative to the attainment of student competencies through the CGCP

For administrators
- Enhances students' academic performance
- Provides a clearly defined role and job description for professional school counselors
- Provides a way to supervise and evaluate professional school counselors
- Encourages administrative input and involvement
- Provides a way to meet Missouri School Improvement Program standards for guidance
- Provides structure for the comprehensive guidance program
- Provides a means of accountability through comprehensive guidance program evaluation
- Enhances the image of the comprehensive guidance program in the community
- Promotes the professional school counselor as a resource/consultant

For professional school counselors
- Provides state-level assistance in the comprehensive guidance program implementation process
- Places guidance in the mainstream of the local curriculum-planning process
- Provides clearly defined roles
- Reduces and strives to eliminate nonguidance activities while retaining fair-share responsibilities
- Offers the opportunity to reach all students
- Provides a tool for program management and evaluation
- Outlines clearly defined responsibilities for helping students master guidance competencies
- Addresses the guidance program standards found in the Missouri School Improvement Program
- Enhances student academic performance

Source: Modified and adapted from Gysbers, N. C., Bragg Stanley, J., Kosteck-Bunch, L., Magnuson, C. S., & Starr, M. F., *Missouri Comprehensive Guidance Program: A Manual for Program Development, Implementation, Evaluation and Enhancement,* Missouri Center for Career Education, University of Central Missouri, Warrensburg, 2008.

connect the work of professional school counselors to the goals of school improvement planning, adding the theoretical and practical applications of a comprehensive, developmental and results-based school counseling program (Gysbers & Henderson, 2001, 2006; Johnson & Johnson, 2001, 2002; Myrick, 2003a; Dahir, 2004; Dahir & Stone, 2003, 2007; Brown & Trusty, 2005; Burnham, Dahir, Stone, & Hooper, 2009; Gysbers, 2004; Lapan, Gysbers, & Kayson, 2007; Sink, 2005a; Stone & Dahir, 2006, 2007; Dahir, Burnham, & Stone, 2009).

COMPREHENSIVE, DEVELOPMENTAL, AND OUTCOME-BASED PROGRAM MODELS

In this era of school reform, everyone must be accountable. A comprehensive, developmental, outcome-based school counseling program provides this measure of accountability. The current educational climate and policy initiatives stress academic achievement and continued success for every student from every socioeconomic strata, race, and ethnicity (No Child Left Behind Act of 2001; Coeyman, 2003; Dollarhide & Lemberger, 2006). However, there are growing concerns about the legislation's effects on the most at-risk students: those students who are from culturally diverse backgrounds, those who are English-language learners, those who live in poverty, and those who live with emotional and behavioral disabilities (Allbritten, Mainzer, & Ziegler, 2004; Leone & Cutting, 2004; Mathis, 2004; Sitlington & Neubert, 2004; Bryan & Holcomb-McCoy, 2007; Myers, Shoffner, & Briggs, 2002). To overcome these barriers to learning, current literature supports a comprehensive, developmental, standards-based school counseling program in which professional school counselors collaborate and team with teachers and administrators as an integral part of the total school improvement initiatives to raise achievement of all students using existing school achievement data (Brigman, Webb, & Campbell, 2007; Gysbers, 2004; Gysbers & Henderson, 2006; Gysbers et al., 2008).

Professional school counselors provide invaluable support for students, teachers, parents/guardians, administrators, school boards, and the greater community (see Table 2.2). These counselors help students and their families improve academic achievement, resolve issues of personal and social development that may become barriers to learning, and plan for meaningful careers and postsecondary alternatives after graduation (ASCA, 2005a; Gysbers, 2004; Gysbers et al., 2008; Johnson & Johnson, 2002). Moreover, the educational reform movement of the late 1999s and the current pressures under the Elementary and Secondary and Education Act (No Child Left Behind Act of 2001) have forced professional school counselors to demonstrate their worth by improving academic achievement or be viewed as merely an ancillary resource that is expendable under tight budgetary constraints, as has been demonstrated in the past (Hayes, Nelson, Tabin, Pearson, & Worthy, 2002; Dollarhide & Lemberger, 2006). Therefore, there is a need to demonstrate results. A results-based model is demonstrated in Figure 2.1.

Johnson and Johnson (2001) developed the results-based model in the early as 1980s, and it is reflective of the CGCP model but also has some distinct differences. Both conceptual models emphasize professional school counseling as a program, not as a service that is expendable, and collectively stress leadership, teamwork, advocacy, collaboration, managing resources, technology, and the use of school achievement and demographic data for decision making regarding prevention and intervention initiatives. The results-based model (Johnson & Johnson, 1981; Johnson, Johnson, & Downs, 2006) also focuses on accountability and consists of 12 distinct elements:

1. Mission statements
2. A philosophy
3. A conceptual model
4. Well-defined goals
5. Student competencies

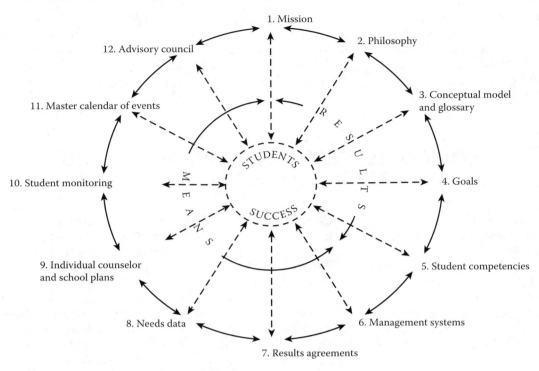

FIGURE 2.1   A systematic approach to achieving student success.

6. A management system
7. Outcome agreements
8. Programs that are developed based on needs gathered from data
9. Individual counselor and school plans
10. Student mentoring
11. A master calendar of events
12. An advisory council.

This model is student driven and represents a systemic approach to achieving student success (Johnson & Johnson, 2003).

TABLE 2.3   Comprehensive Guidance and Counseling Program Components

GUIDANCE CURRICULUM	INDIVIDUAL PLANNING	RESPONSIVE SERVICES	SYSTEM SUPPORT
Provides guidance content in a systematic way to all students K–12	Assists students in planning, monitoring, and managing their academic, personal/social, and career development	Addresses the immediate needs and concerns of students	Includes program, staff, and school support activities and services
Purpose	**Purpose**	**Purpose**	**Purpose**
Student awareness, skill development, and application of skills needed in everyday life	Development and use of Personal Plans of Study	Prevention, intervention	Program delivery and support

TABLE 2.3 Comprehensive Guidance and Counseling Program Components (continued)

GUIDANCE CURRICULUM	INDIVIDUAL PLANNING	RESPONSIVE SERVICES	SYSTEM SUPPORT
Areas and activities addressed *Career development* • Career awareness • Career exploration *Personal/Social Development* • Self-concept • Conflict resolution • Personal responsibilities • Peer friendship • Decision-making skills • Substance abuse prevention program • Cross-cultural understandings • Tolerance for diversity Academic Development • Study skills • Developing personal plans of study • Preemployment skills • Job preparation • Postsecondary • Decision making	**Topics addressed** • Course selection • Transitioning: grade to grade, school to school, school to career • Multiple-year planning • Financial aid • Knowledge of career opportunities • Career awareness • Interest inventories • Career shadowing • Work habits • Setting personal goals • Decision-making skills	**Topics addressed** • Academic concerns • School-related concerns: tardiness, absences and truancy, misbehavior, school avoidance, dropout prevention • Relationship concerns • Physical/sexual/emotional abuse • Grief/loss/death • Substance abuse • Family issues • Sexuality issues • Coping with stress • Suicide prevention • Understanding depression	**Total program** • Comprehensive guidance and counseling program, development and management • School counselor professional development • Advocacy and public relations for comprehensive school counseling program • Advisory committee • Program planning and development • Evaluation and assessment of CGCP, personnel and student results • Documentation of how CGCPs contribute to student achievement • Integral involvement of professional school counselors in school improvement initiatives • Integration of guidance and counseling essential learnings across the school curriculum • Parent/guardian involvement and education • Teacher, administrator, and support staff consultation • Instruction on age-appropriate issues with staff and community • Research and publishing • Community outreach • Public relations • Data analysis
Counselor's role • Structured groups • Classroom presentations • Schoolwide workshops for teachers, students and families	**Counselor's role** • Appraisal • Education and career planning • Transitions • Schoolwide workshops for teachers, students, and families	**Counselor's role** • Individual counseling • Small-group counseling • Consultation • Referral • Crisis intervention • Crisis management	**Counselor's role** • Program management • Professional development • Staff and community relations • Consultation • Committee participation • Community outreach • Evaluation • Self-care

continued

TABLE 2.3   Comprehensive Guidance and Counseling Program Components (continued)

GUIDANCE CURRICULUM	INDIVIDUAL PLANNING	RESPONSIVE SERVICES	SYSTEM SUPPORT
		• Schoolwide workshops for teachers, students, and families	
Time distribution	**Time distribution**	**Time distribution**	**Time distribution**
Elementary 35%–45%	Elementary 30%–40%	Elementary 5%–10%	Elementary 10%–15%
Middle school 25%–35%	Middle school 30%–40%	Middle school 15%–25%	Middle school 10%–15%
High school 15%–25%	High school 25%–35%	High school 25%–35%	High school 15%–20%

Source: Modified and adapted from Gysbers, N. C., Bragg Stanley, J., Kosteck-Bunch, L., Magnuson, C. S., & Starr, M. F., *Missouri Comprehensive Guidance Program: A Manual for Program Development, Implementation, Evaluation and Enhancement,* Missouri Center for Career Education, University of Central Missouri, Warrensburg, 2008; and Schreiber, K., *The Arizona Model: A Framework for School Counseling Programs Handbook, 2009–2020,* Arizona Department of Education, Development and Innovation Group, Phoenix (2008).

In 2003 and 2005, ASCA infused the theoretical frameworks of Gysbers and Henderson with that of Johnson and Johnson to form a single unified framework for a comprehensive developmental school counseling and guidance program. Table 2.3 outlines the components of a CGCP.

OUTCOME RESEARCH AND THEORETICAL IMPLICATIONS FOR COMPREHENSIVE GUIDANCE AND COUNSELING PROGRAMS

Children and adolescents manifest their needs through their behaviors. These behaviors are becoming increasingly self-defeating and self-destructive. For example, youths often join gangs out of their need to belong (Maslow, 1954), become alienated from school because of feelings of inferiority (Erikson, 1963), or fail to maintain relationships with others because of the anxiety that emerges when trying to relate to others more intimately (Sullivan, 1953). Many theories of human development exist, each of which contributes to the understanding of student behavior at various age levels. Children and adolescents progress through almost predictable stages in the specific domains listed in Table 2.4.

TABLE 2.4   Developmental Life Domains

Cognitive development (Piaget, 1950)

Ethical reasoning (justice perspective) (Kohlberg, 1969)

Ethical reasoning (care perspective) (Gilligan, 1982)

Interpersonal understanding (Selman, 1980)

Conceptual level (Hunt, 1975)

Ego development (Loevinger, 1976)

Psychosocial development (Erikson, 1963)

Career development (Super, Savickas, & Super, 1996)

Developmental tasks (Havighurst, 1972)

Source: Paisley, P. O. (2001). Maintaining and enhancing developmental focus in school counseling programs. *Professional School Counseling, 4*(4), 274. Reprinted with permission.

Fundamentally, theories of human development focus attention on the sequence of patterns that occur—biological, social, cognitive, moral, affective, interpersonal, occupational, and so on. From this perspective, the patterns reflect the unfolding of individual development within the life span. The major developmental tasks of youths (see Table 2.5) are to achieve a sense of identity, self-esteem, and autonomy from the family of origin. For youths to accomplish this life transition, they need to acquire skills, knowledge, and attitudes that may be classified into two broad categories: those involving self-development and those involving other people.

Educational and counseling programs should meet the developmental needs of children and adolescents. In order to meet developmental needs, the professional school counselor must have a general knowledge of the cognitive, emotional, and social needs affecting the maturation of children and adolescents. Using this information as a foundation, professional school counselors can create a comprehensive school counseling program that meets the developmental needs of all children and adolescents within the context of school, home, neighborhood, and community.

A growing body of research advocates teaching *social competence* (Greenberg, Kusche, & Mihalic, 1998; Slaby, Roedell, Arezzo, & Kendrix, 1995; Thompson, 1998, 2000, 2006) in the following ways:

- Understanding and recognizing one's own emotions and the emotions of others
- Developing accurate perceptions of a situation to enable correct interpretation of social cues and appropriate responses
- Understanding and predicting the consequences of personal acts, particularly those involving aggression
- Developing the ability to remain calm in order to think before acting, reduce stress and sadness, replace aggression with positive behavior, and control anger
- Using social problem solving and cooperative behavior, understanding and using group processes, and developing and maintaining peer relationships
- Empathizing with others in general, especially with those perceived as different
- Using peer-mediation and conflict-resolution skills
- Selecting positive role models and supportive mentors

TABLE 2.5   Major Developmental Tasks of Adolescence Identified by Traditional Developmental Theorists

THEORIST	DEVELOPMENTAL DOMAIN	DEVELOPMENTAL TASK
Freud	Psychosexual	Sexual energy is invested in socially accepted activities
Erikson	Psychosocial	Self-identity; image of self as a unique individual
Piaget	Cognitive	Formal operations; engaging in abstract thought; consider hypothetical situations
Maslow	Human needs	Ego, esteem needs; confidence; sense of mastery; positive self-regard; self-respect, self-extension
Super	Vocational	Crystallizing a vocational preference; tentative choices are made; appropriate career fields are identified; generalized choice is converted to specific choice
Sullivan	Interpersonal	Personal security with freedom from anxiety; collaboration with others; increased sensitivity to needs of others; establishment of a repertoire of interpersonal relationships
Kohlberg	Moral	Defines moral values and principles; decisions of conscience are congruent with self-held ethical principles
Egan & Cowan	Lifestyle systems	Family, peer group, school, and community are key systems; lifestyle management; gain emotional independence from nuclear family
Havighurst	Stages of childhood development	Gain emotional independence from nuclear family; assimilate appropriate sexual identity; find an educational/vocational direction; set goals; acquire a set of values and ethical systems to guide behavior

There are also significant gender differences that are appearing in the research literature. For example, boys are more vulnerable in the first decade of life, whereas girls become more vulnerable in their second decade. Boys are more susceptible to prenatal stress, more physically vulnerable as infants, and more emotionally vulnerable. They are more adversely affected by growing up in poverty and by disharmony at home and are more likely to be sent to institutions if they cannot be kept at home (Werner, 1987; Werner & Smith, 1982, 1992). Boys have more trouble with social skills in preschool and kindergarten. Until ages 10 or 11, boys are adversely affected by the absence of their father and a change in schools. From 11 to 18, the absence of their mother, conflict with their father, and school failure are more stressful for boys (Werner & Smith, 1992).

For girls between ages 2 and 10, serious risk factors include death of the mother, long-term absence of the father, and chronic conflict between parents (Werner & Smith, 1992). In the second decade, girls become more vulnerable. Dependency is rewarded, and it is often not considered feminine to be assertive and confident (Gilligan, Rogers, & Tolman, 1991). Girls become less assertive and more insecure about themselves (Rutter, 1981, 1984), which has long-term impact on self-esteem and self-efficacy, often contributing to eating disorders.

THINKING, FEELING, AND RELATING: ESSENTIAL DEVELOPMENTAL SKILLS

Thinking, feeling, and relating are essentially cognitive, emotional, and social skills. Dedicated educators, researchers, and professional school counselors feel compelled to create a comprehensive initiative to remediate the broad spectrum of threats to the physical, intellectual, emotional, and social well-being of contemporary youths. This following section gives a more contemporary version of life-stage development for children and adolescents from *thinking, feeling,* and *relating* perspectives (see Tables 2.6, 2.7, and 2.8). Research that outlines growth and development in these three domains has been gleaned from the last two decades and is provided here to support school-based primary prevention and intervention initiatives.

TABLE 2.6   Developmental Tasks for Children and Adolescents in the Domains of Thinking, Feeling, and Relating: Early School Age (4 to 6 Years)

Thinking
- Beliefs and practices followed at home come under scrutiny at school and are challenged by community norms and values.
- Personal hopes and aspirations that parents have for their children are tempered by the reality of school performance.
- Family, school, peer group, neighborhood, and television all influence the child's self-concept.
- Early-school-age children exhibit wide-ranging curiosity about all aspects of life.
- A child's sex-role identity becomes a major cognitive structure that influences a child's interpretation of experiences in developing expectations about what toys, interests, behaviors, dispositions, and occupations are appropriate for each sex (Bern, 1981, 1989; Martin, 1989).
- Learning the moral code of the family and the community guides behavior. Behaviors that are linked to moral principles, such as telling the truth and being respectful of authority figures, become integrated into the child's concepts of right and wrong (J. L. Carroll & Rest, 1982; Damon, 1980; Gibbs, 1979; Kohlberg, 1976; Rest, 1983).
- Young girls are better able to resist temptation than boys and show patterns of decreasing moral transgressions from the toddler years to the early school years (Mischel, Shoda, & Rodriguez, 1989).

TABLE 2.6 Developmental Tasks for Children and Adolescents in the Domains of Thinking, Feeling, and Relating: Early School Age (4 to 6 Years) (continued)

Feeling

- Children are aware of sex-typed expectations for dress, play, and career aspirations (Martin, 1989).
- Significant conceptual and emotional changes give the sex role a greater degree of clarity and highlight the relevance of one's sex in overall self-concept. Major aspects of sex-role identification are an understanding of gender, sex-role standards, identification with parents, and sex-role preference (Baumrind, 1982; Martin, 1989; Spence, 1982).
- Within a family, children are likely to have personality characteristics similar to those of the more dominant parent (Hetherington, 1967).
- Children behave like their parents in order to increase the *perceived similarity* with them, valuing characteristics such as physical size, good looks, special competences, power, success, and respect.
- Early-school-age children can use the social circumstances that may have produced a child's emotional responses, especially responses of anger and distress, to understand and empathize with another child's feelings (Fabes, Eisenberg, McCormick, & Wilson, 1988; Hoffner & Badzinski, 1989).
- Under conditions of peer competition, children begin to experience anxiety about their performance and about the way their abilities will be evaluated in comparison to others' (Butler, 1989).
- Open peer criticism tends to outnumber compliments, and boys tend more than girls to be critical of their peers' performance (Frey & Ruble, 1987).
- Friendships in early-school-age children are based on concrete goods; friendships can be broken by the taking of a toy, hitting, or name-calling (Hetherington, Cox, & Cox, 1979).
- Friendship groups are segregated by sex; boys and girls grow up in quite distinctive peer environments and use different strategies to achieve dominance or leadership in their groups. Boys tend to use physical assertiveness and direct demands; girls tend to use verbal persuasion and polite suggestions (Maccoby, 1988; Maccoby & Jacklin, 1987).
- Some traits of temperament such as attention span, goal orientation, lack of distractibility, and curiosity can affect cognitive functioning because the more pronounced these traits are, the better the child will learn (Campos, Bertenthal, & Kermoian, 1992).
- Some researchers think that external stimuli such as love and nurturing can affect brain chemistry to the extent that seemingly innate negative personality characteristics can be reversed (Embry & Flannery, 1999).
- Securely attached children "demonstrate an expectation of an empathic response," while insecurely attached children tend to be anxious, fearful, or clingy and see the world and other people as threatening (Fonagy, Steele, Steele, Higgitt, & Target, 1994, p. 235).
- Resilient children have a strong ability to make and keep good friends. They are very good at choosing a couple of friends who stick with them, sometimes from kindergarten through middle age (Werner, 1996; Werner & Smith, 1992)

Relating

- Children are most likely to interact with same-sex friends (Maccoby, 1988).
- Preferences for sex-typed play activities and same-sex play companions have been observed among preschoolers as well as older children (Caldera, Huston, & O'Brien, 1989; Maccoby, 1988).
- Girls and boys establish peer friendship groups with members of the same sex and may reject or compete with members of the opposite sex (Maccoby, 1988).
- Children are influenced by the social groups that immediately surround them (Rosenberg, 1979).
- Early-school-age children are aware of the importance of acceptance by adults and peers outside the family, especially teachers and classmates (Weinstein, Marshall, Sharp, & Botkin, 1987). Children's ability to form close relationships becomes highly dependent on their social skills, which include an ability to interpret and understand other children's nonverbal cues such as body language and pitch of voice, to respond to what other children say, to use eye contact, to mention the other child's name often, and to use touch to get attention. If they want to do something that another child opposes,

continued

TABLE 2.6 Developmental Tasks for Children and Adolescents in the Domains of Thinking, Feeling, and Relating: Early School Age (4 to 6 Years) (continued)

they can articulate their reasons for why their plan is a good one. They can suppress their own wishes and desires to reach a compromise with other children and be willing to change. When they are with a group of children, they do not know; they are quiet but observant until they have a feeling for the structure and dynamics of the group (Butler, 1989, 1990; Dodge, 1983; Thompson, 1998).

- Children who lack social skills tend to be rejected by other children. Commonly, they are withdrawn, do not listen well, and offer few if any reasons for their wishes; they rarely praise others and find it difficult to join in cooperative activities (Dodge, 1983). They often exhibit features of oppositional defiant or conduct disorder, such as regular fighting, dominating and pushing others around, or being spiteful (Thompson, 1990).
- It is essential to begin developing prosocial attitudes and behaviors in children at a very young age because aggression in young children that is not remedied nearly always leads to later acts of delinquency (Yoshikawa, 1995).
- The specific antisocial behaviors that young children engage in are learned "through specific and flexible processes of socialization and development" (Slaby et al., 1995, p. 2).
- The most critical factor in promoting children's social development may well be bonding with positive, nurturing adults, including teachers who offer unconditional acceptance and support, model prosocial behavior, live according to positive values, and convey the importance of these values to an individual's well-being (Gregg, 1996).

TABLE 2.7 Developmental Tasks for Children and Adolescents in the Domains of Thinking, Feeling, and Relating: Middle School Age (6 to 12 Years)

Thinking

- The behavior of well-adjusted, competent children is maintained in part by a number of important cognitive abilities such as social perspective taking, interpersonal problem solving, and information processing. These cognitive abilities foster a child's entry into successful peer relations (Asarnow & Callan, 1985; Chalmers & Townsend, 1990; Dodge, Murphy, & Buchsbaum, 1984; Dodge, Pettit, McClasky, & Brown, 1986; Downey & Walker, 1989; Elias, Beier, & Gara, 1989; Patterson, 1982; Pellegrini, 1985; Renshaw & Asher, 1982; Thompson, 1998, 2006).
- At age 6 or 7, a new stage of intellectual development evolves as *concrete operational thought,* in which rules of logic can be applied to observable or manipulative physical relations (Piaget & Inhelder, 1969). Children enjoy classifying and ordering the environment. Addition, subtraction, multiplication, and division are all learned during this stage. Children's performances on tests of cognitive maturity are likely to be inconsistent.
- Children develop metacognition—that is, "thinking about their thinking"—as a means of assessing and monitoring knowledge. They begin to distinguish those answers about which they are confident from those answers about which they have doubts. They are able to review various strategies for approaching a problem to reach the best solution and to select strategies to increase their comprehension of a concept (Butterfield, Nelson, & Peck, 1988; Carr, Kurtz, Schneider, Turner, & Borkowski, 1989; Cross & Paris, 1988)
- Children can learn study techniques that will enhance their ability to organize and recall information. They are also amenable to training both at home and at school. They can master the principles of classification and causality, manipulate techniques for measurement, understanding exploratory hypothesis and evaluating evidence, and consider events that happened long ago. They strive to match their achievements to internalized goals and external standards.
- A high IQ is a powerful predictor of academic competence (Masten et al., 1988; Pellegrini, Masten, Garmezy, & Ferrarese, 1987). In addition, it has been associated with fewer behavior problems, social competence, and successful judgment in general (Garmezy, 1985; Tizard, Schofield, & Hewison, 1982).

TABLE 2.7   Developmental Tasks for Children and Adolescents in the Domains of Thinking, Feeling, and Relating: Middle School Age (6 to 12 Years) (continued)

Feeling

- The need for peer approval becomes a powerful force toward conformity (Ames, Ilg, & Baker, 1988; Pepitone, Loeb, & Murdock, 1977). The peer group establishes norms for acceptance and rejection; children learn to dress, talk, and joke in ways that are acceptable to peers. With the increased emphasis on peer acceptance and conformity comes the risk of peer rejection and feelings of loneliness. The stresses once identified with adolescence have now become prevalent in the lives of children (Ames et al., 1988; Nelson & Crawford, 1990). Increase in stress also increases anxiety, depression, and suicide ideation (Herring, 1990). In childhood, the manifestations of depression often co-occur along with a broader array of behaviors such as aggression, school failure, anxiety, antisocial behavior, and poor peer relations, making the diagnosis of depression in childhood often difficult (Weiner, 1980).
- Many children express loneliness, social dissatisfaction, and difficulty in making friends (Asher, Hymel, & Renshaw, 1984). Being oneself, showing enthusiasm and concern for others, and showing self-confidence but not conceit are among the characteristics that lead to popularity (Hartup, 1983).
- These are the years children have best friends—early same-sex friendships that become building blocks for adult relationships (Berndt, 1981). Children learn to discriminate among different types of peer relationships: best friends, social friends, activity partners, acquaintances, and strangers (Oden, 1987).
- Middle-school-age children focus on self-evaluation. They receive feedback from others about the quality of their performance. At around age 6 or 7, children's thoughts and those of their peers clearly conflict; they begin to accommodate others, and egocentric thought begins to give way to social pressure (Wadsworth, 1989).
- By age 11, children are able to differentiate specific areas of competence that contribute to overall self-evaluation, particularly the domains of cognitive, physical, and social competence, and to weigh their contributions to self-satisfaction in different ways (Harter, 1982; Stigler, Smith, & Mao, 1985).
- Children approach their process of self-evaluation from a framework of either self-confidence or self-doubt.
- Self-efficacy, a person's sense of confidence, is increased with successful experience and decreased with repeated failure. Children who have a low sense of self-efficacy tend to give up in the face of difficulty because they attribute their failure to a basic lack of ability (Bandura, 1982; Bandura & Schunck, 1981; Brown & Inouye, 1978; McAuley, Duncan, & McElroy, 1989; Skaalvik & Hagtvet, 1990).
- Children who have a low sense of self-esteem are more likely to experience intense anxiety about losing in a competitive situation (Brustad, 1988).
- A child's attitude toward work and need to achieve is established by the end of this stage (Atkinson & Birch, 1978; Erikson, 1963).
- Children who are not capable of mastering certain skills will experience feelings of inferiority and inadequacy.

Relating

- Children describe close friends as people who like the same activities, share common interests, enjoy each other's company, and can count on each other for help. Friendships provide social and developmental advantages (Ainsworth, 1989; Hartup, 1989; Youniss, 1980).
- Peers have an important influence on diminishing one another's self-centered outlooks (Piaget, 1948).
- Adults, particularly teachers, lose some of their power to influence children's behavior. Children often play to their peers in class instead of responding to the teacher. Roles of class clown, class snob, and "Joe Cool" serve as ways of gaining approval from one's peer group. The need for peer approval becomes a powerful force toward conformity (Pepitone et al., 1977). Perceived pressure to conform seems stronger in the fifth and sixth grades than later (Gavin & Furman, 1989).
- The structure of the school influences friendship formation. Close friends connect in classes and at extracurricular activities (Epstein, 1983; Hallinan, 1979). Close friendships appear to be influenced by attractiveness, intelligence, and classroom social status (Clark & Ayers, 1988).

continued

TABLE 2.7   Developmental Tasks for Children and Adolescents in the Domains of Thinking, Feeling, and Relating: Middle School Age (6 to 12 Years) (continued)

- The peer group joins the adult world as a source of both criticism and approval. Pressures toward conformity, competition, and the need for approval feed into the evaluation process. Peers identify others' skills and begin to generate profiles of one another.

- Children who relate aggressively with others have a high probability of being rejected by peers, while those who withdraw have a high probability of being neglected by peers (Dodge, 1983).

- To assess their own abilities, children tend to rely on many external sources of evaluation, including grades, teachers' comments, parental approval, and peer approval (Crooks, 1988). By the middle school years, parents develop expectations of how their children will behave, and children develop such expectations of parents. Parents and children tend to label each other in broad categories; for example, a parent is likely to label his or her child as "smart" or "dumb," "introverted" or "extroverted," "mannerly" or "unruly," and "lazy" or "hardworking." The child is likely to label his or her parent as "cold" or "warm," "understanding and easy to talk to" or "not understanding and difficult to talk to," or "too stern" or "too permissive" (Hess, 1981; Maccoby & Martin, 1983).

- Social expectations contribute to children's expectations about their own abilities and behaviors. Evaluative feedback that is associated with intellectual ability or skills reinforces children's conceptualization of their own competence. The pattern of expectations appears to crystallize during the second and third grades. By the end of fifth grade, children are very aware of their teachers' expectations for their performance, and they are likely to reflect those expectations in their own academic achievement (Alexander & Entwisle, 1988; Entwisle, Alexander, Pallas, & Cadigan, 1987; Harris & Rosenthal, 1985; Weinstein et al., 1987).

- A new dimension of play is added to the quality of child's play: team play. Children learn to subordinate personal goals to group goals and learn the principles of the division of labor and elements of competition (Klint & Weiss, 1987).

- Involvement in social activities seems to be as important as academic programs for youth development. Social activities help to foster personality development and socialization (Holland & Andre, 1987). Participation in different social activities is related to low incidence of behavior problems (Rae-Grant, Thomas, Offord, & Boyle, 1989).

- The social environment stimulates feelings of inferiority through the negative value it places on any kind of failure. Failure in school and the public ridicule it brings have been shown to play a central role in the establishment of a negative self-image (Calhoun & Morse, 1977). In general, girls tend to have lower levels of aspiration, more anxiety about failing, and a stronger tendency to avoid risking failure and to accept failure than boys (Dweck & Elliot, 1983; Parsons, Adler, & Kaczala, 1982; Stein & Bailey, 1973).

- Peer relationships contribute to a child's social and cognitive development and socialization (Benard, 1990). Children directly learn attitudes, values, and skills through peer modeling and reinforcement. Peers contribute significantly to one's moral development because the child needs opportunities to see rules of society not only as dictates from figures of authority but also as products that emerge from group agreement (Thompson, 1998).

- In peer interactions, children "learn to share, to help, to comfort, to empathize with others. Empathy (or perspective taking) is one of the most critical competencies for cognitive and social development" (Benard, 1990, p. 2). In peer resource groups, children learn impulse control, communication skills, creative and critical thinking, and relationship skills. Lack of these is a "powerful well-proven early predictor of later substance abuse, delinquency, and mental health problems; social competence is a predictor of life success" (p. 2).

- Positive peer relationships are strongly correlated with liking school, higher school attendance rates, and higher academic performance. Peer relationships exert a powerful influence on a child's development of identity and autonomy. It is through peer relationships that a frame of reference for perceiving oneself is developed.

TABLE 2.8 Developmental Tasks for Children and Adolescents in the Domains of Thinking, Feeling, and Relating: Early Adolescence (12 to 18 Years)

Thinking

- Thinking becomes more abstract. The final stage of cognitive development characterized by reasoning, hypothesis generating, and hypothesis testing evolves (Chapman, 1988; Inhelder & Piaget, 1958; Piaget, 1970, 1972).
- Adolescents learn to manipulate more than two categories of variables simultaneously and to think about changes that come with time. They develop the ability to hypothesize logical sequences of events, to foresee consequences of actions, to detect logical consistency or inconsistency in a set of statements, and to think in realistic ways about self, others, and the world (Acredolo, Adams, & Schmid, 1984; Demetriou & Efklides, 1985; Flavell, 1963; Inhelder & Piaget, 1958; Neimark, 1975, 1982; Siegler, Liebert, & Liebert, 1973).
- The gains in conceptual skill made during adolescence are enhanced by active involvement in a more complex and differentiated academic environment (Kuhn, Amsel, & O'Loughlin, 1988; Linn, Clement, Pulos, & Sullivan, 1989; Rabinowitz, 1988).
- The focus of the adolescent's abstract thinking is on gaining a deeper and more profound self-awareness (Hacker, 1994).
- Adolescent behavior can be viewed as a defense mechanism in response to conflict arising from the existential concerns of isolation, death, meaninglessness, and choice (Hacker, 1994).

Feeling

- Early adolescence is characterized by rapid physical changes, heightened sensitivity to peer relations, a struggle between group identity and alienation (Erikson, 1963), increased autonomy from the family, and the development of a personal identity.
- Generally, girls are more dissatisfied than boys with their physical appearance and overall body image (Petersen, Schulenberg, Abramowitz, Offer, & Jarcho, 1984).
- Boys who mature later than their age-mates experience considerable psychological stress and develop a negative self-image (Blyth, Bulcroft, & Simmons, 1981; Clausen, 1975). Early-maturing girls experience increased stress resulting in heightened self-consciousness and anxiety (Hill, 1988); they are more likely to be identified as behavior problems in school (Blyth et al., 1981).
- Adolescents have fewer daily experiences of overt joy and more experiences of the mildly negative emotions perceived as moodiness or apathy (Larson & Lampman-Petraitis, 1989). The more troublesome of these emotions are anxiety, shame, embarrassment, guilt, shyness, depression, and anger (Adelson & Doehrman, 1980; Garrison, Schoenbach, & Kaplan, 1989; Maag, Rutherford, & Parks, 1988; Robertson & Simons, 1989). Adolescent girls are likely to have heightened awareness of new levels of negative emotions that focus inward, such as shame, guilt, depression, and anxiety. Adolescent boys are likely to have a heightened awareness of new levels of negative emotions that focus on others, such as contempt and aggression (Costello, 1990; Ostrov, Offer, & Howard, 1989; Stapley & Haviland, 1989; Tuma, 1989; Zill & Schoenborn, 1990). A major developmental task is to sustain a tolerance for one's own emotionality. Anxiety and overcontrol of emotions is manifested in such self-destructive behaviors as anorexia nervosa and bulimia or other eating disorders (Yates, 1989).
- As adolescents make their transition from childhood to adolescence, they must resolve the conflict of group identification versus alienation. The absence of peer social support that may result from a negative resolution of this crisis can have significant implications for adjustment in school, self-efficacy, and related psychosocial development. Chronic conflict from one's inability to integrate into a meaningful reference group can lead to lifelong difficulties in areas of personal health and well-being, work satisfaction, and the formation of intimate family bonds (Allen, Weissberg, & Hawkins, 1989; East, Hess, & Lerner, 1987; Spencer, 1982, 1988).

Relating

- With respect to the psychological meaning of bodily changes for males and females, the changes influence the adolescent's identification with the role of man or woman. They become more egocentric and self-involved. The changes produce ambivalence about new aspects of self, and if not supported, negative feelings and conflicts can result.

continued

TABLE 2.8　Developmental Tasks for Children and Adolescents in the Domains of Thinking, Feeling, and Relating: Early Adolescence (12 to 18 Years) (continued)

- The peer group becomes more structured and organized, with distinct subgroups (Thompson, 1998). Peer group friendships, especially for girls, provide opportunities for emotional intimacy, support, self-disclosure, and companionship (Berndt, 1982; Raffaelli & Duckett, 1989; Tedesco & Gaier, 1988).
- Popularity and acceptance into a peer group at the high school level is based on attractiveness; athletic ability; social class; academic performance; future goals; affiliation with a religious, racial, or ethnic group; and special talents.
- Beginning in seventh grade, adolescents perceive their relationship with friends as more intimate than those with parents. Mothers remain at a constant level of intimacy across all ages; intimacy between a child and his or her mother during the middle school years provides a basis for establishing close, affectionate relationships with adolescent friends (Gold & Yanof, 1985; Hunter & Youniss, 1982). Fathers decline in intimacy from seventh to 10th grade and remain constant in intimacy from 10th grade through college (Gold & Yanof, 1985).
- Over the age range 12 to 15, adolescents discuss academic/vocational, social/ethical, and family relations topics more often with their parents than their friends, and they discuss peer relations more with their friends (Hunter, 1985).
- Parental values, educational expectations, the capacity of parents to exercise appropriate control over their child's social and school activities, and the norms of the peer group all play important roles in a young person's willingness to become sexually active (Brooks-Gunn & Furstenberg, 1989; Hanson, Myers, & Ginsburg, 1987; Newcomer & Udry, 1987).
- Adolescents with high self-esteem seldom use avoidance strategies and prefer problem-solving strategies (Dumont & Provost, 1999). Self-esteem is positively correlated with involvement in the community, family, and neighborhood (Dumont & Provost, 1999).
- Adolescents who do not have high self-esteem are more likely to use avoidant coping strategies (Dumont & Provost, 1999). Involvement in negative social or illegal activities (stealing, bullying, illegal use of alcohol or drugs) is positively correlated with depression, stress, and anxiety (Patterson, McCubbin, & Neede, 1983).
- Overly socially incompetent adolescents report increased levels of depression, anxiety, and self-criticism, much more than competent children from low-stress backgrounds (Luthar, 1991; Luthar & Zigler, 1991).

Many youths across the nation are manifesting serious social, emotional, and cognitive deficits. The indicators of emotional deficits appear in the increased incidence of violence, suicide, and homicide. Cognitive deficits place youth at a disadvantage academically, making them more vulnerable to criminal influences. Social deficits manifest themselves in poor peer relations and an inability to resolve conflicts and manage anger.

Social literacy skills are *interpersonal* skills that are essential for meaningful interaction with others. Social skills are those behaviors that, within a given situation, predict important social outcomes such as peer acceptance, popularity, self-efficacy, competence, and self-esteem. These skills fall into categories such as being kind, cooperative, and compliant to reduce defiance, aggression, conflict, and antisocial behavior. They also involve showing interest in people and socializing successfully to reduce behavior problems associated with withdrawal, depression, fearfulness, and anxiety. Social skills include problem solving, assertiveness, thinking critically, resolving conflict, managing anger, and utilizing peer-pressure refusal skills.

Emotional literacy skills are *intrapersonal* skills, such as knowing one's emotions by recognizing a feeling as it happens; managing emotions (i.e., shaking off anxiety, gloom, irritability, and the consequences of failure); motivating oneself to attain goals, delay gratification, stifle impulsiveness, and maintain self-control; recognizing emotions in others with empathy and perspective taking; and handling interpersonal relationships effectively. Emotional skills fall into categories such as knowing the relationships among thoughts, feelings, and actions; establishing a sense of identity and acceptance of self; learning to value teamwork, collaboration, and cooperation; and learning to regulate one's mood, to empathize, and to maintain hope.

Cognitive skills are *thinking* skills, such as knowing how to problem-solve, describe, associate, conceptualize, classify, analyze, evaluate, make inferences, and think critically. Cognitive psychologists advocate teaching youths a repertoire of cognitive and metacognitive strategies using graphic organizers and organizational patterns, self-monitoring, self-questioning, self-regulating, enhancing study skills, and making metacognitions. Inherently, social, emotional, and cognitive skills can be systematically taught and cultivated to give youths advantages with both their interpersonal and intrapersonal adjustment, as well as their academic success.

Concurrently, there is a growing body of knowledge that, in order to overcome risks and adversity, many youths and adults have developed the potential to be resilient. From her work with the International Resilience Research Project, Grotberg (1995, 1998) advocated that people draw upon 15 sources of resilience to overcome adversity (see Table 2.9).

Ideally, the development and implementation of a comprehensive integrated curriculum would be designed for the mastery of daily problem-solving skills such as self-competency, enhancement of interpersonal relationships, communications, values, and the awareness of rules, attitudes, and motivation (Worrell & Stilwell, 1981). Henderson and Milstein (1996) recommend that, to foster resiliency in children, educators:

- Increase prosocial bonding
- Set clear, consistent boundaries
- Teach life skills
- Provide caring and support
- Set and communicate high expectations
- Provide opportunities for meaningful participation in both the school and community

 *educators role in building resiliency*

TABLE 2.9   Fifteen Elements of Resilience

I have:
- People around me I trust and who love me, no matter what.
- People who set limits for me so I know when to stop before there is danger or trouble.
- People who show me how to do things right by the way they do things.
- People who want me to learn to do things on my own.
- People who help me when I am sick, in danger, or need to learn.

I am:
- A person people can like and love.
- Glad to do nice things for others and show my concern.
- Respectful of myself and others.
- Willing to be responsible for what I do.
- Sure things will be all right.

I can:
- Talk to others about things that frighten me or bother me.
- Find ways to solve problems that I face.
- Control myself when I feel like doing something not right or dangerous.
- Figure out when it is a good time to talk to someone or take action.
- Find someone to help me when I need it.

Source: Grotberg, E. H. (1998). I am, I have, I can: What families worldwide taught us about resilience. *Reaching Today's Youth, Spring*, 36–39. Reprinted with permission.

Pikes, Burrell, and Holliday (1998) advocate resilience-building experiences that focus on five themes set forth by Wang, Haertel, and Walberg (1995):

- Competency: feeling successful
- Belonging: feeling valued
- Usefulness: feeling needed
- Potency: feeling empowered
- Optimism: feeling encouraged and hopeful

Life skills training can provide adolescents with supportive services in an attempt to intervene in academic, behavioral, emotional, or interpersonal problems. Education and counseling in life skills can emerge as a comprehensive delivery system designed to facilitate effective functioning throughout the life span (i.e., as a developmental model of helping). The following life-skills descriptors reflect the full spectrum of program components.

- *Interpersonal communication/human relations:* Skills necessary for effective verbal and non-verbal communication, for example, attitudes of empathy, genuineness, clearly expressing ideas and opinions, and giving and receiving feedback.
- *Problem solving/decision making:* Skills of seeking, assessing, and analyzing information, problem solving, implementation, and responsible decision making.
- *Identity development/purpose in life:* Skills that contribute to the ongoing development of personal identity, enhancing self-esteem, and life transitions.
- *Physical fitness/health maintenance:* Skills necessary for nutrition, sexuality, stress management, and wellness.
- *Career awareness:* Skills for obtaining and maintaining desired jobs and giving students opportunities to practice these skills.
- *Conflict resolution:* Skills in effective problem-solving techniques and building more effective interpersonal skills.
- *Study skills:* Skills to improve students' academic work by developing greater academic mastery and enhancing study skills.
- *Family concerns:* Skills to improve students' abilities in communicating with parents, stepparents, and siblings to bring about a more harmonious family life (Wang, Haertel & Walberg, 1994, p. 53).

Such skills, when integrated into instruction and assimilated into a child's cognitive, emotional, and behavioral repertoire, will have long-term implications for the child's future well-being, as well as that of others with whom she or he interacts. These skills should be part of a comprehensive standards-based developmental school counseling model. See Table 2.10 for a comparison between traditional and developmental counseling programs.

TABLE 2.10   Traditional Versus Developmental Counseling Programs

TRADITIONAL COUNSELING PROGRAMS	DEVELOPMENTAL COUNSELING PROGRAMS
Crisis counseling	Primary prevention/early intervention
Information service	Developmental counseling curriculum
Career information service	Career planning and development
Scheduling	Program management
Reactive	Proactive
Clerical-task oriented	Goal/program oriented
Unstructured	Outcome accountability
Maintain status quo	Evaluation and action planning
School as institution	School as community

THE IMPORTANCE OF ACKNOWLEDGING CULTURE AND DIVERSITY

Although many professional school counseling proponents have made concerted efforts to define comprehensive school counseling programs in a systematic manner, some other proponents have recommended that the comprehensive developmental model needs to be reconceptualized to meet the needs of a growing population of diverse students (House & Martin, 1998; Keys, Bemak, & Lockhart, 1998). Culture has a critical influence on human development that cannot be ignored. It influences belief systems; attitudes; values; language skills; nonverbal behavior; social, emotional, and cognitive skills; and assimilation into mainstream culture.

Perhaps it is important to rethink which developmental models clearly address developmental school counseling programs within the context of culture and ethnicity. Urban school settings are impacted by a number of additional school and community issues that become barriers to learning, including substance abuse, unintended teenage pregnancy, higher dropout rates, and gang violence (Thompson, 2006). Moving school counseling programs from a collection of fragmented services to a comprehensive program was a significant achievement in the history of the profession (Gysbers & Henderson, 2006). Yet, the controversial question currently being explored by major proponents in the field is, Do comprehensive school counseling programs adequately meet the growing needs of diverse and urban student populations? *Comprehensive* needs to be redefined and expanded to provide more effective programs for this growing population with many complex needs (Adelman & Taylor, 2005). Working in increasingly culturally diverse school communities will require professional school counselors to more explicitly address dimensions related to culture, gender, and ethnicity.

CONCLUSION

Interpersonal, intrapersonal, and academic achievement should become an integral part of the developmental school curriculum and evolve as a required course that is integrated into the young person's program of studies, much like computer literacy, driver education, or fine arts. Powell, Farrar, and Cohen (1985) lend credence to this perspective, maintaining that along with the horizontal, vertical, and extracurricular components, there must be a *service curriculum,* which is now the fastest growing component within the comprehensive high school. Targeted programs within this curriculum directly address social, psychological, and interpersonal problems such as grief and mourning, child abuse, depression, family dysfunction, alcoholic parents, bulimia, anorexia, underachievement, loss of significant others, or emotional and social problems deemed educationally valid. Some schools provide special services depending on their particular needs, such as day care for children of students; rehabilitation for delinquent teens; services for special-needs students such as the handicapped; remedial services such as tutorials for the underachieving or English-language learners; enrichment programs for the gifted; and resource rooms for students in academic trouble. The effect of such programs is to make counseling and learning available on a larger scale to the many groups that need help but are not currently receiving it.

The Evolution of Accountability

3

Three Current Models of Program Evaluation to Close the Achievement Gaps Among All Students, Including Minority Students and Children of Poverty

> For nearly half a century, the association of social and economic disadvantage with a students and the achievement gap has been well known to economists, sociologists, and educators. Most, however, have avoided the obvious implication of this understanding—raising the achievement of lower-class children requires amelioration of the social and economic conditions of their lives, not just school reform. Today's information economy demands more education and higher levels of skills and knowledge for employment than ever before in history. Children on the lower end of the achievement gap without adequate skills, knowledge, and education have little chance for economic well-being in this country. When a quality education is denied to children at birth because of their parents' skin color or income, it is not only bad social policy, it is immoral.
>
> Richard Rothstein (2004, p. i)

In the current educational climate, the issue of accountability, the disparities in achievement, and the implications of professional school counselors in educational reform issues, especially closing the achievement gap and professional school counselors' impact on the reform movement, are a growing national initiative and continue to be in the forefront of educational reform dialogue across the nation (Dahir, 2004; Isaacs, 2003; Johnson & Johnson, 2002; Myrick, 2003b). Professional school counselors are continually plagued with the question of how students are different because of what they do. Another critical element in the current reform movement is how to measure the change in students through systematic program development and evaluation.

This chapter traces professional school counselors' efforts in various movements within the economic and political landscape to be accountable to the needs of all students and how they have worked to demonstrate credibility, accountability, effectiveness, and efficiency. This has become the professional school counselor's relentless legacy since the evolution of accountability began as early as the 1920s: proving their effectiveness. Several models that demonstrate accountability of professional school counseling programs and services are provided in this chapter.

Table 3.1 represents the concerns and recommendations for accountability throughout the decades. It became increasingly apparent after budget cuts at federal, state, and local levels during the 1980s that the overarching universal initiatives and the national mantra on which the professional school counselor's survival depended has been an emphasis on accountability.

The ever widening achievement gap experienced by minority children and children of poverty, and the theme of closing the achievement gap, is driving the current accountability movement. In an increasingly competitive global arena, the United States and its public schools cannot afford to ignore this problem. Persistent poverty in our society is undermining our economic security and future economic growth potential. Uncertain economic markets are also a threat to professional school counseling programs, because since they are perceived as a resource or ancillary in many school settings, they are vulnerable

TABLE 3.1   Evolution of Professional School Counselor Accountability

DECADE	ACCOUNTABILITY CONCERNS
Before the 1920s, professional school counselors were under the auspices of vocational guidance.	What method do we have of checking the result of our guidance? For particular groups, was it guidance, misguidance, or merely a contributing experience? We simply must work out some definite method of testing and checking the results of our work. If we do not, some other group will, with possibly disastrous results for our work (Payne, 1924, p. 63). Myers (1926) was one of the first to suggest four standards: 1. The number of guidance and counseling activities 2. Distribution and time devoted to each activity 3. Thoroughness revealed by the kinds and quality of work competed 4. Consistency of organization
The 1930s demonstrated extensive work on the issue of accountability.	Proctor (1930) developed a scorecard system designed to assess whether or not certain guidance and counseling activities were in place and functioning accurately. This was the forerunner of today's concept of program evaluation or program audit. Outcomes that were measured included: • Fewer students dropping out of school • Increase in scholarship • Better morale in the student body • Better all-around school life • Fewer student failures • Students better informed about the future • Satisfactory adjustment to community, vocation, or college • Fewer disciplinary cases • Fewer absences • More intelligent selection of subjects • Better study habits (Christy, Stewart, & Rosecrance, 1930; Hinderman, 1930; Rosecrance, 1930) Hutson (1935) aptly stated the need for measuring the results of guidance initiatives by acknowledging that "these days … all school activities are subject to the sharpest scrutiny, and the administrator is called upon to justify every expenditure of time and money in the operation of the school" (p. 21).
The 1940s focused on what kind of training school counselors should receive and how to document evaluation.	Froehlich (1949) proposed the following system of evaluation: 1. External criteria, the do-you-do-this? 2. Follow-up, What happened then? 3. Client opinion, the what-do-you-think? 4. Expert opinion, "The information please?" 5. Specific techniques, the little-little method 6. Within-group changes, the before-and-after method 7. Between-group changes, "This is the difference?" (p. 2)

TABLE 3.1   Evolution of Professional School Counselor Accountability (continued)

DECADE	ACCOUNTABILITY CONCERNS
The 1950s stressed the need to establish better criteria for measuring the results of guidance in the schools.	Cottle (1957), Jones (1951), and Mahoney (1950) stressed the need to establish better criteria for measuring the results of guidance and counseling in the schools and the total impact it had on student's lives.
The 1960s solidified the guidance and counseling movement with the 1958 National Defense Education Act (NDEA) by providing funding for state supervisors, state testing programs, and systematic training of individuals to become school counselors through summer and yearlong institutes.	The 1960s generated the accountability movement in education. School counselors needed to state guidance objectives in measurable terms and demonstrate that these objectives related to the goals of education. Guidance programs increasingly came under scrutiny on how their initiatives made an impact on students. Wellman & Twiford (1961) developed a document for the U.S. Office of Education entitled *Guidance Counseling and Testing Program Evaluation* and provided outcomes, suggestions for data collection, and methods that could be used to measure student outcomes, such as:
	1. Do students develop greater understanding of their abilities, aptitudes, and interests?
	2. Are students and their parents fully aware of opportunities and requirements for education and careers?
	3. Do students select courses, and achieve them, in line with their abilities, aptitudes, interests, and opportunities?
	4. Do those students who are able to do so finish secondary school?
	5. Do those students who are capable of doing so continue education beyond the secondary school?
	6. Are those students who continue education beyond secondary school successful in their educational pursuits?
	7. Are significant numbers of the especially able students getting more expensive background in mathematics, science, and the foreign languages? (p. 26)
	Neidt (1965) identified early on that guidance and counseling should "identify factors of the guidance process that are uniquely related to changes in the behavior of students" (p. 2). Later, Tamminen and Miller (1968) informed the public about the lack of outcome research: "Faith, hope and charity have characterized the American attitude toward guidance programs—faith in their effectiveness, hope that they can meet important if not always clearly specified needs, and charity in not demanding more evaluative evidence that the faith and hope are justified" (p. 3).
In the 1970s, the accountability movement intensified, defining guidance developmentally in measurable individual outcomes.	Multiple initiatives occurred to fulfill the need to demonstrate outcomes:
	1. McDaniel (1970) proposed a model for guidance called Youth Guidance Systems, organized around goals, objectives, programs, implementation plans, and designs for evaluation.
	2. The Comprehensive Career Guidance System (CCGS) developed by the American Institutes for Research (Jones, Helliwell, Ganschow, & Hamilton, 1975) was designed to systematically plan, implement, and evaluate guidance programs.
	3. Concurrently, the National Center for Vocational and Technical Education designed a behavioral model for career guidance based on a systems approach focusing on evaluation.
	4. PLAN (Program of Learning in Accordance with Needs) was advocated by Dunn (1972) as an integral part of the regular instructional program with an emphasis on empirical emphasis to demonstrate program effectiveness (p. 8).

continued

TABLE 3.1   Evolution of Professional School Counselor Accountability (continued)

DECADE	*ACCOUNTABILITY CONCERNS*
	5. In 1971, the University of Missouri–Columbia was awarded a U.S. Office of Education grant to assist each state in developing models or guides for implementing and evaluating career guidance, counseling, and placement programs in schools. Gysbers and Moore (1974) developed a model on how to develop, implement, and evaluate a comprehensive guidance program. The manual was evaluation-based, focusing on both process and outcome evaluation. Four questions were asked: • What do we want to accomplish? • What kind of delivery system is needed? • What did we provide and do? • What was the impact?
	6. In 1975, Pine (1975) wrote: "In this age of accountability the evaluation of school counseling is of paramount concern to all counselors regardless of their theoretical and philosophical biases" (p. 136). Pine identified measurable behavioral changes in students as the result of being involved in counseling: • Academic achievement • Increase in grade-point average • Improvement in reading • Peer relations • Personal adjustment • School attendance • School adjustment • School attitudes • School anxiety • Self-concept • Self-esteem • Self-understanding • Teacher–student relationships • Reduction in inappropriate behavior(s) • Intelligence test scores • Setting realistic goals (p. 138) Typical methods for evaluation the effectiveness of school counseling programs were the experimental approach, or "after-only" design; the "before-and-after design"; the "tabulation approach"; the "follow-up approach"; "opinion surveys"; the "descriptive approach," where counseling practices are analyzed and described; and the "case-study" approach, a longitudinal view of each client (p. 129).
In the 1980s, accountability issues increased due to budget cuts at the federal, state, and local levels.	Numerous articles provided ideas of how to do program evaluation (Lewis, 1983; Lombana, 1985; Pine, 1981).
During the 1990s, the lack of research concerning the impact of guidance and counseling became more apparent, yet professional school counselors had little time in their demanding schedules to fulfill an accountability model.	Lee & Workman (1992) aptly lamented that "school counseling programs seem to have little empirical evidence to support claims to have significant impact on the development of children and adolescents" (p. 15). Borders and Drury (1992b) maintained that "evaluation plans should focus on program results rather than on program services" (p. 493). Whiston & Sexton (1998) reiterated that "in this era of accountability, professional school counselors increasingly are asked to provide information to parents, administrators, and legislators on the effectiveness of school counseling activities" (p. 412).

TABLE 3.1 Evolution of Professional School Counselor Accountability (continued)

DECADE	ACCOUNTABILITY CONCERNS
In the 2000s, the Education Trust began to change the old question of "What do counselors do?" to the new question, "How are students better off because of what professional school counselors do?"	Trevisan and Hubert (2001) reinforced the progress made over the past 20 years regarding the importance of program evaluation and of obtaining accountability data regarding student results. Lapan (2001) stressed the importance of comprehensive programs of guidance and counseling "conceptualized as results-based systems" (p. 289). Professional school counselors should assume the role of counseling, consulting, coordination of services, leadership, advocacy, collaboration and teaming, managing resources, use of data, and use of technology. "What gets measured gets done."

Source: Adapted from Gysbers, N. C., *Professional School Counseling, 8*(1), 1–14. Reprinted with permission.

when budget cuts occur. Research has documented the connection between human capital development and economic growth and brought forward clear evidence that children growing up in poverty have significantly reduced economic prospects stemming from negative impacts on childhood development, reduced educational achievement, and fewer economic opportunities (Castelló & Doménech, 2002). Professional school counselors must become managers of resources and use school improvement data and technology to demonstrate accountability.

PROFESSIONAL SCHOOL COUNSELORS ARE CRITICAL TO THE CURRENT REFORM MOVEMENT

This is a critical time for leaders in school counseling to invest in the future of the profession and support school counseling research. School counselors may believe they make a difference, but without "hard data" to support these claims, school counselors run the risk of losing their positions.

Susan Whiston (2002, p. 153)

For decades, professional school counselors have been trying to define accountability and find ways to monitor it. Despite the new models from the Education Trust (http://www2.edtrust.org/edtrust/) and the American School Counseling Association (ASCA, 2005a) to transform school counseling, traditional ways of operating have persisted and professional school counselors continue to deliver a constellation of isolated services and reactive responses to a small percentage of the student population. Professional school counselors' roles and duties are often determined by others (i.e., administrators, central office personnel) rather than by best-practice initiatives (Borders & Drury, 1992b; Burnham & Jackson, 2000). In addition, time spent on nonguidance and noncounseling activities—scheduling, enrollment of students, high-stakes testing, grading, and so on—detracts from the true roles and responsibilities of professional school counselors, and they are often unable to perform the duties for which they have been trained (Burnham & Jackson, 2000; Gysbers & Henderson, 2006).

The movement toward greater accountability measures entire districts based on student achievement on standardized tests, as well as other accepted indicators such as attendance rates, advanced placement course selection, school safety, violent or disruptive behavior, graduation rates, retention rates, dropout rates, and continuation to postsecondary education by race, ethnicity, and sex. Accreditation for public schools is acutely based on annual yearly progress.

Stone and Dahir (2007) write that data can: *Importance of data*

- Challenge attitudes and beliefs: Data tells the story to staff, faculty, parents, and students in a visual and nonjudgmental manner.

- Develop high expectations: The level of awareness and expectations differ among staff, parents and students.
- Provide career and academic advice: Information is readily available to provide students and parents with current figures on scholarship dollars and financial aid information and how to access the Internet for college and career advice.
- Change enrollment patterns to support success in rigorous academics: Aggregated and disaggregated data graphically show the composition of classrooms and course selection. Using data can influence course enrollment patterns.
- Impact the instructional program: School counselor can support the instructional program by assisting classroom teachers to use data to better understand the issues that achievement and behavior. (p. 21)

TYPES OF DATA COLLECTED

Achievement and Achievement-Related Data

There are many ways to collect data, and it does not have to be complicated. Most school systems have information technology (IT) departments that collect data and report it to stakeholders like the state education department, which in turn reports it to the U.S. Department of Education. It is easy for them to disaggregate data according to category, for example:

- Number of students with a 3.0 or better grade-point average by sex, ethnicity, and socioeconomic status (SES)
- Number of students taking advanced placement (AP) classes by sex and ethnicity
- School safety (e.g., aggressive behavior against staff and students) by sex, ethnicity, and SES
- Performance in core subject areas (math, science, English, and social studies) by sex, ethnicity, and SES
- Attendance rates by sex, ethnicity, and SES
- Graduation rates by sex, ethnicity, and SES
- Dropout rates by sex, ethnicity, and SES
- Number of students with limited English proficiency by race, ethnicity, gender, and SES
- Number of students with disabilities by race, ethnicity, gender, and SES
- Number of students disadvantaged by race, ethnicity, gender, and SES
- Number of AP tests taken by race, ethnicity, gender, and SES
- Number of AP courses enrolled in by race, ethnicity, gender, and SES
- Dual enrollment courses taken by students versus race, ethnicity, gender, and SES
- Enrollment in international baccalaureate (IB) programs by race ethnicity, gender, and SES
- Students receiving different kinds of diplomas (advanced, standard, career, and technical or modified) by race, ethnicity, gender, and SES
- Industry certifications for trade and technical students by race, ethnicity, gender, and SES
- Teacher educational attainment by race, ethnicity, and gender
- Teacher educational achievement (BS, MS, and PhD) by race, ethnicity, and gender

Professional school counselors and student support staff and IT departments can use data to develop a results-based program and report these findings to important stakeholders. In this way, professional school counselors can begin to answer the most important question: "How are students different because of what school counselors do?" Data on student achievement, demographics, perception, and the effectiveness of a program help measure students' gains in attitudes, knowledge, and skills as a result of planned standards-based school curricula or intentional interventions to improve student academic performance and success.

Demographic Data

Demographic data answer the question about the performance of different groups by describing statistical characteristics of a population. How are different groups—African Americans, Latinos, whites, English-language learners, students with disabilities—performing in courses and on achievement tests? They answer questions about race, ethnicity, gender, SES, free and reduced-price lunch recipients, attendance, dropout rates, graduation rates, and family dynamics in a particular school. Demographic data reveal variations among subgroups of students and can identify needed interventions and areas of growth.

Process Data

Process data evaluate the programs, strategies, and practices that have been implemented to meet needs that may have been identified from demographic data. They answer the question "Did the intervention produce the desired outcomes?" Process data are used to evaluate the results of programs such the Advancement via Individual Determination (AVID) program, IB tutoring programs, special academies, mentoring programs, family life education programs, and substance abuse prevention programs. Professional school counselors and student support staff collect process data to show who received certain programs or activities, what programs or activities occurred, when and where programs took place, whether programs followed prescribed practices, and ultimately whether they produced desired outcomes.

Perception Data

Perception data answer the question "Is there a change or improvement in attitudes, knowledge, and skills of students, parents, teachers, and staff?" These data are collected through the use of questionnaires, surveys, interviews, or focus groups. Such data are also derived from students' attainment of certain competencies (e.g., completion of a career interest inventory, taking the Preliminary Scholastic Aptitude Test [PSAT] in the 10th grade for self-assessment purposes, or entering an "early college scholars" program) or by observation (e.g., participation in conflict resolution to reduce anger and negative behavior, participation in an antibullying program that reduced bullying behaviors, a survey on school climate revealing that the majority of teachers are happy). Perception data measure what students and others perceive about changes in attitudes, beliefs, skill improvement, and increased knowledge about decreasing self-defeating behaviors.

Results Data

Results data answer the question "Did school counseling curriculum sessions such as classroom guidance and student support services change students?" Indicators reveal the percentage of students who increased their level of achievement in core-area subjects or improved their behavior after participating in a set of learning experiences such as tutoring or special enrichment programs. Did achievement increase, were failure rates decreased, did attendance improve, and did discipline referrals decline?

Formative Assessment

A formative assessment asks the question "Are students progressing at certain intervals during their participation in a program or course?" to determine whether the program is effective. By assessing the effectiveness of a program's activities, professional school counselors and student support staff can make midterm corrections to improve the implementation of the program or class and to make timely, effective interventions that improve results. For example, a formative assessment can answer these questions:

- Are students with low attendance patterns attending their classes every day?
- Are lower-achieving students performing well at midterm in higher-level classes such as geometry, chemistry, or AP?
- Are English-language learners successful in regular academic classes?
- Are students with disabilities getting the appropriate transition services (i.e., from school to work), so they can become productive members of society?
- Are parents engaged in school activities and has there been a sustained parent involvement since the opening of school?
- Is information about programs and services of the school counseling program being routinely communicated to important stakeholders?

Program Evaluation Data

The goal of a program evaluation is to answer the question "Is the program following its original program design?" It focuses on program interventions. For example, are all students progressing adequately in the AVID, IB, early reading, or lunch buddies program? It is important to gauge any discrepancies between the written program and the implemented program at intervals throughout the life of the program to determine its overall effectiveness. Professional school counselors and teachers have developed benchmarks as standard measures that form the basis for comparison as part of the educational reform movement. Benchmarks are routinely used to assess how well the program has been designed and carried out according to the original design.

Summative Assessment

Summative assessments answer the question "Did the students learn what they were supposed to learn after using a particular instructional intervention?" In a sense, it lets the student know how well he or she performed after a particular intervention. A summative assessment evaluation is typically quantitative, using numeric scores or letter grades to assess student achievement. Professional school counselors and student support staff use this evaluation method to make decisions about whether the program made a positive impact on student academic success. For example, they may ask:

- Did minority students improve on the PSAT or the Scholastic Aptitude Test (SAT) because of a structured PSAT/SAT preparation course?
- Did achievement levels of minority and immigrant students improve in English and mathematics after tutoring sessions or individualized enrichment programs?
- What percentage of English-language learners were achieving at or above grade level after their parents participated in a counseling outreach and community resource program?
- Did mainstream children with disabilities perform better on standards of learning tests after they received accommodations?

Longitudinal Data

Longitudinal data answer the question "Are there patterns and trends or discrepancies in programs and services from year to year?" Established baseline data are compared to yearly progress in the areas of achievement; attendance; test scores in core subject areas (English, mathematics, social studies, science); enrollment of special groups that have an impact on school academic performance such as children with disabilities, immigrants, and minorities; number of highly qualified teachers; SES; and free and reduced-price lunches. Programs and services can be modified or new programs can be introduced to reflect the needs of the changing demographics of the school from year to year. This is the essence of school improvement and using demographic information and other data to demonstrate the strength of interventions, growth, and results. The new role for professional school counselors can be defined by the question "How are students different due to what professional school counselors have done in program planning, targeted interventions, and primary prevention initiatives?" Technology helps provide the necessary data that were not available a decade ago. In the past, professional school counselors implemented programs and services they thought students needed. Now, they have access to data that demonstrate what is actually needed to improve student success.

MODELS OF DATA-BASED DECISION MAKING FOR ASSESSING STANDARDS-BASED SCHOOL COUNSELING PROGRAMS

Three data-based models or outcome models are presented in this chapter:

1. The data-based decision making (DBDM) or IDEAS model (Poynton & Carey, 2006)
2. MEASURE-ing Student Success (Dahir & Stone, 2003a)
3. Get a GRIP! (Brott, 2005, 2006, 2008)

All three demonstrate an effort to market professional school counseling programs in terms of accountability and to answer the perennial question of how students are different as the result of what professional school counselors are doing (ASCA, 2005a). Putting these models in one place makes it easier for the professional school counselor to adapt an accountability model that is most appropriate for his or her particular school setting. It is critical to understand that one size does not fit all when considering counseling initiatives. Professional school counselors must factor in SES, English-language learners, poverty levels, and minority or immigrant needs.

The remainder of the chapter presents the three models for using data to demonstrate accountability in school counseling programs.

FIRST ACCOUNTABILITY MODEL: DATA-BASED DECISION MAKING–IDEAS

Data-based decision making is the "process of collecting, analyzing, reporting, and using data for school improvement" (Dahlkemper, 2002, p. 1). The implicit rationale for implementing DBDM in schools is that "using information to help clarify issues, identify alternative solutions to problems and target resources more effectively will lead to better decisions for all students" (Protheroe, 2001, p. 4). DBDM is an important management tool because using data to plan and evaluate professional school counseling programs and interventions is a significant feature of the *ASCA National Model's* management system. It cannot be emphasized enough that the use of data by professional school counselors today is critical to engage in effective professional school counseling practice (ASCA, 2005a). It is also a fundamental component of the national reform movement to increase student academic success and to close the achievement gap between mainstream students and minorities and students of poverty.

Professional school counselors are now in the position to make a significant impact in school reform and to demonstrate accountability through their efforts to improve student achievement (House & Hayes, 2002; Paisley & Hayes, 2003). What is critical for succeeding in these accountability efforts is that they have to be a team initiative, involving administrators, teachers, and professional school counselors. *The ASCA (2005a) National Model* for students maintains, "Through data analysis, professional school counselors, administrators, faculty and advisory council members are able to create a current picture of students and the school environment" (p. 49).

An overview of Poynton and Carey's IDEAS Model (2006) is shown in Figure 3.1. IDEAS stands for *I*dentify a question, *D*evelop a plan, *E*xecute the plan, *A*nswer the question, and *S*hare results.

Enabling Contextual Conditions

Love (2004) identified four conditions that are necessary for effective DBDM in schools:

1. Collaborative culture
2. Collaborative structures
3. Widespread data-literacy
4. Access to useful data

All members of the working committee need to nurture this mind-set, and it needs to come from a team perspective—that is, lead teachers, the lead professional school counselor, the administrator in charge of instruction, lead special education teachers, lead English–language learner specialists, and other advisory group members and community stakeholders. This is essential in maintaining a mind-set for accountability.

First Stage: Identifying a Question

Using the goals of the professional school counseling program, what areas need to be highlighted and what areas should be the focus? As ASCA (2005a) says:

> Through analysis of data, professional school counselors, administrators, faculty and advisory council members are able to create a current picture of the student population and the school environment. This picture focuses discussion and planning around students' needs and the school counselor's role in addressing those needs. (p. 49)

For example, questions may include:

- Are there a growing population of underachievers?
- Do we have a significant population of English-language learners?
- Is our dropout level increasing?

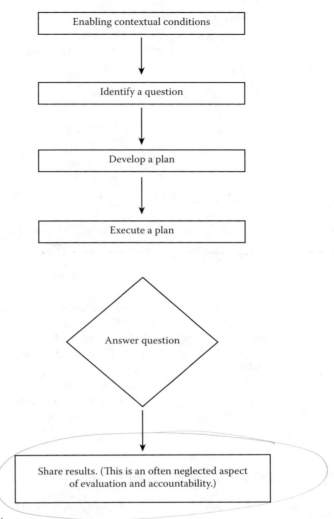

FIGURE 3.1   IDEAS model.

- Are fewer minority males pursuing higher education?
- Are our students in full-day kindergarten struggling behind their peers?

Second Stage: Developing a Plan

1. Develop a plan to address the issues hindering progress toward school counseling goals; and
2. Determine interventions to effect change in problem data. Evidence-based interventions and practices should be considered because they have proven to be effective (Carey et al., 2005).
3. Develop an action plan. "Action plans are useful tools for developing a timeline for intervention implementations, for assigning responsibilities to individuals, for identifying resources needed to effectively implement the intervention, and for identifying the data needed to evaluate the intervention" (Poynton & Carey, 2006, p. 129). ASCA (2005a) provides sample school guidance curricula and closing-the-gap action plans to assist with the planning of interventions.
4. Develop an evaluation plan (see Table 3.2).

TABLE 3.2   Sample Evaluation Planning Tool

Question:	
Process Data	Source(s)
Perception Data	Source(s)
Results Data	Source(s)
Demographic Data	Source(s)
Analysis Plan	Source(s)

Source: Poynton, T. A., & Carey, J. C., (2006). *Professional School Counseling,* *10*(2), 129. Reprinted with permission.

Third Stage: Executing the Plan

The intervention plan (such as closing the achievement gap) is then put into action. "School counselors should develop interventions plans that meet the needs of all students and to close the achievement gap between specific groups of students and their peers" (ASCA, 2005a, p. 10). Counselors should make sure the plans are followed and delivered appropriately. Selected examples of evidence-based plans are provided in Table 3.3.

Counselors should make sure that the action plan is executed appropriately and should check for "treatment fidelity," for instance, making sure that all students experience the Life Skills Program similarly because the program is evidence based. It should also be noted that only *evidence-based* programs should be implemented, because they have empirically demonstrated that they reduce disruptive behavior and are scientifically based research from such disciplines as social science and neuroscience that uses empirical data on student performance and uses it to compare, evaluate, and monitor progress. Finally, a formative evaluation (e.g., pre- and posttests or quizzes) should be conducted to assess student knowledge or to receive preliminary perceptions from teachers, administrators, professional school counselors, and the school's advisory board.

Fourth Stage: Answering the Question

"Data collection provides the professional school counseling program and school's advisory board with the information needed to evaluate the program as it related to students' progress in academic, personal/social and career domains" (ASCA, 2005a, p. 59). The first task is to analyze data gathered before, during, and after the intervention. One resource that Poynton and Carey (2006) "recommend to help organize data is EZAnalyze (http://www.ezanalyze.com) which provides statistical tests and disaggregates data" (p. 128) for special programs that are implemented in the schools. The next task is to interpret the results and to make sure the intervention was a success using short-term perception data and long-term results indicators.

Fifth Stage: Sharing Results

The last stage is perhaps the most overlooked yet critical component of accountability: *sharing the results with important stakeholders* to determine how students are different because of what school counselors do. "Sharing the results with important stakeholders serves as advocacy for the students and the professional school counseling program" (ASCA, 2005a, p. 24). Important stakeholders include teachers, administrators (both in school and from the central office), parents, school board members, Chamber of Commerce members, local businesses, and community agencies. This stage also encompasses using the media, including posting information on the school's website.

TABLE 3.3   Examples of Model/Exemplary Programs for Prevention

PREVENTION TYPE	PROGRAM/AGE GROUP	DESCRIPTION
Universal	Child Development Project (CDP)/ Ages 5–12	Multifaceted, schoolwide improvement program that helps elementary school become "caring communities for learners" for their students. Significantly reduces children's early use of alcohol and marijuana and their involvement in violence-related behaviors. Designed to strengthen connections among peers and between students of different ages, teachers and students, and home and school. Recommended by SAMHSA.
Universal	Dare to Be You/ Ages 2–5	Combines three supporting aspects—educational activities for children, strategies for the parents or teachers, and environmental structures—to enable program participants to learn and practice the desired skills. The program is designed to significantly lower the risk of future substance abuse and other high-risk activities by dramatically improving parent and child protective factors in communication, problem solving, self-esteem, and family skills. Recommended by OJJDP.
Universal	Early Risers "Skills for Success" Program/ Ages 6–10	Multicomponent, high-intensity, competency-enhancement program that targets elementary school children who are at high risk for early development of conduct problems, including substance use (i.e., who display early aggressive, disruptive, or nonconformist behaviors). Recommended by OJJDP.
Universal	The Good Behavior Game (GBG)/ Ages 6–10	A classroom management strategy designed to improve aggressive/disruptive classroom behavior and prevent later criminality. The program is universal and can be applied to general populations of early elementary school children, although the most significant results have been found for children demonstrating early high-risk behavior. It is implemented when children are in early elementary grades to provide them with the skills they need to respond to later, possibly negative, life experiences and societal influences. Recommended by OJJDP.
Universal	Life Skills Training (LST)/ Middle school or junior high school	Three-year intervention designed to prevent or reduce gateway drug use. Implemented by schoolteachers. Targets middle/junior high school students (initial intervention in grades 6 or 7). Recommended by Blueprints, DOE, OJJDP.
Universal	Midwestern Prevention Project/ Early to late adolescents	Comprehensive, community-based, multifaceted program for adolescent drug abuse prevention. It bridges the transition from early adolescence to middle through late adolescence. Recommended by Blueprints.
Universal	Olweus Bullying Prevention Program/ Elementary through middle school or junior high school	Universal intervention for the reduction and prevention of bully/victim problems. Targets students in elementary, middle, and junior high schools. Recommended by Blueprints.

Source: U.S. Department of Health and Human Services. (2009). Identifying and Selected Evidence-Based Interventions. Substance Abuse and Mental Health Services Administration (SAMHSA).
SAMHSA = Substance Abuse and Mental Health Services Administration; OJJDP = Office of Juvenile Justice and Delinquency Prevention; DOE = U.S. Department of Education.

SECOND ACCOUNTABILITY MODEL: ASSESSING SCHOOL COUNSELOR ACCOUNTABILITY THROUGH MEASURE

For the first time in education, teachers, professional school counselors, administrators, and support staff, as well as central office administration, are collectively focusing on the same initiative when it comes to accountability-driven school initiatives. Essentially, what gets measured and publicized to the general public gets accomplished.

It has become common in some communities that new housing developments advertise the location of the "best schools" to lure homeowners to their developments. Parents are actively concerned that their child goes to the best school with the best teachers to get an optimum education. If professional school counselors focus their efforts on the goal of the school improvement, they will widen educational opportunities for every student, too, not just a select few, and they can positively impact the instructional program (Dahir & Stone, 2003a; Stone & Dahir, 2007). This subsequently demonstrates the professional school counselor's *leadership* and *advocacy* skills and the mission of ASCA and the Education Trust to transform school counseling.

> Merely totaling the number of student contacts made, group sessions held, or classroom guidance lessons delivered is *so what* data in the eyes of legislators, school board members, and other critical stakeholders. Counting services as a measure of accountability is no longer acceptable for 21st century professional school counseling programs. (Dahir & Stone, 2003a, p. 261)

Counting services reflects an ancillary or resource role for professional school counselors and sets them up for scrutiny regarding their worth and benefits, making their positions more vulnerable to being cut from the budget. For example, if the reading scores are low at a particular elementary school, school board members faced with a dwindling budget may be forced to choose between funding a school counselor or a reading specialist; the school counselors will probably be the first to be cut because the program will be viewed as fiscally irresponsible and an ineffective use of resources (Whiston, 2002).

Elementary professional school counselor positions are currently threatened in California, and California already has the highest student–counselor ratio in the nation at 966:1. The state's Proposition 13, passed in 1978, cut professional school counselors, librarians, nurses, and other noninstructional staff positions. This legislation sets a precedent for other states. A comprehensive school counseling program that is data driven, proactive, and preventive in focus and is delivered to demonstrate accountability could prevent the discussion of cutting professional school counseling programs.

Essentially, MEASURE is a six-step accountability process. The program is a team effort that requires school counselors to collaborate with teachers, administrators, and support staff as an integral part of important barometers of student success and accomplishment (Dahir & Stone, 2003a). It supports accountability, moving counselors from a "counting tasks" system by aligning the school counseling program with the standards-based reform movement and meeting the reform requirements of the No Child Left Behind Act of 2001. *MEASURE* stands for:

> **M**ission: Connect the comprehensive K–12 professional school program to the mission of the school, and to the goals of the annual school improvement plan. Professional school counselors need to ask how every aspect of the program supports the mission of the school and contributes to student achievement.
>
> **E**lements: Identify the critical data elements that are important to the internal and external stakeholders. Professional school counselors already have ready access to data in areas such as course enrollment patterns, demographics, achievement patterns and attendance that can be framed into accountability publications. Most school divisions have elaborate technology departments that glean data and trends among different subpopulations of students and report them to state departments of education who in turn report them to the U.S. Department of Education.

    Analyze: Discuss carefully which elements need to be aggregated or disaggregated and why? It is critical to disaggregate data elements and to identify success and needs in terms of gender, race/ethnicity, and socioeconomic status (SES) and how they are related to achievement.

    Stakeholder–Unite: Determine which stakeholders need to be involved in addressing these school-improvement issues and unite them to develop strategies to improve achievement. Professional school counselors cannot work in isolation. They need to work in teams to create action plans of the critical data to share with internal and external stakeholders and become an integral part of the school improvement team.

    Reanalyze: Rethink and refine the intervention strategies, refocus efforts needed, and reflect on success. Critical questions to consider are as follows: "Did the results of everyone's efforts show that the interventions and strategies successfully moved critical elements in a positive direction?" "What changes need to be made to the school counseling program to keep the focus on student needs?"

    Educate: Show the positive impact the professional school counseling program has had on student achievement and on the goal of the school improvement plan. Demonstrate how professional school counselors are an integral part of the school improvement plan. (Dahir & Stone, 2003a, p. 263)

Fundamentally, traditional methods of professional school counselors demonstrating their worth by counting counseling sessions and student contacts are referred to as "So what?" data. These methods that have been used to assess and evaluate professional school counseling programs no longer hold the same value or vision for what administrators, faculty, and parents consider important. Advances in technology have allowed everyone to view data and keep up with students' progress on a weekly or even daily basis. MEASURE supports the accountability component of the *ASCA (2005a) National Model* and shifts the counseling program from a *counting-tasks system* to a *standards-based reform* initiative widening the professional school counselors' realm of influence in helping all students become successful learners and productive members of society.

THIRD ACCOUNTABILITY MODEL: GET A GRIP!

Get a GRIP! (Brott, 2005, 2006, 2008) is an accountability framework for succinctly reporting the effectiveness of interventions and strategies that are a part of the professional school counseling program. The GRIP is a one-page document that can easily be shared with others (e.g., counseling colleagues, administrators, parents, other school personnel), can become a system for organizing the success of your program over time, and can generate ideas to improve, strengthen, and maintain a vibrant school counseling program. GRIP stands for *G*oal, *R*esults, *I*mpact statements, and *P*rogram implications.

    The focus of the GRIP is to demonstrate the effectiveness of the professional school counseling program by engaging the professional school counselor in an action research project for continual renewal of the program. The GRIP is formatted as a word-processing document; spreadsheets and charts can be incorporated to provide a visual summary of significant data reflecting the results and impact statements from intervention programs or activities. The format of a GRIP is shown in Table 3.4, and a detailed description of how to format the document in Microsoft Word is contained in the chapter's appendix.

THE LEGISLATIVE PUSH FOR SCHOOL ACCOUNTABILITY

In 2002, a nationally driven accountability system was reinforced and extended by the reauthorization of the Elementary and Secondary Education Act and the No Child Left Behind Act. Without question, the dominant state- and national-level strategy in schools today is standards-driven accountability. Professional school counselors need to play an integral part of this reform movement initiative.

TABLE 3.4   GRIP Template

GOAL
- Goal of the particular program or activity; objectives that the program or activity will address, stated in measurable behavior terms
- A brief, succinct paragraph that describes the program/activity: date, place, participants, facilitators, resources
- Identify types of evaluations used (e.g., needs assessment, pre-/posttests, inventories, assessment instruments)
- Link program/activity to ASCA (2004) National Model: Specify state standards for school counseling programs (2004) that are addressed, identify school district goals or strategic plan objectives addressed, and align with building initiatives

RESULTS
- Relate results of program/activity to standards, district goals, strategic plans, and individual building initiatives
- Short-term results: what is immediately known as a product of the program/activity; process data to report what you did for whom
- Long-term results: increase/decrease of target behavior; impact on participants' behavior, attendance, achievement; what others observe; results data (so what?) to report the difference the program/activity has made for students

IMPACT STATEMENTS
- Bulleted statements
- Quantitative data: lead with a descriptive statistic (e.g., percent versus percent change); perception data to report what others think, know, or can demonstrate
- Qualitative data: gathered from participants' or observers' responses to open-ended questions; identify themes from responses; provide direct participant quotes to illuminate the impact of the program/activity

(insert spreadsheet chart)

(insert spreadsheet chart or pre-/posttest items)

PROGRAM IMPLICATIONS
Bulleted statements to answer the following questions:
- What did/did not work?
- What needs to change?
- What do you need?
- What will happen next?

Source: Brott, P. E. (2006). Counselor education accountability: Training the effective professional school counselor. *Professional School Counseling, 10,* 179–188. Reprinted with permission.

In the last decade, state policy makers have steadily moved toward a system that hinges on explicit performance standards, systematic testing, and consequences for poor results, such as sanctions (e.g., "accredited with warning," replacing school instructional staff and the principal, providing parents with school choice and even transportation to the school of their choice, closing the school and reopening it as a charter school, extending the school year or school day, and other measures). Teachers are being held accountable, administrators are being questioned regarding their leadership role, and professional school counselors are being questioned about whether their program efforts are effective in changing student behaviors in the academic, personal/social, and career domains.

The haunting question remains: "How are students different (positively) as the result of the school counselor's program efforts?" Legislators and policy makers believe that this package of reforms will stimulate teachers and students to focus their efforts in the right direction. But do these high expectations really take into account the changing demographics of the schools, including increasing diversity, more English-language learners, and a growing population of children with disabilities?

COMMUNICATING RESULTS

Communicating results is the most neglected aspect of demonstrating that programs and services have been implemented to improve student success. This is where professional school counselors can answer the question of what they do to increase students' success. Most state departments of education have school accreditation ratings, adequate yearly progress ratings, test results, attendance information, school safety information, and numbers of children with disabilities, limited English proficient students, and disadvantaged students. However, state departments do not list the programs and services that schools have implemented to meet specific needs of individual schools.

Most schools have implemented programs that represent "best practices." Professional school counselors need to share the success and data from these programs and communicate this information to important stakeholders: school administrators, teachers, support staff, central office administrators, parents, school board members, and the greater community. This can be accomplished through various media: fact sheets with easy-to-understand tables, spreadsheets, graphs, easy-to-read brochures, newsletters via email, and school websites. Making a concerted effort to communicate with English-language learners' parents in their native language is also becoming a critical need in some school districts, given the growing population of parents who do not speak English. One of the goals of the No Child Left Behind Act of 2001 is for all children of limited English proficiency to become proficient in English.

Professional school counselors who focus on improving student results will become an integral part of closing the achievement gap if they look at data that are available to them and become active members of their school improvement team. Stone and Dahir (2004) maintain that school counselors can:

- impact student achievement;
- improve student course-taking patterns that increase access to rigorous academic work;
- raise student aspiration and motivation;
- manage and access school and community-based resources;
- motivate students to assume responsibility for their educational and career planning;
- influence the school climate to ensure that high standards are the norm in a safe and respectful environment;
- use date to effectively identify institutional and environmental barriers that can impede student success. (p. 7)

PROFESSIONAL SCHOOL COUNSELORS AND THE USE OF TECHNOLOGY

Computer technology has now become an integral part of professional school counseling programs, significantly affecting the time constraints of professional school counselors by making areas of information retrieval and dissemination easier, sorting and selecting students for special programs, electronically making grading and reporting information available to parents in real time, simplifying career and college exploration, and sharing information via websites, electronic newsletters, and social media. The exchange is rapid and timely, allowing mutual concerns and interests to be shared among teachers, parents, administrators, and professional school counselors and thus promoting effectiveness, efficiency, and accountability.

Professional school counselors should have computer skills and be familiar with applications that make their workload more efficient and accountable, advocate for students, and provide information to students and the families in real time. Time-consuming written notifications and reports, lengthy parent–teacher conferences, and traveling to locations to meet or share information are products of the 20th century. With the advent of the 21st century and modern information technology, professional school counselors are now more visible, accessible, and accountable through the use of technology. Table 3.5

TABLE 3.5   Computer Programs and Services That Are Useful for Professional School Counselors

PROGRAM/SERVICE	DESCRIPTION
Starbase Web Information System	A student information system to centralize all student data on the professional school counselor's desktop. It is used to enroll students, make modifications to student data, post and monitor discipline and attendance in real time, process students' course requests, create a master schedule, change and evaluate student schedules, sort and select students for different programs, provide immediate access to grade-point averages and transcripts, and post and report student performance using the interim and reporting features. Furthermore, test scores can be stored and used for data analysis, and report cards can be produced on a monthly basis for immediate feedback to students and parents.
GradeQuick Web	This Web-based teacher grade book integrates with the Administrator's Plus student information system. GradeQuick Web provides instant access to current grade book data from any computer with an Internet connection. Teachers post grades electronically, rather than using scanable computer sheets that must be sent downtown and then returned. This electronic resource allows teachers to post grades, attendance, and so forth electronically, to send them to the IT department and have them returned to a printer in the school, and to then distribute them to students in home rooms on a monthly basis.
EdLine for parents	Programs like EdLine allows parents into their child's teacher's grade book to look at grades assignments, absences, and so on. Parents can check their child's latest grades. For example, weekly updates may occur every Wednesday, and parents then receive email alerts when new grades are posted; see which assignments were not turned in; and communicate with the child's teacher via email. Parents can also review the "combined calendar" to see all of the events from the school calendar and their child's classes.
School websites	Practically every school district and individual school has a website that lists everything from programs and policies to sporting events. They may even be in different languages. For example, Fairfax County (Virginia) Public Schools has information in العربية • 中文 • فارسی • 한국어 • Español • اردو • Tiếng Việt i.e., Arabic, Chinese, Farsi, Korean, Spanish, Urdu, and Vietnamese.
Familigram	An electronic newsletter provided for parents with a listing of programs and services, often translated into different languages to meet the needs of a diverse student population.
Parent alert system	An automated calling system that alerts parents in the event of a crisis, critical incident, or other emergency.
Calling post	An automated calling system that alerts parents when report cards or special events are occurring.
Email	Email is used by teachers and administrators to communicate to parents regarding student progress or other pertinent information.
Distance learning	Provides opportunities to take courses at other schools that are not offered at the home school via a distance learning platform.
Computer software	Professional school counselors should be able to use word processors, spreadsheets, presentations, publishing, e-mail, and multimedia resources.
Videoconferencing and Skype	Professional school counselors can utilize interactive conferences to meet with parents and colleagues without leaving their offices.
Exploring colleges and careers	Information about financial aid, scholarships, loans, work-study, and the latest information and career trends are available via the Internet, e.g., on O*NET or the Occupational Information Network.

TABLE 3.5   Computer Programs and Services That Are Useful for Professional School Counselors (continued)

PROGRAM/SERVICE	DESCRIPTION
Networking	Professional school counselors can network via email, websites, chat rooms, and social networks like Facebook (e.g., for alumni) and Twitter.
Supervision	Professional school counselors can easily provide supervision of interns via teleconferencing and Skype electronically face-to-face.
Online high-stakes testing	High-stakes testing such as end-of-course tests of content areas are now being conducted online to relieve professional school counselors and educators from time-consuming paper-and-pencil formats.
Webinars	Webinars are Web-based seminars—a presentation, lecture, workshop, or seminar that is transmitted over the Web. The unique feature is that it is more interactive because participants are able to give, receive, and discuss information.
Podcasts	A podcast is a prerecorded audio program that is posted to a website and is made available for download so people can listen to it on a personal computer or mobile device. Special software is not needed other than the audio player, such as Windows Media Player or RealPlayer, which are on most computers.

contains a listing of programs and services that professional school counselors are using in their school systems to make their jobs more effective and efficient.

CONCLUSION

Once again, professional school counselors have been left out of school reform legislation. However, accountability, with its long history, has always been a collective concern and is now at the forefront of professional dialogue among researchers and practitioners. Professional school counselors have struggled with identity issues and how to demonstrate what they do, and they have been responding to social, political, and educational ideation of each era since the 1920s. They are now being actively called upon to demonstrate how they make a difference in the lives of students and families.

Professional school counselors have taken on a lot of noncounseling minutiae and clerical duties that have been thrust on them by administration because they are often conveniently located near administrative suites and have difficulty saying no and don't realize the long-range implications of what saying yes means. But they need to extricate themselves from these collateral duties.

Standards-based education reform seeks to improve education through the following:

1. Clearly specifying desired student outcomes, such as closing the achievement gaps of minority students and students of poverty
2. Measuring student performance so that the students can compete in growing global economy
3. Evaluating the impact of educational practices on actual student performance

Traditionally, professional school counselors have used needs-assessment instruments to gather data from students, parents, and school personnel in order to identify needed interventions (Cook, 1989; R. A. Thompson, 1987), and they have used evaluation data to document the effectiveness of specific interventions and programs (Fairchild & Seeley, 1995). Today, professional school counselors are being urged to use school data to focus on student advocacy initiatives and become integral participants in school improvement planning teams (Hayes et al., 2002) and to use measurable results in the design and improvement of professional school counseling programs and positive student outcomes (Johnson & Johnson, 2002).

The ASCA (2005a) National Model was developed to connect professional school counseling with current education reform movements that emphasize student achievement and success. The ASCA model emphasizes foundation, a delivery system, a management system, and an accountability system that promotes mission statements, a guidance curriculum, agreements with administration, advisory councils, use of data, reporting results, action plans, school counseling performance standards, and program audits.

The Education Trust (1997; Hall, Wiener, & Carey, 2003) has advocated the need to close the achievement gap between minorities and poor students and their middle-class counterparts. It has outlined the roles of professional school counselors as follows:

- Counseling
- Consultation
- Coordination of services
- Leadership
- Advocacy
- Collaboration and teaming
- Managing resources
- Use of data
- Use of technology

Both the ASCA and Education Trust initiatives have been in the forefront of transforming professional school counseling. Essentially, Susan Whiston (2002) says, "professional school counselors may believe they make a difference, but without 'hard data' to support these claims, professional school counselors run the risk of losing their positions" (p. 153). Professional school counselors need to be viewed as an *integral part* of schoolwide accountability and not as an ancillary resource that is expendable during times of fiscal crises and budget constraints. ASCA, the Council for Accreditation of Counseling and Related Educational Programs (CACREP), the Education Trust, and prominent counseling scholars (Adelman & Taylor, 2002; House & Hayes, 2002; Paisley & McMahon, 2001; Sears & Granello, 2002) have challenged the professional school counseling profession to develop new ways for professional school counselors to function in today's educational accountability initiatives, particularly during tight budgets and fiscal constraints. The new role for professional school counselors includes a focus on addressing school system factors that influence student development, including barriers to learning and a growing population of students who are English-language learners, students with disabilities, students with serious mental health issues, and children of poverty.

APPENDIX: GET A GRIP! SETTING UP A WORD DOCUMENT

1. Open a blank Word document.
2. Set margins and page orientation:
   a. Click "File" and the drop-down menu appears.
   b. Click "Page Setup."
   c. From the "margins" tab, set the margins as follows:
      - Top 0.5"
      - Bottom 0.5"
      - Left 0.5"
      - Right 0.5"

    d. Click on the orientation of the page.
- Landscape is 11" × 8.5".
- Portrait is 8.5" × 11".

    e. Click "OK" to close the Page Setup menu.

3. Type a title on first line of document and hit the return to insert a blank line after the title.
4. Insert a table:
   a. Click "Table" and the drop-down menu appears.
   b. Click "Insert" and a menu will open to the right.
   c. Click "Table."
   d. From the Insert Table window, indicate 2 columns and 3 rows.
   e. Click "OK."
5. Enter GRIP.
   a. *Goal:* Place your cursor in the first cell (top left cell) of the table and type your goal statement.
   b. *Results:* Tab to the right one cell (top right cell) and type your results statement.
   c. *Impact statements:* In the same cell as Results, type your impact statements (% increase/decrease).
   d. Tab to the second-row, first-column cell (the cell below Goal) and insert the first chart.
      - Open the Excel file (click on the X file name at the bottom of your computer screen) and open to the chart page.
      - Click in the upper corner of the page, but do not click inside the chart.
      - Click "Edit" and the drop-down menu appears.
      - Click "Copy" or click on the icon in the toolbar for copy.
      - Move to the Word document and place the cursor in the cell below Goal
      - Click the icon in the toolbar for paste, or click "Edit" and then select "Paste" from the drop-down menu.
      - Resize the chart, if necessary:
        1) Click in the upper corner of the chart page, but do not click inside the chart.
        2) Place your cursor in one of the corners of the chart page and a diagonal arrowhead appears.
        3) Press and hold the left mouse button, then move the crosshairs in a diagonal direction to resize the chart page smaller.
        4) Click and hold on any of the edit markers: when the crosshairs appear, resize the chart page.
6. Tab to the next cell to the right and insert another chart or a table displaying your descriptive statistics.
   a. Tab to the last row and merge the two cells in the last row:
      - Place your cursor to the outside of the table and left-click; the row will be highlighted.
      - Go to the toolbar and click "Table."
      - From the drop-down menu, click "Merge Cells."
   b. *Program Implications:* Type in your program implications.
7. Place a footer on the page.
   a. From the toolbar, click "View," and from the drop-down menu, click "Header and Footer."
   b. In the "Header and Footer" menu, click on the icon for "Switch between Header and Footer" so that you are at the bottom of the page.
   c. Select preferred font, font size (smaller the better), and alignment (left, center, right).
   d. Type "Prepared by" and your name; you may also want to include the date in the footer.
   e. Click "Close" on the "Header and Footer" menu to close the menu and return to the page.
8. Save the file!

GET A GRIP! CREATING CHARTS IN EXCEL

Entering Data

1. Open Excel.
2. Spreadsheet basics:
   a.   Columns are vertical and are lettered.
   b.   Rows are horizontal and are numbered.
   c.   Cells are identified by the intersection of a column and row.
   d.   Click in a cell to enter information.
   e.   Use tab, arrow key, enter, or mouse click to maneuver around the spreadsheet.
   f.   Each Excel file consists of multiple "sheets" (i.e., spreadsheets); name each sheet by clicking on "Sheet 1," typing in a new name, and hitting the return.
   g.   Always save your work!
3. Enter data:
   a.   One item/question with a pretest and posttest reported for one group:
      −   Cell A1: Enter a name for the data set.
      −   Cell A3: Type "Pretest."
      −   Cell B3: Enter pretest score average (mean) for group.
      −   Cell A4: Type "Posttest."
      −   Cell B4: Enter posttest score average (mean) for group.
      −   Save the file!
   b.   Multiple items/questions with a pre/post test reported for one group:
      −   Cell A1: Enter a name for the data set.
      −   Across row 2, beginning with cell B2, type in the item/question numbers.
      −   Cell A3: Type in "Pretest."
      −   Across row 3, enter pretest data for each item/question.
      −   Cell A4: Type in "Posttest."
      −   Across row 4, enter posttest data for each item/question.
      −   Save the file!
   c.   One item/question with a pretest/posttest reported for multiple participants:
      −   Cell A1: Enter a name for the data set.
      −   Across row, label columns "Names" (cell A2), "Pretest" (cell B2), and "Posttest" (cell C2).
      −   Beginning in row 3, enter data (e.g., A3 = name of one participant, B3 = pretest score for participant, C3 = posttest score for participant; A4 = name of next participant, B4 = pretest score for this participant, C4 = posttest score for this participant; row 5 and continuing, one row for each participant listing name, pretest, and posttest).
      −   Save the file!
4. Excel can be used to calculate descriptive statistics for data:
   a.   Enter data in one column.
   b.   Click mouse in cell where statistic is to be displayed.
   c.   Click on *fx* (found to the left of the formula bar) to *insert function* (e.g., average, median, mode, sum, count).
   d.   Select a function, then click "OK" at the bottom of the pop-up window.
   e.   In spreadsheet, highlight data for calculation; click "OK" at the bottom of the pop-up window for *function arguments*.
   f.   In the cell preceding the function result, type in a name for the statistic (e.g., Average, Median, Mode, Sum, Count).
   g.   Save the file!

Pretest and posttest can be conveyed to consumers and stakeholders as a column or bar chart, line chart, scatter plot, or pie chart as shown in Figure 3.2.

Creating a Chart

1. Go to the spreadsheet where the data have been entered or open the saved file.

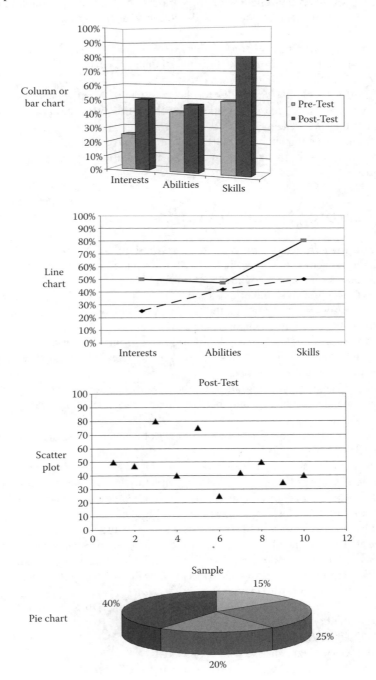

FIGURE 3.2   Types of charts.

2. Place your mouse in the first cell that contains data to be included in the chart.
3. Hold down the button and drag your mouse across cells in a row or down the columns where data are displayed you want to include in the chart; your data should now be highlighted.
4. Click on the "Chart Wizard" icon at the top of the screen (small bar-graph icon); the Chart Wizard window will open.
5. Select your chart type (e.g., bar, line, pie) by clicking on the type in the left-hand column.
6. Select your chart subtype by clicking on the sample to the right of the column. You can sample chart types with your data by clicking and holding your mouse on "Click and Hold to View Sample."
7. Click on "Next" in the Chart Wizard window.
8. You will see a sample of your chart. If displayed data are correct, click "Next"; if not, enter a new data range by highlighting the correct data.
9. Type in the title of your chart and titles for the axes. Click "Next" when done.
10. Click on "As New Sheet" and give a title to the chart; this title will appear on the sheet tab at the bottom of the spreadsheet.
11. Click on "Finish" to complete your chart. You can maneuver between sheets (e.g., data, charts) by clicking on the names that appear on the tabs at the bottom of the spreadsheets.
12. Save the file!

Advanced Features for Excel Charts

1. To change the *appearance of your chart or axes titles*, do the following from your chart:
   a. Highlight the item and double-click; the "Format Title" window will open.
   b. Change colors and borders on the "Patterns" tab.
   c. Change font types, size, and effects on the "Font" tab.
   d. Change the alignment of titles on the "Alignment" tab.
   e. Click on "OK" to apply all changes.
2. To change the *values on your y-axis*, do the following from your chart:
   a. Hold your mouse over the y-axis until "Axis Values" appears, then double-click; the "Format Axis" window will open.
   b. Change pattern, font, and alignment on the tabs as indicated above.
   c. Change the category of your numbers (i.e. percentages, fractions, etc.) on the "Numbers" tab.
   d. Change the scale of your axis by deselecting "Auto" and entering the new scale information on the "Scale" tab.
   e. Click on "OK" to apply all changes.
3. To change the *display of the bars in your bar graph*, do the following from your chart:
   a. Double-click on any bar in the graph. You must repeat the process for each series.
   b. The "Patterns" tab allows you to change colors and borders.
   c. The "Shape" tab allows you to change the shape of your bar (i.e. bar, cone, silo, etc.).
   d. The "Data Labels" tab allows you to place data labels and values on the bars.
   e. The "Series Order" tab allows you to select the order in which series appear (i.e., pretest first).
   f. The "Data Options" tab allows you to change the depth and width of the bars.
   g. Click on "OK" to apply all changes.
4. To *change your legend titles or data range*, do the following from your chart:
   a. From the title bar, click on "Chart."
   b. Click on "Source Data."
   c. From the "Series" tab, change your series labels.
   d. From the "Data Range" tab, edit your data range (i.e., expand or reduce it).
   e. Click on "OK" to apply all changes.

5. To *add your data table to your chart*, do the following from your chart:
   a. From the title bar, click on "Chart."
   b. Click on "Chart Options."
   c. Under the "Data Tables" tab, click on "Show Data Table."
   d. Click on "OK" to apply all changes.
6. To *change the color of your floor or walls*, do the following from your chart:
   a. Double-click on the floor or wall (not on a bar). The "Patterns" window will open up.
   b. Select desired borders and colors.
   c. Click on "OK" to apply all changes.
7. To *rotate* your chart:
   a. Click inside your chart to highlight the chart.
   b. Drag your mouse over a corner until the crossbow appears (+).
   c. Move the mouse to rotate chart to desired angle.

A Profile of Child and Adolescent Well-Being

A Call for Action

4

There can be no keener revelation of a society's soul than the way in which it treats its children.

Nelson Mandela

BARRIERS TO THE HEALTHY DEVELOPMENT OF YOUTH

It is difficult to comprehend how the youth of one of the most affluent nations in the world can be so troubled. Today, within the context of the school and community, the self-defeating, self-destructive potential of youth is an increasing threat to the welfare of our country. The growing concern over suicide rates, substance abuse, violence, alienation, victimization and abuse, family dysfunction, truancy, and dropout rates continues to demonstrate that relationships between youths and adults and among youth peers are significantly strained. All too many American children do not receive consistent, positive, and realistic validation of themselves from the adults on whom they depend. A *Phi Delta Kappan* survey revealed that persons 18 years of age and older believe that the public schools' biggest problems are lack of discipline; lack of financial support; use of drugs; and fighting, violence, and gangs (Rose et al., 1997; Bushaw & McNee, 2009).

Today, children and adolescents spend significantly less time in the company of adults than they did a few decades ago; more of their time is spent in front of the television and video games, with other isolation devices such as iPods, on social networking sites such as Myspace and Facebook or other Internet sites, or with their peers in age-segregated, unsupervised environments. Less time with adults means less time learning from those who can serve as valuable role models and mentors to youths. "The culminating result is what many researchers consider the new morbidities: unprotected sex, drugs, violence, and depression" (Dryfoos, 1994, p. 2).

Significant changes have occurred from 1970 to the present. Risk factors are significant variables in a child's or adolescent's life that make them vulnerable to future self-defeating or dysfunctional behavior. They can be environmental, cultural, or the result of a predisposition in personality. Eleven risk factors have been identified as important variables when considering the well-being of children and adolescents (U.S. Census Bureau, 1997; Child Trends, 2009). These are discussed below.

RISK FACTOR 1: POVERTY

In 2007, according to the U.S. Census Bureau (2008a), 18% of all children ages 0–17 lived in poverty, an increase from 17% in 2006. Compared to their white, non–Latin American peers, the poverty rate was higher for African American children and for Latin American children in 2007: 10% of white, non–Latin American children, 35% of African American children, and 29% of Latino children lived in poverty. The poverty rate for children living in single female households (i.e., no spouse present) had improved. In 1994, 53% of children living in single female households were living in poverty, but by 2007, this proportion was down to 43%. Educational incentives and financial aid provided for single mothers may have contributed to this decrease in poverty rate; however, the rate of poverty among single mothers has a significant impact on the well-being of their children. The poverty rate for Latino children in single female households was 52%. In addition, in 2007, 11% of African American children and 19% of Latino children in married-couple families lived in poverty. For children and adolescents growing up in poverty is associated with lower cognitive abilities, developmental delays, and lower achievement rates, as well as impaired health and development.

RISK FACTOR 2: FAMILY STRUCTURE AND FAMILY SYSTEMS

After decades of decline, the number of children living with both parents has remained relatively stable—69% in 2006. Both parents can play a pivotal role in the growth and development of their children (Child Trends, 2002). The constellation of different family systems (e.g., biological parents, foster-care parents, stepparents, same-sex parents, deployed parents) can have a significant effect on a child's well-being. Parental absence affects many areas of child and adolescent well-being, including income, health, educational attainment, test scores, behavior problems, and psychological well-being (Brown, S. L., 2004; Urban Institute, 2006). Research also continues to demonstrate that youths whose parents are divorced manifest poorer academic performance, social achievement, and psychological adjustment than do children living in two-parent families with a low-conflict marriage (Amato, 2001).

RISK FACTOR 3: ACHIEVEMENT GAP

The achievement gap for African American and Latino students and students of poverty persists, even among middle-class African American and Latino students in suburban communities who do not live in poverty. This revelation is even more distressing because the achievement gap persists regardless of socioeconomic status. Fundamentally, it is imperative that teachers, professional school counselors, and administrators build strong personal relationships with students with a collaborative and consistent message of high expectations regarding achievement.

Very often, teachers' expectations of African American or Latino students are low, assuming that parents do not value an education for their children and do not care to be involved in their child's education. This manifests itself through very little communication, outreach, and support on the part of the school. These teachers' methods fail to address individual differences and cultural and other factors that affect the learning styles, motivation, and behavior of Latino and African American students. With changing demographics and the increasing variables of diversity within public schools, this cavalier approach also significantly impacts students with special needs and English-language learners.

Today, African Americans comprise more than 13% of the population—34,000,000 people—and other minorities make up 32% of the U.S. population and 38% of the public school population (Pratt, 2000). According to Banks (2003), "by the year 2020, the White student population will comprise only 54.5% of the public schools" (p. 60). It is of vital concern that the significant population of 45.5% of the children from diverse racial and cultural backgrounds be given an equal opportunity to succeed in U.S. schools (U.S. Census Report, 2008).

As Banks (2003) and Eck (2001) have maintained, teachers, professional school counselors, administrators, and support staff need to acquire new skills, knowledge, and attitudes that will enable them to effectively relate to and educate all students in multicultural, multiethnic, and multiracial settings. Closing the achievement gap will require educators, professional school counselors, and policy makers to think systematically about their current pedagogical practices and the learning styles of the children they serve and to strive to learn from culturally relevant experiences. It is critical that educators exemplify the virtues they seek to inspire in students: curiosity, tolerance, honesty, fairness, respect for diversity, and appreciation of cultural differences. It is also important that educators examine their instructional practices, seek to expand their instructional delivery repertoire, deepen their knowledge, and adapt their teaching to new research and theories to meet the learning styles of a growing diverse population. For those truly committed to closing the achievement gap, examining their pedagogical practices, learning styles, and level of cultural competence is no longer an option in our nation's schools.

RISK FACTOR 4: DIVERSITY, IMMIGRATION, AND ENGLISH-LANGUAGE LEARNERS

Racial and ethnic diversity in the United States continues to increase rapidly. In 2008, 56% of U.S. children were white, non-Latino; 22% were Latino; 15% were black; 4% were Asian; and 5% were of other races. (Students are identified as African Americans when they are Americans of African descent but are not Latino or Caucasian. Children identified as Latino are of Mexican, Puerto Rican, Cuban, Central or South American, or other Spanish culture or origin, regardless of race.) Obed, Charles, and Bentz (2001) indicated that the "perennial challenge for urban education in the United States is finding effective ways to address the academic achievement gap between African American, Latino and White students" (p. 1).

The percentage of children who are Latino has increased faster than that of any other racial or ethnic group, growing from 9% of the child population in 1980 to 22% in 2008 (U.S. Census Report, 2008). Overall, the percentage of all children living in the United States with at least one foreign-born parent rose from 15% in 1994 to 22% in 2008. In 2007, 21% of school-age children spoke a language other than English at home and one-fourth of those (5%) had difficulty speaking English.

A growing population of immigrants presents new challenges and demands on professional school counselors, teachers, administrators, and support staff, especially when it comes in the wake of an emphasis on higher standards and increased student achievement. The U.S. Census Bureau (2009) found that nearly half (47%) of the nation's children younger than five were minorities in 2008, with 25% representing the Latino population. For all children under 18, 44% were minorities, and 22% were Latino. Concurrently, the number of children who are first- or second-generation immigrants has increased to 22% in 2006, and over one-quarter of these children live in homes where the primary caregiver does not speak English very well (Child Trends, 2009). Communication between school and home in this family constellation can become seriously strained and make children more vulnerable to dropping out of school because of the lack of understanding, home support, and available resources.

RISK FACTOR 5: DROPOUTS AND DISCREPANCIES IN HIGHER EDUCATION ATTAINMENT

In October 2006, approximately 3.5 million 16- through 24-year-olds were not enrolled in high school and had not earned a high school diploma or alternative credential such as the GED (i.e., defined as the General Educational Development, but often referred to as the General Educational Diploma). These status dropouts accounted for 9.3 percent of the 37 million 16- through 24-year-olds in the United States in 2006. (Laird, Cataldi, KewalRamani, & Chapman, 2008, p. 8)

In 2007, 89% of young adults ages 18–24 had completed high school with a diploma or an alternative credential such as a GED certificate. The high school completion rate has increased slightly since 1980, when it was 84% (Forum on Child and Family Statistics, 2009). In 2007, 67% of those completing high school enrolled immediately in a two- or four-year college. Between 1980 and 2007, the rate of immediate college enrollment has increased from 49% to 67%, although the rate has fluctuated from year to year. This increase is perhaps due to the emphasis on higher standards in public schools and the impact of the No Child Left Behind Act of 2001. In addition, each year, nearly half a million people get a high school equivalency GED certificate.

The patterned indicators (e.g., socioeconomic status, family history, family structure, poverty) that place students at risk for dropout are well established (Christenson, Sinclair, Lehr, & Godber, 2001).

> Between October 2005 and October 2006, Latino students in public and private high schools were more likely to drop out than were White and African American students. The event dropout rate for Latinos was 7.0%, compared with rates of 2.9% for Whites and 3.8% for Blacks.... In 2006, the event dropout rates for public and private high school students in the West (5.8%) were higher than for their peers in the Northeast (2.9%) and Midwest (1.8 %), and event dropout rates for students in the South (4.1%) were higher than those for students in the Midwest (1.8%). (Laird et al., 2008, pp. 4, 6)

Dropouts tend to believe they don't have control over their lives. Nearly half felt "useless at times," one-third thought they were "no good at all," and almost one-quarter "didn't have much to be proud of." The most common reason for leaving school was poor academic performance. A variety of studies have identified two major risk variables for a potential dropout: being behind grade level (one year behind in reading and mathematics by fourth grade, two years behind in reading by seventh grade, and not passing the ninth grade) and being older than classmates. Other characteristics of dropouts are listed in Table 4.1.

Girls and students from culturally or linguistically diverse groups may be especially at risk for academic failure if they exhibit poor academic performance (Debold, 1995; Steinberg, 1996b). Not intervening—just letting these students "figure it out" or "take responsibility for their own learning"— may lead to a deeper cycle of failure within the school environment, which is often perceived as less inclusive. Latino students are slightly more likely to drop out of school than African Americans, and both of those groups are more likely to drop out than Asian Americans and white students. Nearly 40% of Latino students who drop out do so before the eighth grade.

Dropouts typically reported the following information about their school experiences, according to Snyder (1995):

- Almost one half missed at least 10 days of school;
- One third cut class at least 10 times;
- One quarter was late at least 10 times;
- One third were put on in-school suspension, suspended, or put on probation;
- Six percent were transferred to another school for disciplinary reasons;
- Eleven percent were arrested;
- Eight percent spent time in a juvenile home or shelter. (p. 34)

Some other common indicators of an adolescent at risk for school failure include:

- Attention problems as a young child: The student had a school history of attention issues or disruptive behavior.
- Retention: The student had been retained for one or more years.
- Poor grades: The student consistently performed below average.
- Absenteeism: The student was absent five or more days per term.
- Lack of connection with the school: The student was not involved in athletics, music, or other extracurricular activities.
- Behavior problems: The student was frequently disciplined.

TABLE 4.1   Characteristics of Dropouts

Social/Family Background
- Low socioeconomic status
- Minority
- Children from single-parent homes
- Parents with poor education
- Primary language other than English
- Punitive, abusive families
- Having a sibling who dropped out
- Being home alone without an adult for long periods on weekdays

Personal Problems Independent of Social/Family Background
- Health problems (mental and physical)
- Substance abuse
- Legal problems
- Trauma from divorce or death in the family
- Pregnancy
- Learning disabilities
- Low self-esteem
- Hostility
- The attractiveness of work

School Factors
- Grade retention
- Course failure
- Truancy
- A perception that school is irrelevant and unchallenging
- Disciplinary infractions: detention, suspension, expulsion
- Low grade-point average
- Feelings of alienation from school authorities
- External academic focus of control
- Poor teacher–student relationships
- Little involvement in extracurricular activities
- Resentment of authority

RISK FACTOR 6: TEEN UNINTENDED PREGNANCY

Each year, almost 750,000 females age 15–19 have an unintended pregnancy. The teenage pregnancy rate in the United States is at its lowest level in 30 years, down 36% since its peak in 1990. However, "the birth rate for teenagers 15–19 years rose 1% in 2007, to 42.5 births per 1,000, up 5% from 2005" (Hamilton, Martin, & Ventura, 2009, p. 1).

A growing body of research suggests that the threat of HIV/AIDS, increased abstinence, and changes in contraceptive practice are responsible for recent declines in teenage pregnancy (Guttmacher Institute, 2006). As of 2002, the teenage abortion rate had dropped by 50% from its peak in 1988, perhaps because of a growing collective interest in giving babies up for adoption rather than terminating pregnancies. During the period 1990–2002, the nationwide pregnancy rate for teenagers age 15–19 fell 40% among African Americans, 34% among whites, and 19% among Latinas. However, in 2007, the adolescent birth rate was 22.2 per 1,000 young women age 15–17, up from the 2006 rate of 22.0 per 1,000. This was the second consecutive year of increase in the teenage pregnancy rate after dropping by almost half from 1991 to 2005 (Forum on Child and Family Statistics, 2009). Risk and protective factors for teenage pregnancy are listed in Table 4.2.

The Centers for Disease Control and Prevention (CDC, 2005) estimates that there are approximately 19 million new sexually transmitted infections (STI) each year—almost half of them among young people 15 to 24 years of age. About one out of four sexually experienced teens acquires a sexually transmitted disease (STD) and will develop long-term complications as a result (Weinstock, Berman, & Cotes, 2004). Women and children suffer a disproportionate amount of the STI burden, with pelvic inflammatory disease,

TABLE 4.2   Risk and Protective Behaviors for High-Risk Sexual Activity and Unintended Pregnancy

RISK FACTORS	PROTECTIVE FACTORS
Community	**Community**
• Greater community social disorganization (e.g., violence, hunger & substance use)	• Higher percent foreign born
Family	**Family**
• Family disruption (e.g., divorce or change to single-parent household)	• Live with two biological parents (vs. one parent or stepparents)
Educational level	*Educational level*
• Transgenerational pattern of teenage childbearing	• Higher level of parental education
Substance abuse	*Family dynamics and attachment*
• Household substance abuse (alcohol or drugs)	• Greater parental supervision and monitoring • Higher-quality family interactions, connectedness, and relationship satisfaction
Family dynamics and attachment	*Family attitudes about and modeling of sexual risk-taking and early childbearing*
• Physical abuse and general maltreatment	• Parental disapproval of premarital sex or teen sex • Parental acceptance and support of contraceptive use if sexually active
Family attitudes about and modeling of sexual risk-taking and early childbearing	*Communication about sex and contraception*
• Mother's early age at first birth • Older sibling's early sexual behavior and early age of first birth	• Greater parent–child communication about sex and condoms or contraception especially before youth initiates sex
Peer	**Peer**
Age	*Peer attitudes and behavior*
• Older age of peer group and close friends	• Positive peer norms or support for condom or contraceptive use • Peer use of condoms
Peer attitudes and behavior	*Romantic partner*
• Peers' alcohol use, drug use, and deviant behavior • Peers' pro-childbearing attitudes or behavior • Peers' permissive values about sex • Sexually active peers	• Partner support for condom and contraceptive use
Romantic partner	
• Having a romantic or sexual partner who is older	
Teen Individual Factors	**Teen Individual Factors**
Biological factors	*Biological factors*
• Being male • Older age	• Being male • Older age • Older age of physical maturity or menarche

TABLE 4.2 Risk and Protective Behaviors for High-Risk Sexual Activity and Unintended Pregnancy (continued)

RISK FACTORS	PROTECTIVE FACTORS
Race/Ethnicity • Being black • Being Latino (Hispanic) *Attachment to and success in school* • Being behind in school or having school problems *Problem or risk-taking behaviors* • Alcohol use • Drug use • Being part of a gang • Physical fighting and carrying weapons • Other problem behaviors or delinquency *Other behaviors* • Working for pay more than 20 hours per week *Emotional well-being and distress* • Thoughts of suicide *Cognitive and personality traits* • Lower level of cognitive development • Greater external locus of control *Sexual beliefs, attitudes, and skills* • More permissive attitudes toward premarital sex • Perceiving more the personal and social benefits than the costs of having sex *Relationships with romantic partners and previous sexual behaviors* • Dating more frequently • Going steady or having a close relationship • Having ever kissed or "necked" • Greater frequency of sex • Having a new sexual relationship • Greater number of sexual partners • Previous pregnancy or impregnation • History of sexually transmitted disease (STD) • History of prior sexual coercion or abuse • Same-sex attraction or behavior • Being married	*Attachment to and success in school* • Greater connectedness to school • Higher academic performance • High educational aspirations and plans for the future *Attachment to faith communities* • Having a religious affiliation • More frequent religious attendance *Other behaviors* • Involvement in sports (females only) *Cognitive and personality traits* • Higher level of cognitive development • Greater internal locus of control *Sexual beliefs, attitudes, and skills* • Greater feelings of guilt about possibly having sex • Taking a virginity pledge • Greater perceived male responsibility for pregnancy prevention • Stronger belief that condoms do not reduce sexual pleasure • Greater value of partner appreciation of condom use • More positive attitude toward condoms and other forms of contraception • Perceiving more benefits and/or fewer costs and barriers to using condoms • Greater self-efficacy to demand condom use • Greater self-efficacy to use condoms or other forms of contraception • Greater motivation to use condoms or other forms of contraception • Greater intention to use condoms • Greater perceived negative consequences of pregnancy • Greater motivation to avoid pregnancy, HIV, and other STDs *Relationships with romantic partners and previous sexual behaviors* • Older age of first voluntary sex • Discussing sexual risks with partner • Discussing pregnancy and STD prevention with partner • Previous effective use of condoms or contraception

Source: Kirby, D., Lepore, G., & Ryan, J., *Factors Affecting Teen Sexual Behavior, Pregnancy, Childbearing and Sexually Transmitted Disease: Which Are Important? Which Can You Change?* National Campaign to Prevent Teen Pregnancy, Washington, DC, 2005.

infertility, ectopic pregnancy, blindness, cancer associated with human papilloma virus, fetal and infant deaths, and congenital defects in their children are among the most serious complications. Ethnic and racial minorities, particularly African American and Latino youths, shoulder a disproportionate share of the STI burden as well, experiencing higher rates of disease and disability than the population as a whole.

Additional facts related to reckless premature sexual activity include:

- "Teen pregnancy rates are much higher in the United States than in many other developed countries—twice as high as in England and Wales or Canada, and nine times as high as in the Netherlands or Japan."
- "Among sexually experienced teens, about 8% of 14-year-olds, 18% of 15- to 17-year-olds, and 22% of 18- and 19-year-olds became pregnant each year. More than half (55%) of the 939,000 teenage pregnancies in 1994 ended in births (two-thirds of which were unplanned)."
- "Raising a child during adolescence is associated with long-term negative effects. Babies born to adolescent mothers are at higher risk of low birth weight and infant mortality. They are more likely to grow up in homes that offer lower levels of emotional support and cognitive stimulation and are less likely to earn a high school diploma. The birth rate of adolescents under age 18 is of particular interest because the mother is of school age."
- "There are significant racial and ethnic disparities in birth rates among young women age 15–17. In 1996, the birth rate was 16% for Asians and Pacific Islanders; 47% for Native Americans, 69% for Latinas, and 65% for African Americans. The rate for non-Latino whites was 22%."
- "Less than one-third of teenagers who begin families before age 18 complete high school."
- "Fourteen percent of high-school-age males report having caused at least one pregnancy."
- "Children of teenage parents often do worse in school than other students and are 50% more likely to repeat a grade."
- "Students cite teachers and professional school counselors as second only to their families as the most reliable sources of sexuality-related information."
- "Girls exposed to multiple types of maltreatment are significantly more likely to become pregnant than girls who experience one type of maltreatment. . . . Maltreated teenage girls are more likely to display a constellation of risk factors in early adolescence, including early substance abuse, early sexual intimacy, and poor academic performance" (Tatem, Thornberry, & Smith, 1997, pp. 8–9).

The outlook for teen parents who have educational deficiencies, episodic work histories, and other barriers to employment is not promising. Rosenheim and Testa (1992) maintain that "the rise in levels of teenage pregnancy may reflect a teenager's decision to deviate from society's age-graded pathway to adulthood" (p. 10). The extension of economic dependency into the mid- or late 20s "requires young people to follow a lengthened social timetable for when they complete their education, enter the labor market, and become parents" (Rosenheim & Testa, 1992, p. 3). High school graduation is strongly dependent on adolescent welfare recipients' remaining in their parental home and delaying marriage. Barriers to employment include family responsibilities, lack of role models and support systems, transportation problems, unfamiliarity with the employment network, criminal records, alcohol, and drugs (Achatz & MacAllum, 1994).

RISK FACTOR 7: ADOLESCENT DRUG AND ALCOHOL ABUSE

The Monitoring the Future survey (Johnston, O'Malley, Bachman, & Schulenberg, 2009) found that for the period 1996–2005 more than half of the students in the United States had tried an illegal drug before they graduated from high school. In 2008, 5.4% of 12th-graders reported daily use of marijuana, up slightly from 5.1% in 2007.

> Marijuana appears to be readily available to almost all 12th graders; in 2005 86% reported that they think it would be "very easy" or "fairly easy" for them to get it—almost twice the number who reported ever having used it (45%). After marijuana, 12th-grade students indicated that amphetamines are among the easiest drugs to obtain (51%). (Johnston, O'Malley, Bachman, & Schulenberg, 2006, p. 401)

"The African American juvenile arrest rate for drug abuse violations, which had already increased dramatically, increased an additional 25% between 1993 and 1997. Between 1997 and 2003, the juvenile drug arrest rate fell marginally (22%), with most of the overall decline attributable to a drop in arrests of African Americans (41%) and males (24%)" (Snyder & Sickmund, 2006, p. 144).

> Juveniles using drugs or alcohol committed 1 in 10 of the nonfatal violent victimizations against older teens. This was 2½ times higher than the percentage of victimizations against younger teens perceived to be committed by a juvenile who was using drugs or alcohol. (Baum, 2005, p. 8)

A federal report by the U.S. Center on Substance Abuse Prevention noted:

> Adolescence is a period in which youth reject conventionality and traditional authority figures in an effort to establish their own independence. For a significant number of adolescents, this rejection consists of engaging in a number of "risky" behaviors, including drug and alcohol use. Within the past few years, researchers and practitioners have begun to focus on this tendency, suggesting that drug use may be a "default" activity engaged in when youth have few or no opportunities to assert their independence in a constructive manner. (Carmona & Stewart, 1996, p. 5)

The Office of National Drug Control Policy Reauthorization Act (2006) and other researchers suggest that local and national strategies should coordinate existing youth programs and expand them to share responsibility for improving family and peer relationships. The board identified 10 factors that increase a child's vulnerability to the lure of drugs:

1. Having parents who use drugs
2. Being the victim of physical, sexual, or psychological abuse
3. Dropping out of school
4. Becoming pregnant
5. Being economically disadvantaged
6. Committing a violent or delinquent act
7. Experiencing mental health problems
8. Attempting suicide
9. Running away from home
10. Being homeless

These same factors place the children and adolescents at high risk for dysfunctional or self-defeating behaviors.

> As the frequency of family dinners increased, reported drinking, smoking and drug use decreased. Compared to teens who have five to seven family dinners per week, those who have fewer than three family dinners per week are more than twice as likely to have used tobacco or marijuana, and one and a half times likelier to have used alcohol. (p. 11) Higher levels of communication between parents and children can significantly reduce drug use or experimentation (QEV Analytics, 2008).

> Within the family domain, higher levels of parental communication about substances were significantly associated with lower odds of past-year marijuana use among Latino youths, but not among youths of

other racial/ethnic groups. Within the peer/individual domain, participation in two or more extracurricular activities was significantly associated with lower odds of past-year marijuana use among whites, African Americans, and Latinos, but not youths in the "other" category. Even after controlling for other factors (e.g., age, gender, family structure, income, past month marijuana use, etc.), there is a relationship between past month alcohol use and emotional and behavioral problems. The relationships were particularly strong among heavy and binge alcohol use and delinquent, aggressive, and criminal behaviors (Greenblatt, 2000, p. 9).

According to Wright & Pemberton (2004, p. 60), "Within the school domain, strong sanctions against illegal drug use were significantly associated with lower odds of past-year marijuana use among" white and Latino, but not African American, youths. Finally, exposure to prevention messages in school was associated with lower odds of past year marijuana use" for whites and Latinos, but not for African Americans or youths in the "other" category (p. 60).

The gateway hypothesis holds that abusable drugs occupy distinct ranks in a hierarchy as well as definite positions in a temporal sequence. Accordingly, substance use is theorized to progress through a sequence of stages, beginning with legal, socially acceptable compounds that are low in the hierarchy, followed by use of illegal "soft" and later "hard" drugs ranked higher in the hierarchy. One of the main findings of this study is that there is a high rate of nonconformance with this temporal order. In a neighborhood where there is high drug availability, youths who have low parental supervision are likely to regularly consume marijuana before alcohol and/or tobacco. Consumption of marijuana prior to use of licit drugs thus appears to be related to contextual factors rather than to any unique characteristics of the individual. Moreover, this reverse pattern is not rare; it was observed in over 20% of the sample. (Tarter et al., 2006, p. 2138)

Research continues to demonstrate that, despite a recent leveling off of substance use by adolescents, the current levels remain high, especially for the newer "designer" drugs such as ecstasy and the abuse of over-the-counter or prescription drugs. Studies suggest that the younger an individual is at the onset of substance use, the greater the likelihood is that a substance-use disorder will develop and continue into adulthood. In fact, more than 90% of adults with current substance-use disorders started using before age 18; half of those began before age 15 (Dennis, Babor, Roebuck, & Donaldson, 2002).

In the area of prevention, researchers have established a list of risk and protective factors that are critical to the development and implementation of effective prevention programs. These risk factors include the availability of drugs in the community, a family history of substance abuse, learning disabilities and other academic problems, associating with friends who engage in problem behaviors, and antisocial norms. Identifying and addressing these factors early is a critical step in the prevention and intervention of substance-use problems, the propensity for delinquency, and other self-defeating behaviors (Arthur, Hawkins, Pollard, Catalano, & Baglioni, 2002). What continues to be true is that drug addiction is a brain disease that can be treated.

The Monitoring the Future program, an ongoing study of the behaviors, attitudes, and values of adolescents and young adults in America, reports trends in substance use and abuse. Some highlights of recent data are:

- Alcohol is still the drug of choice among today's teenagers. "Nearly three quarters of students (72%) have consumed alcohol by the end of high school, and more than one third (37%) have done so by 8th grade. In fact, more than half (57%) of 12th graders and one sixth (17%) of 8th graders in 2009 report having been drunk at least once in their life" (Johnston et al., 2009, p. 7).
- "Nearly half (44%) of American youth have tried cigarettes by 12th grade and one out of five (20%) 12th graders is a current smoker" (Johnston, O'Malley, Bachman, & Schulenberg, 2009, p. 7).

- "After a decade of gradual decline, marijuana use began to increase in 2009 in congruence with the belief that there was less risk involved in smoking marijuana" (Johnson et al., 2009, p. 10).
- "In 2009, there was use of crack cocaine, ecstasy, heroin, narcotics other than heroin, Vicodin, OxyContin, amphetamines, methamphetamine, crystal methamphetamine, tranquilizers, Rohypnol, and ketamine remained steady" (Johnston et al., 2009, p. 11).
- "Since 2007, prescription drugs and over-the-counter cough and cold medicines have been used by many youths to get high" (Johnston et al., 2009, p. 13).

Hawkins, et al. (2004) revealed that there are many *risk factors* for drug abuse, each representing a challenge to the psychological and social development of an individual and each having a different impact depending on the phase of development. Factors that affect early development in the family may be the most crucial, such as:

- "Chaotic home environments, particularly in which parents abuse substances or suffer from mental illness";
- "Ineffective parenting, especially with children having difficult temperaments and conduct disorders"; and
- "Lack of mutual attachments and nurturing" (p. 390).

Other risk factors relate to children interacting with other socialization agents outside of the family, specifically, the school, peers, and the community. Hawkins, et al. (2002) lists some of these factors:

- "Inappropriate shy and aggressive behavior in the classroom"
- "Failure in school performance"
- "Poor social coping skills"
- "Affiliations with deviant peers or peers around deviant behaviors"
- "Perceptions of approval of drug-using behaviors in the school, peer, and community environments" (p. 391)

Additional factors such as the availability of drugs, trafficking patterns, and beliefs that drug use is generally tolerated also influences the number of young people who start to use drugs.

Certain *protective factors* have also been identified. These factors are not always the opposite of risk factors, and their impact varies along the developmental process.

The most profound protective factors that can be influenced for potential future change include:

- Strong bonds with the family
- Experience of parental monitoring with clear rules of conduct within the family unit
- Involvement of parents in the lives of their children
- Success in school performance
- Strong bonds with prosocial institutions such as the family, school, and religious organizations
- Adoption of conventional norms—social norms that have evolved in the last decade, like smoke-free restaurants and designated drivers—about drug use.

Research on factors and processes that increase the risk of using drugs or protect against the use of drugs has identified the following primary targets for preventive intervention: family relationships, peer relationships, the school environment, and the community environment. Each of these domains can be a setting for deterring the initiation of drug use through increasing social and self-competency skills, adoption of prosocial attitudes and behaviors, and awareness of the harmful health, social, and psychological consequences of drug abuse. In addition, helping children become more successful in school helps them form strong social bonds with their peers, the school, and the community, which serve to prevent another barrier to learning.

RISK FACTOR 8: MENTAL ILLNESS AND EMOTIONAL DISORDERS

In 2007, 8% of youths age 12–17 had had a major depressive episode (MDE) in the past year, down from 9% in 2004. The percentage of youths with MDEs receiving treatment for depression in the past year remained stable from 2004 to 2007 (40% in 2004 and 39% in 2007) (Forum on Child and Family Statistics, 2009). Children's mental health needs continue to increase and continue to be largely unmet, even when school/community mental health services are readily available. Yet, schools have increasingly been mandated to serve the needs of all children (e.g., by the Individuals with Disabilities Education Improvement Act of 2004 and No Child Left Behind Act of 2001). Although the provision of basic health care in schools began in the early part of the century, the concept of providing comprehensive services in which mental health services are integrated into primary medical care has been implemented only recently.

RISK FACTOR 9: SCHOOL VIOLENCE, BULLYING, AND RELATIONAL AGGRESSION

The No Child Left Behind Act of 2001 mandates that school systems implement programs to reduce violence, bullying, and relational aggression (U.S. Department of Education, 2002) in an effort to improve academic performance and inhibit disruptive behavior that serve as barriers to learning. Educators are keenly aware that students who fear potential violence in their school or community are more likely to have attendance problems and not to participate in extracurricular activities and are less likely to pursue a college education (Dukes & Stein, 2001).

Violent threats and random attacks in high schools were reported at a rate of 31.2 per 1,000 students in 2005–2006 (Dinkes, Cataldi, & Lin-Kelly, 2007). Risk and protective factors for violence are listed in Table 4.3.

Our nation's schools are not the secure safe havens for teaching and learning that they used to be. Crime and violence are more the norm than the exception in today's society, and schools are a microcosm of this reflection. Any instance of crime or violence at school not only affects the individuals involved but also may disrupt the educational process and affect victims, bystanders, the school itself, and the surrounding community. There is some evidence that student safety has improved. For instance, the victimization rate of students ages 12–18 at school declined between 1992 and 2005. However, violence, theft, drugs, and weapons continue to pose problems in schools.

Violence in the schools erupted most shockingly with the Columbine school shootings in 1999. More recently, 32 people were killed at Virginia Tech on April 16, 2007, by Cho Seung-Hui, one of the deadliest shooting rampages in American history, and five students were killed in a campus shooting at Northern Illinois University on February 14, 2008, when former graduate student Stephen Kazmierczak opened fire in a large lecture hall, killing five and wounding dozens of others before committing suicide on the auditorium stage. Both perpetrators in these tragic events had a history of mental health problems.

The most haunting question in the minds of educators and researchers centers around two issues: school safety and the current emotional well-being of today's youth. Do school uniforms, security officers, metal detectors, camera surveillance, curfews, warning alarms, email systems, and cell phone networks make us feel more secure and protected? Or is there a more deep-seated emotional problem occurring among our youth that is screaming for our attention? Every behavior is a communication, and the communication of many of youths is both extreme and disturbing.

TABLE 4.3 Risk and Protective Factors for Violence

RISK FACTORS	PROTECTIVE FACTORS
Prenatal/perinatal stress	Caring and supportive school and community
Ineffective parenting	Good communication
Family violence	Positive role models
Family gang involvement	Family-connectedness
Community laws and norms favorable toward drug use, firearms, and crime	High expectations
	Resiliency
Learning problems	Emotional health
Substance abuse	Opportunities to participate
Involvement in antisocial groups	School achievement
Media violence	School-connectedness
Culture and history of violence	Connectedness to an adult in the community
Availability and legal access to firearms	Extended day care programs for children
Economic deprivation	Early intervention in declines in academic
Overcrowding	achievement
Prejudice and discrimination	Bonding to school and community
Low neighborhood attachment and community disorganization	Recognition of outstanding performance in multiple areas
Early and persistent antisocial behavior	Gender (girls tend to be less violent although some
Academic failure beginning in late elementary school	research is showing an increase in relational aggression and gang violence)
Friends who engage in problem behavior	Parent involvement

School safety measures may make adults feel better about their environment, but they represent a sense of superficial safety. What if there is a potentially homicidal or suicidal student sitting in a classroom, counseling suite, or administrative office and no one has had a chance to really sit down and hear or understand the student's pain about multiple losses, family rejection, peer harassment, bullying, failure, or not fitting in? The student begins to experience depression, which then turns into anger, and finally into rage. He or she may lash out at the institution (school) or themselves.

For both students and teachers, victimization at school can have long-lasting effects and can create barriers to teaching and learning. In addition to experiencing loneliness, depression, suicide ideation, and adjustment difficulties (Crick & Bigbee, 1998; Crick & Grotpeter, 1996; Nansel et al., 2001; Prinstein, Boergers, & Vernberg, 2001; Storch, Nock, Masia-Warner, & Barlas, 2003), victimized children are more prone to truancy (Ringwalt, Ennett, & Johnson, 2003), poor academic performance, dropping out of school (Beauvais, Chavez, Oetting, Deffenbacher, & Cornell, 1996), and violent behavior (Nansel, Overpeck, Haynie, Ruan, & Scheidt, 2003). For teachers, incidents of victimization may lead to professional disenchantment and disillusionment with their profession, leading to the ultimate decision to exit the teaching profession altogether (Karcher, 2002). Accordingly, teacher attrition has become a national concern (National Center for Educational Statistics, 2007).

The percentage of students who were threatened or injured with a weapon at school fluctuated between 7% and 9% from 1993 through 2005. Males were more likely than females to report being threatened or injured with a weapon on school property. In 2005, some 10% of male students reported such an incident in the past year, compared with 6% of female students. Usually, the lower the grade, the greater risk of being harassed, injured, or bullied especially in middle school. Eleven percent of ninth-graders reported that they were threatened or injured with a weapon on school property in 2005, compared with 9% of 10th-graders and 6% of 11th- and 12th-graders. Latino students were more likely than white students to report a weapon incident at school (Dinkes et al., 2007).

Theft and violence at school and while going to and from school can lead to a disruptive and threatening environment, physical injury, and emotional stress and can be an obstacle to student achievement (Elliot, Hamburg, & Williams, 1998). Data from the National Crime Victimization Survey show that students age 12–18 were victims of about 1.5 million nonfatal crimes (theft plus violent crime) while they were at school and about 1.2 million nonfatal crimes while they were away from school in 2005.

Bullying Behavior

It started out with people calling me names, and then it got worse. They threw things at me, they vandalized my house, and they sang nasty songs about me in school hallways and classrooms. It got so bad that I felt like I was in danger physically.

Erika Harold, Miss America 2003, (Greenya, 2005, p. 114)

Both bullying behavior and being bullied at school are associated with key violence-related behaviors, including carrying weapons, fighting, and sustaining injuries from fighting (Nansel et al., 2003). Twenty-four percent of public schools reported that bullying occurred among students on a daily or weekly basis, and 18% said that student acts of disrespect for teachers took place on a daily or weekly basis during the 2005–2006 school year (U.S. Department of Education, National Center for Educational Statistics, 2006). Undesirable gang activities were reported by 17% of public schools, while 4% reported that undesirable cult or extremist activities had happened during the 2005–2006 year. A higher percentage of middle schools than high schools reported daily or weekly occurrences of student bullying and student sexual harassment of other students.

In 2005, about 28% of students reported having been bullied at school during the prior six months. More specifically, 19% of students said that they had been made fun of, 15% reported being the subject of rumors, and 9% said that they were pushed, shoved, tripped, or spit on (U.S. Department of Justice, 2005).

Of those students who had been bullied in 2005, 79% said that they were bullied inside the school and 28% that they were bullied outside on school grounds. Among the bullied students, 53% reported being bullied once or twice during the previous six months, 25% experienced bullying once or twice a month, 11% once or twice a week, and 8% almost daily (U.S. Department of Justice, 2005). In general, grade level was inversely related to students' likelihood of being bullied: as grade level increased, students' likelihood of being bullied decreased. In 2005, about 37% of sixth-graders, 28% of ninth-graders, and 20% of 12th-graders reported that they had been bullied at school. Clearly, early intervention and prevention programs are critical.

Bullying is an early warning sign that the perpetrators may be headed toward more serious antisocial behavior. Students who engage in aggressive and bullying behaviors during their school years may take part in criminal and aggressive behavior after adolescence. Moreover, victims of repeated bullying can permeate the entire school community in ways that threaten not just the bullies but many others as well. For example, a Secret Service (2002) study of school shootings found that almost three-quarters of the attackers felt persecuted, bullied, threatened, attacked, or injured by others prior to the incident. Bullying victims report feelings of vengefulness, anger, and self-pity after a bullying incident (Borg, 1998). Left untreated, such reactions can evolve into depression, physical illness, and even suicide. In classrooms exhibiting high numbers of bullying problems, students tend to feel less safe and are less satisfied with school life in general (Olweus & Limber, 1999).

Relational Aggression: Mean Girls

Within the past decade, reports and research on relational aggression among girls has increased substantially (Brown, 2003; Crick & Nelson, 2002; Underwood, 2003). *Relational aggression* (RA) is described as any behavior that is intended to harm someone by damaging or manipulating relationships with others (Crick & Grotpeter, 1995), particularly among girls in the fifth through eighth grades. RA refers to any act that actively excludes a person from making or maintaining friendships or being integrated into a peer group by engaging in such behaviors as spreading rumors or socially isolating a person (Bjoerkqvist, Lagerspetz, & Kaukianen, 1992).

There are different ways that males and females express their anger. Studies have found that boys tend to use overt forms of aggression such as physical and verbal aggression and may taunt, punch, kick, grab, and engage in other physical acts. Relational aggression conducted by girls is more insidi-ous. Females tend to use more covert forms of aggression to express their anger. Girls are more likely to taunt their victim, stare at her, tell lies and spread rumors about her, exclude her from the group, or threaten to withdraw friendship. The oppressors in this female social system are more likely to be among the most attractive, popular, and socially prominent girls in the school—often the kind of stu-dent that teachers and school administrators overlook and are often enamored by due to their seemingly stellar behavior. Some of the RA methods used include exclusion, ignoring a victim, malicious gossip and rumor spreading, taunts and insults, teasing, intimidation, manipulative affection, alliance build-ing, and cyberbullying.

There are different roles that are assumed in the RA group, whose main motivation is fear, power, control, popularity, and security (Garbarino & deLara, 2002; Simmons, 2002). There is the *queen*, who appears charming to adults but gets other girls in her crew to do what she wants and whose image is dependent on her relationships with them. The *sidekick* defers to the queen and will lie for her; her power innately comes from the confidence she gains from the queen. The *gossip* manipulates confidential information and shares it with others to improve her position in the group; as a chief manipulator, she gets girls to confide in her and then may casually mention key information in a con-versation. The *floater* moves among and between groups and has many protective characteristics; she doesn't gain anything by creating conflict and insecurity among other girls as the queen does. The *torn bystander* is the peacemaker, who wants everyone to get along and finds she often has to choose between friends; often, the torn bystander may hide her true academic potential to fit into the group. The *wannabe* tries desperately to fit in and uses gossiping, often doing the dirty work of the queen such as text messaging, slamming others on social network sites, or other forms of cyberbullying. The *target* is the girl that doesn't fit in because her personal style is different or she just isn't accepted by the group.

Relational aggression in girls has a negative effect on school climate and culture, as well as on the perpetrators and their victims. According to Crick (1996), relational aggressive girls are disliked more than their peers. Excessive relational aggressiveness among people like the queen can become integrated into the girl's behavioral repertoire and can eventually lead to a lifetime of problematic relationships. Victims may appear sullen and moody and are prone to school absenteeism, anxiety, depression, and long-term mental health concerns. Although indirect in its action, RA is direct in its effectiveness, and it appears to cause both distress and psychological harm (Crick, Casas, & Nelson, 2002; Underwood, Galen, & Paquette, 2001).

Gang Violence: Lost Boys

A relentless resurgence of gang activity—with its concurrent gang-related homicides, aggravated assaults, robberies, drug and weapons trafficking, illegal firearm use, fencing of stolen merchandise, and home invasions—has increased in recent years. The National Youth Gang Survey revealed grow-ing gang problems in 2007. The survey results indicate that an estimated 788,000 gang members and 27,000 gangs were active in the United States in 2007 (Egley & O'Donnell, 2009). This demonstra-tion of antisocial behavior places gang members at high risk for entering the juvenile and criminal justice system and is often precipitated by severe abuse, chronic neglect, high interpersonal conflict, and domestic violence within their families of origin; desperately poor and violent neighborhoods with few employment opportunities and educational options; and serious co-occurring learning disabilities, emotional and behavioral problems, and unmet mental health needs, as well as difficulties with adults in positions of authority.

The prevalence of gang activity in schools increased 21–24% between 2003 and 2005 (Dinkes et al., 2007). Seventeen percent of public schools reported undesirable gang activities and 4% reported cult or extremist activities during 2005–2006. Gang activities were generally less frequent for schools where 20% or fewer of the students were eligible for free or reduced-price lunches than for schools where more than 50% of the students were eligible (U.S. Department of Education, 2006).

The presence of gangs in the school community may incite fear among students and increase the level of school violence (Laub & Lauritsen, 1998). In 2005, some 24% of students reported that there were gangs at their schools. Latino (38%) and African American (37%) students were more likely than white (17%) students to report gangs in their schools. Gangs were reported by 25% of public school students, compared with 4% of students in private schools (U.S. Department of Justice, 2005).

The presence of weapons at school may interfere with teaching and learning by creating an intimidating and threatening atmosphere (Aspy et al., 2004). In 2005, some 19% of students in grades 9–12 reported they had carried a weapon, and about 6% reported having carried a weapon on school property. In both cases, males were more than three times as likely as females to carry a weapon. In 2005, for example, 30% of males carried a weapon (10% on school property), compared with 7% of females (3% on school property) (CDC, 2005).

RISK FACTOR 10: CHILD MALTREATMENT

"Victimization of children in the United States remains at an appallingly high rate, despite some decline over the past decade" (Finkelhor & Jones, 2006, p. 685). Child abuse, exploitation, and neglect are pervasive problems both nationally and internationally. As designated mandatory reporters, professional school counselors often express trepidation and anxiety regarding their procedural responsibility for reporting child abuse, often because of fear of retribution on the part of the perpetrator. They may worry that their name will be released to the perpetrator, regardless of the guarantees of confidentiality as mandatory reporters by the city, county, or town.

Nevertheless, according to the American School Counselor Association's (ASCA, 2010) *Ethical Standards for School Counselors,* a professional school counselor must be "knowledgeable of laws, regulations, and policies relating to students and [strive] to protect and inform students regarding their rights" (A.1.d). These guidelines go on to maintain that professional school counselors must "inform appropriate school officials in accordance with school policy of conditions that may be potentially disruptive or damaging to the school's mission, personnel, and property while honoring the confidentiality between the student and school counselor" (D.1.b).

In addition, ASCA's (2003b) position statement *Child Abuse/Neglect Prevention* stipulates:

> ASCA recognizes it is the absolute responsibility of professional school counselors to report suspected cases of child abuse/neglect to the proper authorities. Responsible action by the professional counselor can be achieved through the recognition and understanding of the problem, knowing the reporting procedures and participating in available child abuse information programs. Professional school counselors are instrumental in early detection of abuse. The association also recognizes that the abuse of children is not limited to the home and that corporal punishment by school authorities can be considered child abuse. (p. 4)

As a specialist in child and adolescent development and family dynamics with training in primary prevention, therapeutic interventions, and crisis intervention and management, professional school counselors are the ideal resource for educating other educators about the risk and protective factors (see Table 4.4) for abuse, neglect, and the exploitation of children (Crosson-Tower, 2002). As a prevention initiation, professional school counselors can facilitate staff development for all school personnel, including school support staff such as bus drivers, custodians, cafeteria workers, and youth service officers, who see students on a daily basis and can observe changes in behavior because they are not distracted by instructional responsibilities that teachers must assume. Consultation with Child Protective Services or related agencies can also be integrated to provide consultation services to all school personnel as needed. Such an initiative reflects the *ASCA (2003c) National Model*, demonstrating a collaborative partnership to support the school's overall mission of nurturing all children and preventing barriers to learning.

TABLE 4.4   Risk and Protective Factors for Child Maltreatment

RISK FACTORS	PROTECTIVE FACTORS
For Victimization	*Family protective factors*
Individual risk factors	• Supportive family environment and social networks
• Children younger than 4 years of age	• Nurturing parenting skills
• Special needs that may increase caregiver burden (e.g., disabilities, mental retardation, mental health issues, chronic physical illnesses)	• Stable family relationships
	• Household rules and child monitoring
	• Parental employment
For Perpetration	• Adequate housing
Individual risk factors	• Access to health care and social services
• Parents' lack of understanding of children's needs and child development and parenting skills	• Caring adults outside the family who can serve as role models or mentors
• Parents' history of child abuse in family of origin	*Community protective factors*
• Substance abuse and/or mental health issues, including depression, in the family	• Communities that support parents and take responsibility for preventing abuse
• Parental characteristics such as young age, low education, single parenthood, large number of dependent children, and low income	
• Nonbiological, transient caregivers in the home (e.g., mother's male partner)	
• Parental thoughts and emotions that tend to support or justify maltreatment behaviors	
Family risk factors	
• Social isolation	
• Family disorganization, dissolution, and violence, including intimate partner violence	
• Parenting stress, poor parent–child relationships, and negative interactions	
Community risk factors	
• Community violence	
• Concentrated neighborhood disadvantage (e.g., high poverty and residential instability, high unemployment rates, high density of alcohol outlets), and poor social connections	

Source: Chaffin, M., & Friedrich, B., *Children and Youth Services Review, 26*, 1097–1113, 2004.

The Most Common Types of Maltreatment, Child Fatalities, and Primary Perpetrators

Child maltreatment can be defined as

> behavior towards [a child] … which (a) is outside the norms of conduct and (b) entails a substantial risk of causing physical or emotional harm. Behaviors included will consist of actions and omissions, ones that are intentional and ones that are unintentional. (Christoffel et al., 1992, p. 1027)

Four types of maltreatment are generally recognized: neglect, physical abuse, sexual abuse, and emotional abuse. The Administration on Children, Youth, and Families of the U.S. Department of Health and Human Services (2008) provided the following statistics for 2006:

- More than 60% (64.1%) of the victims suffered neglect
- More than 15% (16.0%) of the victims suffered physical abuse
- Less than 10% (8.8%) of the victims suffered sexual abuse
- Less than 10% (6.6%) of the victims suffered from emotional maltreatment
- During 2006, an estimated 1,530 children died due to child abuse or neglect
- More than 40% (41.1%) of child fatalities were attributed to neglect; physical abuse also was a major contributor to child fatalities
- More than three-quarters (78.0%) of the children who died due to child abuse and neglect were younger than four years old
- Infant boys (younger than one year) had the highest rate of fatalities, at 18.5 deaths
- Infant girls had a rate of 14.7 deaths per 100,000 girls of the same age
- In 2006, nearly 80% (79.9%) of perpetrators of child maltreatment were parents, and another 6.7% were other relatives of the victim
- Women comprised a larger percentage of all perpetrators than men, 57.9% compared to 42.1%
- More than 75% (77.5%) of all perpetrators were younger than age 40
- Of the perpetrators who maltreated children, less than 10% (7.0%) committed sexual abuse, while 60.4% committed neglect
- Of the perpetrators who were parents, more than 90% (91.5%) were the biological parent of the victim (pp. 1–4)

Vieth, Bottoms, and Perona (2005) profoundly declared that "there is, in the United States today, a culture permitting child abuse to thrive" (p. 5). As indicators of this, they cite:

- Victims do not feel empowered to report their abuses because of fear of retribution.
- Mandated reporters often fail to report abuse, no matter how clear the evidence, because of the fear of retribution.
- Allegations that are reported to child protective services are often screened out with little or no investigation because caseloads are often overwhelming.
- When investigations are conducted, many of the front line responders are inadequately trained and/or inexperienced in handling maltreatment cases and abuse is therefore not well documented or successfully prosecuted.
- When child abuse is eventually documented, the victims are typically older and have needlessly endured years of abuse.
- Child abuse prevention efforts are woefully underfunded and are not present in any meaningful sense in most communities in our country. (p. 2)

The long-term consequences of abuse to victims are devastating and debilitating. Victims are more likely to repeat a grade or dropout of school. The enduring effects include possible brain damage, posttraumatic stress disorder, developmental delays, learning disabilities, problems forming relationships (interpersonal and intrapersonal), aggressive behavior, depression, low academic achievement, substance abuse, teen pregnancy, sexual revictimization, and criminal behavior (Prevent Child Abuse America, 2003). Based on data drawn from a variety of sources, Wang and Holton (2007) estimate the "annual cost of child abuse and neglect" at $103.8 billion (p. 2). Direct costs to support systems include hospitalization, the mental health care system, the child welfare service system, law enforcement, the juvenile justice system, and foster care. Indirect costs include special education services, juvenile justice services, welfare dependency, adult criminal justice services, mental and physical health care, and long-term loss of productivity to society.

Increasingly, attention has been paid to the ramifications of child maltreatment and its long-term impact on subsequent youth development. An accumulation of research is strongly suggesting that being maltreated as a child increases the chances of a variety of developmental problems during childhood, adolescence, and adulthood. A variety of negative teenage outcomes have been identified, such as delinquency, unintended pregnancy, alcohol and other drug abuse, low academic achievement, school failure, and emotional and mental health problems (Tatem et al., 1997; Widom, 1994). Kelly, Thornberry, and Smith (1997) found that youths who experienced maltreatment during childhood were significantly more likely to display a variety of problem behaviors during adolescence. However, it is important to note that Zingraff, Leiter, Johnsen, and Myers (1994) found that adequate school performance appears to substantially reduce the risk of delinquency among maltreated children. Performing well in school fosters adolescent resiliency following childhood maltreatment.

Students who perform poorly in middle school are considered at increased risk for continued academic failure in high school, low educational aspirations, premature school dropout, and reduced educational and economic opportunities. Child victims often have a wide range of maladaptive emotional and interpersonal symptoms such as anxiety, inattentiveness, impulsiveness, anger, aggression, passivity, withdrawal, depression, self-destructiveness, obsessive-compulsive behavior, and unpopularity (Erickson, Egeland, & Pianta, 1989). Child victims are further described as lacking self-confidence, empathy, and joy. Maltreatment has been linked to a number of mental health problems among adolescents, including increased self-destructive and suicidal behavior, fewer interpersonal competencies, and more mood disorders such as anxiety and depression (Downs, 1993; Malinosky-Rummell & Hansen, 1993).

Exposure to violence, including physical abuse, has severe and damaging consequences for many aspects of a child's functioning: physical, developmental, cognitive, social, emotional, behavioral, and academic (Kolko, 1996b). Infants, toddlers, and older children often experience the four hallmark symptoms of posttraumatic stress disorder: reexperiencing the traumatic event, numbing of responsiveness, avoidance of reminders of the trauma, and hyperarousal (American Psychiatric Association, 1994). Other common symptoms include sleep disturbance, night terrors, separation anxiety, fearfulness, aggressiveness, difficulty concentrating, and emotional detachment (Malinosky-Rummell & Hansen, 1993).

Table 4.5 outlines the four categories of child abuse—neglect, physical abuse, sexual abuse, and emotional abuse—and their physical and behavioral characteristics. It is offered as a quick glance into the different categories and behaviors that can be affirmed if the professional school counselor needs additional confirmation on professional observations.

Race and Ethnic Differences

All forms of abuse encompass all socioeconomic groups, races, and religions and range over a continuum from benign neglect to the extremes of human trafficking. Women and children are particularly vulnerable to human trafficking for the sex trade. Human trafficking, however is not limited to sexual exploitation. It also includes persons who are trafficked into forced marriages or into bonded cheap labor markets, such as sweatshops, agricultural work, or domestic service. Neglect continues to be the most common form of child abuse, accounting for more than 60% of all cases of child maltreatment.

TABLE 4.5   Types of Child Abuse, Signs and Symptoms

TYPE OF ABUSE	PHYSICAL SYMPTOMS	BEHAVIORAL SYMPTOMS
Neglect is a pattern of failing to provide for a child's basic needs, such as food, clothing, medical care, or adequate supervision to the extent that the child's physical and/or psychological well-being is damaged or endangered. It falls into three categories: physical, educational, and emotional. Even though physical and sexual abuse receive more public attention because they involve profound physical violence and significant trauma, neglect may be the most common form of child abuse and the most difficult type of abuse to document.	• Clothes that are dirty, ill-fitting, ragged, or unsuitable for the weather • Unwashed appearance; offensive body odor • Indicators of hunger: asking for or stealing food, going through trash for food, eating too fast or too much when food is provided for a group • Apparent lack of supervision: wandering alone in the neighborhood, home alone, left in a car • Colds, fevers, or rashes left untreated; infected cuts; chronic tiredness • In school-age children, frequent absence or lateness; troublesome, disruptive behavior or unusually withdrawn • In babies, failure to thrive; failure to relate to other people or to surroundings *Physical Neglect* • Failure to provide adequate food, clothing, or hygiene • Reckless disregard for the child's safety, such as inattention to hazards in the home, drunk driving with kids in the car, dealing drugs out of the home, leaving a baby unattended in the home or the car • Refusal to provide or delay in providing necessary health care for the child • Abandoning children without providing for their care or expelling children from the home without arranging for their care *Educational Neglect* • Failure to enroll a child in school, i.e., ignoring compulsory school attendance laws • Permitting or causing a child to miss too many days of school, e.g., having them stay home to take care of sick siblings (although there is a need to be culturally	• Poor social skills • An indiscriminate show of affection • Craving for attention • Falling asleep in class • Routinely displaying fatigue • Self-destructive behavior • Begging, stealing, or hoarding food • Frequent school absenteeism or tardiness

TABLE 4.5 Types of Child Abuse, Signs and Symptoms (continued)

TYPE OF ABUSE	PHYSICAL SYMPTOMS	BEHAVIORAL SYMPTOMS
	sensitive to this issue, especially with immigrants who are new to this country) • Refusal to follow up on obtaining services for a child's special educational needs or health needs such as glasses to improve vision	
	Emotional Neglect • Inadequate nurturing or affection and lack of attachment • Exposure of the child to spousal abuse or community violence • Permitting a child to drink alcohol or use recreational or other drugs • Failure to intervene when the child demonstrates antisocial behavior • Refusal of or delay in providing necessary psychological care	
Sexual Abuse is sexual involvement imposed upon a child by a parent or caregiver such as fondling a child's genitals, showing adult genitals, penetration, incest, rape, sodomy, or commercial exploitation through prostitution, human trafficking, or the production of pornographic materials.	• Sleep disturbances or nightmares • Difficulty walking or sitting • Pain, itching, bruising, or bleeding in the genitalia • Venereal disease • Frequent urinary tract infections or yeast infections • Pregnancy	• Being overly affectionate, engaging, or knowledgeable in a sexual way inappropriate to the child's age • Detailed and sophisticated understanding of sexual behavior • Medical problems such as chronic itching, pain in the genitals, venereal diseases • Other extreme reactions, such as depression, self-mutilation, suicide attempts, running away, overdoses, anorexia • Personality changes such as becoming insecure or clinging • Regressing to younger behavior patterns such as thumb sucking, bedwetting, speech loss, or bringing out discarded cuddly toys • Sudden loss of appetite or compulsive eating • Being isolated or withdrawn • Inability to concentrate

continued

TABLE 4.5 Types of Child Abuse, Signs and Symptoms (continued)

TYPE OF ABUSE	PHYSICAL SYMPTOMS	BEHAVIORAL SYMPTOMS
		• Lack of trust or fear of someone they know well, such as not wanting to be alone with a babysitter or child minder • Becoming worried about clothing being removed; unwilling to change clothes or participate in physical education • Suddenly drawing sexually explicit pictures • Adolescents may manifest aggressive behaviors, depression, substance abuse, self-mutilation, suicide ideation, prostitution, and running away
Physical Abuse is nonaccidental physical injury to a child, usually in soft tissue areas, that follows a continuum from minor bruising to severe fractures or even death. Physical abuse includes punching, restraining, kicking, beating, biting, burning, shaking, or stabbing to physically harm the child.	• Unexplained bruises, burns, or welts in various stages of healing • Human bite marks • Ligature marks around the wrists or ankles • Unexplained fractures, abrasions, or other injuries	• Improbable excuses or refusal to explain injuries • Wearing clothes to cover injuries, even in hot weather • Refusal to undress for gym • Bald patches • Chronic running away • Fear of medical help or examination • Self-destructive tendencies • Aggression toward others • Fear of physical contact; shrinking back if touched • Admitting that they are punished, but the punishment is excessive (such as a child being beaten every night to make him study) • Fear of suspected abuser being contacted • Nervous, hyperactive, aggressive, or destructive behavior • Expressing little or no emotion when hurt • Being unusually shy, withdrawn, or passive
Emotional Abuse is concomitant with all forms of child abuse and can be defined as any manifestation of	• Speech disorders • Delayed physical and emotional development • Ulcers, asthma, or severe allergies	• Continual self-depreciation ("I'm stupid," "ugly," "worthless," etc.) • Overreaction to mistakes

TABLE 4.5   Types of Child Abuse, Signs and Symptoms (continued)

TYPE OF ABUSE	PHYSICAL SYMPTOMS	BEHAVIORAL SYMPTOMS
behavior that impairs a child's emotional development or sense of worth, including belittling, embarrassing, constant criticism, threats, rejection along with withholding love, support and direction.		• Extreme fear of any new situation • Inappropriate response to pain ("I deserve this") • Neurotic habit disorders such as rocking, hair twisting, self-mutilation • Extremes of passivity and undemanding demeanor • Low self-esteem • Exceedingly demanding, aggressive, or angry behavior • Conduct disorder such as antisocial or destructive behavior • Depression, suicidal ideation, self-mutilation, and attention-seeking behavior

Source: Adapted from Crosson-Tower, C., *When Children Are Abused: An Educator's Guide to Intervention,* Allyn & Bacon, Boston, 2002; Fisher, L., Schimmel, D., & Stellman, L. R., *Teachers and the Law* (6th ed.), Allyn & Bacon, Boston, 2003; and Lambie, G. W., *Professional School Counseling, 8*(3), 249–258, 2005; and Prevent Child Abuse America, *What Everyone Can Do to Prevent Child Abuse: 2003 Child Abuse Prevention Community Resource Packet,* Chicago, 2003. Reprinted with permission.

Boys and girls suffer physical abuse equally; however, girls are four times more likely to experience sexual abuse (Prevent Child Abuse America, 2003). Prevent Child Abuse America (2003) maintains that at least 20% of American women and 5–16% of American men experienced some form of sexual abuse as children. Based on national sexual abuse statistics (Cole, 1995), if you take the "average case load of a professional school counselor averaging around 477 students" (National Center for Education Statistics [NCES], 2003b, p. 47), approximately 95 of these students have been or will be sexually abused.

RISK FACTOR 11: DEPRESSION AND CHILD AND ADOLESCENT SUICIDE

In 2004, suicide was the third leading cause of death among youths and young adults ages 10–24 years in the United States, accounting for 4,599 deaths (CDC, 2007; Moscicki, 2001). During 1990–2003, "the combined suicide rate for persons aged 10–24 years declined 28.5%, from 9.48 to 6.78 per 100,000 persons, but from 2003 to 2004, the rate increased by 8.0%, from 6.78% to 7.32% (2), the largest single-year increase in years" (Moscicki, 2001, p. 314).

"From 2003 to 2004, suicide rates for three sex/age groups—females age 10–14, females age 15–19, and males age 15–19—departed upward significantly from otherwise declining trends; in particular, results indicated that suicides by hanging/suffocation and by poisoning among females in the 10–14 and 15–19 age groups were significantly in excess of trends in both groups. The results suggest that increases in suicide and changes in suicidal behavior might have occurred among youths in certain sex/age groups, especially females age 10–19" (National Center for Health Statistics, 2007).

In 2005, according to the CDC (Eaton et al., 2006):

1. 16.9% of students, grades 9–12 (21.8% of females and 12.0% of males), had seriously considered suicide in the previous 12 months (p. 6).
2. 8.4% of students (10.8% of females and 6.0% of males) reported making at least one suicide attempt in the previous 12 months (p. 7).
3. 2.3% of students (2.9% of females and 1.8% of males) reported making at least one suicide attempt in the previous 12 months that required medical attention (p. 8).

Closer examination of these disturbing trends is warranted at federal, state, and local levels. Where indicated, health authorities and program directors and all helping professionals should consider focusing suicide-prevention activities on these groups to help prevent suicide rates from increasing further.

Some of the Risk Factors for Potential Suicide

Research has demonstrated the following risk factors for suicide potential:

- Depression and other mental disorders or a substance-abuse disorder (often in combination with other mental disorders)—"more than 90% of people who die by suicide have these risk factors" (Moscicki, 2001, p. 311)
- "Stressful life events, in combination with other risk factors, such as depression. However, suicide and suicidal behavior are not normal responses to stress; many people have these risk factors, but are not suicidal; also everyone stress threshold is different" (Miller, Azreal, Hepburn, Hemenway, & Lippmann, 2006, p. 17)
- Prior suicide attempt
- Family history of mental disorder or substance abuse
- Family history of suicide
- Family violence, including physical or sexual abuse
- Firearms in the home, "the method used in more than half of suicides" (Miller et al., 2006, p. 17)
- Incarceration
- "Exposure to the suicidal behavior of others, such as family members, peers, or media figures" (Moscicki, 1999, p. 345)

Research also shows that the risk for "suicide is associated with changes in brain chemicals called neurotransmitters, including serotonin" (Moscicki, 2001, p. 342). Decreased levels of serotonin have been found in people with depression, impulsive disorders, and a history of suicide attempts, as well as in the brains of suicide victims (Arango, Huang, Underwood, & Mann, 2003).

Risk and Protective Factors and Suicidal Risk among Adolescents

Over the last two decades, an enormous amount of research has examined the epidemic of teenage suicides, suicide ideation, and suicide attempts. Evidence-based practices are now examining risk and protective factors as a means to reduce suicide ideation and attempts, as well as other dysfunctional behaviors such as substance abuse, self-injury, violence, and other self-destructive behaviors, in an effort to reduce these dysfunctional manifestations of behavior. Research has now demonstrated that the following are risk factors for suicide in adolescents:

- Previous suicide attempts or gestures (Borowsky, Resnick, Ireland, & Blum, 1999; Gould, Greenberg, Velting, & Shaffer, 2003; Kaplan, Pelcovitz, Salzinger, Mandel, & Weiner, 1997; Shaffer & Pfeffer, 2001)

- Mood disorder or psychopathology (Borowsky et al., 1999; Gould et al., 2003; Moscicki, 1999; Shaffer et al., 1996; Shaffer & Pfeffer, 2001)
- Substance abuse disorder (Borowsky, Ireland, & Resnick, 2001; Gould et al., 2003; Shaffer et al., 1996; Shaffer & Pfeffer, 2001)
- Family history of suicidal behavior or mental illness (Gould et al., 2003; Moscicki, 1999; Shaffer et al., 2001)
- Relationships, social disrespect, work, or financial loss (Brent, Johnson, & Perper, 1994; Gould et al., 2003; Moscicki, 1999; Shaffer et al., 2001)
- Access to firearms
- Contagion or exposure to individuals who have attempted or completed suicide with exposure through media, television, and direct contact (Moscicki, 1999; Shaffer et al., 2001; Office of the Surgeon General, 1999b)
- History of physical or sexual abuse (Kaplan et al., 1997; Shaffer et al., 2001)
- Conduct disorder (Kaplan et al., 1997; Shaffer et al., 2001)
- Juvenile delinquency (Kaplan et al., 1997; Shaffer et al., 2001)
- Sexual orientation, which has been shown to be correlated with identified risk factors for suicide and is less of a factor after controlling for these risk factors (Borowsky et al., 1999; Gould et al., 2003; Moscicki, 1999; Shaffer et al., 2001)
- Stressful life events (Shaffer et al., 2001)
- Chronic physical illness (Gould et al., 2003; Moscicki, 1999)
- Impulsive or aggressive tendencies (Brent et al., 1994; Gould et al., 2003)
- Living alone/runaways (Shaffer et al., 2001)
- School problems (Borowsky et al., 2001)

Protective factors for suicide prevention are not permanent, just by the nature of adolescents and their fleeting relationships with adults, so the support and maintenance of protection needs to be continuous and ongoing. The following have demonstrated to be protective for suicide:

- Parental/family or extended support and connectedness (religious/cultural beliefs) (Borowsky et al., 2001; Gould et al., 2003; Office of the Surgeon General, 1999b; World Health Organization, 2000)
- Good relationships with other school youths/best friends (World Health Organization, 2000)
- Lack of access to means (Shaffer et al., 2001; Office of the Surgeon General, 2000)
- Support from relevant adults/teachers/professionals (Office of the Surgeon General, 1999b; World Health Organization, 2000)
- Help-seeking behavior/advice seeking (World Health Organization, 2000)
- Conflict resolution abilities (Office of the Surgeon General, 1999b)
- Social integration/opportunities to participate (World Health Organization, 2000)
- Positive sense of worth/confidence (World Health Organization, 2000)
- Access to care for mental/physical/substance disorders (Office of the Surgeon General, 1999b)
- Perceived connectedness to school (Borowsky et al., 2001)

Table 4.6 provides additional risk and protective factors for potential suicide. Table 4.7 provides early warning signs for suicide potential. Table 4.8 provides late warning signs for suicide potential. Table 4.9 identifies significant stressors that could make adolescents more vulnerable and Table 4.10 outlines behavioral manifestations or overt symptoms that help predict a potential suicide. These tables are merely guidelines to confirm the professional school counselor's perceptions of observed behavior and assist when consulting with other helping professionals to ascertain if further intervention, consultation with parents, or a potential referral is needed.

TABLE 4.6   Risk and Protective Factors in Suicide Prevention Initiatives

RISK FACTORS	PROTECTIVE FACTORS
• Previous suicide attempt or gesture • Feelings of hopelessness or isolation • Psychopathology (depressive disorders/mood disorders • Parental psychopathology • Substance abuse disorder • Family history of suicidal behavior • Life stressors such as interpersonal losses (relationships, social work) and legal or disciplinary problems • Access to firearms • Physical abuse • Sexual abuse • Conduct disorders or disruptive behaviors • Sexual orientation (homosexual, bisexual, and transgendered youth) • Juvenile delinquency • School and/or work problems • Contagion or imitation (exposure to media accounts of suicidal behaviors and exposure to suicidal behavior in friends or acquaintances) • Chronic physical illness • Living alone and/or runaways • Aggressive-impulsive behaviors	• Family cohesion (family with mutual involvement, shared interests, and emotional support • Good coping skills • Academic achievement • Perceived connectedness to the school • Good relationships with other school youths • Lack of access to means for suicidal behavior • Help-seeking behavior/advice seeking • Impulse control • Problem-solving/conflict-resolution abilities • Social integration/opportunities to participate in the school/community • Sense of worth/confidence • Stable environment • Access to care for mental, physical, or substance disorders • Responsibilities for others such as pets • Religious affiliation

Source: Doan, J., Roggenbaum, S., & Lazear, K., *Youth Suicide Prevention School-Based Guide—Issue Brief 3b: Risk Factors: How Can a School Identify a Student at Risk?* (FMHI Series Publication #218-3b), Department of Child and Family Studies, Division of State and Local Support, Louis de la Parte Florida Mental Health Institute, University of South Florida, Tampa, 2003.

TABLE 4.7   Early Warning Signs for a Potential Suicide

- Withdrawal from friends and family
- Preoccupation with death
- Marked personality change and serious mood changes
- Difficulty concentrating
- Difficulties in school (decline in quality of work)
- Change in eating and sleeping habits
- Loss of interest in pleasurable activities
- Frequent complaints about physical symptoms, often related to emotions, such as stomachaches, headaches, fatigue, etc.
- Persistent boredom
- Loss of interest in things one cares about

Source: Doan, J., Roggenbaum, S., & Lazear, K., *Youth Suicide Prevention School-Based Guide—Issue Brief 3b: Risk Factors: How Can a School Identify a Student at Risk?* (FMHI Series Publication #218-3b), Department of Child and Family Studies, Division of State and Local Support, Louis de la Parte Florida Mental Health Institute, University of South Florida, Tampa, 2003.

TABLE 4.8   Late Warning Signs for a Potential Suicide

- Actually talking about suicide or a plan
- Exhibiting impulsivity such as violent actions, rebellious behavior, or running away
- Refusing help, feeling "beyond help"
- Complaining of being a bad person or feeling "rotten inside"
- Making statements about hopelessness, helplessness, or worthlessness
- Not tolerating praise or rewards
- Giving verbal hints with statements such as "I won't be a problem for you much longer," "Nothing matters," "It's no use," or "I won't see you again"
- Becoming suddenly cheerful after a period of depression—this may mean that the student has already made the decision to escape all problems by ending his or her life
- Giving away favorite possessions
- Making a last will and testament
- Saying other things like "I'm going to kill myself," or "I wish I were dead."

Source: Doan, J., Roggenbaum, S., & Lazear, K., *Youth Suicide Prevention School-Based Guide—Issue Brief 3b: Risk Factors: How Can a School Identify a Student at Risk?* (FMHI Series Publication #218-3b), Department of Child and Family Studies, Division of State and Local Support, Louis de la Parte Florida Mental Health Institute, University of South Florida, Tampa, 2003.

TABLE 4.9   Types of Stress Experienced by Students (Ages 14 to 18) Ranked by Frequency of Occurrence

SOURCE OF STRESS	RANK
Getting tired for no reason	1
Increased or worse arguments/fights with parents	2
Not doing as well as their parents expect in school	3
Trying to make new friends	4
Feeling that no one cares or understands them	5
No longer enjoying things they used to do	6
Increased or worse arguments/fights with siblings	7
Problems with size	8
Having crying spells or feeling like it doesn't matter	9
Getting grounded	10
Feeling like they are falling apart and going to pieces	11
Change in physical appearance	12
Parent or relative in their family getting very sick	13
Feeling useless and not needed	14
Feeling that things are never going to get better	15
Failing one or more subjects at school	16
Trouble with a teacher or the principal	17
Getting badly hurt or sick	18
Getting into alcohol	19
Feeling there's no one to share concerns with	20
Breaking up with a close friend	21
Losing a favorite pet	22
Taking chances when driving a car	23
Getting into physical fights	24
Feeling that life is not worth living	25
Feeling that others would be better off if you were dead	26

Source: Huff, C. R., *Adolescence, 34*(133), 81–89, 1999.

TABLE 4.10   Behavioral Manifestations or Overt Symptoms That Help Predict a Potential Suicide

MANIFESTATIONS	INTENSITY OF RISK	INDIVIDUAL RATING
Academic progress and attendance	1 Low: Maintains attendance and academic progress concurrent with past performance 2 Moderate: Occasionally fails a class; some concern for school 3 High: Chronic absenteeism; drop in school performance; hostile toward school and administration	_____
Anxiety	1 Low 2 Moderate 3 Severe	_____
Depression	1 Low 2 Moderate 3 Severe	_____
Physical isolation	1 Low: Vague feeling of depression; no withdrawal 2 Moderate: Feelings of helplessness, hopelessness, and withdrawal 3 High: Hopeless, helpless, withdrawn, and self-deprecating	_____
Available resources	1 Low: Resources either intact or able to be restored easily 2 Moderate: Some turmoil regarding trust; strained relationships attainable 3 High: Very limited or nonexistent; student sees himself or herself without resources	_____
Communication	1 Low: Able to communicate directly and nondestructively 2 Moderate: Ambiguous; may use self-injury to communicate and gain attention 3 High: Feels cut off from resources and unable to communicate effectively	_____
Routine interaction	1 Low: Fairly good in most activities 2 Moderate: Moderately good in selected activities 3 High: Not good in most activities	_____
Coping strategies	1 Low: Generally constructive 2 Moderate: Some strategies are self-defeating 3 High: Predominantly destructive	_____
Significant others	1 Low: Several are available 2 Moderate: Few are available 3 High: Only one or none	_____
Previous suicide attempts	1 Low: None, or of low lethality 2 Moderate: One or more of moderate lethality 3 High: Multiple attempts, or of high lethality	_____
Recent loss	1 Low: None or more than one year ago 2 Moderate: One less than 12 months ago 3 High: Recent loss of significant other	_____
Drug abuse	1 Low: Infrequent to excess 2 Moderate: Frequently to excess 3 High: Continual abuse	_____
Suicidal plan	1 Low: Vague, fleeting ideation, but no plan 2 Moderate: Frequent thoughts, occasional plan 3 High: Frequent or constant thoughts with a deliberate plan	_____

Violence produces extensive physical costs and emotional consequences. The long-range implications are that interpersonal violence may become a common part of social interaction in domestic settings as well as a model of behavior adopted by future generations raised in such settings.

THE FULL-SERVICE SCHOOL: THE ULTIMATE RESOURCE FOR YOUTH

The success of wraparound, parallel, or full-service schools includes academic gains, improvement in school attendance, reduction in high-risk behaviors, increased parent involvement, lower incidence of child abuse and neglect, and lower rates of violence in the participating schools and communities. The school component of such a system includes academic, behavioral, and social skills and instructional strategies, as well as consultation and supports for teachers; administrators; professional school counselors; and support staff such as bus drivers, school nurses, youth service officers, and attendance clerks (Scott & Eber, 2003).

The single-issue Band-Aid approach adopted by many school divisions is to treat each problem in isolation from every other program, whether it is alcohol abuse, delinquency, teen suicide, dropouts, or violence. Such an approach has little chance of success, however, since these problems are interrelated, interdependent, and often transgenerational.

Full-service schools represent a holistic approach to meeting children's and adolescents' social, emotional, cognitive, and physical and health needs (Muijs, 2007). This view is based on the assumption that students are more likely to encounter barriers to learning if they encounter health, social, and social problems. Addressing these issues systematically will allow students to maximize their educational achievements as well as to enhance their overall well-being. Youths need safety, support, and opportunity. Innovative programs and community resources must be brought together to ensure that children can grow up to be responsible and productive members of society. Families, the schools, the mental health sector, community organizations, and the media must work in concert to launch all young people on a successful life course (Dryfoos, 1990, 1994; Dryfoos & Maguire, 2002; Scott & Eber, 2003; Muijs, 2007).

A full-service school is a comprehensive, integrated program that addresses the social, emotional, and educational health needs and development of youth. It is a school center in which health, mental health, social, and/or family services may be collaboratively located within the campus, depending on the needs of the particular school and community. Community participation and diverse programming characterize full-service school programs. Collaborative efforts are managed by an advisory board, consisting of some combination of school, government, and health officials, as well as parents, representatives from the community organizations, and youths. Full-service schools require a deep commitment by teachers, administrators, youths, parents, community members, health workers, social workers, and a variety of human services specialists. With goals of improving "academic achievement," along with youth development and family and community well-being, most of the programs showed positive impacts on more than just one outcome (Dryfoos & Maguire, 2002) such as:

- Student achievement and development
- Family engagement
- School environment
- Parental engagement
- School staff engagement
- Community engagement
- Deliberate contracted partnerships with school and community agencies

The full-service school recognizes the value of primary prevention and intervention services by partnering with service providers in the community. School and community partnerships may include community agencies such as the health department, social services, and community services board, along with nationally recognized youth-serving agencies such as the YMCA, Girls and Boys Clubs of America, and Big Brothers and Big Sisters of America. These partnerships provide intervention, social support, and transition services so that students and families do not fall through the cracks in terms of meeting their specific needs (e.g., child care, after-school care, health services, employment). Engaging and partnering with other agencies will help schools become central to the community and involve parents, which in turn empowers students and inhibits barriers to learning. Best practices for full-service schools include the following initiatives:

- Family resource centers or family support centers with services for children and family members
- Youth service centers that include health, mental health, recreational, and employment-related services
- Neighborhood networks of professional agencies to deliver health, mental health, social services, and resources to ensure safe and secure neighborhoods
- Health services centers to provide information and education; immunizations; vision, hearing and dental screenings; mental health resources; testing for sexually transmitted diseases; medication evaluation; physical examinations for participation in school athletic programs; and health screening programs for faculty, students, and families

Such services ensure healthy families and prevent barriers to learning that might otherwise be ignored.

Broad program design allows for the provision of core services and may include academic enrichment and leisure time programs; computer classes; academic remediation; job training; drama, dance, and art classes; music classes; leadership training and support groups; social services; health services and clinics; parenting classes; mental health counseling; family counseling; and employment services. Intramural sports programs can also be a direct means of keeping students out of harm's way.

The vision of the full-service school puts the best of school reform together with all other services that young people and their families need, most of which can be located in a school building. The educational mandate places responsibility on the school system to reorganize and design innovative programs and services. The charge to community agencies is to bring into the schools health, mental health, employment services, child care, parental education, case management, recreation, cultural events, welfare, and community policing. The intent is to create a seamless institution: a community-oriented school with a joint governance structure that allows maximum responsiveness to the community as well as accessibility and continuity for those most in need of services.

School sites are used as the primary facility, so they must be open year-round, before and after school, and on weekends. Lead community agencies provide fiscal, administrative, and programmatic leadership. Challenging activities are tailored to meeting the specific needs of young people and their families in each community and focus on youth development strategies, rather than on youth problems. Finally, school staff and faculty are involved and community-based organizations, service clubs, churches, and local universities are utilized to form a mentoring pool of potential participants.

Schools and community policy makers must quickly move to embrace comprehensive, multifaceted, schoolwide and community-wide models for dealing with factors that interfere with learning and teaching and contribute to violent and aggressive behavior. Restructuring to develop truly comprehensive approaches requires a basic policy shift that moves schools from the inadequate two-component model that dominates school reform to a three-component framework that guides the weaving together of schools, home, and community resources (Adelman & Taylor, 1997, 1998).

Collaboration can encompass a wide range of resources. These include agencies and organizations providing programs and services (e.g., education and youth development, health and human services, juvenile justice, vocational education, and economic development); entities that share facilities (e.g., schools, parks and recreation facilities, and libraries); and various sources of social and financial capital, including youths, families, religious groups, community-based organizations, civic groups, and businesses (Kretzmann & McKnight, 1993). The trend among major demonstration projects is to incorporate health, mental health, and social services into centers (including school-based health centers, family centers, and parent centers). Terms frequently associated with this concept include *school-linked services, wrap-around services, one-stop shopping, full-service schools, parallel schools,* and *community schools* (Center for Mental Health in the Schools, 1999; Melaville & Blank, 1998).

The inherent benefits of these schools could have significant health, social, emotional, and educational benefits for youths, parents, and members of the school and community, such as:

- Engaging youth in meaningful activities for youth risk prevention
- Providing a safe area for youths to meet after school, on weekends, and in the summer
- Providing an opportunity for positive social, emotional, and cognitive development
- Connecting youths with adults and older students in peer helping programs
- Providing mentors and leadership models from service organizations in the community, local universities, and chambers of commerce
- Fostering youth leadership, teamwork, responsibility, and sportsmanship
- Expanding youths' options to learn by augmenting subjects taught during the regular school day
- Improving technology skills by offering relevant courses in spreadsheets, multimedia presentations, digital cameras, and so on;
- Encouraging parents to participate in program offerings with their children
- Promoting wellness and healthy lifestyles by offering wellness clinics (e.g., Family Fun and Fitness), medical screenings, and clinic services to all members of the school and community
- Addressing the community's needs by involving youths in community-building projects such as Arbor Day, Clean the Bay Day, or repair work on homes of the elderly

Given the complexity and magnitude of problems confronting youth today, there is no single solution. Full-service schools provide a broad preventive approach to the serious social problems facing youth, parents, educators, and youth-serving professionals in the community. Promising school/community prevention programs require a comprehensive approach, an early start, a long-term commitment, strong school leadership and disciplinary policies, staff development, parental involvement, community links and partnerships, and a culturally sensitive and developmentally appropriate approach.

Professional school counselors need to generate group work and developmentally oriented activities to improve the way students feel about themselves and interact with each other, particularly during stress and conflict. The goal is to give everyone involved in the school the same skills, language, and terminology for handling stress and conflict in an effort to create an environment that is consistently nonviolent and nurturing. In determining sound prevention and intervention strategies for schools and communities, policy makers, educators, and parents must maneuver through a maze of conventions, focus documents, recommendations, and theories. Educational initiatives must proceed beyond the rhetoric about the maladies of American youth and begin implementing strategies that provide outcomes that can be implemented and evaluated.

Professional school counseling programs should evolve from the different developmental needs of children and adolescents and be preventive, with both an educational and a clinical focus. A case management system should be created that includes a team of school and community staff who can assess the whole student and develop appropriate individual service plans. Transitional support must be provided to students as they move from grade to grade, especially as they move to other school buildings. An example of transitional support is teacher-advisor programs.

Prevention and intervention for youth at risk demand a staff commitment to a student-centered approach that actively involves students in the learning process, both academically and interpersonally. Skilled, compassionate, and knowledgeable professionals are required to meet these challenges.

Schools and school divisions must provide personnel who work with multirisk youths developmental training opportunities in such areas as teaching strategies, positive discipline techniques, establishing cooperative-learning (versus competitive-learning) environments, group counseling procedures, and motivational techniques.

The professional school counselor's role in early intervention strategies is central to the success of all school/community efforts. Professional school counselors have an important role in all dimensions targeted to assist at-risk youth by providing short-term counseling and treatment planning. They also can direct students to critical support services and referral sources in and out of school, which will serve as a pivotal link between the school and the community.

Quantitative evaluations of the literature (Greenwood, Model, Rydell, & Chiesa, 1988; Sherman et al., 1997) have revealed a broad range of primary prevention and intervention programs for youth risk prevention. The underlying component to all of these programs permeates the home, the school, and the community. The key variable is not the need to increase a child's self-esteem or the need to re-create the traditional family; it can't be blamed on faulty parenting or poor schools; and it doesn't cost money or a lot of federally funded or complicated programs. The key variable is *meaningful relationships*. Relationships must be nurtured, cultivated, respected, and maintained. Some evidence-based programs that have demonstrated their worth in enhancing relationships are the following:

- Supervised after-school recreation reduced truancy, aggression, and drug abuse (Grossman & Garry, 1997; Tierney & Grossman, 1995).
- Big Brother and Big Sister programs (more than 1,700 affiliated clubs serve more than 2.2 million children) reduced juvenile crime, drug activity, and vandalism (Schinke, Orlandi, & Cole, 1992; Jones & Offord, 1989). There was also evidence of reduction of alcohol and drug use, particularly in clubs that included parent involvement (St. Pierre, Mark, Kaltreider, & Aikin, 1997).
- Community policing has significantly reduced, neutralized, or eradicated gangs (Bureau of Justice Assistance, 1997). Also, one of the more effective means of preventing firearm-related juvenile crimes has been more stringent enforcement of laws against illegal gun carrying (Kennedy, Piehl, & Braga, 1996; Sherman et al., 1997). The U.S. Department of Justice described 60 methods of responding to gun violence (Sheppard, 1999).
- Family-focused strategies such as parent education have demonstrated their effectiveness when parents are involved in ongoing relationships and training sessions that last from six months to several years (Hawkins & Catalano, 1992). Parent management training has been found to be effective with aggressive and disobedient children (Brestan & Eyberg, 1998; Cedar & Levant, 1990; Kazdin, 1996).
- Parent training for families with aggressive young children and conduct-disordered children is a cost-effective investment of time and effort for preventing future crime (Greenwood et al., 1998; Patterson, Reid, & Dishion, 1992). In addition, the Barkley Parent Training Program has been evaluated as effective for children with severe behavior problems (Barkley, 1997). One well-validated psychosocial intervention program is the Parenting Program for Young Children (Webster-Stratton, 1982, 1992, 1998).
- An important component to parental education for every child is information on the detrimental effects of television violence on children. Exposure to media violence increases aggressive behavior, desensitizes youth to violence, and may promote a positive attitude toward the use of violence to solve problems (American Psychological Association, 1997; Hughes & Hasbrouck, 1996).
- Family therapy improves family relationships and reduces recidivism among adolescents referred by juvenile court for offenses such as truancy, theft, and unmanageable behavior. Multisystemic therapy has demonstrated its effectiveness for high-risk delinquent children and their families (Family Services Research Center, 1995; Henggeler, 1991; Henggeler & Borduin, 1990).
- Preschool programs combined with home visits can have a significant long-term impact on families and the quality of a child's adjustment to school (Tremblay & Craig, 1995; Yoshikawa, 1994).

- School-based strategies such as conflict resolution and peer mediation have demonstrated that students can learn and retain conflict resolution skills and apply those skills to school, family, and peer relationships (Gottfredson, 1997; Johnson & Johnson, 1995a, 1995b; Thompson, 1996). Violence prevention counseling and psychoeducational life-skills training can help both aggressive and mainstream youths cope with their frustration, hostility, and interpersonal and intrapersonal skills to help youth think better, feel better, and relate to others better (Thompson, 1998, 2006).
- "Coping power" teaches aggressive youths to cope with anger, correct distortions in their perceptions of social interactions, and choose nonviolent alternatives to resolving disputes (Lochman, 1992).
- Positive Adolescents Choices Training (PACT) teaches social skills such as strategies for expressing and responding to criticism and negotiating solutions to disputes (Hammond, 1991; Hammond & Young, 1993).
- The Violence Prevention Curriculum for Adolescents: Teenage Health Teaching Modules (THTM) is a school-based program that provides anger management training to combat family violence, media violence, and dating violence (Grossman et al., 1997).
- Cognitive-behavioral approaches have been found to increase school attendance and grades and to decrease aggressive behavior and substance abuse (Bry, 1982; Izzo & Ross, 1990; Lochman, 1992; Rotheram, 1982).

Social and emotional competence development focuses on enhancing interpersonal and intrapersonal development. Children and adolescents are taught how to identify problems, recognize feelings, assess the perspectives of others, consider consequences, and make appropriate decisions. Training improves children's behavior and enhances relationships at school, at home, and with peers (Caplan, Weissberg, Grober, Sivo, & Jacoby, 1992; Cowen et al., 1996; Greenberg, Kusche, Cook, & Quamma, 1995; Shure, 1992, 1996, 1997; Thompson, 1998, 2006).

DEVELOPMENTAL ASSETS: NURTURING PRODUCTIVE ADULTS

Developmental assets focus on looking at the qualities, values, or attributes that youths need to be successful, productive adults. It is an approach that does not look at adolescents through a deficit lens but rather focuses on developing both internal and external assets, improving relationships, and fostering resiliency. The primary focus is on manifesting young people's strengths, skills, and possibilities and the study of resiliency—the capacity for youths to bounce back in spite of adversity. Researchers are consistently finding a cluster of intervention components that make a difference in the well-being of youths:

- Strengthening adult–youth relationships
- Establishing social norms around desired behavior
- Learning social competencies
- Providing youths with opportunities for involvement and leadership (Benson, Scales, Hamilton, & Sesma, 2006, pp. 3–4)

The appendix provides the 40 developmental assets for early childhood, middle childhood, and adolescence. The body of research originated from the Search Institute and is accessible at its website (http://www.search-institute.org). A cross-tabulation of the ASCA National Standards with the 40 developmental assets is provided in Table 4.11.

TABLE 4.11   Cross-Tabulation of the ASCA National Standards With the 40 Developmental Assets

ASCA DOMAINS AND NATIONAL STANDARDS	CORRESPONDING DEVELOPMENTAL ASSETS
Academic Standard A: Students will acquire the attitudes, knowledge, and skills that contribute to effective learning in school and across the lifespan.	*Support:* Caring school climate (5). *Boundaries and Expectations:* High expectations (16). *Commitment to Learning:* Achievement motivation (21), bonding to school (24), reading for pleasure (25).
Academic Standard B: Student will complete school with academic preparation essential to choose from a wide range of substantial postsecondary options, including college.	*Support:* Parent involvement in schooling (6). *Boundaries and Expectations:* High expectations (16). *Constructive Use of Time:* Creative activities (17). *Commitment to Learning:* Achievement motivation (21), school engagement (22), homework (23), bonding to school (24), reading for pleasure (25).
Academic Standard C: Students will understand the relationship of academics to the world of work and to life at home and in the community.	
Career Standard A: Students will acquire the skills to investigate the world of work in relation to knowledge of self and to make informed career decisions.	
Career Standard B: Students will employ strategies to achieve future care success and satisfaction.	*Social Competencies:* Planning and decision-making (32).
Career Standard C: Students will understand the relationship between personal qualities, education and training, and the world of work.	
Personal/Social Standard A: Students will acquire the attitudes, knowledge, and interpersonal skills to help them understand and respect self and others.	*Empowerment:* Community values youth (7), youth as resource (8), service to others (9). *Boundaries and Expectations:* Family boundaries (11), adult role models (14), positive peer influence (15), high expectations (16). *Constructive Use of Time:* Youth programs (18), religious community (19). *Positive Values:* Caring (26), equality and social justice (27), integrity (28), honesty (29), restraint (31). *Social Competencies:* Interpersonal competence (33), cultural competence (34), peaceful conflict resolution (36). *Positive Identity:* Self-esteem (38).
Personal/Social Standard B: Students will make decisions, set goals, and take necessary action to achieve goals.	*Positive Values:* Responsibility (30). *Social Competencies:* Planning and decision-making (32). *Positive Identity:* Personal power (37), sense of purpose (39), positive view of personal future (40).
Personal/Social Standard C: Students will understand safety and survival skills.	*Empowerment:* Safety (10). *Boundaries and Expectations:* School boundaries (12), neighborhood boundaries (13). *Constructive Use of Time:* Time at home (20). *Positive Values:* Restraint (31). *Social Competencies:* Resistance skill (35), peaceful conflict resolution (36).

Source: Stevens, H., & Wilkerson, K., *Professional School Counseling, 13*(4), 231, 2010. Reprinted with permission.

CONCLUSION

To be successful in reducing the debilitating attitudes and destructive behavioral manifestations of today's youth, a school-as-community approach should have long-range implications. The school/community develops distinctive normative patterns that draw students toward or away from particular activities and domains of development (social, academic, physical, emotional, and interpersonal). These normative patterns have a profound long-term effect on the self-concepts, values, and skills that children and youths ultimately develop. Personalities interact within the social system productively or unproductively, with long-lasting effects on motivation and learning style.

Collective efforts centered on structured activities that allow the discussion of adjustment anxieties in a secure environment could enhance the self-esteem and self-sufficiency of struggling youths. Ongoing programs in the schools that provide an opportunity to express feelings are crucial, as is knowing that significant adults care about their well-being, emotionally as well as intellectually. Broad program design allows school/community services to meet the critical needs of children and adolescents. This requires collaborative efforts, school/community accountability, and the willingness to break down "turf and territory" issues often found among helping professionals and service provider entities. Essentially, our youth represents 25% of the population but 100% of the future.

APPENDIX: 40 DEVELOPMENTAL ASSETS

The Search Institute has identified building blocks of healthy development, which it has designated *developmental assets*, that help young children grow up healthy, caring, and responsible. Three sets of 40 developmental assets are listed for different age groups: ages 3–5, 8–12, and 12–18. These are shown in Tables 4.12 through 4.14.

TABLE 4.12   40 Developmental Assets for Early Childhood (Ages 3 to 5)

	EXTERNAL ASSETS
Support	1. *Family support:* Parent(s) and/or primary caregiver(s) provide the child with high levels of consistent and predictable love, physical care, and positive attention in ways that are responsive to the child's individuality.
	2. *Positive family communication:* Parent(s) and/or primary caregiver(s) express themselves positively and respectfully, engaging young children in conversations that invite their input.
	3. *Other adult relationships:* With the family's support, the child experiences consistent, caring relationships with adults outside the family.
	4. *Caring neighbors:* The child's network of relationships includes neighbors who provide emotional support and a sense of belonging.
	5. *Caring climate in child-care and educational settings:* Caregivers and teachers create environments that are nurturing, accepting, encouraging, and secure.
	6. *Parent involvement in child care and education:* Parent(s), caregivers, and teachers together create a consistent and supportive approach to fostering the child's successful growth.
Empowerment	7. *Community cherishes and values young children:* Children are welcomed and included throughout community life.
	8. *Children seen as resources:* The community demonstrates that children are valuable resources by investing in a child-rearing system of family support and high-quality activities and resources to meet children's physical, social, and emotional needs.

continued

TABLE 4.12   40 Developmental Assets for Early Childhood (Ages 3 to 5) (continued)

	9. *Service to others:* The child has opportunities to perform simple but meaningful and caring actions for others. 10. *Safety:* Parent(s), caregivers, teachers, neighbors, and the community take action to ensure children's health and safety.
Boundaries & Expectations	11. *Family boundaries:* The family provides consistent supervision for the child and maintains reasonable guidelines for behavior that the child can understand and achieve. 12. *Boundaries in child-care and educational settings:* Caregivers and educators use positive approaches to discipline and natural consequences to encourage self-regulation and acceptable behaviors 13. *Neighborhood boundaries:* Neighbors encourage the child in positive, acceptable behavior, as well as intervene in negative behavior, in a supportive, nonthreatening way. 14. *Adult role models:* Parent(s), caregivers, and other adults model self-control, social skills, engagement in learning, and healthy lifestyles. 15. *Positive peer relationships:* Parent(s) and caregivers seek to provide opportunities for the child to interact positively with other children. 16. *Positive expectations:* Parent(s), caregivers, and teachers encourage and support the child in behaving appropriately, undertaking challenging tasks, and performing activities to the best of her or his abilities.
Constructive Use of Time	17. *Play and creative activities:* The child has daily opportunities to play in ways that allow self-expression, physical activity, and interaction with others. 18. *Out-of-home and community programs:* The child experiences well-designed programs led by competent, caring adults in well maintained settings. 19. *Religious community:* The child partakes in age-appropriate religious activities and caring relationships that nurture her or his spiritual development. 20. *Time at home:* The child spends most of her or his time at home participating in family activities and playing constructively, with parent(s) guiding TV and electronic game use.
	INTERNAL ASSETS
Commitment to Learning	21. *Motivation to mastery:* The child responds to new experiences with curiosity and energy, resulting in the pleasure of mastering new learning and skills. 22. *Engagement in learning experiences:* The child fully participates in a variety of activities that offer opportunities for learning. 23. *Home-program connection:* The child experiences security, consistency, and connections between home and out-of-home care programs and learning activities. 24. *Bonding to programs:* The child forms meaningful connections with out-of-home care and educational programs. 25. *Early literacy:* The child enjoys a variety of pre-reading activities, including adults reading to her or him daily, looking at and handling books, playing with a variety of media, and showing interest in pictures, letters, and numbers.
Positive Values	26. *Caring:* The child begins to show empathy, understanding, and awareness of others' feelings. 27. *Equality and social justice:* The child begins to show concern for people who are excluded from play and other activities or not treated fairly because they are different. 28. *Integrity:* The child begins to express her or his views appropriately and to stand up for a growing sense of what is fair and right. 29. *Honesty:* The child begins to understand the difference between truth and lies, and is truthful to the extent of her or his understanding.

TABLE 4.12   40 Developmental Assets for Early Childhood (Ages 3 to 5) (continued)

	30. *Responsibility:* The child begins to follow through on simple tasks to take care of her- or himself and to help others.
	31. *Self-regulation:* The child increasingly can identify, regulate, and control her or his behaviors in healthy ways, using adult support constructively in particularly stressful situations.
Social Competencies	32. *Planning and decision making:* The child begins to plan for the immediate future, choosing from among several options and trying to solve problems.
	33. *Interpersonal skills:* The child cooperates, shares, plays harmoniously, and comforts others in distress.
	34. *Cultural awareness and sensitivity:* The child begins to learn about her or his own cultural identity and to show acceptance of people who are racially, physically, culturally, or ethnically different from her or him.
	35. *Resistance skills:* The child begins to sense danger accurately, to seek help from trusted adults, and to resist pressure from peers to participate in unacceptable or risky behavior.
	36. *Peaceful conflict resolution:* The child begins to compromise and resolve conflicts without using physical aggression or hurtful language.
Positive Identity	37. *Personal power:* The child can make choices that give a sense of having some influence over things that happen in her or his life.
	38. *Self-esteem:* The child likes her- or himself and has a growing sense of being valued by others.
	39. *Sense of purpose:* The child anticipates new opportunities, experiences, and milestones in growing up.
	40. *Positive view of personal future:* The child finds the world interesting and enjoyable, and he or she has a positive place in it.

Copyright © 2005 by Search Institute. Reprinted with permission.

TABLE 4.13   40 Developmental Assets for Middle Childhood (Ages 8 to 12)

	EXTERNAL ASSETS
Support	1. *Family support:* Family life provides high levels of love and support.
	2. *Positive family communication:* Parent(s) and child communicate positively. Child feels comfortable seeking advice and counsel from parent(s).
	3. *Other adult relationships:* Child receives support from adults other than her or his parent(s).
	4. *Caring neighborhood:* Child experiences caring neighbors.
	5. *Caring school climate:* Relationships with teachers and peers provide a caring, encouraging environment.
	6. *Parent involvement in child care and education:* Parent(s) are actively involved in helping the child succeed in school.
Empowerment	7. *Community values youth:* Child feels valued and appreciated by adults in the community.
	8. *Children as resources:* Child is included in decisions at home and in the community.
	9. *Service to others:* Child has opportunities to help others in community.
	10. *Safety:* Child feels safe at home, at school, and in his or her neighborhood.
Boundaries & Expectations	11. *Family boundaries:* Family has clear and consistent rules and consequences and monitors the child's whereabouts
	12. *School boundaries:* School provides clear rules and consequences.
	13. *Neighborhood boundaries:* Neighbors take responsibility for monitoring the child's behavior.

continued

TABLE 4.13   40 Developmental Assets for Middle Childhood (Ages 8 to 12) (continued)

	14. *Adult role models:* Parent(s) and other adults in the child's family, as well as nonfamily adults, model positive, responsible behavior.
	15. *Positive peer influence:* Child's closest friends model positive, responsible behavior.
	16. *High expectations:* Parent(s) and teachers expect the child to do her or his best at school and in other activities.
Constructive Use of Time	17. *Creative activities:* Child participates in music, art, drama, or creative writing two or more times per week.
	18. *Child programs:* Child participates two or more times per week in co-curricular school activities or structured community programs for children.
	19. *Religious community:* Child attends religious programs or services one or more times per week.
	20. *Time at home:* Child spends some time most days in both high-quality interaction with parents and doing things at home other than watching TV or playing video games.

INTERNAL ASSETS

Commitment to Learning	21. *Achievement motivation:* Child is motivated and strives to do well in school.
	22. *Learning engagement in learning experiences:* Child is responsible, attentive, and actively engaged in learning at school and enjoys participating in learning activities outside of school.
	23. *Homework:* Child usually hands in homework on time.
	24. *Bonding to school:* Child cares about teachers and other adults at school.
	25. *Reading for pleasure:* Child enjoys and engages in reading for fun most days of the week.
Positive Values	26. *Caring:* Parent(s) tell the child it is important to help other people.
	27. *Equality and social justice:* Parent(s) tell the child it is important to speak up for equal rights for all people.
	28. *Integrity:* Parent(s) tell the child it is important to stand up for one's beliefs.
	29. *Honesty:* Parent(s) tell the child it is important to tell the truth.
	30. *Responsibility:* Parent(s) tell the child it is important to accept personal responsibility for behavior.
	31. *Healthy lifestyle:* Parent(s) tell the child it is important to have good health habits and an understanding of healthy sexuality.
Social Competencies	32. *Planning and decision making:* Child thinks about decisions and is usually happy with results of her or his decisions.
	33. *Interpersonal competence:* Child cares about and is affected by other people's feelings, enjoys making new friends, and, when frustrated or angry, tries to calm her- or himself down.
	34. *Cultural competence:* Child knows and is comfortable with people of different racial, ethnic, and cultural backgrounds and with her or his own cultural identity.
	35. *Resistance skills:* Child can stay away from people who are likely to get her or him in trouble and is able to say no to doing wrong or dangerous things.
	36. *Peaceful conflict resolution:* Child seeks to resolve conflict nonviolently.
Positive Identity	37. *Personal power:* Child feels he or she has some influence over things that happen in his or her life.
	38. *Self-esteem:* Child likes and is proud to be the person that he or she is.
	39. *Sense of purpose:* Child sometimes thinks about what life means and whether there is a purpose for her or his life.
	40. *Positive view of personal future:* Child is optimistic about her or his personal future.

TABLE 4.14   40 Developmental Assets for Adolescents (Ages 12 to 18)

EXTERNAL ASSETS	
Support	1. *Family support:* Family life provides high levels of love and support.
	2. *Positive family communication:* Young person and her or his parent(s) communicate positively, and young person is willing to seek advice and counsel from parents.
	3. *Other adult relationships:* Young person receives support from three or more nonparent adults.
	4. *Caring neighborhood:* Young person experiences caring neighbors.
	5. *Caring school climate:* School provides a caring, encouraging environment.
	6. *Parent involvement in schooling:* Parent(s) are actively involved in helping young person succeed in school.
Empowerment	7. *Community values youth:* Young person perceives that adults in the community value youth.
	8. *Youth as resources:* Young people are given useful roles in the community.
	9. *Service to others:* Young person serves in the community one or more hours per week.
	10. *Safety:* Young person feels safe at home, school, and in the neighborhood.
Boundaries & Expectations	11. *Family boundaries:* Family has clear rules and consequences and monitors the young person's whereabouts
	12. *School Boundaries:* School provides clear rules and consequences
	13. *Neighborhood boundaries:* Neighbors take responsibility for monitoring young people's behavior.
	14. *Adult role models:* Parent(s) and other adults model positive, responsible behavior.
	15. *Positive peer influence:* Young person's best friends model responsible behavior.
	16. *High expectations:* Both parent(s) and teachers encourage the young person to do well.
Constructive Use of Time	17. *Creative activities:* Young person spends three or more hours per week in lessons or practice in music, theater, or other arts.
	18. *Youth programs:* Young person spends three or more hours per week in sports, clubs, or organizations at school and/or in the community.
	19. *Religious community:* Young person spends one or more hours per week in activities in a religious institution.
	20. *Time at home:* Young person is out with friends "with nothing special to do" two or fewer nights per week.

INTERNAL ASSETS	
Commitment to Learning	21. *Achievement motivation:* Young person is motivated and strives to do well in school.
	22. *School engagement:* Young person is actively engaged in learning.
	23. *Homework:* Young person reports doing at least one hour of homework every school day.
	24. *Bonding to school:* Young person cares about her or his school.
	25. *Reading for pleasure:* Young person reads for pleasure three or more hours per week.
Positive Values	26. *Caring:* Young person places high value on helping other people.
	27. *Equality and social justice:* Young person places high value on promoting equality and reducing hunger and poverty.

continued

TABLE 4.14   40 Developmental Assets for Adolescents (Ages 12 to 18) (continued)

	28. *Integrity:* Young person acts on convictions and stands up for her or his beliefs.
	29. *Honesty:* Young person "tells the truth even when it is not easy."
	30. *Responsibility:* Young person accepts and takes personal responsibility.
	31. *Restraint:* Young person believes it is important not to be sexually active or to use alcohol or other drugs.
Social Competencies	32. *Planning and decision making:* Young person knows how to plan ahead and make choices.
	33. *Interpersonal competence:* Young person has empathy, sensitivity, and friendship skills.
	34. *Cultural competence:* Young person has knowledge of and comfort with people of different cultural/racial/ethnic backgrounds.
	35. *Resistance skills:* Young person can resist negative peer pressure and dangerous situations.
	36. *Peaceful conflict resolution:* Young person seeks to resolve conflict nonviolently.
Positive Identity	37. *Personal power:* Young person feels he or she has control over "things that happen to me."
	38. *Self-esteem:* Young person reports having a high self-esteem.
	39. *Sense of purpose:* Young person reports that "my life has purpose."
	40. *Positive view of personal future:* Young person is optimistic about his or her personal future.

PART TWO

Culture, Diversity, Ethics, and Legal Issues

A Profile for Child and Adolescent Well-Being

5

Implications for Primary Prevention and Intervention Initiatives With Evidence-Based Practices

Best practices or *evidence-based procedures*—that is, those programs that have empirically demonstrated that they reduce disruptive or dysfunctional behavior or improve achievement and positive outcomes—were identified by a panel of national experts in a 2004 report (Chadwick Center for Children & Families, 2004). As research has accumulated, evidence-based practices are being advocated and implemented in all fields of education and in mental health prevention and intervention programs and initiatives, including those for prevention of child maltreatment, substance abuse, and violence (Finkelhor & Jones, 2006; Toth & Cicchetti, 2006). These practices are also being used in the development and provision of efficacious prevention and intervention services that improve child and adolescent well-being (Cohen et al., 2006). Best practices and evidence-based programs must be implemented in order to receive federal funding.

Evidence-based programs are programs that have been shown by scientifically rigorous evaluations that are empirically based to be effective in reducing debilitating or self-defeating behavior of children, adolescents, and their families. *Evidence-based practice* is defined by the American Psychological Association (2001) as "the integration of the best available research with clinical expertise in the context of patient characteristics, culture, and preferences" (p. 54) and by the Institute of Medicine (2001) as "the integration of best-researched evidence and clinical expertise with patient values" (p. 5).

IMPLEMENTING ENDURING INTERVENTIONS THAT SIGNIFICANTLY CHANGE BEHAVIOR

A reconceptualization of what constitutes a viable, long-standing intervention is evolving (see Table 5.1). No longer can practitioners and researchers assume that an intervention model will sustain long-term outcomes. To effect long-term change, all dimensions of human behavior and environmental support networks must promote health and well-being. Elias (1989) outlines the necessary aspects of successful stress-related interventions:

TABLE 5.1   Key Tasks Underlying Enduring Interventions for Youth Risk Prevention

1. Program conceptualization
   1a. Use existing theory, research, and intervention information at both personal and environmental levels to specify main program concepts, assumptions, and goals.
2. Program design
   2a. Identify and review potentially appropriate intervention materials and practices.
   2b. Examine these for developmental appropriateness and cultural relevance and modify as necessary.
   2c. Prepare explicit training materials and procedures and guidelines for implementation. Staff development and administrative endorsement is critical for long-term success. Programs implemented in isolation have a tendency not to sustain themselves for the long term.
3. Program implementation
   3a. Conduct a pilot study and adapt the implemented intervention to recipients and environmental realities.
   3b. Fine-tune training and supervision procedures.
   3c. Develop a system to ensure high-quality implementation.
4. Program evaluation
   4a. Select valid, viable approaches to measure extent and quality of implementation, changes in focal attitudes, knowledge, skills, relationships, and mediating factors.
   4b. Design an appropriate, time-framed data gathering and analysis system.
5. Program diffusion
   5a. Conceptualize how the program can be carried out elsewhere by sharing with others with varying degrees of involvement.
   5b. Produce transportable materials and clear and specific training and replication guidelines.
   5c. Determine procedures for minimal program evaluation in new sites and provide relevant materials and training.

Source: Weissberg, R., Caplan, M., & Sivo, P., "A New Conceptual Framework for Establishing School-Based Social Competence Promotion Programs," in Bond, L., & Compass, B. (Eds.), *Primary Prevention and Promotion in the Schools,* Sage, Newbury Park, CA, 255–296, 1989.

- Successful interventions are likely to be those with a multilevel focus, that is, with explicit components at both the individual and environmental levels.
- Successful interventions are likely to be designed with key aspects of the person and environmental levels as defined by the prevention equations.
- Successful interventions are likely to conceptualize the operation of those components over time, particularly as it relates to program goals.
- Successful interventions are likely to follow an action research model (Price & Smith, 1985; Weissberg, Caplan, & Sivo, 1989) and have explicit procedures for addressing the lines of transmission, implementation, and evaluation.

Weissberg et al. (1989) have developed and refined a set of tasks to guide intervention development. Those interested in intervention-related research must reconceptualize the meaning, form, and implications of their work. This is reinforced by evidence-based practices that have proven to make a difference in the lives of children and adolescents.

IMPLICATIONS FOR PRIMARY PREVENTION AND INTERVENTION: UNDERACHIEVEMENT AND POTENTIAL DROPOUTS

Low regard for self or poor self-concept seems to be present in all underachievement, no matter what else is involved. Several special populations should be specifically targeted for dropout prevention:

pregnant and parenting students, substance abusers, disruptive students, truants, students who lack motivation, and immigrants or English-language learners. Influential factors, objectives, and services needed for a successful dropout prevention program from an instructional perspective include the following:

- Provide a caring and mentoring environment for all students.
- Establish a school climate in which achievement is the primary learning culture.
- Recognize the interrelatedness of student self-esteem and successful school performance and take appropriate action as a result.
- Provide a nonthreatening, nonpunitive environment for learning.
- Provide a low student–teacher ratio.
- Provide quality education and an accelerated curriculum.
- Formulate a real-life skills curriculum for problem solving, decision making, and conflict resolution to enhance social, emotional, and cognitive skills that are activity based, not ones that follow repetitive, rote memory or drill and practice paradigms.
- Promote parent involvement.
- Provide cooperative learning opportunities in the classroom.
- Expand counseling and peer counseling services for students.
- Enlist community volunteers as mentors for at-risk youths.
- Create a network of "youth centers" to provide alternative education for all 14- to 21-year-olds who have dropped out of school.
- Combine the last two years of high school with a system of technical and professional training for students who are not interested in obtaining a college education.
- Provide critical services such as individual counseling, job search assistance, job skills training, and GED preparation.
- Encourage individual staff members to take a personal interest in one or two students both in school and outside of school through an advisement or "adopt-a-student program." Have individual staff members adopt a student for the entire time the student attends school in that particular building; then, the staff member can help to ease the transition to the next school the student attends by taking him or her to visit the school, meeting with some teachers, and helping the student identify the next person to "adopt" them.
- Have teachers/counselors help dropout-prone students with study skills and strategies for working around issues like forgetfulness and poor organizational skills.
- Use special events to generate interest in the school and in education (e.g., parent/child dinners, gym nights, art nights, alumni reunions).
- Invite students in dropout prevention programs and students who have left school to talk about their jobs, what they do, the type of people they work with, working conditions, potential promotions, salary and wages, and employer attitudes toward employees. Invite workers to talk to students about their jobs, their need for a high school diploma, the usefulness of an education, and so on.
- Have dropout-prone students assume responsibility for reading newspapers and posting job openings on bulletin boards.
- Use a computer program that calls parents of students who are absent.
- Solicit college students to volunteer to work with, tutor, and develop resources and materials for remedial and/or gifted dropout-prone students.
- Encourage school staff, school board members, advisory committee members, and business and industry to express their support for dropout prevention efforts in writing so that it can be shared with the greater community.
- Establish a home-visit program to improve home–school relations.
- Involve both mothers and fathers in conferences to discuss student progress and problems.
- Have parents participate on advisory committees, task forces, or assessment/evaluation teams.

- Encourage school staff to call parents when the potential dropout has done something "good," not only when there is a problem.
- Hold conferences, visits, and meetings with parents of dropout-prone youths.
- Have staff make presentations to local groups about the dropout problem, share ideas for how people in the community can help the schools, and inform the public what the school is doing to meet the needs of its students.
- Ask school staff members to report and comment on the attendance, attitude, and performance of students participating in the dropout prevention activities.
- Identify "leaders" of various staff groups and work with them to win support and encourage dropout prevention efforts.
- Offer in-service, educational, or awareness activities for school staff to explain dropout prevention programs, activity objectives, and functions.
- Generate an attitude of "caring for students" and a general atmosphere of "I am/we are interested in you as a student and individual" in the school division. (This frequently begins with the school administrators.)
- Conduct meetings and/or cooperative efforts with church groups and utilize and develop parent/family support groups within the church network.
- Initiate cooperative efforts with postsecondary schools, colleges, and universities (e.g., advanced placement, enrollment in courses) to provide services to dropout-prone youths.
- Make services available to dropout-prone youths through vocational, technical, and adult education.
- Increase structured group meetings for high-risk youths within the school setting.

IMPLICATIONS FOR PRIMARY PREVENTION AND INTERVENTION: UNINTENDED TEENAGE PREGNANCY

Ettinger (1991) identifies a number of psychosocial factors that negatively affect the education and training of teen parents: low self-esteem, low aspirations, low motivation, and low expectations; unrealistic goals and ambitions; limited emotional resources for support and maintenance; and lack of role models. To foster self-sufficiency, Ettinger suggests that attention be given to the development of life skills through the following strategies:

- Build up self-concept.
- Build up support systems.
- Learn how to access available child care, transportation, and other support services such as health department resources.
- Learn how to meet the challenge of combining work, family roles, and other responsibilities.
- Learn how to give and receive emotional and social support.
- Network for work opportunities and connections within the community.
- Enhance interpersonal communication and relationships.
- Focus on the teen's child in the school setting and how the teen can be the child's first teacher, child care availability in the school setting, and ways to support and include the father in the entire process of nurturing a child.
- Persuade fathers to establish paternity at the hospital shortly after birth so the child can receive medical benefits, especially if the father enlists in the armed forces (Ettinger, 1991, pp. 5–8).

The following strategies, when implemented, can begin to demonstrate a shared commitment to assisting single mothers, teenage fathers, and their children.

- Increase the emphasis on primary prevention through postponement of sexual activity for teenagers who are not pregnant or not yet sexually active.

- Develop broad-based educational programs that place family life education within the larger context of life-skills development.
- Improve staffing for student services such as counseling, school psychology, and health services, especially elementary school counseling.
- Promote the concept of wellness and the importance of health care of all types, including proper nutrition, exercise, and prevention of substance abuse.
- Increase community mental health services for issues such as poor family communications, single parenting, conflicts between parents and adolescent children, and early identification of abuse and abusive patterns.
- Make maternity programs more accessible by simplifying the eligibility process.
- Develop a system to track high-risk infants from birth, so that case managers can effectively guide them into appropriate services such as early preschool programs.
- Create half-day preschool programs and coordinate child care programs for developmentally delayed 3- and 4-year-olds.
- Create youth health clinics that are school based or accessible before, after, or during school hours.
- Provide critical services for adolescent mothers, such as personal counseling, basic education, assistance in obtaining social services, pregnancy/parental counseling, early childhood enrichment programs for their child, and proper nutrition.
- Provide health and prenatal education for expectant mothers and fathers.
- Provide family life programs for adolescents and encourage responsibility among teenage fathers.
- Implement recruitment strategies to engage teen fathers in counseling.
- Identify the needs of the father from prenatal to postnatal phases.
- Develop extra measures of rapport building to counter the teen father's feelings of blame, guilt, and exclusion attributed by others.
- Promote an open dialogue among all parties to help settle differences of opinion, to identify how family members might help, to clarify role boundaries among family members, and to engender a positive environment of anticipation regarding the birth of a child (Kiselica, Stroud, Stroud, & Rotzien, 1992).
- Provide short-term educational and career planning to inhibit the impulse to drop out of school.
- Provide support for infant–father bonding (the absence of early bonding correlates with subsequent child abuse, neglect, and failure to thrive).
- Provide life-skills training in child rearing, family planning, financial management, conflict resolution, time management, study skills, and anger management.
- Foster professional collaboration among service providers to improve the quality of care for everyone.
- Provide high-quality family life education programs in the schools. The literature suggests that successful programs focus on teaching the skills necessary for responsible and informed decision making, discrepancies between beliefs and actions, the realities of teenage parenting, and the ramifications of the dangers of STDs.

The following collective and collaborative efforts are necessary to demonstrate a commitment to change.

- Coordinate prevention efforts among federal, state, and local programs in education, health, mental health, juvenile justice, and social services. Education in particular offers the ideal non-problem-oriented setting for primary prevention.
- Use community networks and resource centers. Self-help resource centers have grown out of the desire of citizens to be involved in local planning, decision making, and problem solving. Networks and resource centers can operate in a wide variety of local settings: hospitals, schools,

community mental health centers, recreation centers, libraries, community colleges, civic
centers, day care centers, social service agencies, and churches and faith-based organizations.

- Include in the network representatives from the medical, educational, law enforcement, and social
work disciplines, including key leaders from the business, political, and volunteer segments of
the community. Committees of network members should concentrate on areas like those below.
- Develop a system to track high-risk infants from birth, so that case managers can effectively
guide them into appropriate services.
- Advocate that local school districts offer full-day preschool programs and coordinated child
care programs to a percentage of multirisk 4-year-olds.
- Offer parenting and mental health education programs.
- Provide staff for hotlines, crisis nurseries, and/or shelters for victims of family violence.
- Develop self-help groups through churches and community centers.

These systemic changes indicate commitment to improving the well-being of youth.

IMPLICATIONS FOR PRIMARY PREVENTION AND INTERVENTION: ALCOHOL AND OTHER DRUG ABUSE

The National Institute on Drug Abuse (NIDA, 2011), after a decade of research, has identified prevention
principles that represent a useful guide to strategic program development for schools. Prevention programs should be designed to:

- Be based on research and theory
- Enhance "protective factors" and move toward reversing or reducing known "risk factors."
- Target high-risk populations, with more intensive prevention efforts earlier in their particular
developmental stage.
- Be age-specific, developmentally appropriate, and culturally sensitive.
- Be cost-effective—for every dollar spent on drug use prevention, communities can save four or
five dollars in costs for drug abuse treatment and counseling.

According to Hawkins, et al. (2004), such a program should:

- Teach participants to identify and resist social pressures.
- Teach personal skills, social skills, and comprehensive health education.
- Be long-term and in-depth with follow-up.
- Be sensitive to the culture, ethnicity and gender of their participants.
- Be evaluated by an independent evaluator. (p. 392)

Programs to prevent alcohol and drug abuse must be comprehensive and all-inclusive. Schools and
communities must identify ways to integrate the prevention message into multiple service areas. More
innovative ways must be found to include community agencies, health services, the courts, clergy, businesses, and education in providing the leadership and collective commitment to provide comprehensive
services for youths and their families.

*Until the alcohol and drug problem is controlled, we cannot expect other adolescent problems such
as pregnancy, suicide, violence, poor academic performance, and juvenile crime, all of which are often
rooted in drug use, to significantly diminish.* Providing awareness, information, and motivation to "just
say no" is not enough. Programs that emphasize assertive approaches that build resistance skills should
have a longer developmental effect.

Prevention programs should address all forms of drug abuse, alone or in combination, including the under-age use of legal drugs (e.g., tobacco or alcohol); the use of illegal drugs (e.g., marijuana or heroin); and the inappropriate use of legally obtained substances (e.g., inhalants), prescription medications, or over-the-counter drugs. (Johnston, O'Malley, & Bachman, 2009, p. 49)

Prevention programs should address the drug abuse problem in the local community, target modifiable risk factors, and strengthen identified protective factors (Hawkins, Catalano, & Arthur, 2002). They should be tailored to address risks specific to population or audience characteristics, such as age, gender, and ethnicity, in order to improve program effectiveness (Oetting, Edwards, Kelly, & Beauvals, 1997). Prevention programs can be designed to intervene as early as preschool to address risk factors for drug abuse, such as aggressive behavior, poor social skills, and academic difficulties (Webster-Stratton, 1998; Webster-Stratton, Reid, & Hammond, 2001). Programs for elementary school children should target improving academic and social-emotional learning to address risk factors for drug abuse, including early aggression, academic failure, and school dropout.

Education should focus on the following skills (Ialongo, Poduska, Werthamer, & Kellam, 2001):

- Self-control
- Emotional awareness
- Communication
- Social problem-solving
- Academic support, especially in reading (p. 158)

Prevention programs for middle/junior high and high school students should increase academic and social competence with the following skills (Botvin, Baker, Dusenbury, Botvin, & Diaz, 1995; Scheier, Botvin, Diaz, & Griffin, 1999):

- Study habits and academic support
- Communication
- Peer relationships
- Self-efficacy and assertiveness
- Drug resistance skills
- Reinforcement of antidrug attitudes
- Strengthening of personal commitments against drug abuse

To counter the influence of drugs, a number of initiatives have been shown to have an impact on curtailing the negative aspects of drug use:

- Declare drug-free school zones and gang-free zones.
- Use a psychoeducational life-skills training program that teaches drug resistance, self-management, social skills, and emotional and cognitive skills (Thompson, 1998, 2000).
- Develop a critical-thinking curriculum designed to teach students to examine and analyze the media's influence on consumption.
- Establish cooperative programs such as the Adolescent Social Action Program (ASAP).
- Involve parents, for example, through the Parents Association to Neutralize Drug and Alcohol Abuse (PANDAA).
- Train children to resist peer pressure by explaining the nature of peer pressure and teaching students (through role playing) skills to cope with pressure to try drugs. Such training includes didactic descriptions and demonstrations of resistance techniques, accompanied by methods of practicing them. The emphasis is on developing personal coping skills that will be effective in real-life situations.
- Offer normative education that counters the false perceptions of drug use by giving students accurate information about true rates of drug use among peers.

- Inoculate against mass media messages of drug use by teaching youth critical-thinking skills.
- Teach students the simple message that they need not use substances even if their parents choose to do so.
- Implement peer leadership training that uses peer opinion leaders to reach more rebellious youths who are more likely to pay attention to the message if respected peers advocate the goals.
- Use a broad-based approach to deterring drug use by limiting the availability of drugs and enforcing stringent penalties for use, possession, and distribution.
- Start prevention activities early, before youngsters are faced with the decision to use drugs, usually between 12 and 15 years of age.
- Use group counseling, because peer group support is very influential in the process of using and abusing drugs. Structured opportunities to practice peer resistance skills can also be effective. Low self-worth seems to be one predictor of substance use and abuse. Educators and counselors should design treatment modalities to restore or develop a sense of self-worth. Policies that are punitive or those that disenfranchise youth from meaningful participation should be reexamined.
- Train students on impulse control and gratification delay techniques. Poor impulse control and lack of ability to delay gratification correlates with chemical use and abuse. Assisting young people to exert control and postpone satisfaction may provide them with the help they need to overcome drug- and alcohol-related difficulties.
- Improve relationship skills: Youths who are insecure or ambivalent about peer and parental relationships may need help in developing interpersonal trust and socialization skills to initiate and maintain relationships.

IMPLICATIONS FOR PRIMARY PREVENTION AND INTERVENTION: VIOLENCE PREVENTION

"To change a school's culture so all children can learn, we must address the relationships that exist in that school" (Elias, Lantieri, Patti, Walberg, & Zins, 1999, p. 49). Table 5.2 represents best practices in violence prevention initiatives.

The following primary prevention and intervention initiatives are suggested for school violence, bullying behavior, gang violence, and relational aggression:

- Build and reinforce life skills and social competence; health-promotion and problem-prevention skills; coping skills; and social support for transitions, crises, and making positive social contributions.
- Link efforts to building social and emotional skills to developmental milestones and to the need to help students cope with ongoing life events and personal circumstances.
- Emphasize the promotion of prosocial attitudes and values about self, others, and work.
- Integrate social and emotional learning with traditional academics to enhance learning in both areas.
- Build a caring, supportive, and challenging classroom and social climate to assure effective social and emotional teaching and learning.
- Integrate and coordinate social and emotional learning programs and activities with the regular curriculum and the life of the classroom and school.
- Foster enduring and pervasive effects in this type of social and emotional learning through collaboration among home, school, and community agencies.

TABLE 5.2 Best Practices in Reducing School Violence: Types of Interventions

COUNSELING INTERVENTIONS	ENVIRONMENTAL/TECHNOLOGICAL INTERVENTIONS
Peace education	Metal detectors
Listening and maintaining a conversation	Gun-free/Drug-free school zones
Apologizing and expressing feelings	Random locker searches
Negotiating and self-control	Bookbag bans or random checks
Responding to persuasion and to failure	Cell phone bans/limitations to minimize text messaging
Dealing with an accusation and group pressure	Classroom phones
Conflict resolution/peer mediation	Safe corridor/safe haven policies
Gang prevention/reduction	Closed-circuit television
Crime prevention and law-related education	Dress codes
Handgun violence prevention education	Gun- and drug-sniffing dogs
Life-skills training/social competence	Locker removal
Relationship/family/peer violence prevention	Closed campuses
Prejudice reduction/cultural awareness	Magnetic door locks
Stress management/reduction	Student ID cards
Positive anger management	Landscaping
Street-smart skills	School security staff
Personal power/self-esteem	
Dealing with death	*School Policies and Procedures*
Bullying prevention	School safety plans/lockdown procedures
Aggression/Relational aggression reduction	Zero-tolerance policies
Internet safety	Suspension, expulsion, and formal charges
	Staff development
Schoolwide Student Support Services	Multicultural awareness/sensitivity training
Cooperative learning	Gang elimination procedures
Mentors and role models	Student/staff conduct discipline codes
Career exploration	Student arbitration boards
Work experience placements	Personnel diversity
School-based health clinics	Annual safe schools threat assessments
School-linked student services	
Peer counseling	
Student support groups	*Miscellaneous*
Individual and group counseling	Alternative programs and schools
Student leadership	Special programs for youth risk prevention
Dropout prevention	Improvements to school campuses
Extracurricular activities	Youth crime watch
Student recognition programs	Multicultural and diversity education
Boys/Girls Clubs	Crisis management and intervention teams
Interagency support services	Violence hotlines
	Adult development skills
School–Home–Community Linkages	Student forums
Family support programs	Parent forums
Parent skill training	Community forums

continued

TABLE 5.2   Best Practices in Reducing School Violence: Types of Interventions (continued)

COUNSELING INTERVENTIONS	ENVIRONMENTAL/TECHNOLOGICAL INTERVENTIONS
Parent volunteers	Collaborative school/community task force
School–business partnerships	Collaborative agency involvement
Interagency collaboration	
School–community task forces	
School advisory committees	
Email/text messaging services to parents for crisis management and communication	

Source: Adapted from Wilson-Brewer, R., Peer Violence Prevention Programs in Middle and High Schools. *Adolescent Medicine: State of the Art Reviews, 6*(2), 233–250, 1995.

- Promote academic and social competence, especially in the early grades.
- Involve families, peers, media, and faith communities in primary prevention initiatives.
- Foster and develop a climate that does not tolerate violence, aggression, or bullying.

Violence prevention and intervention initiatives include the following:

- Becoming knowledgeable about the different types of violence that commonly occur in families, schools, and communities across the country.
- Learning how to identify the early warning signs of violence.
- Becoming aware of the specific things counselors can do to help children and adolescents refrain from using violence as a way to solve problems or vent anger and hostilities.
- Acquiring new skills that can be used to successfully implement violence prevention strategies in homes, schools, and communities.
- Increasing awareness of other resources (e.g., law enforcement agencies, sexual abuse counselors, domestic violence prevention programs, homeless shelters, antiracist training programs) that are available in the community.

Counseling practitioners in all domains of service must think in comprehensive terms about the ways in which they can help prevent violence from occurring. Avoid implementing short-term, fragmented interventions. Develop and implement comprehensive violence prevention programs that involve all of the school's stakeholders, including administrators, teachers, students, parents, and members of the greater community. Professional school counselors must demonstrate a high level of multicultural competence in assessing the degree to which cultural and racial factors contribute to the problem of youth violence and address these issues in sensitive and respectful ways, such as the following:

- Increase public school funding to create smaller schools, hire more professional school counselors, and provide professional development for teachers that will enable them to provide emotional support to students.
- Reduce the pressure and anxiety that standardized tests place on students and educators by expanding other accountability measures so that test scores are not the primary yardstick of student achievement and school effectiveness.
- Provide in-depth and ongoing professional development to increase all educators' understanding of race, class, and gender bias, anti-Semitism, homophobia, and disabilities.
- Set priorities so that schools' ability to promote young people's good citizenship, honesty, self-confidence, and compassion for others are valued as highly as academic success.
- Institutionalize regular opportunities for educators and students to obtain emotional and intellectual support for reducing student alienation.

- Take time to talk with and listen to your colleagues and exchange emotional support for the daily challenges you face in nurturing our youth.
- Develop caring relationships with students.
- Organize opportunities to engage students in discussions about how to maintain respect for each other; help them learn how to discourage behavior that is disrespectful or hostile.
- Learn ways to intervene effectively (without blaming and punishing) to reduce the harassment, insults, and exclusiveness that are pervasive in many schools.
- When crises occur, take class time to have your students talk and write about their views.
- Encourage students to expand friendships to include people of different genders, socioeconomic classes, races, sexual orientations, interests, and physical disabilities.
- Educate students about harassment and teach how to interrupt racist, sexist, and homophobic jokes, slurs, and demeaning remarks about other people.
- Educate teachers and administrators about the value of students' emotional well-being and insist that it be valued as much as academic learning.
- Implement character education programs.

The following rehabilitative programs and appropriate treatment plans for troubled youth were outlined from a juvenile justice perspective:

- Provide individual/family counseling.
- Provide substance abuse evaluation and treatment.
- Refer the youth to a child development center for multidisciplinary evaluation.
- Implement parenting skills classes for dysfunctional families.
- Implement law-related education or "street law" programs.
- Perform a quarterly probation care review.
- Assign youth to nonprofit community service programs.
- Implement a jail tour as a diversion program.
- Provide residential placements and community-based services.
- Implement volunteer emergency foster care.
- Develop prescriptive teams that include representatives from education, corrections, mental health, and social services agencies to integrate treatment efforts and to coordinate resources.
- Start a Big Brothers/Big Sisters program for troubled youths.
- Coordinate public and private services for school/community programs and services.
- Establish a juvenile justice system that will nurture personal responsibility in juvenile offenders by imposing consistent and appropriate sanctions for every criminal act.
- Support the replication of successful community-based juvenile delinquency programs that foster positive self-esteem and personal and social responsibility.
- Integrate conflict resolution and peer mediation programs in the schools and in youth-serving agencies.
- Create a more positive school climate and a nurturing community environment that empower children and adolescents.
- Implement a mentor program where adults serve as role models for multirisk students.

Many leaders in the field believe that stable parent–child relationships, not stronger juvenile laws, are the best way to prevent teens from breaking the law. They feel parents should encourage their child's participation in community organizations such as the YMCA, sports, recreation, youth-serving organizations, music, and other related activities, so that the child develops self-esteem and a sense of responsibility to the community. Table 5.3 provides best practices for the goals of violence prevention programs for different age groups.

TABLE 5.3   Best Practices in Reducing School Violence: Objectives by Grade Level

	PRESCHOOL/ EARLY ELEMENTARY (K–2) SCHOOL	ELEMENTARY/ INTERMEDIATE	MIDDLE/JUNIOR HIGH SCHOOL	HIGH SCHOOL
		PERSONAL		
Behavior	• Learning self-management (e.g., when waiting one's turn; when entering and leaving classrooms at the start and end of the day and other transition times; when working on something in a group or alone) • Learning social norms about appearance (e.g., washing face and hair, brushing teeth) • Recognizing dangers to health and safety (e.g., crossing street, electrical sockets, pills that look like candy) • Being physically healthy: adequate nutrition; screenings to identify visual, hearing, or language problems	• Understanding safety issues such as interviewing people at the door when home alone; saying no to strangers on the phone or in person • Managing time • Showing respect for others • Asking for, giving, and receiving help • Negotiating disputes, deescalating conflicts • Admitting mistakes, apologizing when appropriate	• Initiating own activities • Emerging leadership skills	
Integration	• Integrating feeling and thinking with language; replacing or complementing that which can be expressed only in action, image, or affectivity	• Ability to calm self down when upset and to verbalize what happened and how one is feeling differently	• Being aware of sexual factors, recognizing and accepting body changes, recognizing and resisting inappropriate sexual behaviors	

TABLE 5.3 Best Practices in Reducing School Violence: Objectives by Grade Level (continued)

	PRESCHOOL/ EARLY ELEMENTARY (K–2) SCHOOL	ELEMENTARY/ INTERMEDIATE	MIDDLE/JUNIOR HIGH SCHOOL	HIGH SCHOOL
	• Differentiating the emotions, needs, and feelings of different people in different contexts—if not spontaneously, then in response to adult prompting and assistance • Recognizing and resisting inappropriate touching or sexual behaviors	• Encouraging perspective-taking and empathetic identification with others • Learning strategies for coping with, communicating about, and managing strong feelings	• Developing skills for analyzing stressful social situations, identifying feelings and goals, carrying out or refusing requests	
Key concepts	Honesty, fairness, trust, hope, confidence, keeping promises, empathy	Initiative, purpose, goals, justice, fairness, friendship, equity, dependability, pride, creativity	Democracy, pioneering, importance of the environment (spaceship Earth, Earth as habitat, ecological environment, global interdependence, ecosystems), perfection and imperfection, prejudice, freedom, citizenship, liberty, home, industriousness, continuity, competence	Relationships, healthy relationships, intimacy, love, responsibility, commitment, respect, love, loss, caring, knowledge, growth, human commonalities, work/workplace, emotional intelligence, spirituality, ideas, inventions, identity, self-awareness
Peer/Social	• Being a member of a group: sharing, listening, taking turns, cooperating, negotiating disputes, being considerate and helpful • Initiating interactions • Resolving conflict without fighting; compromising	• Listening carefully • Conducting a reciprocal conversation • Using tone of voice, eye contact, posture, and language appropriately with peers (and adults)	• Choosing friends thoughtfully but being aware of group norms and popular trends • Developing peer leadership skills	• Exhibiting effective behavior in peer groups • Demonstrating peer leadership/ responsible membership • Using request and refusal skills

continued

TABLE 5.3   Best Practices in Reducing School Violence: Objectives by Grade Level (continued)

PRESCHOOL/ EARLY ELEMENTARY (K–2) SCHOOL	ELEMENTARY/ INTERMEDIATE	MIDDLE/JUNIOR HIGH SCHOOL	HIGH SCHOOL
• Understanding justifiable self-defense Being empathetic toward peers: showing emotional distress when others are suffering; developing a sense of helping rather than hurting or neglecting; respecting rather than belittling, and supporting and protecting rather than dominating others; being aware of the thoughts, feelings, and experiences of others (perspective taking)	• Exhibiting skills for making friends and entering peer groups; judging peers' feelings, thoughts, plans, and actions Learning to include and exclude others • Expanding peer groups • Making friendships based on mutual trust and assistance • Showing altruistic behavior among friends • Becoming assertive, self-calming, and cooperative • Learning to cope with peer pressure to conform (e.g., dress) • Learning to set boundaries and to deal with secrets • Dealing positively with rejection	• Recognizing and accepting alternatives to aggression and violence Recognizing belonging as very important • Dealing with conflict • among friends	• Initiating and maintaining cross-gender friendships and romantic relationships • Understanding responsible behavior at social events • Dealing with drinking-and-driving situations
Family • Being a family member: being considerate and helpful, expressing caring, and developing capacity for intimacy • Making contributions at home with chores and other responsibilities	• Understanding different family forms and structures • Cooperating on household tasks • Acknowledging compliments • Valuing one's own uniqueness as an individual and as a family contributor	• Recognizing conflict between parents' and peers' values (e.g. dress, importance of achievement) • Learning about stages in adults' and parents' lives • Valuing rituals	• Becoming independent • Talking with parents about daily activities; learning self-disclosure skills • Preparing for parenting and family responsibilities

TABLE 5.3   Best Practices in Reducing School Violence: Objectives by Grade Level (continued)

PRESCHOOL/ EARLY ELEMENTARY (K–2) SCHOOL	ELEMENTARY/ INTERMEDIATE	MIDDLE/JUNIOR HIGH SCHOOL	HIGH SCHOOL
• Relating to siblings: sharing, taking turns, initiating interactions, negotiating disputes, helping, caring • Internalizing values modeled in the family • Being both self-confident and trusting—what they can expect from adults; believing that they are important, that their needs and wishes matter, that they can succeed, that they can trust their caregivers, and that adults can be helpful • Being intellectually inquisitive; exploring their home and the world around them • Living in homes (and communities) free from violence • Having a home life that includes consistent, stimulating contact with caring adults	• Sustaining positive interactions with parents and other adult relatives and with friends • Showing affection and negative feelings appropriately • Being close; establishing both intimacy and boundaries • Accepting failure/ difficulty and continuing with an effort		

SCHOOL-RELATED

	PRESCHOOL/ EARLY ELEMENTARY (K–2) SCHOOL	ELEMENTARY/ INTERMEDIATE	MIDDLE/JUNIOR HIGH SCHOOL	HIGH SCHOOL
Reasonable expectations	• Paying attention to teachers • Understanding similarities and differences (e.g., skin color, physical disabilities)	• Setting academic goals, planning study time, completing assignments • Learning to work on teams	• Accepting modified roles • Enjoying novelty over repetition	• Making a realistic academic plan, recognizing personal strengths, persisting to achieve goals in spite of setbacks

continued

TABLE 5.3   Best Practices in Reducing School Violence: Objectives by Grade Level (continued)

PRESCHOOL/ EARLY ELEMENTARY (K–2) SCHOOL	ELEMENTARY/ INTERMEDIATE	MIDDLE/JUNIOR HIGH SCHOOL	HIGH SCHOOL
• Working to the best of one's ability • Using words effectively, especially for feelings • Cooperating • Responding positively to approval • Thinking out loud; asking questions • Expressing self in art, music games, dramatic play • Enjoying starting more than finishing • Deriving security in repetition and routines • Articulating likes and dislikes • Having a clear sense of strengths and areas of mastery, being able to articulate these, and having opportunities to engage in these • Exploring the environment • Being both self-confident and trusting—what they can expect from adults in the school; believing that they are important, that they can succeed, that they can trust adults in school, and that adults in school can be helpful	• Accepting similarities and differences (e.g. appearance, ability levels) • Cooperating, helping— especially younger children • Bouncing back from mistakes • Working hard on projects • Beginning, carrying through on, and completing tasks • Exhibiting good problem solving • Forgiving after anger • Being generally truthful • Showing pride in accomplishments • Being able to calm down after being upset, losing one's temper, or crying • Following directions for school tasks and routines • Carrying out commitments to classmates and teachers • Showing appropriate helpfulness • Knowing how to ask for help • Refusing negative peer pressure	• Learning planning and management skills to complete school requirements	• Planning a career or post–high school path • Demonstrating group effectiveness: interpersonal skills, negotiation, teamwork • Showing organizational effectiveness and leadership: making a contribution to classroom and school

TABLE 5.3 Best Practices in Reducing School Violence: Objectives by Grade Level (continued)

	PRESCHOOL/ EARLY ELEMENTARY (K–2) SCHOOL	ELEMENTARY/ INTERMEDIATE	MIDDLE/JUNIOR HIGH SCHOOL	HIGH SCHOOL
Appropriate environment	• Being given clear classroom and school rules • Having opportunities for responsibility in the classroom • Having authority figures who are clear, fair, and deserving of respect • Receiving frequent teacher redirection • Having classrooms and school locations free from violence and threat • Experiencing school life that includes consistent, stimulating contact with caring adults	• Comforting a peer or classmate in distress; helping a new person feel accepted/included • Participating in groups and group activities • Making/Using effective group rules • Participating in story-based learning • Having opportunities to negotiate • Enjoying time for laughter, occasional silliness	• Having teachers who minimize the lecture mode of instruction and employ varying types of student products (deemphasize written reports) • Having opportunities to participate in setting policy • Understanding expectations about truancy, substance use, and violent behavior • Using opportunities for setting and reviewing personal norms or standards • Participating in group/ academic/ extracurricular activities	• Experiencing guidance/ structure for goal setting, future planning, postschool transition • Participating in school service and other nonacademic activities • Being a role model for younger students
Community	• Being curious about how and why things happen • Recognizing a pluralistic society (e.g., aware of holidays, customs, cultural groups) • Accepting responsibility for the environment • Participating in community events (e.g., religious observances, recycling)	• Joining outside the school • Learning about and accepting cultural community differences • Helping people in need	• Understanding and accepting differences in one's community • Identifying and resisting negative group influences • Becoming involved in community projects • Apprenticing or training for leadership roles	• Contributing to community service or environmental projects • Accepting responsibility for the environment • Understanding the elements of employment • Understanding issues of government

continued

TABLE 5.3   Best Practices in Reducing School Violence: Objectives by Grade Level (continued)

	PRESCHOOL/ EARLY ELEMENTARY (K–2) SCHOOL	ELEMENTARY/ INTERMEDIATE	MIDDLE/JUNIOR HIGH SCHOOL	HIGH SCHOOL
Events triggering preventive services	• Coping with divorce • Dealing with a death in the family • Becoming a big brother or sister • Dealing with family moves	• Coping with divorce • Dealing with a death in the family • Becoming a big brother or sister • Dealing with family moves	• Coping with divorce • Dealing with a death in the family • Dealing with a classmate's drug use or delinquent behavior	• Coping with divorce • Dealing with a death in the family • Dealing with a classmate's drug use or delinquent behavior, injury or death due to violence, pregnancy, suicide, HIV/ AIDS • Transitioning from high school to workplace, college, or living away from home

Source: Adapted from Thornton, T. N., Craft, C. A., Dahlberg, L. L., Lynch, B. S., & Baer, K., *Best Practices of Youth Violence Prevention: A Sourcebook for Community Action* (rev. ed.), Centers for Disease Control and Prevention, National Center for Injury Prevention and Control, Atlanta, 2002.

IMPLICATIONS FOR PRIMARY PREVENTION AND INTERVENTION: GANG PREVENTION

The following is a list of services and strategies for use in combating gangs' negative effects on schools, students and their families, teachers, administrators, and staff.

- Offer Gang Resistance Education and Training (GREAT), a program designed to reduce youth violence and gang membership through a curriculum taught by law enforcement officers to elementary and middle school students. GREAT students are given the opportunity to discover for themselves the ramifications of gang violence. Evaluation of the effectiveness of this program is not conclusive.
- Defuse campus intercultural and gang conflicts by engaging leaders and enlisting their considerable leadership talents in carrying out peaceful, prosocial school programs.
- Institute ongoing professional development programs for all school employees to reduce collective anxiety regarding issues of safety and security.
- Offer classes incorporating curricula on life skills and resistance to peer pressure, value clarification, and cultural sensitivity.
- Design dress codes or school uniforms to eliminate gang colors and clothing and to reduce the competition to fit in.
- Develop partnership academies, schools-within-schools, alternative schools, beacon schools, in-school suspension programs, and school-to-work programs in collaboration with colleges and businesses that relocate and continue the education of students with histories of classroom disruption, lack of motivation, and gang membership.

- Implement victim/offender programs to expose the reality and consequences of delinquent and criminal behavior.
- Foster a climate of school building ownership and school pride.
- Organize regular campuswide graffiti and vandalism cleanup campaigns.
- Counsel students who are coping with troubling violence in and near school.

It is clear that gang involvement and negative outcomes continue to undermine school and community tranquility and safety. Gangs fulfill an inherent need of youth to be valued, to belong, and to be accepted by a unit larger than oneself. These variables perpetuate gang involvement, making the cycle hard to break.

IMPLICATIONS FOR PRIMARY PREVENTION AND INTERVENTION: BULLYING BEHAVIOR

The following is a list of services and strategies for diminishing bullying behavior:

- Publicize rules against bullying and proclaiming zero tolerance for such behavior in the school.
- Institute behavior contracts and behavior codes.
- Organize friendship groups that support children who are regularly bullied by peers.
- Train students, through peer mediation programs and teen courts, to mediate problems among themselves.
- Make conflict and dispute resolution curricula available at all grade levels.
- Maintain cooperative classroom structures and activities.
- Start groups that build children's and adolescents' social, emotional, and cognitive skills.
- Offer the No Bullying program, a Johnson Institute (1996) program that pinpoints the "tell or tattle" dilemma. Teachers are given step-by-step guidelines on how to teach students the difference between telling and tattling and are shown how to establish and use immediate consequences when dealing with bullies.
- Offer the Bully-Proofing Your School program (Garrity, Jens, Porter, Sager, & Short-Camilli, 2004), key elements of which include conflict resolution training for all staff members, social skills building for victims, positive leadership skills training for bullies, and intervention techniques for those who neither bully nor are bullied.
- Offer the Committee for Children's (1987) Second Step curriculum, which teaches positive social skills to children and families, including empathy, impulse control, problem solving, and anger management.

IMPLICATIONS FOR PRIMARY INTERVENTION AND PREVENTION: CHILD MALTREATMENT

While there are no commonly accepted systematic procedures for describing the maltreatment experience, there is an emerging consensus on the dimensions of maltreatment, which need further clarification and examination because the long-term consequences also have long-range implication on the individual and subsequent relationships with others (e.g., the family, the workplace, interpersonal relationships, and the community at large). The commonly accepted dimensions include severity; frequency; intensity; chronicity; duration; type; age of onset; and perpetrator type (e.g., family member, extended family relative, stranger) (English, Shrikant, Bangdiwala, & Runyan, 2005).

The following intervention protocols or treatment plans were identified as best practices by a team of experts assembled from the Best Practices Project, the National Call to Action: A Movement to End Child Abuse and Neglect (http://www.nationalcalltoaction.com), and the Substance Abuse and Mental Health Services Administration's National Child Traumatic Stress Network (http://www.nctsnet.org/nccts/nav.do?pid=hom_mai) (Chadwick Center for Children & Families, 2004):

1. Abuse-Focused Cognitive Behavior Therapy for child physical abuse (AF-CBT)
2. Parent–Child Interaction Therapy (PCIT)
3. Trauma-Focused Cognitive Behavior Therapy for child sexual abuse (TF-CBT)

Each of these are described in detail below.

Abuse-Focused Cognitive Behavior Therapy

Abuse-Focused Cognitive Behavior Therapy (Kolko & Swenson, 2002) was developed for children suffering from physical abuse and represents a combination of behavior therapy and cognitive behavior therapy procedures and techniques to target child, parent, and family characteristics or dynamics that are associated with abusive experiences. Emphasis is placed on altering the family environment and behavioral repertoire that sustains coercive, dysfunctional, or aggressive behavior. Children and parents participate in individual sessions, parent–child sessions, and sessions for the entire family. AF-CBT has been rigorously investigated in randomized controlled clinical trials with school-age children and their parents (Kolko, 1996b). Measures of child, parent, and family intervention outcomes were collected from parents, children, and therapists before and after treatment, as well as at three-month and one-year follow-ups. Social service records also were examined with a one-year follow-up (Kolko, 1996b; Kolko & Swenson, 2002). Results showed significant improvement in child, parent, and family outcomes among persons treated with AF-CBT in comparison to those who received traditional treatment modalities.

Parent–Child Interaction Therapy

Parent–Child Interaction Therapy was designed by Eyberg (1988). This short-term intervention was designed for families of children between the ages of 2 and 7 who were experiencing externalizing behavior problems such as acting out inappropriately as a result of maltreatment. As a primarily parent training program it consists of two distinct interventions: Child-Directed Interaction and Parent-Directed Interaction (Eyberg, 1988; Eyberg & Calzada, 1998; Hembree-Kigin & McNeil, 1995).

In Child-Directed Interaction, parents are taught to integrate traditional play therapy skills with the behavioral principle of differential attention. Specific play therapy skills taught to parents include increasing praise and using reflection, imitation, description, and enthusiasm, while decreasing commands, questions, and criticism. Parents are coached on how to apply the skills in a manner to increase appropriate and decrease inappropriate child behavior by attending to prosocial skills and behavior (e.g., sharing, taking turns, acting politely, asking permission, apologizing) and ignoring mild disruptive behavior (e.g., whining, ignoring, inattention). The goals of this first treatment phase include strengthening the parent–child relationship, building the child's self-esteem, increasing the child's prosocial behaviors, and enhancing the parenting skills of the caregiver. The counselor uses didactic instruction, modeling, and role-play to achieve the goals of PCIT. However, the primary focus is on direct instruction of parents in behavior modification principles such as giving effective commands, encouraging obedience and using time-outs effectively while individualizing skills to the specific needs of each parent–child dyad. Parents must demonstrate mastery of skills for treatment in order to progress in the program.

Typically, the two phases of treatment are completed in 10 to 14 weeks. Outcome research on PCIT has demonstrated decreased behavior problems among children and decreased stress among parents, increases in parental skills, diminished psychopathology, and diminished child maltreatment (Gallagher, 2003; Herschell, Calzada, Eyberg, & McNeil, 2002).

Trauma-Focused Cognitive Behavior Therapy

Trauma-Focused Cognitive Behavior Therapy (TF-CBT) was originally developed for sexually abused children and emerged as a successful treatment alternative with children exposed to multiple traumas (e.g., the terrorist attacks on September 11, 2001) (Hoagwood et al., 2006) and with children who have experienced domestic violence (Cohen, Mannarino, Murray, & Igelman, 2006). It is designed to reduce children's negative emotional and behavioral responses, correct maladaptive beliefs, acknowledge the abusive experiences, provide support and skills to help nonoffending parents cope effectively with their own emotional distress, and assist parents in appropriately responding to their children (Cohen & Mannarino, 1993; Deblinger & Heflin, 1996).

TF-CBT is based on the fundamental behavioral principle that symptoms develop and are maintained by conditioned and learned behavioral responses, coupled with maladaptive emotions and cognitions. The model emphasizes the interdependence of thoughts, behaviors, and feelings, as well as physiological responses, and targets any of these areas of functioning that may indirectly impact the adjustment or impair well-being and appropriate functioning. The treatment focuses on conditioned emotional associations to memories, reminders of the trauma, distorted cognitions about events, and negative attributions about self, others, and the world. Nonoffending parents are included in the treatment process to enhance emotional support for the child, reduce parental distress and confusion, and teach appropriate strategies to collaboratively manage child behavioral reactions. In the latter stages of therapy, family sessions may include all members of the family to enhance communication, understanding, and encourage a climate of support. TF-CBT has been proven effective for children exposed to a variety of traumatic events and has received the strongest empirical support from studies with abused children (American Academy of Child and Adolescent Psychiatry, 1998; Cohen & Mannarino, 1993; Deblinger & Heflin, 1996).

Other Models of Therapy

Table 5.4 lists programs that represent best practices in the treatment of children who have suffered maltreatment. These interventions are provided for the professional school counselor as a resource when collaborating and consulting with agencies and helping professionals in private practice. It is critical that the professional school counselor advocate with community agencies to implement programs that diminish barriers to learning. It is understood that professional school counselors cannot provide all programs to meet the needs of children and adolescents, but they can team and collaborate with community initiatives that are essential to preventing barriers to learning.

GUIDELINES FOR REPORTING CASES OF SUSPECTED CHILD MALTREATMENT AS MANDATORY REPORTERS

As mandatory reporters, professional school counselors are ethically and legally required to report cases of suspected child maltreatment. Because children are among the most defenseless victims of crime, the law is intended to provide special protection for them. There have been few cases of criminal prosecution for not doing so, however, because states require a "knowing" or "willful" failure to report, which is

TABLE 5.4   Best Practice Interventions for Maltreated Children

INTERVENTION FOR CHILDREN	THEORETICAL PROPONENT(S)
Trauma-Focused Integrative-Eclectic Therapy (IET) is an environmental intervention based on data suggesting that persistent effects of trauma and maltreatment are best understood as a function of the child's thoughts, familial relationships, and the environmental context.	Empirical support for IET: Friedrich (1995, 1998); Cicchetti (1989); Hanson & Spratt (2000).
Cognitive-Behavioral and Dynamic Play Therapy for children with sexual behavior problems and their caregivers was designed for children and the caregivers of children ages 6–12 who exhibit sexual behavior beyond normal child sexuality, which causes problems in the child's functioning.	Empirical support: Bonner, Walker, & Berliner (1999a, 1999b, 1999c).
Cognitive Processing Therapy (CPT) is a brief, structured, cognitive behavior treatment designed to treat posttraumatic stress disorder (PTSD) and associated features such as depression.	Empirical support for CPT is summarized by Bonner, Walker, & Berliner (2000); protocols are detailed in Calhoun & Resick (1993) and Resick & Schnicke (1993).
Abuse-focused Cognitive Behavior Treatment (AF-CBT) is a cognitive behavior intervention for children and physically abusive parents that targets beliefs and attributions about abuse and violence, and teaches skills to enhance emotional control and reduce violent behavior.	Evidence in support of this treatment is summarized by Kolko (1996b) and Kolko & Swenson (2002); the treatment protocol is detailed by Kolko & Swenson (2002).
Resilient Peer Training Intervention (RPT) is a school-based intervention for socially isolated, low-income preschool children who have been maltreated. It is based on an ecological model and uses competent peers and parent helpers to increase children's social competence.	Fantuzzo, Sutton-Smith, Atkins, & Meyers (1996); the treatment protocol is detailed by Fantuzzo, Weiss, & Coolahan (1998).
Trauma-Focused Play Therapy is a psychotherapeutic intervention that uses play as a mechanism for allowing abused children to use symbols (toys) to externalize their internal world, project their thoughts and feelings, and process potentially overwhelming emotional and cognitive material from a safe distance.	Gil (1991, 1996, 1998).
Attachment-Trauma Therapy is a multidimensional intervention with the primary goal of creating or restoring a secure primary attachment relationship for the child and caretaker.	Hanson & Spratt (2000); attachment treatment is receiving mounting empirical support (Association for Treatment and Training in the Attachment of Children, 2006; Curtner-Smith et al., 2006; Hanson & Spratt, 2000).
Behavioral Parent Training encompasses several treatment protocols that target behavior disordered children and their families.	Brestan & Eyberg (1998).
Focused Treatment Interventions (FTI) is a protocol of sequential treatment interventions focused on increasing child safety, reducing risk, and clarifying responsibility in child maltreatment cases.	Treatment protocols are articulated by Ralston (1982, 1998); Ralston & Swenson (1996); and Lipovsky, Swenson, Ralston, & Saunders (1998).
Family Resolution Therapy is a protocol that seeks to develop a long-term familial context and functional processes where children can be safe from abuse, yet continue, if possible, to benefit from some type of relationship with their abusive parents.	Protocols and available supportive evidence are detailed by Saunders & Meinig (2000, 2001).
Integrative Developmental Model for Treatment of Dissociative Symptomatology is a multifaceted child and family intervention model.	The treatment protocol and the limited research are described by Silberg (2000, 2001).

TABLE 5.4   Best Practice Interventions for Maltreated Children (continued)

INTERVENTION FOR CHILDREN	THEORETICAL PROPONENT(S)
Multi-Systemic Therapy (MST) is a treatment model that targets key factors within the youth's social ecology that relate to problem behavior and provides multiple, evidence-based interventions.	This protocol is more fully discussed by Henggeler, Schoenwald, Borduin, Rowland, & Cunningham (1998)
Parent–Child Education Program for Physically Abusive Parents is a home- or clinic-based intervention designed to establish positive parent–child interactions and childrearing methods.	This protocol is described in detail by Wolfe (1991). Outcome studies show support for the effectiveness of this intervention (Wolfe, Edwards, Manion, & Koverola, 1988).
Intensive Family Preservation Services is a brief, home-based, multiple-component intervention designed to prevent out-of-home placements of children when it is tenable, and to reduce risk for child maltreatment by changing behaviors and increasing skills of caregivers.	Protocols are presented by Kinney, Haapala, & Booth (1991) and Whittaker, Kinney, Tracy, & Booth (1990).
Parent–Child Interaction Therapy (PCIT) is a behavioral and interpersonal dyadic intervention for children (ages 2–8) and their parents or caregivers that is focused on decreasing externalized child behavior problems (e.g., defiance, aggression); increasing positive parent behaviors; and improving the quality of the parent–child relationship.	Protocols are presented by Hembree-Kigin & McNeil (1995) and Urquiza & McNeil (1996).
Physical Abuse-Informed Family Therapy (FT) is a family systems intervention for children and physically abusive parents that seeks to reduce violence and improve child outcomes by promoting cooperation, developing shared views about the value of noncoercive interactions, and increasing skills of family members.	The protocol is articulated by Kolko & Swenson (2002), who state that the duration of treatment is from 12 to 24 sessions.
Parents United (Child Sexual Abuse Treatment Program) is a clinically based, integrated treatment program that provides direct clinical services as well as a variety of nonclinical support for victims, offenders, adults molested as children and their significant others.	The treatment protocol is subjected to rigorous research (Saunders, Berliner, & Hanson, 2004).

Source: Adapted from Bureau of Legislative Research, Arkansas Legislative Council, *Best Practices in Child Maltreatment Prevention and Intervention,* Little Rock, Arkansas, 2006.

difficult to prove when it has to be validated in court (Cambron-McCabe, McCarthy, & Thomas, 2004; Fischer, Schimmel, & Stellman, 2003; Lambie, 2005).

The professional school counselor should competently perform all duties required under professional ethical guidelines as outlined by child protective services. The professional school counselor, as mandatory reporter, should not investigate or attempt to obtain a detailed or extensive history of abuse; he or she merely needs to obtain enough information to report a "reasonable suspicion" and does not need to provide absolute proof. The counselor should provide a quiet, private place in which to listen to and document the child's disclosure. The following guidelines are helpful:

- Communicate with the child at his or her developmental level.
- Reassure the child that the abuse is not the child's fault.
- Use interpreters, where appropriate, especially with new immigrants; sensitivity to cultural issues should also be considered (e.g., if the child is Muslim and the family is celebrating Ramadan, fasting is part of this ritual and should not be reported to child protective services).
- Use open-ended questions.
- Refrain from making promises to the child that cannot be kept.

- Limit questions to those necessary to complete the required reporting form; do not push the student to give details about the abuse.

Once a disclosure of abuse has been made to child protective services, provide reassurance to the child, but further prodding and questioning about the abuse should not be continued because if may retraumatize the child. If the child continues the disclosure without questioning, permit the child to do so and document all statements made by the child. Follow-up is the responsibility of the designated agency social worker for that particular school. There also may be a school policy to share information with the school principal, or the professional school counselor's immediate supervisor, before reporting to child protective services so that administrators are not blindsided by inquiries about issues of which they have no previous knowledge.

Professional school counselors, as mandated reporters, are not required by law to disclose to the child's parent or guardian that they are making a suspected child abuse or neglect report. Disclosure to a parent sometimes interferes with the fact-finding process, compromises the investigation, or further endangers the child. If the abuse is family related, the child could be subject to further retribution and harm by the abuser. In addition, children are often told by the abuser that what occurred was "their secret," and since the secret is about to be revealed, the child is exposed to further anxiety regarding the impending investigation. An assessment of the risk associated with disclosing the report must be done on a case-by-case basis.

When making the report to child protective services, the following information should be included:

1. Name, address, and gender of the child
2. The name and address of the parent, guardian, or caregiver (including parents who have joint custody)
3. The name and age of any other children/adolescents living in the home
4. The child or adolescent's condition, including the nature and extent of the injury or abuse (particularly sexual abuse on the middle school or high school level)
5. An explanation of the injuries, neglect, or abuse given by the child or adolescent
6. Any information regarding the presence of weapons, alcohol/drug abuse/use or distribution (e.g., potential methamphetamine labs) or other factors that may affect the social worker's safety
7. Action taken by the professional school counselor as mandatory reporter, such as detaining the child until resources are made available
8. Any other information that may be helpful in establishing the causes of injuries and serve to protect the child or adolescent (Cambron-McCabe et al., 2004; Crosson-Tower, 2002; Lambie, 2005).

Most school divisions in all 50 states have procedures and checklists or standardized forms for mandatory reporters to complete. Efforts to help more children are complicated by uncertainty in the recognition of certain types of abuse, such as the long-term insidious emotional abuse with less visible physical indicators. It is imperative that professional school counselors recognize their obligation to advocate on behalf of all children (ASCA, 2003c) and gain the necessary skills to better assist those most vulnerable and in need of their assistance. Thankfully, linkages between maltreatment and long-term adverse effects and other related social, emotional and cognitive problems in the last decade has been discernible by increasing public knowledge, education, and cooperation among public agencies and schools with the primary interest in the health and well-being of children, adolescents, and families.

Maltreatment can have devastating immediate and long-term physical, psychological, and behavioral effects on children and adolescents. Most theories of child maltreatment recognize the root cause can be organized into framework of four principal systems: the child, the family, the community, and society. Within any context, however, child maltreatment, suicide, drug and alcohol abuse, poverty, underachievement, and other risk factors are all considered barriers to learning.

IMPLICATIONS FOR PRIMARY PREVENTION AND INTERVENTION: SUICIDE PREVENTION

The following suggestions for preventing suicide are offered with the understanding that variations will be needed to meet the various maturity and developmental needs of student populations and the needs of various school and communities. This list is not all-inclusive.

- Use more adults in the school as volunteers, aides, paraprofessionals, and mentors.
- Involve students in all major aspects of school operations. Expand students' lines of communication to faculty and administration such as inclusion on advisory boards. Allow for student input and influence on decisions and regulations that affect them.
- Provide more effective counseling programs, including specialized student resource counselors who work exclusively with targeted at-risk student populations such as potential dropouts, substance abusers, and children who are abused or neglected.
- Offer appropriate parent education courses in such areas as preventing drug and alcohol abuse, setting achievement goals, and improving schoolwork habits.
- Develop a "student adoption program" where each member of the instructional staff adopts a vulnerable student (one with behavioral adjustment problems, attendance problems, family problems, etc.) to meet with on a daily basis to discuss problems, progress, or barriers to success; to develop short-term strategies to enhance success rather than failure; and to provide unconditional support.
- Promote clubs and service projects that are altruistic and Other-centered with community service contributions. Students often rediscover their self-importance by learning their value to others. Doing so gives a student an opportunity to feel he or she has worth and can effect change and enhance the quality of life. With this approach, adolescents tend to become "Other-centered" rather than self-centered, and this promotes a realization that they can make a difference in the lives of others.
- Use high school students as academic mentors (tutors) to elementary children from feeder schools. Provide a service project credit to be listed on their high school transcript.
- Weave self-esteem activities across the curriculum and within the educational program.
- Formulate a real-life skills curriculum focusing on such skills as decision making, problem solving, conflict resolution, and interpersonal skills. Focus on a psychoeducational life-skills model that teaches social, emotional, and cognitive skills.
- Institute a peer counseling program. The range of peer helper programs available today includes cross-age tutoring, peer counseling, educational advisement, and special interest self-help groups. Development of a peer counseling program is based on the premise that adolescents invariably turn to their peers for needed support and understanding, as well as a validation of their perceptions and feelings. Expand counseling and peer counseling services for students. Peer counselors are often the first finders of students in distress.
- Implement multicultural programs to counter conflict and prejudice and to increase tolerance for differences.
- Implement an ongoing student support group as part of the student services of the school counseling program. Provide students with the opportunity to share anxieties in a secure environment. To achieve validation, a caring adult in a helping capacity provides needed support for adolescents. Topics could include dealing with life transitions and change; academic pressure; parental separation and divorce; competition and achievement; death, loss, or separation; aptitude, interest, and achievement; maintaining interpersonal relationships; and enhancing social, emotional, and cognitive skills. In addition, school-based after-care groups following

intervention for drug, alcohol, or other self-destructive behaviors can help children and adolescents make the fragile transition to a more productive life, as well as reduce recidivism.

- Establish other support groups to address the multiple needs in the school and the community. These groups can be narrowly targeted such as "Support group for ages 15–18 who want to enhance their self-esteem" or "Support group for survival skills for school." Groups can explore identity issues; peer relationships; emotional awareness; and ways to deal with anger, sadness, and rejection.
- Develop a student stress reduction program that can be preventive and serve to circumvent the direct discussion of suicide, with students focusing on many of the factors found to precipitate self-destructive behaviors. Classes on suicide are often not as successful as student classes and programs about stress, followed by small-group discussion and other group activities. Emphasis should be placed on the social, emotional, and curative factors that adolescents possess as a group to manage personal, social, or academic disappointments or frustrations. Through the mutual sharing of problems in a secure environment, the adolescent discovers a commonality of fears, fantasies, hopes, and needs. Similar problems are no longer unique; they are universal.
- Train volunteer teachers to serve as positive role models and to lead group discussions on time-management, stress, and academic problem-solving strategies. Many caring educators welcome an opportunity to interact with students on a more affective domain. Many teachers are also willing to give one planning bell a week to lead small discussion groups with students.
- Allow mental health professionals to serve as resources to the school, presenting four- to six-week group counseling units in targeted classes on identified needs.

The left column in Table 5.5 lists the evidence-based programs currently recognized by the Substance Abuse and Mental Health Services Administration. The outcomes on the right are changes in behavior that the programs achieved after implementation.

TABLE 5.5   Selected Evidence-Based Programs for Children, Adolescents, and Families as Primary Prevention and Intervention Initiatives

EVIDENCE-BASED PROGRAMS	OUTCOMES
Across Ages	1. Peer pressure refusal reactions to situations involving drug use, 2. Improved attitudes toward school, future, and elders, 3. Improved school attendance, 4. Respectful knowledge about and attitudes toward older adults
Aggressors, Victims, and Bystanders: Thinking and Acting to Prevent Violence	1. Improved social problem-solving skills, 2. Beliefs about the use and consequences of violence, 3. Decreased behavioral intentions as aggressor, 4. Increased behavioral intentions as bystander
AlcoholEdu for High School	1. Current alcohol use and intention to change drinking status, 2. Consequences of underage drinking/drunkenness, 3. Knowledge about alcohol, 4. Riding in a car with a driver who has been drinking, 5. Perceived ability to limit drinking
All Stars	1. Personal commitment not to use drugs, 2. Lifestyle incongruence, 3. School bonding, 4. Normative beliefs, 5. Consequences of cigarette use, 6. Alcohol use, 7. Inhalant use
Al's Pals: Kids Making Healthy Choices	1. Social competence and prosocial behaviors, 2. Antisocial/aggressive behaviors
American Indian Life Skills Development/Zuni Life Skills Development	1. Understanding hopelessness, 2. Suicide prevention skills

TABLE 5.5 Selected Evidence-Based Programs for Children, Adolescents, and Families as Primary Prevention and Intervention Initiatives (continued)

EVIDENCE-BASED PROGRAMS	OUTCOMES
ATLAS (Athletes Training and Learning to Avoid Steroids)	1. Intent to use anabolic steroids and consequences, 2. Anabolic steroid use and consequences, 3. Alcohol and other illicit drug use and consequences
Brief Strategic Family Therapy	1. Engagement in therapy, 2. Understanding conduct problems, 3. Socialized aggression (delinquency in the company of peers), 4. Substance use, 5. Family functioning
Building Assets—Reducing Risks (BARR)	1. Class failure, 2. Bullying at school, 3. School connectedness
CARE (Care, Assess, Respond, Empower)	1. Suicide risk factors, 2. Severity of depression symptoms, 3. Feelings of hopelessness, 4. Anxiety, 5. Anger control problems, 6. Drug involvement, 7. Stress, 8. Sense of personal control
Caring School Community	1. Consequences of alcohol use, 2. Marijuana use, 3. Concern for others, 4. Academic achievement, 5. Student discipline referrals
CASASTART	1. Use of "gateway drugs" (cigarettes, alcohol, inhalants, marijuana), 2. Use of psychedelics, crack, other cocaine, heroin, or nonmedical prescription drugs, 3. Drug trafficking, 4. Violence, 5. School promotion (progression to the next grade), 6. Association with delinquent peers
CAST (Coping and Support Training)	1. Suicide risk factors, 2. Severity of depression symptoms, 3. Feelings of hopelessness, 4. Anxiety, 5. Anger, 6. Drug involvement, 7. Sense of personal control, 8. Problem-solving/coping skills
Celebrating Families!	1. Parenting skills, 2. Parent tobacco and substance use, 3. Parent depressive symptoms, 4. Family environment, 5. Child behaviors, 6. Family reunification
Class Action	1. Tendency to use alcohol, 2. Binge drinking and peer influences
Coping with Work and Family Stress	1. Perceived stressors, 2. Coping strategies, 3. Perceived social support, 4. Alcohol and other drug use/problem drinking, 5. Psychological symptoms of stress
Creating Lasting Family Connections (CLFC)/ Creating Lasting Connections (CLC)	1. Use of community services, 2. Parent knowledge and beliefs about alcohol and other drugs (AOD), 3. Onset of youth AOD use, 4. Frequency of youth AOD use
Critical Time Intervention (CTI)	1. Cost, 2. Homelessness, 3. Mental health, 4. Social functioning
Dialectical Behavior Therapy (DBT)	1. Suicide attempts, 2. Nonsuicidal self-injury (parasuicidal history), 3. Psychosocial adjustment, 4. Treatment retention, 5. Drug use, 6. Symptoms of eating disorders
Early Risers "Skills for Success"	1. Academic competence and achievement (performance and behaviors), 2. Behavioral self-regulation, 3. Social competence, 4. Parental investment in the child, 5. Effective discipline
Familias Unidas (for Latino families)	1. Alcohol, 2. Drugs, 3. Family/relationships, 4. Social functioning, 5. Tobacco, 6. Violence
Families and Schools Together (FAST)	1. Child problem behaviors, 2. Child social skills and academic competencies
Family Behavior Therapy (FBT)	1. Drug use, 2. Alcohol use, 3. Family relationships, 4. Depression, 5. Employment/school attendance, 6. Conduct disorder symptoms

continued

TABLE 5.5   Selected Evidence-Based Programs for Children, Adolescents, and Families as Primary Prevention and Intervention Initiatives (continued)

EVIDENCE-BASED PROGRAMS	OUTCOMES
Family Matters	1. Prevalence of adolescent cigarette use, 2. Prevalence of adolescent alcohol use, 3. Onset of adolescent cigarette use
Incredible Years	1. Positive and nurturing parenting, 2. Harsh, coercive, and negative parenting, 3. Child behavior problems, 4. Child positive behaviors, social competence, and school readiness skills, 5. Parent bonding and involvement with teacher and school, 6. Teacher classroom management skills
JOBS Program	1. Employment, 2. Family/relationships, 3. Mental health, 4. Quality of life
Lifelines Curriculum	1. Knowledge about suicide, 2. Attitudes about suicide and suicide intervention, 3. Attitudes about seeking adult help, 4. Attitudes about keeping a friend's suicide thoughts a secret
LifeSkills Training (LST)	1. Substance use (alcohol, tobacco, inhalants, marijuana, and polydrug), 2. Normative beliefs about substance use and substance use refusal skills, 3. Violence and delinquency
Lions Quest Skills for Adolescence	1. Social functioning, 2. Success in school, 3. Misconduct, 4. Attitudes and knowledge related to AOD, 5. Tobacco use, 6. Alcohol use, 7. Marijuana use
Moral Reconation Therapy (MRT)	1. Recidivism, 2. Personality functioning
Motivational Enhancement Therapy (MET)	1. Substance use, 2. Alcohol consumption, 3. Drinking intensity, 4. Marijuana use, 5. Marijuana problems
Multidimensional Family Therapy (MDFT)	1. Substance use, 2. Substance use-related problem severity, 3. Abstinence from substance use, 4. Treatment retention, 5. Recovery from substance use, 6. Risk factors for continued substance use and other problem behaviors, 7. School performance, 8. Delinquency, 9. Cost-effectiveness
Multisystemic Therapy with Psychiatric Supports (MST-Psychiatric)	1. Mental health symptoms, 2. Family relations, 3. School attendance, 4. Suicide attempts, 5. Days in out-of-home placement
Not on Tobacco (N-O-T)	1. Smoking cessation, 2. Smoking reduction, 3. Cost-effectiveness
Nurturing Parenting Programs (NPP)	1. Parenting attitudes, knowledge, beliefs, and behaviors, 2. Recidivism of child abuse and neglect, 3. Children's behavior and attitudes toward parenting, 4. Family interaction
Parenting Wisely	1. Child problem behaviors, 2. Parental knowledge, beliefs, and behaviors, 3. Parental sense of competence
Peaceful Alternatives to Tough Situations (PATS)	1. Psychological aggression, 2. Physical assault, 3. Forgiveness of others
Positive Action	1. Academic achievement, 2. Problem behaviors (violence, substance use, disciplinary referrals, and suspensions), 3. School absenteeism, 4. Family functioning
Protecting You/Protecting Me	1. Media awareness and literacy, 2. Alcohol use risk and protective factors, 3. Knowledge of brain growth and development, 4. Vehicle safety knowledge/skills, 5. Alcohol use
Reconnecting Youth: A Peer Group Approach to Building Life Skills	1. School performance, 2. Drug involvement, 3. Mental health risk and protective factors, 4. Suicide risk behaviors

TABLE 5.5   Selected Evidence-Based Programs for Children, Adolescents, and Families as Primary Prevention and Intervention Initiatives (continued)

EVIDENCE-BASED PROGRAMS	OUTCOMES
Responding in Peaceful and Positive Ways (RiPP)	1. School disciplinary code violations, 2. Violent/aggressive behavior—self-reports, 3. Victimization, 4. Peer provocation, 5. Life satisfaction
Safe Dates	1. Perpetration of psychological abuse, 2. Perpetration of sexual abuse, 3. Perpetration of violence against a current dating partner, 4. Perpetration of moderate physical abuse, 5. Perpetration of severe physical abuse, 6. Sexual abuse victimization, 7. Physical abuse victimization
Project ALERT	1. Substance use (alcohol, tobacco, and marijuana), 2. Attitudes and resistance skills related to alcohol, tobacco, and other drugs (ATOD)
Project SUCCESS	1. ATOD use, 2. Risk and protective factors for ATOD use
Promoting Alternative Thinking Strategies (PATHS)/PATHS Preschool	1. Emotional knowledge, 2. Internalizing behaviors, 3. Externalizing behaviors, 4. Depression, 5. Neurocognitive capacity, 6. Learning environment, 7. Social-emotional competence
Second Step	1. Social competence and prosocial behavior, 2. Incidence of negative, aggressive, or antisocial behaviors
Strengthening Families Program	1. Children's internalizing and externalizing behaviors, 2. Parenting practices/parenting efficacy, 3. Family relationships
Success in Stages: Build Respect, Stop Bullying	1. Participation in bullying (as bully, bystander, or victim), 2. Achievement of action/maintenance stage of change for bullying behavior
Teaching Students to Be Peacemakers	1. Conflict resolution strategies, 2. Nature of resolutions, 3. Academic achievement and retention of academic learning, 4. Knowledge and retention of conflict resolution and mediation procedures, 5. Attitudes toward conflict
Triple P: Positive Parenting Program	1. Negative and disruptive child behaviors, 2. Negative parenting practices as a risk factor for later child behavior problems, 3. Positive parenting practices as a protective factor for later child behavior problems

Source: Substance Abuse and Mental Health Services Administration, *National Registry of Evidence-Based Programs and Practices,* http://www.nrepp.samhsa.gov, 2010.

CONCLUSION

Evidence-based best-practice programs are not only effective in the services they provide but also represent a very good investment because they can empirically demonstrate outcomes for changing self-defeating or debilitating behaviors. As a result, school and community funding agencies are usually more inclined to fund evidence-based programs because they have consistently demonstrated results and an immediate return in effective service and they serve as a model for future quality program development. "Evidence-based practice" refers to applying the best available research evidence in the provision of increased health, improved behavior, and education services to diminish barriers to learning and living and to increase interpersonal and intrapersonal outcomes. Evidence-based practice originated in the medical field, where thousands of randomized controlled trials have been conducted to demonstrate effectiveness.

The Professional School Counselor's Role

6

Consulting With Teachers, Parents, and Other Support Personnel

> As society has become more complex and demanding, [partnerships between schools and families] have all too often fallen by the wayside. Neither educators nor parents have enough time to get to know one another and establish working relationships on behalf of children. In many communities, parents are discouraged from spending time in classrooms and educators are expected to consult with family members only when a child is in trouble. The result, in too many cases, is misunderstanding, mistrust, and a lack of respect, so that when a child falls behind, teachers blame the parents and parents blame the teachers.
>
> James P. Comer, Maurice Falk Professor, Yale Child Study Center (Comer, 2005, p. 39)

Family involvement in education and school activities has demonstrated a significant impact on a child's well-being and academic achievement. Parental involvement in school is defined as parent-reported participation at least once during the school year attending a general school meeting, a scheduled meeting with their child's teacher, or a school event; volunteering in the school; or serving on a school committee. The outcome research to support family involvement is listed below:

- A synthesis of the research concluded that "the evidence is consistent, positive, and convincing: families have a major influence on their children's achievement in school and through life. When schools, families, and community groups work together to support learning, children tend to do better in school, stay in school longer, and like school more" (Henderson & Mapp, 2002).
- When parents or guardians are involved in education, children do better in school, and as a result, schools improve (Lewis & Henderson, 1998).
- Research has long shown that parents' positive involvement with their children's schooling is related to many positive outcomes such as achievement, belonging, a positive school climate, and engagement in extracurricular activities (After-School Corporation, 2006).
- *Family involvement* is a broader term that refers to the participation of a child's or adolescent's family members in any aspect of an out-of-schooltime program. This participation need not

be limited to a young person's parents but may include any or all adults in a household and extended family members (Shanahan, Mulhern, & Rodriguez-Brown, 1995). Some programs also extend the term to include the involvement of a program participant's siblings, who in many cases can serve as positive role models (After-School Corporation, 2006).

- Children and adolescents whose parents are engaged in out-of-schooltime programs report higher levels of trust and lower levels of disruptive behavior such as lying to and arguing with parents (Harris & Wimer, 2004).
- Children whose parents participate in after-school family literacy initiatives show larger gains on measures of math and reading than do children whose parents do not participate (Garcia & Hasson, 2004).
- Positive parental involvement with adolescents is associated with lower rates of risky sexual behavior, tobacco use, drug use, alcohol use, delinquency, and violent behavior. Youths enrolled in some after-school programs with a parental involvement component have been found to be more likely to refuse alcohol and marijuana, to better understand the dangers of marijuana, and to better understand the health consequences of drug use (St. Pierre, 1998).
- Family members who become involved in programs may offer suggestions for improvements, and studies suggest that programs that respond to such ideas have higher attendance, improved activities, higher youth and family satisfaction, and increased child or adolescent engagement (After-School Corporation, 2006).
- Parents who volunteer with programs report feeling closer to their children, offering further support for the idea that program participation improves relationships between parents and children (Harris & Wimer, 2004).
- One study found that 91% of parents and 89% of program coordinators reported that work schedules precluded parents' regular participation in the school programs (Massachusetts 2020, 2004). Another barrier to participation is that staff members may not know how to work with families and may inadvertently treat parents' contributions and skills as unimportant (Garcia & Hasson, 2004). This is a significant barrier with parents who have students that are English-language learners and may not have adequate English-language skills themselves to acculturate into the school community.
- Parental involvement in education is positively associated with adolescents' academic outcome throughout middle and high school (Hill, Tyson, & Bromell, 2009).

PARENT INVOLVEMENT IN EDUCATION: DEFINITIONS AND THEORETICAL FRAMEWORKS

Parent Involvement

The effort that so many parents make to guide their children's lives repeatedly comes up against the rush of modern living—the "time crunch." The mismatch in how major American institutions—from schools to businesses—carve out time in the day-to-day life of the American family is—to my mind—a serious impediment in how our young people are growing up. We ask families to twist and turn—to grow—to go through every possible contortion to fit into the structure and time needs of schools or businesses or other institutions—instead of the other way around. It is my very strong belief that we really must rethink what we are doing, and how we use our time.

Richard W. Riley, Former U.S. Secretary of Education

Workshops designed to train parents in proper techniques may be perceived as trying to change their values or beliefs regarding methods of child rearing. True support for families occurs by providing such things as babysitting services at PTA meetings; transportation for parents to conferences and meetings, if necessary; booklets for parents on family resources such as homework and grading policies; newsletters and one-page "infobriefs" on parenting and helping children at home; a telephone directory of parent-group representatives and school personnel; extended-day programs for working parents; facilitating foster grandparent programs; mentor programs for children from single-parent families; and greater use of email communication.

True collaboration is responsive to as many as 100 different family constellations and corresponding child and adolescent needs. The following should be understood:

- There are many different forms and levels of involvement. Parents don't have to come to school to be involved. They can be involved in social media to share positive and proactive information with other parents about children with disabilities, gifted education, extracurricular activities, electronic newsletters, and website management for particular events' and groups' Web pages such the swim club, the debate team, student government, and so on. Short training and preparation would be a prerequisite to job assignment, but this would be an investment with multiple returns.
- Parent involvement is a collaborative effort involving families, schools, community agencies, and faith-based groups.
- Parent involvement means family involvement. Growing numbers of grandparents, aunts, uncles, and even friends have taken over the role of surrogate parents for the children of others.

There are many reasons for the lack of parent involvement, including the following:

- Time conflicts between work and school schedules
- Uncertainty about what families should be doing to help their children
- Cultural and language barriers
- Feeling uncomfortable or unwelcome in the child's school
- Lack of support in the community
- Lack of understanding and support in the workplace

Parent involvement in education can be defined as "parents' *interactions with* schools and with their children to promote academic success" (Hill & Taylor, 2004, p. 1491). The No Child Left Behind Act of 2001 (NCLB) defines parent involvement as "the participation of parents in regular, two-way, and meaningful communication involving student academic learning and other school activities" (§ 9101). NCLB also stipulates reinforced guidelines for parent involvement with the central requirement of local educational agencies (LEAs) to produce individual student interpretive, descriptive, and diagnostic reports that allow parents, teachers, and principals to understand and address the specific academic needs of each student, and that also include information regarding achievement on academic assessments aligned with each specific state's academic achievement standards. State educational agencies must provide these reports to parents, teachers, and principals of all public schools as soon as possible after the assessments are given. In addition, the information must be provided to parents in an understandable and uniform format, including alternative formats upon request, especially if they speak a language other than English.

Schools and LEAs are mandated to coordinate and integrate parental involvement programs and activities with the following programs:

- Head Start
- Reading First
- Early Reading First
- Even Start Family Literacy Programs
- Home Instruction Programs for Preschool Youngsters

- Parents as Teachers
- Public preschools
- Other relevant programs that address student achievement

This represents one of the largest federally regulated initiatives in our nation's history. Along with these initiatives, many school systems have also implemented software programs that allow parents or guardians to access their child's attendance, grades, and homework assignments in real time. This initiative has opened communication between teachers, parents, and administrators tremendously and has cut down on teacher–parent conferences. It makes both students and teachers accountable, and parents can view everything from completed assignments and behavior documentation to class requirements. No longer do parents have to be inconvenienced to check on their child's performance. This is particularly beneficial for parents who have joint custody; both parents can check on their son or daughter's progress and talk to their child individually, avoiding blaming each other and exacerbating what may be already strained relationships.

The National Standards for Parent/Family Involvement Programs build upon the six types of parent involvement identified by Joyce L. Epstein of the Center for School, Family and Community Partnerships at Johns Hopkins University. There are six standards (see Table 6.1), which are further elaborated in Tables 6.2 through 6.7. This is the most widely cited parent involvement model among existing frameworks (Epstein, 1987, 2001; Epstein, Salinas, & Jackson, 1995; Epstein & Sanders, 2002; Epstein et al., 2009).

TABLE 6.1   National Standards for Parent/Family Involvement Programs

Standard 1: Communicating—Communication between home and school is regular, two-way, and meaningful.

Standard 2: Parenting—Parenting skills are promoted and supported.

Standard 3: Student Learning—Parents' skills are promoted and supported.

Standard 4: Volunteering—Parents are welcome in the school and their support and assistance are sought.

Standard 5: School Decision Making and Advocacy—Parents are full partners in the decisions that affect children and families.

Standard 6: Collaborating and Community—Community resources are used to strengthen schools, families, and student learning.

It is important to help all families establish environments that support children as students. Best practices include:

- Suggestions for home conditions that support learning at each grade level. For example, suggested appropriate time standards for homework. While it is recognized that homework assignments may vary in length, the following daily homework standards are recommended based on four days of homework per week:
  - Primary grades (1–3): 20–45 minutes
  - Upper elementary (4–5): 30–60 minutes
  - Middle school (6–8): 20–30 minutes per class average
  - High school (9–12): 30–45 minutes per class average
- Workshops, videotapes, and computerized phone messages on parenting and child rearing at each developmental age and grade level.
- Home visits at transition points: preschool, elementary, middle, and high school.
- Neighborhood meetings at schools, churches, or recreation centers to help families understand school policies, procedures, and the various opportunities for their children as well as to help schools understand the unique needs of families from the consumer/community perspective.

Level One: Parenting

Developing school–family–community partnerships using Epstein's theory of the six types of involvement to professional school counseling programs has demonstrated promise in closing the achievement gap that currently exists between low-income students and students of color and their white or Asian counterparts (Griffin & Steen, 2010). "The key to increase student achievement and to ensure more equitable practices in school is to increase parent and community involvement" (Holcomb-McCoy, 2007, p. 66). "Professional school counselors can devote greater attention to communicating, volunteering, learning at home, decision-making and leadership and advocacy practices" (Griffin & Steen, 2010, p. 218).

TABLE 6.2   Epstein's Framework of Six Types of Parent or Guardian Involvement: Parenting

TYPE 1: PARENTING

Help all families establish home environments to support children as students.

Sample Practices
- Suggestions for home conditions that support learning at each grade level
- Workshops, videotapes, computerized phone messages on parent and child rearing at each age and grade level
- Parent education and other courses or training for parents (e.g., GED, college credit, family literacy)
- Family support programs to assist families with health, nutrition, and other services
- Home visits at transition points to preschool, elementary school, middle school, and high school
- Neighborhood meetings to help families understand school and to help school understand families

Challenges
- Provide information to *all* families who want it or need it, not just to the few who can attend workshops or meetings at the school building.
- Enable families to share information with schools about culture, background, and children's talents and needs.
- Make sure that all information for and from families is clear, usable, and linked to children's success in school.

Redefinitions
- *Workshop* to mean more than a meeting about a topic held at the school building at a particular time. It may also mean making information about a topic available in a variety of forms that can be viewed, heard, or read anywhere, anytime, and in a variety of venues (e.g., Internet, email, voice mail, texting, video streaming).

Results for Students
- Awareness of family supervision; respect for parents
- Positive personal qualities, habits, beliefs, and values, as taught by family
- Balance between time spent on chores, on other activities, and on homework
- Good or improved attendance
- Awareness of importance of school

Results for Parents or Guardians
- Understanding of and confidence about parenting, child and adolescent development, and changes in home conditions for learning as children proceed through school
- Awareness of own and others' challenges in parents
- Feeling of support from school and other parents

Result for Teachers, Professional School Counselors, and Administrators
- Understanding families' background, cultures, concerns, goals, needs, and views of their children
- Respect for families' strengths and efforts
- Understanding of student diversity
- Awareness of own skills to share information on child development

Source: Epstein, J. L., Sanders, M. G., Shelton, S. B., Simon, B. S., Salinas, K. C., Jansorn, N. R., . . . Williams, K. J., *School, Family, and Community Partnerships: Your Handbook for Action,* (3rd ed.), Corwin Press, Thousand Oaks, CA, 2009.

Level Two: Communicating

Open and honest communication and effective forms of school-to-home and home-to-school articulation about school programs and children's progress is imperative. Best practices include:

- Holding conferences with every parent at least once a year, with follow-up as needed, on the high school level
- Holding conferences with every parent at least twice a year, with follow-up as needed, on the middle school level
- Holding conferences with every parent at least four times a year, with follow-up as needed, on the elementary school level
- Making time provisions for conferences at the school level and in the workplace
- Providing language translators for immigrant parents
- Sending home weekly (elementary school) and monthly (middle school) academic folders of student work for review and comments
- Conducting parent–student pickup of report cards with conferences commending student performance and conferences on how to improve student performance
- Providing a regular schedule of one-page infobriefs, as well as memos, phone calls, and electronic newsletters, on topics pertaining to learning and discipline
- Routinely providing clear information on courses, programs of study, and student activities (all communication should be provided in the child's native language)
- Increasing use of technology to reach children and their families

TABLE 6.3   Epstein's Framework of Six Types of Parent or Guardian Involvement: Communicating

TYPE 2: COMMUNICATING

Design effective forms of school-to-home and home-to-school communications about school programs and children's progress.

Sample Practices
- Conferences with every parent at least once a year, with follow-up as needed
- Language translators to assist families as needed
- Weekly or monthly folders of student work sent home for review and comments
- Parent–student pickup of report card, with conferences on improving grades
- Regular schedule of useful notices, memos, phone calls, newsletters, and other communications
- Clear information on choosing schools or courses, programs, and activities within schools
- Clear information on all school policies, programs, reforms, and transitions

Challenges
- Review the readability, clarity, form, and frequency of all memos, notices, and other print and electronic communication.
- Consider parents who do not speak English well, do not read well, or need large type.
- Review the quality of major communications (newsletters, report cards, conference schedules, and so on).
- Establish clear two-way channels for communications from home to school and from school to home.

Redefinitions
- *Communications about school programs and student progress* to mean two-way, three-way, and multiple-channel communications that connect schools, families, students, and the community.

Results for Students
- Awareness of own progress and actions needed to maintain or improve grades
- Understanding of school policies on behavior, attendance, and other areas of student conduct
- Informed decisions about courses and programs
- Awareness of own role in partnerships, serving as courier and communicator

Results for Parents or Guardians
- Understanding school programs and policies

TABLE 6.3   Epstein's Framework of Six Types of Parent or Guardian Involvement: Communicating (continued)

- Monitoring and awareness of child's progress
- Responding effectively to students' problems
- Interactions with teachers and ease of communication with school and teachers

Results for Teachers, Professional School Counselors, and Administrators
- Increased diversity and use of communications with families and awareness of own ability to communicate clearly
- Appreciation for and use of parent network for communications
- Increased ability to elicit and understand family views on children's programs and progress

Source: Epstein, J. L. , Sanders, M. G., Shelton, S. B., Simon, B. S., Salinas, K. C., Jansorn, N. R., . . . Williams, K. J., *School, Family, and Community Partnerships: Your Handbook for Action,* (3rd ed.), Corwin Press, Thousand Oaks, CA, 2009.

Level Three: Volunteering

Parental help and support, especially within the school counseling program, are invaluable. Parents can answer phones, help with the career resource room or family center, make copies, stuff envelopes, and help with receptions. (However, there are tasks that would *not* be appropriate for parents, such as filing student records, test scores, or report cards because this information is confidential and requires a release of information from the child's parent in accordance with the Family Education Rights and Privacy Act [FERPA]). Best practices include:

- Counselors sending out annual postcard surveys to identify all available talents, times, and location of volunteers
- Volunteers organizing phone trees or other structures to provide all families with needed information
- Volunteers serving as parent patrols to promote school safety

TABLE 6.4   Epstein's Framework of Six Types of Parent or Guardian Involvement: Volunteering

TYPE 3: VOLUNTEERING
Recruit and organize parent help and support.
Sample Practices
- School and classroom volunteer program to help teachers, administrators, students, and other parents
- Parent room or family center for volunteer work, meetings, and resources for families
- Annual postcard survey to identify all available talents, times, and locations of volunteers
- Class parent telephone tree or other structures to provide all families with needed information
- Parent patrols or other activities to aid safety and operation of school programs

Challenges
- Recruit volunteers widely so that *all* families know that their time and talents are welcome.
- Make flexible schedules for volunteers, assemblies, and events to enable parents who work to participate.
- Organize volunteer work; provide training; match time and talent with school, teacher, and student needs; and recognize efforts so that participants are productive.

Redefinitions
- *Volunteer* to mean anyone who supports school goals and children's learning or development in any way, at any place, and at any time—not just during the school day and at the school building.

Results for Students
- Skill in communicating with adults
- Increased learning of skills that receive tutoring or targeted attention from volunteers
- Awareness of many skills, talents, occupations, and contributions of parent and other volunteers

Results for Parents or Guardians
- Understanding the teacher's job, increased comfort in school, and carryover of school activities at home
- Self-confidence about ability to work in school and with children or to take steps to improve own education

continued

TABLE 6.4   Epstein's Framework of Six Types of Parent or Guardian Involvement: Volunteering (continued)

- Awareness that families are welcome and valued at school
- Gains in specific skills of volunteer work

Results for Teachers, Professional School Counselors, and Administrators
- Readiness to involve families in new ways, including those who do not volunteer at school
- Awareness of parents' talents and interests in school and children
- Greater individual attention to students, with help from volunteers

Source: Epstein, J. L. , Sanders, M. G., Shelton, S. B., Simon, B. S., Salinas, K. C., Jansorn, N. R., . . . Williams, K. J., *School, Family, and Community Partnerships: Your Handbook for Action,* (3rd ed.), Corwin Press, Thousand Oaks, CA, 2009.

Level Four: Learning at Home

Schools need to routinely provide information and ideas to families on how to help students at home with homework or other curriculum-related activities, such as how to prepare for tests. Best practices include:

- Educating families on skills required for students in all subjects at each grade level. Because of the emphasis on higher academic standards, many teachers in core subject areas (English, mathematics, science, and social studies) have pacing guides that designate what is to be taught week to week. This information can easily be shared and reinforced by parents.
- Informing parents about homework policies and how to monitor and discuss schoolwork at home.
- Informing parents on how to help students improve skills on various class and school assignments.
- Regularly scheduling homework that requires students to discuss with their families what they are learning in class.
- Holding family fun nights that focus on mathematics, science, reading, or health and fitness.
- Providing summer learning packets or suggested summer enrichment activities in a June–August calendar.

TABLE 6.5   Epstein's Framework of Six Types of Parent or Guardian Involvement: Learning at Home

TYPE 4: LEARNING AT HOME
Provide information and ideas to families about how to help students at home with homework and other curriculum-related activities, decisions, and planning.
Sample Practices
- Information for families on skills required for students in all subjects at each grade
- Information on homework policies and how to monitor and discuss schoolwork at home
- Information on how to assist students to improve skills on various class and school assessments
- Regular schedule of homework that requires students to discuss and interact with families on what they are learning in class
- Calendars with activities for parents and students at home
- Family math, science, and reading activities at school
- Summer learning packets or activities
- Family participation in setting student goals each year and in planning for college or work
Challenges
- Design and organize a regular schedule of interactive homework (e.g., weekly or bimonthly) that gives students responsibility for discussing important things they are learning and helps families stay aware of the content of their children's classwork.
- Coordinate family-linked homework activities, if students have several teachers.
- Involve families and their children in all-important curriculum-related decisions.

TABLE 6.5   Epstein's Framework of Six Types of Parent or Guardian Involvement: Learning at Home (continued)

Redefinitions
- *Homework* to mean not only work done alone but also interactive activities shared with others at home or in the community, linking schoolwork to real life. *Help at home* to mean encouraging, listening, reacting, praising, guiding, monitoring, and discussing—not "teaching" school subjects.

Results for Students
- Gains in skills, abilities, and test scores linked to homework and classwork
- Homework completion
- Positive attitude toward schoolwork
- View of parents as more similar to teacher and of home as more similar to school
- Self-concept of ability as learner

Results for Parents and Guardians
- Knowing how to support, encourage, and help student at home each year
- Discussions of school, classwork, and homework
- Understanding of instructional program each year and of what the child is learning in each subject
- Appreciation of teaching skills
- Awareness of child as a learner

Results for Teachers, Professional School Counselors, and Administrators
- Better design of homework assignments
- Respect for family time
- Recognition of equal helpfulness of single-parent, dual-income, and less formally educated families in motivating and reinforcing student learning
- Satisfaction with family involvement and support

Source: Epstein, J. L. , Sanders, M. G., Shelton, S. B., Simon, B. S., Salinas, K. C., Jansorn, N. R., & Williams, K. J., *School, Family, and Community Partnerships: Your Handbook for Action,* (3rd ed.), Corwin Press, Thousand Oaks, CA, 2009.

Level Five: Decision Making

It is important to include parents in school decisions by establishing a school counseling advisory board (ASCA, 2005a). Allow parents to be informed of school/community demographics and identify areas that need improvement. Best practices include:

- Local and district-wide advisory boards advising the schools regarding coordination of activities, programs, and services to students and their families
- Including on the advisory board local government officials, businesspeople, parents, students, teachers, representatives of community agencies, medical professionals, and representatives from law enforcement and community-based organizations
- Having the advisory board meet on a regular basis, making participation broad-based, and fostering a sense of ownership of programs and services for youth
- Having the advisory board conduct a thorough assessment of needs based on objective data

TABLE 6.6   Epstein's Framework of Six Types of Parent or Guardian Involvement: Decision Making

TYPE 5: DECISION MAKING

Include parents in school decisions, developing parent leaders and representatives.

Sample Practices
- Active PTA or other parent organizations, advisory councils, or committees (e.g., curriculum, safety, personnel) for parent leadership and participation
- Independent advocacy groups to lobby and work for school reform and improvements
- District-level councils and committees for family and community involvement

continued

TABLE 6.6   Epstein's Framework of Six Types of Parent or Guardian Involvement: Decision Making (continued)

- Information on school or local elections for school representatives
- Networks to link all families with parent representatives

Challenges
- Include parent leaders from all racial, ethnic, socioeconomic, and other groups in the school.
- Offer training to enable leaders to serve as representatives of other families, with input from and return of information to all parents.
- Include students (along with parents) in decision-making groups.

Redefinitions
- *Decision making* to mean a process of partnership, of shared views and actions toward shared goals, not just a power struggle between conflicting ideas. *Parent leader* to mean a real representative, with opportunities and support to hear from and communicate with other families.

Results for Students
- Awareness of representation of families in school decisions
- Understanding that student rights are protected
- Specific benefits linked to policies enacted by parent organizations and experienced by students

Results for Parents and Guardians
- Input into policies that affect their child's education
- Feeling of ownership of school
- Awareness of parents' voices in school decisions
- Shared experiences and connections with other families
- Awareness of school, district, and state policies

Results for Teachers, Professional School Counselors, and Administrators
- Awareness of parent perspectives as a factor in policy development and decisions
- View of equal status of family representatives on committees and in leadership roles

Source: Epstein, J. L. , Sanders, M. G., Shelton, S. B., Simon, B. S., Salinas, K. C., Jansorn, N. R., . . . Williams, K. J., *School, Family, and Community Partnerships: Your Handbook for Action,* (3rd ed.), Corwin Press, Thousand Oaks, CA, 2009.

Level Six: Collaboration with the Community

Identifying and integrating resources and services from the community (health, social services, substance abuse, juvenile justice, recreation, service clubs and organizations) can strengthen school programs, family practice, student learning, and personal development. Best practices include:

- Developing a full-service school
- Providing information on community activities that link learning skills and talents, including summer programs and enrichment activities
- Promoting service learning projects through partnerships with the chamber of commerce and civic, cultural, health, recreational, and other agencies, organizations, and businesses

Schools need to rethink their traditional schedules in terms of parent needs and consider a range of times to meet, including early mornings, evenings, and weekends. Some more innovative ways to reach parents and guardians include:

- Internet networking to provide parenting information and increase interactive discussion among parents
- Building trust and openness by reaching out to families through multiple approaches such as workshops, encouragement from teachers, phone calls, voice mail, memos, school-based parent resource centers, and home visits
- Reaching out to include fathers, especially single-parent fathers
- Providing transportation to conferences and programs by organizing parent carpools and providing child care for siblings

- Translating written material and having a person who speaks the parents' language make a telephone call or home visit
- Using alternative places for conferences or programs, such as churches or community centers
- Considering early morning breakfast meetings, which may be more convenient than after school
- Providing in-service programs for teachers to prepare them to build partnerships with families and communities
- Networking through community organizations
- Providing year-round day care, after- and before-school programs, and summer enrichment programs

Dunst and Trivette (1994, 2005) found that parenting programs embrace a common set of principles:

1. a focus on prevention and optimization rather than treatment
2. a recognition of the need to work with the entire family and community
3. a commitment to regarding family as an active participant in the planning and execution of the program rather than as a "passive client" waiting to receive services
4. a commitment to nourishing cultural diversity
5. a focus on strength-based needs analysis, programming, and evaluation
6. flexible staffing

These principles of contemporary parent education and support programs empower families with the primary responsibility for their child's development and well-being.

TABLE 6.7   Epstein's Framework of Six Types of Parent or Guardian Involvement: Collaboration With Community

TYPE 6: COLLABORATION WITH COMMUNITY

Identify and integrate resources and services from the community to strengthen school programs, family practices, and student learning and development.

Sample Practices
- Information for students and families on community health, cultural, recreational, social support, and other programs or services
- Information on community activities that link to learning skills and talents, including summer programs for students
- Service integration through partnerships involving schools; civic, counseling, cultural, health, recreation, and other agencies and organizations; and businesses
- Service to the community by students, families, and schools (e.g., recycling, art, music, drama, and other activities for seniors or others)
- Participation of alumni in school programs for students

Challenges
- Solve turf problems of responsibilities, funds, staff, and locations for collaborative activities.
- Inform families of community programs for students, such as mentoring, tutoring, and business partnerships.
- Assure equity of opportunities for students and families to participate in community programs or to obtain services.
- Match community contributions with school goals, and integrate child and family services with education.

Redefinitions
- *Community* to mean not only the neighborhoods where students' homes and schools are located but also any neighborhoods that influence their learning and development. A community is rated not only by low or high social or economic qualities but also by strengths and talents to support students, families, and schools. The community includes all who are interested in and affected by the quality of education, not just those with children in the schools.

continued

TABLE 6.7   Epstein's Framework of Six Types of Parent or Guardian Involvement: Collaboration With Community (continued)

Results for Students
- Increased skills and talents through enriched curricular and extracurricular experiences
- Awareness of careers and of options for future education and work
- Specific benefits linked to programs, services, resources, and opportunities that connect students with community

Results for Parents or Guardians
- Knowledge and use of local resources by family and child to increase skills and talents or to obtain needed services
- Interactions with other families in community activities
- Awareness of school's role in the community and of community's contributions to the school

Results for Teachers, Professional School Counselors, and Administrators
- Awareness of community resources to enrich curriculum and instruction
- Openness to and skill in using mentors, business partners, community volunteers, and others to assist students and augment teaching practices
- Knowledgeable, helpful referrals of children and families to needed services

Source: Epstein, J. L. , Sanders, M. G., Shelton, S. B., Simon, B. S., Salinas, K. C., Jansorn, N. R., . . . Williams, K. J., *School, Family, and Community Partnerships: Your Handbook for Action,* (3rd ed.), Corwin Press, Thousand Oaks, CA, 2009.

SCHOOL-AS-COMMUNITY OR SCHOOL-AS-INSTITUTION

Raywid (1993; Raywid, Schmerler, Phillips, & Smith, 2003) highlights six common attributes of healthy and vital school communities: respect, caring, inclusiveness, trust, empowerment, and commitment. Communication is open, participation is widespread, teamwork is prevalent, and diversity is incorporated. Members share a vision for the future of the school, a common sense of purpose, and a common set of values. Trust and respect as well as recognition of efforts and accomplishments are part of an important ethos. A strong sense of community facilitates instructional efforts and enhances student and staff well-being.

Faculty, professional school counselors, and support staff members experiencing a strong sense of community tend to be clearer about the expectations that others at school have for them and tend to report feeling less burned out, overwhelmed, or confronted with conflicting demands (Rossi & Stringfield, 1995; Royal & Rossi, 1996). Schools whose teachers work with one another model important behaviors such as collaboration and cooperation to their students as well (Smith & Scott, 1990). Students' sense of community is related to their engagement in school activities. They experience less anxiety about being unprepared for class and are less prone to drop out of school.

Westheimer and Kahne (1993) maintain that training programs should be provided to help staff members understand the benefits of community and to supply them with the pedagogical tools and technical support to foster a shared commitment. Furthermore, unless a sound fabric of interpersonal relationships can be integrated into school improvement initiatives, the long-term commitment of everyone within the school community may be lost to tension and dissention.

Social and economic conditions have a larger effect on the educational system's ability to perform its task than most people understand or expect. Hungry, emotionally disturbed, abused, or unhealthy students are obviously unable to focus their full attention to learning. Premature, low-birthweight babies born into poverty have a poorer prognosis of functioning within normal academic expectations (Bradley et al., 1994), and family income and poverty are powerful predictors of the cognitive development and behavior of young children (Duncan, Brooks-Gunn, & Klebanov, 1994). Economically deprived single mothers are more likely to abuse their children physically (Gelles, 1989). However, when services such as parent education and support are offered, outcomes for children, siblings, and families improve (Roberts & Wasik, 1990; Seitz & Apfel, 1994).

CONSULTATION

Consultation is a function well within the competencies of professional school counselors. As shown in Figure 6.1 and 6.2 (see the Appendix), professional school counselors possess many skills. A fundamental consultation course is required in many counselor educational programs, and consultation experiences have been included in the Council for Accreditation of Counseling and Related Educational Programs (CACREP) standards for accreditation of such programs. Many states now require a course in consultation for school counselor certification. Adopting a counselor-as-consultant model is one alternative to enhancing counselor accountability. Adopting that model and providing targeted services could revitalize existing professional school counselor programming, especially when services are consumer/community oriented.

Annual needs assessments are a critical component of a comprehensive school counseling program. Directors of school-based professional school counseling programs cannot make assumptions about client needs. For example, one might assume that all parents want their child to go to college, yet, upon closer examination, the reality may be that most students in a particular community are first-generation, college-bound students whose parents don't understand the intricacies of getting into college, which prevents them from seeking information. Community pride may also make parents reluctant to ask for help. What continues to be true is that the best indicator of a student getting into college is his or her parent(s) having gone to college. With this in mind, the consumers in this particular community may need services that target first-generation, college-bound students.

Professional school counselors are human behavior and relationship specialists who make use of the following helping processes:

- counseling
- coordination of services
- consultation
- leadership
- advocacy
- collaboration and teaming
- management of resources
- use of data
- use of technology

Consultation is "a cooperative process in which the counselor-consultant assists others to think through problems and to develop skills that make them more effective in working with students" (ASCA, 1990, p. 1; Otwell & Mullis, 1997).

Consulting has become a preferred activity for many counselors (Dustin & Ehly, 1992). Professional school counselors believe that changes in a student's behavior are more likely to be accomplished through changes in the behavior of the significant adults in the student's life than through direct counseling services (Campbell, 1992; Myrick, 2003b), and many teachers regard consultation as the most beneficial service provided by counselors (Bundy & Poppen, 1986; Hall & Lin, 1994; Wilgus & Shelley, 1988). Consulting is an efficient method of affecting the well-being and personal development of many more students than can be seen directly by a single professional school counselor (Campbell, 1992). With increasing demands upon teachers' management and therapeutic skills, teachers often welcome the professional school counselor's skills, especially in areas that increase cooperative efforts between teacher and parent.

Relationships among parent, teacher, student, and professional school counselor can benefit from consultation that focuses on problem solving. A consultation model that follows a problem-solving approach focuses on three stages:

1. Establishing the relationship
2. Identifying the problem
3. Facilitating change

Counselor skills that focus on areas such as active listening, feedback, empathy, genuineness, concreteness, and action planning help ease the elimination of the problem. These skills promote a more positive attitude on the part of the teacher, which in turn promotes the greatest gains in learning.

Numerous consultation models and/or theories have been discussed in the literature (Brack, Jones, Smith, White, & Brack, 1993; Bundy & Poppen, 1986; Dustin & Ehly, 1992; Erchul & Conoley, 1991; Fuqua & Kurpius, 1993; Hall & Lin, 1994; Kern & Mullis, 1993; Stoltenberg, 1993; Zins, 1993). The four general models characterized as most applicable to school consultation are process consultation, mental health consultation, behavioral consultation, and advocacy consultation (Conoley & Conoley, 1982). All have problem solving as a primary goal, while prevention of problems is secondary (Medway, 1989; Zins, 1993).

Consultation as Problem Solving

Fostering intellectual, interpersonal, and affective growth of children and adolescents through consultation with teachers has long been considered one of the primary roles of the professional school counselor. Because of its efficiency and efficacy, teacher consultation has become increasingly desirable. Effective consultation with parents, teachers, and other helping professionals is an important step in developing a proactive, responsive professional school counseling program. Profession school counselors represent a wealth of resources and skills that can enhance any staff development program. An added dimension occurs when staff development goals are school based rather than school *system* based. School system–based goals tend to be generic in nature, reflecting a broad spectrum of needs. School-based staff development reflects the targeted needs of the school, the community, and the consumer.

Mathias (1992) maintains that "group consultation may be the most effective, efficient, and powerful approach to a problem" (p. 193). Some good examples of group consultation are developing positive relationships with students (Rice & Smith, 1993); working with parents of children with disabilities (Berry, 1987); enhancing communication skills (Hawes, 1989); fostering positive self-esteem (Braucht & Weime, 1992; Maples, 1992); preventing sexual abuse (Allsopp & Prosen, 1988); and promoting suicide awareness (Klingman, 1990). Selected examples of staff development or parent education topics could include the following:

- Maximizing achievement of the marginalized student
- Closing the achievement gap
- Developing positive student–teacher relationships
- "Carefronting" the parent of a student in trouble with drugs and alcohol
- Enhancing student self-esteem
- Creating a more nurturing school climate
- Managing stress and information overload
- Uncloseting the cumulative record
- Helping students reach higher standards
- Diversity training
- Preventing cyberbullying
- Making sure children are safe when they are home alone
- Communicating more effectively to all parents and different family constellations

Benefits of Consultation

A number of benefits are received through employing a systematic consultation model. In addition to gaining increased assistance from families and school personnel, it provides:

- Improved relationships among teachers, administrators, parents, students, and the school
- Improved referral linkages with human service organizations and agencies
- Concrete strategies for enhancing the personal development of the child or adolescent at home and in school

Systematic consultation serves to provide inherent accountability in light of large student–counselor ratios and more diverse student populations. It increases the credibility of the professional school counselor as a viable resource for parents, teachers, administrators, and other support personnel. Furthermore, it reinforces the value of the professional school counselor to administrators and teachers in the realm of primary prevention by reducing such things as the number of parent conferences.

COUNSELORS AND TEACHERS AS PARTNERS IN NURTURING STUDENTS' SUCCESS

Teaching may be defined as the art and craft of persuading, coercing, cajoling, threatening, enticing, entertaining, outwitting, and disciplining others, usually younger, into the dawning of a suspicion that knowledge may be preferable to ignorance.

William O. Dough

Implementing a Teacher Advisor Program

Teacher advisor (TA) programs integrate the professional school counseling program into the total school arena. Teachers and professional school counselors working together as team members is an investment with multiple returns for student-centered environments. By having both a teacher and a professional school counselor as advisors, students can be encouraged to perform to their fullest potential, knowing that they are nurtured and supported outside of the classroom. TA programs are beginning to experience a revival in many school systems (Anfara, 2006; MacLaury, 2002; Spear, 2005; James & Spradling, 2001).

Selection of Advisors Cool

Each spring, all students list, in order of preference, five members of the professional staff they would like to act as their advisor. After review by the professional staff or advisor selection committee, each student is assigned an advisor. (This can be accomplished effectively and efficiently with current technology.) Students who wish to remain with their current advisor are encouraged to do so and are assured of assignment to the same advisor for the following year. During the school year, if a student desires to change advisors, a formal request must be made.

Advisee groups are composed of 8 to 15 students from all grade levels and meet each morning during the school year. The TA system is designed to augment the counseling services available to students by providing regular individual attention to every student and increasing communication between the home and the school. During TA period, time is allotted for two kinds of communication: general school communications (student activities, counseling information) and personal communications (academic progress, school/community activities, special recognition, problem solving).

The TA's Role as Advocate for All Students

The purpose of the teacher advisor program is to provide a comfortable nonteaching arena for the student and the teacher. The TA performs a variety of services, including:

- Orienting new students to the school
- Assisting students with school adjustment
- Serving as a central staff member with whom students can discuss their adjustment concerns without a grade tied to their performance
- Settling misunderstandings between students or with other staff members
- Organizing and participating in group discussions regarding personal/social, academic, and career issues
- Knowing each student's academic potential
- Identifying students who need help and assisting them in getting the services they need such as special accommodations
- Providing an opportunity for students to work in groups representing different grade levels
- Helping students recognize and accept individual differences
- Encouraging communication and cooperation

The TA provides the student with an advocate and another means of nurturing communication with other adults. Within this framework, another significant adult builds a relationship with a student that is characterized by caring, trust, honesty, and communication. It fosters a sense of belonging and responsibility by providing activities that focus on increasing social skills and interpersonal understanding to prevent self-defeating behaviors.

MOTIVATING AND ENCOURAGING THE "KIDS IN THE MIDDLE"

THE AVERAGE CHILD

I don't cause teachers trouble
My grades have been okay.
I listen in my classes
And I'm in school every day.
My teachers think I'm average
My parents think so, too.
I wish I didn't know that
'Cause there's lots I'd like to do.
I'd like to build a rocket.
I have a book that tells you how.
Or start a stamp collection.
Well, no use trying now.
'Cause since I found out I'm average

I'm just smart enough to see
To know there's nothing special
That I should expect of me.
I'm part of that majority
That hump part of the bell.
Who spends his life unnoticed
In my "only average" shell.

Anonymous

Parents, teachers, administrators, and professional school counselors frequently contemplate how to motivate students more effectively. The techniques of encouragement increase motivation among recipients and lessen feelings of inadequacy. Encouragement communicates trust, respect, competence, and ability. Encouragement that increases motivation involves some of the following tenets:

- Valuing individuals as they are, not as their reputation indicates or as one hopes they will be
- Having faith in the abilities of others
- Showing faith in others to help them believe in themselves
- Giving recognition for effort as well as performance
- Planning for success and assisting in the development of skills that are sequentially and psychologically paced
- Identifying and focusing on strengths and assets rather than on mistakes
- Using the interests of the student to motivate learning and instruction

SKILLS TO FOSTER AFFECTIVE GROWTH

In a survey of expert opinion, Stein and French (1984) identified the key skills, concepts, and attitudes necessary for teachers to foster the affective growth of students. The skills listed in Table 6.8 were identified as being essential to this effort.

To encourage social and emotional growth, it is essential that those who work with children and adolescents understand the special needs and psychological development of children and adolescents, are knowledgeable about the typical emotional problems of normal development, and understand the positive and negative effects that praise has on emotional growth.

PARENT–TEACHER CONFERENCING: THE PROFESSIONAL SCHOOL COUNSELOR'S ROLE

The parent–teacher conference has the potential to be one of the most effective means of strengthening the home–school relationship, while serving to enable information exchange, solve problems, and make educational plans for an individual student or an entire family. Yet, very few studies contain empirical data about parent conferences. One of the few studies measured the effects of establishing a parent–counselor conference relationship prior to the student's entry into middle school (Wise & Ginther, 1981). Its significant findings included increased student attendance, increased grade-point averages, and additional parent contact with the school. Dropout rate and disciplinary referrals

TABLE 6.8   Skills, Concepts, and Attitudes for Fostering Students' Affective Growth

Skills for the affective growth of students
- Using reflective listening
- Using "I" messages
- Using problem-solving and decision-making techniques
- Helping learners to increase self-control
- Helping learners to learn acceptable outlets for strong emotions
- Crisis counseling and intervention
- Using role-playing in the classroom
- Deliberate modeling of acceptable behavior

Concepts for the affective growth of students
- Structuring learners' work so as to ensure an adequate amount of success
- Integrating social, emotional, and cognitive skills in the classroom
- Increasing cooperation and cooperative work among learners in the classroom
- Using creative writing for affective development
- Using children's literature as a resource for affective development

Attitudes for the affective growth of students
- Increasing learners' involvement with making rules in the classroom
- Using nonpunitive discipline methods
- Using classroom activities designed to increase learners' self-esteem
- Increasing learners' acceptance of other children and adults
- Helping learners accept themselves, their families, and their own cultures
- Establishing trust between the teacher and the learner
- Having the ability to laugh at oneself

significantly decreased, and parent–child communication tended to increase for those who partici-pated in the conferences.

Parenting and teaching share many of the same pressures. Both parents and teachers are inter-ested in children's and adolescents' growth and development. Both seek to create and structure a learning environment that fosters lifelong learning. Successful parent–teacher conferences depend on interpersonal communication skills and a shared goal of the continued growth and develop-ment of youth (Fielding, 2000; McLeod, & Yates, 2006; O'Loughlin, 2006). Strother and Jacobs (1986) provided the following systematic step-by-step procedure for an effective conference (see also Figure 6.4 in the Appendix):

- *Initial contact:* Set the tone with the initial contact to the home. Convey a message of coopera-tion and indicate that you value the parents' input. A statement like "We need your opinion" or "The information you could provide us would be valuable" demonstrates a spirit of equality and openness.
- *Perception check:* Assess the parents' initial feelings about coming to school. Engage them in a dialogue that covers questions such as the following:
  - Have they had previous contact with the school?
  - Was the contact positive or negative?
  - Do the parents understand the role of the professional school counselor?
  - What are their feelings toward the school and their child's school experiences?
  - Are they willing to be part of the helping process?
- *Information delivery:* Introduce the critical information concerning the child, such as academic, behavioral, or social difficulties. Explanations should be simple and concrete. Cooperation and encouragement should be the mutual goal. The focus should be on the problem, not on the personalities of individuals who may be involved. The focus should be in the "here and now," not the "then and there." Bringing up the past is disrespectful, leaving the child with a sense of helplessness to observe opportunities to change current behavior.

- *Perception check:* Respond to the parents' feelings, thoughts, and reactions. Ask, "How are you feeling about what I've told you?" Assess their commitment and understanding. Be prepared with alternative methods of presenting information since parents differ in their knowledge, level of understanding, and school experiences. Elicit suggestions from them about potential strategies to explore.
- *Assessment of family dynamics:* Explore relationships in the family in a nonthreatening way to assess if strategies can be realistically carried out by the parent(s). Questions might include: "Are there any problems that the parents are aware of in the family regarding other children?" "Is the home atmosphere calm or tense?" "Are work schedules erratic?" "Is supervision reliable and consistent?" and "Do other family members get along?"
- *Education and strategy implementation:* Assess if the parents are willing to work cooperatively to help the child. Involve the child at this stage of the process.
- *Summarization, confirmation, and clarification:* Summarize the information discussed and presented, repeat strategies to be used to help the child, and restate what each person has agreed to do in terms of behavior changes, homework assignments, and family/school responsibilities. This may also be reinforced with a written contract signed by all parties involved, helping to solidify the agreement. Provide your name and telephone number, as well as the best time to reach you in the event the family needs some reinforcement or needs to amend the contract. Check for final questions and set a time for a follow-up meeting.
- *Follow-up for follow-through:* Follow up on plans discussed in the conference two or three days later. Express positive feelings about the conference, and offer support and encouragement. Confirm the date and time for the next meeting.

Urban and Sammartano (1989) have outlined an excellent way of turning negative comments into positive ones, which decreases defensiveness and confusion and fosters an important transition to changing children's behavior. (See Figure 6.5 in the Appendix for more discussion of positive and negative approaches to conferences.) Meyers and Pawlas (1989) maintain that for a successful conference, counselors and teachers must adhere to three main steps: preconference homework, positive communication during the conference, and follow-up, as described in Table 6.9.

STUDENT-LED CONFERENCES

Little and Allen (1989; see also Stiggins, 1994; Picciotto, 1996) maintain that professional school counselors can demonstrate support for teachers by initiating and implementing student-led conferences, especially at the elementary or middle school level. Guyton and Fielstein (1989); Conderman, Ikan, and Hatcher (2000); and Bailey and Guskey (2002) have further outlined the educational objectives of the student-led conference:

1. To foster a sense of accountability within the student for academic progress
2. To encourage students to take pride in their work
3. To allow more flexible conference time to meet the needs of all families and their children
4. To encourage student–parent communication with regard to school performance

A schedule of events prior to the parent conference could involve developing minilessons to prepare the student to handle his or her conference. Topics for the lessons could be explaining the report card and grading system, selecting examples of classroom work to support the letter grade, making subject folders for displaying daily work, identifying strengths and weaknesses, keeping a log of homework assignments and time spent on task, using effective communication for leading a conference, or discussing appropriate

TABLE 6.9 Steps for Conducting a Successful Conference

Preconference Homework
- Gather data: report cards, discipline records, and samples of student work to demonstrate improvements or declines in performance.

The Conference
- Maintain continuity and focus. If an issue comes up that was not planned for, redirect the dialogue back to current issues and note the concern on the conference sheet as a reminder. Tell the parents that notes provide a record for the meeting and that they will receive a copy. Include records of agreed-upon solutions and action plans involving the teacher and student at school and the parents at home.
- Keep the parents involved and included by limiting the amount of time the teacher talks. Teachers have been found to monopolize parent–teacher conferences by talking 75% to 98% of the allotted time (Meyers & Pawlas, 1989). It is the professional school counselor's role to keep parents involved.
- Use the conference form to make thorough notes. Before making notes, consider, "Is this in the best interest of the child, and will it help him or her succeed?" Also consider: "Is this a reasonable expectation for the teacher to carry out?" and "Is there enough commitment between the child, the parent, the teacher, and the counselor to realistically accomplish the action plan?"
- If needed, set another day for a further conference, and thank all parties for participating.

Follow-up
- Assess the conference using an evaluation tool such as that shown in Figure 6.6 (see the Appendix).
- To follow up, the teacher should contact the parents regarding progress or impediments.
- If the action plan went as planned, a simple postcard (predesigned with school logo) can be sent by the professional school counselor acknowledging progress.
- In the case of a more structured home–school intervention, weekly progress reports may be needed to exchange information and evaluate progress. To gain commitment and responsibility from the student, he or she should be responsible for picking the report up from the professional school counselor on Thursday, giving it to the teachers involved, and bringing it home on Friday so the parents can evaluate progress.
- If the conference did not go well, a phone call to the parents after the meeting could be the first step in reestablishing rapport and gaining home–school collaboration.
- Keep administrators informed of conference resolutions, action plans, and commitments and provide them with a copy of the conference report.

social conduct. Talk with students ahead of time, and have them focus on two questions: "What work are you the most proud of?" and "What areas do you think you would like to improve?"

Student-led conferences have the potential to:

- Improve student–parent communication and foster greater understanding of the child's progress and academic record
- Encourage the student to assume greater ownership and responsibility for grades and academic progress, as well as teach the student the process of self-evaluation
- Facilitate the development of the student's organizational and oral communication skills and increase self-confidence
- Increase student accountability for daily work as well as homework prior to, and in preparation for, the conference
- Eliminate the negative connotation that parent–teacher conferences often project, increase parent attendance at conferences, and strengthen parent–teacher bonds

Conflict resolution skills and mediation techniques may be needed if parents have joint custody so that the blame does not shift to one parent's sole responsibility when their child was with that parent.

The students' benefits from the student led-conferences include:

- Accountability and responsibility for being responsible for their own learning
- More productive student–teacher relationships and clarification of expectations

- Learning to be responsible for evaluating their own progress and leading the conference by doing most of the talking
- Becoming more vested in school and gaining a greater commitment to schoolwork and their own learning
- Sharing work samples, identifying strengths and areas for growth, and preparing ahead of time for the conference
- Increasing their competence, self-confidence, and self-esteem
- Encouraging student–parent communication
- Empowering them to make positive change
- Placing greater ownership and responsibility on the student and the parent
- Allowing both students and parents to become actively involved in their achievement and progress

From the parents' point of view, the benefits are that student-led conferences:

- Systematically give increased amounts of information to the parents and generally in a more positive way. Discussion is about strengths and weaknesses and areas of improvement and doesn't concentrate only on the negative attributes of student effort, behavior, and lack of follow-through. The parent listens to the child, notices students' successes and areas of growth, and avoids dominating the conference.
- Help parents learn more about their child's learning style and study skills and attitudes.
- Give parents and their child an opportunity to set positive goals that can be achieved in reasonable timeframes.
- Allow parents to become active participants and partners in their child's learning.

Teachers also benefit from student-led conferences:

- With expectations clearly outlined, the teacher helps collect samples of the students work.
- At a preconference, the teacher helps the student reflect on and analyze specific assignments, outlining strengths and areas of improvement that they would like to accomplish.
- The student-led conference is less confrontational regarding what is wrong with student performance, focusing on strengths and opportunities for achievement growth. Questions that facilitate the conference may include: "What can you tell us about this assignment?" "What did you have to do to complete this assignment?" "What skills did you have to use to complete this assignment?" and "What goals or strategies do you need to use next to time to feel more successful with your assignment?"

What continues to be true is that what parents do at home has twice as strong an influence on children's achievement as does the family's socioeconomic status. Effectively engaging parents and families in the education of their children has the potential to be far more transformational than other types of educational reform.

DEALING WITH HOSTILE PARENTS

There will always be the parent who, despite everything we may have done to be positive, helpful and involve them in the educational process, turns into a hostile person who meets you with all guns blazing. (Mamchak & Mamchak, 1980, p. 77)

The key to working with an angry parent is to avoid responding in a hostile or defensive way. Such responses contribute to a spiraling negative encounter in which both parties accuse each other of negligence and neither person listens to the other. (Seligman, 2000, p. 228)

With the increased use of technology, information—whether correct or not—often flies off the computer with very little thought of the consequences of things that were said. Social network sites contribute to both positive and negative press. Also, things that happen in the community often spill over to the school setting for resolution. Unfortunately today, schools spend more money on high-stakes testing and security than they do trying to improve interpersonal relationships among students, teachers, parents, administrators, and support staff. Seligman (2000), Whitaker and Fiore (2001), and Mamchak and Mamchak (1980) offer the following do's and don'ts for holding a parent–teacher–counselor conference that may turn hostile or volatile.

Things to Do to Promote a Positive Rather than Hostile Parent Conference

A number of helpful ideas to use when dealing with hostile, angry parents can be reduced to a few short reminders. This is the "do" list:

- First, thank the parents for coming and taking time out of their busy schedule to meet.
- Sit with them as partners—don't let your desk serve as a barrier in the conference, sending a message of superiority to the parents.
- Provide adult-size chairs for all adults, especially if meeting in an elementary classroom.
- Listen, and resist the temptation to interrupt or become defensive. Parents just want to be heard.
- Focus on problems, not personalities. Seek solutions as the primary goal.
- Ask each parent how the situation could be improved. Apologize if there was any harm done, and assure the parent that it will not happen again.
- Make only those promises you can realistically keep; for example, changing classes to a favorite teacher may not be fair for that particular teacher, and students need to learn to get along with all kinds of people in life.
- Be open to practical suggestions from parents as possible solutions (e.g., having the child sit at a new location in the lunchroom may avoid tensions with other students).
- Remember that parental anger may be due to *interaction* with a specific staff member—a secretary, attendance clerk, youth service officer, or bus driver—who may have had a bad day and not to the actions of the professional school counselor or the teacher. The parent may just need to vent.
- Suggest a neutral place to meet if the parent seems to be hostile to "everything" about the school. Neutral locations include a coffeeshop, a fast-food restaurant or food court, the public library, or a community center. Sometimes a home visit may be appropriate. Let the parent(s) know that this is not usually done (you can't be out of the building all the time), but in this case, an exception is being made.
- Emphasize the "we" in the situation as a partnership of working together for mutual satisfaction. Say things like: "We all want what's best for your child" or "What do you think we can do to deal with this problem?"
- Always document. If an incident is not documented, it technically didn't happen. Be careful about FERPA issues of confidentiality and about where you store documentation. In this age of litigation, parents are quick to take even petty issues to a higher level, such as the school administration, the school board, or a lawyer. Should you anticipate a potential problem, report your meeting and your notes to your immediate supervisor—usually the principal, the director of counseling services, or the appropriate assistant superintendent that is charge of guidance and counseling services. They appreciate knowing beforehand if a critical issue is about to come in their direction for resolution.
- Many angry, hostile parents want a listening ear as much as, if not more than, they want answers, so listen.

Things Not to Do in a Potentially Hostile Parent Conference

Just as there are helpful behaviors to use when confronting hostile parents, there are a number things to avoid:

- Do not take the parent's anger personally. The parent is probably upset about other events like child care, someone that is ill in the family, a job situation, or financial issues.
- Do not attribute motives to the parents. Undoubtedly, there are factors you know nothing about. Deal with the presenting problem and don't try to read anything else into it.
- Do not try to defend yourself or your position before the parents are finished speaking. It is counterproductive and only intensifies anger and tension. The very act of becoming defensive impedes communication.
- Do not feel that you have to meet as soon as possible at the parent's insistence. Delaying the meeting for a day will give time to collect information and perhaps let the parent's anger dissipate to a degree.
- Do not meet with the parents alone, especially if they are potentially violent or threatening. Having another administrator or counselor present will give you validation of what you heard; having another person take notes to document the meeting is acceptable. Do not be afraid to show parents any notes you have taken during the meeting.
- Do not be afraid to terminate the conference if the parents become verbally abusive or appear to be on the verge of a physical attack. Call security, and tell the parents you will meet them later when they calm down.
- Do not arrange the seating so that the parent is between you and the door. You may want to be close to the door if things get out of hand. If you are a male and meeting with a female, you might consider keeping the door open to avoid any kind of sexual harassment allegations.
- Do not have a meeting in an isolated area of the building or meet alone with parents when everyone else has left the building.
- Do not get sidetracked. The parent may attempt to steer the conversation to negative comments about other counselors, teachers, or other parents. Don't succumb to that trap. Stay on track and keep on the subject.

Finally, it is critical to create an atmosphere of warmth, openness, trust, hopefulness, respect, advocacy, collaboration, and cooperation. These are skills that the professional school counselor can model for other adults from their unique training. Teachers must display empathy and be responsive and sensitive to feelings of guilt, anger, defensiveness, or hostility on the part of the parent. A positive atmosphere can be achieved through such nonverbal skills as making eye contact, smiling, warmly shaking hands, leaning forward, nodding, and touching the parent's arm. Listening, attending, perceiving, responding, and initiating are also important interpersonal skills.

INVOLVING PARENTS IN THEIR CHILD'S ACADEMIC PERFORMANCE

Professional school counselors, by themselves, cannot bring about students' academic achievement or career development. However, the counselor can capitalize on the existing interest and commitment that parents have for their children. Although many parents may have unrealistically high expectations for their child, career counseling and academic achievement are top priorities for students and their families. Many times, constituents want a structured arena to discuss some of their anxieties about academic preparation and career planning.

Parents want validation that the program of study their child has chosen is appropriate and congruent in terms of ability, aptitude, and interest. The following suggestions are provided as interventions for counselor involvement with academic performance and career development. Methods for building parent involvement in their child's academic achievement include:

- Programs using the model of parents as tutors or home-teachers, which can increase academic performance
- Opportunities for families to supplement and reinforce their child's academic performance
- A systematic communication network for parents, particularly on the high school level, with a dual accountability strategy: (1) regular and timely newsletter communication of important dates, programs, and enrichment opportunities, and (2) early notification whenever possible if academic or interpersonal problems arise
- Explanation of a cumulative record and what it contains
- Discussion of ability as measured by standardized tests and given by category
- Discussion of achievement as measured by standardized tests and interpreted by national and/ or local percentile rank
- Examination of interests and tentative career choices, giving the student and parent an opportunity to share expectations and interests and providing fact sheets with general information on occupational job clusters and differentiated preparation programs offered at the district's high schools (honors, academic, vocational, or technical), including prerequisite grade-point averages and percentile ranks for each program and the student's potential eligibility

Strategies to Improve Academic Performance

Sometimes some very simple things can be implemented to improve student performance. Some suggestions include:

- Systematically doing homework at a specific time of day, every day.
- Doing homework in a specific study area.
- Having a study partner for difficult subjects.
- Recopying notes in an organized manner for systematic memorization.
- Following a daily schedule for the completion of work.
- Following a weekly schedule for the completion of assignments.
- Implementing a contract between teacher, students, and parents. A homework contract encourages young people to accept responsibility for an agreement made between parent and child contingent upon the completion of teacher requirements. Complying with academic requirements and performing appropriately provides certain rewards agreed upon prior to the goal.
- Incorporating time-management strategies for school, family, extracurricular, and leisure activities often creates insight in itself. Time-management skills are a critical component of anyone's maximum performance.
- Implementing a weekly "progress report" from the teacher whose subject is most difficult for the student helps to align goals, objectives, and expected performance.
- Identifying a specific academic study skill problem that a student may have, and as a team focusing on specific strategies that may remedy the problem.

Involving Parents as Career Counselors

Parents play a primary role in their child's career development, and school counseling can benefit significantly by tapping into this resource (Birk & Blimline, 1984; Daniels, Karmos, & Presely, 1983; Noeth,

Engen, & Noeth, 1984; Otto & Call, 1985; Prediger & Sawyer, 1985; Grobe, Niles, & Weisstein, 2001; Henderson, & Mapp, 2002). The following activities have a direct and indirect influence on families:

- Providing parent study groups to share current information about emerging careers, nontraditional careers, income projections, occupational outlook, and local training opportunities. These study groups could be provided through community employment services or by local colleges on a quarterly basis on the school premises. Professional school counselors merely need to coordinate the activity and "get the word out" to parents. Many agencies in the community would welcome the chance to participate, because it also increases their visibility.
- Using parents as career resource people in parent–student workshops to facilitate discussion and understanding of a particular career choice.
- Conducting student sessions of family influence on their careers to process issues such as independence and family differentiation. Techniques that can facilitate this process include family systems reviews, paradigms of family interaction, family sculpting, family constellation diagrams, occupational family trees, and exploration of family work values (Splete & Freeman-George, 1985).

CULTURAL DIVERSITY IN THE UNITED STATES: A PHENOMENON THAT CAN'T BE IGNORED

According to 2008 U.S. Bureau of the Census figures:

> Minorities, now roughly one-third of the U.S. population, are expected to become the majority in 2042, with the nation projected to be 54% minority in 2050. By 2023, minorities will comprise more than half of all children. The Latino population is projected to nearly triple from 46.7 million to 132.8 million during the 2008–2050 period. The Latino share of the nation's total population is projected to double from 15%–30%. The African-American population is projected to increase from 41.1 million, or 14% of the population in 2008, to 65.7 million, or 15% in 2050. The Asian population is projected to climb from 15.5 million to 40.6 million to rise from 5.1% to 9.2% of the nation's population. American Indians and Alaska Natives are projected to rise from 4.9 million to 8.6 million or from 1.6–2% of the total population, Native Hawaiian and Other Pacific Islander populations are expected to more than double from 1.1 million to 2.6 million. In addition, people who identify themselves as being of two or more races is projected to more than triple, from 5.2 million to 16.2 million. (U.S. Census Bureau, 2008b, p. 3)

Projections into the 21st century reveal that by 2020, most school-age children attending public schools will come from diverse cultural and ethnic backgrounds (Campbell, 1994). Non-Latino whites will no longer represent the majority of the population, but rather will constitute another minority group among the host of racial and ethnic groups composing America's growing mosaic of diversity. This represents a significant shift in demographics and will require innovation and flexibility in programs and services to meet the needs of a diverse population.

Research supports the idea that children's early childhood experiences are powerful in influencing their cultural understanding (Banks, 1993, 2004). Children develop ideas about racial identity and the attributes of cultural groups other than their own as early as age 3. One of the most critical challenges facing the field of school counseling today, therefore, is the preparation of professional school counselors who are able to address the needs of an increasingly diverse student population and their families (Coleman, 1995; House & Martin, 1998; Lee, 1995; Lewis & Hayes, 1991; Banks, 2004; Durodoye, 1998; Hobson & Kanitz, 1996; Johnson, 1995). Multicultural counseling competence refers to counselors' attitudes, beliefs, knowledge, and skills in working with individuals from different cultural groups, including racial, ethnic, gender, social class, and sexual orientation (Arredondo et al., 1996; Sue & Sue, 2003).

A useful model for working with diverse learners is the ecological model developed by Bronfenbrenner (1979) and enhanced by Knoff (1986) and Nuttall, Romero, and Kalesnik (1992). The proponents of this model maintain that to understand or evaluate a student, one must assess the student—conceptualized as a microsystem—in the context of his or her mesosystems (immediate family, extended family, friends, and network); macrosystems (culture or subculture); and exosystems (social structures). The ability to conceptualize and integrate culture and issues of diversity within a developmental perspective is also important. The changes in developmental tasks at each life stage and the various ways that these "tasks" are expressed and resolved within various cultural groups are also important (Lee, 1995). These issues must be integrated within the specialized early intervention programs offered to children with developmental issues. Early intervention services are critical for this population in the schools because such learners are more vulnerable to developmental concerns.

Work with specific cultural groups, such as Lock's (1995) work on interventions with African American youth, Jackson's (1995) on counseling youth of Arab ancestry, Thomason's (1995) on counseling Native Americans, Zapata's (1995) on working with Latinos, and Yagi and Oh's (1995) on interventions with Asian American youth, provide valuable guidelines on working with specific populations and generate awareness of the specific cultural factors relevant to that particular cultural group. Knowledge and the potential to assess specific factors such as acculturation, language proficiency, and sociocultural history further enhance the provisions of culturally affirming treatment strategies (Paniagua, 1994; Vazquez-Nuttall, DeLeon, & Valle, 1990). The need to deal with diverse groups also includes work with sexual minority youths who have developmental issues regarding openness and peer tolerance (LaFontaine, 1994).

Strategies that support children's multicultural learning within a context of family involvement fall into three categories: parent education and support, school–family curriculum activities, and teacher–parent partnership efforts (Banks, 1993, 2004, 2005; Swick & Graves, 1993; Bank Street College of Education. 2006; Barrera, 2003; Derman-Sparks, 2006; Grant, 2007; and Howard, 2006).

Parent education and support includes offering a lending library of books, articles, and videos; bulletin boards of events, ideas, and suggestions; parenting programs; and newsletters. It is difficult for immigrant parents to become actively involved in the school because of their lack of familiarity with American school systems. The need for direct work with parents and communities has been stressed by Atkinson and Juntunen (1994): "School personnel must function as a school–home–community liaison, as an interface between school and home, school and community, and home and community" (p. 108). Casas and Furlong (1994) stress the advocacy role professional school counselors play to both "increase parent participation and facilitate increased empowerment" (p. 121) of parents and the community.

School–family curriculum activities include discussion groups on racial or cultural issues; events in which parents as well as teachers and children celebrate their cultural diversity; parent participation in specific classroom curriculum activities (Ramsey & Derman-Sparks, 1992); and field trips and classroom presentations with discussion to explore concerns and ideas (Neugebauer, 1992). Displays throughout the classroom that include representatives of people from diverse racial, ethnic, and cultural backgrounds engaged in meaningful activities are also important. Original class books should include class directories; friendship or family books; activity books; collections of photographs, drawings, and writings; or music and drama to support children's ethnic, racial, and cultural understandings. Specific objectives for school counselors to ease the transition of students could include the following:

- Develop and display family trees for students. Note and celebrate the differences and origins of each child (nation, language, culture). Encourage parents, grandparents, and other relatives to come to the classroom to speak with children.
- Encourage and support discussions about individual differences. Answer the curious questions children inevitably ask about physical characteristics of their classmates. Use this as an opportunity to talk about different family structures (e.g., foster parents, adoptive, two-parent, single-parent, skip-generation parents, interracial, extended and multicultural families).

- Expand the concept of one's cultural background to include multiple cultural heritages. Become aware of the unspoken message in some cultural heritage celebrations that communicates that each child needs to identify with one cultural group; encourage pride in multicultural families and societies.
- Emphasize that diversity goes beyond the acknowledgment of racial groups to include biracial individuals, different lifestyles, and gender orientation. The more children are exposed to the notion that "different" does not mean "abnormal," the more opportunity there is to promote tolerance.
- Be sensitive to the dilemmas of biracial children when topics pertaining to personal and group identity are being presented. Maximize cultural sensitivity and provide children with the opportunity for self-examination.
- Avoid curriculum materials, discussions, and activities that divide the country and world into neat, distinct racial and ethnic groups. Support the richness and diversity of humanity in the classroom.
- Provide many activities where students can learn about their physical characteristics and feel positive about these traits. Drawing, painting, and making collages with flesh-tone colors and realistic qualities will help reinforce natural differences in a positive manner.
- Develop activities that help children understand ways in which all kids are the same. Discuss the things that unite all children worldwide.

Parent–teacher partnerships—classroom study teams, school advisory groups, multicultural planning sessions for input on school policy—are empowering (Ramsey & Derman-Sparks, 1992). Storytelling by parents, grandparents, neighbors, and teachers about a culture and its development and about struggles to achieve respect in the community is genuinely helpful.

> As human development specialists, professional school counselors will be called upon to be proactive, collaborative, and integrative in providing services to students and their families. In terms of multicultural relationships, school counselors must be multifaceted, inclusionary, developmental, continuous, and community supported. (Johnson, 1995, p. 124)

Locke (1990) articulated basic guidelines regarding the attitudes and behaviors associated with culturally responsive counseling:

- Be open to culturally different values and attitudes.
- Learn about different cultures and their mores.
- Retain the uniqueness of each child by avoiding stereotyping within cultural groups.
- Encourage students to be open about their cultural backgrounds.
- Learn about one's own culture and cultural values.
- Participate in activities in students' cultural community.
- Eliminate all personal behaviors that suggest bias or prejudice.
- Hold high expectations for students across all cultural groups.

The following strategies provide responsive and proactive approaches to meet the needs of an increasingly diverse student population (Johnson, 1995):

- *Human relations training.* Establish human relations training opportunities for all students to promote understanding and acceptance of differences.
- *Recognition and acknowledgment.* Produce a calendar of religious holidays and ethnic festivals to be used in schools as a means of promoting recognition and respect for divergent cultures represented in the school.
- *Orientation and transition services.* Work with English as a second language (ESL) or English-language learner (ELL) teachers and community resources to provide significant

support in their transition to a new environment by assessing prior academic background, determining course equivalencies, testing for placement, and advising about current academic standards.

- *Peer helper programs.* Address school/community multicultural needs by establishing a peer helper program and train the participants to work with other students on issues relating to adjusting to their new school experience.
- *Conflict resolution and peer mediation programs.* Implement a peer mediation program to teach students alternative ways of resolving conflicts through discussion and mediation rather than by aggression and violence.
- *Small group counseling.* Plan small group counseling activities that explore and nurture the importance of self-identity and interpersonal relationships. Groups that emphasize self-appreciation through heritage in which members share family cultural traditions, their fears, and their goals can provide much-needed support to minority students.
- *Bibliotherapy.* Students can gain greater understanding of their own situations or the situations of others by reading about characters or conflicts with which they can identify.
- *Classroom guidance and Teacher Advisor (TA) programs.* Incorporate multicultural awareness units into classroom, group guidance, and TA programs to increase sensitivity and acceptance of cultural diversity as students confront social, educational, and career development concerns.

Professional school counselors, as human relations specialists, can use their unique training to assist teachers, administrators, and students and their families attain optimum adjustment and acceptance in their new community.

PREVENTION AND INTERVENTION FOR FAMILIES UNDER STRESS

In the past, children and adolescents with school-related problems were often understood to be anxious, acting-out, depressed, immature, passive-aggressive, or emotionally disturbed. Today, however, children's and adolescents' classroom behaviors are explained as a function of the levels of health and stress in their family systems. Minuchin, Nichols, and Lee (2007); and Spencer, Jordan, and Sazama (2004) offer lists of the differences in behavior between functional and dysfunctional families.

Functional families:

- Use humor, praise, and encouragement
- Respect and prize each other
- Communicate clearly
- Solve family problems effectively and democratically
- Perform fairly and consistently
- Use effective disciplinary methods
- Touch affectionately

Dysfunctional families:

- Use criticism, put-downs, and sarcasm
- Devalue or envy each other
- Communicate poorly and infrequently
- Cannot solve family problems without resorting to power and autocratic decisions
- Perform autocratically and inconsistently

- Use ineffective corporal punishment methods
- Use touch as a control method

The amount of stress and family dysfunction has increased proportionally with the number of school-age youth from single-parent and disrupted families. Primary prevention strategies need to focus on education through parent support groups. Concurrently, early intervention strategies should focus on counselor-assisted procedures to empower parents in caring for their children.

Baruth and Burggraf (1983) have suggested that parent study groups be developed for the purpose of helping families. They have developed the following guidelines for helping professionals start such study groups:

- Inform parents about study groups by providing basic information, such as the time and place for the group's meeting. Letters sent home with children or public announcements in local media can be helpful in keeping parents informed, as can the Internet, websites, and email.
- Limit the size of the group to between 8 and 12 parents to foster better parental communication.
- Set the time and place for the meetings, preferably around the parents' schedule.
- Plan meetings to last two hours on a weekly basis for 10 sessions.
- Establish a deadline by which parents can enter the study group, and add no new members after two sessions have been completed.
- Before teaching a parent study group, first participate as a group member, and then co-lead a group with supervision.

Parent networks and support groups aimed at restoring supportive family interactions by promoting positive communication are gaining momentum in every community across the nation. Small grassroots groups of parents have generated enormous attention as they empower parents to intervene in their child's life. Combating peer pressure and its lure toward alcohol and drug abuse is one example of such initiatives.

The school and the professional school counselor should focus on extending the parent groups' potential to operate independently. Definition of community goals and activities should be parent generated. The professional school counselor should lend support and resources such as:

- Speaking or assisting with arrangements for other speakers
- Providing films, articles, brochures, and resource lists of materials and curricula
- Training groups in planning, evaluation, and prevention of self-destructive behaviors among adolescents
- Assisting in the design and implementation of community needs assessment
- Facilitating interagency cooperation
- Maintaining a community calendar and mailing list
- Coordinating information in the community newspaper

GUIDELINES FOR DECIDING WHETHER TO COUNSEL OR REFER TO FAMILY THERAPY

Differentiating families experiencing reactions to recent stress from those with chronic, long-standing problems is important. The former are probably appropriate to counsel, the latter should be referred to other helping professionals. All families experience temporary stress associated with typical life crises in the family cycle (e.g., birth, loss, separation, deployment). Healthy families may need only supportive counseling during these times, whereas unhealthy families probably need referral because they have fewer coping mechanisms. In general, it is appropriate to offer supportive counseling to families in transition (e.g., adjusting to a birth or remarriage) and to families of children with behavior problems of recent origin (e.g., a child who is just beginning to show behavior problems).

Situations that reflect more chronic problems, and therefore referral for more intensive help, include families exhibiting chemical dependency or abuse (therapy for this problem is highly specialized and the problem is often transgenerational); families with long-standing problems (e.g., chronic marital difficulties or a child with serious behavioral problems); families with a history of psychiatric disturbance in the family (e.g., debilitating depression, anxiety, psychosis, or other conditions requiring medications and/or hospitalization); and families with serious, acute problems, particularly child abuse, spouse abuse, or incest. These are life-threatening situations, which are more appropriately managed by professionals with special training.

CONCLUSION

Consultation by professional school counselors is an effective, preventive intervention to enhance overall academic achievement, increase self-esteem in students, and improve classroom management skills (Bundy & Poppen, 1986; Cecil & Cobia, 1990; ASCA, 2005a). Helping children with learning and/or behavioral difficulties, assisting individual children with special needs, developing appropriate learning activities, and encouraging a productive classroom environment are fundamental roles for professional school counselors to play. Parent involvement is crucial to a comprehensive school counseling program. Empowering parents to interact with the school and assessing their children's needs for programs and services cannot be understated. Positive experiences help to prove the value of a school counselor when administrators and important stakeholders confront budget constraints that force them to make choices about resources for their particular schools. When addressing the critical issues of school safety, a superintendent shouldn't have to decide between a school resource officer and a professional school counselor. Schools need both—one for intervention (the resource officer) and one for primary prevention (the professional school counselor). As the old saying goes, "It's easier to build a child than repair a man."

APPENDIX

TABLE 6.10 Professional School Counselor as Consultant and Advocate: An Adjective Checklist

Collaborator	Conceptualizer
Stabilizer	Facilitator
Educator	Inquirer
Synthesizer	Evaluator
Innovator	Energizer
Change agent	Organizer
Analyzer	Catalyst
Reframer	Data gatherer
Advocate	Liaison
Negotiator	Skilled helper
Conflict manager	Mediator
Team player	Motivator
Transformer	Ambassador

TABLE 6.11 Stages of Consultation

STAGE	SKILL	FUNCTIONS
Establishing the Relationship	Acceptance	Consultant expresses concern.
	Active Listening	Teacher presents more data.
	Acknowledging Strengths	Teacher has had success in the past and the counselor recognizes that the setback is temporary.
	Active Listening	Consultant is beginning to grasp the magnitude of teacher's problem.
Identifying the Problem	Feedback	Based on information obtained from the classroom.
	Active Listening and Feedback	
	Concreteness	The consultant wants the teacher to be more specific.
	Commitment	The teacher has stated readiness to do something and a specific behavior has been identified.
	Active Listening	Clarification of the problem.
	Test Alternatives	The consultant and teacher together develop a list of strategies that might work.
Facilitating Change	Support	The consultant agrees and reinforces what the teacher has been saying.
		A summary plan of what the teacher is going to do is developed.
	Action	

TABLE 6.12 Consultation Activities

ADMINISTRATORS	TEACHERS	PARENTS	STUDENTS
Plan school/community needs assessment	Implement teacher advisor (TA) program	Facilitate positive home–school partnerships	Develop peer counseling, peer tutoring, peer listening, peer mediation programs
Identify students with special needs	Identify and intervene in deficiencies in academic or personal development	Join in volunteer program	Provide leadership training
Support instructional partnerships	Provide in-service in life skills, crisis intervention, logical consequences, classroom management, special education, primary prevention, early intervention	Conduct parent education groups	Provide groups on life skills, communication, stress management, decision making, time management, conflict resolution, study skills, self-esteem, wellness, children of alcoholics
Facilitate community and parent–school relations		Provide workshops on developmental needs of children, college planning, financial aid, postsecondary training, adolescent stress, parenting skills, drug education	
Assist in promoting a positive school climate	Develop remedial or prescriptive program for target populations		
Integrate the counseling program into school goals and objectives	Provide a team effort in home–school partnerships		

TABLE 6.13   Elements of Effective Parent–Teacher Conferencing

TEACHER INITIATED	COMMON ELEMENTS	PARENT INITIATED
Prepare for conference in advance.	Allow enough time.	Positively identify parent requesting meeting.
Give parent(s) some idea of topic.	Determine whether student should be present.	If parent shares topic, collect necessary background information.
Specify points to be made.	Do not become defensive; maintain open mind.	Have pertinent student records accessible for conference.
Prepare written progress report to include: 1. survey of student 2. areas of concern 3. areas of strength.	Listen to what parent is saying, specifically and implicitly.	Do not make assumptions; ask teacher(s) or administrators to express concern.
Don't wait for regularly scheduled conference if a matter arises; deal with it.	Seek clarification when necessary.	Get complete story before suggesting actions or solutions.
Structure conference for parent(s): why, what, when; explain purpose.	Avoid overwhelming parent(s) with irrelevant material or use of jargon; be thorough.	
Allow parent(s) time to read and/or discuss written summary.	Meet parent(s) at building entry point if possible.	
	Show parent concern and respect—respect as person, concern as patron of school; maintain positive, professional demeanor.	
	Make environment for conference conducive to open communication; avoid physical barriers.	
	Attempt to part on positive note; set up future conference or referral procedures before parent leaves.	
	Be sure to carry out any promised follow-up.	

Source: Rotter, J. C., & Robinson, E. H., *Parent–teacher conferencing,* National Education Association, Washington, DC, 1982. Reprinted by permission.

TABLE 6.14   Positive and Negative Approaches to Parent–Teacher Conferencing

NEGATIVE APPROACHES	POSITIVE APPROACHES	SUPPORTING DETAILS
He/she wastes half the morning fooling around.	He/she has so much energy and curiosity that he/she sometimes has trouble keeping focused on classwork.	He/she talks to his/her friends and looks around to see what others are doing.
When something is difficult to understand, he/she won't even try.	He/she is a good worker when familiar with the material. It's important to apply the same habit to material that he/she is less familiar with.	When the work is difficult, he/she asks to leave the room, tears up papers, and throws the book on the floor.

TABLE 6.14   Positive and Negative Approaches to Parent–Teacher Conferencing (continued)

NEGATIVE APPROACHES	POSITIVE APPROACHES	SUPPORTING DETAILS
If he/she doesn't know or like you, you know it. He/she teases and makes fun of children.	He/she is very perceptive regarding other children's strengths as well as their weaknesses, but he/she uses that edge to taunt others.	He/she knows what makes others self-conscious (weight, height, braces) and points it out, calling them names (porky, shorty, metal head).
He/she is disrespectful to adults.	He/she often challenges and debates well, which is appropriate in some academic classes, but it's important to learn the limits of an appropriate debate.	He/she questions why he/she has to put a book away, line up for a fire drill, and sit quietly in his/her seat.
He/she is immature.	He/she relates better with younger children in the group.	He/she is very shy around more confident children and clowns around to get attention. When disciplined, he/she cries easily.
Peers tease and taunt him/her, making him/her the scapegoat and the victim of humiliation.	He/she works hard and is very polite, but seems to have trouble gaining the respect of classmates.	The others tease him/her about glasses and front teeth.

Source: Adapted from Urban, D., & Sammartano, R., *Learning, 18*(3), 47, 1989.

TABLE 6.15   Effective Conference Continuum

	ALWAYS	SOMETIMES	NEVER
Was the tone and "opening" of the conference designed to help all members feel comfortable?	—	—	—
Were parents given some idea in advance of the topic to be discussed?	—	—	—
Was enough time allowed for the conference?	—	—	—
Was the emotional climate of the conference positive?	—	—	—
Was problem solving directed at personalities or behavior?	—	—	—
Was there a balance between positive and negative remarks?	—	—	—
Did colleagues avoid becoming defensive when parents question judgment or procedures?	—	—	—
Did colleagues and parents maintain an open mind to problem-solving ideas?	—	—	—
Were the goals of the conference understood by all persons present?	—	—	—
Were the goals of the conference met?	—	—	—
Were efforts made to include the student in the conference to establish goals and to reinforce resolutions?	—	—	—
Were efforts made to avoid overwhelming parent(s) with the presence of other school personnel?	—	—	—
Were efforts made to avoid overwhelming parent(s) with irrelevant material or use of "educanese"?	—	—	—
Was the closure of the conference appropriate?	—	—	—
Were there provisions made to follow up on commitments?	—	—	—

The Professional School Counselor's Role in Academic and Career Planning

7

> To maintain and enhance our quality of life, we must develop a leading-edge economy based on workers who can think for a living. If skills are equal, in the long run wages will be, too. This means we have to educate a vast mass of people capable of thinking critically, creatively, and imaginatively.
>
> Donald Kennedy, President, Stanford University (Stanford University News Service, 1991)

THE NEGATIVE OUTCOMES OF DROPPING OUT OF SCHOOL

Dropping out of high school is related to a number of negative outcomes, among them unemployment, welfare dependence, poor health, and a vulnerability for criminal activity because of the lack of legitimate employment opportunities for unskilled and uneducated workers. To demonstrate economic disparities, the median income of persons age 25 or older who did not complete high school was roughly $23,400 in 2007 (Baum & Ma, 2007). By comparison, the median income of persons age 25 or older who did complete their high school education—including those with a General Educational Development (GED) certificate—was approximately $31,500 (Cataldi, Laird, & KewalRamani, 2009). Persons with some college but no degree earned $37,100; those with an associate's degree earned $40,600; with a bachelor's degree, $50,900; with a master's degree, $61,300; with a doctoral degree, $79,400; and with a professional degree, $100,000 (Baum & Ma, 2007). Essentially, education pays in terms of improved health, wealth, well-being, and capacity to be a productive member of society.

Ninety percent of the fastest growing jobs in America require a postsecondary credential for training (Snyder, Dillow, & Hoffman, 2009), yet only 38% of all 18- to 24-year-olds are currently enrolled in postsecondary education (Berkner & Choy, 2008). In addition, about 60% of manufacturing companies say high school graduates are poorly prepared for entry-level jobs (Amos, 2008). What continues to emerge is a tremendous gap between job preparation and postsecondary education that is having a tremendous impact on the economy and American society. The percentage of 25- to 34-year-olds in the United States who have completed a postsecondary education or training program is lower than the percentage of graduates in Canada, Japan, Korea, Sweden, Belgium, Ireland, and Norway (Baum & Ma, 2007).

The poverty rate for families of college graduates is only 3.6, but for families with less than a high school diploma, the rate increases to 24%. For single mothers without a high school diploma, the poverty rate doubles to 49% (Amos, 2008). Further, dropouts make up disproportionately higher percentages of the nation's prison and death-row inmates (Pleis & Lethbridge-Çejku, 2006). Approximately 75% of state prison inmates and 59% of federal inmates did not complete high school, and many of them cannot even read (Harlow, 2003; Baum & Ma, 2007). It costs approximately $26,000 annually to care for a prisoner

(Harlow, 2003)—about the same as for a four-year public education. Essentially, in the long run, it is cheaper to send a student to "Penn State than the state pen."

INCOME, RACE, AND ETHNICITY GAPS

With regard to income, race, and ethnicity gaps, the disparities in postsecondary enrollment rates continue to be problematic. Regrettably, African American and Latino students, as well as low-income students, are less likely to matriculate from a college or university with a baccalaureate degree (Baum & Ma, 2007). Latinos have been continually overrepresented in low-skill and service sector jobs. One of the cultural variables accounting for this is the educational experience of the Latino community, which has been characterized by low high school graduation rates, substandard school environments, and subsequent low college/university completion rates (Chapa & De la Rosa, 2004; Fry, 2002, 2003).

This situation is exacerbated by the barrier of low income that many first-generation college students encounter. Many do not have the same access to college and postsecondary school information or the support needed to navigate the college application process, financial aid applications, and SAT or ACT preparation. This lack of information and support is a significant barrier (Roderick et al., 2008). Low-income students and minorities require greater access to structured social and academic support groups, with programs like AVID (Advancement via Individual Determination), peer support, mentoring, parent involvement, and early college preparation and planning opportunities and experiences that are systematically delivered by teachers specially trained to motivate and teach this population.

PROFESSIONAL SCHOOL COUNSELORS' ROLE IN BRIDGING THE GAP

Professional school counselors need to change the current mind-set of providing postsecondary and career services to only a select few advanced students. Research has demonstrated that when professional school counselors are available consistently and frequently to students and their families, they can significantly expand students' educational aspirations, increase students' academic achievement, and increase college enrollment and graduation rates (McDonough, 2005). The single most consistent predictor of whether students took action to prepare for college was whether their school fostered a postsecondary education college/university culture for all students (Roderick et al., 2008).

Professional school counselors provide a wide range of services to students, including academic advising, career planning, career/postsecondary pathway counseling, mental health and personal counseling, drug abuse and violence prevention, and parent and teacher consultation. Retaining a concerted focus on these responsibilities is essential to improving student achievement and eliminating barriers to learning. To accomplish all of this, it is imperative that professional school counselors eliminate administrative and other duties unrelated to school counseling.

CAREER THEORIES 101: THE NEED FOR ACCURATE CAREER AND OCCUPATIONAL INFORMATION

A *career theory* is a cognitive map to make sense of occupational interests, abilities, and aptitude as well as career experiences and opportunities. Theories help describe, explain, generalize, and summarize what counselors do in helping students and their families make informed responsible career decisions.

Career development and selection is an interaction of psychological, sociological, economic, cultural, and chance factors that shape the sequence of jobs, occupations, or careers a person may have throughout a lifetime. (*Career development, occupational development,* and *vocational development* are used interchangeably in the literature.) Career development is a significant aspect of human development and often influences economic status, self-worth, career roles, and meaning and relatedness in life. Feller and Whichard (2005) define *career development* as "expanding from a focus on mechanistic matching of people to a list of existing choice to creating opportunities from things that don't presently exist" (p. 15).

Theories give counselors a foundation for organizing information about the student in order to formulate appropriate career and educational goals. Career development theory has the following objectives:

- To understand the relationship between further education and training and the occupational outlook of the potential job market
- To bridge gaps between knowledge and the unknown about career opportunities
- To explain current timely information, summarize information, and make informed decisions
- To understand the financial implications, cost/benefits, and resources that are currently available for further training and the current job market
- To understand one's strengths, weaknesses, goals, and responsibilities to make informed, responsible, and realistic decisions

What continues to be constant in the current career climate today is change. The number of adults in career transition has significantly increased over the last three decades, and the unemployment rate has soared to the highest it has been in the past 25 years. As adults search for meaningful work, they have experienced downsizing in the workplace, outsourcing of their jobs to foreign countries whose employees will work for less pay, disparity between current work content and reformulated company goals, feelings of isolation in the work environment, despair about the future, and a slowing economy. Many people fear they may no longer have marketable skills, while others lack basic skills for an increasingly technology-savvy workplace.

There is a significant relationship between skill development and employment opportunities, and there is a critical skill gap between current and emerging job requirements. Loyalty is no longer valued as it was in the past, since employers would rather rely on temporary workers or contract workers. The company no longer feels the need to nurture and guide individual career paths. Therefore, the onus is on the individual. Those workers who have developed ongoing career transitions skills and are lifelong learners will feel more empowered and more in control of their lives in an uncertain global economy.

A solid knowledge base in a theory provides a meaningful conceptual framework for working with clients. However, economic climate and potential career opportunity changes are always a factor, so there is a need to be flexible when looking for an initial job and to be creative in marketing oneself in the current job climate. The ability to use a number of theories and career approaches equips aspiring professional school counselors to determine and meet the unique needs of each individual. Table 7.1 provides a quick reference to current career theories and perspectives.

Professional school counselors must be cautious because a monocultural perspective of universally shared beliefs, attitudes, and worldviews has dominated career counseling practice and research and does not consider the growing diversity of our current society. It is important to acknowledge that no single theory of career development is all-inclusive and comprehensive. At best, it is a conceptual map, like the 16 career clusters included in the chapter. Using a more holistic approach to students and their families means pulling from a combination of career development theories and strategies and making students aware of their potential and their opportunities.

TABLE 7.1　Career Theories at a Glance

THEORY	MAJOR PROPONENT(S)	APPROACH TO CAREER COUNSELING AND ASSESSMENTS
STRUCTURAL THEORIES		
Trait and Factor Theory	Frank Parsons and Edmund G. Williamson	Trait and factor theory focuses on the match between an individual's aptitude, achievements, interests, and values and the requirements and conditions of particular occupations. It is possible to identify a fit or match between individual traits and job factors using a straightforward problem-solving/decision-making process between counselor and client.
Theory of Work Adjustment (TWA)	Rene V. Dawis and Lloyd H. Lofquist	Work is an interaction between an individual and a work environment and a clearer application of trait and factor theory. An individual's abilities and values can be predictive of work adjustment and length of time on a particular job, if the ability requirements and reinforce patterns are known satisfaction is achieved between both parties especially if work personality and work environment match. Major assessment contribution: Minnesota Importance Questionnaire, which measures an individual's work needs.
Holland's Theory of Types	John Holland 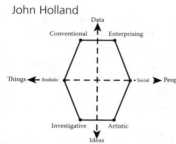	Holland's career typology theory focuses on individual characteristics and occupational tasks. A typology theory of six personality types, it focuses on six broad categories: Realistic, Investigative, Artistic, Social, Enterprising, and Conventional (RIASEC). These six personality types can be matched to respective work environments. Assessment contributions: Holland's *Self-Directed Search*, the *Vocational Preference Inventory,* and the *Strong Interest Inventory.*
DEVELOPMENTAL THEORIES		
Life-Span Theory of Career Development	Donald Super	Super has generated a life-span vocational choice theory that has five life and career development stages. It formalizes stages and developmental tasks over the life span. People change over time, in their life roles, and in their experience, and they progress through the following developmental stages. • *Growth* (Birth to age 14 or 15): Form self-concept; develop capacity, attitudes, interests, and needs; and form a general understanding of the world of work. • *Exploratory* (15–24): "Try out" through classes, work experience, hobbies; collect relevant information. Tentative choice and related skill development. • *Establishment* (25–44): Entry skill-building and stabilization through work experience. • *Maintenance* (45–64): Continual adjustment process to improve position.

TABLE 7.1   Career Theories at a Glance (continued)

THEORY	MAJOR PROPONENT(S)	APPROACH TO CAREER COUNSELING AND ASSESSMENTS
		• *Decline* (65+): Reduced output, preparing for retirement. These stages change as the current economic and job market changes. Since people are living longer, they have a tendency to work longer and stay active, which has proven a contributing factor to longevity.
Krumboltz's Social Learning Theory of Career Choice	John D. Krumboltz	Krumboltz's theory of career development was based on making career decisions via social learning experiences between encounters with significant people, institutions, and events in one's particular community or environment. Essentially, the four factors that influence career choice are 1.) genetic factors and special abilities, 2.) community or environmental conditions, 3.) learning experiences, and 4.) task approach skills, i.e., the skills the individual applies to new tasks. The influence of significant others in the life of youths (coaches, teachers, positive role models) have a powerful influence on career decisions.
Constructivist Theory: An Existential Approach	Mark L. Savickas, Vance Peavy, and Pam Brott	This is more of a philosophical framework. It holds that there are multiple meanings and multiple perspectives in the career world and that people "construct" their own meaning or reality from the interpretations they make and the experiences they take from it. The client and counselor explore new constructs of one's life/work/self through a number of techniques, including: life-space map, life line, life-space genogram, life roles circles, life roles assessment, life role analysis, and goal map (Brott, 2001) as a means for looking at life roles and career satisfaction.
Contemporary Cultural Context in Career Theory		The long-standing emphasis in career psychology on person variables, trait and factor theory, and neglecting community and environmental variables' relevance across cultural groups (i.e., race, culture, and ethnicity) is beginning to raise considerable debate when looking at career theories as they currently exist. According to Leong and Brown's (1995) evaluation, "The central problem with most, if not all, of the majority of career theories is their lack of cultural validity for racial and ethnic minorities in this country" (p. 145). Osipow and Fitzgerald (1996) further stated that "possibly the most profound challenge to the generalizability of career development theories and counseling practices is posed by the assertion that many racial/ethnic minority individuals do not share the value systems on which the traditional career explanations are based" (p. 275).

THE SUPERFLUITY OF THE INFORMATION AGE: TODAY'S REALITY

The explosion of knowledge and technology in mathematics, science, and information technology and a rapidly emerging global economy require systemic reforms at all levels of education K–16. New performance standards and advanced technologies have changed the educational requirements of the workforce. Many formerly middle-class jobs, particularly those that can be outsourced outside of the United States, are more at risk. Friedman (2006) maintains that "in a flat world there is no such thing as an American job. There is just a job, and in more cases than ever before it will go to the best, smartest, most productive or cheapest worker—wherever he or she resides" (p. 277).

Skills once demanded only of white-collar workers and technical elites are now required for everyone. International competition and new technologies dictate the need for a well-educated workforce. In a recent report entitled "Are They Really Ready to Work?" (Conference Board, Partnership for 21st Century Skills, Corporate Voices for Working Families, & Society for Human Resource Management, 2006), researchers wrote:

> Creativity/Innovation is projected to "increase in importance" for future workforce entrants, according to more than 70% of employer respondents. Currently, however, more than half of employer respondents (54.2%) report new workforce entrants with a high school diploma to be "deficient" in this skill set, and relatively few consider two-year and four-year college-educated entrants to be "excellent" (4.1% and 21.5%, respectively). (p. 10)

Participatory management, sophisticated quality control, decentralized production services, and increased use of information-based technology are now common practice in both large and small businesses. These changes have increased the autonomy, responsibilities, and value of personnel at all organizational levels, which in turn calls for workers with higher levels of academic competencies and broader technical knowledge. These new skills are categorized as follows:

- Academic basics: reading, writing, computing
- Adaptability skills: learning to learn, creative thinking, problem solving
- Self-management skills: self-esteem, goal setting, motivation, employability, and career development
- Social skills: interpersonal, negotiation, teamwork
- Communication skills: listening, oral communication
- Influencing skills: organizational effectiveness, leadership

The workplace of the 21st century has demonstrated more varied avenues and pathways to careers than in the past. The difference between high-paying and low-paying jobs will become more pronounced and will be based on the employee's ability to learn new information and act quickly on that information. *Self-directed learners* (i.e., people who can select what to learn and then teach themselves) will be expected in this new work environment. This is an important skill now, but it will be even more vital in the future. *Problem solvers* who can look at vast amounts of data and information and select the important points, put them together, and evaluate their own results are always in demand, but in the 21st century, those skills will be expected of all individuals. Changes in the workplace from the present to the future include:

- A shift from task to project
- An increase in teamwork
- An ability to work without direct supervision

- Increased opportunities to work from home
- An increase in worker flexibility
- A requirement that workers be willing to learn on an ongoing basis
- A mastery of traditional basic academic skills as a starting point for job success
- A higher level of cognitive ability, creativity, and ability to articulate career assets in creative ways will be required for all workers
- A movement toward individual responsibility and toward workers as stakeholders
- An increased understanding of global economic principles

THE PROFESSIONAL SCHOOL COUNSELOR AS CAREER DEVELOPMENT SPECIALIST

The professional school counselor will assume a greater role in career development and in the relationship between educational preparation and career preparation. To improve course sequence planning, counselors will rewrite student literature concerning school requirements to reflect a course of study adequate for employment and postsecondary learning. Responsibilities include:

- Developing programs orienting students, parents, and teachers to the skills needed in postsecondary education and within the workplace
- Providing students with annual interest and aptitude assessments to help them plan their academic and career options
- Establishing a comprehensive, developmental school counseling program with a curriculum that enhances career development knowledge, skills, and abilities

CAREER EXPLORATION AND COUNSELING INITIATIVES

Career exploration and counseling will transcend the curriculum, the school, and the community, as well as business and industry. Career awareness activities are essential for promoting the relationship of academics and the world of work. A comprehensive, coordinated career counseling network is essential to increasing intelligent career choices and educational planning, as well as providing transitional services and programs. This effort includes familiarizing students with many different job/career options, providing information on requirements for success, and leading students to explore their own interests and aptitudes. Every student should receive an individualized career and educational plan that specifically outlines coursework and academic options.

In addition, all teachers, professional school counselors, and support staff will need to become career path advisors to students, providing information on career possibilities and the relationship to curriculum and instruction in their particular discipline. For example, what career opportunities are available for a student with interests in such subjects as English, mathematics, science, or technology? It is important to make the connection between coursework and potential career opportunities systematically throughout the curriculum. The primary goals will be to

- Accelerate academic learning
- Organize around a career theme to prepare for further study

- Motivate students who have ability but may lack effort
- Involve parents and the community at large

The Internet and significant websites have evolved as a viable resource for college information, career information, and financial aid and scholarship opportunities. Professional school counselors should link these resources and websites to the school's own website.

SCHOOL-TO-WORK SYSTEMS

Change in the workplace continues at a rapid pace, affecting careers and career development. Mergers, acquisitions, reengineering, and downsizing are influencing employment patterns and altering career pursuits. The rapidly changing skills required in the American labor market and the effectiveness of school-to-career in other global networks has spanned a number of reform initiatives, such as the Blueprint for High Performance (Secretary's Commission on Achieving Necessary Skills, 1992), America's Choice (National Center on Education and the Economy, 1990), and the No Child Left Behind Act of 2001 (NCLB).

America's Choice: High Skills or Low Wages was developed to accelerate interest in linking education to economic competitiveness and the employability and marketability of contemporary American workers. In response, in 1994, Congress passed Public Law 103-239 to establish a national framework for each state to create school-to-work opportunities systems that

- are part of a comprehensive educational reform;
- are integrated with the systems developed under the Goals 2000: Educate America Act; and
- offer opportunities for all students to participate in a performance-education and training program.

Within this framework, all students should be prepared to earn transferable credentials; to prepare for their first jobs in high-skill, high-wage careers; and to pursue further education.

This was reinforced by the federal Carl D. Perkins Vocational and Technical Education Improvement Act of 2006, also known as Perkins IV, which aimed at helping today's students gain the academic and technical skills and knowledge necessary for high demand, high-wage jobs. The legislation requires states to outline a logical sequence of high school and college courses leading to industry certification, while maintaining a strong academic focus that promotes instruction and accountability consistent with NCLB.

High Schools That Work in 1987 was another national initiative that recommended higher standards with an academic core of courses consisting of four college-preparatory English/language arts courses; at least four credits in mathematics, including Algebra I, geometry, Algebra II, and a fourth higher-level course; at least three college-preparatory, lab-based science courses; and at least three college-preparatory social studies courses.

School-to-work partnerships must consist of employers, representatives of local educational agencies and postsecondary institutions, and representatives from business, labor, and industry. Local partnerships must include special compacts that detail the responsibilities and expectations of students, parents, employers, and school personnel. These local partnerships are charged with implementing programs that have three key components: school-based learning, work-based learning, and connecting and integrating school and career activities.

School-based learning focuses on career exploration and counseling, student identification of a career major, a program of study based on high academic and skill standards, a program of instruction that integrates academic and vocational learning, and procedures that facilitate student participation in additional training or postsecondary education.

Work-based learning is a planned program of job training or experience, paid work experience, workplace mentoring, and instruction in general workplace competencies in all aspects of business and industry.

Connecting activities include matching a student with work-based learning opportunities; providing a school site mentor to act as a liaison for the student; providing technical assistance and services to the school site mentor to act as a liaison for the student; providing technical assistance and services to employers; training teachers, mentors, and counselors; integrating academic and occupational education; linking program participants with community services; collecting and analyzing information regarding program outcomes; and linking youth development activities with employer and industry strategies to upgrade workers' skills.

Academic and career planning is an ongoing process beginning in elementary school and does not necessarily culminate with one's first job. Professional school counselors also have been consistently charged with the responsibility of helping students discover their interests, aptitudes, abilities, achievements, and values. Inherently, all students must realize that their personal characteristics are unique and that they can influence their decisions about future life goals.

Career planning cannot stand alone. It is an important element of the total counseling program and total school curriculum. Educational and career planning is the shared responsibility of schools, students, families, employers, and communities. Table 7.2 outlines student outcomes for the world of work to increase their career awareness and to do in-depth career exploration related to personal interests, values, and abilities. It also includes how to make effective educational plans so that students may achieve their career goals.

Career planning is an essential component that all students must undertake, and many factors should be taken into consideration in career exploration, academic preparation, and the life-planning process. The academic and career-planning aspects of the professional school counselor's role must be embraced and shared by the entire educational community. All teachers are role models to students, and many students choose a field of education because of the influence of a significant role model during their school experience. Nearly 80% of today's young people graduate from high school, and of these, well over half enter a college, university, or postsecondary institution of some kind. Everyone is rapidly becoming a lifelong learner, for whom learning does not cease with the final chord of "Pomp and Circumstance."

Professional school counselors are continually being called on to assume the role of advocate, catalyst, and conduit for programs, services, and changing information. They assume responsibility for varying degrees of college counseling, scholarship and financial aid planning, career planning, interest and aptitude testing, and consulting with parents, teachers, and administrators. The professional school counselor also advocates for students with college admissions officers and often mediates resolutions of conflicts or misunderstandings with parents, faculty, and significant others over programs of study, future aspirations, and educational expectations. Academic and career planning needs to be a comprehensive system of services and programs in the school setting (reflecting the needs of students and the community) designed to assist the student in attaining academic adjustment, educational competence, and career exploration. Empirically, such things as higher grade-point average (GPA), increased test scores, or follow-up studies of graduates can measure traditional outcomes.

Prospectively, such concepts as skilled workers, information-handling technologies, flexibility, inventiveness, and portfolio workers create a new mosaic of variables that will influence educational and occupational decisions in a changing economy punctuated by increasing technology and shifting demographics. National and local economic trends also seem to direct the focus and the thrust of programs and services to students and their families.

The National Career Development Association (NCDA, formerly the National Vocational Guidance Association) maintains that the application of life stages to career development education provides a means for describing the development of career competence. A founding division of the American Counseling Association, the NCDA's mission is "to promote the career development of all people over the life span" (National Career Development Association, 2011).

TABLE 7.2   Student Outcomes for a Comprehensive Career Counseling Program

Pre-K and kindergarten students will:
- Identify workers in the school setting
- Describe the work of family members
- Describe what they like to do as part of a group

First-grade students will:
- Describe workers in various settings
- Describe different work activities and their importance
- Distinguish work activities in their environment that are done by specific people and or a group of people

Second-grade students will:
- Describe the diversity of jobs in various settings
- Define *work* and recognize that all people work
- Identify groups with which they work

Third-grade students will:
- Explain why people choose certain work activities and that those choices may change
- Describe different types of rewards obtained for work
- Describe behaviors that contribute or detract from successful group work

Fourth-grade students will:
- Define *stereotype* and indicate how stereotypes affect career choices
- Analyze how their basic study skills relate to career
- Explain how attitudes and personal beliefs contribute to individual group work

Fifth-grade students will:
- Compare their interests and skills to familiar jobs
- Predict how they will use knowledge from certain subjects in future life and work experiences
- Identify their own personal strengths and weaknesses and how they relate to career choices and work style

Sixth-grade students will:
- Compare their interests and skills to familiar jobs
- Predict how they will use knowledge from certain subjects in future life and work experiences
- Identify their own personal strengths and weaknesses and how these relate to career choices and work style

Seventh-grade students will:
- Know sources of information about jobs and careers
- Describe the importance of good work habits for school and future jobs
- Assess their own interests as they apply to career fields

Eighth-grade students will:
- Explore career fields in which they are interested
- Apply what they have learned about themselves to career choices
- Apply what they have learned about themselves to educational choices

Ninth-grade students will:
- Analyze academic plans and experiences relevant to the future
- Demonstrate skills for locating, evaluating, and interpreting information about career opportunities

Tenth-grade students will:
- Analyze the multiple career/educational options and opportunities available upon completion of high school
- Determine how career concerns change as situations and roles change

TABLE 7.2   Student Outcomes for a Comprehensive Career Counseling Program (continued)

Eleventh-grade students will:

- Demonstrate understanding of the need for personal and occupational flexibility in an ever-changing world
- Explain how a changing world demands lifelong learning

Twelfth-grade students will:

- Anticipate and manage the changes experienced entering postsecondary training and employment
- Use decision making and goals setting to manage the post–high school transition

The goal of career development is to stimulate the student's progress through four stages. A step-by-step description, combining the notions of life stages and career management tasks appropriate to each stage, provides a way of ordering curricula by enabling the counselor or teacher to anticipate the kinds of learning experiences students will most likely respond to and profit from (Herr & Cramer, 1984).

The National Consortium of State Career Guidance Supervisors (1999) outlined the "seven *C*'s of career planning," Which encapsulate the common practices in the field of career counseling. As described by Hayslip and VanZandt (2000), the seven *C*'s are:

1. *Clarity of Purpose:* Shared understanding of the program's purpose by school, family, business, and community.
2. *Commitment:* Ongoing investment of resources in the program by school, family, business, labor, industry, and community.
3. *Comprehensiveness:* The degree to which the program addresses all participants and ensures that all career and educational opportunities are fairly presented.
4. *Collaboration:* The degree to which schools, family, business, and community share program ownership.
5. *Coherence:* The degree to which the program provides a documented plan for all students and furnishes specific assistance and progress assessment.
6. *Coordination:* The degree to which the program ensures that career planning is developmental and interdisciplinary.
7. *Competency:* Evidence of student competency attainment. (pp. 82–83).

Career planning cannot stand alone. It is an important element of the total counseling program and school curriculum. Educational and career planning is the shared responsibility of schools, students, families, employers, and communities.

COLLEGE AND UNIVERSITY EXPECTATIONS

Nearly all colleges and universities continue to offer remedial programs in writing, reading, mathematics, and study skills for underprepared students. Almost all will also incorporate systematic testing and placement into remedial, regular, and honors courses to insure matriculation.

Crouse and Trusheim (1988), in their book *The Case against the SAT,* used data on nearly 3,000 students to compare the selection decisions that would have been made using high school GPAs alone or using GPAs combined with SAT scores. From their thorough critique, they concluded:

Colleges make identical admissions decisions, either to admit or reject, on a great majority of their applicants whether they use the SAT along with the high school record, or the high school record alone. The SAT, therefore, has very little impact on who is in college freshman classes and who is not. It is, in effect, statistically redundant. (p. 257)

The American Association of College Registrars and Admissions Officers (AACRAO) and the College Board designed a survey for all institutions of higher education. Responses were obtained from 1,463 institutions. "When asked what single characteristics or credentials they considered most important in making their admissions decisions, 40% of all four-year institutions indicated academic performance, as measured by grade-point average and class rank" (Conner, 1983, p. 36). The survey also revealed other factors institutions considered most important or very important. The findings reinforce the idea that a student's academic record has more influence than any other factor on a college or university admissions decision. Admission tests are important, but ultimately, it is a student's course history that seems to matter most. Without additional exceptions, it is probably safe to say that measures of an applicant's academic success in high school (grades, rank in class, and courses taken) and measures of how well the applicant compares with other students across the state and nation (with SAT or ACT scores) are the factors given the most emphasis by college admissions personnel.

ENHANCING THE COLLEGE ADMISSIONS PROCESS

Another critical study of the college admissions process selection (Matthay, 1989; Matthay & Nieuwenhuis, 1995) revealed the following perceptions regarding decision making for college:

- Visits to college campuses were significantly more helpful to students attending highly competitive four-year private liberal arts colleges than to students attending all other types of institutions.
- Use of computer information systems was significantly more helpful to students attending all other types of institutions.
- College fairs were significantly more helpful to students who wanted to attend a highly competitive four-year private liberal arts college or a competitive four-year private secular institution.
- Satisfaction with choice of college was significantly higher for students attending highly competitive four-year, private liberal arts colleges than for students attending any other type of college. The least satisfied students were those who attended a four-year public nonresearch university.

Matthay (1989) and Matthay and Nieuwenhuis (1995) concluded that the four most helpful resources for students deciding which college to attend are college visits, college catalogs, parent involvement, and information provided by the professional school counselor. The data suggest that college planning should begin in the middle school years and that professional school counselors should emphasize the importance of visiting colleges and should prepare students and their families to critically evaluate college selections. Regional education centers can provide libraries of catalogs and videos, and high schools should ensure their students' access to visiting college representatives.

Even with brochures, letters, college fairs, college catalogs, and campus visits, high school students and their families still feel inadequately informed or lacking enough facts to make an informed decision. When univariate analysis was used to determine statistically significant differences in perceptions of helpfulness based on type of college attended, the following findings emerges from the study:

- The college catalog was more helpful to students who wanted to attend a competitive four-year private secular college than to those who wanted to attend a noncompetitive public community college.
- Parents and family were more helpful to students attending a highly competitive four-year private liberal arts or a state two-year technical college than to students attending a four-year public nonresearch university.

- Interviews with admission representatives on college campuses were significantly more helpful to students at a competitive four-year private secular college than to students at all other types of colleges (Matthay, 1989; Matthay & Nieuwenhuis, 1995).

Fundamentally, students who need the most guidance for making decisions about attending college are those whose parents may not have had the college experience. Parents with a college education tend to have children who attend college. This relationship has a stronger correlation than SAT scores.

The professional school counselor's college-advising responsibility is especially important for low-income and minority families, where parents are unable to share the experience of college with their children. Parents without a college education often don't know how to play the college admissions game. Yet, Chapman, O'Brien, and DeMasi (1987) found low-income students indifferent to the professional school counselor's role in assisting with postsecondary decision making.

Lee and Ekstrom (1987) found that professional school counselors often devote more time to college-bound, middle- and upper-income, white students than to others. They concluded that family income is the major determinant of the education a student receives. Many researchers have warned that current trends might eventually lead to a dual school system in the United States, one for the rich and one for the poor.

First generation students are at the highest risk for having difficulty making the transition from high school to post-secondary options (Pike & Kuh, 2005; Ishitani, 2006).

- School size greatly influences the availability of resources devoted to college counseling, especially the number of counselors with college counseling duties versus ancillary responsibilities.
- The patterns of college attendance are affected dramatically by the family income and the overall profile of the school. Fewer students from lower-income schools attend a four-year institution than do students from upper-income schools. Much of this has to do with first-generation college students whose parents do not have the knowledge of college/university entrance requirements, financial aid information, and scholarship application processes and deadlines.
- High schools drawing students from more affluent families offer more exposure to colleges through programs such as fairs, visits from college representatives, parent meetings, and new information technologies. Professional school counselors at upper-income schools spend a large portion of their time on college counseling duties.
- There is a need to help expand student horizons, that is, to consider more college options, to think more independently, and to strive for higher goals by instituting special intervention programs such as Gear-up, Upward Bound, and AVID, because peer support is an important factor in making the transition to college (Hurtado, Carter, & Spuler, 1996, p. 153).
- Financial resources are insufficient, resulting in small staffs, student–counselor ratios that are too high, and small operating budgets.
- There is widespread student apathy and indifference toward taking responsibility and meeting deadlines, filling out applications, and registering for college entrance examinations.
- Scholarship requirements change and federal financial aid fluctuates, and professional school counselors sometimes have difficulty keeping up to date with financial aid developments, college admissions requirements, and career information.
- The academic achievement gaps that differentiate Latino and African American students from their white counterparts is significantly wider today than in 1975, and the gap between low-income and high-income students has doubled (U.S. Census Bureau, 2006).
- Attrition after entering college is significant for minority students. Nationally about six in 10 white students matriculate with a bachelor's degree within six years, compared to four in 10 minority students (Knapp, Kelly-Reid, & Ginder, 2007).
- It was also found in a recent report by the Education Trust that only 7% of minority students who enter two-year colleges earn a bachelor's degree within ten years (Engle & Lynch, 2009).

Effective college counseling programs share a number of common characteristics. First, they start working early with students and their families. Second, they help families find creative ways to finance higher education. It is increasingly important for professional school counselors to assist in dismantling the financial aid barrier for all income levels. To do so will necessitate coordinating community resources. Third, successful programs require the full support and commitment of policy makers. Finally, effective college counseling involves the larger community in the success of the students. Community goals, school mission, and college counseling or other postsecondary training alternatives should be fully integrated into the total school program.

Many students come into counseling offices pressured by family and friends to declare a major course of study for a career field that they might know little about, to choose a school from glossy brochures or enticing videos, to sort through an abyss of acronyms, and to fill out form after form to qualify for scholarships from organizations ranging from Daughters of the American Revolution to the local recreational athletic association. For the first-generation college student, this can create deception and false hopes. Missed deadlines and missteps along the way can be frustrating to the student. "You are not college material" is perhaps the worst sentence that any student or parent wants to hear from a person in a position of educational authority.

Studies on attrition continue to reveal that most students leave colleges and universities for one or more of the following reasons: inadequate academic preparation, lack of finances, or poor college choice. It is of paramount importance that students and their families be appropriately counseled so that, as they approach the end of high school, all of their postsecondary options are commensurate with their ability, aptitude, achievement, and aspirations.

Many observers support the development of an explicit sequence of activities designed to carry students through their school academic experiences and career possibilities. The goals of the curriculum would include challenging student potential and enhancing self-esteem, broadening experiences and aspirations, and preparing students to make comprehensive and flexible decisions. The college preparation curriculum should be intricately woven into the academic curriculum.

SCHOOL-BASED INITIATIVES TO MEET THE ACADEMIC AND CAREER NEEDS OF ALL STUDENTS

Several student-focused initiatives are available that professional school counselors can design or implement to meet local needs. They include:

- Encourage more minority students to take college entrance examinations. SAT, ACT, and PSAT preparation programs are a natural extension of the counseling office, in cooperation with academic disciplines such as English and mathematics. Minority students make up only 7% of the million high school students who take the SAT annually. Taking the PSAT as early as the 10th grade can provide the counselor and counselee with a diagnostic tool to assess areas (such as vocabulary or reading comprehension) that may need remediation. Having the school division pay for the registration fee would be an added incentive to encourage participation.
- Develop programs to help students discover alternatives for financing their education and ways they can support themselves while in college.
- Provide in-service programs for mathematics and English teachers on PSAT/SAT content. For example, mathematics scores increase with credits earned in algebra and geometry.
- Increase options for postsecondary education and occupations through repeated counseling sessions spent on planning programs of study by concentrating on pathways to colleges, universities, and postsecondary training opportunities.
- Mail PSAT information to parents of all 10th- and 11th-grade students who are taking geometry or algebra.

- Promote summer enrichment programs at local universities for rising ninth-grade students to learn critical thinking skills, problem solving, test-taking strategies, vocabulary, computer technology, and high school program planning and to prepare students to become National Merit Semifinalists. National Merit Semifinalists are only identified one time, as part of the PSAT/NMSQT (National Merit Scholarship Qualifying Test).
- Develop a systemwide item analysis of the PSAT and give the results to home schools to develop individual academic improvement plans.
- Provide greater recognition of student academic achievement in each secondary school through honors banquets and receptions for Presidential Academic Fitness Award nominees, National Merit Scholarship winners, the National Achievement Scholarship for Outstanding African American Students winners, National Hispanic Scholarship Awards Program winners, and other similar achievers.
- Have a school bulletin board showing median SAT achievement and Advanced Placement scores of the previous freshman class at various colleges and universities.

Inherently, professional school counselors must ensure that students are not academically stereotyped or tracked in such a way that will endanger future college/university admission or success. In addition, professional school counselors can:

- Develop programs with alumni to educate potential college-bound students about college life, coping skills, and survival strategies.
- Offer tutorial assistance, career planning, and an active career counseling program.
- Link choice of classes tightly with career and college preparation.
- Network with local colleges and universities that offer precollege programs or summer enrichment institutes for minority students or first-generation college students.
- Implement an academic or homework hotline (a local cable television or radio station could provide help to students having trouble with homework). Students could call and receive help from honors students and teachers. Such a program is not only good public relations, it also demonstrates to students and their families a community interest in their academic success and well-being.
- Develop a school website with pertinent information and updates and implement such programs as *Pinnacle Internet Viewer,* sometimes referred to as "Parent Internet viewer," where parents can log on to the Internet and view their child's grades, assignments, homework, and attendance anytime in real time for each one of their child's teachers.
- Encourage English composition teachers to focus on critical thinking skills, analogies, vocabulary, and reading comprehension as early as the seventh grade.

Analyses of data by the National Longitudinal Survey of Young Americans (William T. Grant Commission on Work, Family, and Citizenship, 1988) also revealed significant correlations between levels of academic skills and youth prospects for participation in society. The research confirms the high cost of failure in school. For example:

- Girls who, at age 15, have basic skill scores in the bottom fifth of the skills distribution are five times as likely to become mothers before age 16 as those scoring in the top half.
- Young women who, at age 17 or 18, have very weak basic skills are 2½ times as likely to be mothers before age 20 as those in the top half of the basic skills distribution.
- Young men who, at age 17 or 18, have very weak basic skills are three times as likely to become fathers before age 20 as those scoring in the top half.
- Young adults ages 18 to 23 with basic academic skills in the bottom fifth of the distribution relative to their peers in the top half are:
  - 8.8 times more likely to have left school without a diploma

- 8.6 times more likely to have a child out of wedlock
- 5.4 times more likely to be receiving some form of public assistance
- 5.0 times more likely to be at poverty level in income and not in school of any type
- 3.6 times more likely to be not working, not in school, and not taking care of a child
- 2.2 times more likely to have been arrested in the previous year

Some strategies that employers, schools, and youth-serving organizations can collectively undertake to facilitate the transition from school to work include the following:

- Expand the hiring of recent high school graduates directly into career-ladder positions rather than low-wage, dead-end jobs.
- Reevaluate hiring criteria, making certain that ability to do the job is considered more important than age, credentials, dress, or diction.
- Make apprenticeship training available to 16- to 20-year-olds.
- Have potential employers work with schools to provide better cooperative education placements for students.
- Establish a career information center to provide job-hunting skills, educational and training opportunities, and financial aid possibilities.
- Create incentives such as guaranteed employment, training opportunities, and financial aid incentives.

THE NATIONAL CAREER TECHNICAL EDUCATION FOUNDATION AND CAREER CLUSTERS: A NATIONAL INITIATIVE

The National Career Technical Education Foundation (NCTEF) is a supporting arm of the National Association of State Directors of Career Technical Education Consortium (NASDCTEC). Under NASDCTEC, NCTEF receives grants to develop products and provide research to support the states' Career Cluster Initiative under the Perkins IV legislation passed by the 109th Congress. This legislation was aimed at helping today's students gain the academic and technical skills and knowledge necessary for high demand, high-wage jobs while maintaining a strong academic focus that promotes instruction and accountability consistent with No Child Left Behind.

Career Clusters is a national initiative that helps students investigate careers and design their courses of study to advance their career goals. Most states have adopted the nationally accepted structure of career clusters, career pathways, and sample career specialties or occupations. There are 16 career clusters, providing opportunities for learners in new areas such as Human Services or Law, Public Safety, Corrections, and Security. Within each career cluster, there are multiple career pathways that represent a common set of skills and knowledge, both academic and technical, necessary to pursue a full range of career opportunities within that pathway—ranging from entry level to management, including technical and professional career specialties. The organization and structure of Career Clusters provides a place for all learners, linking them to their career goals.

The Career Clusters initiative is a state and national effort to increase the influence of the STEM (Science, Technology, Engineering, and Math) educational environment through community and industry partnerships as well as to strengthen the core curriculum (English, science, math, and social studies). It serves to strengthen college-preparatory and career-based internship and apprenticeship programs at the secondary level to show the relationship between course work, college, and career preparation.

Career Clusters and its curriculum frameworks reflect the higher state academic standards required of learners to be successful as they transition to postsecondary education and future careers. Career

Clusters represents a partnership formed between the states, secondary and postsecondary education, and employers to provide a more uniform curriculum integration and contextual learning opportunities that reflect the career goals and interests of all students—those pursuing a postsecondary education and those going directly into the workforce after high school. Relevant learning opportunities create the motivation for many students to stay in school longer and enroll in more challenging courses.

In some states, there are partnerships with technical schools that are part of the secondary program, and certification programs with local community colleges. It has long been recognized that too many students do not graduate from high school and many more who do graduate lack preparation for further study and the recognized credentials to get good jobs. There have been some national initiatives such as High Schools That Work which emphasize more rigorous standards for all students, not just for a select few.

THE STATES' CAREER CLUSTERS INITIATIVE

The States' Career Clusters Initiative (SCCI) is a national initiative intended to help states and schools organize their programs and guidance activities around clusters of similar occupations. The 16-cluster format used by the U.S. Department of Education and the U.S. Department of Labor's Employment and Training Administration encompasses all 970+ occupations identified by O*net and the Standard Occupational Classification (SOC) codes. By adopting this cluster philosophy, schools expand their content and offerings to better prepare students for their future career opportunities.

SCCI has three major objectives:

1. Increase students awareness of career options so that they may make better informed decisions.
2. Increase student understanding of the structure and function of businesses so they can be more productive, value-added employees.
3. Increase student learner achievement by setting high standards of expectations and by teaching academics in a context that interests students.

The career service is free and online at http://onetcenter.org.

The 16 career clusters of the SCCI are:

1. *Agriculture, Food, and Natural Resources Cluster:* The production, processing, marketing, distribution, financing, and development of agricultural commodities and resources, including food, fiber, wood products, natural resources, horticulture, and other plant and animal products or resources.
2. *Architectural and Construction Cluster:* Careers in designing, planning, managing, building, and maintaining the existing or new building and development environment.
3. *Arts, Audio-Visual Technology, and Communication Cluster:* Designing, producing, exhibiting, performing, writing, and publishing multimedia content, including visual and performing arts and design, journalism, media, and other entertainment services.
4. *Business Management and Administration Cluster:* Planning, organizing, directing, and evaluating business functions essential to efficient and productive business operations. Business management and administration career opportunities are available in every sector of business, health services, technology, and industry.
5. *Education and Training Cluster:* Planning, managing, and providing education and training services and related learning support services for business, education, industry, and health services.
6. *Finance Cluster:* Financial and investment planning, banking, insurance, and financial management of personal and business transactions.

7. *Government and Public Administration Cluster:* Executing governmental functions—governance, national security, foreign service, planning, revenue and taxation, regulation, and management and administration at the local, state, and federal levels.

8. *Health Science Cluster:* Planning, managing, and providing therapeutic services, diagnostic services, health information and education, support services, and biotechnology research and pharmacology.

9. *Hospitality and Tourism Cluster:* Management, marketing, and operations of restaurants and other food services, hotel and motel management, amusement attractions, recreation events, and travel-related services.

10. *Human Services Cluster:* Career pathways that relate to families and human needs such as social services, court services, group homes, and in-home counseling.

11. *Information Technology Cluster:* Entry-level, technical, and professional careers related to the design, development, support, and management of hardware, software, databases, multimedia, and systems integration services, as well as security of data and communication.

12. *Law and Public Safety Cluster:* Planning, managing, and providing legal, public safety, protective services, and homeland security for individuals, cities, and counties as well as institutions, including professional and technical support services.

13. *Manufacturing Cluster:* Planning, managing, and performing the processing of materials into intermediate or final products and related professional and technical support activities such as production planning and control, maintenance, manufacturing, and process engineering and services.

14. *Marketing Cluster:* Planning, managing, and performing marketing activities to reach organizational objectives of businesses, institutions, and organizations.

15. *Science, Technology, Engineering, and Mathematics Cluster:* Planning, managing, and providing scientific research and professional and technical services (e.g., physical science, social science, engineering), including laboratory and testing services and research and development services.

16. *Transportation, Distribution, and Logistics Cluster:* Planning, management, and movement of people, materials, and goods by road, pipeline, air, rail, and water and related professional and technical support services such as transportation infrastructure planning and management, logistics services, mobile equipment, and facility maintenance.

Table 7.3 demonstrates career pathways and plans of student study for the "Information Technology" career cluster. Each pathway and course of study is detailed and sometimes complicated; however, they are well planned in order to give the student many options and opportunities in class preparation and course of study.

TABLE 7.3   Information Technology Cluster

INFORMATION SHEET: Information and tips for instructional leaders, administrators, counselors, and teachers/faculty for creating a Career Pathway Plan of Study

1. The following pathway course sequence options for the Information Technology Cluster. Use these options to identify any middle school CTE courses offered in your school division that complement the secondary sequence, but middle school courses are not a required component of the plan of study. CTE courses listed in the middle and secondary sections must use state course titles.

2. For the postsecondary section of the Plan of Study, the template provides the recommended certificate programs associate degree program using the VCCS state code for the degree program as shown below. Degree specialization is available at some community colleges. Registered apprenticeships can be developed in almost all program areas. School divisions and postsecondary institutions should identify specific courses as provided for in the blank template.

TABLE 7.4 Commonwealth of Virginia Sample Study Plan

Cluster: Arts, Audio/Video Technology & Communications
This Career Pathway Plan of Study can serve as a guide, along with other career planning materials, as learners continue on a career path. Courses listed within this plan are only recommended coursework and should be individualized to meet each learner's educational and career goals. This Plan of Study, used for learners at an educational institution, should be customized with course titles and appropriate high school graduation requirements, as well as college entrance requirements.

EDUCATION LEVEL	GRADE	ENGLISH/ LANGUAGE ARTS	MATHEMATICS	SCIENCE	HISTORY AND SOCIAL SCIENCE	RECOMMENDED ELECTIVES IN VISUAL ARTS PATHWAYS	RECOMMENDED CAREER AND TECHNICAL COURSES	SAMPLE – OCCUPATIONS RELATING TO THE PATHWAY
						Use state course titles	*Source: Administrative Planning Guide* http://www.cteresource.org/apg/	http://www.doe.virginia.gov/instruction/career_technical/career_clusters/sample_plans_study/index.shtml http://www.careerclusters.org http://www.cteresource.org/cpg/
		Graduation Requirements: http://www.doe.virginia.gov/instruction/graduation/index.shtml						
MIDDLE	7	English 7	Mathematics 7	Life Science	Civics and Economics	9105 Art Grade 7 9106 Art Exploratory/18 Weeks	6110/6111 (BIT); 8109/8112/8113/8114 (MKT) Make It Your Business 6150 Keyboarding 6160/6161 Digital Input Technologies 8240 Family and Consumer Sciences Exploratory II	– Advertiser – Animator – Architect – Art Broker – Art Buyer (corporate) – Art Critic – Art Historian – Art Preservationist – Art Restorer – Art Therapist – Arts Administrator – Artist – CAD Technician – Cartoonist, Caricaturist – Cinematographer – Commercial Printer

continued

TABLE 7.4   Commonwealth of Virginia Sample Study Plan (continued)

	English	Mathematics	Science	Social Studies	Electives	Electives	Career Options
8	English 8	Mathematics 8	Physical Science	World History & Geography I	9115 Art Grade 8 9120 Art I / Art Foundations	6115/6116 (BIT); 8115/8116 (MKT) Principles of Business and Marketing 6609/6610 Computer Solutions 6670 Information Technology (IT) Fundamentals 8241 Family and Consumer Sciences Exploratory II 9093 Exploring Entrepreneurship	– Curator/Gallery Manager – Designer – E-Commerce Specialist – Educator – Fashion Designer – Fashion Illustrator – Game Designer – Graphic Designer – Illustrator – Interior Designer (commercial/residential) – Jeweler – Makeup Designer – Media Marketer – Medical, Scientific Illustrator – Performance Artist – Photographer – Print Maker – Set Designer – Stylist – Textile Designer – Videographer – Web Designer
	Career Assessment: Administration of a career assessment instrument is appropriate at the middle school level to help students and their parents plan for high school (Virginia's Career Planning System or other assessment product).						
9	English 9	Algebra I	Earth Science	World History & Geography II	9130 Art II/Intermediate 9153 Graphic Arts Design I 9160 Craft Design I 9175 Ceramics I 9180 Computer Art Graphics I 9193 Photography I	6120/6121 Finance 6612/6614 Computer Information Systems 8248/8247 (FACS); 8148/49 (MKT) Intro to Fashion Design and Marketing 8415/8418 Communication Systems 8434/8435 Technical Drawing and Design 8455 Imaging Technology 8459 Digital Visualization	

SECONDARY

7 · The Professional School Counselor's Role   219

10	English 10	Geometry	Biology	World Geography		
					9140 Art III / Adv. Intermediate	6135/6136 Business Management
					9151 AP Art History	6613/6615 Computer Information Systems, Advanced
					9154 Graphic Arts Design II	6630/6632 Design, Multimedia, Web Technologies
					9161 Craft Design II	8280 Fashion Design I
					9170 Art History	8295 Interior Design I
					9176 Ceramics II	8436/8493 Engineering Drawing and Design.
					9181 Computer Art Graphics II	8458/8494 Graphic Communications Systems
					9194 Photography II	8527 Cosmetology I
						8530 Drafting I
						8570 Advertising Design I
						8600 Basic Carpentry
						8601 Carpentry I'
						8607 Commercial Photography I
						8610 Basic Photography
						8660 Graphic Imaging Technology I
						8672 Welding I
						8688 Television Production I

TABLE 7.4   Commonwealth of Virginia Sample Study Plan (continued)

11	English 11	Algebra II	Chemistry	Virginia and US History	9145 Art IV / Adv.	6631/6633 Design, Multimedia, and Web Technologies, Advanced
					9148 AP Studio Art: 2-D Design	8120 Marketing
					9149 AP Studio Art: 3-D Design	8125 Internet Marketing
					9150 AP Studio Art: Drawing Portfolio	8140 Fashion Marketing
						8281 Fashion Design II
					9155 Graphic Arts Design III	8296 Interior Design II
					9162 Craft Design III	8438 Advanced Drawing and Design
					9177 Ceramics III	8528 Cosmetology II
					9182 Computer Art Graphics III	8531 Drafting II
						8571 Advertising Design II
					9195 Photography III	8602 Carpentry II
					IB#### IB Studio Art (Year 1)	8608 Commercial Photography II
						8661 Graphic Imaging Technology II
						8673 Welding II
						8689 Television Production II
						9094 Entrepreneurship Education
12	English 12	Trigonometry/Advanced Algebra	Physics/Principles of Technology I and II	Virginia and US Government	9147 Art V/Portfolio Preparation	8130 Advanced Marketing
					IB#### IB Studio Art (Year 2)	8145 Adv, Fashion Marketing
						8603 Carpentry III

Other required Secondary Courses: Economics and Personal Finance, Health & PE (2 years)
The following courses may be required depending on the diploma sought: Foreign Language (3 years)

High School Courses in the pathway offered locally for college credit should coded: Advanced Placement (AP), International Baccalaureate (IB), Dual Enrollment (DE), and/or VC (Validated Credit)

List related certifications/credentials approved by VDOE and offered locally:
http://www.cteresource.org/apg (Go to Certification - License Section)

Administrative Assisting Assessment (NOCTI); Adobe Certified Associate (Adobe Systems, Inc.); Advertising and Design Assessment (NOCTI); Advertising Design Examination; Apple Pro Certification Program (Apple, Inc.); Architectural Drafting Assessment (NOCTI); Auto CAD Certifications (Brainbench); Autodesk Application Certification Program (Autodesk); Banking and Related Services Assessment; Basic Principles of Construction; Residential Construction Academy Examination (Thomas Delmar Learning/Home Builders Institute); Brainbench Desktop Publishing Certifications (Brainbench); Brainbench Software Development Certifications (Brainbench); Brainbench Web Administration Certifications (Brainbench); Brainbench Web Design and Development Certifications (Brainbench); Business Financial Management Assessment; CAD Assessment (NOCTI); Carpentry Assessment (NOCTI); Carpentry Level One, National Construction Career Test (NCCER); Carpentry: Residential Construction Academy Examination (Thomas Delmar Learning/Home Builders Institute); Certified Internet Webmaster Associate (ProSoft Learning); Certified SolidWorks Professional (SolidWorks Corporation); Concepts of Finance Examination; Concepts of Entrepreneurship and Management Examination; Core: Introductory Craft Skills, National Construction Career Test (NCCER); Cosmetology Assessment (NOCTI); Cosmetology (Virginia Board of Barbers and Cosmetology, Department of Professional and Occupational Regulations); Drafter Certification (American Design Drafting Association); Financial and Investment Planning Assessment; Financial Literacy Certification; Fundamental Business Concepts (ASK Institute, DECA/MarkED); Fundamental Marketing Concepts (ASK Institute); General Drafting and Design Assessment (NOCTI); Graphic Communication Technology Assessment (NOCTI); IC3 Certification (Certiport); Microsoft Certified Application Specialist (MCAS); Microsoft Office Specialist (MOS)(Microsoft); National Professional Certification in Customer Service (National Retail Federation Foundation); Pre-Skills Assessment for Mastercam Certification (NOCTI); PrintED Certification (all exams) (Graphic Arts Education and Research Foundation); Retail Trades Assessment (NOCTI); Sales Certification (National Retail Federation Foundation); SENSE Training Program Certification (Level 1, Entry-level Welder) (American Welding Society); Television Broadcasting Assessment (NOCTI); Virginia Workplace Readiness Assessment (NOCTI) and IC3 Certification (Certiport); Visual Communications Assessment (NOCTI); Welding Assessment (NOCTI); Welding, National Construction Career Test (NCCER)

Additional Learning Opportunities:

CTSO Organization(s): X DECA X FBLA X FCCLA ___ FFA X FEA ___ HOSA X SkillsUSA X TSA
Other: National Art Honor Society; National Junior Art Honor Society; Alliance for Young Artists and Writers

Work-Based Learning

X Career Research X Cooperative Education X Internship X Mentorship X Job Shadowing X Service Learning Project ___ Student Apprenticeship

continued

TABLE 7.4 Commonwealth of Virginia Sample Study Plan (continued)

POSTSECONDARY

SAMPLE POSTSECONDARY PROGRAMS RELATED TO THIS CAREER PATHWAY

Individual plans must include locally agreed upon courses at the postsecondary level (See page 2)

Pathway	Associate Degree, College Certificate, or Apprenticeship	Bachelor's Degree	Postgraduate Degree
Visual Arts	Fine Arts – AA	(Determined Locally)	(Determined Locally – Optional)

Postsecondary: Placement Assessments such as COMPASS & SAT Subject Tests | College Entrance exams such as ACT & SAT

POSTSECONDARY PLANS OF STUDIES MUST INCLUDE POSTSECONDARY ACADEMIC, CTE, AND OTHER ELECTIVE COURSES APPROPRIATE FOR AN ASSOCIATE DEGREE

Semester	English	Mathematics	Science	Social Studies	Required Courses or Recommended Electives
Year 1 1st Semester					
Year 1 2nd Semester					

POSTSECONDARY – COMMUNITY COLLEGE OR APPRENTICESHIP – DETERMINED LOCALLY

College courses offered locally in high school for college credit should be coded: DE (Dual Enrollment) and/or VC (Validated Credit)

		Year 2 1st Semester	Year 2 2st Semester

Related Industry Certifications Available:

Additional Suggested Learning Opportunities:

Work-Based Learning:

___ Cooperative Education ___ Internship ___ Mentorship ___ Job Shadowing ___ Service Learning Project ___ Registered Apprenticeship

University/College:

Degree or Major:

Number of Articulated CC Credits:

UNIVERSITY

Notes:

Source: *Virginia Department of Education, Office of Career and Technical Education,* http://www.doe.virginia.gov/VDOE/Instruction/CTE/careerclusters/.

THE EMERGENCE OF THE PORTFOLIO WORKER

The "career is dead." The world of stable, long-term employment is coming to an end (Kotter, 1995; Rifkin, 1995). Marketability in employment is increasingly based on skills and knowledge rather than titles, loyalty, and seniority. Handy (1989) reported on the emergence of the "portfolio worker" and the "portfolio career," where individuals maintain portfolios of their skills, abilities, and achievements with which they obtain temporary assignments in a variety of organizations, rather than securing permanent jobs. The downsizing and reorganizations of the past decade have caused organizations to rely on a core group of full-time employees complemented by part-timers and networks of flexible staffing through outsourcing (Logan & Kritzell, 1997; National Alliance of Business, 1996; Yate, 1995). This represents a fundamental change of attitude and worker identity.

People who are versatile, can handle many types of challenges, and can consider different kinds of employment can be portfolio workers. The work portfolio is a diverse collection of abilities and knowledge. Individuals should consider themselves a collection of attributes and skills, not a job title. They are flexible and mobile. The critical skills of the portfolio will be versatility, flexibility, creativity, self-direction, interpersonal and communication skills, facility with computer and information technology, ability to learn continuously, and ability to manage work, time, and money (Lemke et al., 1995; The New Economy, 1996). Fundamentally, the portfolio workers' loyalty is to themselves rather than to an employer. It requires a unique attitude of going where the skills are needed and being resourceful, innovative, and able to take risks.

The new workplace will reward the "specialized generalist" who has a solid basic education plus professional and technical skills that are in demand across a range of companies or industries. Putting skills, achievements, and interests together can begin with the educational and career portfolio given in Figure 7.1. The portfolio is a record of a student's educational experiences in school. It includes information about his or her efforts, progress, and achievement. The portfolio can begin in middle school and follow the student through his or her senior year. It can provide a conceptual map for redefining the traditional resume with documentation of marketable skills and work experiences.

APPENDIX: THE NATIONAL CAREER DEVELOPMENT GUIDELINES FRAMEWORK

The National Career Development Guidelines (NCDG) is a framework for building and evaluating comprehensive career development programs for youths and adults in schools, colleges, universities, and institutions. The NCDG framework, which has taken two decades to come to fruition, reinforces both the No Child Left Behind initiatives and the American School Counselor Association's framework of career, academic, and personal social domains.

In terms of NCLB and ASCA standards, the NCDG promotes the following:

- *High-quality academic assessments, curricula, and instructional materials aligned with challenging state academic standards.* The NCDG seeks to align personal/social, academic, and career goals with standards-based curricula and state standards.
- *Accountability.* The NCDG can increase program accountability because it encourages self-assessment, which leads to aligning student learning outcomes with instructional materials.
- *Improving teaching quality.* The NCDG gives teachers, administrators, and counselors the skills and knowledge they need to help students and their families make career choices and plan their education with concrete information, resources, and assessments.

A **portfolio** is a visual presentation of your skills, abilities, achievements, and goals. We all have many talents and skills, experiences, and achievements that can be presented to give others a more comprehensive understanding of our potential.

Begin with your cover—something that makes a statement about you. Or design a formal cover. Employers and college representatives will probably be impressed.

Start to build your portfolio by focusing on the following steps.

1. *Develop or review* your five-year educational and career plan—your school-to-work development plan.
2. Decide how you are going to *organize* your portfolio.
3. Decide *what* and *how* you want to document your accomplishments.
4. You will eventually highlight your accomplishments in your resume.

Initially, review the plan you developed in the seventh or eighth grade. Your plan should include:

- ☐ A short-term career goal
- ☐ A long-term career goal
- ☐ Educational and training goals
- ☐ Your greatest interests
- ☐ Your best abilities

Areas you would like to improve (there is always room for improvement)

- ☐ Required classes
- ☐ Career-related elective classes
- ☐ School activities
- ☐ Outside school experiences
- ☐ Volunteer experiences
- ☐ Paid work experiences

My short-term career goal is _____.
Eventually, I would like to be a _____.
The way I plan to reach these goals is by _____.
My three favorite career clusters are _____.
I made these decisions because my interests are _____.
My best abilities are _____.
Areas I need to improve are _____.
Classes I can take in high school that relate to my career goals are _____.
Vocational programs that would be helpful are _____.
Helpful work experiences include _____.
After I graduate, I will probably _____.

Academic skills are the skills that help you prepare for future training and education. They include communicating, planning, understanding, and problem solving.

- ☐ Read and understand written materials.
- ☐ Understand charts and graphs.
- ☐ Understand basic math.
- ☐ Use math to solve problems.
- ☐ Use research/library skills.
- ☐ Use tools and equipment.
- ☐ Speak in the language in which business is conducted.
- ☐ Write in the language in which business is conducted.
- ☐ Use scientific method to solve problems.
- ☐ Use specialized knowledge to get a job done.

FIGURE 7.1 Managing your career and educational portfolio.

Personal management skills are the skills or habits that help you develop responsibility and dependability. They include accomplishing goals, doing your best, making decisions, acting honestly, and exercising self-control.

- ☐ Attend school/work daily and on time.
- ☐ Meet school/work deadlines.
- ☐ Know personal strengths and weaknesses.
- ☐ Demonstrate self-control and self-discipline.
- ☐ Pay attention to details and commitments.
- ☐ Follow written and verbal instructions.
- ☐ Learn new skills.
- ☐ Demonstrate personal values.

Teamwork skills are the skills that help you work cooperatively with a group. They include organizing, planning, listening, sharing, flexibility, and leadership.

- ☐ Actively participate.
- ☐ Follow the group's rules and values.
- ☐ Listen attentively to other group members.
- ☐ Express ideas to other group members.
- ☐ Be sensitive to the group members' ideas and views.
- ☐ Be willing to compromise to accomplish group goals.
- ☐ Work in changing settings and with different people.

Identify your accomplishments at school and outside of school. Decide *what* to display and *how* to set up your portfolio. Use:

- ☐ Pictures
- ☐ Computer disks
- ☐ Work samples
- ☐ Awards
- ☐ Drawing
- ☐ Diagrams

Document accomplishments:
Accomplishments
Examples
If you're in a vocational-technical program, you could list skills you've completed, or you could paste in photographs of your projects or high-tech equipment you can use.

Achievements
Projects
Try to include some of the awards you have received. Even if you received them in elementary school, they are still good ways to validate your accomplishments. Ask your parents or guardians for information on your past activities.
Include examples of teamwork. You can use sports, clubs, student government, class projects, or group activities outside of school. Band, chorus, and yearbook are examples.
You may want to include results from tests you have taken. You could use local, state, or national exam results. You can also use your high school transcript.
Hobbies and other outside interests demonstrate your accomplishments, too! Volunteer activities should be included.

Hobby/Volunteer Activities
Responsibilities
- ☐ What were your duties?
- ☐ What were your best accomplishments?
- ☐ Make a list of all your personal references who can vouch for all your portfolio claims.
- ☐ Include teachers, counselors, principals, coaches, employers, minister, rabbi, or club sponsor.

FIGURE 7.1   (Continued)

- *A comprehensive developmental, preventive approach to career and academic counseling.* Career development activities and lessons based on the NCDG help students make connections between their school subjects and occupations, so they better understand the relationship between educational achievement and future career opportunities—that course work relates to work and to postsecondary education.
- *Increased parental options and choice.* The NCDG gives parents information, activities, and resources, so they can support their children's education and career development as well as understanding the occupational outlook and potential pathways to a career.

The National Career Development Guidelines were first released in 1989. The most recent revision of the guidelines was completed in September 2004. They are provided in Table 7.5 at the end of this appendix as the national standards with continuity of language and format.

Domains and Goals

Domains, goals, and indicators organize the NCDG framework. There are three *domains:* Personal Social Development (PS), Educational Achievement and Lifelong Learning (ED), and Career Management (CM). Under each domain are *goals* (11 in total). The goals define broad areas of career development competency.

Personal Social Development Domain

- GOAL PS1: Develop understanding of self to build and maintain a positive self-concept.
- GOAL PS2: Develop positive interpersonal skills including respect for diversity.
- GOAL PS3: Integrate growth and change into your career development.
- GOAL PS4: Balance personal, leisure, community, learner, family, and work roles.

Educational Achievement and Lifelong Learning Domain

- GOAL ED1: Attain educational achievement and performance levels needed to reach your personal and career goals.
- GOAL ED2: Participate in ongoing, lifelong learning experiences to enhance your ability to function effectively in a diverse and changing economy.

Career Management Domain

- GOAL CM1: Create and manage a career plan that meets your career goals.
- GOAL CM2: Use a process of decision making as one component of career development.
- GOAL CM3: Use accurate, current, and unbiased career information during career planning and management.
- GOAL CM4: Master academic, occupational, and general employability skills in order to obtain, create, maintain, and/or advance your employment.
- GOAL CM5: Integrate changing employment trends, societal needs, and economic conditions into your career plans.

Indicators and Learning Stages

Under each goal in the framework are *indicators of mastery* that highlight the knowledge and skills needed to achieve that goal. Each indicator is presented in three *learning stages* derived from Bloom's taxonomy: knowledge acquisition, application, and reflection. The stages describe learning competency. They are not tied to an individual's age or level of education.

- *Knowledge acquisition* (K). Children and adolescents at the knowledge acquisition stage expand knowledge awareness and build comprehension. They can recall, recognize, describe, identify, clarify, discuss, explain, summarize, query, investigate, and compile new information about the knowledge.
- *Application* (A). Children and adolescents at the application stage apply acquired knowledge to situations and to self. They seek out ways to use the knowledge. For example, they can demonstrate, employ, perform, illustrate, and solve problems related to the knowledge.
- *Reflection* (R). Children and adolescents at the reflection stage analyze, synthesize, judge, assess, and evaluate knowledge in accord with their own goals, values, and beliefs. They decide whether or not to integrate the acquired knowledge into their ongoing response to situations and adjust their behavior accordingly.

Coding System

The NCDG framework has a simple coding system to identify domains, goals, indicators, and learning stages. The coding system makes it easy to use the NCDG for program development and to track activities by goal, learning stage, and indicator. However, you do not need to know or include the codes to use the NCDG framework.

Domains

- PS—Personal Social Development (ASCA: Personal/Social)
- ED—Educational Achievement and Lifelong Learning (ASCA: Academic)
- CM—Career Management (ASCA: Career)

Goals
Coded by domain and then numerically. For example, under the Personal Social Development domain:

- Goal PS1: Develop understanding of yourself to build and maintain a positive self-concept.
- Goal PS2: Develop positive interpersonal skills including respect for diversity.

Indicators and Learning Stages:
Coded by domain, goal, learning stage, and then numerically. The learning stages are:

- K—Knowledge Acquisition
- A—Application
- R—Reflection

The second indicator under the first goal of the Personal Social Development domain, for example, is then coded as follows:

- PS1.K2: Identify your abilities, strengths, skills, and talents.
- PS1.A2: Demonstrate use of your abilities, strengths, skills, and talents.
- PS1.R2: Assess the impact of your abilities, strengths, skills, and talents on your career development.

TABLE 7.5 National Career Development Guidelines

PERSONAL SOCIAL DEVELOPMENT DOMAIN

GOAL PS1 *Develop understanding of yourself to build and maintain a positive self-concept.*

PS1.K1	Identify your interests, likes, and dislikes.
PS1.A1	Demonstrate behavior and decisions that reflect your interests, likes, and dislikes.
PS1.R1	Assess how your interests and preferences are reflected in your career goals.
PS1.K2	Identify your abilities, strengths, skills, and talents.
PS1.A2	Demonstrate use of your abilities, strengths, skills, and talents.
PS1.R2	Assess the impact of your abilities, strengths, skills, and talents on your career development.
PS1.K3	Identify your positive personal characteristics (e.g., honesty, dependability, responsibility, integrity, and loyalty).
PS1.A3	Give examples of when you demonstrated positive personal characteristics (e.g., honesty, dependability, responsibility, integrity, and loyalty).
PS1.R3	Assess the impact of your positive personal characteristics (e.g., honesty, dependability, responsibility, integrity, and loyalty) on your career development.
PS1.K4	Identify your work values/needs.
PS1.A4	Demonstrate behavior and decisions that reflect your work values/needs.
PS1.R4	Assess how your work values/needs are reflected in your career goals.
PS1.K5	Describe aspects of your self-concept.
PS1.A5	Demonstrate a positive self-concept through your behaviors and attitudes.
PS1.R5	Analyze the positive and negative aspects of your self-concept.
PS1.K6	Identify behaviors and experiences that help to build and maintain a positive self-concept.
PS1.A6	Show how you have adopted behaviors and sought experiences that build and maintain a positive self-concept.
PS1.R6	Evaluate the affect of your behaviors and experiences on building and maintaining a positive self-concept.
PS1.K7	Recognize that situations, attitudes, and the behaviors of others affect your self-concept.
PS1.A7	Give personal examples of specific situations, attitudes, and behaviors of others that affected your self-concept.
PS1.R7	Evaluate the affect of situations, attitudes, and the behaviors of others on your self-concept.
PS1.K8	Recognize that your behaviors and attitudes affect the self-concept of others.
PS1.A8	Show how you have adopted behaviors and attitudes to positively affect the self-concept of others.
PS1.R8	Analyze how your behaviors and attitudes might affect the self-concept of others.
PS1.K9	Recognize that your self-concept can affect educational achievement (i.e., performance) and/or success at work.
PS1.A9	Show how aspects of your self-concept could positively or negatively affect educational achievement (i.e., performance) and/or success at work.
PS1.R9	Assess how your self-concept affects your educational achievement (performance) and/or success at work.
PS1.K10	Recognize that educational achievement (performance) and/or success at work can affect your self-concept.
PS1.A10	Give personal examples of how educational achievement (performance) and/or success at work affected your self-concept.
PS1.R10	Assess how your educational achievement (performance) and/or success at work affects your self-concept.

continued

TABLE 7.5   National Career Development Guidelines (continued)

GOAL PS2	*Develop positive interpersonal skills including respect for diversity.*
PS2.K1	Identify effective communication skills.
PS2.A1	Demonstrate effective communication skills.
PS2.R1	Evaluate your use of effective communication skills.
PS2.K2	Recognize the benefits of interacting with others in a way that is honest, fair, helpful, and respectful.
PS2.A2	Demonstrate that you interact with others in a way that is honest, fair, helpful, and respectful.
PS2.R2	Assess the degree to which you interact with others in a way that is honest, fair, helpful, and respectful.
PS2.K3	Identify positive social skills (e.g., good manners and showing gratitude).
PS2.A3	Demonstrate the ability to use positive social skills (e.g., good manners and showing gratitude).
PS2.R3	Evaluate how your positive social skills (e.g., good manners and showing gratitude) contribute to effective interactions with others.
PS2.K4	Identify ways to get along well with others and work effectively with them in groups.
PS2.A4	Demonstrate the ability to get along well with others and work effectively with them in groups.
PS2.R4	Evaluate your ability to work effectively with others in groups.
PS2.K5	Describe conflict resolution skills.
PS2.A5	Demonstrate the ability to resolve conflicts and to negotiate acceptable solutions.
PS2.R5	Analyze the success of your conflict resolution skills.
PS2.K6	Recognize the difference between appropriate and inappropriate behavior in specific school, social, and work situations.
PS2.A6	Give examples of times when your behavior was appropriate and times when your behavior was inappropriate in specific school, social, and work situations.
PS2.R6	Assess the consequences of appropriate or inappropriate behavior in specific school, social, and work situations.
PS2.K7	Identify sources of outside pressure that affect you.
PS2.A7	Demonstrate the ability to handle outside pressure on you.
PS2.R7	Analyze the impact of outside pressure on your behavior.
PS2.K8	Recognize that you should accept responsibility for your behavior.
PS2.A8	Demonstrate that you accept responsibility for your behavior.
PS2.R8	Assess the degree to which you accept personal responsibility for your behavior.
PS2.K9	Recognize that you should have knowledge about, respect for, be open to, and appreciate all kinds of human diversity.
PS2.A9	Demonstrate knowledge about, respect for, openness to, and appreciation for all kinds of human diversity.
PS2.R9	Assess how you show respect for all kinds of human diversity.
PS2.K10	Recognize that the ability to interact positively with diverse groups of people may contribute to learning and academic achievement.
PS2.A10	Show how the ability to interact positively with diverse groups of people may contribute to learning and academic achievement.
PS2.R10	Analyze the impact of your ability to interact positively with diverse groups of people on your learning and academic achievement.
PS2.K11	Recognize that the ability to interact positively with diverse groups of people is often essential to maintain employment.
PS2.A11	Explain how the ability to interact positively with diverse groups of people is often essential to maintain employment.
PS2.R11	Analyze the impact of your ability to interact positively with diverse groups of people on your employment.

TABLE 7.5   National Career Development Guidelines (continued)

GOAL PS3	*Integrate personal growth and change into your career development.*
PS3.K1	Recognize that you will experience growth and changes in mind and body throughout life that will impact on your career development.
PS3.A1	Give examples of how you have grown and changed (e.g., physically, emotionally, socially, and intellectually).
PS3.R1	Analyze the results of your growth and changes throughout life to determine areas of growth for the future.
PS3.K2	Identify good health habits (e.g., good nutrition and constructive ways to manage stress).
PS3.A2	Demonstrate how you have adopted good health habits.
PS3.R2	Assess the impact of your health habits on your career development.
PS3.K3	Recognize that your motivations and aspirations are likely to change with time and circumstances.
PS3.A3	Give examples of how your personal motivations and aspirations have changed with time and circumstances.
PS3.R3	Assess how changes in your motivations and aspirations over time have affected your career development.
PS3.K4	Recognize that external events often cause life changes.
PS3.A4	Give examples of external events that have caused life changes for you.
PS3.R4	Assess your strategies for managing life changes caused by external events.
PS3.K5	Identify situations (e.g., problems at school or work) in which you might need assistance from people or other resources.
PS3.A5	Demonstrate the ability to seek assistance (e.g., with problems at school or work) from appropriate resources, including other people.
PS3.R5	Assess the effectiveness of your strategies for getting assistance (e.g., with problems at school or work) from appropriate resources, including other people.
PS3.K6	Recognize the importance of adaptability and flexibility when initiating or responding to change.
PS3.A6	Demonstrate adaptability and flexibility when initiating or responding to change.
PS3.R6	Analyze how effectively you respond to change and/or initiate change.
GOAL PS4	*Balance personal, leisure, community, learner, family, and work roles.*
PS4.K1	Recognize that you have many life roles (e.g., personal, leisure, community, learner, family, and work roles).
PS4.A1	Give examples that demonstrate your life roles, including personal, leisure, community, learner, family, and work roles.
PS4.R1	Assess the impact of your life roles on career goals.
PS4.K2	Recognize that you must balance life roles and that there are many ways to do it.
PS4.A2	Show how you are balancing your life roles.
PS4.R2	Analyze how specific life role changes would affect the attainment of your career goals.
PS4.K3	Describe the concept of lifestyle.
PS4.A3	Give examples of decisions, factors, and circumstances that affect your current lifestyle.
PS4.R3	Analyze how specific lifestyle changes would affect the attainment of your career goals.
PS4.K4	Recognize that your life roles and your lifestyle are connected.
PS4.A4	Show how your life roles and your lifestyle are connected.
PS4.R4	Assess how changes in your life roles would affect your lifestyle.

EDUCATIONAL ACHIEVEMENT AND LIFELONG LEARNING DOMAIN

GOAL ED1	*Attain educational achievement and performance levels needed to reach your personal and career goals.*

continued

TABLE 7.5   National Career Development Guidelines (continued)

ED1.K1	Recognize the importance of educational achievement and performance to the attainment of personal and career goals.
ED1.A1	Demonstrate educational achievement and performance levels needed to attain your personal and career goals.
ED1.R1	Evaluate how well you have attained educational achievement and performance levels needed to reach your personal and career goals.
ED1.K2	Identify strategies for improving educational achievement and performance.
ED1.A2	Demonstrate strategies you are using to improve educational achievement and performance.
ED1.R2	Analyze your educational achievement and performance strategies to create a plan for growth and improvement.
ED1.K3	Describe study skills and learning habits that promote educational achievement and performance.
ED1.A3	Demonstrate acquisition of study skills and learning habits that promote educational achievement and performance.
ED1.R3	Evaluate your study skills and learning habits to develop a plan for improving them.
ED1.K4	Identify your learning style.
ED1.A4	Show how you are using learning style information to improve educational achievement and performance.
ED1.R4	Analyze your learning style to develop behaviors to maximize educational achievement and performance.
ED1.K5	Describe the importance of having a plan to improve educational achievement and performance.
ED1.A5	Show that you have a plan to improve educational achievement and performance.
ED1.R5	Evaluate the results of your plan for improving educational achievement and performance.
ED1.K6	Describe how personal attitudes and behaviors can impact educational achievement and performance.
ED1.A6	Exhibit attitudes and behaviors that support educational achievement and performance.
ED1.R6	Assess how well your attitudes and behaviors promote educational achievement and performance.
ED1.K7	Recognize that your educational achievement and performance can lead to many workplace options.
ED1.A7	Show how your educational achievement and performance can expand your workplace options.
ED1.R7	Assess how well your educational achievement and performance will transfer to the workplace.
ED1.K8	Recognize that the ability to acquire and use information contributes to educational achievement and performance.
ED1.A8	Show how the ability to acquire and use information has affected your educational achievement and performance.
ED1.R8	Assess your ability to acquire and use information in order to improve educational achievement and performance.
GOAL ED2	*Participate in ongoing, lifelong learning experiences to enhance your ability to function effectively in a diverse and changing economy.*
ED2.K1	Recognize that changes in the economy require you to acquire and update knowledge and skills throughout life.
ED2.A1	Show how lifelong learning is helping you function effectively in a diverse and changing economy.
ED2.R1	Judge whether or not you have the knowledge and skills necessary to function effectively in a diverse and changing economy.

TABLE 7.5 National Career Development Guidelines (continued)

ED2.K2	Recognize that viewing yourself as a learner affects your identity.
ED2.A2	Show how being a learner affects your identity.
ED2.R2	Analyze how specific learning experiences have affected your identity.
ED2.K3	Recognize the importance of being an independent learner and taking responsibility for your learning.
ED2.A3	Demonstrate that you are an independent learner.
ED2.R3	Assess how well you function as an independent learner.
ED2.K4	Describe the requirements for transition from one learning level to the next (e.g., middle school to high school, high school to postsecondary).
ED2.A4	Demonstrate the knowledge and skills necessary for transition from one learning level to the next (e.g., middle school to high school, high school to postsecondary).
ED2.R4	Analyze how your knowledge and skills affect your transition from one learning level to the next (e.g., middle school to high school, high school to postsecondary).
ED2.K5	Identify types of ongoing learning experiences available to you (e.g., two- and four-year colleges, technical schools, apprenticeships, the military, on-line courses, and on-the-job training)
ED2.A5	Show how you are preparing to participate in ongoing learning experiences (e.g., two- and four-year colleges, technical schools, apprenticeships, the military, on-line courses, and on-the-job training).
ED2.R5	Assess how participation in ongoing learning experiences (e.g., two- and four-year colleges, technical schools, apprenticeships, the military, on-line courses, and on-the-job training) affects your personal and career goals.
ED2.K6	Identify specific education/training programs (e.g., high school career paths and courses, college majors, and apprenticeship programs).
ED2.A6	Demonstrate participation in specific education/training programs (e.g., high school career paths and courses, college majors, and apprenticeship programs) that help you function effectively in a diverse and changing economy.
ED2.R6	Evaluate how participation in specific education/training programs (e.g., high school career paths and courses, college majors, and apprenticeship programs) affects your ability to function effectively in a diverse and changing economy.
ED2.K7	Describe informal learning experiences that contribute to lifelong learning.
ED2.A7	Demonstrate participation in informal learning experiences.
ED2.R7	Assess, throughout your life, how well you integrate both formal and informal learning experiences.

CAREER MANAGEMENT DOMAIN

GOAL CM1	*Create and manage a career plan that meets your career goals.*
CM1.K1	Recognize that career planning to attain your career goals is a lifelong process.
CM1.A1	Give examples of how you use career-planning strategies to attain your career goals.
CM1.R1	Assess how well your career planning strategies facilitate reaching your career goals.
CM1.K2	Describe how to develop a career plan (e.g., steps and content).
CM1.A2	Develop a career plan to meet your career goals.
CM1.R2	Analyze your career plan and make adjustments to reflect ongoing career management needs.
CM1.K3	Identify your short-term and long-term career goals (e.g., education, employment, and lifestyle goals).
CM1.A3	Demonstrate actions taken to attain your short-term and long-term career goals (e.g., education, employment, and lifestyle goals).
CM1.R3	Reexamine your career goals and adjust as needed.

continued

TABLE 7.5　National Career Development Guidelines (continued)

CM1.K4	Identify skills and personal traits needed to manage your career (e.g., resiliency, self-efficacy, ability to identify trends and changes, and flexibility).
CM1.A4	Demonstrate career management skills and personal traits (e.g., resiliency, self-efficacy, ability to identify trends and changes, and flexibility).
CM1.R4	Evaluate your career management skills and personal traits (e.g., resiliency, self-efficacy, ability to identify trends and changes, and flexibility).
CM1.K5	Recognize that changes in you and the world of work can affect your career plans.
CM1.A5	Give examples of how changes in you and the world of work have caused you to adjust your career plans.
CM1.R5	Evaluate how well you integrate changes in you and the world of work into your career plans.
GOAL CM2	*Use a process of decision making as one component of career development.*
CM2.K1	Describe your decision-making style (e.g., risk taker, cautious).
CM2.A1	Give examples of past decisions that demonstrate your decision-making style.
CM2.R1	Evaluate the effectiveness of your decision-making style.
CM2.K2	Identify the steps in one model of decision making.
CM2.A2	Demonstrate the use of a decision-making model.
CM2.R2	Assess what decision-making model(s) work best for you.
CM2.K3	Describe how information (e.g., about you, the economy, and education programs) can improve your decision making.
CM2.A3	Demonstrate use of information (e.g., about you, the economy, and education programs) in making decisions.
CM2.R3	Assess how well you use information (e.g., about you, the economy, and education programs) to make decisions.
CM2.K4	Identify alternative options and potential consequences for a specific decision.
CM2.A4	Show how exploring options affected a decision you made.
CM2.R4	Assess how well you explore options when making decisions.
CM2.K5	Recognize that your personal priorities, culture, beliefs, and work values can affect your decision making.
CM2.A5	Show how personal priorities, culture, beliefs, and work values are reflected in your decisions.
CM2.R5	Evaluate the effect of personal priorities, culture, beliefs, and work values in your decision making.
CM2.K6	Describe how education, work, and family experiences might impact your decisions.
CM2.A6	Give specific examples of how your education, work, and family experiences have influenced your decisions.
CM2.R6	Assess the impact of your education, work, and family experiences on decisions.
CM2.K7	Describe how biases and stereotypes can limit decisions.
CM2.A7	Give specific examples of how biases and stereotypes affected your decisions.
CM2.R7	Analyze the ways you could manage biases and stereotypes when making decisions.
CM2.K8	Recognize that chance can play a role in decision making.
CM2.A8	Give examples of times when chance played a role in your decision making
CM2.R8	Evaluate the impact of chance on past decisions.
CM2.K9	Recognize that decision making often involves compromise.
CM2.A9	Give examples of compromises you might have to make in career decision making.
CM2.R9	Analyze the effectiveness of your approach to making compromises.
GOAL CM3	*Use accurate, current, and unbiased career information during career planning and management.*
CM3.K1	Describe the importance of career information to your career planning.

TABLE 7.5   National Career Development Guidelines (continued)

CM3.A1	Show how career information has been important in your plans and how it can be used in future plans.
CM3.R1	Assess the impact of career information on your plans and refine plans so that they reflect accurate, current, and unbiased career information.
CM3.K2	Recognize that career information includes occupational, education and training, employment, and economic information and that there is a range of career information resources available.
CM3.A2	Demonstrate the ability to use different types of career information resources (i.e., occupational, educational, economic, and employment) to support career planning.
CM3.R2	Evaluate how well you integrate occupational, educational, economic, and employment information into the management of your career.
CM3.K3	Recognize that the quality of career information resource content varies (e.g., accuracy, bias, and how up-to-date and complete it is).
CM3.A3	Show how selected examples of career information are biased, out-of-date, incomplete, or inaccurate.
CM3.R3	Judge the quality of the career information resources you plan to use in terms of accuracy, bias, and how up-to-date and complete they are.
CM3.K4	Identify several ways to classify occupations.
CM3.A4	Give examples of how occupational classification systems can be used in career planning.
CM3.R4	Assess which occupational classification system is most helpful to your career planning.
CM3.K5	Identify occupations that you might consider without regard to your gender, race, culture, or ability.
CM3.A5	Demonstrate openness to considering occupations that you might view as nontraditional (i.e., relative to your gender, race, culture, or ability).
CM3.R5	Assess your openness to considering nontraditional occupations in your career.
CM3.K6	Identify the advantages and disadvantages of being employed in a nontraditional occupation.
CM3.A6	Make decisions for yourself about being employed in a nontraditional occupation.
CM3.R6	Assess the impact of your decisions about being employed in a nontraditional occupation.
GOAL CM4	*Master academic, occupational, and general employability skills in order to obtain, create, maintain, and/or advance your employment.*
CM4.K1	Describe academic, occupational, and general employability skills.
CM4.A1	Demonstrate the ability to use your academic, occupational, and general employability skills to obtain or create, maintain, and advance your employment.
CM4.R1	Assess your academic, occupational, and general employability skills and enhance them as needed for your employment.
CM4.K2	Identify job-seeking skills such as the ability to write a resume and cover letter, complete a job application, interview for a job, and find and pursue employment leads.
CM4.A2	Demonstrate the following job-seeking skills: write a resume and cover letter, complete a job application, interview for a job, and find and pursue employment leads.
CM4.R2	Evaluate your ability to write a resume and cover letter, complete a job application, interview for a job, and find and pursue employment leads.
CM4.K3	Recognize that a variety of general employability skills and personal qualities (e.g., critical thinking; problem solving; resource, information, and technology management; interpersonal skills; honesty; and dependability) are important to success in school and employment.
CM4.A3	Demonstrate attainment of general employability skills and personal qualities needed to be successful in school and employment (e.g., critical thinking; problem solving; resource, information, and technology management; interpersonal skills; honesty; and dependability).

continued

TABLE 7.5   National Career Development Guidelines (continued)

CM4.R3	Evaluate your general employability skills and personal qualities (e.g., critical thinking; problem solving; resource, information, and technology management; interpersonal skills; honesty; and dependability).
CM4.K4	Recognize that many skills are transferable from one occupation to another.
CM4.A4	Show how your skills are transferable from one occupation to another.
CM4.R4	Analyze the impact of your transferable skills on your career options.
CM4.K5	Recognize that your geographic mobility impacts on your employability.
CM4.A5	Make decisions for yourself regarding geographic mobility.
CM4.R5	Analyze the impact of your decisions about geographic mobility on your career goals.
CM4.K6	Identify the advantages and challenges of self-employment.
CM4.A6	Make decisions for yourself about self-employment.
CM4.R6	Assess the impact of your decision regarding self-employment on your career goals.
CM4.K7	Identify ways to be proactive in marketing yourself for a job.
CM4.A7	Demonstrate skills that show how you can market yourself in the workplace.
CM4.R7	Evaluate how well you have marketed yourself in the workplace.
GOAL CM5	*Integrate changing employment trends, societal needs, and economic conditions into your career plans.*
CM5.K1	Identify societal needs that affect your career plans.
CM5.A1	Show how you are prepared to respond to changing societal needs in your career management.
CM5.R1	Evaluate the results of your career management relative to changing societal needs.
CM5.K2	Identify economic conditions that affect your career plans.
CM5.A2	Show how you are prepared to respond to changing economic conditions in your career management.
CM5.R2	Evaluate the results of your career management relative to changing economic conditions.
CM5.K3	Identify employment trends that affect your career plans.
CM5.A3	Show how you are prepared to respond to changing employment trends in your career management.
CM5.R3	Evaluate the results of your career management relative to changes in employment trends.

Source: Perkins Collaborative Resource Network, The National Career Development Guidelines (NCDG) Framework, http://cte.ed.gov/acrn/ncdg/ncdg, retrieved December 1, 2010.

Special Programs for Academically Disenfranchised Students

8

Promoting Achievement and Advancement of First-Generation College and University Students

In the early 1980s, seminal and controversial educational reform reports on the state of American education by the National Commission on Excellence in Education (1983), the Carnegie Foundation for the Advanced of Teaching (Boyer, 1983), and the National Association of Secondary School Principals, in collaboration with the Commission on Educational Issues of the National Association of Independent Schools (Sizer, 1984), all vehemently called for educational reform and greater accountability of student achievement and teacher effectiveness. In the wake of the national movement toward standards-based reform, professional school counselors were not viewed as an integral part of the most recent systematic national initiative, the No Child Left Behind Act of 2001 (NCLB).

Yet, professional school counselors need to embrace a standard-based school counseling program to be school improvement specialists to close the achievement gap affecting minority students and students of poverty. The American School Counselor Association (ASCA, 2005a) has developed a model that significantly changes the school counselor's role from being a broker of isolated services to being a catalyst for systemic change by providing leadership, advocacy for all students, collaboration, and involvement with teachers, parents, and the greater community. A standards-based school counseling model serves to demonstrate how school counseling programs are central to the school's mission, while defining the responsibilities and standards for school counseling delivery and evaluation. The potential benefits include, but are not limited to:

- Programs that assist in identifying and removing barriers to student achievement and success, thus closing the achievement gap for minority, poor students, and first-generation students whose parents/caregivers do not have information on how to maneuver the process to postsecondary education and further training
- Increased equity in access to school counseling services and interventions for all students (not just the brightest or those with discipline problems)

- Increased student motivation to enroll in and complete rigorous course work to be more prepared and competitive in an increasingly global society
- Support and training for teachers in school counseling principles and strategies to address learning and behavior problems in the classroom as well as the school community
- Programs and services that develop essential attitudes, knowledge, and skills and the propensity for student achievement and successful postsecondary transition to adulthood
- Programs and services that assist students with education and career planning and decision making
- Organized program coordination with staff, parents/caregivers, community resources, and advisory boards
- Data analysis of school counseling program outcomes and variables for school improvement planning and leadership
- Partnerships with business and industry to design programs that enhance students' workplace readiness and flexibility in a changing global economy
- Well-defined and well-articulated roles, responsibilities, programs, and services for school counselors distinct from other student support service personnel, with written agreements between principals and professional school counselors
- Student learning benchmarks and school counselor performance standards that guide the preparation and professional development of counselors, including a model for field placement and practice (Carey & Dimmitt, 2006).

Essentially, professional school counselors must work to as leaders and change agents to advocate the elimination of systemic barriers and individual barriers that impede academic success for all students, not for a chosen few students. Closing the achievement gap between poor and minority children and their more advantaged peers becomes the primary goal of every school counselor in the standards-based school counseling initiative. The changes outlined by ASCA (2006) are listed in Tables 8.1 and 8.2.

> We pass through this world but once. Few tragedies can be more extensive than the stunting of life, few injustices deeper than the denial of an opportunity to strive or even to hope, by a limit imposed from without, but falsely identified as lying within.
>
> Stephen Jay Gould (1981, pp. 28–29)

Public schools today continue to respond to economic, social, and political pressures. Schools have often been accused of following the latest educational fad to try to improve educational achievement and performance. Waves of reform have been well documented (Oakes, 1985; Cuban, 1990; Darling-Hammond, 1996), often in response to national or international events. For example, the National Defense Education Act of 1958 was a response to *Sputnik,* the Cold War, and the need to make our students stronger in math and science so we could compete with the Soviet Union. Yet more than 50 years later, our students are outperformed in mathematics and science by majority of their peers around the world (NCES, 2007).

School reform proposals have focused largely on the structure and content of schools, but not on the changing circumstances—such as family dynamics, social change, and the influence of popular culture, English-language learners, immigration, the achievement gap, and poverty—that affect the development

TABLE 8.1   Needed School Counseling Changes

FROM COUNSELORS WHO:	TO COUNSELORS WHO:
Focus on good intentions	Focus on accomplishments
Talk about how hard they work	Talk about outcomes
Feel little need to change behavior	Know that the future depends on continued improvement
Use intuition to design programs	Use data to design and evaluate programs

TABLE 8.2 Needed School Counseling Program Changes

FROM A PROGRAM THAT:	TO A PROGRAM THAT:
Is student centered and serves some students	Is program centered and serves all students well
Focuses on activities	Focuses on outcomes
Measures activities	Measures progress toward goals
Works to maintain the system	Works to help the system adapt and change

Source: American School Counselor Association (2002). Reprinted with permission.

of children and youth. Sociocultural factors have also influenced schooling. The stratified, unequal society that has existed for affluent white, nonwhite, and poor students has been perpetuated in educational practice. Thus, differentiated schooling, cultural bias, and differences between family and school perspectives have contributed to creating a significant achievement gap for African American students, Latino students, and children of poverty.

The most significant educational problem in the 21st century is the fact that the achievement of minority children lags behind that of nonminority children in the United States. In this era of educational reform, "school counselors like all educators are being held accountable for the academic achievement because a disproportionate number of minority and poor students are invariably at risk for school failure" (Wang, Haertel, & Walberg, 1998, p. 74). Professional school counselors need to assume the role of facilitator, resource manager, collaborator, and advocate when working with all students, but particularly those who are most at risk for dropping out of school or falling behind.

Recent student demographics, shown in Table 8.3, provide a depiction of the student population across the nation with educational attainment by race. Comparing the demographic distribution of students across each educational level shows what happens to children as they journey through the education system in the United States. Significant differences should raise questions about educational equity and educational opportunity, which in term affect career success. For example, Latinos represent 8.6% of the United States college-going population compared with 73.2% for whites (NCES, 2005b, 2002). In addition, Latinos are more likely to attend a two-year college than either African American or white students (NCES, 2005b).

Differentiated schooling evolved as a means to create "a socially efficient schooling system that would select the *minds best suited for mental training* and the *bodies best suited for manual training*" (Nasaw, 1979, p. 137). Ultimately, the high school as we know it today, with both career and technical programs and academic program tracks, emerged, and it continues to perpetuate barriers to learning for minorities and poor students. High schools "were called upon to do the impossible: to uphold the myths of the 'classless' community while at the same time preparing young people for their future lives in a society based on class divisions" (Nasaw, 1979, p. 157).

TABLE 8.3 Student Progression Through Educational Attainment by Race

	POPULATION, AGE 5–24*	PUBLIC K–12	TWO-YEAR COLLEGES	FOUR-YEAR COLLEGES
African American	14%	17%	14%	12%
Asian	4%	4%	6%	5%
Latino	15%	19%	14%	10%
Native American	1%	1%	1%	1%
White	57%	58%	58%	62%
Other	10%	N/A	7%	10%
Total	87,671,193	48,344,926	10,301,501	10,291,784

Source: Education Trust, *EdWatch Online 2005 State Summary Reports*, http://www.edtrust.org, retrieved April 15, 2009. American School Counselor Association (2002). Reprinted with permission.

In the past, although public schools did not deliberately create racism and class bias, they "often reinforced social injustice for some students at the same time that they offer[ed] opportunity to other students" (Tyack, 1974, p. 4). Career and technical tracking and academic tracking continue to exist, relegating minority, disadvantaged, and poor children to classes that have low expectations—for example, language skills instead of English, or consumer math instead of Algebra I. Because public schools are steeped in the traditions of a Euro-American, white, middle-class culture and heritage, some researchers believe this white dominance is ingrained in the public school system in the United States.

White dominance and white privilege perpetuate bias and discrimination through institutional racism and socioeconomic class structures (Howard, 2006; Jensen, 1998; McIntosh, 1990). In addition, teachers generally expect students to change to fit into the mold of the school rather than adapting the school structures to the different learning styles of children (Delpit, 1995; Greenfield, Raeff, & Quiroz, 1996; Howard, 2006; Lipman, 1998). Students who do not conform have been described or labeled as *deficient, disadvantaged, culturally deprived,* and *at risk of failure.* These labels are disabling and convey that the students and their families are to "blame." The use of such terms "constructs reality for those children, and for the professionals who are responsible to them" (Fennimore, 2000, p. xi). Essentially, the expectation of academic and career success of poor students and students of color is not nurtured and is often ignored. There are also artificial gatekeepers that prevent students from engaging in college outreach programs; for example, a certain grade-point average (GPA) is required for participation in National Collegiate Athletic Association (NCAA), Upward Bound, or Advancement via Individual Determination (AVID) programs. Yet, the literature shows overwhelmingly that African Americans (regardless of social status) universally view education as the most promising means for attaining higher socioeconomic status. This creates both dissonance and disconnect between minority parents and teachers, and reveals the *misperceptions* they have of one another. (Ashton & Webb, 1986, p. 21)

Many authors have described the internal segregation that occurs in the form of assignment of disproportionate numbers of children of color—particularly African American male students—to slower, remedial tracks and to programs for students with behavioral problems (Darling-Hammond, 1997; Oakes, 1985). The reverse occurs as well: disproportionately few students of color are enrolled in gifted and talented classes, enrichment programs, or other challenging classes or programs such as Advanced Placement (AP) courses. Students of color are overrepresented in special education programs and students of color, particularly African American students, are disproportionately subject to harsh disciplinary action. Studies commissioned by the Civil Rights Project (Sunderman, 2008) suggest that this overrepresentation is due to many complex and interacting factors that include racial bias, inequities in resources, overreliance on intelligence quotient (IQ) and other evaluation tools, pressures of and inappropriate responses to high-stakes testing, and an imbalance of power between minority parents and school officials (Losen & Orfield, 2002). "African-American students nationwide are nearly three times as likely to be classified as intellectually disabled, nearly twice as likely to be identified as having an emotional disturbance and nearly a third more likely to be diagnosed with a specific learning disability" (Land & Legters, 2001, p. 101). For example:

African-American children represent 16% of the school population nationally but 21% of the enrollments in special education, 25% of those identified by schools as having emotional and behavioral disorders, 26% of those arrested, 30% of the cases in juvenile court, 32% of out-of-school suspensions, 40% of youth in juvenile detention, 45% of cases involving some form of detention, and 46% of the cases waived to criminal court. (Osher, Woodruff, & Sims, 2001, p. 16)

THE CHANGING DEMOGRAPHICS OF THE PUBLIC SCHOOL

Unfortunately, such views of school reform do not factor into their propositions that, in many cases, because of deteriorating situations in homes, schools have become child-rearing institutions, one of the few places in their lives where many children find predictability, safety, support, and food. Schools are one of the few places that allow children to escape violence in the home and in the community, the increasing lawlessness of gangs and cults, physical or psychological neglect in their home, a lack of family presence and support as they return home from school to empty apartments and houses, or to homes where chemical dependency robs parents of their ability to be responsible for their children. Many children are experiencing the multiple conditions of disintegrating families, the special tensions associated with the rise of blended families, the growing pockets of child poverty and child malnutrition, and the growth in the number of single parents and grandparents raising children.

Edwin L. Herr (2002, p. 230)

According to the 2000 United States census, Latinos are the largest minority racial/ethnic group in the United States, comprising 12.5% of the population (Grieco & Cassidy, 2001). As of July 2006, there were 44.3 million Latinos living in the United States (U.S. Census Bureau, 2008). Latinos accounted for one-half of the nation's growth, with a growth rate (24.5%) more than three times that of the total population (6.1%) (U.S. Census Bureau, 2008). If this rate continues, by 2010, this group will represent 20% of the nation's population (Marotta & Garcia, 2003). Not only is the Latino population disproportionately young (U.S. Census Bureau, 2001), but Latino children are also disproportionately poor. An estimated 28% of Latinos under the age of 18 live in poverty, a poverty rate almost three times that of non-Latino whites and comparable to the poverty rate (30%) of African American children and adolescents (U.S. Census Bureau, 2003). Latino Americans are a diverse population, including individuals of Cuban, Mexican, Puerto Rican, South or Central American, or other Spanish origin (Grieco & Cassidy, 2001).

THE PRECONCEIVED NOTIONS AND ATTITUDES TEACHERS AND ADMINISTRATORS HAVE TOWARD POOR AND MINORITY YOUTHS

Teachers often treat low-income students and students of color significantly differently than they do their white, middle-class counterparts. Teacher confidence in their own professional competence, lack of cultural sensitivity, and attitudes about student ability appear to be mutually reinforcing an attitude of low expectations. As a result, many teachers leave the profession within the first five years because of the lack of skills, knowledge, or training on how to deal with more diverse populations of students. However, Ferguson (1998) has concluded that "African American students respond more strongly to teachers' beliefs than do White students" (p. 320). This suggests that students of color are more affected by both negative and positive attitudes and by the treatment they receive from the teachers they encounter.

Ashton and Webb (1986) report differences in teacher perception of and behavior toward low-achieving students and state that students' personal characteristics—socioeconomic status, race, attractiveness, and classroom conduct—are often related to these expectations. Teachers' expectations about students' ability appear to be the single most influential characteristic affecting students' academic achievement.

> If teachers have low expectations of their students' ability to learn, these low expectations insidiously emerge to foster a learning environment that perpetuates a low sense of teacher efficacy and lesser commitment to effectively teach the students they believe to have low ability. (Ashton & Webb, 1986, p. 14)

R. F. Ferguson (2003) drew four conclusions based on a review of research on current conditions in schools and teacher expectations:

1. Teachers have lower expectations for African-American and other minority students than for White students.
2. Teachers' expectations have more impact on African-American and other minority students' performance than on White students' performance.
3. Teachers expect less of African-American and other minority than of White students because African-American and other minority students' past performance and behavior have been worse.
4. By basing their expectations on children's past performance and behavior, teachers perpetuate racial disparities in achievement and performance and contribute to creating the achievement gap. (p. 462)

These conditions can be observed in many impoverished classrooms at all levels across the United States. Haberman (1991) "described these practices as certain ritualistic acts that maintain order by occupying students in routine busy work (i.e., drill and practice) and leaving them intellectually unengaged and ultimately bored with education" (p. 292). Other researchers have reported that low-achieving students are typically given more routine, highly structured classwork focused on low-level intellectual activity. Consequently, low-achieving students continue to fall behind their high-achieving counterparts in the classroom and in life.

Haberman's (1991) theory of perpetuating poverty describes classroom practice that reflects poor teaching practices and low expectations. The instructional practices, such as giving information, asking questions, giving directions, checking homework, assigning homework, monitoring seatwork, giving tests, reviewing tests, settling disputes, and punishing students' noncompliance continue to be the norm rather than the exception. Land and Legters (2001) speculate that "white school personnel may perceive disrespect from African American youth when none is intended" (p. 36). This preconceived notion about discipline and subsequent behavior may also convey to students that they are more "deviant and less worthy of education" than their white peers (Land & Legters, 2001, p. 21). These discrepancies in achievement will have long-term implications for academic achievement and economic success. For example, African American youths are twice as likely and Latino youths three times more likely to drop out of school than their white non-Latino counterparts (U.S. Census Bureau, 2008).

Oakes (1985) contrasted the student behavior required by high school teachers in "high-track" versus "low-track" English and mathematics classes. Teachers of high-track classes were more likely

> to emphasize such behaviors as critical thinking, independent work, active participation, self-direction, and creativity than were teachers of low-track classes. At the same time, teachers of low-track classes were more likely than others to emphasize student conformity, students getting along with one another, working quietly, improving study habits, being punctual, and conforming to classroom rules and expectations. (p. 85)

A boring, drill-and-practice classroom climate generates low-achieving student performance.

Darling-Hammond (1997, 1999) found that teachers who were sent to the poorest schools were often poorly trained. These students

> too often sit at their desks for long periods of the day matching the picture in column "a" to the word in column "b," filling in the blanks, copying off the board. They work at a lower cognitive level on boring tasks profoundly disconnected from the skills they need to learn to be successful in the 21st century, such skills as: collaboration, team work, critical thinking, research, and public speaking. Rarely are students in these classes given opportunities to talk about what they know, to read interesting books, to construct and solve problems in mathematics or science. (Darling-Hammond, 1997, p. 272)

Fletcher and Cardona-Morales (1990) found that Latino students "tend to be instructed in whole-class instruction with students participating passively (i.e., watching or listening to the teacher) in teacher-assigned and teacher-generated activities" (p. 152). Teachers also spend more time in these classrooms explaining things to students rather than questioning, cueing, or prompting students to respond. Teachers were not often observed encouraging extended student responses or pushing students to help themselves or help each other. "In these classrooms, teachers typically used direct instruction to teach to the whole class at the same time and they controlled all of the classroom discussion and decision making" (Padron,

Waxman, & Rivera, 2002, pp. 70–71). All these methods need to be challenged because they represent barriers to learning.

In addition to poverty, many Latino youths are exposed to developmental risks both within and outside the home. Within-home risks include being born to an adolescent mother, being raised by parents with limited English skills, and living with a single or in large family households. Outside risks include attending low-quality segregated schools and residing in disadvantaged neighborhoods that are most vulnerable to the drug trafficking, gang activity, and other self-defeating behaviors (Bumpass & Lu, 2000; Leyendecker & Lamb, 1999). With these multiple risk factors, Latinos tend to score lower on academic achievement tests (Ainsworth, 2002; Roscigno, 2000), attain fewer years of education (U.S. Department of Education, 2003), and do progressively worse on subsequent economic indicators such as earnings, postsecondary education, and family income (Marotta & Garcia, 2003). Consequently, students who attend schools with high percentages of poor and minority students, coupled with serious crime problems, low instructional expenditure, and few opportunities to enroll in advanced courses, have lower achievement scores (Catsambis & Beveridge, 2001; Roscigno, 2000).

> Lack of appropriate role models and adult supervision, parentifying older children in the family, restricted career and employment opportunities, and unsupportive or unhelpful social networks are among the explanations for the influence of disadvantaged neighborhoods on academic achievement. (Ainsworth, 2002, p. 132)

Research continues to support the idea that "addressing the entire family system might be particularly insightful for professional school counselors when working with Latinos because of the strong values that many Latinos hold regarding the importance of family, cooperation, and positive interactions" (Leyendecker & Lamb, 1999, p. 257). Further, because Mexican Americans are the largest Latino subgroup in the nation (Marotta & Garcia, 2003; U.S. Census Bureau, 2008), educational policies and interventions that help Mexican American youths in achieving academic success appear to be particularly important. School environments can improve their environment by assisting teachers in becoming more sensitive to and prepared for the different learning styles and needs of Latino students, establishing tutoring and mentoring programs (instead of placing Latino youths in lower-level course work), holding high academic expectations, providing counseling and support services, and enhancing parental involvement and communication between parents and schools (McEvoy & Welker, 2000; Slavin & Calderon, 2001).

Certain attitudes—such as educational aspirations, occupational expectations, and attitudes toward school—are related to students' achievement (Ainsworth-Darnell & Downey, 1998; Dumais, 2002). Both African Americans and Latinos have higher educational aspirations than do whites, especially when differences in family (socioeconomic status) are taken into account (Cheng & Starks, 2002), yet even national college outreach initiatives such as AVID, EAOP (Early Academic Outreach Program), and Upward Bound are exclusionary. They all require a 3.0 GPA and reserve the right to exclude a student based on behavioral or emotional problems (Gibson & Bejines, 2002; Upward Bound, 2001).

According to Ainsworth-Darnell and Downey (1998), "African American students have higher occupational expectations and more pro-social attitudes than do White students" (p. 560). However, Farkas, Lieras, and Maczuga (2002) suggest that African American students who hold prosocial attitudes and optimistic beliefs about education are chastised by their peers for wanting to achieve in predominantly African American schools (Ainsworth-Darnell & Downey, 1998; Ainsworth, 2002; Downey & Ainsworth-Darnell, 2002). This represents a sociocultural disconnect between a student's expected academic role and peer expectations for achievement.

The research is replete with evidence that such issues as poverty, immigration status, language issues, school-related problems, and parental educational background all impact the lives of Latinos (Garcia, 2003; Gibson & Bejines, 2002; Tornatzky, Cutler, & Lee, 2002). Furthermore, perhaps more significant than the growing achievement gap between students is the growing "preparation gap" of some subpopulations of students. "Recent research demonstrates that young children are capable of learning far more complex skills and ideas than previously believed, and developing pre-academic skills helps them succeed later in school" (Mead, 2008, p. 6). But many minority students come to school less prepared than their white counterparts. They fall behind in basic skills needed for success, such as reading and mathematics. To compensate for the lack of preparedness, many poorer schools have established full-day kindergarten programs, but this has not been a national initiative. Approximately two-thirds of African American fourth-graders, and about as many Latinos and Native American children in that grade, perform below the basic level in reading on the National Assessment of Educational Progress (NAEP). This gap between students' current level of performance and what they are expected to know and be able to do continues to persist through middle school and high school, and as a long-term consequence these students are unable to enter college or secure high-paying jobs. This gap subsequently produces the "economic apartheid" for adult income levels and employment rates along racial and ethnic lines (Rothman, 2002, p. 6).

According to the American Council on Education (Harvey, 2003), "African-American students earned only 12,149 bachelor's degrees in social sciences, 4,851 degrees in biological/life sciences, and 4,324 degrees in engineering during 2000–01" (p. 26). The figures are even more alarming on the graduate level. With respect to doctoral degrees, African Americans earned only 80 degrees in physical sciences, 190 in life sciences, 299 in social sciences, and 82 in engineering during 2000–2001 (Harvey, 2003). These figures are cause for concern in light of the fact that minority students represent approximately 11% of all students enrolled in higher education (Wilds, 2000).

EMPIRICALLY BASED STRATEGIES TO CLOSE THE ACHIEVEMENT GAP

> Schools can become islands of hope in otherwise devastated neighborhoods. When schools and communities work together to give poor children the supports typically enjoyed by children in middle-class neighborhoods, they help children avoid a culture of failure.
>
> Lisbeth B. Schorr (1997, p. 289)

The following strategies can be implemented to close the achievement gap between minority children and children of poverty and their white counterparts. Doing so will take bold leadership and collective commitment and understanding, such as putting the best teachers at the poorest schools, engaging students in exciting curricula, and promoting parent involvement. Professional school counselors are being urged to take leadership roles in education reform aimed at reducing the barriers to learning and academic achievement (ASCA, 2003a, b, c; Bemak, 2000; Butler, 2003; Taylor & Adelman, 2000).

Central to change are teacher expectations, caring demeanors, efficacy, and persistence in teaching, learning, and professional school counseling initiatives. A teacher's perception of student performance and the expectations for higher academic standards is particularly critical for minority and poor students. Essentially, no one rises above low academic expectations in an environment that promotes barriers to success. Other critical elements include genuine caring for students, higher expectations for *all* students, professional efficacy among teachers, consistency and fairness in discipline practices, cultural competence, learning environments that are challenging and motivating, a vibrant curriculum, and school–family–community partnerships.

Genuine Caring for Students

When teachers genuinely care, they value the individual student and convey belief and confidence in his or her capacity to learn and ability to succeed. Caring entails listening sincerely to students, knowing something about the students and their families, and developing positive relationships with them. When explicit caring occurs between students and significant adults, it promotes and creates the relationships, the "bonds," necessary to ensure learning. Comer (2001), Darling-Hammond (1997), Delpit (1995), Gay (2000), Noddings (1992), and Wilson and Corbett (2001) are among the authors who have discussed this essential prerequisite quality in the learning environment. According to Delpit (1995), "Children of color value the social aspects of an environment to a greater extent than do 'mainstream' children, and tend to put an emphasis on feelings, acceptance, and emotional closeness" (p. 102).

Gay (2000) has also showed that motivation in African American children from low socioeconomic groups is more influenced by the need for "affiliation than for achievement" (p. 140). She extends this notion of caring to include being culturally responsive and sensitive teaching to close the achievement gap.

> Teachers demonstrate caring for children as students and as people. This is expressed in concern for their psycho-emotional well-being and academic success; personal morality and social actions; obligations and celebrations; communality and individuality; and unique cultural connections and universal human bonds ... students, in kind, feel obligated to be worthy of being honored. (p. 46)

The attitude that drives this kind of caring "accepts, embraces, and leads upward; it questions, it responds, it sympathizes, it challenges, it delights" (p. 48). Teachers who attempted to close the achievement gap

> created classroom climates of emotional warmth; consistently and clearly demanded high-quality academic performance; spent time establishing positive interpersonal relationships between themselves and students, and among students; extended their relationships with and caring for students beyond the classroom; and communicated with students through nonverbal cues, such as smiles, a gentle touch, teaching, and establishing a "kinesthetic feeling of closeness." (p. 50)

Darling-Hammond (1999) describes school organizational structures that support caring relationships. These structures include student groupings and teacher assignments that personalize the educational setting (e.g., "looping," a concept where teachers stay with their students for multiple years), small schools, interdisciplinary clusters, family or advisory groups, and school environments that promote respect and caring.

Higher Expectation for All Students

Research over the past two decades has revealed that teacher expectations on student achievement have a tremendous impact on barriers to learning (Bamburg, 1994; Ferguson, 1998; Good & Brophy, 2000). Professional staff development programs can help teachers examine their current instructional practices in order to raise expectations for student learning. Good and Brophy (2000) have demonstrated how breaking the cycle of low expectations helps increase both teacher and student perceptions of student capacity to learn.

Ferguson (1998) maintains that what teachers communicate to students about ability is important because positioning in the hierarchy of perceived ability has social significance for both individuals and groups. Essentially, the more inviting and responsive instruction is to students' individual efforts to improve, the less teachers' initial perceptions and expectations predict later success. Professional school counselors can use their team-building and group-counseling skills to assist in this school improvement initiative.

Teacher Expectation and Professional Efficacy

"Teacher expectations and sense of professional efficacy are interrelated" (Gay, 2000, p. 60). According to Ashton and Webb (1986), a teacher's sense of efficacy impacts student achievement. Those with a high sense of efficacy positively impact students and those with low sense of efficacy do not feel competent to teach low-achieving students. Therefore, a low sense of efficacy negatively affects a teacher's relationship with minority students and students from poverty.

Rosenholtz (1989) found that teachers in "moving schools," (i.e., those with a positive professional working environment) positively impacted student achievement. Teachers in these schools were encouraged to learn together and developed more assurance about their instructional capacity and classroom management skills. Professional development that increases knowledge and skill can increase teachers' confidence in their capacity to meet student needs. Professional development in cultural competence and understanding of diversity issues are embedded in professional school counselors' training and ongoing personal and professional growth. The professional school counselor can play a pivotal role in the school climate by enhancing an understanding of diversity issues among faculty, administration, and staff.

Consistence and Persistence in Discipline, Policy, and Equality

Consistence and persistence are qualities that enhance the achievement of students who are academically behind their peers. Gay (2000) "described successful teachers as 'tough' and 'took no stuff' and who were respected and revered by their students" (p. 223). Good teachers, according to students in one of Gay's case studies, are "respectful of them, care about them, provide choices, and are tenacious in their efforts to make the information taught more understandable for them" (p. 49). Middle school students interviewed by Wilson and Corbett (2001) emphasized the importance of their teachers who never quit or gave up on them. Effective teachers adhered to a "no excuses" policy; there were no good reasons to give up on a child. Persistence is connected to teacher confidence and feelings of efficacy. Teachers who hold themselves and their teaching accountable for the achievement of all students, including those who have difficulty learning, are more successful (Gay, 2000).

Cultural Responsiveness and Cultural Competence

Teachers, professional school counselors, administrators, and support staff need to activate a child's prior learning and cultural orientation to teach and counsel. Using the context of a child's culture is fundamental to good teaching, and to a good school climate. Cultural responsiveness requires more than good intentions. Educators must have the instructional strategies, knowledge, and skills, as well as courage, to change inappropriate routines and instructional practices in order to educate students of color and poverty more successfully.

Many researchers provide guidance in creating classrooms and schools to better respond to students from diverse backgrounds (Antunez, DiCerbo, & Menken, 2000; Feng, 1994; Goodwin, 2000; Kim & Yeh, 2002; Lewis & Palk, 2001; Lockwood & Secada, 1999; Noguera, 1999, 2001; Pang & Cheng, 1998). Gay (2000) defines "culturally responsive teaching" as "using the cultural knowledge, prior experiences, frames of reference, and performance styles of ethnically diverse students to make learning encounters more relevant to and effective for them, by teaching to and through the strengths of these students" (p. 29). She further characterizes culturally responsive teaching by the following:

- It acknowledges the legitimacy of the cultural heritages of different ethnic groups, both as legacies that affect students' dispositions, attitudes, and approaches to learning and as worthy content to be taught in the formal curriculum.
- It builds bridges of meaningfulness between home and school experiences as well as between academic abstractions and lived sociocultural realities.
- It uses a wide variety of instructional strategies that are connected to different learning styles.
- It teaches students to know and praise their own and each other's cultural heritages.
- It incorporates multicultural information, resources, and materials in all subjects and skills routinely taught in schools. (Gay, 2000, p. 29)

Opportunities for More Learning Time
That Is Motivating and Challenging

Opportunities for more motivating and challenging learning time include before and after school, summer, and modified school calendars so that knowledge and skills are not lost during long summer breaks. This includes reducing or eliminating pull-out programs that interrupt regular instructional time, increasing the focus on learning during scheduled class time by reducing extraneous activities, and scheduling longer blocks of time for classes to reduce fragmentation and provide for more in-depth, hands-on study. Modifying the school year by rearranging the school calendar to shorten summer vacation and intersperse breaks through the year provides continuous learning opportunities. The breaks, called *intersessions,* create opportunities for students to receive supplemental instruction and enrichment while retaining information for longer periods of time. Another strategy that many suburban and urban schools are moving toward is having full-day kindergarten programs, especially if students are coming from lower economic areas. All of these strategies have the potential to increase opportunities to learn and, consequently, to improve student achievement.

High Expectations and a Rigorous Curriculum for Everyone

The standards-based movement emphasizes educational goals to include rigorous content that all students are expected to learn. This expectation requires a shift in the type of curriculum that is often provided for students of color and poverty. Haycock (2001), Oakes (1985), Haberman (1991), Gay (2000), Good and Brophy (2000), Goodlad (1984), and Darling-Hammond (1997) are among the educational researchers who have reported the inequities suffered by low-status and low-achieving students. These children are often relegated to low-curriculum tracks because of preconceived notions about their achievement potential. In order to reduce the achievement gap, students of color and poverty must have access to cognitively rich, relevant curriculum content that is appropriate for their grade level.

Research indicates that when students of similar achievement levels are exposed to more and less challenging materials, those given the richer curriculum systematically outperform those placed in less challenging classes (Alexander, Entwisle, & Olson, 2001; Oakes, 1985). For students who have the opportunity to take similar courses, achievement test score differences by race or ethnicity narrow substantially (Johnson, 1984; Johnson & Kritsonis, 2006; Jones, Burton, & Davenport, 1984). This is the ultimate goal of closing the achievement gap. However, it will take bold leadership and the willingness to change the instructional attitude, programs, services, and school–community initiatives.

Enriched and Varied Programs Instead
of Remedial Punitive Programs

Opportunities to learn include enrichment programs, arts programs, collaborative learning, and extracurricular activities. Students of color and poverty are underrepresented in many of these programs and activities. Research has provided evidence of the relationship between student participation in extracurricular and co-curricular activities and success in school and in later life (Camp, 1990; Holloway, 2002; NCES, 2002; National Federation of State High School Associations, 2002). Intentional outreach to involve students of color and poverty in clubs, sports activities, academic associations, and other school-based activities benefits individuals through the learning that occurs, service to the school and community, and the deep relationships that grow among students and between adults and students in this type of school environment.

Participation in afterschool programs, academic associations like language clubs, and school-sponsored social activities contributes to academic performance, reduces high school dropout rates and discipline problems, and enhances interpersonal skills among students from different ethnic backgrounds. (Banks et al., 2001, p. 8)

A Vibrant Curriculum That Connects Learners with Maximum Engagement

The new science of learning and brain-based research (Bransford, Brown, & Cocking, 2000) provides insights into effective teaching practices that have the potential to increase the learning of students of color and of poverty. The literature on the achievement gap specifically describes instructional practices that often relegate such students to low-level content that is focused on basic skills and activities emphasizing drill and practice, memorization, recitation, and meaningless worksheets. This approach to instruction implies that these students must first master low-level work before they can engage in thinking, understanding, and critically applying what they learn. The current research questions this assumption and supports the teaching of advanced skills along with basic skills (e.g. critical thinking along with basic skills).

The concepts of *teaching for understanding* and *teaching for meaning* include strategies that dramatically improve performance of students who are traditionally underachieving (Knapp, Shields, & Turnbull, 1995; Newmann & Associates, 1996; Wiske, 2004). Marzano, Pickering, and Pollock (2001) describe instructional strategies that have demonstrated success in improving student performance. They also provide guidance for implementing these "research-based strategies." They include the following topics:

- Identifying similarities and differences
- Summarizing and note taking
- Reinforcing effort and providing recognition
- Homework and practice
- Nonlinguistic representation
- Cooperative learning
- Setting objectives and providing feedback
- Generating and testing hypotheses
- Cues, questions, and advance organizers (Marzano, Pickering, & Pollock, 2001, p. 169)

The achievement of students of color and poverty would increase demonstrably if high-quality instruction for deep understanding were in place in all classrooms and not differentiated. All children can learn if they are given quality instruction, a caring environment, and parent involvement in their future.

PARENT INVOLVEMENT AND SCHOOL–FAMILY–COMMUNITY PARTNERSHIPS

Educational achievement is important for all students. Professional school counselors are being urged to take a leadership role in education reform aimed at reducing the barriers to academic achievement (ASCA, 2005a; Bemak, 2000; Butler, 2003; Taylor & Adelman, 2000), and school–family–community partnership involvement is considered a central aspect of this role (ASCA, 2003c; Bemak, 2000; Bryan & Holcomb-McCoy, 2004, 2006; Taylor & Adelman, 2000; Walsh, Howard, & Buckley, 1999). In addition, NCLB and the U.S. Department of Education have mandated the development of school–family–community partnerships in Title I schools. Under NCLB, Title I schools are required to work jointly with family and community members to develop a systematic school–family–community involvement policies and procedures.

S. Ferguson (2003) has revealed, however, that the provision concerning school–family–community partnerships is being overlooked, even though such partnerships may hold the solution to significantly reducing the achievement gap between white and poor and minority students in public schools. When students do not fully develop their academic skills or drop out of school, they take with them educational deficiencies that significantly decrease their economic and social well-being over their life span, especially within a rapidly changing economy replete with career uncertainty and global instability (Santrock, 2002).

The achievement gap among student subpopulations (Dworkin & Dworkin, 1999) and the resulting high dropout rates among minority groups have been well documented in the literature (NCES, 2002). Not only are the lives of a disproportionate number of racial and ethnic minority children characterized by oppression and a lack of privilege, but, too often, they are also "neglected, labeled, and left to wither in the lowest tracks in our schools" (Lewis & Arnold, 1998, p. 263). Research continues to demonstrate that school–family–community partnerships improve school programs and school climate, increase parents' skills and leadership, connect families with others in the school and the community, and improve children's chances of success in school and life (Epstein, 1995; Henderson & Mapp, 2002).

Professional school counselors cannot increase students' educational outcomes alone; neither can they build partnerships alone. They must team and collaborate with family, community, and school staff members to develop and implement comprehensive programs of partnerships to meet the needs of students vulnerable to academic failure, many of whom are minorities or have recently immigrated to the United States. School–family–community partnerships are collaborative initiatives among school personnel, families, community members, and community-based organizations, including businesses, churches, libraries, and community service agencies. Partners need to work together to accomplish mutual goals aimed at increasing the academic, emotional, and social success of students (Bryan & Holcomb-McCoy, 2004, 2006; Epstein, 1995).

School–family–community partnerships lead to increased educational outcomes for students, empowerment for parents, and ultimately successful academic and career success for all youth (Bryan, 2005; Henderson & Mapp, 2002; Lapan, Osana, Tucker, & Kosciulek, 2002). Such partnerships are effective means of addressing barriers to learning (Ramirez, 2003; Roffman, Suarez-Orozco & Rhodes, 2003; Shields & Behrman, 2004). *The ASCA National Model*, the Education Trust Transforming School Counseling Initiative, and recent professional school counseling literature promote teaming and collaboration roles for school counselors in building school–family–community partnerships to help children succeed academically (ASCA, 2005a; Bryan, 2005; Bryan & Holcomb-McCoy, 2006; Cicero & Barton, 2003). These partnerships are a critical component in successful urban schools attended largely by racially and ethnically diverse students and a growing population of immigrant students (Bryan, 2005). The professional school counselor's role is to advocate to remove systematic barriers to student success, especially for students who have been disenfranchised due to racism and discrimination (House & Martin, 1998).

Parenting Interventions

Parenting interventions are initiatives that assist families with parenting skills and with understanding the school's policies, procedures, and learning strategies that can enhance their child's academic, social, and emotional success (Epstein, 1995; Simon & Epstein, 2001). Parenting interventions involving families in schools have been linked to higher student achievement (Henderson & Mapp, 2002; Shields & Behrman, 2004). Examples of such partnership practices are parent education workshops and support groups, family life centers, home visits, and neighborhood meetings to provide parents with the skills and knowledge to help their child succeed in school (Cicero &

Barton, 2003). It is also important to understand that within some families, the "parent" may refer to grandparents, other members of the extended family, or even people who are not family members but play a parenting role in the child's life. Sometimes it is necessary to ask a student who they live with rather than ask them who their parents are because of changing family dynamics and family arrangements.

In addition, parents are also face multiple barriers that may prevent them from school involvement, including lack of child care and transportation, long work hours, multiple jobs, language barriers, and unfamiliarity with the schools and school dynamics. To eliminate these barriers, school counselors may have to be more assertive and reach out to faith communities or community centers, or even make home visits accompanied by a parent liaison who can act as a cultural broker to assist the school in learning more about the needs of families (Cicero & Barton, 2003; Hiatt-Michael, 2001; Johnson, 2001). Parent centers or family resource centers within the school are also beneficial (Johnson, 2001). Parent volunteers can be enlisted to help coordinate these centers (Cicero & Barton, 2003).

Communication Interventions to Encourage Understanding

Communicating and learning-at-home interventions involve initiatives to help parents understand the school's policies, programs, and school-to-home communication and expectations and learn about community services and resources that could meet their needs (Epstein, 1995, 2009; Lapan, Osana, et al., 2002; Shields & Behrman, 2004; Simon & Epstein, 2001). Conferences, fliers, newsletters, activity calendars, and other media that contain clear, readily available information in the parents' primary language on school policies, programs, and activities and on community services and resources are vital to instill involvement. For example, enlisting the help of a Spanish teacher in the school or school system to develop information in Spanish would be most helpful to Latino immigrant parents. Family literacy nights; interactive homework involving family members; workshops on skills and information that students need to succeed; and special reading, math, and science activities at home and at school from someone who speaks the parents' native language would also be beneficial. Programs and services designed to enhance communication and understanding between parents and the school and to engage parents in their children's learning at home have led to higher educational outcomes for children (Henderson & Mapp, 2002; Hiatt-Michael, 2001). Furthermore, higher student achievement has been demonstrated in schools with high levels of outreach to parents and extended family members (Henderson & Mapp, 2002).

Linkages with the Community: Promoting Interprofessional Collaboration

Parent or community volunteers are valuable resources to the school counseling program, enabling school counselors to meet the needs of larger numbers of students and their families (Bryan, 2005; Epstein, 1995; Simon & Epstein, 2001). Family and community members should be recruited as volunteers to assist in the classroom or career center, to coordinate the parent center, to be tutors and mentors, to assist with field trips or special programs such as Career Day, to work as clerical assistants, and to assist on the playground or in the cafeteria. Collaboration with businesses, local police, social service workers, libraries, churches, radio and television stations, and any other youth-serving community organization to implement activities that will help children and families to learn and develop is also valuable. Community-based organizations increasingly are partnering with schools to provide a range of services—tutoring, mentoring, advocacy, leadership training, health services, literacy programs, college and career services, school-to-work career programs, counseling, prevention programs, and more (Adger, 2000).

Professional school counselors can also invite professionals from local health, mental health, or counseling agencies to inform family members about their services and to provide consulting services in the schools. For example, counselors from community mental health agencies often collaborate with school counselors to provide family therapy, support groups, family life education, and other mental health services in schools (Keys, Bemak, Carpenter, et al., 1998; Shields & Behrman, 2004). School-to-work transition programs or community career partnerships appear to be successful in helping immigrant and minority adolescents gain access to career development skills, knowledge, and competencies that enhance their transition into the world of work and productive careers (Fuligni & Hardway, 2004; Lapan, Osana, et al., 2002). Because of the Carl D. Perkins Vocational and Technical Education Act of 1998 (Pub. L. 105-332), most schools systems already have these programs in place because of designated categorical federal funds.

In addition, faith-based organizations and spiritual leaders are valuable resources of support. Spiritual leaders have a significant leadership status and a collective commitment to their parishioners. Professional school counselors can use community asset mapping to learn where the resources (e.g., the social service agencies, mentoring program, and libraries) and the community meeting places are located.

> Community asset mapping is a useful tool that school counselors can use to learn the point people, or people of influence in the local community, that is which persons and organizations who have the respect of the people (e.g., pastors, priests, heritage centers, churches), and who the active advocates and voices of the community. (Dudley-Grant, 2001, p. 50)

Colleges and universities are another resource for potential mentoring and tutoring opportunities. Many colleges and universities partner with schools to provide academic enrichment, precollege academic preparation, and orientation programs for students at risk for school failure. They often participate by offering service learning activities as preemployment preparation (Fenske, Geranios, Keller, & Moore, 1997).

EVIDENCE-BASED SCHOOL PROGRAM INITIATIVES THAT HAVE IMPROVED STUDENT ACHIEVEMENT AND ACCESS TO POSTSECONDARY OPPORTUNITIES

Before proceeding with initiatives to enhance the postsecondary attendance of minorities and youths of poverty, one must be well acquainted with the Ethical Standards for School Counselors (2010), which expressly states in the preamble:

- Each person has the right to be respected, be treated with dignity and have access to a comprehensive school counseling program that advocates for and affirms all students from diverse populations regardless of ethnic/racial status, age, economic status, special immigration status, sexual orientation, gender, gender identity/expression, family type, religious/spiritual identity and appearance.
- Each person has the right to receive the information and support needed to move toward self-direction and self-development and affirmation within one's own group identities, with special care being given to students who have historically not received adequate educational services: students of color, low socio-economic students, students with disabilities and students with nondominant language backgrounds. (p. 1)

This brings professional school counseling programs full circle: to advocate for all children, to be a catalyst for leadership and change, to integrate a standards-based program of services and initiatives to meet the needs of all students within the counselors' care, and to maintain a viable and formidable force in the current educational reform movement.

Professional school counselors, as well as policy makers and administrators, need to continue to be alarmed by the relentlessly high dropout rates—estimated be 29% nationally and much higher among African American and Latino students (Greene & Winters, 2005). Those in critical leadership positions are concerned about the low academic achievement of many high school students and the large numbers of high school graduates who do graduate yet require remedial classes in college. An estimated 28% of all students entering higher-education institutions in fall 2000 required remediation in reading or mathematics (Parsad & Lewis, 2003). This revelation is particularly disturbing when you factor in the parallel research that has revealed that more than two-thirds of new jobs created between 2000 and 2010 require a postsecondary education, with the most rapidly growing, best-paying jobs requiring the most education (Carnevale & Desrochers, 2003). These profound economic changes both limit individual potential and threaten America's competitive position in the global economy. The technological and scientific advances of the 21st century require that high school graduates be both competent in high-level skills and prepared to successfully secure a postsecondary education.

Martinez and Klopott (2003, 2005) identify four practices that are most commonly given credit for the success of low-income and minority high school students:

1. Access to a rigorous academic core curriculum for all students
2. The prevalence, in school structure and climate, of personalized learning environments for students
3. A balance of academic and social support for students in developing important social networks and instrumental adult relationships
4. Alignment of curriculum between various levels, such as high school and postsecondary and within the K–12 system, in a K–16 approach

They conclude that high school reform efforts that integrate these practices have the greatest potential to improve college accessibility and overall success for underserved minority and low-income students (Martinez & Klopott, 2005). Concurrently, the authors make seven recommendations regarding the future of school reform:

1. Tracks that are not academically rigorous should be eliminated. Essentially, no one rises from low expectations. A common core curriculum should be implemented that stresses high-order mathematical skills.
2. Students should implement a support system for academically unprepared high school freshmen—those most vulnerable to dropping out if experiencing failure—and should provide a system to help accelerate their learning.
3. High schools should facilitate a system of supportive and instrumental relationships between students and adults to assure that the students do not get lost in the system and are able to accessible valuable information that would enhance their future opportunities.
4. There should be a K–16 orientation so that both school and university systems work together to align high school curricula with college enrollment requirements.
5. There should be a collectivist mentality between students, parents/caregivers, and counselors, sharing information systematically about college entrance requirements, placements tests, costs, financial aid, and other issues pertaining to attending higher education.
6. Reform initiatives for college preparedness should be continuously evaluated to assess outcome measures of high school achievement, graduation rates, and college matriculation rates.
7. Review College Readiness for All, a toolbox developed by the Pathways to College Network was developed to help school and college advocates increase college preparation and access to all students.

Predictors of Engaging First-Generation College Students

Recent studies (Adelman, 1999; Cabrera & La Nasa, 2000; Horn & Kojaku, 2001) have determined the following to be the strongest predictors of college attendance and matriculation, particularly among minority and low-income students:

- Academic preparation
- Social support
- Access to critical information
- Parental involvement and knowledge about college
- Financial aid

Out of all of these variables, academic preparation is the most significant predictor of college success. Adelman (1999) aptly stated that college completion is most likely to occur when students take academically intense and high-quality course work during high school, such as AP courses and mathematics classes beyond Algebra II. Another study demonstrated that taking Precalculus and Calculus produced positive effects on postsecondary completion for white and Latino students (Swail, Carbera, Lee, & Williams, 2005).

First-generation college students also need a variety of forms of social support in order to be successful (King, 1996; McDonough, 1997). Often minority students, those from low-income families, and students whose parents/caretakers did not attend college do not understand how to maneuver through the system to a postsecondary education (i.e., the application process, deadlines, scholarship information, financial aid, entrance requirements, testing requirements) (Noguera, 2001; Wimberly & Noeth, 2004). In addition, students who have good relationships with teachers, where there is genuine support and caring, are more likely to attend college (Lee & Burkham, 2003; Croninger & Lee, 2001; McLaughlin, 2000).

The national standards-based educational reforms are the most significant efforts to improve student achievement in 20 years. Standards-based education has four overall components:

1. The standards, usually in the form of a framework, are developed by an overseeing authority.
2. The curriculum is taught in the classroom.
3. The assessment is provided by the overseeing authority.
4. The accountability component rewards or sanctions schools and teachers according to student performance (Howard, 1995; Meier, 2000; Martinez & Klopott, 2005).

A college preparatory curriculum should be the default curriculum for all students (Wimberly & Noeth, 2004; Barth, 2003; Center for State Scholars, 2003; NCES, 2005b).

Model Programs That Promote Advanced Academic Achievement of All Students

Equity 2000, an initiative by the College Board, was specifically designed to provide access to advanced mathematics courses for minority and low-income students. Teachers in Equity 2000 schools use the standards developed by the National Council of Teachers of Mathematics as a basis of instructional practice, and students are expected to have completed Geometry by the 10th grade. After six years of implementation, more students reported that they intended to attend college than had done so before the program was implemented (College Board, 2000).

The *Urban Systemic Initiative* was launched by the National Science Foundation in 1991 to provide low-income and minority students with increased access to rigorous curricula in mathematics and science.

It is interesting that the National Defense Education Act of 1958 was instituted primarily to stimulate the advancement of education in science and mathematics, and it took more than 30 years for anyone to develop a systematic program to address these needs. Under this initiative, the disparity between African American and white student enrollment and between Latino and non-Latino white student enrollment in biology, chemistry, and physics decreased. Almost all schools showed increases in the number of minority students taking the PSAT, SAT, or ACT, and nearly all exceeded the national test-taking average (Kim et al., 2001).

Advanced Placement is structured across 20 subject areas and assesses the student's knowledge and ability to analyze complex ideas within each subject's core disciplinary framework (College Board, 2001). Taking AP courses is a strong predictor of college attendance because they reflect some of the same academic rigor (Adelman, 1999), and is also a strong predictor of college success (Camara, 2003).

The *International Baccalaureate* (IB) has emerged as a worldwide exemplary program that promotes high achievement, rigorous secondary education, and college preparation. The IB program has been systematically aligned with college curricular expectations. All grades and examinations are based on criterion-referenced rubrics that are the same for students throughout the world. Initially, the majority of IB programs were located in wealthy communities; however, a growing number of programs are emerging in more urban districts with the goal of offering rigorous programs to traditionally underserved, low-income, and minority students (Gehring, 2001).

Model Reform Programs That Address Both Academic and Social Support

Emotional learning and academic achievement are intrinsically linked. Meaningful social relationships among students and staff create a system through which students are able to develop strong networks of adults and peers to support them through their high school years. This is critical for first-generation college students whose parents do not know how to maneuver the postsecondary entrance requirements.

America's Choice was designed by the National Center for Education and Economy to raise achievement and prepare all students for college through a rigorous standards-based curriculum, along with the provision of safety nets to provide social support (Supovitz, Poglinco, & Snyder, 2001). The program systematically identifies students who are falling behind and provides interventions to help them catch up with peers. The old comprehensive high school model is redesigned to incorporate small schools or house systems within the larger school, promoting a core academic curriculum and a strong college and career-based technical preparation program. Another goal is to inculcate students with the expectation that *not* attending college is not an option (National Clearinghouse for Comprehensive School Reform & Northwest Regional Educational Laboratory, 2001). In grades 4–8, students in America's Choice schools have averaged slightly more than two months of additional learning time per year when compared to students from other school districts (May, Supovitz, & Perda, 2004).

AVID (Advancement via Individual Determination) was developed to identify underachieving students with a C average and prepared them for a four-year college education. The intent is to give the students strong academic and social support, so they can succeed at completing high-level course work. The AVID program revolves around an AVID class, where students learn basic academic survival skills such as note taking, test taking, study skills, time management, organizational skills, research skills, and college entrance examination preparation (Walker, Jurich, & Estes, 2001). Students also receive instruction in an AVID-developed writing-to-learn process, critical inquiry, and techniques for collaborating with other students. AVID students are guided to take high school courses that are more rigorous than peers who did not participate in the program (AVID Center, 2003; Watt, Yanez, & Cossio, 2003).

The goal of the *Coalition of Essential Schools* (CES) is to create strong relationships between and among students and adults that provide academic and social support to students (CES, 2001). The learning environment seeks to increase academics and college attendance, particularly among low-income and minority students (Raywid, 1994). CES (2001) reports that 82% of African American and 84% of Latino CES graduates were enrolled in college compared to national averages of 59% and 42%, respectively. Researchers attribute the success CES to its principles of focusing on the small class size and the personalization afforded by the size, formal advisement structures, and an intense focus on curriculum and instruction, including an emphasis on explicit teaching of academic skills (Darling-Hammond, Ancess, & Wichterle-Ort, 2002).

First Things First (FTF) was developed by the Institute for Research and Reform in Education to improve educational outcomes for all students, particularly students from high-poverty communities. The FTF model is based on the principles of developmental psychology, which embrace the need for students to feel competent, autonomous, and related. Meeting their needs within the social context of the school environment promotes positive development. Quint (2001) and Quint, Bloom, Black, and LaFleur (2005) found that student attendance, graduation rates, and academic achievement increased with FTF. A unique attribute of FTF is a family advocacy program implemented to improve the affective relations within the school by bringing adults (at home and at school) into more long-standing, respectful, and mutually accountable relationships with students.

High Schools That Work (HSTW) is sponsored by the Southern Regional Education Board, whose design intent was to improve the communication, mathematics, science, technical and problem-solving skills of career bound youth and to close, by one-third, the gap in reading, mathematics and science achievement between career bound students and college-preparatory students nationally (Bottoms & Mikos, 1995). HSTW strives to serve students who were routinely tracked in vocational and general education programs and to change the propensity to enroll children of color and those from low-income families disproportionately in lower, noncollege-preparatory academic tracks (Lee & Bryk, 1988).

Talent Development High Schools (TDHS), developed by the Johns Hopkins Center for Research and Education of Students Placed at Risk (CRESPAR), targets schools that face serious problems with student attendance, discipline, achievement scores, and dropout rates. What is unique about TDHS is its Ninth-Grade Success Academies, which give students the social and academic support and opportunities that this very vulnerable population need to transition to high school. The ninth-grade academies have a common core curriculum consisting of preparatory courses that are supported by instructional techniques and extra learning opportunities to help students successfully complete these courses. The number of credits earned during the freshman year is a strong predictor of whether or not a student will graduate on time (Allensworth & Easton, 2005). Another unique component of TDHS is the Twilight School, an after-hours program offered to disruptive, truant, or incarcerated students in an effort to keep them in school and give them a second chance rather than becoming another statistic of the juvenile justice system. The TDHS program has demonstrated positive effects on school climate and student attendance, achievement, promotion, and dropout rates (McPartland, Balfanz, Jordan, & Legters, 1998).

The *GE Foundation College Bound Program* is a whole-school change initiative near General Electric facilities to increase the college-bound rate (Brandeis University, 2000). Graduates of GE Foundation College Bound high schools were 27% less likely than students at other schools to dropout of college without completing a degree (Brandeis University, 2000). The key component is more social support both in and out of school, particularly those attended by low-income and minority youths (McDonough, 1997).

Personalized learning and the opportunity to build strong relationships are critical to the academic success of minority and low-income students (Nathan & Febey, 2001; Wasley et al., 2000). *Smaller and more personal learning environments* foster closer relationships and stronger academic achievement (Ancess & Ort, 1999). *Schools-within-schools* are career academies that provide students with high-quality, rigorous, and relevant courses as well as experiential opportunities in their fields of interest, such as in the health sciences (Elliot, Hanser, & Gilroy, 2002). Career academies have demonstrated an ability to raise achievement, significantly reduce dropout rates, and increased both attendance rates and the number of credits earned to graduation among students considered most at risk (Kemple & Snipes, 2000).

Aligning curriculum between high school and postsecondary levels creates a more seamless education and ensures that students are prepared for the challenges of each subsequent grade. Aligning K–12 and postsecondary education to create a K–16 framework also reduces the number of students who arrive at college needing remedial course work (Kirst, 2001). The following selected programs and models primarily focus on aligning curricula K-16 to prepare students for college.

Dual enrollment encourages college preparedness by having students take classes at college at the same time they are in high school during their junior or senior year. It serves to reduce the cost of higher education and the number of remedial enrollments in state university systems (Martinez & Bray, 2002). Dual enrollment has become very popular in preparing high school students for college, saving money in earning a college degree while enhancing admission to postsecondary education (NCES, 2005a). Dual enrollment opportunities are most prevalent at public two-year community college systems. Clark (2001) found that four-year college students who participated in a high school dual enrollment program have, on average, a higher college GPA and a higher four-year graduation rate than students who did not participate.

The purpose of the Carl D. Perkins Vocational and Technical Education Improvement Act of 2006 (Perkins IV, Pub. L. 109-270) was to develop more fully the academic and career and technical skills of secondary and postsecondary education students who elect to enroll in career and technical education programs during high school and continue on to community college systems. Career and Technical Preparation, or *Tech Prep,* programs have seven elements:

1. An articulation agreement between secondary and postsecondary consortium participants
2. A two-plus-two or a four-plus-two (only four- or six-year programs are authorized) design with a common core of proficiency in math, science, communication, and technology
3. A specifically developed Tech Prep curriculum
4. Joint in-service training of secondary and postsecondary teachers to implement the Tech Prep curriculum effectively
5. Training of counselors to recruit students and to ensure program completion and appropriate employment
6. Equal access for special populations to the full range of Tech-Prep programs
7. Preparatory services

Tech Prep utilizes common academic and participation expectations to keep all students on track to graduation and to enable willing students to go on to college (Bragg et al., 1997).

Project GRAD (Graduation Really Achieves Dreams) is designed to increase graduation and college attendance rates of at-risk students (Project GRAD, 2003). Students at Project GRAD schools are eligible for $1,000 to $1,500 college scholarships for each year of college, provide they fulfill a number of requirements, including on-time high school graduation, maintenance of a 2.5 GPA in college-preparatory courses, attendance at Summer Institutes, and enrollment in higher-level courses, including Algebra II (Project GRAD, 2003).

GEAR UP (Gaining Early Awareness and Readiness for Undergraduate Programs) is a federally funded early-intervention program developed to increase the number of low-income students in postsecondary education and prepare them to enter college and succeed. GEAR UP starts in middle school, providing students and families with necessary information regarding college access. Because course-taking decisions made on the high school level are important for college entrance and success (McDonough, 1997; Cabrera, La Nasa, & Burkum, 2001), the early intervention provided by this program is critical for this underserved population.

Table 8.4 summarizes model programs that have specific practices to encourage advancement to college.

TABLE 8.4 Model Practices That Enhance Advancement to College or University Opportunities

MODEL PROGRAM	PRACTICES THAT ENHANCE ADVANCEMENT TO COLLEGE OR UNIVERSITY OPPORTUNITIES
Advanced Placement	• Rigorous curriculum • High expectations • Alignment with higher education
America's Choice	• Access to rigorous courses for all students • Early identification of struggling students to provide adequate support • Expectation that all students will enroll in college
AVID	• Elimination of remedial classes • Students taught academic skills necessary for success in rigorous courses and college • Close relationships between students and teachers and among students, and close ties to students' families, to ensure strong academic and social support
Coalition of Essential Schools	• Access to a rigorous curriculum for all students • Individual attention and strong social support • Development of critical thinking skills • Personalized learning
Dual enrollment	• Exposure to college expectations and experiences • Access to college information • Increased rigor of academic program • Alignment between K–12 and higher education
Equity 2000	• Increased rigor of mathematics classes • Increased availability of high-level mathematics classes • Increased academic support • Improved counseling and academic support
First Things First	• Close relationships between adults and students and between school and families that lead to strong social support • Academic support in the form of low student-to-teacher ratios during core instruction • High academic standards for all students
GEAR UP	• Early information to students regarding the college application process • Expectation of college attendance established early • Alignment between K–12 and higher education
GE Foundation College Bound	• Access to more rigorous courses • Increased counseling for students • Academic and social support provided by mentors
High Schools That Work	• High expectations • College-preparatory curriculum
International Baccalaureate	• Access to rigorous courses • High expectations • Alignment with higher education
Middle College and Early College High Schools	• High common expectations with accelerated learning opportunities • College-preparatory curriculum • Strong academic and social support for students • Alignment of high school and college curricula

continued

TABLE 8.4   Model Practices That Enhance Advancement to College or University Opportunities (continued)

MODEL PROGRAM	PRACTICES THAT ENHANCE ADVANCEMENT TO COLLEGE OR UNIVERSITY OPPORTUNITIES
Smaller learning environments	• Mission-driven • Academic and social support for students • High common expectations
Talent Development High Schools	• High common expectations • Family and community participation that leads to strong social support • Small learning communities that lead to strong social and academic support
Tech Prep/2+2 Articulation	• Alignment of high school and college curricula • Increased rigor of academic course work • Guidance for students with regard to postsecondary options
Urban Systemic Initiative	• Enrollment in gatekeeping and upper-level mathematics courses • Improved instruction in mathematics and science courses with increased rigor
Project GRAD	• Alignment of K–12 curricula to improve academic preparation • Financial assistance to students • Transition programs • Family included to increase support for students and to increase parents' access to college information

Source: Adapted from Martinez, M., & Klopott, S., *Link between High School Reform and College Access and Success for Low-Income and Minority Youth,* American Youth Policy Forum and Pathways to College Network, Washington, 2005. Reprinted with permission.

CONCLUSION

Across all the reform initiatives presented in this chapter, four practices were a common variable for student achievement and success:

- Access to a rigorous academic core curricula for all students
- The prevalence, in school structure and climate, of personalized learning environments for all students
- A balance of academic and social support for students in developing important social network and instrumental adult relationships
- Alignment of curriculum between various levels, such as high school and postsecondary and within the K–12 system, in a K–16 approach (Martinez & Klopott, 2005)

Research on effective practices in middle and high school restructuring aimed at increasing student attendance, reducing dropout rates, and closing the achievement gap for minority and poor youths are well documented. Multiple studies on school reform consistently show that student achievement and equity improve with high expectations, academic rigor, and social support (Lee & Burkam, 2002; Lee, Smith, & Croninger, 1995). Low expectations and the absence of academic rigor in schools with minority children of color and poverty tend to limit students to lives without the knowledge and skills they need to exist anywhere except on the margins of society and in minimum-wage careers (Williams, 1996).

Nettles (2002) found that individual students from low-income families perform better when they are in wealthier schools that have the best teachers, high expectations of all students, and a rigorous curriculum. The exposure to a higher overall level of teacher quality and more resources is a contributing factor in this educational outcome. Schools themselves have deeply embedded practices that provide different educational experiences for children of color and children of poverty. Currently, attention is beginning to be focused on the manner in which school culture and organizational practices unconsciously act to maintain the racial inequities in academic achievement and the effect that these assumptions, fears, attitudes, and stereotypes of school personnel have on both the interactions and the academic success of minority children and their families (Noguera, 1999, 2001).

The underrepresentation and inequalities of African American and Latino students among the ranks of high achievers on standardized tests, among the honor graduates of most American colleges and universities, and among the practitioners of mathematics and science professions have been well documented and tragically ignored (Borman, Stringfield, & Rachuba, 2000). One of the most urgent concerns among education stakeholders and policy makers today is the underrepresentation of African Americans, Latinos, and Native Americans among high-achieving students. New reform initiatives for closing the achievement gap have evolved to eliminate this academic disparity among underrepresented students and to ensure that no child is left behind.

Educational stakeholders and policy makers have been working relentlessly to maximize educational outcomes and to respond to the unprecedented challenge of educating increasingly multicultural, multilingual, and socially disadvantaged students. Although focusing and bringing these issues to the forefront of global educational initiatives indicates some signs of progress, more efforts are necessary to continue to improve the academic performance of all students and to decrease these cultural, social, and economic disparities.

The issue of the achievement gaps between minority and nonminority populations is a national travesty (Huang, Reiser, Parker, Muniec, & Salvucci, 2003) and will have long-range consequences for society, the economy, and those who continue to remain marginalized in society. The lure of the underground economy (e.g., dealing in the drug trade, joining gangs, fencing stolen goods, perpetrating home invasions) becomes more attractive than trying to maintain two part-time minimum-wage jobs to make a living to support a oneself or one's family. Regrettably, this is the path this group of disenfranchised students ultimately faces unless a dramatic change to the educational system immediately occurs to systematically close the achievement gaps across the nation.

PART THREE

Applications

Children with Disabilities

The Long and Winding Road to a Free and Appropriate Public Education

9

Between the mid-1960s and 1975, parent advocates, state legislatures, the federal courts, and the U.S. Congress outlined the first comprehensive initiative for the educational rights for children with disabilities to finally obtain a free and appropriate education in the public schools with the least restrictive environment. This occurred in the midst of the civil rights movement and was also a civil rights issue that was significantly ignored. Strategically adopting the tactics of other civil rights movements, advocates for children with disabilities turned to the judicial system to garner their own endowed civil rights (Martin, Martin, & Terman, 1996).

Before this tumultuous era in U.S. history, children with disabilities were hidden from the public, abandoned by the public schools, and denied adequate educational programs or services. Hundreds of thousands of children with disabilities were condemned to live their lives in institutions, often deprived not only of love and attention but even of the most basic physical care, emotional nurturing, and intellectual stimulation. Throughout history, children with disabilities were denied access to education, family life, adequate health care, opportunities for play or for training, and the right to participate in "normal" activities of childhood. They were viewed as "uneducable" and routinely barred from attending public schools (U.S. Department of Education, 2000). Their experience in effect was a form of social exclusion or ostracism that represented a denial of their basic human and civil rights. Worse, these children were the most vulnerable population in terms of abuse, neglect, and exploitation by the adults in institutions who were responsible for them, since children with disabilities are the least able to assert their rights on their own behalf and are dependent on the caregivers who surround them. Children with disabilities continue in many ways to remain invisible and marginalized in our society. This is a national travesty.

Even today, despite the depth of the problem, the increasing identification of children with disabilities, and the extent of discrimination, the plight and rights of children with disabilities are rarely high on the national, state, or local agenda. Parents and other activists must continue to be vocal and advocate for the rights of their children to a free and appropriate education. Many supporters have developed advocacy groups across the nation, such as the Center for Special Education Advocacy (CSEA), the Council of Parents, Attorneys, and Advocates (COPPA), and the Parent Educational Advocacy Training Center (PEATC) in order to provide adequate programs and services.

After securing some initial government support for special education efforts, advocates shifted to an emphasis on educational rights—an orientation strongly influenced by the of the remnants of the civil rights movement. In the 1960s, advocates for children with disabilities wanted:

- A single entity that would coordinate federal educational efforts for children with disabilities;
- Increased categorical funding for the exclusive purpose of educating students with disabilities; and
- An enforceable entitlement, which was eventually obtained through federal legislation.

In 1975, Congress passed the most significant piece of legislation for children with disabilities, the Education of the Handicapped Act (Pub. L. 94-142). It required an individualized educational plan (IEP) for students with a disability, to be rewritten every year with new goals and objectives. Individualized designed instruction must be in writing to meet the unique needs of each student and agreed upon between teacher and parent or guardian. The written goals are to address the following important issues:

- An account of the student's present educational performance levels;
- A statement of annual goals, including short-term instructional objectives;
- A statement of the specific educational services that are to be provided to the student;
- An account of the extent to which the student will be able to participate in regular educational programs;
- The projected date for the beginning of services and expected length of services; and
- Appropriate evaluation procedures and schedules for determining, on at least an annual basis, whether instructional objectives are being achieved. (Nauert, 2002, p. 19)

In 1980, the American School Counselor Association (ASCA) developed a position statement concerning school counselor roles with students with disabilities. This position statement was revised in 1986, 1993, 1999, and 2004b (Baumberger & Harper, 1999). ASCA adopted two more focused position statements that discuss school counselor roles in relation to working with students with attention deficit disorder (ADD) and attention deficit hyperactivity disorder (ADHD) (ASCA, 2000b) and with students with special needs (ASCA, 1999d). In those statements, ASCA suggested that professional school counselors:

- Advocate for students with disabilities in the school and/or community
- Assist students with disabilities in planning for transitions to careers or to postsecondary institutions
- Assist with the establishment and implementation of behavior modification plans for students with disabilities
- Counsel parents and families of students with disabilities
- Make referrals to other appropriate specialists for students with disabilities

Interventions in which the professional school counselor participates may include but are not limited to the following:

- Serving on the school's multidisciplinary team to identify the special needs student
- Collaborating with other pupil support specialists in the delivery of services
- Providing social-skills training in a classroom setting, in small groups or individually
- Leading group guidance activities to improve self-esteem through the comprehensive counseling and guidance program
- Providing group and individual counseling
- Advocating for special needs students in the school and in the community
- Assisting with the establishment and implementation of behavior modification plans
- Providing guidance and counseling for career planning and a smooth postsecondary transition from school to career
- Working with staff and parents to understand the special needs of these students
- Counseling parents and families
- Making referrals to other appropriate specialists within the school system and in the community

ASCA (1999d) cautioned, however, that it is not the professional school counselor's responsibility to be the sole source of information or administrative representative in a district in preparing IEPs for students with disabilities, other than those portions relating to counseling services to be rendered.

> Further, school counselors should not make decisions regarding placement or retention and should not serve in any supervisory capacity in relation to the implementation of IDEA [the Individuals with Disabilities Education Improvement Act of 2004] nor should they serve as a member of a multidisciplinary team reviewing placement referrals for those students not usually part of the counselor's caseload. (ASCA, 1999d, p. 1)

In addition, it said, the school counselor should not be responsible for the coordination of the 504 planning team or supervision of the implementation of the 504 plan.

The 2004 version of the ASCA position statement makes even more specific the role of the school counselor and the special education program at his or her school:

> The professional school counselor advocates for students with special needs and is one of many school staff members who may be responsible for providing information as written plans are prepared for students with special needs. The professional school counselor has a responsibility to be a part of designing portions of these plans related to the comprehensive school counseling program, but it is inappropriate for the professional school counselor to serve in supervisory or administrative roles such as:

> - Making decisions regarding placement or retention
> - Serving in any supervisory capacity related to the implementation of IDEA
> - Serving as the LEA [local educational agency] representative for the team writing the IEP
> - Coordinating the 504 planning team
> - Supervising of the implementation of the 504 plan (ASCA, 2004b, p. 1)

This is a clear delineation of the professional school counselor's role and function. Professional school counselors are service providers when it comes to assisting students with disabilities. They are not to be used as a quasi-administrator of the special education program in the school.

THE STEPS IN THE SPECIAL EDUCATION PROCESS

Two federal education laws—the Elementary and Secondary Education Act (ESEA), more commonly called the No Child Left Behind Act of 2001 (NCLB), and the Individuals with Disabilities Education Improvement Act of 2004 (IDEA)—have had a major implications on instruction, assessment, evaluation, identification, and eligibility of students with disabilities. Under these laws, comprehensive assessment and evaluation of individual students with disabilities must be conducted by a multidisciplinary team for the identification and diagnosis of students. This assessment requires the use of multiple data sources such as standardized tests, informal measures, observations, student self-reports, parent reports, and monitoring of academic progress. The purpose of the comprehensive assessment and evaluation is to accurately identify each individual student's patterns of strengths and needs. Gathering information from many sources of assessment data ensures that the assessment accurately reflects how the student is performing, in an effort to create a profile of his or her strengths and needs and to determine decisions about identification, eligibility, services, and individualized instruction as outlined by the student's IEP.

The steps in the special education process include:

1. Identification and referral of a child with a disability
2. Evaluation of the child's disability
3. Determination of eligibility for special education services
4. Development of an IEP and determination of services
5. Reevaluation of the child's progress and the need for continued services

The process is further outlined in Figure 9.1.

The Individuals with Disabilities Education Act as renewed in 2004 (Pub. L. 108-446) gives specific requirements to ensure that students with disabilities receive the services they need to achieve their educational goals and become productive members of society. IDEA outlines broad mandates for services to all children with disabilities, yet these children are a large and heterogeneous group—incorporating the three-year-old with a developmental delay, the first-grader with a speech or hearing impediment, the junior high student with emotional disorders and a history of school suspensions, and the college-bound high school student who needs a technical assistance device to complete assignments because he has dysgraphia, among many others. IDEA is a comprehensive set of guidelines set forth by the U.S. Congress to

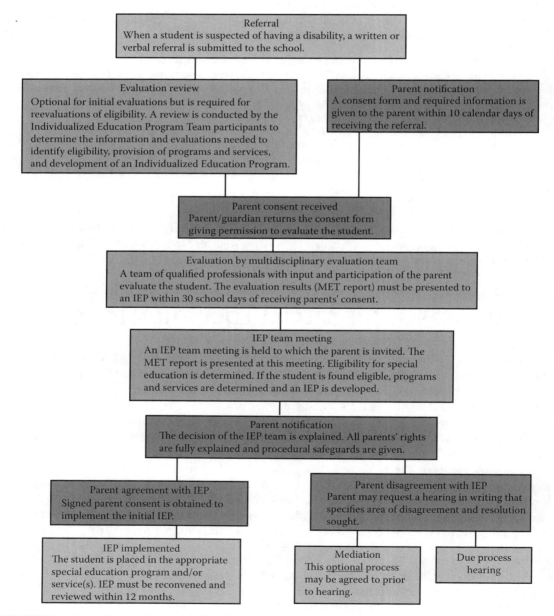

FIGURE 9.1 Evaluating students with disabilities: The process. (From Plymouth Educational Center, *Student Support Services,* retrieved from http://www.plymouthed.org/studentServices.htm.)

aid the states in complying with their constitutional obligations to provide a free and appropriate public education for all children age 3–21 with disabilities.

Some of the more salient points of IDEA that were emphasized in the authorization of the law were the following:

A. Purposes [§ 1482 (d)]

1. To ensure that children with disabilities have a Free Appropriate Public Education (FAPE) available to meet their unique needs and prepare them for further education, employment, and independent living.
2. To ensure that the rights of children with disabilities and their parents are protected.
3. To assist states, localities, educational service agencies, and Federal agencies in providing for the education of all children with disabilities.
4. To assist states in the implementation of a statewide, comprehensive, coordinated, multidisciplinary, interagency system of early intervention services for infants and toddlers with disabilities and their families.
5. To ensure that educators and parents have the necessary tools to improve educational results for children with disabilities.
6. To assess and ensure the effectiveness and efforts to educate children with disabilities.

B. Aims [§ 1482 (c)(5) – (13); related to Congress's findings]

1. To improve educational results for students with disabilities.
2. To ensure that states align their accountability systems for students with disabilities to NCLB accountability and require IEPs to specifically address academic achievement.
3. To support early intervention by giving school divisions flexibility to use up to 15 percent of their funds for early intervening services for students before they are identified as needing special education.
4. To require school divisions with significant over-identification of minority students to operate early intervening programs.
5. To reduce paperwork; focus resources on teaching and learning.
6. To establish a six-year path to reach the 40 percent funding goal. Further, to allow schools to redirect a share of their own local resources for educational purposes, consistent with activities in NCLB.
7. To strengthen the role and responsibility of parents to ensure that families of students with disabilities have meaningful opportunities to participate in the education of their children at school and at home.
8. To support high-quality, intensive pre-service preparation and professional development for all personnel who work with students with disabilities in order to ensure that such personnel have the skills and knowledge necessary to improve the academic achievement and functional performance of students with disabilities, including the use of scientifically based instructional practices, to the maximum extent possible.
9. To provide incentives for whole-school approaches, scientifically based early reading programs, positive behavioral interventions and supports, and early intervening services.
10. To support the development and use of technology, including assistive technology devices and assistive technology services, to maximize accessibility for students with disabilities. (Virginia Department of Education, 2005, pp. 1–2)

DISABILITY BY CATEGORY

In general, a *child with a disability* is a person age 3 through 21 who has been evaluated in accordance with §§300.304 through 300.311 of IDEA as needing special education and related services because he or she falls into one or more of the 11 different disability categories:

1. Autism Spectrum Disorder
2. Developmental Delay

3. Emotional Disability
4. Intellectual Disability
5. Learning Disability
6. Multiple Disabilities
7. Other Health Impairment
8. Orthopedic Impairment
9. Sensory Disabilities
10. Speech and language impairment
11. Traumatic brain injury (Virginia Department of Education, 2010)

IDEA provides the definitions of these 11 categories that make children eligible for special education services. These federal definitions are universal across the nation and guide states and localities in determining who is eligible for a free and appropriate education according to their disability and must receive appropriate accommodations because of that disability.

Autism Spectrum Disorder

Autism/Pervasive Developmental Disorder (PDD) is a neurological disorder that affects a child's ability to communicate, understand language, play, and relate to others. PDD represents a distinct category of developmental disabilities that share many of the same characteristics.

The different diagnostic terms that fall within the broad meaning of PDD include:

- Autistic Disorder
- Asperger's Disorder
- Rett's Disorder
- Childhood Disintegrative Disorder
- Pervasive Developmental Disorder Not Otherwise Specified (PDD-NOS), including Atypical Autism

In the *Diagnostic and Statistical Manual of Mental Disorders* (*DSM-IV-TR;* American Psychiatric Association, 2000a), autistic disorder is listed under the heading of Pervasive Developmental Disorders. A diagnosis of autistic disorder is made when an individual displays 6 or more of 12 symptoms across three major areas: social interaction, communication, and behavior. When children display similar behaviors but do not meet the specific criteria for autistic disorder (or the other disorders listed above), they may receive a diagnosis of PDD-NOS.

Autism is one of the disabilities specifically defined in the Individuals with Disabilities Education Act, the federal legislation under which infants, toddlers, children, and youth with disabilities receive early intervention, special education, and related services. IDEA defines the disorder as

> a developmental disability significantly affecting verbal and nonverbal communication and social interaction, generally evident before age 3, that adversely affects a child's educational performance. Other characteristics often associated with autism are engagement in repetitive activities and stereotyped movements, resistance to environmental change or change in daily routines, and unusual responses to sensory experiences. (34 CFR §300.8[c])

Developmental Delay

The federal code implementing IDEA includes in the definition of *child with a disability* "children aged three through nine experiencing developmental delays." It elaborates that this may...include a child—

1. Who is experiencing developmental delays as defined by the State and as measured by appropriate diagnostic instruments and procedures in one or more of the following areas: Physical development, cognitive development, communication development, social or emotional development, or adaptive development; and
2. Who, by reason thereof, needs special education and related services. (34 CFR §300.8[b])

Emotional Disability

Many terms are used to describe emotional, behavioral, or mental disorders. Currently, students with such disorders are categorized as having an emotional disturbance, which is defined under IDEA as:

a condition exhibiting one or more of the following characteristics over a long period of time and to a marked degree that adversely affects a child's educational performance—

(A)   An inability to learn that cannot be explained by intellectual, sensory, or health factors.
(B)   An inability to build or maintain satisfactory interpersonal relationships with peers and teachers.
(C)   Inappropriate types of behavior or feelings under normal circumstances.
(D)   A general pervasive mood of unhappiness or depression.
(E)   A tendency to develop physical symptoms or fears associated with personal or school problems. (34 CFR §300.8[c])

As defined by IDEA, emotional disturbance includes schizophrenia, but does not apply to children who are socially maladjusted, unless it is determined that they have an emotional disturbance.

Intellectual Disability

Intellectual disability is the currently preferred term for the disability historically and formerly referred to as mental retardation. IDEA defines *mental retardation* as "significantly subaverage general intellectual functioning, existing concurrently with deficits in adaptive behavior and manifested during the developmental period, that adversely affects a child's educational performance" (34 CFR §300.8[c]). The term *intellectual disability* covers the same population of individuals who were diagnosed previously with mental retardation in number, kind, level, type, and duration of the disability and the need of people with this disability for individualized services and supports. Many school districts used the term *educable mentally retarded* or EMR, which is no longer tolerated.

Intellectual disability is diagnosed by looking at two main things. These are:

* The ability of a person's brain to learn, think, solve problems, and make sense of the world (called *IQ* or *intellectual functioning*)
* Whether the person has the skills he or she needs to live independently (called *adaptive behavior* or *adaptive functioning*)

Intellectual functioning is measured by an intelligence quotient (IQ) test. The average score is 100. People scoring below 70 to 75 are designated with an intellectual disability and qualify for services. To measure adaptive behavior, professionals look at what a child can do in comparison with other children of his or her age. Certain skills are important to adaptive behavior. These are:

* Daily living skills, such as getting dressed, going to the bathroom, and feeding oneself
* Communication skills, such as understanding what is said and being able to answer
* Social skills with peers, family members, adults, and others

Learning Disability

IDEA defines a specific learning disability as

> a disorder in one or more of the basic psychological processes involved in understanding or in using language, spoken or written, that may manifest itself in an imperfect ability to listen, think, speak, read, write, spell, or do mathematical calculations, including conditions such as perceptual disabilities, brain injury, minimal brain dysfunction, dyslexia, and developmental aphasia (34 CFR §300.8[c]).

However, learning disabilities do *not* include, "learning problems that are primarily the result of visual, hearing, or motor disabilities, of mental retardation, of emotional disturbance, or of environmental, cultural, or economic disadvantage" (34 CFR §300.8[c]).

Multiple Disabilities

A child may be eligible for special education and related services because of multiple disabilities or simultaneous impairments, such as an intellectual disability coupled with blindness or a learning disability coupled with an orthopedic impairment.

Other Health Impairment

Many students with ADHD may qualify for special education services under the "Other Health Impairment" category within IDEA. *Other health impairment* (OHI) is defined as:

> having limited strength, vitality, or alertness, including a heightened alertness to environmental stimuli, that results in limited alertness with respect to the educational environment, that—
>
> (i) Is due to chronic or acute health problems such as asthma, diabetes, epilepsy, a heart condition, hemophilia, lead poisoning, leukemia, nephritis, rheumatic fever, sickle cell anemia, and Tourette's syndrome; and
> (ii) Adversely affects a child's educational performance. (34 CFR §300.8[c])

Orthopedic Impairment

Orthopedic impairment means

> a severe orthopedic impairment that adversely affects a child's educational performance. The term encompasses impairment caused by congenital anomaly, impairments caused by disease (e.g., poliomyelitis, or bone tuberculosis), and impairments from other causes (e.g., cerebral palsy, amputations, and fractures or burns that cause contractures). (34 CFR 300.8[c])

Sensory Disabilities

Sensory disabilities can involve any of the five senses, but generally refers to a disability related to hearing, vision, or both hearing and vision.

Deaf-Blindness

There are approximately roughly 45,000 to 50,000 individuals in the United States who are deaf-blind, and according to the 2007 National Deaf-Blind Child Count, more than 10,000 of these are under the age of 21 (Malloy & Killoran, 2007; National Consortium on Deaf-Blindness, 2008). The term *deaf-blindness* does not necessarily mean a person who cannot hear or see *at all*. It actually describes a person who has some degree of loss in both vision and hearing. The amount of loss in either will vary from person to person. The "key feature of deaf-blindness is that the combination of losses limits access to auditory and visual information" (National Consortium on Deaf-Blindness, 2008, p. 2). This can severely limit an individual's natural opportunities to learn and communicate with others.

IDEA defines *deaf-blindness* as simultaneous:

> hearing and visual impairments, the combination of which causes such severe communication and other developmental and educational needs that they cannot be accommodated in special education programs solely for children with deafness or children with blindness. (34 CFR §300.8[c])

Deafness and Hearing Loss

IDEA includes "hearing impairment" and "deafness" as two of the categories under which children with disabilities may be eligible for special education and related services programming. While the term *hearing impairment* is often used generically to describe a wide range of hearing losses, including deafness, the regulations for IDEA define hearing loss and deafness separately.

Hearing impairment is defined by IDEA as "an impairment in hearing, whether permanent or fluctuating, that adversely affects a child's educational performance," while *deafness* is defined as "a hearing impairment that is so severe that the child is impaired in processing linguistic information through hearing, with or without amplification" (34 CFR §300.8[c]). Thus, deafness may be viewed as a condition that prevents an individual from receiving sound in all or most of its forms. In contrast, a child with a hearing loss can generally respond to auditory stimuli, including speech.

Visual Impairment and Blindness

"Visual impairment including blindness means an impairment in vision that, even with correction, adversely affects a child's educational performance. The term includes both partial sight and blindness" (34 CFR §300.8[c]). According to the National Dissemination Center for Children with Disabilities (2004):

> Students with visual impairments ... are defined as follows:
>
> - "Partially sighted" indicates some type of visual problem has resulted in a need for special education;
> - "Low vision" generally refers to a severe visual impairment, not necessarily limited to distance vision. Low vision applies to all individuals with sight who are unable to read the newspaper at a normal viewing distance, even with the aid of eyeglasses or contact lenses. They use a combination of vision and other senses to learn, although they may require adaptations in lighting or the size of print, and, sometimes, braille;
> - "Legally blind" indicates that a person has less than 20/200 vision in the better eye or a very limited field of vision (20 degrees at its widest point); and
> - Totally blind students learn via braille or other non-visual media.
>
> Visual impairment is the consequence of a functional loss of vision, rather than the eye disorder itself. Eye disorders which can lead to visual impairments can include retinal degeneration, albinism, cataracts, glaucoma, muscular problems that result in visual disturbances, corneal disorders, diabetic retinopathy, congenital disorders, and infection.

Speech-Language Impairment

"Speech-language impairment can impact the way a student communicates. Impairments include dysfluency (stuttering) or motor speech issues. Students may also receive therapy for improving the understanding and use of spoken or written language, pragmatics, meta-linguistic skills" (Virginia Department of Education, 2010).

Traumatic Brain Injury

IDEA defines traumatic brain injury as

> an acquired injury to the brain caused by an external physical force, resulting in total or partial functional disability or psychosocial impairment, or both, that adversely affects a child's educational performance. The term applies to open or closed head injuries resulting in impairments in one or more areas, such as cognition; language; memory; attention; reasoning; abstract thinking; judgment; problem-solving; sensory, perceptual, and motor abilities; psycho-social behavior; physical functions; information processing; and speech. The term does not apply to brain injuries that are congenital or degenerative, or to brain injuries induced by birth trauma. (34 CFR §300.8[c])

ASSESSMENT OF CHILDREN WITH DISABILITIES

Slowly increasing numbers and proportions of children are being served in programs for children with disabilities. During the 2003–2004 school year, 14% of students were served in these programs, compared with 12% in 1993–1994. Some of this rise may be attributed to the increasing proportion of children identified as having speech or language impairments, which rose from 2.3% of enrollment to 3.0%; other health impairments (having limited strength, vitality, or alertness due to chronic or acute health problems, such as a heart condition, tuberculosis, rheumatic fever, nephritis, asthma, sickle cell anemia, hemophilia, epilepsy, lead poisoning, leukemia, or diabetes), which rose from 0.2% of enrollment to 1.0%; and autism and traumatic brain injury, which rose from 0.1% of enrollment to 0.4% (NCES, 2008). Table 9.1 provides a glimpse of what is assessed and what services are provided for children with disabilities.

THE ROLE OF THE PROFESSIONAL SCHOOL COUNSELOR WITH CHILDREN WITH DISABILITIES

There is an increasing interest in public education in involving all school personnel with students with disabilities. As Williams and Katsiyannis (1998) point out, "A primary implication of the 1997 Amendments to the Individuals with Disabilities Education Act is the need for all educators to share in the responsibility for services provided for all students including those with disabilities" (p. 17). However, little research has been conducted to examine the actual roles that professional school counselors perform for those students. Helms and Katsiyannis (1992) surveyed elementary school counselors in Virginia and found that professional school counselors were providing individual, group, and classroom counseling for students with disabilities. The most common counseling issues involved self-concept, social skills, behavior, study skills, and career awareness.

NCLB AND THE ASSESSMENT OF CHILDREN WITH DISABILITIES AND ENGLISH-LANGUAGE LEARNERS

Researchers continue to find that the performance levels of students with disabilities are lower than those of students without disabilities (Klein, Wiley, & Thurlow, 2006; Thurlow, Bremer, & Albus, 2008). This is problematic, especially in an era of high-stakes testing and the need to achieve and close the achievement

TABLE 9.1   Assessment and Services for Children With Disabilities

TESTS OF A STUDENT'S POTENTIAL DISABILITIES PERFORMED BY QUALIFIED PERSONNEL	POTENTIAL DEVELOPMENTAL, CORRECTIVE, OR SUPPORTIVE SERVICES AVAILABLE FOR STUDENTS WITH DISABILITIES
• Overall health assessment • Vision screening and evaluation • Hearing screening and evaluation, including an audiology test • Evaluation of the child's social and emotional status (e.g., evidence of developmental delays or mental illness) • Evaluation of general intelligence measured by standardized intelligence tests • Academic performance measured by pass/failure rates and grade-point average • Communicative abilities such the ability to articulate and pronounce words appropriately • Motor abilities (e.g., are there discrepancies between fine motor and gross motor skills?) • Adaptive behavior (i.e., ability to function well in the school setting; not being aggressive, disruptive, or unable to follow rules)	• Counseling services, including rehabilitation counseling • Early identification and assessment (e.g., developmental delays) • Interpreting services, especially for student who are English-language learners • Medical services required for diagnosis and evaluation purposes (e.g., vision screening, hearing) • screening, audiology services, and transportation, etc.) • Orientation and mobility services (e.g., special transportation, mobility assistant devices) • Parent counseling, training, consultation, and support networking • Physical, occupational, or speech therapy • Psychological services or support groups and advocacy networks • Recreation, including therapeutic recreation such as equi-kids (a therapeutic program that offers horseback riding lessons to individuals with mental and physical disabling condition) • School health services and school nurse services, along with collaborative relationships with the community health department • Social work services in schools and collaborative partnerships with social service agencies within the community • Partnerships with organizations such as the Community Services Board, Boys and Girls Clubs, and YMCA

gap, along with annual yearly progress and the stipulations of the No Child Left Behind Act of 2001 for schools across the nation.

Based on the Individuals with Disabilities Education Act Part B Child Count data, the largest group receiving special education services in public schools is those with specific learning disabilities, accounting for 45.5%. This category has a significant reading disability revealed in Figure 9.2. The incidence of SLDs has increased by more than 300% over the past 30 years (President's Commission on Excellence in Special Education, 2002). The second largest disability group is speech or language impairments, totaling 18.9%, followed by intellectual disability at 8.9% and emotional disabilities at 7.7%. Students with autism represent 3.2% of students served in special education, and students with multiple disabilities make up 2.2% of students in special education. Students with developmental delay represent 1.3%, hearing impairments 1.2%, orthopedic impairments 1.0%, and visual impairments and traumatic brain injury each 0.4%. The remaining 9.2% of students served by special education have other health impairments, a category that now includes students with ADHD (Thurlow et al., 2009).

It has been estimated that nearly 200,000 English-language learners (ELLs) received special education services for specific learning disabilities, totaling approximately 55.9% of school-age ELLs with disabilities in 2001–2002 (Zehler, Fleischman, Hopstock, Pendzick, & Stephenson, 2003). Almost 84,000 ELLs received special education services for speech or language impairments, comprising approximately 23.5%

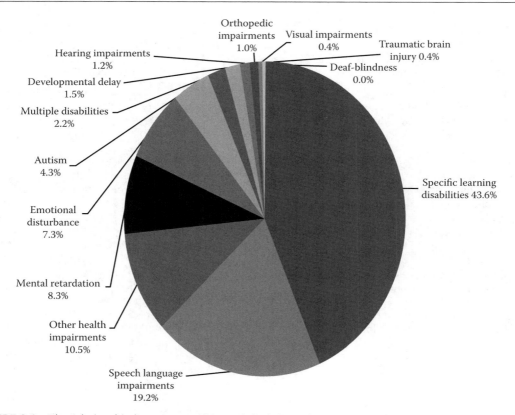

FIGURE 9.2 The relationship between reading and disabilities. (From Thurlow, M. L., Moen, R. E., Liu, K. K., Scullin, S., Hausmann, K. E., & Shyyan, V., *Disabilities and reading: Understanding the effects of disabilities and their relationship to reading instruction and assessment,* Minneapolis: University of Minnesota, 2009.)

of ELLs with disabilities. Typically, to qualify for these services, ELLs must demonstrate difficulties with communication that are not related to the second language acquisition process and demonstrate that those difficulties are present in both the first and second language. Some 8,723 ELLs received special education services for emotional or behavioral disabilities, approximately 2.4% of school-age ELLs with disabilities.

With the increase in immigration rates in the schools, this has created an additional strain on the schools with compliance issues with NCLB and the need to make annual yearly progress. How can schools compete with other schools that do not have large numbers of ELL students and students with disabilities?

ADJUSTMENT DIFFICULTIES AND SCHOOL CONFLICT

It is essential that the professional school counselor advocate for children with disabilities and help with their individual adjustment and peer relations. Children in elementary school generally do well with the support system and current structure of remaining with their teachers and getting services. By middle school, however, as the system changes to more teachers, changing classes, dressing for physical education classes, and being unleashed in settings like a massive cafeteria, some children with disabilities fall prey to teasing and bullying by their peers. By high school, the stigma of having a disability becomes psychologically stressful. This is compounded with classes that focus on basic skills and not being able to pass standardized tests necessary for graduation. School participation for many becomes an exercise in futility.

The constant feeling of failure is prevalent and often relentless. As a result, many students receive a modified diploma or certificate of attendance with no real marketable skill to make it in today's economy.

Under IDEA, there is more of a focus on legalities, student and parent rights, IEPs, least restrictive environment, mainstreaming, inclusion, and due process than there is on the potential career future or productivity of this fragile population. Children with mild disabilities, such as learning disabilities, specific disabilities, or intellectual disabilities may also be socially immature (Heward, 2006; Sciarra, 2004). In addition, children with visible disabilities may be concerned that their classmates will reject them because of their differences (Mattingly, 2004). Essentially, "labeling is disabling," because students cannot rise above the disability label they have been given. Professional school counselors need to be sensitive to this problem in the school setting.

PER-PUPIL COST AND OVERREPRESENTATION OF MINORITY STUDENTS IN SPECIAL EDUCATION CLASSES

Research demonstrates that per-pupil expenditures are almost twice as high for the average child with disabilities compared to the general education student ($15,030 versus $7,867, respectively). Average spending levels for more severe, although less prevalent, disability categories can reach three times those for general education (Chambers, Shkolnik, & Perez, 2003). In addition, the overall rate at which students have been diagnosed with disabilities has steadily increased over the past three decades, perhaps due to better awareness and diagnosis. When viewed as a share of public school enrollment, recipients of special education services now comprise almost 14% of individuals age 3 to 21, compared with about 8% in 1976 (Snyder et al., 2009).

Three-quarters of the increase in identification, diagnosis, and enrollment among high-school-age students can be attributed to just two disability categories: specific learning disabilities and other health impairments, which account for one-half and one-quarter, respectively, of the increase in enrollment in these programs. The SLD category comprises a wide variety of diagnoses that do not fit under other existing classifications. OHI includes attention deficit hyperactivity disorder, a widely debated phenomenon among professionals and laypeople. A 1991 memorandum issued by the U.S. Department of Education explicitly stated that ADHD could qualify as a disability under OHI, which inadvertently may have contributed to increasing diagnoses of this category (Davila, Williams, & MacDonalt, 1991).

More recently, concerns have been repeatedly debated about the overrepresentation of particular student subpopulations in special education programs. In particular, African American and Native American students are more likely to receive special education services than their white or Asian counterparts. Rates of special education among Latino and white students are close to the national average (Swanson, 2008), while African American students receive special education services at a rate about 40% higher than the national average. In particular, rates of diagnosis of mental retardation and emotional disturbance are extremely elevated within the African American population, roughly twice the national average (Swanson, 2008).

Gender disparities have also become a significant concern in debates over special education placements. Males are diagnosed with disabilities nearly twice as often as female students. Data from the U.S. Department of Education's Office for Civil Rights on specific learning disabilities, intellectual disabilities, and emotional disabilities show that males from every racial and ethnic group are more likely than females to be in special education. This raises questions as to whether instruction is meeting the needs of every learning style and if perhaps behavior has some implications in this diagnosis. Considerable public attention has been concentrated on the high rates of disability diagnosed for minority males, especially African Americans (Losen & Orfield, 2002).

Concerns of subjectivity and bias have also entered the area of closer scrutiny within special education placements. Is there a need for clearer systematic guidelines for diagnosing disabilities and more uniform referral procedures for special education services to reduce the potential for subjective judgments often cited for certain diagnoses, especially SLDs? Weak academic performance can also be an indicator of better early education intervention programs, especially for those students who come to school less prepared than their peers. Poverty and lack of early educational stimulation must be factored into the special education diagnostic equation. Many school districts are going to pre-K programs and full-day kindergartens to intercede for achievement gaps early on in the student's academic experience.

DISRUPTIVE BEHAVIOR AND DISCIPLINARY INFRACTIONS

Students exhibiting atypical behavior—particularly those with emotional disabilities, autism, or OHI—often succumb to negative encounters with peers and school authority. The National Longitudinal Transition Study 2 (NLTS2; SRI International, 2000) found that about one in five secondary-school-age students with disabilities exhibit problems with self-control, appropriately controlling behavior, or fighting with classmates. Forty-five percent of disabled youths argued with other students in class. This frequently occurs because they are teased, bullied, or taunted due to their atypical disability. Not adhering to norms or rules can lead to disciplinary actions from suspension or expulsion to homebound instruction. This vicious cycle can lead to patterned behavior that becomes integrated into the child's daily repertoire.

According to the NLTS2, one-third of special education students were suspended or expelled at some point during their school careers, compared with 21% of nondisabled youth. This has become so exasperating for some school systems with large populations of children with disabilities that they have assigned administrators whose primary responsibility is to work with the special education population in their school. Again, male students and historically disadvantaged minorities are more often subject to this disciplinary action than are their female and white counterparts. Within the category most often implicated in disciplinary actions, students with emotional disabilities, 73% have been suspended or expelled. The rate of disciplinary action is also high (41%) among students with OHI, the classification that includes ADHD (Swanson, 2008).

ACHIEVING COMPETITIVELY WITH PEERS ON STANDARDIZED ACHIEVEMENT TESTS

Historically, students with disabilities have had difficulty keeping up with their peers in school or state assessment programs. The movement in recent years, however, has been toward greater inclusion of special education students in school assessment programs with numerous accommodations. Table 9.2 contains a listing of the accommodations suggested by the U.S. Department of Education.

GRADUATION RATES OF STUDENTS WITH DISABILITIES

Graduation rates have been a national concern for all students during the last decade. Some have called the dilemma a "graduation crisis," asserting that only 70% of all students graduate from high school across the nation. But, this finding has led to some controversy among statisticians and researchers on how graduation rates are calculated. If you have an entering freshman class of 540 and a graduating senior

TABLE 9.2   Common Testing Accommodation for Students With Disabilities

PRESENTATION FORMAT	RESPONSE FORMAT	SETTING FORMAT	TIMING
• Direction read aloud/ repeated • Assistance interpreting directions • Directions signed • Test items signed • Occasional words or phrases read aloud • Braille version of test • Large-print version of test • Magnifying equipment	• Respond in sign language • Braille typewriter • Point to answers • Respond orally • Tape-record answers • Computer or typewriter • Use template to respond • Large marking pen • Special writing tool	• Take test in small group • Take test one-on-one • Take test in study carrel • Preferential seating (e.g., special lighting) • Test administered by familiar person	• Receive extended time • Breaks during test • Test session over several days

Source: Kitmitto, S., & Bandeira de Mello, V., *Measuring the Status and Change of NAEP State Inclusion Rates for Students with Disabilities,* National Center for Education Statistics, U.S. Department of Education, Washington, DC, 2008.

class of 340, where did those students go? Did they drop out or move? Tracking this information has become very difficult as society becomes more transient.

Some researchers maintain that state-reported statistics tend to inflate the graduation rate, although the size of that discrepancy differs across states (Hall, 2007). According to federal data collected under the sponsorship of IDEA, about 7 out of every 10 students with disabilities who exited high school during the 2005–2006 school year left with either a regular diploma or an alternative credential—which includes certificates of attendance that are issued by most states and account for 21% of all completers (Swanson, 2008). Of course, certificates of attendance are not given the same weight as diplomas by potential employers; students, including those with disabilities, face diminished prospects for postsecondary access and desirable employment with alternative credentials that are not highly valued by college officials, employers, or the armed services.

Among students with disabilities, those with visual or hearing impairments are the most likely to leave high school as completers, with about 85% earning a diploma or other certificate. On the other hand, students diagnosed with emotional disabilities face the greatest challenges finishing high school, with only 54% earning a diploma or credential, which is problematic for both the student and his or her career future. Students with disabilities need to be provided with more transition services for further school or career and technical skills, partnerships with business and industry, and sheltered workshops. They need to feel like meaningful and productive citizens that can contribute to society.

CONCLUSION

With more than 6.6 million students in the United States—13.7% of students—currently served under the Individuals with Disabilities Education Improvement Act of 2004 (National Center for Educational Statistics, 2005b), professional school counselors as advocates can have a significant impact in the lives of students. Some districts are even designating professional school counselors and administrators to work exclusively with this population in their schools to ensure that they are supporting the success of students with disabilities and meeting their required goals and objectives as designated by their individualized educational plans.

Perhaps the greatest void in the current efforts for the self-efficacy of adolescents with disabilities is not providing adequate training and transition services in the public schools so that these students can graduate and become productive citizens, earning a living and becoming more self-sufficient in their communities. Adolescents with disabilities can become the most loyal employees, because they take pride in their job and their responsibilities. The legislators who developed IDEA included transition components in the legislation with the goal of preparing students with disabilities to access the supports and services they will need to become as independent and self-sufficient as possible as productive citizens.

The Appendix provides definitions and acronyms in special education. It also contains a resource list of organizations and websites to consult to get the transition component of IDEA moving forward in communities.

APPENDIX: SPECIAL EDUCATION TERMS AND RESOURCES

A Primer of Common Terms Definitions and Acronyms in Special Education

Educators from preschool to higher education, like the armed services, health care, and other agencies, employ acronyms to describe various programs, services, regulations, and other stipulations when it comes to describing what they are doing and tracking programs and services. To the layperson, to a parent whose first language is not English, to a first-year teacher, or to a professional school counselor, knowing the definitions of all these terms can be overwhelming, so it is beneficial to have them in one place. Table 9.3 provides a comprehensive list of these terms and acronyms and their definitions.

Different agencies or systems that interface with the schools such as child protective services, juvenile justice, and the medical community have their own language for communicating to those who work within their systems. People who work in systems such as schools, the courts, community agencies, city hall, law enforcement, and the medical community, to name a few, naturally establish their own language to make meaning of rules, regulations, and policies easier to understand.

TABLE 9.3   Special Education and Other Mental Health Terms: Vital Information for the Professional School Counselor

ABC model	"A behavioral way to select interventions by analyzing events that occur antecedent to (A) the target behavior, the target behavior (B) itself, and events that occur consequent to (C) the target behavior" (Smith, 2004, p. 479).
Ability grouping	"Placing students with comparable achievement and skill levels in the same classes or courses; an approach used in education of the gifted" (Smith, 2004, p. 479).
Absence seizure	"A type of epileptic seizure in which the individual loses consciousness, usually for less than half a minute; can occur very frequently in some children" (Heward, 2006, p. G-1).
Access to records	"Public Law (PL) 94-142 states that all agencies that provide services to disabled children must allow parents complete access to their child's educational records, including those used for evaluation and class placement" (Wilson, 1992, p. 239).
Accessibility	"A quality or condition wherein people with disabilities have access to ordinary activities of daily life, including employment, transportation, recreation, and education, without being limited by architectural or attitudinal barriers" (Wilson, 1992, p. 239).

TABLE 9.3   Special Education and Other Mental Health Terms: Vital Information for the Professional School Counselor (continued)

Accommodation	(1) "A change in teaching methods to meet the educational needs of a child with special needs" (Wilson, 1992, p. 239). (2) "Modifications or supports to the instructional or the assessment situation to help compensate for disabilities" (Smith, 2004, p. 479).
Accountable	"A term in law meaning agencies, including schools, report on special education spending" (Wilson, 1992, p. 239).
Adaptive behavior	"The ability of an individual to meet the standards of personal independence as well as social responsibility appropriate for his or her chronological age and cultural group" (Gargiulo, 2006, p. 619).
Adaptive skill areas	"Targets of instruction that focuses on the ability of an individual to function in a typical environment and on successful adult outcomes (independent living, employment, and community participation)" (Smith, 2004, p. 479).
Adventitious hearing loss	"Hearing loss that is acquired after birth, not inherited" (Gargiulo, 2006, p. 619).
Advocate	"Someone who pleads the cause of a person with disabilities or group of people with disabilities, especially in legal or administrative proceedings or public form" (Heward, 2006, p. G-1).
AIDS (acquired immunodeficiency syndrome)	"A usually fatal medical syndrome caused by infection from the human immunodeficiency virus (HIV)" (Smith, 2004, p. 479).
Albinism	"A congenital condition marked by deficiency in, or total lack of, pigmentation. People with albinism have pale skin; white hair, eyebrows, and eyelashes; and eyes with pink or pale blue irises" (Heward, 2006, p. G-1).
Amblyopia	"Dimness of sight without apparent change in the eye's structures; can lead to blindness in the affected eye if not corrected" (Heward, 2006, p. G-1).
American Sign Language (ASL)	"A visual-gestural language with its own rules of syntax, semantics, and pragmatics; does not correspond to written or spoken English. ASL is the language of the Deaf culture in the United States and Canada" (Heward, 2006, p. G-1).
Americans with Disabilities Act (ADA)	"Federal legislation passed in 1990 to guarantee basic civil rights to people with disabilities; Public Law (PL) 101-336" (Smith, 2004, p. 479).
Anencephaly	"Cranial malformation; large part of the brain fails to develop" (Gargiulo, 2006, p. 619).
Angelman syndrome	"A genetic disorder characterized by congenital mental retardation, the absence of speech, unprovoked laughter, unusual facial features, and muscular abnormalities" (Gargiulo, 2006, p. 619).
Annual goal	"An IEP contains annual goals that the child should attain in a year and short-term objectives or goals" (Wilson, 1992, p. 240).
Anorexia nervosa	"Refusal to maintain body weight at or above a minimally normal weight for age and height; obsessive concern with body weight or shape and intense anxiety about gaining weight, even though severely underweight. Two subtypes: restricting food intake by starving oneself down to an abnormal weight and binge-eating/purging (see bulimia nervosa)" (Heward, 2006, p. G-1).
Anoxia	"Lack of oxygen severe enough to cause tissue damage; can cause permanent brain damage and mental retardation" (Heward, 2006, p. G-1).
Anxiety disorders	"Conditions causing painful uneasiness, emotional tension, or emotional confusion" (Smith, 2004, p. 479).

continued

TABLE 9.3   Special Education and Other Mental Health Terms: Vital Information for the Professional School Counselor (continued)

Aphasia	"Loss or impairment of language ability as a consequence of brain injury" (Smith, 2004, p. 479).
Apraxia of speech	"Speech and language disorder comprised of both a speech disorder, caused by oral-motor difficulty, and a language disorder, characterized by the resultant limitation of expression" (Gargiulo, 2006, p. 619).
Aptitude tests	"These tests provide information about a child's ability to learn in school. They measure understanding, use of language, and other skills" (Wilson, 1992, p. 240).
Array of services	"A constellation of special education services, personnel, and educational placements" (Smith, 2004, p. 479).
Asperger's syndrome (or Asperger syndrome)	"Developmental disorder characterized by normal cognitive and language development with impairments in all social areas, repetitive and stereotyped behaviors, preoccupation with atypical activities or items, pedantic speech patterns, and motor clumsiness; included in autism spectrum disorder" (Heward, 2006, p. G-1).
Assessment	"The process of gathering information and identifying a student's strengths and needs through a variety of instruments and products; data used in making decisions" (Gargiulo, 2006, p. 619).
Assistive listening devices	"Devices such as FM or sound field systems that improve the clarity of what is heard by an individual with hearing impairments by reducing background noise levels" (Gargiulo, 2006, p. 619).
Assistive technology	"Any item, piece of equipment, or product system that increases, maintains, or improves functional capabilities of individuals with disabilities" (Gargiulo, 2006, p. 619).
Assistive technology specialists	"Related service providers who determine, and sometime create, assistive devices that reduce barriers to the physical and learning environments for students with disabilities, with the goal of increasing each student's access to the general education curriculum and the typical school environment" (Smith, 2004, p. 480).
Astigmatism	"One or more surfaces of the cornea or lens are cylindrical, not spherical, resulting in distorted vision" (Gargiulo, 2006, p. 619).
Ataxic cerebral palsy	"A type of cerebral palsy that is characterized by poor balance and equilibrium in addition to uncoordinated voluntary movement" (Gargiulo, 2006, p. 619).
Athetoid cerebral palsy	"A type of cerebral palsy in which movements are controlled, abnormal, and purposeless" (Gargiulo, 2006, p. 619).
Attention deficit	"A characteristic often associated with learning disabilities in which students either do not pay attention to the task or do not focus on the features of a task that are relevant to learning how to perform skills" (Smith, 2004, p. 480).
Attention deficit hyperactive disorder (ADHD)	"A condition now included in the special education category 'other health impairments'; students display hyperactive behaviors, have difficulty attending to task at hand or focusing on relevant features of tasks, and tend to be impulsive; not all students with ADHD qualify for special education services" (Smith, 2004, p. 480).
Audio neuropathy/ dys-synchrony	"A hearing loss in which the cochlea is functioning normally but with loss of neural function" (Gargiulo, 2006, p. 619).
Augmentative and alternative communication devices (AAC)	"Alternative methods of communicating, such as communication boards, communication books, sign language, and computerized voices" (Smith, 2004, p. 480).

TABLE 9.3   Special Education and Other Mental Health Terms: Vital Information for the Professional School Counselor (continued)

Authentic assessments	"Performance measures that use work generated by the student or observational data on social behaviors for assessment and evaluation purposes" (Smith, 2004, p. 480).
Autistic savant	"Individual who exhibits extraordinary ability in a specific area such as memorization, mathematical calculations, or musical ability while function at the intellectual disability mental level in all other areas" (Heward, 2006, p. G-2).
Autistic spectrum disorders (ASD)	"Group of five related developmental disorders that share common core deficits or difficulties in social relationships, communication, and ritualistic behaviors; differentiation from one another primarily by the age of onset and severity of various systems; includes autistic disorder, Asperger syndrome, Rett syndrome, childhood disintegrative disorder, and pervasive developmental disorder not otherwise specified (PDD-NOS)" (Heward, 2006, p. G-2).
Automatic speech recognition (ASR)	"Technology that allows the computer to convert speech (at rates below 160 words per minute) to text" (Smith, 2004, p. 480).
Behavioral contract	"A written agreement between two parties in which one agrees to compete a specified task (e.g., a child agrees to complete a homework assignment by the next morning) and in return the other party agrees to provide a specific reward (e.g., the teacher allows the child to have 10 minutes of free time) upon completion of the task" (Heward, 2006, p. G-2).
Behavioral disorder	"A disability characterized by behavior that differs markedly and chronically from the current social or cultural norms and adversely affects educational performance" (Heward, 2006, p. G-2).
Behavioral inhibition	"A characteristic common in persons with ADHD; impacts executive functions. Typically affects the ability to (1) withhold a planned response; (2) interrupt an ongoing response; and (3) protect an ongoing response from distractions" (Gargiulo, 2006, p. 620).
Behavioral intervention plan	"The plan developed for any student with disabilities who engages in violent or dangerous behavior; includes a functional behavioral assessment and describes individually determined procedures for both prevention and intervention; developed as a result of disciplinary action" (Smith, 2004, p. 480).
Best practices	"Instructional techniques, scientifically based practices, or methods that have been proved through research to be effective" (Smith, 2004, p. 480).
Bilingual education	"An educational approach whereby students whose first language is not English are instructed primarily through their native language while developing competency and proficient in English" (Gargiulo, 2006, p. 620).
Bilingual special education	"Strategy whereby a pupil's home language and culture are used along with English in an individually designed program of special instruction" (Gargiulo, 2006, p. 620).
Bilingual transitional approach	"Teaching students primarily in English and partly in their home language until they know enough English to learn academic subjects" (Smith, 2004, p. 481).
Bilingual-bicultural approach	"The application of ESL [English as a second language] and bilingual techniques to education of the deaf, where ASL [American Sign Language] is the native language and reading and writing in English are taught as a second language" (Smith, 2004, p. 481).

continued

TABLE 9.3   Special Education and Other Mental Health Terms: Vital Information for the Professional School Counselor (continued)

Bipolar disorder	"(Formerly called manic-depressive disorder) Represents alternative episodes of depressive and manic states; during manic episodes person is in an elevated mood of euphoria and exhibits three or more of the following symptoms: excessive egotism; very little sleep is needed; incessant talkativeness; rapidly changing thoughts and ideas in uncontrolled order; easily distracted; agitated, and may participate in personally risky activities" (Heward, 2006, p. G-2).
Blind	"An impairment in which an individual may have some light or form perception or be totally without sight" (Gargiulo, 2006, p. 620).
Braille	"A system of writing letters, numbers, and other language symbols with a combination of six raised dots. A person who is blind reads the dots with his fingertips" (Heward, 2006, p. G-2).
Brain injury	"Actual or assumed trauma to the brain" (Gargiulo, 2006, p. 620).
Bulimia nervosa	"Recurrent episodes of binge eating and inappropriately compensatory behavior to prevent weight gain (e.g., self-induced vomiting, misuse of laxatives or other medications, fasting, excessive exercise)" (Heward, 2006, p. G-2).
Case manager	"The coordinator of services, a case manager works with the family in implementing an IFSP [individualized family service plan] or other intervention plan" (Wilson, 1992, p. 241).
Central auditory processing disorder (CAPD)	"A problem in the processing of sound not attributed to hearing loss or intellectual capacity, involving cognitive and linguistic functions that directly affect receptive communications skills" (Gargiulo, 2006, p. 620).
Cerebral dysfunction	"Many terms are used to describe children with learning disorder: cerebral dysfunction, minimal brain dysfunction (MBD), minimal brain injury, hyperkinetic impulse disorder, dyslexia, specific dyslexia or specific learning disability, neurologically handicapped (NH), hyperkinetic syndrome, maturational lag, educational handicap, performance disability, problem learner, psychoneurological learning disorder, underachiever, central nervous system disorder, word blindness, congenital alexia, agraphia, dysgraphia, acalculia, dyscalculia, agnosia, aphasia, language disability, ADD or attention deficit disorder, and SDD or specific developmental disorder" (Wilson, 1992, p. 241).
Cerebral palsy (CP)	"A neuromotor impairment cause by insufficient oxygen getting to a child's brain before, during, or immediately after birth; results in motor impairments; often associated with multiple disabilities, communication problems, and mobility difficulties" (Smith, 2004, p. 481).
Chaining	"A strategy to teach the steps of skills that have been task analyzed, either first step first (forward chaining) or last step first (backward chaining)" (Smith, 2004, p. 481).
Child find	"School districts are to locate and identify all children, newborn to age twenty-one, in the district who have disabilities or are at risk for needing special education" (Wilson, 1992, p. 241).
Childhood disintegrative disorder (CDD)	"A marked regression in multiple areas of functioning following a period of at least two tears of apparent normal development. After the first two years of life (but before ten years), the child has a clinically significant loss of previously acquired skills in at least two of the following areas: expressive or receptive language, social skills or adaptive behavior, bowel or bladder control, play, or motor skills" (Gargiulo, 2006, p. 620).
Classification	"A child is given a term that describes his or her special education needs. Sometimes called labeling" (Wilson, 1992, p. 241).

TABLE 9.3   Special Education and Other Mental Health Terms: Vital Information for the Professional School Counselor (continued)

Cleft lip/cleft palate	"A congenial defect in which the upper lip is split or there is an opening in the roof of the mouth. Can often be surgically corrected. Hypernasality is common" (Gargiulo, 2006, p. 620).
Closed head injury	"Caused by the head hitting a stationary object with such force that the brain slams against the inside of the cranium; stress of this rapid movement and impact pulls apart and tears nerve fibers or axons of the brain" (Heward, 2006, p. G-3).
Cluster grouping	"The practice of placing five or more students who have similar needs and abilities with one teacher; promotes challenging cognitive development and positive social-emotional development" (Gargiulo, 2006, p. 620).
Cluttering	"A type of fluency disorder in which speech is very rapid, with extra sounds or mispronounced sounds; speech may be garbled to the point of unintelligibility" (Heward, 2006, p. G-3).
Cochlea	"Main receptor organ for hearing located in the inner ear: tiny hairs within the cochlea transform mechanical energy into neural impulses that then travel through the auditory nerve to the brain" (Heward, 2006, p. G-3).
College Board testing for learning-disabled students	"LD [learning-disabled] students can take college admissions tests under special conditions, such as extended test times, readers, and separate testing rooms" (Wilson, 1992, p. 241).
Communication disorder	"An impairment in the ability to receive, send, process, and comprehend concepts or verbal, non-verbal and graphic symbols systems; ... disorder may be evident in the processes of hearing, language, and/or speech" (ASHA, 1993, p. 40, as cited in Heward, 2006, p. G-3).
Community-based instruction (CBI)	"Teaching functional skills in the environments in which they occur; for example, shopping skills are taught in the local market instead of in a classroom 'store'" (Smith, 2004, p. 482).
Complex partial seizure	"A type of seizure in which an individual goes though a brief period of inappropriate or purposeless activity (also called psychomotor seizure). Usually lasts from two to five minutes, after which he person has amnesia about the entire episode" (Heward, 2006, p. G-3).
Conduct disorder	"A common psychiatric disorder among children and youth characterized by disruptive and aggressive behavior as well as other actions that violate societal rules" (Gargiulo, 2006, p. 621).
Consent	"Parent must give written consent before their child is evaluated for special education or before he or she receives special education services" (Wilson, 1992, pp. 241–242).
Consultation/teaching	"General education and special education teachers working together to teach students with special needs" (Smith, 2004, p. 482).
Contingency contract	"A document that specifies an if-then relationship between performance of a specified behavior(s) and access to or delivery of a specified reward" (Heward, 2006, p. G-3).
Continuum of services	"A progressive system of special education services, each level of service leading directly to the next, which is more restrictive that the one before" (Smith, 2004, p. 482).
Cortical visual impairments (CVI)	"Decreased vision or blindness due to known or suspected damage or malfunction of the parts of the brain that interpret visual information" (Heward, 2006, p. G-3).

continued

TABLE 9.3 Special Education and Other Mental Health Terms: Vital Information for the Professional School Counselor (continued)

Cri-du-chat syndrome	"A chromosomal abnormality resulting from deletion of material from the fifth pair of chromosomes. It usually results in severe retardation. Its name is French for 'cat cry,' name for the high-pitched crying of the child due to a related larynx dysfunction" (Heward, 2006, p. G-3).
Criterion referenced	"An assessment procedure in which a student's performance is compared to a particular level of mastery" (Gargiulo, 2006, p. 621).
Cross-cultural dissonance	"Conflict between the home culture and the school cultures" (Smith, 2004, p. 482).
Cued speech	"Hand signals that accompany oral speech and make it easier to lip-read 'difficult to see' speech sounds; manual communication system used by people with severe hearing loss" (Smith, 2004, p. 482).
Cultural pluralism	"The practice of appreciating and respecting ethnic and cultural differences" (Gargiulo, 2006, p. 621).
Cultural sensitivity	"A perspective adopted by professionals when working with families in which there is an awareness of and respect for the values, customs, and traditions of individual and families" (Gargiulo, 2006, p. 621).
Culture	"The attitudes, values, belief systems, norms, and traditions shared by a particular group of people that collectively form their heritage" (Gargiulo, 2006, p. 621).
Curriculum-based measurement (CBM)	"A method of evaluating students' performance by collecting data on their academic performance directly and frequently" (Smith, 2004, p. 482).
Cystic fibrosis	"An inherited disorder that causes a dysfunction of the pancreas, mucus, salivary, and sweat glands. Cystic fibrosis causes severe long-term respiratory difficulties. No cure is currently available" (Heward, 2006, pp. G-3–G-4).
Cytomegalovirus (CMV)	"A common virus that infects most people worldwide; can remain alive but dormant in the body for life; usually harmless, but in a very small percentage of children infected at birth, CMV may later develop and lead to various conditions including mental retardation, visual impairment, and most often, hearing impairment" (Heward, 2006, p. G-4).
Day treatment program	"A daytime program that conducts a clinical assessment of a person's disability and develops an individual treatment plan. Treatment can include physical therapy, occupational and speech therapy, nursing care, vision or hearing services, and/or behavior modification" (Wilson, 1992, p. 242).
Decoding	"Reading and listening skills" (Wilson, 1992, p. 242).
Deinstitutionalization	"Process of removing disabled people from institutions to integrate them in normal community settings" (Wilson, 1992, p. 242).
Developmental delay	"A term defined by individual states referring to children ages 3 to 9 who perform significantly below developmental norms" (Gargiulo, 2006, p. 621).
Developmental disability	"A term applied to children who exhibit problems in development before age 18. Children in our society are expected to perform, within limits, at a set rate. Those who cannot perform physically and/or mentally within these limits are said to have developmental disabilities. Their disabilities include mental retardation, cerebral palsy, neurologically based conditions, autism, and developmental imbalance" (Wilson, 1992, p. 242).
Developmental language delay	"Slowness in the development of adequate vocabulary and grammar, or when a child's language age does not correspond to the child's chronological age" (Gargiulo, 2006, p. 621).
Diagnosis	"The science of identifying disease, defects, conditions, and disorders in order to treat them" (Wilson, 1992, p. 242).

TABLE 9.3 Special Education and Other Mental Health Terms: Vital Information for the Professional School Counselor (continued)

Differentiation	"A modification of the curriculum that enables students who are gifted to learn at a level appropriate to their ability" (Gargiulo, 2006, p. 621).
Disability	"An inability or incapacity to perform a task or activity in a normative fashion" (Gargiulo, 2006, p. 621).
Down's syndrome (or Down syndrome)	"A genetic condition due to chromosome error that causes moderate to severe intellectual disability. Down syndrome children have 47 rather than 46 chromosomes. Originally called mongolism, children born with this condition are characterized by a broad facial structure and a slanted appearance to the eyes. The disorder is named after Langdon Down, a mid-nineteenth century physician" (Wilson, 1992, p. 242).
Duchenne muscular dystrophy	"An inherited disease that is characterized by progressive muscle weakness from the degeneration of the muscle fiber" (Gargiulo, 2006, p. 621).
Due process hearing	"A noncourt proceeding before an impartial hearing officer that can be used if parents and school personnel disagree on a special education issue" (Smith, 2004, p. 483).
Dysarthia	"A group of speech disorders caused by neuromuscular impairments in respiration, phonation, resonation, and articulation" (Heward, 2006, p. G-4).
Dyscalculia	"A learning disorder affecting the ability to do arithmetic" (Wilson, 1992, p. 243).
Dysfluencies	"Aspects of speech that interrupt that pattern of speech; typical of normal speech development in young children; in older children, dysfluency is more likely to be a speech impairment" (Smith, 2004, p. 483).
Dysgraphia	"A learning disorder affecting the ability to write" (Wilson, 1992, p. 243).
Dyslexia	"A medical/educational term for specific language disability affecting reading. Sometimes referred to as 'word blindness,' dyslexia means a person cannot read with ability or comprehension because he sees printed words upside down, reversed, blurred, or backward. A person with dyslexic tendencies may confuse meanings of word and phrases. Dyslexia is a condition not related to general intelligence but often occurs with other symptoms of learning disorders, such as hyperactivity and poor attention span. It can be caused by neurological, emotional, constitutional (physical), genetic, or developmental factors or a combination of these" (Wilson, 1992, p. 243).
Dysphasia	"Partial ability to use spoken and/or written language" (Wilson, 1992, p. 243).
Echolalia	"The repetition of what other people say as if echoing them, characteristic of some children with delayed development, autism, and communication disorders" (Heward, 2006, p. G-4).
Educable mentally retarded	"Classification of a person with mild mental retardation who typically develops functional academic skills at the third- or fourth-grade level; IQ range generally between 50/55 and 70/75" (Gargiulo, 2006, p. 621).
Educational handicap (EH)	"If a child fails to learn within the school environment for any reason—medical, social, neurological, or emotional—he or she is said to be educationally handicapped" (Wilson, 1992, p. 243).
EEG (electroencephalogram)	"A neurological test made by painlessly placing electrodes on the scalp with a special glue to measure electrical activity within the brain. Often called a 'brain wave test,' it is used as part of tests and evaluations for children suspected of having epilepsy or brain injury" (Wilson, 1992, p. 244).

continued

TABLE 9.3   Special Education and Other Mental Health Terms: Vital Information for the Professional School Counselor (continued)

EKG (electrocardiogram)	"A record of heart action taken from a graph recording electrical currents in the heart" (Wilson, 1992, p. 244).
Emotional or behavioral disorders	"A condition characterized by disruptive or inappropriate behaviors that interfere with a student's learning, relationships with others, or personal satisfaction to such a degree that intervention is required" (Smith, 2004, p. 483).
Encephalitis	"Inflammation of the brain; can cause permanent damage to the central nervous system and mental retardation" (Heward, 2006, p. G-4).
Encoding	"Expressing ideas with symbols; expressing oneself through verbal or warren language and body expression" (Wilson, 1992, p. 244).
English as a second language (ESL)	"Instructing students in English in their classrooms or in special classes until English proficiency is achieved; does not provide support in the student's native or primary language" (Smith, 2004, p. 483).
English-language learner (ELL)	"The preferred term for students who are learning English as their second language; these students are also sometimes called limited English proficient (LEP) students" (Smith, 2004, p. 483).
Epilepsy	"A condition marked by chronic and repeated seizures, disturbances of movement, sensation, behavior, and/or consciousness caused by abnormal electrical activity in the brain. Can usually be controlled with medication, although the drugs may have undesirable side effects. May be temporary or lifelong" (Heward, 2006, pp. G-4–G-5).
Equal protection	"Legal concept included in the 14th amendment to the Constitution of the United States, stipulating that no state may deny any person equality or liberty because of that person's classification according to race, nationality, or religion. Several major court cases leading to the passage of PL 94-142 (IDEA) found that children with disabilities were not provided with equal protection if they were denied access to an appropriate education solely because of their disabilities" (Heward, 2006, p. G-5).
Ethnocentrism	"A perspective whereby a person views his or her cultural practices as correct and those of other groups as inferior, peculiar, or deviant" (Gargiulo, 2006, p. 622).
Evaluation	"Assessment or judgment of special characteristics such as intelligence, physical abilities, sensory abilities, learning preferences, and achievements" (Smith, 2004, p. 483).
Exceptional children	"Children who deviate from the norm to such an extent that special educational services are required" (Gargiulo, 2006, p. 622).
Executive functions	"Internal regulations of one's behavior through control of emotions, inner speech, working memory, arousal levels, and motivation. Considered impaired in individuals with attention deficit hyperactivity disorder" (Gargiulo, 2006, p. 622).
Expressive language	"The formation and production of language, verbal and non-verbal, that is understood by and meaningful to others" (Gargiulo, 2006, p. 622).
Facilitated communication (FC)	"A type of augmentative communication in which a 'facilitator' provides assistance to someone in typing or pointing to vocabulary symbols; typically involves an alphanumeric keyboard on which the user types out his message one letter at a time. To date, research designed to validate FC has repeatedly demonstrated either facilitator influence (correct or meaningful language is produced only when the facilitator 'knows' what should be communicated) or no unexpected language competence compared to the participants' measured IQ or a standard language assessment" (Heward, 2006, p. G-5).

TABLE 9.3   Special Education and Other Mental Health Terms: Vital Information for the Professional School Counselor (continued)

Family system	"Potential sources of support for people with disabilities, including sons and daughters, spouses, parents, siblings, in-laws, aunts and uncles, grandparents, extended family members, and step-family members" (Smith, 2004, p. 483).
Family systems model	"A model that considers a family as an interrelated social system with unique characteristics and needs" (Gargiulo, 2006, p. 622).
Family-centered early intervention (approach)	"A philosophy of working with families that stresses family strengths and capabilities, the enhancement of skills, and the development of mutual partnerships between service providers and families" (Gargiulo, 2006, p. 622).
Family-directed assessment	"A form of assessment, useful for infants, toddlers, and preschool-age youngsters, that focuses on information that families choose to provide regarding needs, concerns, resources, and priorities" (Gargiulo, 2006, p. 622).
Fetal alcohol effect	"Term used to identify the suspected etiology of developmental problems experienced by infants and toddlers who have some but not all of the diagnostic criteria for fetal alcohol syndrome (FAS) and have a history of prenatal alcohol exposure" (Heward, 2006, p. G-5).
Fetal alcohol syndrome	"Results from mother's consumption of alcohol while pregnant; mild to moderate mental retardation is common, along with physical deformities. A leading cause of mental retardation, although completely preventable" (Gargiulo, 2006, p. 622).
Finger spelling	"A form of manual communication that assigns each letter of the alphabet a sign; one form of sign language used by deaf people" (Smith, 2004, p. 483).
Fluency encoding	"Talking" (Wilson, 1992, p. 244).
Formal diagnosis	"After a child is tested by professionals from the fields of psychology, medicine, and education, their assessment of his or her strengths and weaknesses is called a formal diagnosis. Not to be confused with screening" (Wilson, 1992, p. 244).
Fragile X syndrome	"A chromosomal abnormality leading to mental retardation along with physical anomalies; believed to be the most common form of inherited mental retardation" (Gargiulo, 2006, p. 622).
Free appropriate public education (FAPE)	"One provision of IDEA; states that students with disabilities must receive necessary education and services without cost to the child and family" (Smith, 2004, p. 484).
Full inclusion	"An interpretation of the principle of least restrictive environment advocating that all pupils with disabilities are to be educated in the general education classroom" (Gargiulo, 2006, p. 623).
Functional behavior assessment (FBA)	"Systematic process of gathering information about the purposes (functions) a problem behavior serves for an individual; that information then guides the design of three basic types of interventions: indirect assessment (structured interviews with significant others), direct descriptive assessment (systematic observation), and functional analysis" (Heward, 2006, p. G-5).
Functional skills	"Personal living skills that enable persons with disabilities to become a 'functioning' part of the community. Functional skills depend on the individual, but for a younger child, they usually include dressing, bathing, and finding one's way independently. Adult functional skills may include reading public signs, finding public restrooms, eating out, or counting change" (Wilson, 1992, p. 244).

continued

TABLE 9.3   Special Education and Other Mental Health Terms: Vital Information for the Professional School Counselor (continued)

GED	"General Educational Development. A high school equivalency diploma" (Wilson, 1992, p. 244).
Generalized anxiety disorder	"Excessive, unrealistic worries, fears, tension that lasts six months or more; in addition to chronic anxiety, symptoms include restlessness, fatigue, difficulty concentrating, muscular aches, insomnia, nausea, excessive heart rate, dizziness, and irritability" (Heward, 2006, p. G-5).
Generalized tonic-clonic seizure	"The most severe type of seizure, in which the individual has violent convulsions, loses consciousness, and becomes rigid. Formally called grand mal seizure" (Heward, 2006, p. G-5).
Gifted and talented	"Persons who possess abilities and talents that can be demonstrated, or have the potential for being developed, at exceptionally high levels" (Gargiulo, 2006, p. 623).
Grade one Braille	"A beginning level of Braille in which a word is spelled out with a Braille letter corresponding to each printed letter" (Gargiulo, 2006, p. 623).
Grade two Braille	"A more complex level of Braille in which contractions are used to represent parts of words or whole words" (Gargiulo, 2006, p. 623).
Group home	"A community based residential alternative for adults with disabilities, most often person with mental retardation, in which a small group of people live together in a house with one or more support staff" (Heward, 2006, p. G-6).
Handicapism	"Prejudice or discrimination based solely on a person's disability, without regard for individual characteristics" (Heward, 2006, p. G-6).
Handicap	"Difficulties imposed by the environment on a person with disability" (Gargiulo, 2006, p. 623).
Hard of hearing	"Refers to a person who has a hearing loss but uses the auditory channel as the primary avenue of oral communication, with or without a hearing aid" (Gargiulo, 2006, p. 623).
Hemiplegia	"Paralysis (or spasticity) on the left or right side of the body" (Gargiulo, 2006, p. 623).
Hemophilia	"An inherited deficiency in blood-clotting ability, which can cause serious internal bleeding" (Heward, 2006, p. G-6).
High-stakes testing	"Placing incentives and disincentives on teachers, schools, and school districts for their students' academic achievement" (Smith, 2004, p. 484).
HIV (human immunodeficiency virus)	"A microorganism that infects the immune system, impairing the body's ability to fight infections" (Smith, 2004, p. 484).
Hydrocephalus	"A condition in which the head is unusually large due to accumulation of excessive cerebrospinal fluid; brain damage often minimized by surgically implanting a shunt to remove excess fluid" (Gargiulo, 2006, p. 623).
Hyperactivity	"Overactivity with no apparent need or goal. A hyperactive child is restless and constantly on the move. He or she may exhibit symptoms or learning disabilities, attention deficit disorder (ADD), distractibility, impulsiveness, and excitability. He or she may react to a situation by becoming happier, angrier, and more fearful than the average child. He or she has a harder time settling down in active classroom and home situations. A hyperactive child is not necessarily learning disabled. Other physical, emotional, and environmental factors can contribute to hyperactivity" (Wilson, 1992, p. 245).
Hyperkinetic	"Synonym for hyperactive or overactive" (Wilson, 1992, p. 245).
Hyperlexia	"The ability to read prior to formal instruction, which can be manifested as early as 2 to 5 years of age" (Gargiulo, 2006, p. 623).

TABLE 9.3   Special Education and Other Mental Health Terms: Vital Information for the Professional School Counselor (continued)

Hypoxia	"Insufficient amount of oxygen to the brain; can result in brain damage" (Gargiulo, 2006, p. 623).
IDEA	"Individuals with Disabilities Education Act. In September 1990, the reauthorization of the Education for the Handicapped Act changed the name from EHA to IDEA. The term 'handicapped' in the law was replaced with 'children with disabilities'" (Wilson, 1992, p. 245).
Identification	"Process of locating and identifying children who need special services" (Wilson, 1992, p. 245).
IEP Team	"The multidisciplinary team of education and related services professionals that develops and evaluates, along with students with disabilities and their parents, the individualized education program [IEP] for each student with disability" (Smith, 2004, p. 484).
IHO	"Impartial hearing officer" (Wilson, 1992, p. 245).
Implement	"To carry out procedures, as in implementing special education services" (Wilson, 1992, p. 245).
Impulsivity or Impulsiveness	"Responding to a situation or stimulus while lacking verbal and/or physical controls. A child may respond impulsively in social situations when he or she grabs or handles objects or asks inappropriate questions" (Wilson, 1992, p. 245).
Individualized education program (IEP)	"A written detailed plan developed by a team for each pupil ages 3–21 who receives a special education; a management tool" (Gargiulo, 2006, p. 623).
Individualized family service plan (IFSP)	"A written plan developed by a team that coordinates services for infants and toddlers and their families" (Gargiulo, 2006, p. 623).
Individualized health care plan (IHCP)	"IEP component for students with special health care needs; specifies health care procedures and services administered by school personnel and a plan for emergencies" (Heward, 2006, p. G-6).
Individualized transition plan (ITP)	"Specifies desired post-school outcomes in four areas (employment, postsecondary education, residential, and recreation/leisure) and instructional programming and supports to help student attain those outcomes; required part of student's IEP by age 16" (Heward, 2006, p. G-6).
Informal diagnosis	"A teacher works with a child on a daily basis. He or she formulates an informal diagnosis while evaluating the child's needs and learning patterns. A child does not receive special services, however, without a formal diagnosis arrived at through appropriate evaluations" (Wilson, 1992, pp. 245–246).
Interdisciplinary	"Resources and information combining several fields of study, including medicine, psychology, and education" (Wilson, 1992, p. 246).
Internalizing disorders	"Behavior disorders characterized by anxiety, withdrawal, fearfulness, and other conditions reflecting an individual's internal state" (Gargiulo, 2006, p. 624).
Interpersonal problem solving	"Teaching pupils the cognitive skills needed to avoid and resolve interpersonal conflicts, peer pressure, and ways of coping with stress and their own feelings" (Gargiulo, 2006, p. 624).
Intervention	"A modification, teaching technique, or special material used to help a child learn. Educationally, the term means children with disabilities are identified at an early age and strategies initiated to help them" (Wilson, 1992, p. 246).
Job coach	"An individual who supervises a person with a disability for all or part of the day to provide training, assistance, or support to maintain a job" (Gargiulo, 2006, p. 624).

continued

TABLE 9.3   Special Education and Other Mental Health Terms: Vital Information for the Professional School Counselor (continued)

Joint attention deficits	"Inability to interact mutually or to share interest in events or objects with another person; a problem for many individuals with autism" (Smith, 2004, p. 485).
Juvenile rheumatoid arthritis	"A chronic arthritic condition affecting the joints that occurs before 16 years of age" (Gargiulo, 2006, p. 624).
Klinefelter syndrome	"A chromosomal anomaly in which males receive an extra X chromosome; associated with frequent social retardation, sterility, underdeveloped male sex organs, developed secondary female sex characteristics, and bordering or mild levels of intellectual disabilities" (Heward, 2006, pp. G-6–G-7).
Kurzweil Reader	"One of the first computerized systems designed for people with visual disabilities that translates print into synthesized speech" (Smith, 2004, p. 485).
Language delay	"Development of language skills that is slower than in the majority of peers; may signal that the child will require the assistance of a specialist to use language proficiently" (Smith, 2004, p. 485).
Language impairment	"Difficulty mastering or inability to master the various systems of rules in language, which then interferes with communication" (Smith, 2004, p. 485).
Learning disability (LD)	"A disability in which there is a discrepancy between a person's ability and academic achievement; individual possesses average intelligence" (Gargiulo, 2006, p. 624).
Least restrictive environment (LRE)	"A standard principle that each student should be educated in the maximum appropriate environment with classmates who are typical of their disability" (Gargiulo, 2006, p. 624).
Legally blind	"A visual acuity of 20/200 or less in the better eye with correction or a visual field that is no greater than 20 degrees" (Gargiulo, 2006, p. 624).
Life skills	"Those skills used to manage a home, cook, shop, and organize personal living environments" (Smith, 2004, p. 486).
Limited English proficient (LEP)	"A person with a reduced or diminished fluency in reading, writing, or speaking English" (Gargiulo, 2006, p. 624).
Low-incidence disability	"A disability that occurs infrequently; that is, the prevalence and incidence are very low. Examples include visual disabilities, deaf, and hard of hearing, deafblindness, autism, multiple-severe disabilities, and traumatic brain injury" (Smith, 2004, p. 486).
Mainstreaming	"An early term for the practice of integrating students with special needs into a general education classroom for all or part of the school day" (Gargiulo, 2006, p. 624).
Maturation lag	"A child is behind his or her peers in development" (Wilson, 1992, p. 247).
Medically fragile	"A term that was formerly used to describe children with special health care needs but now reflects an individual's health status" (Smith, 2004, p. 486).
Meningitis	"An inflammation of the membranes covering the brain and spinal cord; can cause problems with sight and hearing and/or mental retardation" (Heward, 2006, p. G-7).
Mental age (MA)	"A means of describing an individual's mental ability, derived from a contrived comparison between an individual's measured IQ score and current chronological age; not [the] preferred means of describing an individual's abilities" (Smith, 2004, p. 486).

TABLE 9.3   Special Education and Other Mental Health Terms: Vital Information for the Professional School Counselor (continued)

Mentally ill	"A generic term often used by professionals outside of the field of special education to refer to individuals with emotional or behavioral disorders" (Gargiulo, 2006, p. 624).
Microcephaly	"A condition in which the head is unusually small, leading to inadequate development of the brain and resulting in an intellectual disability" (Gargiulo, 2006, p. 624).
Minimal brain injury	"A once popular term referring to individuals who exhibit behavioral signs of brain injury (such as distractibility of impulsivity) but with no neurological evidence" (Gargiulo, 2006, p. 624).
Minimal hearing loss (MHL)	"Technically not a hearing loss; however, individual experiences difficulty hearing spoken language at a distance or when background noise is present" (Gargiulo, 2006, p. 624).
Mixed cerebral palsy	"Cerebral palsy that consists of combinations of different types. A person who has both spastic and athetoid cerebral palsy would be considered to have mixed cerebral palsy" (Gargiulo, 2006, p. 624).
Modality	"The sensory path through which a person receives information; visual modality and auditory modality" (Wilson, 1992, p. 247).
Monoplegia	"Paralysis affecting one limb" (Heward, 2006, p. G-7).
Multidisciplinary	"A group of professionals from different disciplines who perform their roles independent of one another but function as a team when making special education placement decisions." (Gargiulo, 2006, p. 625).
Multidisciplinary evaluation	"PL 94-142 requires that each disabled child receive an evaluation gathered from a variety of disciplines, i.e., professional fields" (Wilson, 1992, p. 247).
Multiple-severe disabilities	"Exceptionally challenging disabilities where more than one condition influences learning, independence, and the range of intensive and pervasive supports the individual and the family require" (Smith, 2004, p. 486).
Muscular dystrophy	"A group of diseases that gradually weakens muscle tissue; usually becomes evident by the age of 4 or 5" (Heward, 2006, p. G-8).
Myopia	"Elongation of the eye that causes extreme nearsightedness and decreased visual acuity" (Gargiulo, 2006, p. 625).
Native language	"Parents have the right to establish the native language of their child" (Wilson, 1992, p. 247).
Neurological impairment	"Damage to the central nervous system resulting in limitations in the ability to control muscles and motor movement" (Smith, 2004, p. 486).
Neuromotor impairments	"Several types of impairments involving abnormality of, or damage to, the brain, spinal cord, or nerves that send impulses to the muscles of the body" (Gargiulo, 2006, p. 625).
NIH	"The National Institute for Health coordinates and support biomedical research into cause, prevention, and cure of disease. A division of Health and Human Services" (Wilson, 1992, p. 247).
Norm-referenced	"Refers to standardized tests on which a pupil's performance is compared to that of his or her field" (Gargiulo, 2006, p. 625).
Obsessive/compulsive disorder (OCD)	"Persistent, recurring thoughts (obsessions) that reflect exaggerated anxiety or fears; typical obsessions include worry about being contaminated, behaving improperly or acting violently. Obsessions may lead an individual to perform compulsive rituals or routines—such as washing hands, repeating phrases or hoarding—to relieve the anxiety caused by the obsession" (Heward, 2006, p. G-8).

continued

TABLE 9.3   Special Education and Other Mental Health Terms: Vital Information for the Professional School Counselor (continued)

Occupational therapy (OT)	"Treatment provided by an occupational therapist to help a child with daily living skills. OT includes improving or restoring functions impaired or lost through illness, injury, or deprivation, improving ability to perform functions leading to independence, or preventing further loss of function" (Wilson, 1992, pp. 247–248).
Optic nerve atrophy	"Degenerations of the optic nerve, which may be congenital or hereditary, causing loss of central vision, color vision, and reduced visual acuity" (Gargiulo, 2006, p. 625).
OSEP	"Office of Special Education Programs, U.S. Department of Education" (Wilson, 1992, p. 248).
OSERS	"Office of Special Education and Rehabilitative Services" (Wilson, 1992, p. 248).
Outreach services	"Specialized programs offered in local communities by residential school or centralized agencies serving student with special needs" (Smith, 2004, p. 487).
Overrepresentation	"Too many students from one cultural or ethnic group participating in a special education category, beyond the level one might expect from that group's representation of the overall school population" (Smith, 2004, p. 487).
Paraplegia	"Paralysis (or spasticity) of the legs" (Gargiulo, 2006, p. 625).
Pediatric neurologist	"A physician who specializes in diseases of children's nervous systems" (Wilson, 1992, p. 248).
Percentile rank	"A number that indicates how the child compares with other children who took the tests at the same time" (Wilson, 1992, p. 248).
Perception	"Understanding. A perceptual disorder is a deficiency in understanding one's environment" (Wilson, 1992, p. 248).
Perseveration	"A child who perseverates has difficulty changing to new activities and may continue with old ones long after peers have discontinued. The child repeats words, phrases, and motions after they are appropriate" (Wilson, 1992, p. 248).
Personality disorder	"A group of behavior disorders, including social withdrawal, anxiety, depression, feelings of inferiority, guilt, shyness, and unhappiness" (Heward, 2006, p. G-8).
Pervasive developmental disorder not otherwise specified (PDD-NOS)	"Label applied when there is a severe and pervasive impairment in the development of reciprocal social interaction associated with impairment in wither verbal or non-verbal communication skills or with the presence of stereotyped behavior, interests, and activities" (Gargiulo, 2006, p. 625).
Phenylketonuria (PKU)	"A hereditary condition that cases mental retardation and can be avoided by eliminating from the diet, shortly after birth, foods (such as milk) that contain an amino acid that, in these individuals, can built up to toxic levels" (Smith, 2004, p. 487).
Phoneme	"Any one of a set of small sounds that represent a language. Sets of phonemes are different for each language" (Wilson, 1992, p. 248).
Phonological disorder	"A language disorder in which the child produces a given sound correctly in some instances but does not produce the sound correctly at other times" (Heward, 2006, p. G-9).
Photophobia	"Extreme sensitivity of the eyes to light; occurs most notably in albino children" (Heward, 2006, p. G-9).
Physical therapist (PT)	"A professional trained to help people with disabilities develop and maintain muscular and orthopedic capabilities and make correct and useful movement" (Heward, 2006, p. G-9).

TABLE 9.3 Special Education and Other Mental Health Terms: Vital Information for the Professional School Counselor (continued)

Physical therapy	"Treatment of physical disabilities to help an individual improve the use of bones, muscles, joints, and nerves. Techniques used by physical therapists include the use of heat, cold, water, massage, and exercise" (Wilson, 1992, p. 248).
Placement	"A class, program, and/or related services for a child with disabilities" (Wilson, 1992, p. 249).
Posttraumatic stress disorder (PTSD)	"Prolonged and recurrent emotional reactions after exposure to a traumatic event (e.g., sexual or physical assault; unexpected death of a loved one; witnessing or being a victim of a natural disaster, acts of war, or terrorism). Symptoms: flashbacks and nightmares of the traumatic event; avoiding places or things related to the trauma; emotional detachment from others; difficulty sleeping, irritability, or poor concentration" (Heward, 2006, p. G-9).
Prader-Willi syndrome	"A condition linked to chromosomal abnormality that is characterized by delays in motor development, mild to moderate mental retardation, hypogenital development, an insatiable appetite that often results in obesity, and small features and stature" (Heward, 2006, p. G-9).
Prenatal asphyxia	"A lack of oxygen during the birth process usually caused by interruption of respiration; can cause unconsciousness and/or brain damage" (Heward, 2006, p. G-9).
Primary prevention	"Activities aimed at eliminating a problem or condition prior to its onset; may also refer to reducing the number of new instances of problematic behavior" (Gargiulo, 2006, p. 626).
Procedural safeguards	"IDEA guarantees students with disabilities and their parents the right to a free appropriate public education (FAPE) in the least restrictive environment (LRE) possible through a process to resolve disagreements and disputes that begins with mediation and ends with civil action" (Smith, 2004, p. 488).
Prognosis	"Projected outcome of disease or condition" (Wilson, 1992, p. 249).
Projective tests	"Psychological tests that require a person to respond to a standardized task or set of stimuli (e.g., draw a picture or interpret an ink blot). Responses are thought to be a projection of the test taker's personality and are scored according to the given test's scoring manual to produce a personality profile" (Heward, 2006, p. G-9).
Prosthesis	"An artificial body part to aid function" (Wilson, 1992, p. 249).
Psychostimulants	"Medications typically prescribed for persons with ADHD. These drugs activate or enhance specific aspects of neurological functioning that in turn affect executive functions" (Gargiulo, 2006, p. 626).
Pull-in programming	"Rather than having students with disabilities leave general education classes for special education or for related services, delivering those services to them in the general education classroom" (Smith, 2004, p. 488).
Pull-out programs	"Providing special services outside of the general education classroom; often called a resource room for students with disabilities; the most common educational placement for the gifted students" (Smith, 2004, p. 488).
Raw score	"In testing, the number of right answers on a test" (Wilson, 1992, p. 249).
Readiness	"A child's growth and experiences enable him or her to undertake new learning experiences. As in 'reading readiness'" (Wilson, 1992, p. 249).
Recognition	"To know again. Cognition is to know or comprehend" (Wilson, 1992, p. 249).
Referral	"A process of directing a person to an agency for services" (Wilson, 1992, p. 249). "A formal request by a teacher or parent that a student be evaluated for special education services" (Gargiulo, 2006, p. 626).

continued

TABLE 9.3   Special Education and Other Mental Health Terms: Vital Information for the Professional School Counselor (continued)

Regular education initiative (REI)	"An approach that advocates that general educators assume greater responsibility for the education of students with disabilities" (Gargiulo, 2006, p. 626).
Rehabilitation	"Planned program to help a disabled person develop his or her abilities to the fullest" (Wilson, 1992, p. 250).
Related services	"Supports to help a child benefit from special education" (Wilson, 1992, p. 250).
Remediation	"An educational program designed to teach a person to overcome a disability through training and education" (Heward, 2006, p. G-10).
Resource room	"Classroom in which special education students spend part of the school day and receive individualized special education services" (Heward, 2006, p. G-10).
Respite	"Substitute care in order to provide relief and rest for a parent, guardian, or caregiver" (Wilson, 1992, p. 250).
Retinitis pigmentosa	"Pigmentation of the retina that can result in night blindness, photophobia, and eventual loss of vision in various parts of the periphery" (Gargiulo, 2006, p. 626).
Retinopathy of prematurity (ROP)	"An interruption in the vascular system of the eye, due to premature birth, in which veins and arteries begin to grow in an unorganized manner and cause bundles, that pull together and detach the retina, resulting in loss of peripheral vision or total blindness" (Gargiulo, 2006, p. 626).
Rett's disorder	"Neurodevelopmental disorder of childhood characterized by normal early development followed by loss of purposeful use of the hands, gait abnormalities, seizures, and mental retardation; affects females almost exclusively; included in autism spectrum disorders" (Heward, 2006, p. G-10).
Reyes's syndrome	"A relatively rare disease that appears to be related to a variety of viral infections; most common in children over the age of 6. About 30% of children who contract it die; survivors sometimes show signs of neurological damage and mental retardation. The cause is unknown, although some studies have found an increased risk after the use of aspirin during a viral illness" (Heward, 2006, p. G-10).
Schizophrenia	"A severe disorder characterized by psychotic symptoms, including hallucinations, delusions, disorganized thinking and catatonic motor behaviors. These signs and symptoms are associated with marked social or occupational dysfunction" (Gargiulo, 2006, p. 627).
School nurses	"Professionals who participate in delivering FAPE [free appropriate public education] to students with disabilities by assisting with medical services at school and designing accommodations for students with special health care needs" (Smith, 2004, p. 488).
School psychologist	"A psychologist trained to test and evaluate individual students' abilities" (Smith, 2004, p. 488).
Screening	"A group examination given in order to identify those children in need of diagnostic evaluations" (Wilson, 1992, p. 250).
SEA	"The state education agency" (Wilson, 1992, p. 250).
Section 504 of the Rehabilitation Act of 1973	"This law set the stage for both the Individuals with Disabilities Education Act, passed in 1975, and the Americans with Disabilities Act, passed in 1990, by outlining basic civil rights of people with disabilities" (Smith, 2004, p. 488).
Seizure	"A sudden, temporary change in the normal functioning of the brain's electrical system due to excessive, uncontrolled electrical activity in the brain" (Gargiulo, 2006, p. 627).

TABLE 9.3 Special Education and Other Mental Health Terms: Vital Information for the Professional School Counselor (continued)

Term	Definition
Selective mutism	"Speaking normally in some settings or situations and not speaking in others" (Heward, 2006, p. G-10).
Self-advocacy	"A social and political movement started by and for people with mental retardation who wish to speak for themselves on important issues such as housing, employment, legal rights, and personal relationships" (Smith, 2004, p. 488).
Self-contained class	"A classroom for children who cannot function comfortably in normal settings" (Wilson, 1992, p. 250).
Self-injurious behavior	"Self-inflicted actions that can cause tissue damage, such as bruises, redness, and reopen wounds. The most common self-injurious behaviors are head banding, finger-, hand-, or wrist-biting, excessive scratching, cutting, or burning oneself." (Gargiulo, 2006, p. 627).
Semantic disorder	"Language difficulty associated with poor vocabulary development, inappropriate use of word meaning, and/or inability to comprehend word meanings" (Gargiulo, 2006, p. 627).
Sensorineural hearing loss	"The loss of sound sensitivity produced by abnormalities of the inner ear or nerve pathways beyond the inner ear to the brain" (Gargiulo, 2006, p. 627).
Sensory perception disorder	"A problem with the function of the brain that is responsible for producing the composite picture of who we are physically, where we are, and what is going on around us" (Gargiulo, 2006, p. 627).
Seriously emotionally disturbed (SED)	"Also known as 'serious emotional disorder' and/or 'severely emotionally disturbed.' In PL 94-142, the term does not include children who are socially maladjusted unless it is determined that they are seriously emotionally disturbed" (Wilson, 1992, p. 250).
Service delivery options	"Various ways in which special education services are provided to students with disabilities (e.g. full inclusion programs, special classes, center schools)" (Smith, 2004, p. 489).
Severe disabilities	"Challenges faced by individuals with severe and profound mental retardation, autism, and/or physical/sensory impairments combined with marked developmental delay. Persons with severe disabilities exhibit extreme deficits in intellectual functioning and need systematic instruction for basic skills such as self-care and communicating with others" (Heward, 2006, p. G-10).
Sheltered workshop	"A structured work environment where persons with disabilities receive employment training and perform work for pay. May provide transitional services for some individuals (e.g., short-term training for competitive employment in the community) and permanent work setting for others" (Heward, 2006, p. G-10).
Shunt	"A tube used in a medical procedure that draws excess fluid from the brain and head area and disposes of it in a safe area in the body, such as the stomach; used to prevent cognitive disabilities resulting from hydrocephaly" (Smith, 2004, p. 489).
Sickle cell anemia	"A heredity blood disorder that inhibits blood flow; African Americans are most at risk for this health impairment" (Smith, 2004, p. 489).
Simple partial seizure	"A type of seizure characterized by sudden jerking motions with no loss of consciousness. Partial seizure may occur weekly, monthly, or only once or twice a year" (Heward, 2006, p. G-11).
Social skills training	"Using direct instruction to teach students appropriate social behaviors; goal is to increase individual's social competency and acceptance" (Gargiulo, 2006, p. 627).

continued

TABLE 9.3   Special Education and Other Mental Health Terms: Vital Information for the Professional School Counselor (continued)

Socialized aggression	"A group of behavior disorders, including truancy, gang membership, theft, and delinquency" (Heward, 2006, p. G-11).
Socially maladjusted	"Individuals whose social behaviors are atypical; often regarded as chronic social offenders" (Gargiulo, 2006, p. 627).
Socioeconomic status (SES)	"The status an individual or family unit holds in society, usually determined by job, level of education, and the amount of money available to spend" (Smith, 2004, p. 489).
Spastic cerebral palsy	"A type of cerebral palsy in which the person has very tight muscle occurring in one or more muscle groups, resulting in stiff, uncoordinated movements" (Gargiulo, 2006, p. 627).
Special education	"Specially designed instruction to meet the unique needs of an individual recognized as exceptional" (Gargiulo, 2006, p. 627).
Special Olympics	"A sports program for disabled people. Special Olympics games include competitions in track and field, swimming, gymnastics, basketball, volleyball, floor hockey, bowling, ice-skating, soccer, winter activities, wheelchair events, and other sports" (Wilson, 1992, p. 251).
Specialized instructional strategies	"Teaching techniques specifically designed for a particular special education population to assist with learning specific material" (Gargiulo, 2006, p. 627).
Specific developmental disorder (SDD)	"A new term for learning disability. Specific developmental disorders include developmental reading disorder and developmental arithmetic disorder" (Wilson, 1992, p. 250).
Speech recognition threshold (SRT)	"A measure of threshold sensitivity for speech. The SRT represents the softest sound level at which a listener can identify the stimuli 50 percent of the time" (Gargiulo, 2006, p. 627).
Speech/language pathologist (SLP)	"A professional who diagnoses and treats problems in the area of speech and language development; a related services provider" (Smith, 2004, p. 489).
Spina bifida	"Failure of the neural tube to completely close during fetal development. In its most severe form, the baby is born with a sac on his or her back containing part of the spinal cord" (Gargiulo, 2006, p. 627).
Spina bifida occulta	"A type of spina bifida that usually does not cause serious disability. Although the vertebrae do not close, there is no protrusion of the spinal cord and membranes" (Heward, 2006, p. G-11).
Stay-put provision	"The legal mandate that prohibited students with disabilities from being expelled because of behavior associated with their disabilities" (Smith, 2004, p. 489).
STORCH infections	"Many different congenital viruses fall under this group of congenital infections; the term stands for syphilis, toxoplasmosis, other, rubella, cytomegalovirus, and herpes" (Smith, 2004, p. 489).
Syndrome	"A group of symptoms or signs that, appearing together, indicate a condition, disease, or disability" (Wilson, 1992, p. 252).
System of support	"The network of supports that each individual develops to function optimally in life" (Smith, 2004, p. 489).
Systems of care model	"Providing an individually tailored and coordinated system of services and care to students with emotional or behavioral disorders; developed by family members and service providers" (Gargiulo, 2006, p. 628).
Tay-Sachs disease	"A progressive nervous system disorder causing profound mental retardation, deafness, blindness, paralysis, and seizures. Usually fatal by age 5. Caused by a recessive gene; blood test can identify carrier; analysis of enzymes in fetal cells provides prenatal diagnosis" (Heward, 2006, p. G-11).

TABLE 9.3 Special Education and Other Mental Health Terms: Vital Information for the P
Counselor (continued)

Telecommunication device for the deaf (TDD)	"An instrument for sending typewritten messages over telephone received by a person who is deaf or severely hearing impaired as a p message. Sometimes called TT, TTY, or TTD" (Gargiulo, 2006, p. 628).
Telecommunications relay service (TRS)	"A telephone system required by federal law where an operator at a relay center converts a print-telephone message into a voice-telephone message" (Smith, 2004, p. 490).
Tertiary prevention	"Efforts that attempt to limit the adverse consequences of an existing problem while maximizing a person's potential; in regard to persons with emotional or behavioral disorder, refers to an intense level of intervention using strategies and supports designed for individuals with chronic and intense behavior problems" (Gargiulo, 2006, p. 628).
Time out	"A behavior management technique that involves removing the opportunity for reinforcement for a specific period of time following an inappropriate behavior; results in a reduction of the inappropriate behavior" (Heward, 2006, p. G-11).
Token economy (token reinforcement systems)	"An instructional and behavior management system in which students earn tokens (e.g., stars, points, poker chips) for performing specified behaviors. Student accumulate their tokens and exchange them at prearranged time for their choice of activities or items from a menu of backup rewards (e.g., stickers, hall monitor of a day)" (Heward, 2006, pp. G-11–G12).
Total immersion	"The student is taught entirely in English; all the other students are also non-native English speakers and the teacher can speak the student's home language" (Smith, 2004, p. 490).
Tourette's syndrome	"A neurological disorder characterized by motor tics and incontrollable verbal outbursts" (Gargiulo, 2006, p. 628).
Trainable mentally retarded	"Classification of a person with moderate mental retardation who is capable of learning self-care and social skills; IQ range generally between 35/40 and 50/55" (Gargiulo, 2006, p. 628).
Transition services	"Individualized and coordinated services that assist an adolescent with a disability to successfully move from school to post-school activities" (Gargiulo, 2006, p. 628).
Treatment and Education of Autistic and Communication-Handicapped Children (TEACCH)	"An individualized program that helps children with autism compensate, through visual supports and other forms of structure, for skills they cannot learn" (Smith, 2004, p. 490).
Turner's syndrome	"A sex chromosomal disorder in females, resulting from an absence of one of the X chromosomes; lack of secondary sex characteristics, sterility, and short stature are common. Although not usually a cause of mental retardation, it is often associated with learning problems" (Heward, 2006, p. G-12).
Twice exceptional	"Students who are gifted and talented but also have a disability" (Gargiulo, 2006, p. 628).
Type I diabetes (formally called juvenile diabetes or early onset diabetes)	"A disease characterized by inadequate secretion or use of insulin and the resulting excessive sugar in the blood and urine. It can be managed with diet and/or medication but can be difficult to control. It can cause coma and eventually death if left untreated or treated improperly. Can also lead to visual impairments and limb amputation. The disease is not curable at the present time" (Heward, 2006, p. G-12).
Usher syndrome	"A genetic syndrome that includes a nonprogressive sensorineural hearing loss, retinitis pigmentosa and a progressively restricted field of vision, loss of the sense of smell, mental retardation, and impaired balance and motor" (Smith, 2004, p. 490).

continued

d Other Mental Health Terms: Vital Information for the Professional School

A rare genetic disorder characterized by mild mental retardation, developmental delays, language delays, problems in gross motor skills, and hypersensitivity" (Gargiulo, 2006, p. 629).

A coordinated interagency effort at providing supports and services to a student and his or her family in natural environment—school, home, or community" (Gargiulo, 2006, p. 629).

Resources for School to Work or Further Education

Alliance for Technology Access (ATA), 2175 E. Francisco Blvd., Suite L, San Rafael, CA 94939. Telephone: (800) 455-7970; (415) 455-4575; (415) 455-0491 (TTY). Email: atainfo@ataccess.org. Web: http://www.ataccess.org.

Americans with Disabilities Act Disability and Business Technical Assistance Centers (DBTACs). Telephone: (800) 949-4232. Web: http://www.adata.org. (The DBTACs provide information, referral, teaching assistance, and training on the Americans with Disabilities Act.)

Association on Higher Education and Disability (AHEAD), University of Massachusetts Boston, 100 Morrissey Blvd., Boston, MA 02125. Telephone: (617) 287-3880; (617) 287-3882 (TTY). Email: AHEAD@umb.edu. Web: http://www.ahead.org.

Beach Center on Families and Disability, University of Kansas, 3111 Haworth Hall, Lawrence, KS 66045. Telephone: (785) 864-7600. Email: beach@dole.lsi.ukans.edu. Web: http://www.beachcenter.org.

Council for Exceptional Children, Division on Career Development and Transition, 1110 N. Glebe Rd., Suite 300, Arlington, VA 22201-5704. Telephone: (703) 620-3660; (703) 264-9446 (TTY). Web: http://www.cec.sped.org.

Easter Seals National Headquarters, 230 W. Monroe St., Suite 1800, Chicago, IL 60606. Telephone: (312) 726-6200; 1-800-221-6827. Email: info@easter-seals.org. Web: http://www.easter-seals.org.

Easter Seals Project ACTION, 700 13th St., NW, Suite 200, Washington, DC 20005. Telephone: (202) 347-3066; (202) 347-7385 (TTY). Email: project_action@opa.easter-seals.org. Web: http://www.projectaction.org.

Employer Assistance Referral Network (EARN). Telephone: (866) 327-6669. Email: earn@earnworks.com. Web: http://www.earnworks.com.

HEATH Resource Center (National Clearinghouse on Postsecondary Education for Individuals with Disabilities), George Washington University Graduate School of Education and Human Development, 2121 K St., NW, Suite 220, Washington, DC 20037. Telephone: (800) 544-3284 (Voice/TTY); (202) 973-0904. Email: help@heath.gwu.edu. Web: http://www.heath.gwu.edu.

Job Accommodation Network (JAN), 918 Chestnut Ridge Rd., Suite 1, P.O. Box 6080, Morgantown, WV 26506. Telephone: (800) 526-7234 (Voice/TTY); (800) 232-9675 (V/TTY, information on the ADA). Email: jan@icdi.wvu.edu. Web: http://www.jan.wvu.edu.

Mobility International USA (MIUSA), P.O. Box 10767, Eugene, OR 97440. Telephone: (541) 343-1284 (Voice/TTY). Email: info@miusa.org. Web: http://www.miusa.org.

National Center on Secondary Education and Transition, University of Minnesota, 6 Pattee Hall, 150 Pillsbury Dr. SE, Minneapolis, MN 55455. Telephone: (612) 624-2097. Email: ncset@icimail.coled.umn.edu. Web: http://www.ncset.org.

National Center on Workforce and Disability/Adult, Institute for Community Inclusion, University of Massachusetts Boston, 100 Morrissey Blvd., Boston, MA 02125. Telephone: (888) 886-9898 (Voice/TTY). Email: contact@onestops.info. Web: http://www.onestops.info.

National Collaborative on Workforce and Disability/Youth, Institute for Educational Leadership, 1001 Connecticut Ave., NW, Suite 310, Washington, DC 20036. Telephone: (877) 871-0744. Email: collaborative@iel.org. Web: http://www.ncwd-youth.info.

National Council on Independent Living (NCIL), 1916 Wilson Blvd., Suite 209, Arlington, VA 22201. Telephone: (703) 525-3406; (703) 525-4153 (TTY). Email: ncil@ncil.org. Web: http://www.ncil.org.

National Dissemination Center for Children with Disabilities (NICHCY), P.O. Box 1492, Washington, DC 20013. Telephone: (800) 695-0285; (202) 884-8200 (Voice/TTY). Email: nichcy@aed.org. Web: http://www.nichcy.org.

National Rehabilitation Information Center (NARIC), 4200 Forbes Blvd., Suite 202, Lanham, MD 20706. Telephone: (800) 346-2742. Email: naricinfo@heitechservices.com. Web: http://www.naric.com.

Office of Disability Employment Policy (formerly the President's Committee on Employment of People with Disabilities), U.S. Department of Labor, 200 Constitution Ave., NW, Washington, DC 20210. Telephone: (202) 376-6200. Email: infoodep@dol.gov. Web: http://www.dol.gov/odep/.

Research and Training Center on Independent Living, University of Kansas, 4089 Dole Building, Lawrence, KS 66045. Telephone: (913) 864-4095 (Voice/TTY). Email: rtcil@ukans.edu. Web: http://www.lsi.ukans.edu/rtcil/rtcil.htm.

Technical Assistance Alliance for Parent Centers, PACER Center, 8161 Normandale Blvd., Minneapolis, MN 55437. Telephone: (888) 248-0822; (952) 838-9000; (952) 838-0190 (TTY). Email: alliance@taalliance.org. Web: http://www.taalliance.org.

Transition Research Institute at Illinois (TRI), College of Education, University of Illinois at Urbana-Champaign, 113 Children's Research Center, 51 Gerty Dr., Champaign, IL 61820. Telephone: (217) 333-2325. Web: http://www.ed.uiuc.edu/SPED/tri/institute.html.

U.S. Equal Employment Opportunity Commission, 1801 L St., NW, Washington, DC 20507. Telephone: (800) 669-4000; (800) 669-6820 (TTY). Web: http://www.eeoc.gov.

The Professional School Counselor's Role in Understanding Cultural Diversity and Sexual Minority Youth

10

CULTURAL DIVERSITY

A professional school counselor is holding an evening parenting series at her school on the role of parents in supporting academic success as part of the collective literacy initiatives of her school system. At the first session, the professional school counselor emphasizes the importance of creating a separate, undisturbed quiet space for elementary school students to do their homework at night. She tells parents they should take their children to the library once a week and should read books to them in English each night. At the end of the session, each parent is asked to sign a "Parent Contract for Academic Success" as a personal commitment to their agreement to create supportive learning conditions in their home. A number of parents leave before signing the document and never return: One mother feels embarrassed, unable to imagine how a separate homework space could be arranged in her family's overcrowded apartment, which is shared by three generations in her extended family (nine people). Another father feels embarrassed and ashamed because he never learned to read in his native language and is just beginning to learn English. Another parent has to juggle two part-time jobs to make a living and has to rely on public transportation, which is time consuming. The school counselor is disappointed that attendance is dwindling and feels frustrated that some parents weren't even willing to sign the agreement. (Adapted from Olsen, Bhattacharya, & Scharf, 2006, p. 1. Adapted and reprinted with permission.)

This vignette is a typical example of the kinds of cultural challenges and misunderstandings counselors, teachers, and administrators encounter when working with children and families whose cultural backgrounds differ from their own without first acknowledging their own insensitivity to those with whom they are serving. Sometimes these situations cause discomfort; occasionally, they are explosive. Sometimes they are viewed mistakenly as merely a lack of connection between cultures. In any case, they often result in disappointing outcomes.

In diverse communities, cultural differences, conflicts, and misunderstandings are powerful forces that shape whether people are able to access services and to participate in the school community outreach initiatives or become alienated from this viable resource and become marginalized. Misunderstanding and discord also determine to a large extent the degree to which programs are able to succeed in reaching their intended audiences and meeting their intended goals. To increase the likelihood of their effectiveness, school and community service providers should be sensitive and responsive to cultural and ethnic differences when planning programs and services.

Schools and community agencies must operate in ways that are inclusive and equitable for the various cultural, ethnic, and language groups for whom they need to provide primary prevention and intervention initiatives. Part of the answer lies in the development of cultural competency and responsive services. For example, Fairfax County Schools in Virginia, the 12th largest school system in the nation, provides services for students in seven different languages: Arabic, Chinese, Farsi, Korean, Spanish, Urdu, and Vietnamese. It has also established a Hispanic/Latino Council for parents and students and resources for English Speakers of Other Languages (ESOL).

CULTURAL COMPETENCY

Cultural competency can be defined as a set of congruent behaviors, attitudes, and policies that come together in a system, community, or among professionals that enables them to work effectively in cross-cultural situations. Cultural competency is the acceptance and respect for difference, a continuous self-assessment regarding culture, an attention to the dynamics of difference, the ongoing development of cultural knowledge, and the resources and flexibility within service models to meet the needs of minority populations. (Cross, Bazron, Dennis, & Isaacs, 1989, p. 33)

Different authors define the term *cultural competency* in a variety of ways and involve a series of five skills:

1. Awareness and acceptance of cultural differences
2. Self-awareness of one's own culture and cultural blind spots
3. Understanding and working with the dynamics of cultural difference
4. Gaining knowledge of the clients culture
5. Adapting skills to cultural contexts (Diller, 2007, p. 289)

Competency refers to understanding more explicitly the mores, traditions, customs, formal and informal helping networks, customs, and mastery of the English language so that parents can be helped to understand the integral systems and dynamics of the schools. Knowledge about various cultures and the development of specific skills and attitudes in providing services in a manner consistent with the client's (both students' and parents') needs are essential. The cultural appropriateness of counseling and educational services may be the most important factor in making services accessible to people of diverse backgrounds.

Developing culturally sensitive practices can help reduce barriers to learning and acculturalization to a new country. Rapport building is a critical component of competency development. The professional

TABLE 10.1   Diversity Considerations of Individuals or Groups

CULTURAL IDENTITY	ETHNIC IDENTITY	NATIONALITY
• Acculturation to the U.S. • Family configuration or constellations • Gender and ordinal position in family • Political orientation • Social networks • Educational level • Housing resources and home environment	• Assimilation and acceptance in society • Language (English-language learners) • Social history • Sexuality • Entry status to the U.S. • History of place of origin • Understanding of the educational system	• Social class and financial resources • Language literacy and economic opportunity • Perception of time • Religion and spiritual views • Stress experience • Employment experience of parents • Motivation, aspirations, and resilience

Source: Adapted from National Center for Cultural Competence (2006).

school counselor needs to know who the client perceives as "natural helpers" and who he or she views as traditional helpers (e.g., elders in the church). This knowledge can facilitate the development of trust and enhance the individual's investment and continued participation in school programs. "Cultural competence requires that organizations have clearly defined, congruent set of values and principles, and demonstrate behaviors, attitudes, policies, structures and practices that enable them to work effectively cross-culturally" (National Center for Cultural Competence, 2006, p. 26). The diversity of individuals or groups may be influenced by the factors listed in Table 10.1.

ESSENTIAL COUNSELOR CHARACTERISTICS

Ensuring the provision of culturally competent services to students places a great deal of responsibility on the school system and school personnel, especially the service and resource responsibilities that professional school counselors assume. In particular, there are a number of generally expected levels of knowledge, skills, and attributes that are essential to providing culturally competent school and community, including those discussed below.

Essential Knowledge

- The knowledge of a counselees' culture (history, religion, traditions, values, family systems, sibling relationships, discipline of children, and relationships of children to their father or their mother and extended kinship relationships).
- The knowledge of the impact of racism, ethnicity, immigration, and poverty on behavior, attitudes, values, disabilities, and employment and educational opportunities.
- The knowledge of counselee's help-seeking behaviors and availability of employment, educational opportunities, transportation, health services, and social services and their accessibility to ethnically diverse and immigrant counselors.
- The knowledge of the roles of language, speech patterns, and communication style, as well as communication hierarchy, in different families that come from diverse and immigrant backgrounds. It is important to understand that in some cultures, it is inappropriate to bring concerns of the family to school personnel. Cultural pride and self-sacrifice take precedence over asking for assistance or help.
- The knowledge of the impact of the policies and procedures of social services, department of motor vehicles, health services, mental health services, and other community agencies on the needs of students and families who come from diverse backgrounds or have recently immigrated to the United States.
- The knowledge of community resources (e.g., agencies, persons, social networks, informal helping networks, temporary shelters, places of worship) available for diverse students, families, and communities.
- The recognition of how professional values and personal beliefs of community helping professionals and colleagues may either conflict with or accommodate the needs of counselees from different cultures. It is critical to assess personal bias and preconceived notions held by counselors about counselees from diverse backgrounds or immigrants and to serve as a catalyst for education awareness and understanding.
- The knowledge of how power struggles, political hierarchies, and relationships within and outside communities, institutions, and schools may impact different cultures by creating open or closed systems. This creates a level of frustration among new students and families and fosters barriers to learning.

Essential Communication Skills

The Center for Immigration Studies, a research organization provides a detailed picture of the numbers and socioeconomic status (SES) of the nation's immigrant or foreign-born population, both legal and illegal. The data were collected by the U.S. Census Bureau in March 2007. Among the report's findings:

- The nation's immigrant population (legal and illegal) reached a record of 37.9 million in 2007. Compared to the great wave of immigration at the turn of the 19th century, the immigrant population then was much less than half what it is today.
- Immigrants account for one in eight U.S. residents, the highest level in 80 years. In 1970, it was one in 21; in 1980, one in 16; and in 1990, one in 13.
- Overall, nearly one in three immigrants is an illegal alien. Half of Mexican and Central American immigrants and one-third of South American immigrants are illegal.
- Between 2000 and 2007, 10.3 million immigrants arrived—the highest seven-year period of immigration in U.S. history. More than half of post-2000 arrivals (5.6 million) are estimated to be illegal aliens (Camarota, 2007, p. 1).

This wave of immigration will have long-range implications on education, employment, and economics and represents something that the educational reform legislation of the No Child Left Behind Act of 2001 (NCLB) did not anticipate, namely, "How do you get a growing population of immigrants to achieve at high levels on standards of learning tests when they have not mastered the English language?"

Nonetheless, it is imperative that professional school counselors meet this challenge and advocate for this population, because it is an investment in our economic future. With this in mind, the following skills are necessary to feel comfortable learning about cultures of ethnic and immigrant minority student groups and helping them to acculturate and assimilate into our society:

- The ability to communicate accurate information on behalf of culturally different students, their families, and their communities and to help them access this information routinely and in their native language.
- The ability to openly discuss racial and ethnic differences or issues and to respond to culturally biased cues such eye contact, touching when greeting a person, and communication style (i.e., who talks to whom or who talks for whom in the family system is important to know and understand).
- The ability to assess the meaning that ethnicity has for individual clients. For example, are clients assimilating to this culture, or are they trying to maintain both cultures in a new environment? Are they having difficulty accessing child care, health services, and other community resources?
- The ability to understand the difference between the symptoms of emotional stress from trying to assimilate into a new culture or feelings of prejudice or stigma because of the association with a particular ethnic group when coming to the United States. For example, hatred or suspicion toward Arabs after the September 11, 2001, attacks or other acts of terrorism such as the 2009 massacre at Fort Hood, Texas, is a reality for some people in the United States because of lack of education or understanding about Muslim culture and traditions.
- Interviewing techniques that help the professional school counselor understand and accommodate the role of language in the client's culture by using professional interpreters rather than relying on children to be interpreters for their parents if English is not understood or spoken. It must be understood that in any culture, children can be manipulative and interpret less-than-flattering reports in a better light to their parents when there is a language barrier between teacher and parent or counselor and parent.
- The ability to utilize the concepts of empowerment, advocacy, and resourcefulness on behalf of culturally different clients and navigate the various systems within the community such as

health care, housing, employment, education, and transportation. For example, it can be important to understand that transportation may be a huge consideration, especially if mass transit is not easily available or is time consuming, when coupled with child care issues. Coordinating child care, employment responsibilities, and public transportation can be an insurmountable task for those living on the margins of society.

- The ability to recognize and combat racism, racial stereotypes, and myths among individuals and institutions through programs that serve to educate and to desensitize groups within the school and the community. Professional school counselors can provide a pivotal resource in terms of educating and providing faculty, administration, and support staff with diversity training and education. This is critical in order to make the transition of those from diverse backgrounds into mainstream society as productive citizens.

Essential Verbal and Nonverbal Nuances in Cultural Behaviors

Obviously, the most fundamental function of any counseling or educational initiatives among diverse populations is communication. Verbal and nonverbal ways of expression have been fundamentally influenced by the culture in which the student was raised. Nonverbal behavior can be dynamic, spontaneous, or very subtle, but it is patterned by the culture from which it originated and often transcends into mainstream society. It is crucial that there be a shared knowledge of the rules and codes of nonverbal communication among different ethnic and cultural groups—even if they just represent generalities. These styles can vary dramatically because each ethnic, cultural, and SES group has its own nuances. For example:

- *Personal space:* In the United States, it is common for people to stand about three feet apart when having a personal conversation. In other cultures, such as Arab cultures, people typically stand closer than three feet, which may feel awkward to someone unfamiliar with this style of engaging in a smaller realm of personal space.
- *Eye contact and feedback behaviors:* In the United States, individuals are encouraged to look each other directly in the eye and to participate actively in feedback behaviors (e.g., leaning forward, smiling, nodding—the kind of Rogerian listening that we have been used to when responding to someone). In contrast, people from other ethnic and racial backgrounds may show respect or deference by *not* engaging in eye contact or by participating more passively in their body language. This is often true in Asian cultures. Professional school counselors need to be sensitive to these nuances in attending behavior.
- *Interruption and turn-taking behaviors:* Most Americans have come to expect a conversation to progress linearly (i.e., going from point A to point B to point C), whereas in other cultures, it may be more natural for several people to be talking at the same time, with no one seemingly listening to anyone intently. Listening skills to deal with different turn-taking rules must be developed and understood if professional school counselors are to adjust to conversations with people from diverse cultures. The hierarchy of who talks *to* whom, who talks *for* whom, and who talks *with* whom is also important in many cultures, and this needs to be understood at the initial intake of counselor and counselee, especially in family relationships where the male may seem to be the dominant leader in that culture no matter what his socioeconomic status, which is often held in higher esteem in the United States.
- *Gesturing:* Hand and arm gesturing can vary quite a bit in different cultural backgrounds, as well as cultural subcultures such as gangs. In general, extra gesturing should not necessarily be interpreted as excitement—it might just be an ordinary manner of communication, depending on the speaker and the speaker's race and ethnicity. It is critical to understand these nuances.
- *Facial expression:* Variance in this form of communication is also common, and again, it is important to not assume that someone is cold or distressed by merely judging facial expression.

For example, in Asian culture, not maintaining eye contact demonstrates a form of respect toward the speaker.

- *Silence:* Americans are often uncomfortable with silence and find it harder to tolerate prolonged periods between conversational exchanges than do others from different cultures, and they may try to fill in what they perceive as an awkward pause by speaking. Other cultures may require more time to think things through before accepting a solution or resolution, however, and take more time in their response. Time and patience may need to be tolerated.
- *Dominance behaviors:* Prolonged eye contact; a strong, deliberate, erect posture; looking down at someone with lowered lids; hands on hips; and holding the head high are all examples of behavior that may be interpreted as assertive or even aggressive in the United States but can vary in different cultures. In addition, sitting behind a desk (demonstrating authority) or sitting on top of a desk (demonstrating superiority) when talking to parents can be intimidating, even in the American culture.
- *Conversation volume:* Confusion often occurs when culturally different speakers speak at differing levels of volume. It is important to remember that individuals may be reacting based on the rules learned in their own culture and what is considered normal by their peers. For example, in some cultures, children "should be seen and not heard" and are told to "only speak when spoken to" or to "respond in a whisper" when answering adults, demonstrating respect for parental figures or those in authority.
- *Touching:* Persons from cultures outside the United States may perceive someone as cold and aloof if there is not much touching during a conversation. Americans, on the other hand, may find someone from a different culture who touches excessively to be a bit abrasive, intrusive, or rude.

It is important for the professional school counselor to note that a great deal of meaning is conveyed nonverbally as well as verbally. Even before a word is spoken, the listener observes the body gestures and facial expressions of the speaker in an effort to make sense of these symbolic messages. They are unconscious and often speak louder than the words the speaker is trying to convey. People try to make sense of the nonverbal behavior of others by attaching meaning to what they observe them doing. Consequently, these symbolic messages help the listener to interpret the speaker's intention, and this substantiates the importance of nonverbal communication in the field of interpretation among both U.S. citizens and newly arriving immigrants.

Essential Counselor Attributes That Build Rapport

Counselor qualities that reflect genuineness, empathy, unconditional positive regard, warmth, and a capacity to respond flexibly to a range of possible solutions are among the greatest attributes most professional school counselors naturally possess. Acceptance and understanding of ethnic differences between people creates an inclusive school climate. This needs to be accomplished by ongoing education and cultural awareness activities. A willingness to work with counselees of different ethnic and cultural backgrounds and to provide viable school and community resources to the student and family provides a sense of stability and fosters cultural assimilation and acculturation.

The following are some guidelines to promote rapport with students and parents from other cultures:

- Engage immigrant or diverse students and their families in a respectful and warm atmosphere. Learn to pronounce names correctly and understand the family hierarchy, especially who talks to whom or for whom. Decide if an interpreter or translator is need before trying to use their child as an interpreter.
- Take into account and understand the student's cultural background, recognize who in the family holds authority, and use this in understanding the student's current academic functioning

and any special needs for special services such as English-language learning or the need for a free and appropriate education because of intellectual or other disabilities.

- Briefly describe any special programs and explain the role of each participant in the program, from accelerated programs to children with intellectual disabilities. Acknowledge that this may differ from the counselee's and the family's prior experience in a school setting. For example, parents may think their son should be in the hard sciences and their daughter should be more concerned with domestic classes. Some other cultures may stereotype the sexes into different career goals, which our culture does not support.
- Explain confidentiality, what it does and does not cover, and how it will or will not be affected by residency and immigrant status. Immigrants who are illegal present another issue for professional school counselors.
- Assess possible problems in light of other factors such as the need for food, shelter, and employment or stressful interactions with community agencies. Provide the necessary assistance in developing and maintaining environmental and social supports.
- Discuss possible consequences of achieving the goals for the student, the family, and the community.
- Simplify language. Slang or acronyms can be unfamiliar and confusing to a student and/or family. Be especially careful about using specialized language or jargon that may be unfamiliar to those outside the school setting (e.g., ESL, ELL, IEP, inclusion, etc.).
- If using preprinted pamphlets to help explain a condition, service, or resource,
- underline or highlight important passages. This way, the student and family do not have to read the entire text in order to refer back to the most significant information.
- Any information written by hand should be printed, not in longhand. It is preferable to write using both upper- and lowercase letters, as opposed to all capitals; in some situations, this may be viewed as "flaming" or threatening to the receiver. Also, keep the instructions in short, simple sentences and avoid abbreviations.

Fundamentally, professional school counselors play a critical role in a growing multicultural society by promoting higher academic standards and helping all students reach their full academic, career, and personal/social potential. Professional school counselors should be skilled multicultural consultants for parents, students, teachers, and support staff.

SELECTED MINORITY STUDENTS IN THE SCHOOLS

African American, Latino, and Native American Indian students continue to lag far behind their white and Asian peers academically. This section focuses on these groups and their performance.

African American Students

In 2005, the African American population in the United States was estimated to be 34,361,740 representing about 12.2% of the total population. Another 1.9 million people reported being black and one or more other races (U.S. Census Bureau, 2005a). Of the increase since 1980, 16% was due to immigration to the United States from countries such as Jamaica, Haiti, and Nigeria. Poverty and unemployment among African Americans remains two times higher than that of white Americans. African American men are also overrepresented in the prison system, and African American youths are overrepresented in special education programs and street gangs. In the 25–29 age group, nearly 12% of black men were in prison or jail, compared to just 1.7% of white males (Associated Press, 2006, May 21). Much of this data is based on lower end of the spectrum of social class (Holmes & Morin, 2006).

There is great diversity among African Americans, who may vary greatly from one another on variables such as socioeconomic status, educational attainment, cultural identity, family structure, and reaction to discrimination and racism. By 2000, the high school graduation rate for African Americans had increased to 74.2%, versus 80% for white Americans. However, African Americans trail behind in graduating from college with a bachelor's degree (14.3% versus 24.3% for whites; U.S. Census Bureau, 2005a). The educational environment and the educational system itself are often exclusive rather inclusive, which creates many barriers to full participation in academic offerings, from kindergarten to postsecondary education. African American children are two to five times more likely to be suspended from school and receive harsher consequences than their white peers (Monroe, 2005). In addition, many schools systems have predominantly white teaching staffs, and little multicultural or diversity training is taking place as the student population grows more diverse. Underprepared teachers may see communication patterns or nonstandard movements and walking styles as aggression or misbehavior (Monroe, 2005) and may respond negatively or inappropriately. Academically, African American students are overrepresented in special education and underrepresented in academically gifted programs (Ford, 1997; Gutman & McLoyd, 2000).

American Indians and Alaskan Natives

American Indians and Alaskan Natives belong to a highly heterogeneous group composed of "562 federally recognized tribes, some of which have only four or five members today" (Bureau of Indian Affairs, 2008, p. 1). In 2005, the American Indian, Eskimo, and Aleut population was approximately 2,500,000; an additional 1.81 million claim to have Indian roots (U.S. Census Bureau, 2006c).

The experience of the Native Americans is unique. Their language, culture, beliefs, resources, family structure, and land were gradually eroded and diminished by state and federal laws. In attempts to "civilize" Native Americans, many tribes were forced from their homes onto reservations that disrupted cultural traditions. Many Native American children were removed to be educated in English-speaking boarding schools and had to relinquish their tribal values, beliefs, and traditions. These practices had a tremendous negative impact on family and tribal cohesion, impeded the transmission of values from parents to children, and undermined the original cultural and family dynamics of many tribal communities. Still, "American Indians differ in their level of acculturation" (Trimble, Fleming, Beauvais, & Jumper-Thurman, 1996, p. 179).

More than 60% of Native Americans are of mixed heritage, some with combinations of black, white, and Latino backgrounds. What constitutes a true American Indian remains an area of controversy. It is imperative for professional school counselors to understand the history of oppression regarding this group of people as well as understand local issues, policies, specific tribal histories, and placement issues established by law (Dana, 2000).

> Fewer American Indians are high school graduates than the general U.S. population; their income level is only 62% of the U.S. average, and the poverty rate is twice as high.... Only 11% percent of Native American Indians and Alaskan have a bachelor's degree versus 24% of the general U.S. population. (U.S. Census Bureau, 2006c, p. 8)

Secondary and postsecondary schools need to become more culturally sensitive to accommodate some of the social and cultural differences between Native Americans and the general student population, especially if the youths view schools and further education as hostile and uninviting institutions of learning. "Native American youth who drop out of school often report having felt disenfranchised, and essentially 'pushed out' by the dominant Euro-American culture" (Deyhle & Swisher, 1999, p. 115). Teachers should understand and accommodate the sociocultural history regarding education and utilize a curriculum that reflects more closely the students' cultural background (Reyhner, 2002).

Health and wellness statistics regarding Native Americans are also staggering, with the alcoholism mortality rate six times higher than that of the U.S. population as a whole (Frank, Moore & Ames,

2000). In addition, motor vehicle fatalities, suicides, and homicides are much higher than that of the overall U.S. population (CDC, 2003). American Indian youths have twice the rate of attempted and completed suicide than other youths. The mental health dynamics are also complicated. For example, suicide ideation among the Pueblo Indians has been associated with a friend's suicidal behavior (e.g., overidentification with the youth that suicide and copycat behavior), while it is associated with lower self-esteem and depression among the Northern Plains adolescents (LaFromboise, 2006). A contributing factor to these behaviors is substance abuse. This is one of the greatest problems faced by Native Americans, although this should not be considered a stereotype of all Native Americans, because abstinence is high among certain tribes, such as the Navajo (Myers, Kagawa-Singer, Kumanyika, Lex, & Markides, 1995).

Asian Americans and Pacific Islanders

When you're growing up as an Asian, you get called names and it makes you feel like you're not wanted. "Can I get some fried rice?" That's all I used to hear, and still do. I walk down the street and people I don't even know make fun of me. They call me Chink and Ching Chong. I hate those words so much. It makes me feel so low. When I was younger, all the other kids who weren't Asian seemed to be having a good time and I wondered why I couldn't. I concluded that it was because I was Asian. I thought if I were Black or White people would like me more and I wouldn't get teased, so I used to wish I were Black or White.

A. Lin Goodwin (2003, p. 4)

They [whites] will have stereotypes, like we're smart. They are so wrong, not everyone is smart. They expect you to be this and that and when you're not.... (shook her head) And sometimes you tend to be what they expect you to be and you just lose your identity ... just lose being yourself. Become part of what ... what someone else want[s] you to be. And it's really awkward, too! When you get bad grades, people look at you really strangely because you are sort of distorting the way they see an Asian. It makes you feel really awkward if you don't fit the stereotype.

Stacey J. Lee (2005, p.34)

Although members of the Asian American population currently constitute only about 5% of the U.S. population, they make up one of the fastest growing racial/ethnic groups in terms of percentage growth (Le, 2006). Between-group differences within the Asian American population can be confusing, since the population is composed of at least 40 distinct subgroups—Indian, Bangladeshi, Cambodian, Vietnamese, Chinese, Filipino, Hmong, Japanese, Korean, Pakistani, Taiwanese, Thai, Laotian, Pacific Islander (Hawaiian, Guamanian, and Samoan), and others—that differ in language, religion, values, and attitudes toward other Asians (Sandhu, 1997). For example, refugees and immigrants from Southeast Asia (Vietnamese, Laotians, Cambodians, and Hmongs) often lack English proficiency and are at a higher risk for not completing their high school education.

Asian Americans have been described as the "model minority" because they comply with dominant social norms and achieve well academically. However, there is a large disparity in the area of education, with extraordinarily high educational attainment among current Asian Americans and a growing undercurrent of an undereducated mass of Asian immigrants that are coming to the United States. "Among the Hmong, only 40% have completed high school, and fewer than 14% of Tongans, Cambodians, Laotians and Hmongs 25 years or older have a bachelor's degree" (U.S. Census Bureau, 2005b, p. 1).

Latinos

The term Latino is preferred to Hispanic [which] excludes racial and cultural differences. Latino (from Latin American) is a more inclusive term accounting for those who come or descend from a specific geographical area where the Spanish and Portuguese legacy is dominant but not exclusive. It recognizes the presence and importance of nonwhite populations and cultures (Amerindian and African) in the group.

Xavier F. Totti

The term Hispanic, coined by technomarketing experts and by the designers of political campaigns, homogenizes our cultural diversity (Chicanos, Cubans, and Puerto Ricans become indistinguishable), avoids our indigenous cultural heritage and links us directly with Spain. Worse yet, it possesses connotations of upward mobility and political obedience.

Guillermo Gomez-Pena

U.S. Census Bureau (2003) data indicate that the 44-million-member Latino community is the fastest growing minority group in the United States, accounting for as much as half of the total population growth. The Latino population is expanding at a rate three to five times faster than the general population (Casas & Vasquez, 1996; Clemente & Collison, 2000; Garcia & Marotta, 1997; Pew Hispanic Center, 2005). "The U.S. Latino population more than doubled between 1980 and 2000, accounting for 38% of total U.S. population growth, and is expected to account for 46% of total U.S. population growth over the next two decades" (Pew Hispanic Center, 2005, p. 1). Births to Latino immigrants, rather than immigration itself, will be the key source of this growth: By 2010, Latino Americans are projected to number 47.7 million, a number that will swell to 60.4 million by 2020 (Pew Hispanic Center, 2005).

Today, Latino students represent the largest minority school-age population (Pew Hispanic Center, 2005; U.S. Census Bureau, 2003). The group's rapid growth has dramatically changed the demographics of U.S. schools. In the past, Latinos were concentrated primarily in the Southwest. In the near future, however, Latino population growth will begin to impact communities that had relatively few Latinos. By 2030, Latino students age 5–18 will constitute 25% of the total school population (Fracasso & Busch-Rossnagel, 1992; President's Advisory Commission on Educational Excellence for Hispanic Americans, 1996).

According to the President's Advisory Commission on Educational Excellence for Hispanic Americans (1996), Latino students are at greater risk for failure and dropping out of school in the current U.S. educational system and represent a significant proportion of the achievement gap. Only half of Latinos age 25 or older have completed high school, and the population's dropout rate is higher than any other minority group in the United States; Latino students drop out twice as often as non-Latino white students (Casas & Vasquez, 1996; Garcia & Marotta, 1997). Their overall level of participation in the educational system is lower than other minority populations (Dana, 1998; Fracasso & Busch-Rossnagel 1992; Santiago-Rivera, 1995). Therefore, it is critical that Latino youths and their families obtain the needed assistance and intervention from professional school counselors, teachers, administrators, and the wider community to promote school success and to prevent barriers to learning.

Cultural responsiveness in school counseling programs involves providing access, equity, equality, and educational justice, as well as outreach services, to disenfranchised families (Lee, 2001). Varying levels of English proficiency and a lack of understanding of how to maneuver in a predominantly Euro-American academic institutional environment can foster and can unwittingly lead Latino parents and children to feelings of mistrust, anxiety, discomfort, and shame toward school, school policy, and school officials or other persons in authority positions (Zapata, 1995). Latino students also are susceptible to a variety of psychosocial difficulties due to the impact of language barriers, poverty, poor housing, lack of community services, and discrimination in educational systems that can leave educators inadequately informed and ill equipped to deal with the distinctive needs of this growing population within the school and community (Alva & de los Reyes, 1999; Clemente & Collison, 2000; Koss-Chioino & Vargas, 1999).

For example, Latino children, as well as other minorities, are less likely than white children to ask for federal assistance programs even though they may qualify for such programs (e.g., free and reduced-price breakfast and lunch programs, or tuition assistance with textbooks) and even when assistance is needed (Sue & Sue, 2003). Further, counseling services that are available often are underused or not used at all by Latino students and their families because they do not know they are available, do not know how to access them, or don't have the transportation to get these resources and services (Gopaul-McNicol &

Thomas-Presswood, 1998; Clemente & Collison, 2000). Many Latino parents report wanting to be a part of their child's education but feel they are not listened to or welcomed by school personnel (Ramirez, 2003). Clearly, a growing population that feels alienated and disenfranchised from public education will have long-range consequences and implications for maintaining an economically productive society and for the overall well-being of this population.

Effective outreach services must extend beyond the Latino student and family to include the Latino community (Koss-Chioino & Vargas, 1999). The first contact with the student's family ideally should be in Spanish (Fracasso & Busch-Rossnagel, 1992; Preciado & Henry, 1997). In the United States, 8.3 million Latinos do not speak English at all or do not speak it fluently (Clemente & Collison, 2000). Gopaul-McNicol and Thomas-Presswood (1998) suggest that reading materials and information from the school and community be written in Spanish to assist family members who cannot read English. In some regions with high populations of Latino students, speaking Spanish may be an employment requirement for teachers and professional school counselors or at the minimum is an employment advantage. Furthermore, Casas, Furlong, and Ruiz de Esparza (2003) suggest using Spanish television and radio stations to encourage families to take part in their children's academic, career, and personal/social development. Reaching out to faith communities and conducting home visits may also be helpful.

Professional school counselors need to step out of their current comfort zones of reaching a few selected students, develop unique services to meet the needs of all diverse populations within their school setting, and become more active as community liaisons. Professional school counselors with similar ethnicity and language can help in establishing trust between the counselor and client (Teyber & McClure, 2000). In particular, Altarriba and Bauer (1998) report that Latino students and families who are less acculturated are more open to Latino professional school counselors, and as a result, these counselors are perceived as a more favorable resource than Anglo-American counselors. However, Latinos are currently underrepresented in the school counseling profession.

Providing direct counseling services to raise school administrators', teachers', and professional school counselors' awareness of the barriers to Latino students' learning success—particularly in areas where the numbers of Latino families are growing and where there are large numbers of these families with low English proficiency, in such surprising geographical areas as Arkansas, Georgia, North Carolina, northern Virginia, South Carolina, and Tennessee—should be a primary prevention initiative to prevent further underachievement (Hamann, Wortham, & Murillo, 2002). Higher expectations can be encouraged by implementing a nationwide public service motivation campaign to change attitudes, intentions, and behavior toward increasing Latino educational attainment at every opportunity, from pre-kindergarten to postsecondary education.

Arab Americans

At least 3.5 million Americans are of Arab descent. Arab Americans live in all 50 states, but two-thirds reside in 10 states and half of those live in California, New York, and Michigan. Approximately 94% live in metropolitan areas, the top five being Los Angeles, Detroit, New York, Chicago, and Washington, D.C.. Arab Americans value education; 85% of Arab Americans possess at least a high school diploma. More than 4 out of 10 Americans of Arab descent have a bachelor's degree or higher, compared with 24% of Americans at large, and 17% of Arab Americans have a postgraduate degree, nearly twice the American average (9%). Of the school-age population, 13% are in preschool, 58% are in elementary or high school, 22% are enrolled in college, and 7% are conducting graduate studies. The desire for Arab Americans for education is impressive and steadfast (Cruz & Brittingham, 2003).

Arab Americans are relatively more likely than other Americans to be self-employed and relatively less likely to work in the government sector (Zogby, 1990). Arab Americans in United States schools represent more than 20 countries in the Middle East and North Africa. Some Muslim Arab American parents send their children to private Muslim schools so they can receive an education consistent with the family's religious beliefs, but most seek their education from the public schools (Zehr, 1999). Unfortunately, many schools have not actively acknowledged Arab culture and history or have actively counteracted Arab stereotyping (Suleiman, 1999).

As educators and professional school counselors, it is an inherent responsibility to be proactive to ensure that our schools are safe places, physically and psychologically, for all children. Since the terrorist acts of September 11, 2001, students from Arab, South Asian, and Muslim backgrounds have a special need for a sense of safety, security, and acceptance at school and the community. Because prejudice against Arab Americans increases when political events involve Arabs, educators need to be prepared to respond to possible harassment of Arab American students resulting from negative news reporting or rumors and to invoke school policies against hate crimes and discrimination as appropriate for all students who are in a minority group (Suleiman, 1999). With increasing diversity come increasing controversy, suspicion, prejudice, and doubt. Professional school counselors are the first line of defense in providing accurate knowledge, understanding, and tolerance.

Administrators, teachers, professional school counselors, and support personnel need to correct erroneous information when confronted with it, such as popular myths "that all Arabs are … wealthy … barbaric and backward, and … have harems" (Farquharson, 1988, p. 4). New negative stereotypes have emerged in and permeated advertising, television, movies, and the daily news, particularly those of the subversive terrorist. The Arab as villain has been a favorite scapegoat of popular American culture, thereby setting the stage for acts of discrimination and bigotry that have affected Arab Americans in the United States. They face a range of reactions from other students, from anxiety to fear, especially since the 9/11 attacks. Professional school counselors, and educators in general, can help students understand that Arab Americans should not be held personally accountable for events in the Middle East. They can confront scapegoating by allowing students to air their views and then helping them to understand why such judgments are inaccurate and hurtful (American-Arab Anti-Discrimination Committee, 2003).

Nearly one in three (30%) Arab Americans reports personal experiences with discrimination, and 40% know someone who has been discriminated against since 9/11; one-fifth of these report the discrimination as having been against themselves (Arab American Institute Foundation, 2002b). Even Arab Americans who do not regard themselves as particularly religious are influenced positively by Islam through their culture, beliefs, and values such as dignity, honor, and reputation; family loyalty versus personal gain; piety; and a belief in God and God-determined fate (Nydell, 1987).

The ethnic identity of Arab Americans is impacted negatively by the stereotype of Arabs, or Middle Easterners or Muslims generally, being collectively perceived as terrorists. That stereotype is among the strongest of the characterizations held by mainstream culture. Chomsky (1986) has said that the United States literally equates the Middle East with terrorism.

The current federal classification system defines Arab Americans as white, putting them in the same category as the European-origin majority, which has created some cultural confusion. The "Asian/Pacific Islander" category often is used mistakenly to describe Arab American students and clients (Samhan, 1999). This is the same dilemma that occurs when classifying all Latinos as Hispanic. Defining Arab Americans and other groups within the school setting in terms of origin, race, and ethnicity is a daunting task, contributing to the intercultural confusion of individuals and communities.

Schools must take care not to discriminate against Muslims. They should not enforce dress codes or showering requirements that violate the Muslim tradition of modesty and should not require Muslim students to participate in coed physical education classes. Educators should ensure that girls are not ridiculed for their head covering (hijab). They should not schedule tests on major Islamic holidays and should allow fasting students to go to the library instead of the cafeteria during Ramadan. Federal law permits students to organize prayer services, and schools should accommodate such requests from Muslims (Council on Islamic Education, 2002). Muslims across the country are now petitioning schools to label cafeteria food containing pork products, and some schools are already doing so (Zehr, 1999).

Among Arab Americans, the family is more important than the individual and more influential than nationality. People draw much of their identity from their role in the family. Muslims often name their children after prophets in the Qur'an. Some Arab women wear garments that cover their faces or heads; this is a religious practice, rooted in Islamic teachings about *hijab*, or modesty, but its form is culturally influenced. On the other hand, some Arab men wear a checked garment on their heads called a *kafiyyeh;* it is traditional, not religious. Wearing the kafiyyeh is similar to an African American wearing traditional African attire, or an Indian wearing a sari. The kafiyyeh shows identity and pride in one's culture.

The five pillars of Islam are minimum sacred obligations for followers who are able to observe them. They are:

1. Belief in the *shehada,* the statement that "There is no god but God, and Muhammad is his prophet"
2. *Salat,* or prayer five times a day
3. *Zakat,* charity given to the poor
4. Fasting during the holy month of Ramadan
5. The Hajj, or pilgrimage to Mecca in Saudi Arabia

"Ramadan, the ninth month of the Muslim calendar, is a month of fasting whose end is marked with the celebration of Eid al-Fitr" (McGoldrick, Giordano, & Pearce, 1996, p. 336). During this month, self-discipline and purification are a religious requirement and should be respected much like Christian or Jewish holidays. Professional school counselors need to be keenly aware of these rituals. For example, many students will fast during lunch at school, and this may be falsely interpreted as child neglect on the part of school personnel. Allah means Godthe same word is used by Arabic-speaking Christians, Muslims, and Jews (*Detroit Free Press*, 2001). The majority of Arab Americans are in fact Christian: 42% are Catholic, 23% Orthodox, 12% Protestant, and just 23% Muslim (Zogby, 2001).

In working with Arab American students and their families, the power and politics of race and religion in contemporary social and political contexts must be addressed to effectively explore issues of ethnic and cultural self-identity (Abu El-Haj, 2002, 2006). By serving as social justice advocates in this growing arena of diversity, professional school counselors will enhance the mental health and well-being of Arab Americans and, in so doing, will ensure tolerance and acceptance among all Americans.

Some Arab Americans suffer from an understandable level of cultural confusion. The terms "Arab nation" (Abudabbeh, 1996; Gray & Ahmed, 1988) and "Arab world" are more accurate in defining the region of origin of Arab peoples. To put things in perspective, the League of Arab States includes Algeria, Bahrain, the Comoros, Djibouti, Egypt, Iraq, Jordan, Kuwait, Lebanon, Libya, Mauritania, Morocco, Oman, Palestine, Qatar, Saudi Arabia, Somalia, Sudan, Syria, Tunisia, United Arab Emirates, and Yemen. This knowledge can be both overwhelming and controversial, generating heated debates and diverse opinions among citizens and educators. Even within scholarly Arab American circles, there is debate over which of these countries should be included as countries of origin for Arab Americans. Famous Arab Americans in the United States include Kahlil Gibran, Ralph Nader, Danny Thomas, Paul Anka, Paula Abdul, and Doug Flutie.

A second point of potential confusion is the unique separation, or connectedness, of culture and religion in the Arab world. Although development of Arab culture historically was heavily influenced by Islam, the terms *Muslim* and *Arab* are not synonymous, and professional school counselors must keep this in the forefront of their cultural understanding. The Middle East represents only about 15–20% of the world's Islamic adherents (Council on Islamic Education, 2002). Further, Arab Americans equate their life satisfaction in the United States with their religiosity (Faragallah, Schumm, & Webb, 1997).

THE IMPLICATIONS OF INCREASING DIVERSITY IN THE SCHOOL SETTING

The United States has a long history of ethnic and racial diversity. However, the current increase in the percentage of immigrants will have long-range implications for schools, community resources, and society at large on education, employment, welfare, and health care. It has been well documented that diversity has accelerated in recent decades, and this is expected to continue into the future. Race and ethnicity are important for many reasons, including relationships, culture, identity, assessment of resources, opportunity, and overall well-being. Children of different races and ethnicities often show vast differences in areas of well-being—health, mortality, academic achievement, educational attainment—as well as access to family and community resources and services. These and similar disparities are also evident in adulthood (Blank, 2001).

It is critical that professional school counselors, teachers, administrators, and support personnel recognize this trend and become more culturally competent. Toward this goal, Holcomb-McCoy (2004)

> identified 51 competencies that are necessary for working with culturally diverse students in 9 areas of competence: (1) multicultural counseling, (2) multicultural consultation, (3) understanding racism and student resistance, (4) multicultural assessment, (5) understanding racial identity development, (6) multicultural family counseling, (7) social advocacy, (8) developing school–family–community partnerships, and (9) understanding cross-cultural interpersonal interactions. (p. 178)

Take a moment to assess your multicultural competence with the self-assessment shown in Table 10.2.

INTERVENTION IMPLICATIONS FOR PROFESSIONAL SCHOOL COUNSELORS WHEN DEALING WITH DIVERSE CLIENTS

There are a number of implications for professional school counselors in helping diverse populations and several techniques that can be used to integrate these often fragile groups into the mainstream of American culture. Three techniques that can be used to obtain family information in order to provide necessary programs and services are migration narratives, genograms, and ecograms. The assessment process and procedures depend upon the mutual engagement and participation of the entire family.

A *migration narrative* of a family can be constructed by asking them the following questions:

1. How long has the family resided in the United States?
2. Who immigrated first, who was left behind, and who came later or is yet to be reunited?
3. What stresses and/or stressors and new learnings were experienced by various family members over time, and what strengths and resources were discovered?

Family systems theory (Bowen, 1978) has produced a useful way of assessing families in which they can actively participate. Using diagrams to describe complex family relationships can provide a visual representation of the hierarchy and relationships in a family (e.g., distant, close, strained). Two methods of diagramming can be used to understand the dynamics in families:

- *Genograms* to describe and gain insight into relationships and roles within the family unit
- *Ecomaps* to document the family unit's relationship to outside systems.

By using these methods of diagramming, the professional school counselor can innocuously learn something about the relationships within the family, the location of the family's boundaries, and the variety and quality of the family's connections to outside systems. In addition to assessment, these diagramming methods may be useful as:

TABLE 10.2   Nine Areas of Multicultural Competence: An Individual Assessment

Self-Assessment: As a professional school counselor how many of these competencies can you meet?

I. Multicultural Counseling

1. I can recognize when my attitudes, beliefs, and values are interfering with providing the best services to my students.
2. I can identify the cultural biases of my communication style.
3. I can discuss how culture affects the help-seeking behaviors of students.
4. I can describe the degree to which a counseling approach is culturally inappropriate for a specific student.
5. I use culturally appropriate interventions and counseling approaches with students.
6. I can list at least three barriers that prevent ethnic minority students from using counseling services.
7. I can anticipate when my helping style is inappropriate for a culturally different student.
8. I can give examples of how stereotypical beliefs about culturally different persons impact the counseling relationship.

II. Multicultural Consultation

9. I am aware of how culture affects traditional models of consultation.
10. I can discuss at least one model of multicultural consultation.
11. I recognize when racial and cultural issues are impacting the consultation process.
12. I can identify when the race and/or culture of the client is a problem for the consultee.
13. I discuss issues related to race/ethnicity/culture during the consultation process, when applicable.

III. Understanding Racism and Student Resistance

14. I can define and discuss white privilege.
15. I can discuss how I (if European American/white) am privileged based on my race.
16. I can identify racist aspects of educational institutions.
17. I can define and discuss prejudice.
18. I recognize and challenge colleagues about discrimination and discriminatory practices in schools.
19. I can define and discuss racism and its impact on the counseling process.
20. I can help students determine whether a problem stems from racism or biases in others.
21. I understand the relationship between student resistance and racism.
22. I include topics related to race and racism in my classroom guidance units.

IV. Multicultural Assessment

23. I can discuss the potential bias of two assessment instruments frequently used in the schools.
24. I can evaluate instruments that may be biased against certain groups of students.
25. I am able to use test information appropriately with culturally diverse parents.
26. I view myself as an advocate for fair testing and the appropriate use of testing of children from diverse backgrounds.
27. I can identify whether or not the assessment process is culturally sensitive.
28. I can discuss how the identification of the assessment process might be biased against minority populations.

V. Understanding Racial and/or Ethnic Identity Development

29. I am able to discuss at least two theories of racial and/or ethnic identity development.
30. I use racial/ethnic identity development theories to understand my students' problems and concerns.
31. I have assessed my own racial/ethnic development in order to enhance my counseling.

continued

TABLE 10.2   Nine Areas of Multicultural Competence: An Individual Assessment (continued)

VI. Multicultural Family Counseling

32. I can discuss family counseling from a cultural/ethnic perspective.
33. I can discuss at least two ethnic groups' traditional gender-role expectations and rituals.
34. I anticipate when my helping style is inappropriate for an ethnically different parent or guardian.
35. I can discuss culturally diverse methods of parenting and discipline.

VII. Social Advocacy

36. I am knowledgeable of the psychological and societal issues that affect the development of ethnic minority students.
37. When counseling, I consider the psychological and societal issues that affect the development of ethnic minority students.
38. I work with families and community members in order to reintegrate them with the school.
39. I can define "social change agent."
40. I perceive myself as being a social change agent.
41. I can discuss what it means to take an "activist counseling" approach.
42. I intervene with students at the individual and systemic levels.
43. I can discuss how factors such as poverty and powerlessness have influenced the current conditions of at least two ethnic groups.

VIII. Developing School–Family–Community Partnerships

44. I have developed a school–family–community partnership team or some similar type of group that consists of community members, parents, and school personnel.
45. I am aware of community resources that are available for students and their families.
46. I work with community leaders and other resources in the community to assist with student (and family) concerns.

IX. Understanding Cross-Cultural Interpersonal Interactions

47. I am able to discuss interaction patterns that might influence ethnic minority students' perceptions of inclusion in the school community.
48. I solicit feedback from students regarding my interactions with them.
49. I verbally communicate my acceptance of culturally different students.
50. I nonverbally communicate my acceptance of culturally different students.
51. I am mindful of the manner in which I speak and the emotional tone of my interactions with culturally diverse students.

Source: Holcomb-McCoy, 2004, p. 178. Reprinted with permission.

- Interviewing tools that can be used with individuals, couples, or the entire family
- A way to facilitate participation by providing a clear structure and to assist people who might have difficulty entering into discussion because of language difficulties
- Tools for organizing information to assist in the identification of resource needs and to prepare diverse populations' integration into school, employment, health services, housing, social services, and other resources.

The use of these assessment methods recognizes that the family is the most knowledgeable source of information about themselves. The information requested is concrete, and this method encourages an interviewing style that tends to be nonthreatening and assists in rapport building.

Visual representations of family dynamics and relationships can offer a sense of pride, especially when difficulties have been resourcefully resolved and viable connections have been made with community resources. Having the family members sit beside the professional school counselor to complete the diagram builds rapport and an alliance between the school and the professional school counselor. It also promotes open communication and insight into the family's past and present circumstances. As Thomas and Schwarzbaum (2006) explain, through these methods the professional school counselor and the family (along with interpreter if needed) can learn about the following:

- Family members: Who are the members of the family: their names, ages, relationships, hierarchy, identity occupations, and religion;
- Family roles: What roles are differentiated in the family and who is responsible for them: For example, are grandparents, older children or others involved in the parenting? Do members identify any unfulfilled tasks or specific needs (e.g., special education services; need for employment training; needs for learning English)? Who is perceived as having the most power in this family or who is the dominant leader?
- Family rules: What are the family rules regarding decision making; child care; discipline; intimacy/distance; expressions of love and anger? What are the rules with respect to relationships between generations?
- Family communication: Are there identifiable channels of communication? Who communicates to whom and how? Do children defer to parents? Does the entire family defer to the father?
- Family system: How do members of this family feel about the other members? Who is close to whom in this family? Are there identifiable alliances? What are the major conflicts within the family from the point of view of each member?
- Family timeline: What is the significant history about the development of the family (e.g., marriage, separation, divorce, children, extended family, etc.)? What are the significant themes, patterns, events in the family history, major losses, and changes, and how has the family handled them?
- Family network and support system: What persons or systems are important to the family? Outside the immediate family, where does the family turn for support?
- Family assimilation: How does the family "fit" in relation to larger society? Are there problems with other organizations, (e.g., schools, work, and church)? (pp. 298–299)

CONCLUDING REMARKS ABOUT CULTURAL DIVERSITY

It is important to consider that immigrant students and their families face multiple stressors when they come to the United States. Skilled and knowledgeable interpreters are paramount when negotiating the various systems that immigrants encounter. These include employment, language barriers, the school system, housing, health care, adult education, and social services, to name a few. They must also understand new social, economic, and sociopolitical conditions and the potential for prejudice and discrimination in a country that is foreign to them. The professional school counselor needs to work as a bridge to programs and services in the community and to serve as an educator and advocate helping access local resources.

Children may assimilate into the U.S. culture easier than their parents and extended family. The educational experience and performance of diverse and immigrant students depend on multiple factors, including:

- Their age on arrival
- Previous schooling
- Home language and literacy
- Family education and aspirations
- Economic circumstance
- Whether their immigration was voluntary or involuntary
- Current level of English language proficiency

The resources in this section have explored the complex and multilayered issues affecting the education of students in American schools and provide helpful information on intervention methods, approaches, and styles that are sensitive to the needs of immigrant students. For those immigrant students who arrive as adolescents with limited English proficiency and limited formal schooling, academic success depends on having the time and support necessary to develop essential learning and literacy (Mace-Matluck, Alexander-Kasparik, & Queen, 1998).

Promoting understanding of U.S. culture does not necessarily mean that the student's native culture must be ignored or erased; it just means that these students must learn how to function in both cultures, as they are now bicultural individuals. Concurrently, native-born U.S. citizens have a responsibility to learn about, and to respect, other cultures. The professional school counselor provides a pivotal role in this school/community initiative.

SEXUAL MINORITY YOUTH IN TODAY'S SCHOOLS

Does It Matter?
My father asked if I am gay
I asked *Does* it matter?
He said No not really
I said *Yes.*
He said get out of my life
I guess it mattered.
My boss asked if I am gay
I asked *Does* it matter?
He said No not really
I told him *Yes.*
He said you're fired faggot
I guess it mattered.
My friend asked if I am gay
I said *Does* it matter?
He said No not really
I told him *Yes.*
He said *Don't* call me your friend
I guess it mattered.
My lover asked *Do* you love me?
I asked *Does* it matter?
He said *Yes.*
I told him I love you
He said, let me hold you in my arms
For the first time in my life something matters.
My God asked me *Do* you love yourself?
I said *Does* it matter?
He said *YES*
I said How can I love myself? I am gay
He said That is the way I made you
Nothing will ever matter again.

An anonymous high school student

A growing body of research has identified the health, mental health, and safety risks gay, lesbian, bisexual, transgendered, and questioning (GLBTQ) youths—sexual minority youths—experience in the school setting (Herr, 1999). (*Sexual minority youth* is the term that will be used consistently throughout this chapter.) Without appropriate supports, and more importantly policy, in school settings, sexual minority youths often struggle in isolation with important developmental tasks such as intimacy issues, being valued for who they are, and self-esteem (Savin-Williams, 1990).

These unique stressors for sexual minority youths often manifest in self-defeating behaviors such as alcohol or drug abuse, risky or premature sexual behaviors, depression, suicide ideation, self-injurious behavior, academic underachievement, social withdrawal from the mainstream culture, running away from home, and dropping out of school (Savin-Williams, 1990; Zera, 1992). Physical safety and social and emotional support have been identified as paramount to stress reduction and psychological well-being among sexual minority youths (Hershberger & D'Augelli, 1995; Levy, 1992).

The dominant perception in our culture is that it simply is better to be heterosexual than a sexual minority. This belief, called *heterosexism* (Herek, 2004), denies and denigrates nonheterosexual forms of behavior, identity, relationships, and family constellations. However, popular culture, especially in the entertainment industry, continues to challenge this perception. Entertainment celebrities such as Ellen DeGeneres, Rosie O'Donnell, Clay Aiken, Melissa Etheridge, Wanda Sykes, and Elton John have popularized sexual minorities in the media.

BEING A SEXUAL MINORITY: A MORAL ISSUE OR A CIVIL RIGHTS ISSUE?

The issue of how sexual orientation is determined is both a provocative and confusing debate enveloped in both strong emotion and profound convictions. Conservative religious and political groups tend to view homosexuality as a moral issue, while proponents see it as a civil rights issue. It cannot be separated easily from either context. Thus, a person's sexual orientation has political, religious, and moral implications.

One example that demonstrates the polarization between religious and professional organizations involved in this issue is research conducted by Nicolosi (1991) on *reparative therapy* (RT), which claims to change sexual orientation (always from gay to straight, never the reverse). RT parallels another "treatment" called *conversion therapy* (CT), hailed by conservative Christian groups as proof that prayer and meditation can drive the sin out and bring the sexual minority youth back to a heterosexual orientation. Sexual minority youths often find themselves the victims of misguided efforts to change their sexual orientation or gender identity. Such "conversion" or "reparative" efforts are extremely harmful psychologically, causing low self-esteem with no real effect on sexual orientation. For this reason, RT and CT have been condemned as unethical by a number of mainstream psychological, medical, and child welfare organizations, such as the American Psychological Association (DeLeon, 1998), the American Psychiatric Association (1999, 2002, 2004; American Psychiatric Association, 1993), the American Academy of Pediatrics (2001; Frankowski & American Academy of Pediatrics Committee on Adolescence, 2004; Perrin & American Academy of Pediatrics Committee on Psychosocial Aspects of Child and Family Health, 2002), and the American Medical Association (2005), as well as the National Association of Social Workers (1997), the National Association of School Psychologists, the American School Health Association, the American Federation of Teachers, and the National Education Association. Many mental health workers believe it is unethical for mental health professionals to practice CT or RT (Barret & Logan, 2001). Even some conservative religious groups now acknowledge sexual minority youths as long as they practice abstinence.

Sexual minorities are becoming more open with their sexual orientation in all aspects of their lives. This cultural shift toward more positive statements about sexual minority youth can be observed in the media, from national and local political candidates, and in the debates within virtually all Christian denominations about the role of sexual minorities within the church (Barret & Logan, 2001; Boswell,

1980). The American Academy of Pediatrics (2001) in its policy statement on homosexuality and adolescence states:

> Confusion about sexual orientation is not unusual during adolescence. Counseling may be helpful for young people who are uncertain about their sexual orientation or for those who are uncertain about how to express their sexuality and might profit from an attempt at clarification through a counseling or psychotherapeutic initiative. Therapy directed specifically at changing sexual orientation is contraindicated, since it can provoke guilt and anxiety while having little or no potential for achieving changes in orientation. (p. 499)

Sexual minority youths may also be the victims of the damaging and unfounded myth that they are sexual predators (Jenny, Roesler, & Poyer, 1994; Stevenson, 2000). Those caring for young people need to apply professional standards and information, not stereotypes, in their work. The prejudice sexual minority youths face often takes its psychological toll, affecting their core sense of self by forcing them to deny and repress their identities. A number of studies show that stigma and prejudice based on sexual orientation place sexual minority youths at a higher risk for stress-related mental illness than their heterosexual counterparts (Meyer, 2003; Proctor & Groze, 1994; Savin-Williams, 1994).

Sexual minority youths need to feel that they are not condemned and stigmatized for something they cannot change and that is an important part of them—their sexual orientation or gender identity. They need to be cared for in an environment that shields them from, rather than exposing them to, bias and prejudice. They need to be free from bullying behavior and harassment. They need to be accepted, not hated, for who they are as young people.

In its 2001 report *Hatred in the Hallways,* Human Rights Watch, an international nongovernmental organization dedicated to protecting the rights of people around the world, documents attacks in the United States on the human rights of sexual minority youths who:

> are subjected to abuse on a daily basis by their peers and in some cases by teachers and school administrators. These violations are compounded by the failure of federal, state, and local governments to enact laws providing students with express protection from discrimination and violence based on their sexual orientation and gender identity, effectively allowing school officials to ignore violations of these students' rights. Gay youth spend an inordinate amount of energy plotting how to get safely to and from school, how to avoid the hallways when other students are present so they can avoid slurs and shoves, how to cut gym class to escape being beaten up—in short, how to become invisible so they will not be verbally and physically attacked. Too often, students have little energy left to learn. [The] vast majority of lesbian, gay, bisexual, and transgender youth trying to escape the hostile hallways of their schools confront school officials who refuse to recognize the serious harm inflicted by the attacks and to provide redress for them. In fact, there is not even a token consensus among public school officials that gay youth deserve to be treated with dignity and respect. (Human Rights Watch, 2001, pp. 2–3)

Thirty-eight states administer the Centers for Disease Control and Prevention (CDC) Youth Risk Behavior Survey (YRBS), a biannual survey administered to students in grades 9–12. Since 1995, Massachusetts has included two questions on its YRBS to identify issues relating to sexual minority youth. The Massachusetts YRBS demonstrates that:

- Sexual minority students were more than twice as likely to report being in a physical fight at school in the prior year (31.5% of sexual minority students versus 12.9% of others).
- Sexual minority students were three times likelier to report having been threatened or injured with a weapon at school in the past year (23.5% of sexual minority students versus 7.8% of others).
- Sexual minority students more often reported that they had missed school in the past month because they felt unsafe (19.1% of sexual minority versus 5.6% of others) (Goodenow, 2003, p. 9)

In 2003, the Gay, Lesbian and Straight Education Network (GLSEN) issued findings from its National School Climate Survey, which mirrored those of the Massachusetts YRBS. Key findings of this survey include:

- Harassment continues at unacceptable levels and is too often ignored: 84% of sexual minority students report being verbally harassed because of their sexual orientation and gender identity; 82.9% of students report that faculty never or rarely intervene when present.
- Unchecked harassment correlates with poor performance and diminished aspirations: sexual minority youth who report significant verbal harassment are twice as likely to report they do not intend to go to college.
- Supportive teachers can make a difference: 24.1% of sexual minority students who cannot identify supportive faculty report they have no intention of going to college. That figure drops to just 10.1% when sexual minority students can identify supportive staff at their school.
- Policy makers have an opportunity to improve school climates: Sexual minority students who did not have (or did not know of) a policy protecting them from violence and harassment were nearly 40% more likely to skip school because they were simply too afraid to go. (Kosciw, 2004, p. 14)

Another recent survey done by Kosciw and Diaz (2006) found:

- 33% of sexual minority students reported attempting suicide in the previous year; 8% of their heterosexual peers reported attempting suicide.
- 84% of sexual minority students were called names or had their safety threatened as a result of their sexual orientation or gender expression.
- 45% of sexual minority youth of color experienced verbal harassment and/or physical assault in response to perceived sexual orientation and race/ethnicity.
- 39% of sexual minority students and 55% of transgendered students were shoved or pushed. Transgendered youth were one third more likely to endure physical harassment than sexual minority students.
- 64% of sexual minority students felt unsafe at school. In the most recent month; 29% missed one or more days of school because they felt in danger.
- 25–40% of homeless youth may identify as sexual minority. Parents and caregivers often throw them out of their homes after they discover or are told of their child's sexual orientation. (Kosciw & Diaz, 2006, p. 27)

It is currently recognized that harassment and bullying put gay youths at risk:

- Sexual minority youths hear antigay slurs such as "homo," "faggot," and "sissy" about 26 times a day or every 14 minutes (Bart, 1998).
- Sexual minority youths are at high risk because their distress is a direct result of the hatred and prejudice that surround them, not because of their inherently sexual minority identity orientation (Norton & Vare, 2002).
- Sexual minority youths in U.S. schools are often subject to such intense bullying that they are unable to receive an adequate education (Chase, 2002).
- Sexual minority youths are more prone to skip school due to the fear, threats, and property vandalism directed at them (Garofalo, Wolf, Kessell, & Palfrey, 1998). One survey revealed that 22% of sexual minority respondents had skipped school in the past month because they felt unsafe there (Chase, 2002).
- Twenty-eight percent of sexual minority students will drop out of school. This is more than three times the national average for heterosexual students (Bart, 1998).
- According to several surveys, four out of five sexual minority students say they do not know one supportive adult at school (Sessions Stepp, 2001).

SEXUAL MINORITY YOUTH: A PHYSICAL, EMOTIONAL, SOCIAL, AND MEDICALLY NEGLECTED AT-RISK POPULATION

The problems that sexual minority youths face in our schools are overwhelming. D'Augelli, Pilkington, and Hershberger (2002) studied 350 sexual minority youths who were at least 21 years old. More than half, they found, "reported verbal abuse in high school as a direct result of their sexual orientation. Eleven percent (11%) had been physically assaulted" (p. 152). Young people who were more open about their sexual orientation in high school and had a history of more gender atypical behavior were victimized more often. Males reported being targeted more often than females. Their current mental health symptoms, especially traumatic stress reactions, were directly associated with having experienced more verbal abuse in high school. D'Augelli and colleagues (2002) also found in another study that young people who had experienced more victimization and who had lost friends reported more mental health symptoms.

There seems to be a direct relationship between being on the receiving end of at-school victimization and high-risk health behaviors. Bontempo and D'Augelli (2002), in a study of 9,188 high school students, found that "the combined effect of sexual minority status and high levels of at-school victimization was associated with the highest levels of health risk behaviors, even higher than a similar sample of their heterosexual peers" (p. 372). Sexual minority youth is an at-risk population and deserves the same kinds of support and assistance that other at-risk populations now routinely receive (Pope, Bunch, Szymanski, & Rankins, 2003). Harassment, victimization, and bullying by peers and adults can no longer be tolerated because it has evolved into a civil rights issue. Litigation is beginning to emerge, holding schools responsible for allowing unsafe environments to perpetuate.

Sexual minority youths face stigmatization, prejudice, and a significant number of stressors in the school environment, including social ostracism, humiliation, physical violence, and verbal as well as Internet harassment on websites and social networks. This is a growing problem for all students (Benvenuti, 1986; Gustavsson & MacEachron, 1998; Jordan, Vaughan, & Woodworth, 1997; Pope, 2000). Schools can be very cruel environments, especially when a student veers from the mainstream culture. The search for one's sexual identity is an important part of adolescence (Sexuality Information and Education Council of the United States, 1995), but when that search is intertwined with a minority status—race or sexual orientation or ethnicity—it is even more complex and often more devastating emotionally, socially, and cognitively (Chung & Katayama, 1998; Dube & Savin-Williams, 1999; Herring, 1998; Sanchez, 1995).

Adolescents who are different face a variety of barriers to healthy social, emotional, cognitive, and psychological development, generated by their peers, their family, their culture, and their society (Pope, 2000; Thompson, 2006). According to Gibson (1989), "suicide is the leading cause of death among gay youth" and "gay male adolescents are six times more likely to attempt suicide than their heterosexual counterparts" (pp. 111, 112). Sexual minority youths are three to five times more likely to attempt suicide than their heterosexual peers (Brown, 1991; Gibson, 1989; Mondimore, 1996). However, after further study, many of the attempts were not considered truly life threatening, suggesting that these suicide reports were merely attempts to communicate the current angst in the student's life and should be recognized as a cry for help and a need for intervention. McDaniel, Purcell, and D'Augelli (2001) have explored issues of psychological resilience in sexual minority youth, giving them the resources and social support to resist their current negative environment.

Some of the findings of the 2005 National School Climate Survey (Kosciw & Diaz, 2006) include the following:

- "Three-quarters (75.4%) of students reported hearing derogatory homophobic remarks, such as 'dyke' or 'faggot,' often or frequently at school."
- "Three-quarters (73.1%) of students heard sexist remarks often or frequently in school."

- "Many students (28.3%) also reported that school personnel made sexist remarks at least some-times while in school."
- "Over half (55.5%) had often or frequently heard comments about students not acting 'mascu-line enough.' In contrast, 38.3% heard comments frequently about students not acting 'femi-nine enough.'"
- "Nearly two-thirds of students (64.3%) reported that they felt unsafe in school because of their sexual orientation."
- "More than a third of students (40.7%) reported feeling unsafe in school because of how they expressed their gender."
- "Nearly two-thirds (64.1%) of respondents reported having been harassed at least some of the time in the past year because of their sexual orientation, and more than a quarter (27.0%) reported that it occurred more frequently."
- "A third of sexual minority youths reported at least some experience of physical harassment (e.g., being pushed or shoved) because of their sexual orientation (37.8%); a quarter of students (26.1%) had been physically harassed because of their gender expression. Half of the students (51.4%) had their property deliberately damaged or stolen."
- "About two-thirds of sexual minority youths had been sexually harassed."
- "Relational forms of aggression—that is, harm caused by damage to peer relationships by spreading lies or mean rumors—were reported by over a third of students. In addition, cyber-bullying is becoming an increasing form of peer harassment, with four out of ten (41.2%) sexual minority youths reporting that they had experienced this type of harassment."
- "More than half of the students who were harrassed said that they had never told school authori-ties (58.6%), a parent or guardian (55.1%), or another family member (62.6%). Only a quarter (28.1%) of students said that their parent or guardian intervened on their behalf with school personnel." (p.26)

These findings truly paint a picture of victimization, harassment, lack of support, humiliation, degradation, and lack of school safety—which also is a violation of the Safe and Drug-Free Schools and Communities Act (SDFSCA; Title IV, Part A, of the Elementary and Secondary Education Act). Higher incidence of depression, suicide ideation, isolation, high-risk sexual behavior, and dropping out of school are an inevitable consequence of trying to survive in this type of hostile, uncaring, unsafe environment.

HOMOPHOBIA AND RACISM OF SEXUAL MINORITY YOUTH OF COLOR

Sexual minority youths who are also racial/ethnic minorities must bear the dual psychosocial burdens of racism and homophobia. Greene (1997) points to several important cultural factors to consider in under-standing the experience of sexual minority youths of color. These include:

> Attitudes, values and beliefs related to sexuality; the importance of procreation; the role of religious values; the importance of one's ethnic community; the degree of acculturation of the individual into the dominant culture; and historical experiences with acknowledgement of discrimination or oppression from the domi-nant culture. (pp. 3–5)

Youths of color are significantly less likely to have told their parents they are a sexual minority. For example, Chan (1989) found that "while 80% of sexual minority White adolescents told their parents, only 71% of Latinos, 61% of African Americans, and 51% of Asians and Pacific Islanders told their parents"

(p. 18). Like their white counterparts, they also suffer suicidal thoughts, depression, and low esteem. In many Latino communities, machismo and Catholicism combine to portray homosexuality as wrong and sinful (Battle, Cohen, Warren, Fergerson, & Audam, 2000). Chan (1989) found that Latino cultures view being a sexual minority as rejecting traditional culture or, in the words of Espin (1993), as "an act of treason against the culture and one's family" (p. 408).

Parks (2001) revealed that the African American church, a cultural cornerstone for the community, represents a source of both strength and conflict for sexual minority youths. Basic identities revolve around role expectations that support heterosexual family life. The church also reinforces heterosexual norms, often with distinct gender roles within the church (e.g., male deacons and female deaconesses) and the church leadership, that affect the self-esteem and self-concept of members.

Asian American and Pacific Islander sexual minority youths often feel that they have shamed their families when they diverge from cultural expectations that they marry and have children (Wong, 1996). Chung and Katayama (1998) maintain that "the intensity of heterosexualism and homophobia is much stronger in Asian cultures than the mainstream U.S. culture" (p. 23). The conflict of choosing between one's ethnic or sexual minority identity is an ongoing concern for sexual minority Asians. Fundamentally, there is a dearth of research on sexual minority youth of color in primary areas such as sexual and transgender identity development, sexuality, sexual behaviors, cultural discrepancies, and experiences related to families, coping, and the propensity for self-destructive behaviors.

"COMING OUT" AND ADOLESCENT SEXUALITY DEVELOPMENT

Deciding to "come out to self and others"—accepting one's own same-sex feelings, attraction, and orientation—is an important and necessary developmental task for a sexual minority youth and is especially important for the adolescent because of the developmental ramifications of delaying this acknowledgment and the need for understanding and acceptance by significant others (Pope, 1995). For example, delaying acknowledgment often leads to high-risk sexual experimentation in an effort to confirm or deny sexual orientation and makes males in particular vulnerable to exploitation by older gay men. "Males tend to define themselves as gay in the context of same-sex erotic contact, but females experience lesbian feelings in situations of romantic love and emotional attachment" (Troiden, 1979, p. 365).

A large study of Minnesota junior and senior high school students found that about "11% reported that they were still unsure about their sexual orientation" (Remafedi, Resnick, Blum, & Harris, 1992, p. 715). Twenty percent of self-identified gay and bisexual men surveyed on college campuses say that they knew about their sexual orientation in high school, and another 17% knew as far back as grade school that they were gay. "The figures for sexual orientation are 6% and 11%, respectively, for lesbians" (Fontaine, 1998, p. 12).

Chung and Katayama (1998) report that the formation of sexual identity is a developmental process with these stages: "awareness of same-sex feelings, feeling confused because one's assumed sexual orientation differs from one's perceived orientation, tolerance and acceptance of a lesbian or gay identity, and integration of a sexual identity with other aspects of one's life" (p. 24). Omizo, Omizo, and Okamoto (1998) found that common sentiments among sexual minority youths included confusion, fear of not being understood, fear of negative or violent reactions from others, concerns about what kind of college or career future they might have, poor self-esteem, and internalized feelings of self-doubt and self-hatred. Not all sexual minority adolescents accept themselves, which is understandable given the constant battering they receive within the context of culture and religious values as well as from their peers, family, and society. The fear of rejection and isolation, along with parental sanctions, tend to be ever present; therefore, some sexual minority youths decide to not disclose their sexual orientation at all, especially if they are still in high school or living with their parents or other family members (Newman & Muzzonigro, 1993).

THE NEED FOR SCHOOL-BASED INTERVENTIONS

Although often controversial, there is a growing moral obligation for school-based interventions and educational training for school faculty and staff to create a safe, supportive, and nondiscriminatory environment for sexual minority youth from a social justice perspective. First, harassment and discrimination should never be tolerated. Second, comparing 2005 data with a study of the general secondary school population, sexual minority youths were twice as likely as the national sample to say they were not planning to complete high school or to attend college. This is a tremendous loss in terms of educational opportunities and talent. In this era of accountability, this is an invisible minority group that needs to be included in closing the achievement gap. Sexual minority students who experience more frequent verbal or physical harassment are more likely to report that they do not plan to go to college. This disparity is significant in the case of physical harassment: the average grade-point average for students who were physically harassed because of their sexual orientation was half a grade lower than that of other students (2.6 versus 3.1; Murdock & Bolch, 2005).

For many sexual minority students, however, schools are notoriously unsafe and hostile places where everyday survival is the prevailing priority rather than excelling academically. Many school districts omit sexual orientation language from antibullying programs or schoolwide codes of conduct. Others fail to enforce existing codes, which are merely paper policies without consequences. Even though students are taught that the use of hate speech, such as the use of religious, racial, or ethnic slurs, will not be tolerated, homophobic name-calling and antigay taunts, such as "fag" or "you're so gay," are rampant in most schools and are often ignored by adults. A climate survey by GLSEN (Kosciw, 2004) found that 83% of sexual minority students experienced verbal, physical, sexual harassment, and assault at school. Specific acts of school violence against sexual minority youth included being urinated and ejaculated on, being attacked with weapons, receiving death threats, having their clothes pulled off or possessions destroyed, and being gang-raped.

WHAT SEXUAL MINORITY YOUTHS SHOULD CONSIDER IN COMING OUT TO OTHERS

The Human Rights Campaign Foundation's (2004) National Coming Out Project issued the following guidelines for sexual minority youths. These are important for the professional school counselor to know when he or she encounters a sexual minority youth who wants to make his or her sexual identity public. It is critical, however, that the professional school counselor not initiate these steps unless the student persists and is experiencing extreme emotional distress. The professional school counselor should also be knowledgeable about the ethical responsibilities and limitations of working with a minor in the school setting. The guidelines for students are:

1. Take your time and think about what you want to say and choose the time and place carefully. For example, gathering the family around a holiday or family reunion could be a very explosive situation because everyone is at different levels of acceptance and understanding.
2. Be cognizant of what the other people are going through. For example, if a parent just lost a promotion or is ill, this is not the best time. The best time for you may not be the best time for someone else, so be mindful of current circumstances.
3. Present yourself honestly and assure the other person that you are the same individual you were yesterday, and they merely know something else about you. Essentially, it is part of you, but it does not represent you as a total person.

4. Be prepared for an initial negative reaction from some people (e.g., if it is your parents, they may first think he or she will never have grandchildren, which may be a tremendous loss for them, especially if they want you to carry on the family name). Remember, it took time for you to come to terms with your own sexual orientation, so it is important to give others the time and space they need to process the new information.

5. Have trusted friends as a support network or a counselor to talk with you after you reveal your information. You will want to process reactions and feelings with someone in a safe environment.

6. If you do not get the original reaction that you wanted to receive, don't give up hope. Sometimes it takes time and distance for people to come to terms about what they have heard. Providing family and friends with reading resources and materials may be helpful.

7. Finally, do not let your self-esteem depend on the approval of others. You can't live up to everyone's expectations. Always keep in mind that you have the right to be who you are because all aspects of your identity should be acknowledged, including your sexual orientation. Being rejected is part of living. Another person's rejection of you is not evidence of your lack of self-worth or human value. (Human Rights Campaign Foundation, 2004)

LEGAL RAMIFICATIONS AND PROFESSIONAL POSITION STATEMENTS

Within the past decade, professional school counselors have been confronted regularly with elementary, middle, and secondary school students who are sexual minorities, including those who are questioning their sexual orientation (Cooley, 1998). Fontaine (1998) surveyed school counselors and found that

> more than half (51%) of both middle and high professional school counselors had worked with at least one student who was questioning his/her sexual orientation and that 42% had worked with at least one self-identified lesbian or gay student. Twenty-one percent (21%) of elementary professional school counselors also reported that they were aware of students in their schools who were identifying as gay or lesbian, or were questioning their sexual orientation. (p. 9)

Professional school counselors often feel conflicted when confronted with a student who comes to them and says, "I think I am a lesbian." Immediately, values and issues of privacy and confidentiality come into the equation, along with the dilemma of whether or not the counselor should counsel them.

Sawyer, Porter, Lehman, Anderson, and Anderson (2006) conducted a national-level needs assessment of high school psychologists, social workers, professional school counselors, and nurses to identify training and educational resource material needs of these staff members relevant to providing health and mental health services to sexual minority youth. Results revealed:

> Most staff acknowledged the presence of sexual minority youth in their schools; reported "accepting" attitudes toward these students; perceived sexual minority youth to be at much higher risk, than their heterosexual counterparts, for several health and mental health problems; indicated that they should be providing more services to these students; and identified a number of barriers related to school climate, lack of staff training, and community/parental opposition that hamper service provision to sexual minority youth. (p. 2)

Many other factors could lead to the reluctance of professional school counselors to get involved, from lack of training and preparation to school board policy and community norms to the personal religious orientation and values of the professional school counselor.

It should be cautioned that professional school counselors are bound by the policies of their individual schools and districts. Their role is further limited by state laws and regulations that govern the credentialing of professional school counselors (McFarland & Dupuis, 2001). However, the shift toward the protection of sexual minority students in the schools is gaining momentum. In 1993, Massachusetts became the first state to ban antigay discrimination in its schools and created a statewide "safe schools" program. Court decisions have consistently supported the right of sexual minority youths to attend school free from harassment and the responsibility of the school to protect them. Schools have a legal, ethical, and moral obligation to provide equal access to education and equal protection under the law for all students. Any educational program or activity that receives federal financial assistance cannot discriminate on the basis of sex or choose which students will be safe or which will not.

Many schools, even those that have safe school programs in place, fail to recognize the needs of sexual minority youth and implicitly assume that heterosexuality is the norm, neglecting to address stressors that affect the safety and education of sexual minority students. These practices have a negative effect on students and significant legal and financial implications for school districts.

According to the 14th Amendment of the U.S. Constitution, all students are entitled to equal protection under the law. The interventions described below will help ensure that all students are able to receive the education they deserve. Federal law (Title IX of the Education Amendments of 1972) also protects student in public schools, or any educational institutions that receive federal funds, from discrimination on the basis of sex. Sexual harassment and discrimination is covered by Title IX. If they are so severe, persistent, or pervasive that they interferes with a student's education or create a hostile or abusive educational environment, then school districts can be held liable. Although the language of Title IX does not mention sexual orientation, the U.S. Department of Education has stated that harassment based on sexual orientation can be a violation of Title IX if the harassment is sexual in nature.

In the 2003 decision *Lawrence v. Texas,* the U.S. Supreme Court declared such laws unconstitutional, holding that sexual minority individuals are entitled to government "respect for their private lives" (539 U.S. 558, 578 [2003]; Wardenski, 2005). Fourteen states now offer protections for sexually minority students. Nine states (California, Connecticut, Maryland, Massachusetts, Minnesota, New Jersey, Vermont, Washington, and Wisconsin) have laws that prohibit harassment and discrimination on the basis of sexual orientation. Maryland enacted its law in 2005, which also includes gender identity in their coverage. Five states (Alaska, Florida, Pennsylvania, Rhode Island, and Utah) have regulations, policies, or ethical codes that prohibit harassment or discrimination on the basis of sexual orientation.

SCHOOL-BASED INTERVENTIONS: THE ADMINISTRATOR'S ROLE

Schools typically do not have the information, interest, or comfort level to address the needs of sexual minority students. However, school principals are responsible for the safety of all students, including sexual minority youths. School personnel may be their only support system and, with effective intervention, can have a positive impact on the lives of sexual minority students.

An affirmative environment is more likely when school personnel are knowledgeable about protective factors and the needs of sexual minority students, provide them with support and understanding, and become their advocates and allies. Principals, moreover, are in the position of potentially having to confront the same kinds of issues among faculty and staff who may be sexual minorities. This could create tensions in both the school and community.

The suggestions that follow have been drawn from real-life scenarios and may be helpful in understanding different issues the administration may be prepared to confront and eliminate doubt or controversy.

- Administrators should have a firm policy of nondiscrimination at their school.
- Harassment against sexual minority teachers or students should not be tolerated, whether it is among students, between students and teachers, or among teachers themselves.

- Disclosing one's sexual orientation is a right that most teachers and students have if they choose to exercise it. Administrators should respect this right and protect both staff and students from a hostile environment.
- Court cases have generally upheld the right of same-sex couples to attend school dances as long as their behavior is not disruptive. The conventional wisdom is "Don't make a big issue out of it."
- Discussing sexual minority issues in a classroom is not the same as having a lesson on family life education, as some people may believe. Teachers should be careful that the classroom discussion does not evolve into sexually explicit conversation or disrespectful debate.
- If a parent complaint should arise, ask that the complaint be put in writing, specifically stating the objections and the reasons for them. The administrator can then, calmly but firmly, review the complaint, in view of the suggestions mentioned above and according to school district policy. This will give the parents the satisfaction that their concerns have been heard and also give the administrator time to respond in an objective manner.

Improve School Safety and School Climate

Antigay epithets, harassment, violence, and relational aggression create a negative school climate and reinforce the message that hate speech and violence is permitted. A schoolwide policy of zero tolerance for harassment, hate epithets, and slurs must be incorporated into an overall school safety effort. The policy should apply to students and staff members and include incidents from name-calling, cyberbullying, harassment on social networking sites, and property damage to physical and sexual assault. Most importantly, the policy must be consistently enforced by *all* staff members. Creation of a nondiscrimination school policy for sexual minority students and staff members extends additional protections. Including staff members in the nondiscrimination policy demonstrates to sexual minority students that their role models will not be discriminated against because they were involved in the policy and procedures process.

Educate, Teach Tolerance, and Affirm Diversity

In addition to preventing antigay behavior, it is important to represent and celebrate diversity throughout the school year. Accurate information regarding sexual identity development, sexual minority issues, and famous sexual minority individuals could be infused into the curriculum. There are many examples in history, literature, and science as well as in politics and current events of famous people who are or were sexual minorities. Other ways to create a positive environment include displaying posters about sexual minority students, reading literature by sexual minorities, and providing library resources and information. The use of gender-neutral and inclusive language indicates that sexual orientation is not assumed. Co-curricular activities, such as after-school clubs, sports teams, and social events, need to be explicitly open to all students. Proms and other "couple" events can be particularly uncomfortable for sexual minority students. Students at some schools prefer to organize their own dances, but this should be a student choice and not a result of being unwelcome at the annual prom. Such a measure could also fuel further divisiveness among faculty, staff, and mainstream students.

Provide a Support Network for Sexual Minority Students

Identify at least one trained staff member to serve as a resource for sexual minority students. In many cases, this would be the professional school counselor, but a teacher or other staff member may be a more effective resource, demonstrating a more collaborative spirit among professional school counselors and faculty. Having someone other than a mental health professional act as a resource for students can help normalize sexual minority issues and prevent them from being viewed as a mental health issue. The staff member should be trained to be knowledgeable about effective strategies for working with sexual minority students; familiar with the best practices for implementing antibias and diversity programs in schools; and knowledgeable about the resources available in the community. The National Association of School Psychologists and GLSEN are just two of the organizations offering training for educators. Students should know which personnel they can turn to; hanging rainbow posters or placing "safe zone" stickers on doors are good ways to help identify where staff members are located. Another effective way to improve the school climate is to establish a school-based Gay-Straight Alliance, which provides support and companionship, improves self-esteem, and promotes positive school change.

Be Prepared for Some Controversy

Issues of sexuality, just like religion and politics, can provoke strong emotions, controversy, debate, opinion, and opposing perspectives. Be sure to engage students, faculty and staff members, parents, and school board members in developing codes of conduct and diversity programming initiatives. It is also critical to have an understanding of the cultural perspectives and biases within the community. Be cognizant of the ramification about sexual orientation, affirm the need for equality and social justice, and communicate these concepts to all groups within and outside of the school. Talk to colleagues in other school districts who have successfully created safe and supportive school cultures for sexual minority students. Affirm the need to embrace diversity, and ensure a safe, healthy learning environment for everyone that promotes social justice.

Train All Staff Members in How to Understand Sexual Minority Students and Use Effective Interventions

Provide staff members with ongoing antibias and diversity training, as well as education regarding the legal responsibility to protect and treat all sexually minority students respectfully. Such training should provide a protocol for responding to students who reach out for help and should include all members of the school community. Another effective way of raising awareness is to bring in guest speakers who are willing to share their school experiences, such as sexual minority graduates from the school or representatives from Parents, Families, and Friends of Lesbians and Gays (PFLAG), a national organization with local chapters.

It is important to know that many heterosexual youths have had sexual experiences with peers of their same gender as an experiential exercise, but are not a sexual minority. Today, adolescents are engaging in their first sexual encounter earlier than generations before them. Other researchers have offered various suggestions for discussing emerging sexuality with all adolescents. What follows are some guidelines from the American Academy of Pediatrics's Committee on Psychological Aspects of Child and Family Health and Committee on Adolescents (2001) for discussing emerging sexual minority issues with adolescents:

- Assure the adolescent that his or her confidentiality is protected. Help the adolescent think through his or her feeling carefully; strong same-sex feelings and even sexual experiences can occur at this age and do not necessarily define sexual orientation.
- Labeling an adolescent as homosexual who has over-identified with a same sex peer, who has sexual experiences with persons of the same sex, or who is questioning his or her sexual orientation could be inappropriate, premature, counterproductive, and offensive to the adolescent. Sometimes it is wise to let experimentation run its course as long as it not endangering the well-being, such as high risk sexual behavior or exploitation from older sexual predators.
- Deal with feelings first and foremost. Most sexual minority youth feel alone, afraid, and guilty. It is helpful to listen, allowing the opportunity to unburden uncomfortable feelings and thoughts.
- Be supportive. Assure sexual minority youth that they are okay. Help them understand that many people have struggled with the issue of homosexuality. Acknowledge that dealing with one's sexuality is often a struggle. Keep the door open for further dialogue, information and assistance.

- Use gender-neutral language in discussing sexuality with both youth and adults; use the word "partner" rather than "boyfriend" or "girlfriend." In addition, focus on "protection" rather than "birth control."
- Give evidence of support, acceptance, congruence and unconditional positive regard. These are the primary relationship skills that were promoted from Carl Rogers and it works with this population as well as all parents and adolescents. Also, ensure that the client's confidentiality is protected.
- Provide information and resources regarding sexual minority youth issues to all interested adolescents including health issues such as risky behaviors, depression, substance abuse, isolation, and suicidal thoughts.
- Like most school-based family life or sex education programs in the schools today, encourage abstinence, discourage multiple partners, clubbing in high risk arenas, and provide "safer sex" guidelines to all adolescents.
- Counsel and educate all adolescents about the vulnerable connection between substance use (alcohol, marijuana, and other drugs) and unsafe sexual encounters.
- Frankly engage the adolescent about personal experience with violence or abuse regarding violence including sexual or intimate-partner violence, parental violence and violence from peers.
- Counsel all adolescents about the increased vulnerability between substance use (i.e., alcohol, marijuana, club drugs and other drugs) and the risk for unsafe sexual intercourse.
- Connect youth with support groups or student organizations that allow them to interact with other sexual minority youth. This will assist in diminishing feelings of alienation and isolation.
- Learn about stages of sexual identity development for sexual minority youth. When professional school counselors take the time to educate themselves they can better understand the developmental needs of their counselees. Professional school counselors can explore safeguards with sexual minority youth and serve to help lessen their personal risk factors through each of these stages.
- Be aware that the revelation of an adolescent's sexual minority status (i.e., "coming out") has the potential for intense family disruption and discord. In many families, it generates physical and/or emotional abuse and in extreme measures kicking the adolescent out of the home. Parents, siblings and other family members may require professional counseling to deal with their confusion, anger, guilt, and feelings of loss and betrayal.
- Have critical literature on hand and referral resources for screening for STDs, HIV, hepatitis B, pregnancy testing and counseling.
- Fundamentally, a counseling intervention has been successful whenever an adolescent is willing to be vulnerable to a caring adult and process challenging material. Providing a safe place for sexual minority youth may very well be a life line and an opportunity to reduce the risk of future traumas.
- Above all, refer adolescents' care if you have personal barriers talking with sexual minority youth. Even discomfort expressed in a subtle manner through body language can send a damaging message to sexual minority youth who are subject to harassment and victimization. (American Academy of Pediatrics, 2001, pp. 498–502).

CONCLUDING REMARKS ABOUT SEXUAL MINORITY YOUTH

The stigma, tensions, and stressors of being a member of a marginalized community makes sexual minority youths more vulnerable to using mind-altering substances and engaging in other high-risk behaviors such as irresponsible sexual activity. Creating safe and affirmative schools for all students, including sexual minority and gender-nonconforming students, is an essential role of principals, professional school counselors, teachers, and support staff. When educators do not intervene in antigay abuse, they deny the existence and unique needs of sexual minority student population and place their mental health and well-being, as well as their education and future productivity, at risk. Conversely, educators can improve the physical, social, and psychological functioning of sexual minority students through support and advocacy. Prevention programs call for staff development, sensitivity, and access to nonjudgmental information.

The American Counseling Association and American School Counselor Association have begun to take strong, concerted action to address school violence and to protect students in general, and especially those categories of students who are most at risk of physical and emotional violence from this bullying behavior; this includes the sexual minority youth in the schools (American Counseling Association, 2000; ASCA, 2000a; Coleman & Remafedi, 1989; Nichols, 1999; Pope, 2000; Pope et al., 2003; Sandhu & Aspy, 2000). Administrators and professional school counselors need to support these efforts to the maximum extent possible.

APPENDIX A: IMPORTANT DEFINITIONS AND TERMS RELATING TO SEXUAL MINORITY YOUTH

The term *sexual minority* includes a variety of young people who are in various stages of their psychosocial, gender, sexual, and cultural identity development processes. The term includes *gays* (males who identify with a same-sex sexual or affectional orientation), *lesbians* (females who identify with a same-sex sexual or affectional orientation), *bisexuals* (males or females who identify with both a same-sex and opposite-sex sexual or affectional orientation), *transgender* (individuals who are physiologically one gender but psychologically the opposite gender), *intersex* (individuals who have biological characteristics of both males and females), *queer* (individuals who identify as "different" sexually than the majority culture), and *questioning* (individuals who are unsure of their sexual or affectional orientation or gender identity). All gay and lesbian youths are members of a sexual minority, but not all sexual minority persons are gay.

Professional school counselors should also be familiar with the following terms (Reis, 2004) to increase their own personal awareness and education.

- *Ally:* A member of a historically more powerful identity group who stands up against bigotry, discrimination, or harassment, for example, a man who confronts his friend about harassing women, a Christian who helps paint over a swastika, or a heterosexual person who confronts an antigay joke among his or her peers.
- *Bisexual:* Being romantically and sexually attracted to people of both genders. Often shortened to *bi.*
- *Coming out:* The process of acknowledging and accepting a nonheterosexual orientation or a sexual minority identity to oneself and then sharing it with others. Adolescents typically come out to friends first, as a means to test the level of acceptance of their peers, before finding the courage to tell their family. Coming out means dropping the secrecy and pretense and becoming more emotionally integrated. Many will acknowledge to those who they trust that "I am still the same person I was yesterday."
- *Co-parents or co-partners:* Adults who are raising a child together and who may or may not be biologically related to the child. Sometimes they may refer to themselves as *partners, parents, stepparents,* or *guardians.* It is important to acknowledge and respect their preferred role description.
- *Failure to report:* Certain professionals are required by law to contact child protective services and/or law enforcement when they know or suspect that a child or teen has been neglected or physically or sexually assaulted.

- *Failure to protect:* The Equal Protection Clause of the 14th Amendment to the Constitution states that all citizens are due equal protection under the law and cannot be discriminated against through selective enforcement. This means that schools are responsible for equally protecting all students. Sexual harassment policies, for instance, must be applied consistently, regardless of a student's gender, race, religion, sexual orientation, or gender expression.
- *Gender identity:* One's understanding or feeling about whether one is emotionally or spiritually male or female, both, or neither. Youths can be heterosexual and congruent in gender identity and physical gender, or transsexual and conflicted, feeling biologically one gender but emotionally and spiritually the other.
- *Gender role:* One's gender expression and one's beliefs and feelings about the appropriate and/or comfortable expression of one's gender.
- GLBTQ: Acronym for Gay, Lesbian, Bisexual, Transgender, and Questioning. Much of the current research simply calls GLBTQ youth sexual minority.
- *Heterosexism:* The presumption that heterosexuality is superior to homosexuality or bisexuality. Also, prejudice, bias, or discrimination based on that presumption.
- *Homophobia:* A bias against or dislike of gay, lesbian, bisexual, and transgender people or of stereotypically gay/lesbian behavior, or discomfort with one's own same-sex attractions or being perceived as gay or lesbian.
- *Internalized homophobia:* The fear and self-hate an individual experiences of one's own homosexuality or bisexuality that occurs for individuals who have learned negative ideas about homosexuality throughout childhood. Once gay and lesbian youths realize that they belong to a group of people that is often despised and rejected in our society, many internalize and incorporate the stigmatization of homosexuality and fear or hate themselves.
- *Invisibility:* The constant assumption of heterosexuality renders sexual minority youth invisible and seemingly nonexistent. Sexual minority youths are usually not seen or portrayed in society, especially not in schools and classrooms.
- *Malicious harassment:* Physical injury, damage to property, or threats based on a person's (real or perceived) sexual orientation, race, color, religion, ancestry, national origin, gender, or mental, physical, or sensory handicap.
- *Outing:* Publicly revealing the sexual orientation or gender identity of someone who has chosen not to share it. With the popularity of the Internet, middle school males are often bullied on-line regarding their gender orientation.
- *Pink triangle:* During World War II, the Nazis forced homosexuals to wear pink triangles on their clothing when they were imprisoned in concentration camps and targeted for extermination. Now, the downward-pointing, equilateral, pink triangle is a symbol of sexual minority pride and the struggle for civil rights.
- *Rainbow flag:* A flag of six equal horizontal stripes in six symbolic colors: (1) red for life, (2) orange for healing, (3) yellow for sun, (4) green for nature, (5) blue for harmony, and (6) lavender or violet for spirit. It has been adopted to signify the diversity of the sexual minority youth community.
- *Sexual orientation:* One's core sense of the gender(s) of people toward whom one feels romantically and sexually attracted; the inclination or capacity to develop intimate emotional and sexual relationships with people of the same gender, a different gender, or more than one gender. Sexual orientation doesn't presume sexual experience or activity (i.e., sexual minority people are as capable as heterosexual people of choosing to abstain). It refers to an individual's pattern of physical and emotional arousal toward other persons (Friedman & Downey, 1994; Stronski Huwiler & Remafedi, 1998). Some youths may overidentify with someone of their same sex during the developmental transition of "identity versus role confusion." These can be confused with having homosexual feelings when in fact they may be

merely infatuated with the person's demeanor, interests, and self-efficacy traits and want to emulate that person.

APPENDIX B: A STAFF DEVELOPMENT MODEL FOR TRAINING TEACHERS AND OTHER SUPPORT STAFF

This model, developed by Friends of Project 10, can be adapted to fit a 90-minute workshop up to a full-day module.

GOALS AND OBJECTIVES

Goals:

- Create a safe environment that will foster student achievement.
- Provide an environment that respects the diversity of the school community, with a focus on lesbian, gay, bisexual, transgendered, and questioning (GLBTQ)—that is, sexual minority—youth.

Objectives:
By the end of the session, participants will have:

- Increased competence in addressing sexually minority issues in a school setting
- Increased knowledge of school, community, state, and national resources
- Increased understanding and comfort level in addressing harassment and equity issues as they relate to district policies and state laws (if applicable).
- The opportunity to develop a site-specific plan that:
  - addresses harassment based on actual or perceived sexual orientation and gender identity; and
  - creates a safer learning environment that fosters student achievement

Preparation for Training

The training should be tailored according to the target audience (i.e., school administrators, teachers, professional school counselors, or parents). Some areas may be emphasized more than others depending on the needs of the group.

Prior to the training, request that the school select an administrator, professional school counselor, or teacher to answer the questions in a School Self-Assessment. This will help you understand specific issues and needs to be addressed in the training.

The School Self-Assessment might include the following questions:

1. Why are you asking for this presentation?
2. Have you had bias-motivated incidents targeted towards members (student or staff) of the sexual minority community?
3. Do you have a Gay-Straight Alliance or other support programs for sexual minority youth at your school?

4. Are there supportive persons in the administration and teaching staff?
5. On a scale of 1 (no support) to 10 (adequate support), how would you assess the school climate around sexually minority issues?

Each participant should receive a packet upon entering the training. Suggested contents include the following:

- Goals and objectives
- School district and community resources
- One news article that is relevant to sexual minority youth

Additional resource information such as school district policies, state laws (if applicable), and school and community resources can be put on tables for participants to take as they exit the training. It is best not to give them too much at once.

It is suggested that the facilitator not stop during the presentation for questions and answers (Q&A) except for clarification. Leave Q&A until the end of the presentation. The training can get bogged down very easily and you may not be able to get through your program.

Section 1: Introduction

- Overview of the training.
- Review purpose and goals.
- Request that participants take a self-evaluation (not to be shared).
- Review major points from sexual minority youth as an at-risk group (see Tables 10.3 and 10.4).

TABLE 10.3   Sexual Minority Youth as a High-Risk Group

The Stressors
- Devaluation by family, community and religious institutions, and schools
- Family rejection
- Poor peer relationships
- Verbal and physical abuse
- Low self-esteem
- Social stigmatization
- Isolation
- Racial, ethnic, and cultural conflicts

The Possible Outcomes
- School-related problems
- Runaway and homelessness
- Conflict with the law or other points of authority
- Alcohol and substance abuse
- Survival sex (i.e., trading sex for food, money, or shelter)
- Poor mental health
- Self-devaluation
- Depression and suicide
- Unintended pregnancy
- Unprotected sexual experimentation
- Depression
- Powerlessness

Source: Uribe, V., Friends of Project 10, Inc., 2002. Reprinted with permission.

TABLE 10.4   Risk Factors for Sexual Minority Youth

General

- Awareness/identification of sexual minority orientation at an early age
- Self-acceptance of sexual minority orientation
- Conflicts with others related to sexual minority orientation
- Problems in sexual minority relationships

Family

- Rejection of child due to sexual minority orientation
- Abuse/harassment of child due to sexual minority orientation
- Failure of child to meet parental/societal expectation
- Perceived rejection of child due to sexual minority orientation

School

- Abuse/harassment of sexual minority youth by friends and peers
- Lack of accurate information about sexual minority youth

Substance abuse

- Self-medication to relieve the pain of oppression
- Substance abuse to reduce inhibitions on sexual minority feelings

Relationship problems

- Inability to develop relationship skills like heterosexual youth
- Extreme dependency needs due to prior emotional deprivation
- Absence of social supports in resolving relationship conflicts

Society

- Discrimination/oppression of sexual minority youth in society
- Portrayal of sexual minority youth as self-destructive by society
- Poor self-esteem
- Internalization of image of sexual minority youth as sick and bad
- Internalization of image of sexual minority youth as helpless and self-destructive
- Identity conflicts
- Denial of sexual minority youth orientation
- Despair in a recognition of a sexual minority youth orientation

Religion

- Child's sexual minority orientation seen as incompatible with family religious beliefs
- Youth feels sinful, condemned to hell due to sexual minority youth orientation

Social isolation

- Rejection of sexual minority youth by friends and peers
- Social withdrawal of sexual minority youth
- Loneliness and inability to meet others like themselves

Professional help

- Refusal to accept sexual minority orientation of youth
- Refusal to support sexual minority orientation of youth
- Involuntary treatment to change sexual minority youth orientation

Independent living

- Lack of support from family
- Lack of support from adult sexual minority community
- Involvement of street life
- Unsafe sexual practices
- Despair about the future

Source: Adapted from Gibson, P., "Gay Male and Lesbian Youth Suicide," in *Report of the Secretary's Task Force on Youth Suicide*, U.S. Department of Health and Human Services, Washington, DC, Vol. 3, 110–142, 1989. Terms were changed to reflect current research perspective, e.g., *sexual minority youth*, not *homosexuals*.

Section 2: Background Information

Select one or a combination of activities depending on time constraints and available resources:

- Have a student or a recent graduate of the school speak to the group about their experience as a sexually minority student at that school.
- Have a small panel of sexual minority youths and parents of sexual minority youths speak to the group.

- Show a video or clips of videos that are appropriate. See Gay, Lesbian, & Straight Education Network (http://www.glsen.org) and Parents, Families, & Friends of Lesbians and Gays (http://www.pflag.org) for video listings and educational resources.

Section 3: District Policies and State Laws

- Review district policies and state laws as they apply to your district. It is advisable to have either a district representative (Title IX officer, general counsel) or attorney (e.g., from the American Civil Liberties Union [ACLU], Lambda Legal Defense, or Education Fund) address information and issues related to policies and laws as they apply to sexual minority students. Visit http://www.aclu.org or http://www.lambda.org for chapters near you.
- Emphasis on safety and equity issues needs to be made clear to the audience. This is not a discussion about homosexuality. Students who do not feel safe in school and who do not have equal access to learning cannot achieve academically. It is everyone's duty to facilitate learning in a safe and equitable environment for all.
- If time permits, use scenarios on prejudice reduction. Allow the audience to brainstorm the situation(s) presented to them.

Establish a Code of Discipline

Name-calling, which has its basis in poor self-esteem, has the spiral effect of further lowering self-esteem, making it difficult for learning to take place. A systemwide Code of Discipline will assist in controlling name-calling when this behavior is addressed directly. A phrase in one school's Code of Discipline defines the unacceptable behavior as: "Willful obscene, abusive, or profane language or gestures (including racial, religious, ethnic, gender, disability, or sexual slurs)." This definition is followed by specific consequences for transgressions. With systemwide support and commitment, a discipline code is very effective in eliminating name-calling not only in the classroom but also in the hallways where it is most prevalent (Uribe, 1994).

See the Model Anti-Harassment Policy published by the ACLU at http://www.aclu.org/issues/gay/schoolpolicy.html.

A sample policy under the Massachusetts General laws, Chapter 76, Section 5: states:

> No person shall be excluded from or discriminated against in admission to a public school of any town, or in obtaining the advantages, privileges and courses of study of such public school on account of race, color, sex, religion, national origin, or sexual orientation.

Students in the Springfield, Massachusetts, Gay-Straight Alliance developed this safe schools pledge that members of the school community were asked to sign during their annual Safe Schools Week:

> I pledge from this day onward to do my best to interrupt prejudice and stop those who, because of hate, would harass or violate the civil rights of anyone. I will try at all times to be aware of my biases against people who are different than myself. I will speak out against anyone who mocks, seeks to intimidate, or hurt someone of a different race, religion, ethnic group, or sexual orientation. I will reach out to support those who are targets of harassment.

Uribe (1990) developed the following bill of rights for sexual minority students:

1. The right to attend schools free of verbal and physical harassment; where education, not survival, is the priority.
2. The right to attend schools where respect and dignity for all is a standard set by the Boards of Education and enforced by every school administrator.
3. The right to have access to accurate information about themselves, free of negative judgment and delivered by adults who not only inform them, but affirm them.
4. The right to positive role models, both in person and in the curriculum.

5. The right to be included in all support programs that exist to help teenagers deal with the difficulties of adolescence.
6. The right to legislators who guarantee and fight for their constitutional freedom, rather than ones who reinforce hate and prejudice.
7. The right to a heritage free of crippling self-hate and unchallenged discrimination. (Reprinted with permission)

Section 4: Educational Resources and Strategies

- Review school district resources, community resources, and GLBTQ Links.
- Review "How to Handle Harassment in the Hallways in Three Minutes or Less" below.
- Review "Name-Calling in the Classroom" below.

How to Handle Harassment in the Hallways in Three Minutes or Less
1. Stop the harassment

- Interrupt the comment or halt the physical harassment.
- Do not pull student aside for confidentiality unless absolutely necessary.
- Make sure all the students in the area hear your comments.

2. Identify the harassment

- Label the form of harassment: "You just made a harassing comment based upon race [or ethnicity, religion, sex, sexual orientation, socioeconomic status, size, age, etc.]."
- Do not imply that the victim is a member of that identifiable group.

3. Broaden the response

- Do not personalize your response at this stage. Say: "We, at this school, do not harass people" or "Our community does not appreciate hateful, thoughtless behavior."
- Reidentify the offensive behavior: "This name-calling can also be hurtful to others who overhear it."

4. Ask for change in future behavior

- Personalize the response: "Chris, please pause and think before you act."
- Check in with the victim at this time: "Please tell me if this continues. We can take future action to work out this problem. We want everyone to be safe at this school."

Name-Calling in the Classroom: What Can Be Done?
Everyday denigrating names are echoed down the corridors of school and often explode in the classroom. The sense of pain, humiliation, and insult affects children and adolescents and takes many forms. Racial, ethnic, and sexual slurs are particularly abusive because they reflect a history of oppression and therefore there is more power to inflict damage with such slurs. Do youths need to be reminded that they are members of a denigrated class? Sometimes slurs don't even get recognized as being hurtful and may be considered socially acceptable. Many young people use terms such as "faggot," "lezbo," and "queer" because they know the effectiveness of their hurtful nature. The use of slurs attacks another's self-esteem and teaches young people that hatred of one group is condoned by our society. As educators, it is important to create a cooperative learning environment where students are safe to express themselves in all their diversity. It is also the responsibility of educators to teach children that diversity is something to be celebrated rather than ridiculed.

Exercise for Establishing Classroom Rules
Even without a Code of Discipline, name-calling can be controlled within the classroom using the following exercise:

- Have students brainstorm names they have heard or have been called.
- List all suggestions on the board.
- Discuss the following categories and categorize names accordingly: racial, ethnic, sexual, gender, or religious bias.
- Make students aware that all name-calling involves prejudice and is equally bad.
- State that none of the listed names are acceptable in your classroom.
- Make it clear that you will not tolerate any form of name-calling.
- Explain why, and discuss the consequences for failure to adhere to this rule.

You can control behavior in your classroom. It you react immediately to any transgressions, students will feel safe in the classroom.

Section 5: Wrap-Up and Evaluation
Conduct an evaluation of the training.

PART FOUR

Consultation, Accountability, and Self-Care

Advocating for the Mental Health Needs of Children and Adolescents

11

A Silent Scream

*"Cell and bell" reflects the rigorous
structure of the school,
A six hour logic is the rigid "golden rule."
A silent scream echoes from impersonal, sterile walls,
Illusion, bleak despair lurk in estranged halls.*

*"Time-on-task" and pacing guides evolve
as the teacher's arduous chore,
Promoting content over feeling is
the fundamental class core.
A silent scream reluctantly sits in a desk alone there,
Haunting a young troubled mind and yearning to share.*

*"Clocking-in and dropping-out" marks
a parent's rushed demeanor,
"Perhaps I'll get to know him better,
when he becomes a senior!"
A silent scream desperately lives disillusioned here,
New defenses, repression and
depression mask unshed tears.*

*A caring nature and welcome shelter is the
professional school counselor's role,
But schedule changes, crisis management, and
clerical tasks consume their daily toll.
A silent scream beckons a critical therapeutic source,
perchance, I'll see him discussing
the new elective course.*

*Content, task, and structure punctuate
our institutional norms,
Depression and alienation succumb
as interpersonal forms.
What if ... the silent scream decided it was time to quit,
called an unsuspecting friend, and
then slit his fragile wrist?*

Rosemary A. Thompson

PROFESSIONAL SCHOOL COUNSELORS AS MENTAL HEALTH ADVOCATES, CONSULTANTS, AND REFERRAL AGENTS

The next decade must mark a turning point for how schools and communities address the problems of children and youth. Needed in particular are initiatives to reform and restructure how schools work to prevent and ameliorate the many learning, behavioral, and emotional problems experienced by students. The end product must be schools where everyone—staff, students, families, and community stakeholders—feel supported. This will require reshaping the functions of the school personnel who have a role to play in addressing barriers to learning and promoting healthy development. And, it requires fully integrating all this into school improvement planning.

School Mental Health Project/Center For Mental Health in the Schools, Department of Psychology, UCLA

The decades of the 1960s and 1970s were a distinctive, discernible, and turbulent period of social history that reflected significant social changes such as the long-range implications of the civil rights movement, the women's movement, the sexual revolution, and the emerging drug culture, coupled with a dramatic rise in the divorce rate and the disintegration of the traditional family structure. This turmoil created a need for professional school counselors to provide interventions in personal and social development more than academic and career guidance (Gysbers & Henderson, 2006).

The Federal Community Mental Health Centers Construction Act of 1963 was instrumental in allocating federal funding to states to build local centers so that clients could live closer to home and not be institutionalized in state mental hospitals (Governing, 2004). This Act promoted the National Institutes of Mental Health as a recognized federal bureau in 1967; the creation of the Alcohol, Drug Abuse, and Mental Health Administration in 1973; and the formation of the President's Commission on Mental Health in 1977 (New York State Archives, 2007).

The burden of suffering experienced by children with mental health needs and their families has created a health crisis in this country. Growing numbers of children are suffering needlessly because their emotional, behavioral, and developmental needs are not being met by those very institutions, systems and agencies which were explicitly created to take care of them. It is time that we as a Nation took seriously the task of preventing mental health problems and treating mental illnesses in youth. (U.S. Public Health Service, 2000, p. 1)

Emotional health in children as a part of healthy child development must be a national priority. Both the promotion of mental health in children and the treatment of mental disorders should be major public health and educational goal. To achieve these goals, the Surgeon General's National Action Agenda for Children's Mental Health (Office of the Surgeon General, 2000) takes as its guiding principles a commitment to:

1. Promoting the recognition of mental health as an essential part of child health;
2. Integrating family, child and youth-centered mental health services into all systems that serve children and youth;
3. Engaging families and incorporating the perspectives of children and youth in the development of all mental healthcare planning; and
4. Developing and enhancing a public-private health infrastructure to support these efforts to the fullest extent possible.

Its primary goals are to:

1. Promote public awareness of children's mental health issues and reduce stigma associated with mental illness

2. Continue to develop, disseminate, and implement scientifically-proven prevention and treatment services in the field of children's mental health
3. Improve the assessment of and recognition of mental health needs in children
4. Eliminate racial/ethnic and socioeconomic disparities in access to mental healthcare services
5. Improve the infrastructure for children's mental health services, including support for scientifically-proven interventions across professions
6. Increase access to and coordination of quality mental healthcare services
7. Train frontline providers to recognize and manage mental health issues, and educate mental health-care providers about scientifically-proven prevention and treatment services
8. Monitor the access to and coordination of quality mental healthcare services (Office of the Surgeon General, 2000)

Professional school counselors represent the largest single group of mental health professionals working in the schools today with extensive training in the developmental needs of youth and family dynamics. Professional school counselors therefore have an important part to play in helping schools respond to the increasing number of students whose mental health needs place them at risk for school failure and poor interpersonal relationships.

The Center for Mental Health Services (CMHS) has been established to provide a leadership role in delivering mental health services, generating new knowledge, and establishing national mental health policy. Section 1912(c) of the Public Health Service Act, as amended by Public Law 102-321, states:

> Children with a serious emotional disturbance are persons: from birth up to age 18, who currently or at any time during the past year, have had a diagnosable mental, behavioral, or emotional disorder of sufficient duration to meet diagnostic criteria specified within *DSM-III-R*, that resulted in functional impairment which substantially interferes with or limits the child's role or functioning in family, school, or community activities. (p. 2)

CMHS is a branch of the Substance Abuse and Mental Health Services Administration (SAMHSA) of the U.S. Department of Health and Human Services. A 2002 survey by SAMHSA found that "two-thirds of school districts reported an increased need for mental health services" (p. 2). During the same period, 60% of districts reported that referrals to community-based providers increased, while one-third of those surveyed reported that the availability of outside providers to deliver services to students in need had decreased (U.S. Department of Health and Human Services, 2008).

As schools move forward into the 21st century, they face the considerable challenge of educating a growing population of students at risk for school failure (Carlson, 1996; Dryfoos, 1990; Kirst, 1991). Too many children and adolescents grow and develop in an environment characterized by poverty, substance abuse, child abuse and neglect, family instability, domestic violence (Kirst, 1991; Weist, 1997), and inadequate child care or supervision (Schorr, 1997). In addition, many children with serious emotional disturbances and their families attempt to maneuver through fragmented, confusing, and overlapping configurations of services in education, mental health, health, substance abuse, social service, youth services, juvenile justice, and community-related agencies. These children and their families encounter and must endure competing definitions, regulations, and jurisdictions in a delivery system marked by bureaucracy, categorical funding, and regulatory roadblocks. To effectively plan, administer, finance, and deliver the necessary educational services, mental health services, social services, health services, and other support services to students and their families, coordination among numerous agencies concerned with the well-being of children and adolescents must increase and improve because this is an investment in society's future and the well-being of its citizens.

A report from the National Institute of Medicine (National Advisory Mental Health Council, 1990) indicated that in 1990 15–22% of children and adolescents in the United States had mental health problems severe enough to warrant treatment, yet estimates suggest that fewer than 20% of this group were receiving any type of mental health services (Costello, 1990; Tuma, 1989; Zill & Schoenborn, 1990). The first Surgeon General's report on mental health (Office of the Surgeon General, 1999a) estimated that between 3 million and 6 million children suffer from clinical depression and are at high risk for suicide.

Complex emotional problems put children and youths at risk for school failure, and therefore, new methods and models for assisting students to achieve school success are both necessary and needed. More and more school districts are recognizing the need for responsive services, such as individual or group counseling, implementation of a trauma protocol, consultation, and referral to meet the immediate needs and concerns of students. At the school level, issues that warrant responsive services include family crises, death, divorce, school failure, peer conflicts, interpersonal difficulties, relational aggression, bullying, cyberbullying, depression, suicide, self-mutilation, drug and alcohol abuse, eating disorders, disciplinary problems, child abuse or neglect, pregnancy, STDs, rape, illness, and violence. The professional school counselor assumes a critical role in helping students with these serious nondevelopmental issues that serve as barriers to learning and deplete self-sufficiency and hamper their potential for developing resiliency skills and developmental assets.

Counseling, consultation, and coordination advocacy are three of the primary functions of a school counselor (Borders & Drury, 1992a; Paisley & Borders, 1995), and these require redefinition in light of the complex needs of at-risk youth. Additional roles include collaboration, teamwork, the use of technology, and accountability (ASCA, 2005a). The broad spectrum of this pervasive problem is evident from the data that follow:

- Ten million children and adolescents suffer from a diagnosable psychiatric disorder.
- Two million adolescents suffer from depression.
- Anxiety disorders are the most common mental health problems children face; it is estimated that 5–20% of all children are diagnosed with them.
- More children suffer from psychiatric illness than from leukemia, diabetes, and AIDS combined.
- Every year, at least three million children are victims of posttraumatic stress disorder.
- Between 1980 and 1996, the suicide rate among children age 10–14 increased by 100%.
- Close to 50% of all adolescents with eating disorders will also have a predisposition for an obsessive-compulsive disorder.
- Fifty-nine percent of those with bipolar disorder report suffering their first symptoms during childhood or adolescence.
- Someone who experiences an episode of depression in adolescence carries a 20% risk of developing a manic episode within 3–4 years.
- The percentage of high school students who report they have thought seriously about attempting suicide has dropped substantially, from 29% in 1991 to 17% in 2003, where it remained in 2005 (Child Trends, 2003).

Child welfare agencies estimate that between 60% and 70% of all parents and children involved in foster care have a diagnosable substance abuse disorder (Center on Addiction and Substance Abuse, 1999; Young, Gardner, & Dennis, 1998; Anderson, Frissell, & Brown, 2007; August et al., 2006; Ballon & Chaim, 2006). In addition, between 40% and 60% of children in the custody of juvenile justice systems have a diagnosable substance abuse disorder, and another 20–30% have a primary mental health diagnosis (Abt Associates, 1994; American Psychiatric Association, 1994; Otto, Greenstein, Johnson, & Friedman, 1992; Ulzen & Hamilton, 1998).

It has long been recognized that mental health and psychosocial problems must be addressed if schools are to function satisfactorily and students are to learn and perform effectively. Thus, school-based and school-linked mental health and psychosocial programs have been developed for the purposes of early intervention, treatment, crisis management, and primary prevention in some school systems that recognize the value of primary prevention and early intervention initiatives to decrease barriers to learning.

Professional school counselors can no longer allow counseling skills to languish. They must provide a wide range of counseling services to meet school, community, and consumer needs. Professional school counselors need to become more visible service delivery providers. Some of the most commonly known psychiatric disorders of children and adolescents are the following:

- Anxiety disorders
- Major depression
- Bipolar disorder
- Attention deficit/hyperactivity disorder (ADHD)
- Learning disorders
- Conduct disorders
- Oppositional defiant disorders
- Attachment disorders
- Eating disorders
- Autism

It is the professional school counselor's responsibility to be familiar with these disorders in an effort to advocate for all students and to coordinate and advocate for community services. Support systems need to be available from a school community perspective and linkages between the school and community must be easily accessible.

CHARACTERISTICS OF EFFECTIVE PROGRAMS

The mission of public schools is to educate all students. However, children with serious emotional disturbances have the highest rates of school failure. Fifty percent of these student drop out of high school, compared to 30% of all students with disabilities. While schools are primarily concerned with education, mental health is essential to learning as well as to social and emotional development. Because of this important interplay between emotional health and school success, schools must be partners in the mental health care of our children.

President's New Freedom Commission on Mental Health (2003, p. 58)

Effective intervention programs take into account the developmental and sociocultural risk factors that lead to antisocial, dysfunctional, or self-defeating behavior. They must be theory based and empirically demonstrate outcome-based intervention strategies that are known to be effective in changing behavior and tested program designs and validated measurement techniques to assess intervention outcomes. Prevention programs that empirically demonstrate intervention outcomes that significantly reduced drug use, violence, or disruptive behaviors are usually designed to enhance "protective factors" and to reduce "risk factors." *Protective factors* are those associated with reduced potential for dysfunctional or disruptive behaviors. *Risk factors* are precipitating variables in the individual, school, or family that make drug use, dysfunction, or disruptive behaviors more likely. Research has shown that many of the same factors apply to other behaviors such as youth violence, delinquency, school dropout, risky sexual behaviors, and teen pregnancy.

Protective factors that buffer youths from risky behaviors include:

- Strong and positive family bonds
- Parental monitoring of children's activities and peers
- Clear rules of conduct that are consistently enforced within the family
- Involvement of parents in the lives of their children
- Success in school performance
- Strong bonds with institutions, such as school and religious organizations
- Adoption of conventional norms about drug use

Among the risk factors that increase the vulnerability of youths to engaging in risky behavior are:

- Chaotic home environments, particularly in which parents abuse substances or suffer from mental illnesses
- Ineffective parenting, especially with children who have difficult temperaments or conduct disorders
- Lack of parent–child attachments and nurturing
- Inappropriately shy or aggressive behavior in the classroom or home
- Failure in school performance
- Poor social or emotional coping skills
- Affiliations with peers who also display deviant behaviors
- Perceptions of approval of drug-using behaviors in family, work, school, peer, and community environments

It is important to begin interventions with children as early as possible to interrupt and redirect processes related to the development of disruptive behavior. For example, early intervention programs must address the aggressive and violent behavior of a child within the context of other difficulties that the child is experiencing, such as low academic achievement, poor peer relationships, and social, emotional, and cognitive deficits. Effective intervention strategies target the many social causal of the child such as family, school, peers, media, and community. They also work toward creating a safe, cooperative school environment by eliminating factors that promote aggressive and violent behaviors. Increasing children's and adolescents' abilities to resist violence as a perpetrator, victim, or bystander is paramount.

There is intervention research that offers support for a classroom and role-taking discussion approach to violence prevention. Interpersonal cognitive problem-solving skills are related to social behavior. Generating alternative solutions, consequential thinking, means–ends thinking, social-causal thinking, sensitivity to problems, and dynamic orientation is a necessary intervention. Improving perspective-taking skills, focusing on the negative consequences of violence, teaching how to negotiate nonviolent solutions to conflict, and recognizing the escalating process of conflict and what to do if things cannot be resolved is a process that can be learned.

Early intervention for children has demonstrated savings in expenditures for special education, welfare assistance, and the juvenile justice system (Fleming et al., 2005). Early intervention also leads to better social, emotional, and decision-making skills and higher standardized test scores (Fleming et al., 2005). Project Achieve, a national model prevention program from the U.S. Department of Health and Human Services (SAMHSA, 2004), is a school-effectiveness or school-improvement process that uses an effective whole-school design and reform process with schools and school districts to:

- Maximize students' academic achievement
- Create safe school environments and positive school climates
- Build effective teaching and problem solving teams that speed successful interventions to challenging students
- Increase and sustain effective classroom instruction
- Increase and sustain strong parent involvement
- Develop and implement effective strategic plans
- Organize building committees and student learning clusters and
- Develop effective data management systems for outcome evaluations (Knoff, 2004, p. 5)

Empirical research for Project Achieve has demonstrated the following results:

- Overall discipline referrals to the office decreased 16%
- School-based discipline referrals to the office decreased 10%
- School bus discipline referrals to the office decreased 26%
- Out-of-school suspensions decreased 29%

- Grade retentions decreased 47%
- Special education referrals decreased 61%
- Special education placements decreased 57% (Knoff, 2004, p. 2)

Behavioral change was attributed to the influence of beliefs and behaviors of other group members. Social problem-solving programs where youths are trained to follow specific steps in solving interpersonal problems have been found to be effective. Components of effective interventions have included general problem solving, decision-making skills, general cognitive skills for resisting interpersonal or media influences, skills for increasing self-control and self-esteem, adaptive coping strategies for relieving stress and anxiety through the use of cognitive coping skills or behavioral relaxation techniques, general interpersonal skills, and general assertive skills (Thompson, 1998, 2006).

UNADDRESSED MENTAL HEALTH PROBLEMS

Unaddressed mental health problems and the lack of adequate services become profound barriers to learning. However, with heightened awareness of the potential advantages of school-based mental health (SBMH) services, "there has been a growing progressive movement toward developing more comprehensive programs and services to meet the needs of all students that may have barriers to learning because of mental health issues" (Flaherty & Osher, 2003, p. 12). A recent longitudinal study provided strong empirical evidence that "interventions that strengthen students' social, emotional, and decision-making skills also positively impact their academic achievement, both in terms of higher standardized test scores and better grades" (Fleming et al., 2005, p. 342). Lower test scores and lower grades were predictive of elevated levels of attention problems, negative behavior among peers, and disruptive and aggressive behavior. Prevention programs that reach all students and early identification and intervention that focus on youth risk prevention are both crucial and essential. Examples include education on mental health issues, school violence prevention, social skills training, bullying prevention, suicide prevention, conflict resolution, and screening for emotional and behavioral problems. A school-based social developmental program that focuses on mental health issues has the potential to curtail early manifestations of antisocial behavior and promote school bonding and social and emotional skills (Fleming et al., 2005).

School-based violence prevention programs concentrate efforts on risk variables such as poor impulse or emotional control, learned violent responses, and poor peer relations. Theories of aggression show that since aggression is a learned behavior; it can be unlearned and replaced with prosocial, nonaggressive behavior. The most effective research-based violence prevention programs have been multidimensional, including components to address the following topics:

- Self-esteem or positive self-affirmation
- Awareness of the negative consequences of violence on peers, family, and community
- Improvement of social perspective-taking skills and communication enhancement
- Anger-management, conflict-resolution, and stress-management techniques
- Generation of nonviolent solutions to interpersonal and intrapersonal problems
- Training of youth to follow specific steps to solve interpersonal problems, that is, social problem-solving skills training

Such programs aim at addressing a wide variety of mental health and psychosocial problems (school adjustment and attendance problems, dropout, physical and sexual abuse, substance abuse, relationship difficulty, emotional upset, teen pregnancy, delinquency, and violence, including gang activity). They encompass efforts to help students, schools, parents, and communities establish ways to deal with emergency situations and enhance social and emotional well-being, resiliency, self-esteem, intrinsic motivation, empathy, and prosocial skills.

MENTAL HEALTH VERSUS MENTAL ILLNESS

> Mental health is how we think, feel, and act as we face life's situations. It is how we look at ourselves, our lives, and the people in our lives. It is how we evaluate options and make choices. Mental health includes how we handle stress, relate to others, and make decisions.
>
> American Psychiatric Association

Mental health is a state of successful performance of mental function, resulting in productive activities, rewarding relationships with other people, and the ability to adapt, change, and cope with adversity. It provides the internal anchor for positive relationships, learning, emotional growth, resilience, competence, confidence, self-efficacy, and self-esteem.

Kessler and colleagues (2005) report that "half of all lifetime cases of mental disorders start by age 14" (p. 594). Among the 2.2 million adolescents age 12–17 who reported a major depressive episode in 2004, "nearly 60% did not receive any treatment" (Hallfors, Waller, Bauer, Ford, & Halpern, 2005, p. 164). However, students are more likely to seek counseling when services are available in schools (Slade, 2004). In many states, schools have become the major providers of mental health services to children (Rones & Hoagwood, 2000; Weist, Paternite, & Adelsheim, 2005).

The UCLA Center for Mental Health in the Schools suggests that policy makers and school staff must work with families and community providers to create a cohesive and integrated continuum of interventions and services that meets the universal needs of students and those with severe problems. Too often, the mental health concerns of students are not assigned a high priority on a daily basis and gain stature only in the event of a crisis such as a school shooting, homicide, or suicide (Adelman & Taylor, 2005).

Numerous data support the need for mental health services in schools, including the following findings:

- "Approximately 20% of children and adolescents in the U.S. reported experiencing symptoms of a mental health problem and 5% reported experiencing extreme functional impairment" (Office of the Surgeon General, 1999a, p. 20).
- "Untreated mental illness can result in a lack of school-to-work success, substance abuse, violence and even suicide" (National Institute for Healthcare Management Research and Education Foundation, 2005, p. 36).
- "The dropout rate for students with severe emotional and behavioral problems is nearly two times higher than it is for other students" (Lehr, Johnson, Bremer, Cosio, & Thompson, 2004, p. 124).
- "Epidemiological studies indicate that 12% to 30% of school-aged children in the U.S. experience at least moderate behavioral, social or emotional problems" (Juvonen, Le, Kaganoff, Augustine, & Louay, 2004, p. 164).
- "Nearly three quarters (73%) of the schools reported that social, interpersonal, or family problems were the most frequent mental health problems for both male and female students; for males, aggression or disruptive behavior and behavior problems associated with neurological disorders were the second and third most frequent problems; for females, anxiety and adjustment issues were the second and third most frequent problems" (Foster et al., 2005, p. 61).
- "According to the U.S. Surgeon General's report on children's mental health (1999) 20% of children need active mental health interventions, 11% have significant functional impairment, and 5% have extreme functional impairment." These data were derived from the Methodology

for Epidemiology of Mental Disorders in Children and Adolescents study, which also found that "13% of children and adolescents have anxiety disorders, 6.2% have mood disorders, 10.3% have disruptive disorders, and 2% have substance abuse disorders, for a total of 20.9% having 1 or more mental health disorders" (Office of the Surgeon General, 1999a, p. 45).

- "Students in need of mental health services who receive emotional support and preventive care perform better in school" (SAMHSA, 2007, p. 7).
- Elementary schools that have recently expanded mental health services have reported reductions in "special education referrals, … disciplinary referrals, suspensions and grade retentions" and "improved school climate" (SAMHSA, 2007, p. 8).
- Evidence supplied by the Institute of Medicine indicates that "early childhood mental health interventions for at risk and low-income children have resulted in savings in public expenditures for special education, welfare assistance and the criminal justice system" (Shonkoff & Phillips, 2000, p. 266).
- It is estimated that nearly "$200 billion a year in economic loss could be avoided by improving the quality of schooling; investing more in education and reducing the dropout rate" (Teachers College, 2005, p. 5).
- During 2005, "approximately three in ten high school-aged children reported feeling sad or hopeless almost every day for a two-week period" (Centers for Disease Control and Prevention, 200, p. 14). The 2005 Youth Risk Behavior Surveillance System corroborates this finding, reporting that 36.7% of females and 20.4% of male high school students reported sadness. Latino students reported higher rates of depressive symptoms (46.7% of females and 26.0% of males) (Eaton et al., 2006, p. 9).
- Researchers from the National Institute of Mental Health (NIMH) concluded that "there are often long delays between the first onset of symptoms and the time people seek and receive treatment" (Juvonen, Kaganoff, Augustine, & Louay, 2004, p. 46).

Mental illness encompasses all diagnosable mental disorders that are health conditions characterized by alterations in thinking, mood, emotion, or behavior associated with distress and/or impaired functioning (Office of the Surgeon General, 1999a). Persons suffering from any of the severe mental disorders manifest a variety of symptoms that may include inappropriate anxiety disturbance of thought, perception, mood, and cognitive dysfunction. For example, depression exemplifies a mental disorder largely marked by alterations in mood, whereas ADHD exemplifies a mental disorder largely marked by alterations in behavior (i.e., overactivity) and/or thinking (i.e., inability to concentrate). Alteration in thinking, mood, or behavior contributes to a host of adjustment problems such as distress, impaired functioning, or heightened risk of death, pain, disability, or loss of independence (American Psychiatric Association, 1994). Table 11.1 represents the most prevalent mental disorders among children and adolescents.

The causes of mental health problems are complicated. There are biological causes, such as genetics, chemical imbalances in the body, damage to the central nervous system, fetal alcohol syndrome, prenatal crack/cocaine use, HIV, and intellectual disabilities. There are also environmental causes such as attachment disorder; exposure to environmental toxins (e.g., lead, alcohol, and other drugs); exposure

TABLE 11.1   Mental Disorders and Their Prevalence

MENTAL DISORDER	PREVALENCE
Anxiety disorders	13.0%
Mood disorders	6.2%
Disruptive disorders	10.3%
Substance abuse disorders	2.0%
Any disorder	20.9%

Source: Shaffer, D., et al., *Journal of the American Academy of Child and Adolescent Psychiatry, 35*, 865–877, 1996.

TABLE 11.2   Critical Adolescent Mental-Health-Related Problems

PROBLEM	MALES	FEMALES
Disabling sadness, unhappiness, or depression	33.0%	34.0%
Suicide attempts requiring medical attention	2.1%	3.1%
Drinking and driving	17.0%	9.5%
Alcohol consumption (prior to age 13)	24.0%	34.0%
Physical fights	43.0%	33%
Carrying a weapon at school	10.0%	3.0%
STDs	15.7%	12.2%

Source: Elster, A. B., & Marcell, A. V., *Adolescent Medicine, 14*(3), 525–540, 2003.

to violence; and stress related to chronic poverty, discrimination or other hardships, or the loss of primary caregiver through death, divorce, or broken relationships.

The Surgeon General has estimated that as many as 6.5 million emotionally disturbed and 3.5 million severely disturbed children are not getting the help they need. This translates to the prospect that four out of five youths will not get help before their disorder becomes more debilitating (Office of the Surgeon General, 2000). With the growing incidence of violence in children and adolescents, more co-occurring disorders are emerging that further hinder their well-being. Elster and Marcell (2003) examined mental-health-related problems that presented themselves in adolescent health care. The current prevalence of significant mental-health-related problems facing physicians and pediatricians are presented in Table 11.2.

This lack of care will have long-term costs on society in terms of extended services, as well as loss of productivity on the part of youth in an employment venue that is changing dramatically from the secure factory worker to the portfolio worker. What continues to be true, however, is that half of lifetime diagnosable mental health disorders start by age 14; this number increases three-fourths by age 24 (Kessler et al., 2005).

THE LONG-TERM INVESTMENT OF PROVIDING MENTAL HEALTH SERVICES IN THE SCHOOLS

The burden of suffering experienced by children with mental health needs and their families has created a health crisis in this country.

David Satcher (U.S. Public Health Service Report of the Surgeon General's Conference on Children's Mental Health, 2000)

To promote a healthy learning environment, schools need to provide a cohesive and coordinated school health and wellness program that promotes healthy development, engages in preventive initiatives, allows for early interventions, and provides assistance to those with severe and persistent problems (Fieldman, Backman, & Bayer, 2002). Evidence has demonstrated that students are much more likely to seek help when school-based programs are available and when these programs promote confidentiality and anonymity (Slade, 2004). Though schools are not responsible for meeting every need of every student, schools need to address the barriers that directly affect learning (Office of the Surgeon General, 1999a). Untreated mental disorders can lead to more severe and more difficult-to-treat illnesses and can disrupt the progression through normal child and adolescent development. It is even possible that an untreated mental illness can develop into an additional mental condition or co-occuring disorder (Juvonen et al., 2004).

There is compelling evidence not only that there are strong positive associations between mental health and academic success but also that emotional, social, and behavioral health problems are significant barriers to learning; consequently, full-service schools are becoming the norm rather than the exception (Adelman & Taylor, 2000; Atkins, Frazier, Adil, & Talbott, 2003; Bishop et al., 2004; Catalano, Haggerty, Oesterle, Fleming, & Hawkins, 2004; Greenberg et al., 2003; Klern & Connell, 2004; Libbey, 2004; McNeely & Falci, 2004; Weist, 1997; Wilson, 2004). Fundamentally, the stigma associated with mental health issues has diminished through education, awareness, and understanding.

SCHOOL-BASED MENTAL HEALTH SERVICES: DELIVERY METHODS AND SYSTEMIC RESISTANCE

School-based mental health programs offer the promise of improving identification, diagnosis, and treatment options for the mental health needs of children and adolescents. Increasingly, SBMH services are being collectively delivered in a multiplicity of ways in a need-based program—school-based, agency-based, community-based, in-home, or through individual consultation and counseling (Weist, Evans, & Lever, 2003)—without an explicit "best practice" model that current program development and evaluation models require for most health service programs. Best practices demonstrate that the program or service empirically demonstrate desired outcomes. However, the idea of expanded school mental health services recognizes that there is a growing need among children and adolescents for services that would prevent barriers to learning and create for them a climate of nurturing and well-being (Weist, 1997; Weist et al., 2005).

SBMH programs and services that incorporate key elements for success are highlighted and documented in numerous reports (President's New Freedom Commission on Mental Health, 2003; Office of the Surgeon General, 1999a; American Academy of Pediatrics, 2004). The key elements for SBMH programs and services include:

- School–family–community agency and service partnerships;
- Commitment to a full continuum of mental health education, mental health promotion, assessment, problem prevention, early intervention, and treatment; and
- Services for all youth, including those in general and special education (Weist et al., 2005).

Expanded programs and services also mean moving an entire community toward a system of care—as linkages between schools and community agencies, and opportunities for developing more comprehensive and responsive programs and services—to meet all the needs of youth and families (Leaf, Schultz, Kiser, & Pruitt, 2003). SBMH services recognize that mental health, just as with disabilities, is an area that must be addressed in order to serve the whole child. Mental health is fundamentally important and cannot be ignored. Mental, emotional, and behavior disorders such as anxiety disorders, depression, bipolar disorder, conduct disorders, and autism are sources of stress and can be disabling for children and their families, schools, and communities.

In addition, SBMH programs and services, involving effective, collaborative strategies to promote the mental health and school success of youth, offer significant potential to substantially address the mandates of the 2002 Elementary and Secondary Education Act (No Child Left Behind) and the reauthorized Individuals with Disabilities Education Act (IDEA) (School Mental Health Alliance, 2005; Weist et al., 2005). In their review of research on SBMH services, Rones and Hoagwood (2000) suggest that schools' fulfillment of the mandate to educate all children necessitates attention to mental health issues, thus supporting SBMH programs.

Weist and colleagues (2005) highlight a number of strategies that are important to address school indifference or resistance to SBMH initiatives, including:

- Ensuring strong coordination and collaboration among families, school administrators, and community mental health program providers as programs are being planned,
- Ensuring that school mental health clinicians are well trained, closely supervised, and socially skilled, and that they understand the culture of schools in order to work as collaborative partners in them (Paternite & Johnston, 2005),
- Emphasizing high quality and empirical support of school mental health services (Weist et al., 2009),
- Framing SBMH services as effective means for reducing barriers to learning and creating positive conditions that promote school success (Adelman & Taylor, 1999), and perhaps most important,
- Being able to empirically demonstrate viable and positive outcomes to youth, families, and schools (Prodente, Sander, & Weist, 2002).

ANXIETY DISORDERS IN CHILDREN AND ADOLESCENTS

Anxiety for most adults is a fact of contemporary life. However, children with an anxiety disorder experience anxiety, or excessive worry, more intensely—to the degree that it interferes with their daily functioning. They often experience significant and long-term psychosocial and cognitive impairment, such as poor school performance, poor relationships with peers and school adults, and familial conflict (Langley, Bergman, McCracken & Piacentini, 2004). The internal mechanisms that regulate anxiety may deteriorate in a wide variety of circumstances, leading to excessive or inappropriate expressions of anxiety such as phobias, panic attacks, or obsessive-compulsive disorders. The onset of anxiety disorders can be differentiated by age. *Separation anxiety disorder* and *specific phobias* have the earliest average onset in elementary school (around age 7), while *generalized anxiety disorder* and *obsessive-compulsive disorder* typically have their onset in middle childhood (age 9–10). *Social phobias* typically emerge in adolescence, and the onset of panic disorder comes later, around the age of 15 during high school (Morris & March, 2004).

Children experience anxiety over test scores, school performance, peer and adult expectations, and getting up in front of the class to speak (i.e., communication apprehension). They may also obsessively worry about family discord or the absence of a parent deployed in the armed forces. With the increased violence exhibited in some schools and communities, children and adolescents may worry about their own personal safety and well-being, as well. Terrorism has increased feelings of free-floating anxiety exponentially since the September 11, 2001, attacks on the United States.

If not treated, anxiety disorders can lead to:

- Missed school days or the inability to finish school. such as school phobia
- Impaired relationships with peers and adults
- Low self-esteem and low self-worth
- Alcohol or other drug abuse in an effort to self-medicate in order to diminish feelings of anxiety
- Problems adjusting to work situations or difficulty obtaining a job
- Anxiety disorders in adulthood

Studies have also suggested that teens with anxiety disorders are at risk for developing major depression.

Children and adolescents who have anxiety disorders are very self-conscious, feel tense, have a strong need for reassurance, and complain about somatic illnesses that do not appear to have any physical basis. Anxiety disorders are the most common disorder among children and adolescents. Some of the more common anxiety disorders are described below.

Panic Disorder

Panic disorder manifests with a sudden onset of intense apprehension, fearfulness, or terror, often associated with feelings of impending doom. Symptoms include shortness of breath, heart palpitations, dryness of the mouth, chest pain or discomfort, choking or smothering sensations, fear of losing control, and terror when in certain situations or places. During a panic attack, the child or adolescent feels intense fear or discomfort and sensations of unreality. Children and adolescents with panic disorder may avoid certain school situations such as riding the bus, dressing for physical education classes, or speaking in front of a class or may refuse to attend school altogether. Rates of panic disorder are higher for females and increase in late adolescence, although 10–20% of youths who have panic disorder report that their first manic attack occurred before age 10 (Ollendick & March, 2004).

Specific Phobias

Specific phobias manifest when provoked by exposure to a specific feared object or situation and often lead to avoidance behaviors. Some typical phobias center on animals, storms, water, heights, and closed places. One must differentiate between the normal fears of childhood and the severe, impairing fears associated with specific phobias. Estimates of the prevalence of youths with a specific phobia are between 3% and 10% (Ollendick & March, 2004). The disorder is more common among females and younger children than among boys and older children (King, Muris, & Ollendick, 2004).

Social Phobias

Social phobias or social anxiety manifests as excessive fear of being negatively evaluated, rejected, humiliated, or embarrassed in front of others. Children and adolescents with social phobia fear such things as giving an oral report; changing clothes in gym class; initiating a conversation; eating, drinking, or writing in public; and taking tests. Feelings of anxiety in these situations produce physical reactions such as heart palpitations, tremors, sweating, diarrhea, blushing, or muscle tension.

Children and adolescents suffering from social anxiety disorders fall behind in school, avoid school completely, or avoid social activities among peers their age. They may find it impossible to speak in social situations or in the presence of unfamiliar people (American Psychiatric Association, 1994; Thompson, 1998, 2006). Some studies have shown that youths with social phobia, who are often painfully shy, may have a heightened risk in adulthood for problem drinking and depression, resulting in part from social isolation and limited social contact. Alcohol abuse is a form of self-medication to decrease social anxiety.

Social anxiety can also develop as an ongoing reaction to repeated failure, mistreatment, or rejection by peers and adults. Some students may show good peer group adjustment and ability to interact socially with a teacher, but display communication apprehension when asked to answer academic questions, perform in public, or engage in an activity that they know will be evaluated.

Obsessive-Compulsive Disorder

Obsessive-compulsive disorder (OCD) manifests as obsessions in thought that cause significant anxiety or distress and a compulsion in behavior that serves to neutralize anxiety. A child with OCD is consumed with obsessions of repeated, unwanted, recurrent, and persistent ideas, thoughts, impulses, or images that intrude into his or her thinking. These obsessions produce tremendous anxiety or feelings of discomfort, disgust, and guilt. Common obsessions are fear of contamination, harm, disease, illness, or death. In children and adolescents, they may include aggressive or violent images. Common compulsions include repetitive washing, checking, ordering, and arranging (March et al., 2007; Piacentini & Langley, 2004).

The earlier age of onset of OCD has also been associated with an increased risk of ADHD and other anxiety disorders, including specific phobias, general anxiety disorders, and separation anxiety (March et al., 2007).

Approximately 1–2% of children and adolescents meet the criteria of the *Diagnostic and Statistical Manual of Mental Disorders* (*DSM-IV;* American Psychiatric Association, 1994) for OCD with age of onset between 7 to 10 years of age (Piacentini & Langley, 2004). Males outnumber females with OCD in childhood and early adolescence, but over time this gender difference disappears.

Compulsions are repetitive, purposeful behaviors that are carried out in response to the obsession and include washing and cleaning rituals; checking compulsions (doors, windows, light switches, faucets, and other objects); repeating compulsions (an action must be repeated a certain number of times to get things "just right"); touching and counting rituals; and symmetry rituals (e.g., tying shoes so that both shoes are balanced, or symmetrically arranging books on a shelf or items on a desk).

Treatment usually involves behavior therapy treatment, exposure, and response prevention. *Exposure* consists of having the child or adolescent come into contact with a stimulus that prompts obsessions and provokes compulsions, while providing simultaneous response prevention. For example, a child whose fear of contamination has resulted in compulsive hand washing may be asked to pick up and handle a pile of dirt (exposure) and then helped to resist hand washing for an hour (response prevention).

Children may qualify for services under IDEA as "seriously emotionally disturbed" if OCD-related symptoms adversely affect the child's educational performance and are characterized by one or more of the following: an inability to learn, an inability to build or maintain satisfactory interpersonal relationships, exhibition of inappropriate types of behavior or feelings under normal circumstances, a general pervasive mood of unhappiness or depression, or a tendency to develop physical symptoms of fears associated with personal or school problems.

Posttraumatic Stress Disorder

Posttraumatic stress disorder (PTSD) manifests by reexperiencing an extremely traumatic event accompanied by symptoms of increased arousal and by avoidance of stimuli associated with the trauma. PTSD is considered to be a consequence of exposure to "early onset, multiple, extended and sometimes highly invasive traumatic events, frequently of an interpersonal nature, often involving a significant amount of stigma or shame" (Briere & Spinazzola, 2005, p. 401). If a child or adolescent has experienced a disturbing or frightening event, PTSD often begins within three months of the event, although for some children and adolescents it doesn't appear until much later.

Four hallmark symptoms of PTSD are reexperiencing the traumatic event, numbing of responsiveness, avoidance of reminders of the trauma, and hyperarousal (American Psychiatric Association, 1994). An estimated 5.2 million Americans (including children and adolescents) suffer from PTSD (SAMHSA, 2010). Co-occurring problems—such as hyperactivity, aggressiveness, social withdrawal, depression, anxiety, desperation anxiety, dissociative experiences, substance abuse, runaway behavior, and risky sexual acting out—may in reality be reactions to PTSD. One in every four children reports experiencing at least one event of high-magnitude stress by the time he or she has reached 16 years of age. Anyone can react adversely when high-magnitude stressors intrude on his or her life (Fletcher, 2003), but past experience with high-magnitude stressors can predispose a child to react with symptoms of posttraumatic stress to a current stressful circumstance. This is important for the professional school counselor to understand—that a history of stressful life events has repeatedly been associated with higher levels of PTSD in children and adolescents after exposure to high-magnitude stressors; for example, current stressful events such as competition tryouts, comprehensive end-of-semester examinations, and so forth can trigger previous PTSD symptoms.

A child or adolescent with PTSD develops such symptoms as intense fear, anxiety, disorganized and agitated behaviors, emotional numbness, depression, and intrusive thoughts as a result of being exposed to or witnessing an extreme traumatic situation involving threatened death, serious injury, or significant loss.

PTSD can occur from witnessing violence; from being a victim of physical, sexual, or emotional abuse; or from a catastrophic environmental episode such as a hurricane, earthquake, or tornado. Reactions and recovery are affected by the length and intensity of the traumatic event.

Posttraumatic stress disorder can also be differentiated into Type I acute and Type II traumatic stress. Type I PTSD disorders stem from acute high-magnitude stressors that have a tendency to occur only once and have a short duration; these include natural disasters such as hurricanes and earthquakes and man-made disasters such as fires. Type II traumatic events tend to be more intense and prolonged, with multiple repetitions such as interpersonal violence, sexual and physical abuse, and domestic violence. When evaluating a student's situation, the professional school counselor needs to take into account the kinds of stressful events involved; the child or adolescent's culture, support networks, age and developmental stage, gender, and ethnicity; how soon after the exposure the student's reactions were assessed; and other variables of the impact of the stressful events on survivors.

A recent meta-analysis found incidence rates of stress as high as 39% for preschool children, 33% for elementary school children, and 27% for adolescents. Those who have suffered from PTSD are also more likely to show signs of other disorders such as substance abuse (Kilpatrick et al., 2000); adjustment, panic, and depressive disorders (Kilpatrick et al., 2003); anxiety, dissociative, and attention deficit disorders (Saigh, Yasik, Sack, & Koplewicz, 1999); and eating disorders (Cloitre, Chase, Stovall-McClough, Miranda, & Chemtob, 2004).

General Anxiety Disorder

General anxiety disorder manifests with at least six months of persistent and excessive nonspecific anxiety that is most often experienced as excessive worrying, restlessness, and tension. Children and adolescents may worry excessively about all manner of upcoming events and occurrences, such as academic performance, sporting events, and being on time.

Separation Anxiety

Separation anxiety manifests with intense anxiety to the point of panic as the result of being separated from a loved one or other parental figure. Children with separation anxiety experience recurrent anxiety when separated from home or major attachment figures. They often become preoccupied with irrational fears of accidents or illness. Children with this disorder often express anxiety about being lost and never being reunited with their parents.

DISTURBANCE OF MOOD IN CHILDREN AND ADOLESCENTS

Disturbance of mood manifests as a sustained feeling of sadness or a sustained elevation of mood. Persistent sadness is called *major depression,* whereas fluctuations in mood from periods of sadness to periods of elation is designated *bipolar disorder.* Disorders of mood are associated with an array of related symptoms that include disturbances in appetite, sleep patterns, energy level, concentration, and memory. The most frequently diagnosed mood disorders are major depressive disorder, dysthymic disorder, and bipolar disorder.

Mood disorders such as depression increase the risk of suicide, especially among adolescents. The incidence of suicide attempts reaches a peak during the midadolescent years, and mortality increases steadily through the teens (CDC, 1999; Hoyert, Kochanek, & Murphy, 1999). Over 90% of children and adolescents who commit suicide have a mental disorder before their death (Shaffer & Craft, 1999), the most common of these being mood disorders, substance abuse, and anxiety disorder (Shaffer, Fisher, et al., 1996).

Mood disorders are marked by changes in:

- Emotion: The child or adolescents feels sad, cries, looks tearful, and feels worthless.
- Motivation: Schoolwork declines, and the child shows no interest in play or interactions with others.
- Physical well-being: There may be changes in appetite or sleep patterns and vague physical complaints.
- Thoughts: The child or adolescent has feelings of helplessness and believes that he or she is physically undesirable, that he or she is unable to do anything right, or that life is hopeless.

Depression

Recent studies have revealed that as many as one in every 33 children may have depression. Depression affects a significant number of youths during critical developmental stages, particularly during adolescence (Lewinsohn & Essau, 2002) and is usually best conceptualized along a continuum rather than a specific age or stage (Hankin, Fraley, Lahey, & Waldham, 2005). However, major depression is most likely to appear during midadolescence, around ages 13–15 (Lewinsohn & Essau, 2002). Risk for a chronic episode can be predicted by a variety of factors such as severity, personal or family history of depression, suicide ideation, negative beliefs, and family or environmental adversity (Birmaher, Arbelaez, & Brent, 2002; Rohde, Lewinsohn, Klein, & Seeley, 2005). There is also a significant correlation between depression and anxiety disorder, conduct/oppositional disorder, ADHD, and substance abuse disorders in adolescents (Lewinsohn, Hops, Roberts, Seeley, & Andrews, 1993).

Major depression is one of the mental, emotional, and behavior disorders that affect a child or adolescent's thoughts, feelings, and interpersonal relationships (Center for Mental Health in the Schools, 1999). Signs of depression include:

- Sadness that won't go away
- Helplessness and hopelessness
- Loss of interest in usual activities
- Changes in eating and sleeping patterns
- Deteriorating school performance
- Thoughts and ruminations about death and suicide
- Passive and lethargic behavior or affect
- Uncaring physical state and lack of concern about appearance

Depressed children can have trouble paying attention, feel tired or angry, isolate themselves, and stop participating in their favorite activities. Associated anxiety symptoms, such as fears of separation or reluctance to meet people, and somatic symptoms such as stomachaches or headaches, are more common in depressed children and adolescents than in adults with depression (Birmaher, Ryan, Williamson, Brent, & Kaufman, 1996; Kolvin et al., 1991).

After age 15, depression is twice as common in girls and women as in boys and men (Linehan, Heard, & Armstrong, 1993; McGee et al., 1990). As many as two-thirds of children and adolescents with major depressive disorder also have another mental disorder such as dysthmic disorder, anxiety disorder, disruptive or antisocial disorder, or a substance abuse disorder (Anderson & McGee, 1994; Angold & Costello, 1993). Children and teens most at risk are those who have difficulty seeing a solution to their problems. Family history of depression, particularly a parent who had depression at an early age, increases the chances of a child or adolescent developing depression. Research has indicated that between 20% and 50% of depressed children and adolescents have a family history of depression (Kovacs, Devlin, Pollock, Richards, & Mukerji, 1997). Medications may not be as effective in treating children and adolescents. NIMH is currently evaluating the effectiveness of individual therapy, family therapy, and group therapy.

Some research suggests that ethnic minority youths have higher rates of depression, but socioeconomic status and assessment instruments that are not culturally sensitive may factor into these higher numbers (Chang, 2002). It is commonly assumed that African American, Latino, and Asian adolescents have significantly more depressive symptoms than do their white counterparts. However, focusing on race or ethnic status exclusively to examine group differences in depression among youth can be misleading, because it does not account for how symptoms manifest among different cultures or ethnic groups or how youths describe their symptoms to someone that does not represent their race or culture (Choi, 2002). For example, in some Asian groups, cultural norms may include suppressing emotions and keeping problems within the family constellation, which may also restrict expression or self-disclosure and cause confusion for the counselor (Yeh, 2002). In addition, many Asian cultures might describe their depressive symptoms as physical (somatic) rather than emotional (affective) concerns (Ying & Han, 2007).

Professional school counselors should be sensitive to these cultural variables. Nonetheless, what continues to be true, regardless of culture, is that depressed youth manifest the following barriers to learning: decreased academic performance; social, emotional, and cognitive difficulties; negative perceptions of self; and the potential for dropping out of school, self-medicating with substances, and early unintended pregnancy.

Dysthymic Disorder

Dysthymic disorder is a more chronic condition than depression, with onset in childhood and adolescence (Akiskal, 1983; Klein, Lewinsohn, & Seeley, 1997). The child is depressed on most days, and the symptoms continue for several years (Kovacs, Obrosky, Gastonis, & Richards, 1997). Seventy percent of children and adolescents with dysthymia eventually experience an episode of major depression (Kovacs, Akiskal, Gastonis, & Parrone, 1994). The prevalence of dysthymic disorder in adolescence has been estimated at around 3% (Garrison et al., 1997). Before puberty, major depressive disorder and dysthymic disorder are equally common in boys and girls (Rutter, 1987).

Bipolar Disorder

Bipolar disorder is a brain disorder that is characterized by unusual swings in a person's mood, energy level, and ability to function. About 5.7 million adults in the United States have bipolar disorder (NIMH, 2009). Bipolar disorder, also known as *manic-depressive disorder,* is characterized by intense, persistent mood swings between two distinct poles, depression and mania, that is inconsistent with the child's or adolescent's usual personality. The depressive pole of the manic-depressive illness includes:

- Persistent, sad, anxious, or empty mood
- Feeling helpless, guilty, or worthless
- Hopeless or pessimistic feelings
- Loss of pleasure in usual activities
- Decreased energy
- Loss of memory and concentration
- Irritability or restlessness
- Sleep disturbances
- Loss of or increase in appetite
- Thoughts of death

The manic pole of manic-depressive illness includes:

- Extreme irritability and distractibility
- Excessive "high" or feelings of euphoria
- Sustained periods of unusual behavior
- Increased energy, activity, rapid talking and thinking, and overall agitation
- Decreased sleep
- Unrealistic beliefs in one's own abilities
- Poor judgment
- Increased sex drive
- Provocative or obnoxious behavior
- Denial of the problem

Bipolar disorder is rare in children under the age of 12 and is most often diagnosed during adolescence, between the ages of 15 and 18. Often children can inherit this disorder from their parents. The adolescent may talk nonstop, need very little sleep, and show unusually poor judgment. An early sign of bipolar illness may be hypomania, characterized by high energy, moodiness, and impulsive or reckless behavior. A multisite Course and Outcome of Bipolar Illness in Youth (COBY) study funded by NIMH revealed that bipolar disorder affects children and adolescents more severely than adults, with longer symptomatic stages (i.e., between manic and depressive episodes) and more frequent cycling from one mood to another (Birmaher et al., 2006). Younger age of onset, low socioeconomic status, and psychotic symptoms were common factors that predicted poorer outcomes for children and adolescents.

Major differences in the course of illness between youths and adults may have serious implications for their emotional, cognitive, and social well-being, since this disorder occurs during formative stages of their overall development. Left untreated, bipolar disorder can reoccur, with increasingly severe episodes of mania and depression. In the early stages, alcohol or other drug abuse may occur in an effort to self-medicate.

Bipolar disorder is genetic. The physiological basis of the disorder is supported by neuroimaging studies that reveal that the two sides of the brain are different. Neurochemical imbalances in the brain—in particular, excessive dopamine and a disregulation of norepinephrine—are the probable causes. Mood swings can be stabilized with medication, psychotherapy, and family support.

SUICIDE AND SELF-INJURIOUS BEHAVIORS IN CHILDREN AND ADOLESCENTS

The common purpose of suicide is to seek a solution. Suicide is not a random act. It is never done without purpose. It is a way out of a problem, a dilemma, a bind, a difficulty, a crisis, an unbearable situation.

Edwin Shneidman (1996, p. 103)

Suicide remains the third leading cause of death among 10- to 24-year-olds (accidents and homicide rank as the first two) (Eaton et al., 2006). In the school setting, suicide often has traumatic implications for survivors (Jordan & McMenamy, 2004). Attempted suicides are as high as one in 12 high school students on a yearly basis (Grunbaum et al., 2004). Yet, the newest self-defeating behavior on the adolescent mental health landscape is self-harm, self-injury, or self-mutilation (Laye-Gindhu & Schonert-Reichl, 2005). Self-harm behavior, which is on the rise, can be differentiated from suicidal behavior in that it is not associated with the intent to die, but rather with the intent to relieve emotional pain. Self-harm behavior has garnered the attention of school personnel, who feel ill equipped to deal effectively with self-harming youth.

Suicide

Suicide ideation and deaths are very rare prior to age 15 but increase between 15 and 18 years of age. Suicide attempt rates are less than 1% for 5- to 11-year-olds (Lewinsohn, Rohde, Seeley & Baldwin. 2001). On the other hand, the Youth Risk Behavior Survey, conducted routinely by the Centers for Disease Control and Prevention (CDC, 2007), found that 8.4% of high school students had attempted suicide within the last year, and 2.3% reported that their attempt had required medical attention; moreover, 13% reported having a suicidal plan, and 16.9% said they were seriously considering a suicide attempt.

Males are more likely to die from a suicide attempt than females, with 3.6 completed suicides among males for every suicide death among females among 15- to 19-year-olds (CDC, 2007). Suicidal methods used by 10- to 24-year-olds in 2004 were firearms (47.0%), hanging or suffocation (often provoked by a choking game in an effort to get a quick high) (37.4%), poisoning or overdose (directions are available on the Internet) (8.2%), or jumping (2.4%; CDC, 2007).

Suicidal behaviors are often co-occuring with more severe substance abuse and dependence (Goldston, 2004). Other researchers investigating disruptive disorders have found that risk factors for suicide attempts include ADHD and conduct disorders (Goldston, Reboussin, & Daniel, 2006), oppositional defiant disorder and conduct disorder (Gould et al., 2005), and sexual abuse (Molnar, Berkman, & Buka, 2001). Nonetheless, a history of engaging in suicidal behavior is the best predictor of future suicide behavior.

Self-Injury or Self-Mutilation

A growing number of adolescents are engaging in nonsuicidal self-harm behavior such as cutting with a sharp object, burning, hitting, pinching, scratching, and biting (Ross & Heath, 2002). Adolescents engage is this type of self-destructive behavior for a variety of reasons to cope with depression, anxiety, and difficult feelings. They may also be experiencing unbearable tension, have a need to feel physical pain to distract attention away from unpleasant memories, or want to punish themselves to stop suicidal ideation (Nixon, Cloutier, & Aggarwal, 2002). Such adolescents often have friends who also engage in self-injury, and the behavior is often impulsive rather than planned out (Nock & Prinstein, 2004). Depression appears to be an underlying factor in both suicidal and nonsuicidal self-harm behaviors among adolescents (Nixon et al., 2002).

ATTENTION DEFICIT/HYPERACTIVITY DISORDER

Attention deficit/hyperactivity disorder is the most commonly diagnosed behavior disorder of childhood, occurring in 3.0–7.8% of school-age children in the United States (Biederman, 2005; Esser, Schmidt, & Woerner, 1990; Pelham, Gnagy, Greenslade, & Milich, 1992; Schaffer et al., 1996; Wolraich, Hannah, Pinnock, Baumgaertel, & Brown, 1996). In a typical classroom of 25, at least one student will have ADHD. It is 10 times more common in boys than girls and is most often diagnosed when the child is between ages 8 and 10.

The child with ADHD has difficulty finishing any activity that requires concentration at home, school, or play. He or she acts before thinking, frequently calls out in class, is excessively active, runs or climbs all the time, has serious difficulty waiting his or her turn in games or groups, and is often restless even during sleep. A child with ADHD requires close and constant supervision. Children with ADHD endure significant impairment in many of life's domains, including school, family, and peer relationships. The disorder may manifest in such self-defeating behaviors as high-risk activities to impair personal safety, criminal behavior, and substance abuse (Barkley, Fischer, Smallish, & Fletcher, 2004, 2006). These children have difficulty paying attention to details and are easily distracted by events around them. They find it difficult to finish their schoolwork and put off anything that requires sustained mental effort. They are disorganized, losing books and assignments, and fail to follow through on tasks (American Psychiatric Association, 1994; Waslick & Greenhill, 1997).

Children with ADHD have two distinct sets of symptoms: inattention and hyperactivity-impulsivity; it is important to determine whether the disorder is predominantly related to either category or is a combination of both. Children with the inattentive type manifest the following behaviors and characteristics:

- Have a short attention span and are easily distracted by surroundings
- Do not pay attention to details or systematic guidelines, directions, or assignments
- Make lots of mistakes because of lack of tolerance to double-check their work
- Fail to finish things because of distraction
- Forget things because of sustained concentration
- Don't seem to listen because they become distracted or preoccupied with other things
- Cannot stay organized because of failure to learn organizational skills

Children with the hyperactive-impulsive type manifest the following behaviors and characteristics:

- Fidget and squirm and are unable to stay seated and play quietly
- Run and climb with reckless abandon and often with disregard for the rights of others
- Blurt out answers to questions even before the question is asked
- Have trouble taking turns and following social protocols
- Interrupt others without considering appropriate social skills

Children with combined ADHD, the most common type, demonstrate both the inattentive and hyperactive-impulsive behaviors.

The etiology of ADHD is still inconclusive, although neurotransmitter deficits, genetics, and perinatal complications have been implicated. ADHD also runs in families. The scope of treatment includes support and education of parents, appropriate school placement, and pharmacology (American Academy of Child and Adolescent Psychiatry, 1991). Inattention is most dramatically evident in situations requiring the child to sustain attention to dull, boring, repetitive tasks in their schoolwork (Fischer, Barkley, Smallish, & Fletcher, 2005). Further research suggests that impaired attention may be part of a larger domain of cognitive activities known as *executive functioning* in addition to working memory, that is, the ability to hold onto information in order to reach a goal (Martinussen, Hayden, Hogg-Johnson, & Tannock, 2005).

Smith, Barkley, and Shapiro (2007) outline the following key concepts of the *DSM-IV* criteria for ADHD:

1. Individuals with ADHD may have problems related to inattention, hyperactivity, impulsivity or both.
2. These deficits are significantly inappropriate for the person's age.
3. The disorder should have an onset in childhood.
4. The condition is generally chronic or persistent over time.
5. The core symptoms are significantly pervasive or cross-situational in nature.
6. The deficits are not the direct result of severe language delay, deafness, blindness, or another psychiatric condition, such as autism, depression, or psychosis, that may better explain the symptoms.
7. The core symptoms of ADHD must be causally associated with significant impairment in major life activities, such as educational, familial, social, vocational, adaptive (self-sufficiency), or other significant areas of life functioning. (pp. 60–61)

Children with ADHD are at high risk for other problems. Many experience learning difficulties such as dyslexia and language-processing difficulties. Anxiety and depression may also be more common than in the general population. Medication does not cure ADHD; however, it does make the child more receptive to learning in the classroom and for other types of treatment, such as behavioral management techniques, social skills training, and educational modifications.

During the 1980s, the use of Ritalin and other prescription drugs in the treatment of ADHD more than doubled (Borr, 1988; National Education Association, 1989). Today, ADHD medications for children and adolescents include methylphenidate (Ritalin), dexmethylphenidate (Focalin), pemoline (Cylert), amphetamine (Adderall), and dextroamphetamine (Dexedrine, Dextrostat). There is overwhelming evidence of the efficacy of these medications in the treatment of children and adolescents with ADHD (Barkley & Murphy, 2006; Smith, Barkley, et al., 2006). The medications appear to improve attention span, decrease impulsivity, decrease disruptive behavior, increase productivity on academic assignments, improve peer relationships, and decrease reprimands or punishment by adults around them.

Stimulant medication without the support of psychoeducational and social interventions, however, is an incomplete treatment approach. It subdues the behavior via medication but often does not provide education or training to redirect inappropriate impulses or behavior. Combined treatment (i.e., medication and psychosocial intervention) is most effective in treating coexisting problems associated with ADHD (Smith, Barkley, et al., 2006). In particular, Pelham, Fabiano, and Massetti (2005) found three psychosocial treatments that are well established in treating ADHD in children and adolescents: behavioral parent training, behavioral classroom management, and summer treatment programs that focus on peer relationships in recreational settings.

When children are capriciously placed on a regimen of medication and continue to do poorly in school, they may begin to attribute their behavior problems to factors beyond their control (McGuiness, 1985). They may come to believe that external events, such as luck, fate, or other people, are responsible for their successes or failures. Such an attitude leads to low self-esteem, depression, and feelings of ineffectiveness.

Information about nutritional approaches, behavior modification, self-control training, and the importance of encouragement and motivation in treating ADHD must be communicated systematically to teachers, parents, and administrators. Professional school counselors can help to coordinate programs in which cooperation and communication between home and school are maximized.

AUTISM SPECTRUM DISORDER

Autism spectrum disorder (ASD) is a pervasive developmental disorder characterized by a severely compromised ability to engage in, and by a lack of interest in, social interactions (Bryson & Smith, 1998). The American Psychiatric Association (2000a) lists five pervasive developmental disorders that are used synonymously with ASD: autistic disorder, Asperger's disorder, Rett's disorder, childhood disintegrative disorder, and pervasive developmental disorder not otherwise specified; the last three of these are relatively rare.

Autistic Disorder

It is estimated that 3.4 of every 1,000 children 3–10 years old in the United States have autism (Yeargin-Allsopp et al., 2003). The onset of autistic disorder always occurs before age 3, with two-thirds of children manifesting developmental abnormalities within the first two years of life (Mandell, Novak, & Zubritsky, 2005), with the average onset of regression between 14 and 24 months (Fombonne & Chakrabarti, 2001). Loss of language is the most common salient manifestation of regression (Siperstein & Volkmar, 2004), along with loss of social behaviors such as eye contact, social interest, and engagement with others (Ozonoff, Williams, & Landa, 2005). A majority of children and adolescents with autism (roughly 75%) are intellectually disabled, with mild to moderate intellectual disabilities. In addition, one-third of children with autism develop seizures (Danielsson, Gillberg, Billstedt, Gillberg, & Olsson, 2005).

Children and adolescents with autism typically have a difficult time communicating with others, exhibit repetitive behaviors like rocking back and forth or twirling objects, have a limited range of interests or activities, and become easily upset by a change in daily routine. Symptoms of autistic disorder include:

1. Deficits in reciprocal social interaction: difficulty with nonverbal behavior to regulate social interaction, failure to develop age appropriate peer relationships, little sharing of pleasure, achievements, or interests with others, lack of social or emotional reciprocity;
2. Deficits in communication: delay or total development of language, difficulty holding conversations, unusual or repetitive language, play that is not appropriate for developmental level;
3. Interests that are narrow in focus, overly intense, and/or unusual, unreasonable insistence on sameness and following familiar routines, repetitive motor mannerisms, and preoccupation with parts of objects (Ozonoff, Goodlin-Jones, & Solomon, 2005, pp. 488–489)

To meet the criteria of autistic spectrum disorder, the child or adolescent must exhibit the symptoms listed above (Ozonoff, Goodlin-Jones, et al., 2005).

Autistic disorder might be caused by a combination of biological factors, including genetic factors (Bailey et al., 1995), or by an abnormal slowing down of brain development before birth. In addition, autism has been reported in children with fetal alcohol syndrome and in children whose mothers took a variety of medications that are known to damage the fetus.

Once diagnosed with ASD, the majority of children and adolescents retain this diagnosis into adulthood, with functional impairment throughout life (Billstedt, Gillberg, & Gillberg, 2005). Further, ASD often manifests additional psychiatric and behavioral problems such as anxiety and depressed mood (Kim, Szatmari, Bryson, Streiner, & Wilson, 2000), aggressive outbursts and irritability (Gillberg & Coleman, 2000), bipolar disorder (Frazier, Doyle, Chiu, & Coyle, 2002), and hyperactivity.

Asperger's Disorder

Asperger's disorder shares some of the same social disabilities and restrictive behaviors and interests of a child with autistic disorder; however, language abilities are well developed with Asperger's, and intellectual functioning is not impaired. Children with Asperger's disorder also manifest at older ages (Mandell et al., 2005). The *DSM-IV* (American Psychiatric Association, 2000a) criteria for Asperger's disorder specify that the individual must have "severe and sustained impairment in social interaction, and the development of restricted, repetitive patterns of behavior, interests and activities that must cause clinically significant impairment in social, occupational or other important areas of functioning" (p. 80). Children and adolescents with Asperger's may have limited eye contact, seem to be unengaged in a conversation, and not understand the use of gestures or the meaning of social interactions. They often have an eccentric or obsessive interest in a topic or object, to the exclusion of everything else. Although socially awkward, many go on to finish high school and attend college or university programs.

CONDUCT PROBLEMS: CONDUCT AND OPPOSITIONAL DISORDERS

Conduct problems are the most common reasons that children and adolescents are referred to mental health services (Frick & Silverthorn, 2001). Conduct problems include a broad spectrum of "acting out" behaviors on a continuum from minor oppositional behaviors such as yelling and temper tantrums to more serious forms of antisocial behavior such as violent aggression, physical destructiveness, and stealing. They are often referred to in literature as "oppositional," "antisocial," "conduct disordered," or "delinquent" (Hinshaw & Lee, 2003, p. 12).

This growing behavioral problem is demonstrated by data on juvenile delinquency cases in the court system—which probably underrepresents the severity of the problem. For example, more than 110,000 children under age 13 were arrested for felonies in 1994; 12,000 of these felonies were crimes against people, including murder, rape, robbery, and aggravated assault. An estimated 1.7 million delinquency cases were handled in juvenile courts nationwide in 2005, with the number of delinquency cases climbing sharply to 61% from 1997 through 2005. With regard to race and ethnicity, 64% of delinquency cases handled in 2005 involved white youths, 34% African American youths, 1% Asian youths, and 1% Native American youths. The most common offenses were simple assault, property offenses, larceny/theft, vandalism, drug violations, obstruction of justice, and disorderly conduct (Snyder & Sickmund, 2006).

Many youths enter the juvenile justice system because they are not engaged in school or work and may be dealing with learning, mental health, or family issues that thwart their academic success. There is a disproportionate representation of children of color in the juvenile justice system. In addition, the vast majority of these children suffer from undiagnosed attachment disorders, have histories of abuse and neglect, live in single-parent homes with highly stressed mothers, and had a parent with a criminal record (Levy & Orlans, 1999). Therefore, many processes may be involved in the development of severe conduct problems (Dodge & Pettit, 2003; Raine, 2002). Young offenders will become the reckless predators of tomorrow, desensitized by violence and with personality demeanors that lack remorse.

Attachment Disorder

Attachment-disordered youths develop aggressive, controlling, and conduct-disordered behaviors with personalities that exhibit a lack of responsibility, dishonesty, and a blatant disregard for the rules of school and community, family, and society (Raine, Brennan, & Mednick, 1997). As early as 1969, Bowlby identified these youth as exhibiting an "affectionless psychopathology" marked by an inability to form meaningful emotional relationships, coupled with chronic anger, poor impulse control, and lack of remorse. This is a behavioral phenomenon that has become commonplace in both schools and communities.

Attachment disorder affects many aspects of a child's functioning, and manifests in the following ways:

- Behavior that is oppositional, defiant, impulsive, destructive, aggressive, and abusive (fire setting and cruelty to animals are not uncommon)
- Intense anger, anxiety, depression, moodiness, hopelessness, and inappropriate emotional reactions
- Thoughts that are negative with regard to relationships, self, and life in general
- Lack of cause-and-effect thinking
- Attention and learning problems
- Relationships that lack trust
- Behaviors that are bossy, unstable, manipulative, and superficial
- Tendency to blame others for their problems
- Health issues that manifest themselves as poor hygiene, enuresis and encopresis, high pain tolerance, and tactile defensiveness
- Moral and spiritual deficits such as lack of empathy, faith, compassion, and other prosocial values
- Identification with satanic principles and embracing the evil or dark side of life

The most common causes of attachment disorders are abuse, neglect, multiple out-of-home placements (e.g., moves in the foster care system), and other prolonged separations from a primary attachment figure. Other risk factors include domestic violence, poverty, substance abuse; a history of maltreatment in the parents' childhood; and depression and other serious psychological disorders of the primary attachment figure.

Oppositional Defiant Disorder

Children with oppositional defiant disorder (ODD) repeatedly lose their temper, argue with authority figures, refuse to comply with requests or rules of adults, and blame others for their own mistakes. ODD "is diagnosed when a child displays a persistent or consistent pattern of defiance, disobedience, and hostility toward various authority figures, including parents, teachers, and other adults" (Office of the Surgeon General, 1999a, p. 164). These behaviors cause significant relationship problems with peers, school personnel, friends, and family (American Psychiatric Association, 1994; Weiner, 1997). ODD is often the harbinger of conduct disorders and a growing population of attachment-disordered children.

Conduct Disorder

Conduct-disordered "children behave aggressively by fighting, bullying, intimidating, physically assaulting, sexually coercing, and/or being cruel to people and animals" (Office of the Surgeon General, 1999a, p. 165). Conduct disorders occur in 9% of boys and 2% of girls under the age of 18. Girls with conduct disorders tend to run away from home and may become involved in prostitution and living on the street. Symptoms are socially unacceptable, violent, or criminal behavior such as:

- Stealing without confrontation, such as forgery or lying
- Using physical force, as in muggings, armed robbery, purse-snatching, or extortion
- Deliberately setting fires
- Often being truant from school
- Breaking into homes, offices, or cars
- Forcing someone into sexual activity
- Using a weapon in more than one fight
- In childhood, avoiding cuddles, stiffening, and resisting affection
- Failing to develop normal relationships with anyone, including parents
- Exhibiting repetitive behaviors, such as rocking and head banging

Rates of depression, suicidal thoughts, and suicide attempts are higher in children diagnosed with conduct disorders (Shaffer, Gould, et al., 1996). Other problems with adjustment include ADHD, depressive and anxiety disorders, substance abuse problems (Waschbusch, 2002), language impairment, learning difficulties, underachievement (Wakschlag & Danis, 2004), and peer rejection in elementary school (Fergusson, Swain, & Horwood, 2002). Types of parenting practices that have been closely associated with the development of conduct problems include inconsistent or irritable parenting, explosive discipline, low supervision and involvement, and inflexible, rigid discipline (Chamberlain, Reid, Ray, Capaldi, & Fisher, 1997).

Children with early onset of conduct disorder have a bleak prognosis and are predisposed to adult antisocial personality disorder (American Psychiatric Association, 1994; Hendren & Mullen, 1997; Rutter & Giller, 1984). Certain children have a genetic vulnerability to this disorder (Hendren & Mullen, 1997), but environmental and social factors are more common causes. Environmental and social factors for conduct disorder include early maternal rejection; family neglect, abuse, or violence; a parent's psychiatric illness; parental discord; and parental alcoholism (Loeber & Stouthamer-Loeber, 1986). These factors lead to a lack of attachment to the primary caregiver or to the family unit, which evolves into a lack of regard for the rules and boundaries of school and community (Sampson & Laub, 1993).

EATING DISORDERS

Eating disorders are serious, life-threatening conditions that often become chronic (Herzog et al., 1999). They are considered psychiatric disorders with an obsessive concern to control shape and weight, marked by abnormal eating behaviors. The three eating disorders recognized in the literature are anorexia nervosa, bulimia nervosa, and binge-eating disorder. About 3% of adolescents have one of these three main eating disorders (Becker, Grinspoon, Klibanski, & Herzog, 1999). The causes of eating disorders are not known conclusively but are thought to be a combination of genetic, neurochemical, psychodevelopmental, and sociocultural factors (Becker et al., 1999; Kaye, Strober, Stein, & Gendall, 1999).

Anorexia Nervosa

The criteria for anorexia nervosa is refusal to maintain body weight above 85% of what is expected for age, intense fear of gaining weight or becoming fat, and disturbance in the perception of body weight or shape (American Psychiatric Association, 2000a). Common symptoms associated with anorexia nervosa include the relentless pursuit of thinness and overevaluation of body shape, which usually result in extreme dietary restriction and high levels of physical activity (Fairburn & Harrison, 2003). During episodes of semistarvation, individuals may experience mood disturbances, preoccupation with food, and ritualistic and stereotyped eating patterns (Wilson, Becker, & Heffernan, 2003). Anorexia is also associated with the highest rates of suicidal ideation and mortality of any psychiatric condition of adolescents (Herzog et al., 2000). Physical symptoms that manifest themselves are yellowish skin, fine downy hair, hypersensitivity to cold, hypotension, bradycardia (i.e., slower than normal heart rate), and other cardiovascular complications (Wilson et al., 2003). Approximately 1.4–2.0% of females (and just 0.1–0.2% of males) experience anorexia nervosa during their lifetime (Favaro, Ferrara, & Santonastaso, 2003).

Interestingly, the onset for anorexia peaks at ages 14 and 18, which correspond to two developmental transition periods in the life span: from grade school to high school and from high school to postsecondary roles (American Psychiatric Association, 2000a). There is little evidence of ethnic differences in the rates of eating disorder symptoms (Shaw, Ramirez, Trost, Randall, & Stice, 2004). However, African American females report less body dissatisfaction than their white counterparts (Smolak & Striegel-Moore, 2001).

Risk factors for anorexia include norepinephrine abnormalities, serotonin abnormalities, childhood sexual abuse, negative life events, low self-esteem, perfectionism, need for control, disturbed family dynamics, internalization of a thin ideal self, dietary restraint, and mood disturbances (Fairburn & Harrison, 2003; Wilson, Becker, et al., 2003). Adolescents who develop anorexia are more likely to come from families with a history of weight problems, physical illness, depression, and alcoholism. Among adolescents with anorexia, 50–70% will recover, 20% will show improvement but have residual symptoms, and 10–20% will not recover from this eating disorder (Commission on Adolescent Eating Disorders, 2005). Anorexia nervosa has one of the highest mortality rates of any psychiatric disturbance, with suicide rates 57 times greater than that for the general population (Keel et al., 2003).

Bulimia Nervosa

Bulimia nervosa consists of recurrent episodes (usually twice a week) of binge eating during a discrete period of time, with a lack of a sense of control over eating during this episode. This is paired with inappropriate means to correct the excessive consumption of food with expunging behaviors such as induced vomiting, misuse of laxatives or diuretics, fasting, or excessive exercise. Self-evaluation is influenced by self-criticism of body shape or weight. Bulimia is secretive and is kept from the knowledge of family and friends, coupled with feelings of guilt and shame regarding eating behaviors (Wilson, Becker, et al., 2003). Rigid rules regarding eating and an overevaluation of thinness are also present.

Adolescents with bulimia are typically distressed about their behavior and thus more receptive to receiving treatment. This disorder may be associated with physical complaints, including fatigue, headaches, and erosion of dental enamel from excessive gastric fluids (Wilson, Becker, et al., 2003). Approximately 1.1–4.6% of females experience bulimia nervosa during their lifetime (Favaro et al., 2003); some evidence suggests that male athletes may also be at elevated risk for eating disorders (Wilson, Becker, et al., 2003). The onset for bulimia is between 14 and 19 years of age. Adolescents who develop bulimia are more likely to have a close family relative with the disorder, suggesting a biochemical predisposition; the neurochemical serotonin has also been implicated in the diagnosis of bulimia (About Our Kids Mental Health, 1999).

Individuals with bulimia have elevated rates of agoraphobia, social phobia, major depression, alcohol dependence, marijuana dependence, and antisocial personality disorder (Stice, Presnell, Shaw, & Rohde, 2005). Bulimia increases the risk for future onset of depression, suicide attempts, anxiety disorders, substance abuse, obesity, and other health problems (Johnson, Cohen, Kasen, & Brook, 2002; Striegel-Moore, Seeley, & Lewinsohn, 2003).

Binge-Eating Disorder

Binge-eating disorder is a recently recognized condition of uncontrolled consumption, as in bulimia, but without purging activities to avert weight gain (Devlin, 1996). Bulimia manifests as both binge eating and compensatory activities, such as vomiting or use of laxatives, to eliminate consumption.

SUBSTANCE ABUSE DISORDERS

Substance use and abuse problems among children and adolescents have been a public health problem since the 1970s when the drinking age in many states was lowered to 18 years of age. According to the nationwide survey Monitoring the Future (Johnston, O'Malley, Bachman, & Schulenberg, 2005), 51% of 12th-graders and 30% of eighth-graders had used illicit drugs (including inhalants) and almost half (44%) had used alcohol in their lifetime.

Substance use disorder (SUD) has several health and social implications, including school failure, risky sexual behavior (Jainchill, Yagelka, Hawke, & De Leon, 1999); delinquency, incarceration, suicide ideation (Bolognini, Plancherel, Laget, & Halfon, 2003), motor vehicle accidents and injuries (Kokotailo, 1995), and significantly related medical health care costs (King, Gaines, Lambert, Summerfelt, & Bickman, 2000). Some subpopulations have high risk for SUD, such as homeless youths, youths in the juvenile justice system, and those in psychiatric settings (Baer, Ginzler, & Peterson, 2003).

Children and adolescents who suffer from social anxiety, stress-related disorders, and depression may begin abusing drugs in an attempt to lessen their feelings of distress or heightened discomfort. Stress can play a major role in initial drug use, continuing drug abuse, or relapse in children and adolescents recovering from addiction because they not only are dealing with important developmental issues but also must deal with peer pressure, school demands, and family dynamics that may not be positive or nurturing. Risk of drug abuse increases greatly during times of transition, such as changing schools, moving, or divorce because the easiest group to join, fit into, and be accepted by is a drug-using peer group.

Drug and alcohol abuse can disrupt brain function in areas critical to motivation, memory, learning, judgment, and behavior control (National Institute for Drug Abuse, n.d.). So, it is not surprising that teens who abuse alcohol and other drugs often have co-occurring family and school difficulties, poor academic performance or underachievement, mental and health-related problems, and involvement with the juvenile justice system. Indicators of more positive substance use outcomes include a lower severity level of substance abuse at treatment admission (Maisto, Pollock,

Lynch, Martin, & Ammerman, 2001), an attitude with a greater readiness to change (Kelly, Myers, & Brown, 2000), fewer co-occurring problems such as conduct disorders (Grella, Hser, Joshi, & Rounds-Bryant, 2001); longer length of treatment with family involvement (Hser et al., 2001), after-care program participation (Winters, Stinchfield, Opland, Weller, & Latimer, 2000), and low levels of substance abuse among peers (Winters et al., 2000). Increased drug use among adolescents was found when parents failed to provide supervision or set boundaries regarding self-destructive behavior as well as with parents who demonstrated inconsistent parenting (Cleveland, Gibbons, Gerrard, Pomery, & Brody, 2005).

Other co-occurring disorders also had implications for adolescent substance abuse, such as ADHD, anxiety disorders, PTSD, and mood disorders and adolescents who had parents with SUDs (Clark & Miller, 1998). In addition, neurobiology may play a significant role in adolescent SUD because the brain does not fully develop until early adolescence and the developing adolescent brain may be highly vulnerable to the effects of drug use, with adolescents less capable than adults of moderating their alcohol intake. Further, Hsieh and Hollister (2004) found that female adolescents who were entering a substance abuse treatment program exhibited more psychological difficulties, poorer self-image and self-esteem, increased family problems, and more incidences of sexual abuse than males who entered treatment.

National estimates indicate that approximately 11% of children and adolescents use drugs enough to meet the criteria for either a substance abuse or substance dependence disorder during the precarious developmental period of adolescence (Winters et al., 2007). Table 11.3 provides risk and protective factors for the potential for succumbing to or averting a substance abuse disorder. Protective factors are those associated with reduced potential for drug use; risk factors are precipitating variables in the individual, school, or family that make drug use more likely.

Project ALERT, a drug education and prevention curriculum, has been nationally recognized to reduce drug use, violence, and disruptive behavior (BEST Foundation for a Drug Free Tomorrow, 2005). Designed for middle school, Project ALERT has demonstrated that it is effective in curbing cigarette and marijuana use and alcohol misuse and in reducing pro-drug attitudes.

DIAGNOSIS AND TREATMENT: THE DECADE OF THE BRAIN AND ITS IMPLICATIONS ON MENTAL HEALTH

The last decade of the previous millennium was declared the "decade of the brain." The brain is the integrator of thought, emotion, behavior, and health, and it has emerged as the central focus for studies of mental health and mental illness. Mental functions are carried out by the brain, and mental disorders are reflected in physical changes in the brain (Kandel, 1998).

TABLE 11.3   Risk and Protective Factors for Potential Substance Abuse Disorders

RISK FACTOR	DOMAIN	PROTECTIVE FACTOR
Early aggressive behavior	Individual	Self-control
Poor social skills	Individual	Positive relationships
Lack of parental supervision	Family	Parental monitoring and support
Substance abuse	Peer	Academic competence
Drug availability	School	Antidrug use policies

Source: NIDA Note (2002). Drug Abuse Prevention Research Update, 16, 6, Author.

New scientific disciplines, technologies, and insights have begun to outline a concurrent model of the way in which the brain mediates the influence of biological, psychological, and social factors on human thought, behavior, and emotion in mental health or mental illness. (Office of the Surgeon General, 1999a, p. 13)

Many mental disorders in children such as ADHD, depression, and disruptive disorders respond to pharmacological treatments.

Diagnosis

The standard manual used for the diagnosis of mental disorders is the *Diagnostic and Statistical Manual of Mental Disorders* (*DSM-IV-TR;* American Psychiatric Association, 2000a). The *DSM-IV-TR* is organized into 16 major diagnostic classes. Within each class, it outlines specific criteria for making a diagnosis, as well as subtypes for some disorders to confer greater specificity. No other health care entity has taken the responsibility to provide practitioners with such an extensive compendium of all disorders with such explicit diagnostic criteria, although,

> One caveat on the use of the *DSM-IV-TR* is the limitation that cultural differences (i.e., emotional expression and social behavior) can be misinterpreted as "impaired" if helping professionals are not sensitive to the cultural context and meaning of exhibited symptoms. (Office of the Surgeon General, 1997, p. 12)

The *Diagnostic and Statistical Manual of Mental Disorders,* first published by the American Psychiatric Association in 1952, is among the most important diagnostic documents in the history of clinical counseling, psychology, psychiatry, and social work. The counseling profession has clearly recognized the importance of the use of the diagnostic system in counselor education programs and requires demonstration of *DSM-IV-TR* competency in licensure examinations. The *DSM* maximizes its use for case conceptualization, treatment planning, and educating clients and their families about their disorders and treatment planning.

The *DSM* provides a common language, which facilitates communication among mental health specialists for the purposes of treatment and research. As the most widely used system for the diagnosis of mental disorders in this country, it provides a diagnosis system that is used by insurance companies for third-party payments, by various government agencies for accounting purposes, and by mental health professionals practicing in agencies, private practice, and hospitals (Mead, 1994).

The *DSM* enhances the selection of effective treatment procedures. It is now possible to identify treatment approaches most likely to be effective in treating specific problems or mental disorders (Seligman & Moore, 1995). *DSM* diagnoses provide a foundation for the evaluation of counseling effectiveness when the counselor considers whether the symptoms that led to the diagnosis have been reduced or alleviated and whether the client's functioning has improved (Hohenshil, 1993; Seligman & Moore, 1995).

Treatment Approaches

About 20% of children are estimated to have mental disorders with at least mild functional impairment. Mental health problems influence the way children and adolescents think, feel, and act. These problems can lead to school failure, school and family conflict, drug abuse, violence, or suicide. Cognitive-behavioral therapy that provides a systematic approach to addressing problem-solving and social skills shows promise in treating symptoms of disorders such as ODD, depression, and anxiety disorders (Hinshaw & Erhardt, 1991; Lochman, 1992). The premise is that mental disorders represent maladaptive behaviors that were learned and can be unlearned through behavior modification (Kazdin, 1996, 1997).

Treatment of Anxiety Disorders

For childhood phobias, contingency management has been most successful (Ollendick & King, 1998). Contingency management attempts to alter behavior by manipulating its consequences through the behavioral principles of shaping, positive reinforcement, and extinction. A cognitive-behavioral-therapy approach pioneered by Kendall and associates (Kendall, 1994; Kendell et al., 1992; Kendall, Hudson, Gosch, Flannery-Schroeder, & Suveg, 2008) treats anxiety with four components:

1. Recognizing anxious feelings
2. Clarifying cognitions in anxiety-provoking situations (i.e., understanding how cognitions can be distorted)
3. Developing a plan for coping
4. Evaluating the success of the coping strategy

Silverman & Hinshaw (2008) found the following treatments to be effective with children and adolescents:

- Individual cognitive behavioral therapy
- Group cognitive behavioral therapy (GCBT)
- Group cognitive behavioral therapy with parents
- Group cognitive behavioral therapy for social phobia
- Social effectiveness training for children with social phobia

Treatment of Depression

Relieving symptoms of depression in children and adolescents has promising results with self-control therapy, which consists of social skills training, assertiveness training, relaxation training, imagery, and cognitive restructuring (Stark, Reynolds, & Kaslow, 1987; Stark, Rouse, & Livingston, 1991). Adolescents who received cognitive-behavioral therapy had lower rates of depression, less self-reported depression, improvement in cognitions, and increased activity levels (Clark et al., 1992; Kaslow & Thompson, 1998; Lewinsohn, Clark, Rohde, Hops, & Seeley, 1996). Other treatments for depression include:

- Recognizing depressive feelings
- Increasing activity levels and a pleasant events schedule
- Positive self-talk
- Limiting inappropriate attention
- Using deliberate internal affirmations
- Increasing physical activity
- Relaxation and meditation
- Recalling past successes
- Saying no to unreasonable requests
- Teaching interpersonal communication skills
- Teaching decision-making and problem-solving skills
- Helping youths assume responsibility for choices and actions
- Encouraging self-disclosure, self-responsibility, and self-management

Treatment of Autism

The goal of treatment for autism is to promote the child's social interactions and language development and to minimize behaviors that interfere with the child's functioning and learning. Intensive, sustained special education programs and behavior therapy early in life can enhance the ability of the child to acquire language and to learn and relate to the environment.

Treatment of ADHD

Children with ADHD are unable to stop, look, listen, and use good judgment. Part of their treatment should include teaching and practicing appropriate social responses. Cognitive therapy and behavior therapy have been explored as potential adjuncts to medication because they focus on strategic problem-solving skills and age-appropriate behavior. Pelham and Fabiano (2008) found that three psychosocial or psycho-educational treatments were well established for treating ADHD in children and adolescents: behavioral parent training, behavioral classroom management, and summer treatment programs that focus on peer relationships in recreational settings at summer-camplike settings.

Treatment of Conduct Disorders

Intervening with high-risk children on social interaction, social competence, and academic help to reduce rates of failure can help prevent some of the negative educational consequences of conduct disorder in children (Johnson & Breckenridge, 1982). Training parents how to reduce problem behaviors through operant conditioning principles (i.e., rewarding desirable behaviors and ignoring or punishing deviant behaviors) has been successful (Spaccarelli, Coder, & Penman, 1992). Behavioral and cognitive therapies that provide the child with social skills and teach self-reflection, planning, decision making, and logical consequences could also render the child more socially competent.

Treatment of Eating Disorders

Most studies conducted with adult women find cognitive-behavior therapy and interpersonal therapy to be effective for bulimia and binge-eating disorders (Becker et al., 1999; Devlin, 1996; Fairburn, Jones, Peveler, Hope, & O'Connor, 1993). Individual and family multifaceted treatment has the greatest potential for treating eating disorders. Individual cognitive therapy can teach the adolescent to have a more realistic body image, and family counseling can be used to improve communication and expression of feeling. Group therapy can also be an integral component of a treatment plan.

A SYSTEM OF CARE

To treat the full range of problems associated with "serious emotional disturbances," a system of care in which multiple service sectors work in an organized and collaborative way to meet the mental health needs of these youths has been found to be the most effective. Collaboration that links services to vulnerable youths is the critical component. Professional school counselors have an important role to play in helping schools respond to the increasing number of students whose mental health needs place them at risk for school failure. Too many children and adolescents grow and develop in an environment characterized by poverty, alcohol and other drug abuse, family instability, and domestic, community, and school violence. Counseling, consultation, coordination, advocating, and teaming are the primary function of the school counselor. Many students and their families need multiple services.

Professional school counselors can further validate their own effectiveness by having a positive attitude about referring students and their families, treating referrals as a professional responsibility, and improving their referral procedures. This requires more collaborative relationships with school and community agencies. The benefits gained by collaboration include increased visibility, reduction of competition for diminishing resources, elimination of duplication of services, a diversified approach to solving problems, and a provision of services needed by students. Integrated service models in which several providers—school counselors, school psychologists, school social workers, community agencies—work together enhance the possibility for student success (see Table 11.4).

By working with the needs of the whole student through a comprehensive developmental counseling program focused on critical life skills, the professional school counselor emerges as a coordinator of the delivery of school-linked and community-linked services. The professional school counselor becomes the site-based professional best positioned and trained to coordinate comprehensive health and human service programs.

The American School Counselor Association supports the role of the professional school counselor as facilitator and change agent in local school community initiatives. The school counselor is the most appropriate educator to facilitate a "culture of collaboration" in the local community. However, this is increasingly difficult to do, given the large numbers of students that professional school counselors must currently serve. At the elementary level, there is hope for prevention and intervention initiatives, because group work can be planned and followed through. At the secondary level, however, most counselors play the role of crisis manager on a daily basis.

Also, the recommendation of the American Academy of Pediatrics for school-based mental health programs is very clear. Just as we should have programs and services for children with disabilities and children with great academic potential, we cannot ignore the growing population of children and adolescents with serious emotional disorders. The mental health program (preventive strategies and mental health services) should be coordinated with educational programs and other school-based health services. School social workers, professional school counselors, school psychologists, school nurses, and all mental health therapists should plan preventive and intervention strategies together with school administrators and teachers, as well as with families and community stakeholders such as employers, because ignoring the problem will have dire implications for the economy, society, welfare dependency, and future employee assistance programs. The American Academy of Pediatrics (2004) recommends the following:

1. "Preventive mental health programs should be developed that include a healthy social environment, clear rules, and expectations that are well publicized. Administrators, teachers and support staff (from school secretaries, to bus drivers, to custodians) should be trained to recognize stresses that may lead to mental health problems as well as early signs of mental illness and refer these students to trained professionals within the school setting."

TABLE 11.4 Coordinated Systems of Care for Children and Adolescents

Case management/service coordination	Protection and advocacy
Community-based psychiatric care	Psychiatric consultation
Counseling	Recreation therapy
Crisis outreach teams	Residential treatment
Crisis residential care	Respite care
Day treatment	Small therapeutic group care
Education/special education services	Support groups
Family support	Therapeutic foster care
Family-based in-home counseling	Transportation
Health services	Tutoring
Independent living supports	Vocational counseling

Source: Rosenblatt, A. (1998). Assessing the child and family outcomes of systems of care for youth with serious emotional disturbance. In Epstein, M. H., Kutash, K., & Duchnowski, A. (Eds.), *Outcomes for children and youth with behavioral and emotional disorders and their families*, 329–362, Austin, TX: PRO-ED, Inc.

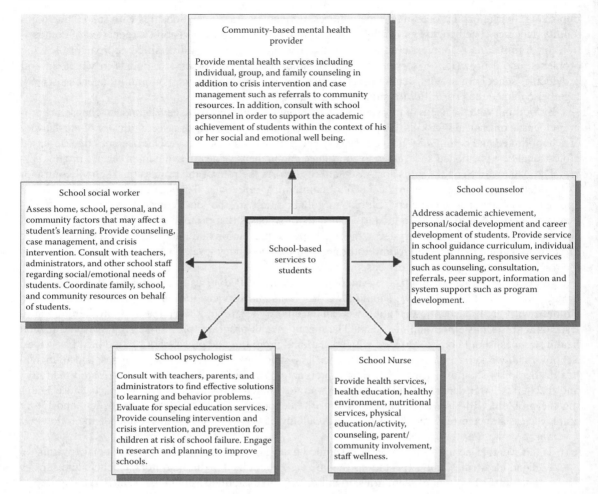

FIGURE 11.1 The roles of school-based personnel and community-based providers in the provision of mental health services.

Source: Center for Community Solutions, *School-Based Mental Health Tool Kit for Cuyahoga County School Districts,* Cleveland, OH, 2008.

2. "Mental health referrals (within the school system as well as to community-based professionals and agencies) should be coordinated by using written protocols, should be monitored for adherence, and should be evaluated for outcome effectiveness." Parents, guardians, group homes, foster care, and social service should be an integral part of this initiative.

3. "School-based specific diagnostic screenings, such as for depression, should be implemented at school only if they have been supported by peer-reviewed evidence of their effectiveness in that setting." One caveat from the author is that screenings should not be conducted unless there are affordable therapeutic services and enough clinicians to serve the population (i.e., rural, inner city, suburban).

4. "Roles of all the various mental health professionals who work on campus with students should be defined so that they are understood by students, families, all school staff members, and the mental health professionals themselves." Boundary issues among helping professionals continue to be a problem in many school and community settings.

5. "Group, individual, and family therapies should be included as schools arrange for direct services to be provided at school sites. Alternatively, referral systems should be available for each

of these modes of therapy so that students and families receive the mode of therapy most appropriate to their needs." These services can be school based, community based, or home based.

6. "It should be documented that mental health professionals providing services on site in schools (whether hired, contracted, or invited to school sites to provide services) have training specifically in child and adolescent mental health (appropriate for students' ages) and are competent to provide mental health services in the school setting."

7. "Private, confidential, and comfortable physical space should be provided at the school site. Often, this is not difficult for schools if mental health services are provided after school hours. Having school-based services should not preclude the opportunity for mental health services to be provided at nonschool sites for situations in which therapy at school for a student may be ill advised (e.g., a student who feels uncomfortable discussing a history of sexual abuse at the school setting). During extended school breaks, schools must provide continued access to mental health services."

8. "Staff members should be provided with opportunities to consult with a child psychiatrist or clinical psychologist (on or off the school site) so that they may explore specific difficult situations or student behaviors and review school policies, programs, and protocols related to mental health."

9. "Quality-assurance strategies should be developed for mental health services provided at school, and all aspects of the school health program should be evaluated, including satisfaction of the parent, student, third-party payers, and mental health professionals."

10. "Confidentiality of health information should be maintained, as mandated by law" (pp. 1839–1845).

CONCLUSION

This chapter provided a tremendous amount of insight into child and adolescent disorders, especially the implications of coexisting disorders, family dynamics, and peer influences. If the goal is to eliminate barriers to learning that have the potential to have long-term effects on a child's social, emotional, and cognitive skills, then it is critical to both establish a system of care and eliminate the stigma associated with mental illness and mental disorders. Ideally, developing a manageable culture of collaboration has the potential to unite students and their families, teachers and administrators, and schools and communities in a common vision and mission to prepare each student to be successful in school and to acquire the essential skills for successful employment, responsible citizenship, and lifelong learning.

Transcending and transforming barriers to collaboration requires five primary strategies:

1. *Multidisciplinary team meetings.* Professional school counselors can provide leadership in scheduling meetings to decide on prevention and remedial interventions for youth risk prevention (Adelman & Taylor, 2005; Flaherty et al., 1998).

2. *Cross-cultural training.* Train all mental health staff to be sensitive to race, ethnicity, class, and gender to reduce the level of racial and cultural tension in an effort to foster open and honest dialogue (Weist et al., 2005).

3. *Cross-disciplinary training and supervision.* When this takes place among school and community organizations, it can facilitate the development of a common language and change the hierarchy and turf issues that often exist between helping professionals (Flaherty et al., 1998; Flaherty & Osher, 2003).

4. *An open and flexible organizational culture.* This is especially important with helping professionals who share the goal of helping children but have different methods of achieving the goal.

TABLE 11.5   Guidelines for Mental Health in the Schools

1. **General domains for intervention in addressing students' mental health issues**
   1.1 Ensuring academic success and also promoting healthy cognitive, social, and emotional development and resilience including promoting opportunities to enhance school performance and protective factors; fostering development of assets and general wellness; enhancing responsibility and integrity, self-efficacy, social and working relationships, self-evaluation and self-direction, personal safety and safe behavior, health maintenance, effective physical functioning, careers and life style roles, as well as creativity.
   1.2 Addressing barriers to student learning and performance (including educational and psychosocial problems, external stressors, and psychological disorders).
   1.3 Providing social/emotional support for students and their families, as well as administration, faculty, and support staff.
2. **Major areas of concern related to barriers to student learning**
   2.1 Addressing common educational and psychosocial problems (e.g.. learning problems; language difficulties, attention problems; school adjustment; other life transition problems; attendance problems and dropouts; social, interpersonal, and familial problems; conduct and behavior problems; delinquency and gang-related problems; anxiety problems; affect and mood problems; sexual and/or physical abuse; neglect; substance abuse; psychological reactions to physical status and sexual activity).
   2.2 Countering external stressors (e.g., reactions to objective or perceived stress/demands/crises/deficits at home, at school, and in the community; inadequate basic resources such as food, clothing, shelter, and a sense of security; inadequate support systems; hostile and violent conditions).
   2.3 Teaching, serving, and accommodating disorders/disabilities (e.g., learning disabilities; attention deficit hyperactivity disorder; school phobia; anxiety disorders; anorexia nervosa/bulimia; suicidal or homicidal behavior; post-traumatic stress disorder; substance abuse disorders; special-education-designated disorders such as emotional disturbance and developmental disabilities).
3. **Type of functions provided related to individuals, groups, and families**
   3.1 Assessment for initial (first-level) screening of problems, as well as for diagnosis and intervention planning (including focus on needs and assets).
   3.2 Referral, triage, and monitoring/management of care.
   3.3 Direct services and instruction (e.g., primary prevention programs, including enhancement of wellness through instruction, skills development, school counseling, advocacy, schoolwide programs to foster safe caring climates, and liaison connections between school and home; crisis intervention, management, and assistance, including psychological first aid, prereferral interventions; accommodations to allow for differences and disabilities, transition, and follow-up programs; short- and longer-term treatment, remediation, and rehabilitation).
   3.4 Coordination, development, and leadership related to school-owned programs, services, resources, and systems—toward evolving a comprehensive, multifaceted, and integrated continuum of programs and services.
   3.5 Consultation, supervision, and in-service instruction with a transdisciplinary focus.
   3.6 Enhancing connections with and involvement of home, community resources, and faith communities.
4. **Timing and nature of problem-oriented interventions**
   4.1 Primary prevention.
   4.2 Intervening early after the onset of problems.
   4.3 Interventions for severe, pervasive, and/or chronic problems.
5. **Assuring quality of interventions**
   5.1 Systems and interventions are monitored and improved as necessary.
   5.2 Programs and services constitute a comprehensive, multifaceted continuum.
   5.3 Interventionists have appropriate knowledge, skills, and training for their roles and functions and provide recommendations for continuing professional development.

TABLE 11.5   Guidelines for Mental Health in the Schools (continued)

5.4   School-owned (which are also public-owned) programs and services are coordinated and integrated.

5.5   School-owned (which are also public-owned) programs and services are connected to home, community, and faith-based resources.

5.6   Programs and services are integrated with instructional and governance/management components at schools.

5.7   Programs and services are available, accessible, advertised, and attractive.

5.8   Empirically supported, evidence-based, and best-practices prevention and interventions are used when applicable.

5.9   Differences among students/families are appropriately accounted for (e.g., diversity, disability, developmental levels, motivational levels, strengths, weaknesses).

5.10 Legal and ethical considerations are appropriately accounted for (e.g., mandated services, mandatory reporting, confidentiality, privacy, and privileged communication).

5.11 Contexts for intervention are appropriate (e.g., office, clinic, classroom, home).

6. Outcome evaluation and accountability

6.1   Short-term outcome data are systematically collected.

6.2   Long-term outcome data are systematically collected.

6.3   Data results are reported to key stakeholders (i.e., school board members, parents, community leaders) to enhance and to garner support for intervention quality).

Source: Adapted from Policy Leadership Cadre for Mental Health in Schools, *Mental Health in Schools: Guidelines, Models, Resources and Policy Considerations,* Center for Mental Health at UCLA, Los Angeles, 2001. Reprinted with permission.

5. *Instituting standardized procedures.* Standardized methods for collecting and reviewing information can reduce potential professional conflicts and accelerate the process of developing and providing best-practice interventions. Inherently, school counselors are in the best position to ensure that processes and procedures are institutionalized.

As a change agent, human relations specialist, facilitator of team building, resource broker of services, information and promoter of positive student outcomes, the professional school counselor develops and nurtures collaborative relationships by facilitating change through programs of prevention and intervention for all students. Collaborative efforts, when properly initiated and carefully nurtured, will improve school counseling programs and promote student success and well-being. See Table 11.5 for guidelines from the Policy Leadership Cadre for Mental Health in the Schools. Table 11.6 lists medications typically given to children and adolescents with mental health disorders.

TABLE 11.6   Common Medications Given to Children and Adolescents

TRADE NAME	GENERIC NAME	FDA APPROVED AGE
Combination antipsychotic and antidepressant medications		
Abilify	aripiprazole	13–17 for schizophrenia and bipolar disorder
Haldol	haloperidol	3 and older
Orap (for Tourette's syndrome)	primozide	12 and older
Resperdal	risperidone	13 and older for schizophrenia; 10 and older for bipolar mania and mixed episodes; 5–16 for irritability associated with autism
[generic only]	thioridazine	2 and older

continued

TABLE 11.6   Common Medications Given to Children and Adolescents (continued)

TRADE NAME	GENERIC NAME	FDA APPROVED AGE
Antidepressant medications (also used for anxiety)		
Anafranil (tricyclic)	clomipramine	10 and older (for OCD only)
Luvox (SSRI)	fluvoxamine	8 and older (for OCD only)
Prozac (SSRI)	fluoxetine	8 and older
Sinequan (tricyclic)	doxepin	12 and older
Tofranil (tricyclic)	imipramine	6 and older (for bedwetting)
Zoloft (SSRI)	sertraline	6 and older (for OCD only)
Mood stabilizing and anticonvulsant medications		
Depakote	divalproex sodium (valproic acid)	2 and older (for seizures)
Eskalith	lithium carbonate	12 and older
[generic only]	lithium citrate	12 and older
Lithobid	lithium carbonate	12 and older
Tegretol	carbamazepine	any age (for seizures)
Trileptal	oxcarbazephine	4 and older
ADHD medications (all of these ADHD medications are stimulants, except Strattera.)		
Adderall	amphetamine	3 and older
Adderall XR	amphetamine (extended release)	6 and older
Concerta	methylphenidate (long lasting)	6 and older
Daytrana	methylphenidate patch	6 and older
Desoxyn	methamphetamine	6 and older
Dexedrine	dextroamphetamine	3 and older
Dextrostat	dextroamphetamine	3 and older
Focalin	dexmethylphenidate	6 and older
Focalin XR	dexmethylphenidate (extended release)	6 and older
Metadate ER	methylphenidate (extended release)	6 and older
Metadate CD	methylphenidate (extended release)	6 and older
Methylin	methylphenidate (oral solution and chewable tablets)	6 and older
Ritalin	methylphenidate	6 and older
Ritalin SR	methylphenidate (extended release)	6 and older
Ritalin LA	methylphenidate (long-acting)	6 and older
Strattera	atomoxetine	6 and older
Vyvanse	lisdexamfetamine dimesylate	6 and older

Source: Adapted from National Institute of Mental Health, "Alphabetical List of Medications," 2011, retrieved from http://www.nimh.nih.gov/health/publications/mental-health-medications/alphabetical-list-of-medications.shtml.

Real Counseling in the Schools

12

Implementing Solution-Focused Brief Counseling, Problem-Solving Groups, Psychoeducational Groups, and Student Success Skills to Meet the Needs of All Students

---

SOLUTION-FOCUSED BRIEF COUNSELING

The potential mismatch between professional school counselors' training and the realities of counseling in schools can foster a feeling of inadequacy and frustration when trying to meet the needs of all students within the reality of fiscal constraints and large student caseloads. Professional school counselors frequently report that they are overwhelmed by a number of factors that limit their counseling effectiveness because for decades professional school counselors have allowed themselves to be ancillary and fragmented services in the schools rather than an integral part of school improvement efforts and their role in assisting to close the achievement gap between minority and children of poverty.

Factors that impede professional school counselor effectiveness include heavy caseloads, inadequate resources, lack of professional development in the *ASCA (2005a) National Model*, and the emerging diversity among student populations with multiproblem families that often leave students and teachers as well as administrators feeling powerless to effect significant change with limited resources to remediate debilitating situations that are out of their control. One viable counseling alternative is to integrate the Solution-Focused Brief Counseling (SFBC) model into the professional school counseling program.

Professional school counselors and therapists have reported using SFBC with various clients in diverse settings, including community mental health centers, state and private hospitals, private psychiatric practices, and schools (de Shazer, 1985; de Shazer & Berg, 1997; David-Ferdon & Kaslow, 2008). SFBC has already been proven beneficial in schools (Murphy, 1997; Metcalf, 2008; Cooley, 2009).

Solution-Focused Brief Counseling was originally conceptualized by Steve de Shazer and colleagues (de Shazer et al., 1986; de Shazer, 1991, 1994; Walter & Peller, 1992) as a set of clinical assumptions and strategies in response to the question "What works in counseling?" SFBC emphasizes wellness: individuals are seen as having the resources to solve their own problems in a practical, immediate way, and problems are not seen as evidence of an underlying pathology (Berg & Miller, 1992; Fisch, Weakland, & Segal, 1982). The model is future oriented and solution focused to resolve current complaints rather than to find the cause of the problem. The professional school counselor's job, therefore, is to help get the solution started and then "get out of the way" (Berg & Miller, 1992; de Shazer, 1985). SFBC is also cooperative (Berg & Miller, 1992). Table 12.1 captures the characteristics of SFBC chronologically.

Professionals in the field of counseling and education have benefited from using the SFBC model in terms of their perceptions of professional efficacy, the time constraints on service delivery, and a clear sense of increased professional direction in the therapeutic process. The practical nature of the model can offer professional school counselors a usable and succinct, yet effective and highly practical approach to meeting the various needs of students by enhancing their coping skills, focusing on solutions to problems rather than magnifying problems, and looking at problems and life circumstances through a deficit lens.

TABLE 12.1 Characteristics of Solution-Focused Brief Counseling

Koss and Shiang (1994)
1. The focus of counseling is clearly stated and maintained throughout the process.
2. There is a high level of counselor activity and involvement.
3. The counselor remains receptive and flexible.
4. Interventions are introduced in a timely manner.
5. The expectations of termination are addressed throughout the counseling process.

Bloom (1992, 1997)
1. Interventions are introduced immediately.
2. There is a high level of counselor involvement.
3. Specific, realistic, but limited goals are established.
4. A clear focus for counseling change is identified and maintained.
5. A solution-focused limit for the counseling process is set.

Bruce (1995)
1. The school counselor and student establish a strong working alliance.
2. The school counselor recognizes and uses the student's strengths and resources.
3. A high level of counselor and student affective and behavioral involvement is achieved.
4. Counselor and student establish clear and concrete goals.

Metcalf (2008)
1. Using a nonpathological approach makes problems solvable.
2. There is no need to attempt to understand or promote insight to solve problems.
3. It is not necessary to know a great deal about the complaint.
4. Students, teachers, administrators, and parents have complaints, not symptoms.
5. The student defines the goal.
6. Motivation is a key ingredient for change.
7. There is no such thing as resistance when all cooperate.
8. If it works, don't fix it; if it doesn't, do something different.
9. Focus on the possible and the changeable.
10. Rapid change is possible.
11. Every complaint pattern contains some sort of exception.
12. Look at problems differently and redescribe them. (pp. 16–23)

Source: Metcalf, L., *Counseling toward Solutions: A Practical Solution-Focused Program for Working with Students, Teachers, and Parents,* (2nd ed.), Jossey-Bass, San Francisco, 2008.

The SFBC model can be used with students as well as parents. Professional school counselors perceive themselves to be more effective when they used this model. Helping professionals trained in the use of SFBC would be an effective first line of defense in any crisis situation affecting both the physical and psychological well-being of children and adolescents in schools. SFBC has the following attributes:

- Goals are chosen in part by the student.
- Attention is directed at one focused issue.
- Counseling is directed at clarifying feelings, thoughts, and behavior manifestations in the here and now. Diagnosis, history taking, and exploration of the problem are minimized.
- Emphasis is placed on the student identifying the change that is needed or the coping goals related to the problem.
- The student is encouraged to both actively search for exceptions to the problem and identify strengths in his or her coping repertoire.

The stages of SFBC proceeds as follows:

Stage 1: Define the problem (for example, student is experiencing panic attacks).
- Communicate an expectancy of change.
- Reframe the problem situation as normal and modifiable. This can be accomplished by using systematic questions. For example, the presenting problem may be that the student is experiencing "panic attacks in his or her English class."
- Systematic questions include:
  - "What is different about the times when you are *not* having a panic attack?"
  - "Who else noticed your panic attack?"
  - "How do you respond when you have a panic attack during a presentation?"

Stage 2: Establish treatment goals.
- The process of setting goals initiates the intervention. Critical questions include:
  - "What will be the first signs that things are moving in the right direction?"
  - "Who will be the first to notice?"
  - "What do you need to do to make it happen more?"

Stage 3: Design the intervention. This involves three integral steps:
- *Reframing the problem* in a more positive light to provide a mechanism that encourages change.
- *Utilization* of whatever the student presented, including a rigid belief system, behaviors, demands, or characteristics to motivate the student to act differently.
- *Assigning a strategic task* to be carried out between sessions. The primary goal is to get the student to do something different to fulfill the goals that were outlined in the first stage. This homework assignment the professional school counselor gives the counselee to complete before the next meeting is also called the Formula First Session Task (FFST). For example: "Between now and the next meeting, I would like you to observe what happens in your family, life, friends that you want to continue to happen" (de Shazer, 1985, p. 137). The goal of the FFST is to promote optimism by framing for the student that positive things will happen and change will occur.

Stage 4: Deliver a strategic task.
- The task is clearly outlined. The student writes certain instructions down that may be critical to the task performance and completion.

Stage 5: Emphasize positive new behavior.
- This stage is enhanced by questions that encourage positive change and solutions:
  - "What is happening that you would like to continue to happen?"
  - "Who else will notice your progress?"
  - "How did it make things go differently?"

- The most engaging intervention is termed the "miracle question" (de Shazer, 1991): "Imagine tonight while you sleep, a miracle happens and your problem is solved. What will be happening the next day, and how will you know your problem has been solved?" Often the answers are specific and concrete, because the focus is on what will be *present* when the problem is *absent*.

Stage 6: Terminate the intervention. Typically, the student recognizes problem resolution and initiates termination.

One way to change self-defeating, self-deprecating behavior is to reframe the presenting problem into "solution talk." Table 12.2 lists some common complaints experienced in schools as problem talk and then reframed as solution talk.

This simple approach has some enduring interventions because it empowers students to maximize their own resources to effect change. This model integrates theory and technique by providing a comprehensive, empirical approach from proponents of strategic and solution-focused counseling. Professional school counselors have a growing interest in becoming more efficient and effective with students, especially with growing caseloads and increasing diversity among student populations.

FOSTERING ACADEMIC DEVELOPMENT THROUGH LARGE AND SMALL GROUP INTERVENTIONS

Research-based resources and structured frameworks for intervening with early adolescents who are in a critical developmental phase that may hinder or enhance their academic domain are currently available in the literature, but they have not yet been systematically implemented in middle school (Brown, Anfara, & Roney, 2004). With the passage of the No Child Left Behind Act of 2001, the large disparity in achievement between minority and economically disadvantaged students and their white counterparts has brought this educational travesty to forefront of reform initiatives among professional school counselors (e.g., ASCA, 2005a; Carey & Dimmitt, 2004; Dahir & Stone, 2003b; Fitch & Marshall, 2004; Gysbers, 2003; House & Hayes, 2002; Lapan, 2005; Paisley & Hayes, 2003).

Comprehensive school counseling programs (CSCP) can have a significant impact on the academic development and the learning mastery of early adolescents (Ripley et al., 2003). Counselors have both a

TABLE 12.2 Problem Talk Versus Solution Talk

PROBLEM TALK	SOLUTION TALK
Hyperactive	Very energetic at times
Attention deficit disorder	Short attention span sometimes
Anger issues	Gets upset sometimes
Depressed	Sad or unhappy sometimes
Oppositional defiant	Argues a point often
Rebellious	Prefers to develop his or her own way
Family problems	Worries about home life
Disruptive	Often forgets the rules
Shy	Takes time to know people
Negative peer pressure	Allows other people influence him or her
Feelings of rejection	People forget to notice him or her
Isolating	Prefers to be alone

Source: Metcalf, L., *Counseling toward Solutions: A Practical Solution-Focused Program for Working with Students, Teachers and Parents*, Jossey-Bass, San Francisco, 2008.

professional and ethical responsibility to establish academic development and learning as a foundation of their CSCP.

Key developmental domains are outlined in the *ASCA's National Model*, which describes how professional school counselors can "become catalyst for educational change," "call attention to situations within the schools that hinder students' academic success," and "use effective strategies to meet stated student success and achievement" (ASCA, 2005a, pp. 15–16; Sink, 2005a). In addition, from an ethical standpoint, professional school counselors' role statement (ASCA, 2004b) and ethical standards (ASCA, 2004a) posit that professional school counselors must effectively assist students to pursue their academic and educational goals, as well as comprehensive program competencies associated with this developmental domain, to enhance the learning process and academic achievement of *all* students (ASCA, 2005a; Sink, 2005b). Table 12.3 summarizes helpful middle school counseling interventions and their effects on student achievement.

Professional school counselors have the responsibility to focus on educating students in critical academic skill areas (Lapan, Kardash, & Turner, 2002; National Middle School Association Research Committee, 2003; Paisley & Hayes, 2003). Following a CSCP, the foundation for interventions should embrace the five *C's*—collaboration, coordination, consultation, individual and group counseling, and classroom guidance—especially as they correspond with academic development and learning (ASCA, 2005a). Large- and small-group interventions should help students develop self-regulation, that is, how to self-manage and self-monitor their learning (Rudolph, Lambert, Clark, & Kurlakowsky, 2001), as well as ways of using memory strategies, seeking information, planning and organizing their learning activities, and studying (Lapan, Kardash, et al., 2002). Professional school counselor–directed activities should also include topics such as enhancing achievement, motivation, self-efficacy, social problem solving, listening, teamwork, and positive learning attitudes (McGannon, Carey, & Dimmitt, 2005; Sears, 2005; Webb et al., 2005; Whiston, 2003). Finally, Student Success Skills (Brigman & Campbell, 2003; Brigman, Campbell, & Webb, 2004; Brigman & Webb, 2004; Campbell & Brigman, 2005; Webb et al., 2005) and Solution Shop (Cook & Kaffenberger, 2003) are research-based curricula that will be discussed further in this chapter.

SOLUTION SHOP: A DATA-DRIVEN COUNSELING AND STUDY-SKILLS PROGRAM BASED ON SOLUTION-FOCUSED COUNSELING STRATEGIES

Solution Shop is a systematic counseling and study-skills program specifically designed to address the academic needs of minority students and economically disadvantaged students who are entangled in the disparities of the achievement gap. One key indicator of perpetuating the achievement gap is not completing algebra in middle school. Students who have not completed this pivotal course are at a serious disadvantage in high school, because they lack the preparation that would qualify them for more rigorous course work at the high school level. This, in turn, puts students at a disadvantage on the SAT, which requires knowledge of algebra and geometry, and fuels the achievement gap, perpetuating the disparity between the achievement of white and Asian students and other minority students and children of poverty.

This initiative is consistent with the new role for professional school counselors. Solution Shop combines all the necessary components of an exemplary school counseling program:

(a) program development is based on an analysis of school data; (b) the school leadership, administration, school counseling department and teachers support the development and implementation of the program; (c) the program is based on counseling theory; (d) the program advocates for underserved students; and (e) program effectiveness is continually being assessed and evaluated. (Cook & Kaffenberger, 2005, p. 118)

TABLE 12.3   Summary of Helpful Middle School Counseling Interventions and Their Effects on Student Achievement

RESEARCH REVIEWED	ACTIVITIES COLLEGIALITY INTERVENTIONS LEADERSHIP	KEY INSTRUCTIONAL OUTCOMES	QUALITIES OF HIGH-PERFORMING MIDDLE SCHOOLS		
			ACADEMIC	EMPHASIS	AFFILIATION
Gerler & Herndon (1993)	Classroom guidance on school success behaviors	High school success awareness ratings	X	X	X
Dunham & Frome (2003); Hughes & Karp (2004); Mau (1995); Peterson et al. (1999)	Classroom guidance on academic planning	Enhanced course planning	X		
Fouad (1995)	Classroom guidance on career and academic development	Higher teacher ratings of students' math and science achievement and effort	X	X	X
Edmondson & White (1998); Lapan et al. (2001); Vargis (2004); Cook & Kaffenberger (2003); Fitch & Marshall (2004)	Systematic interventions programs (e.g., tutoring, counseling, coordination, consultation)	Improvement on a variety of measures related to academic development (e.g., self-report surveys, higher GPAs)	X	X	
Brigman & Campbell (2003); Webb et al. (2005)	Group counseling using Student Success Skills program curriculum	Higher math and reading standardized test scores	X	X	X

Source: Adapted from Brown, K. M., Anfara, V. A., Jr., & Roney, K., *Education and Urban Society, 36*(4), 428–456, 2004, as cited in Sink, C. A., *Professional School Counseling, 9*(2), 128–135, 2005b. Reprinted with permission.

The specific goals of the Solution Shop program are to:

(a) introduce and reinforce study skills; (b) establish specific academic goals; (c) involve parents or caregivers; (d) monitor progress on a daily, weekly, bi-quarterly basis; (e) develop a positive attitude about academic achievement and understand future benefits; and (f) provide encouragement. (Cook & Kaffenberger, 2003, p. 119)

Solution Shop procedures are as follows: Ten students with two or more failing grades are chosen for the program. They meet with the program director once a week for nine weeks during an elective class. Each student in the program develops individual academic and personal goals. Students participate in solution-focused group counseling and study-skills instruction for a portion of the class period and receive individualized tutoring during the remainder of the period. Solution-focused counseling is future-oriented, positive focused, and its goal is to use strengths to solve problems (Metcalf, 2008). Solution-focused strategies such as scaling are used to review student progress. Program leaders also teach communication skills such as "I" messages and specific study skills such as using a homework notebook.

According to the *ASCA's National Model* for School Counseling Programs, a comprehensive school counseling program should be data driven (ASCA, 2005a) and demonstrate how students are different because of what professional school counselors do. Solution Shop uses data already available at the school such as grade-point average, report cards, attendance records, truancy records, achievement scores, and behavioral referrals to understand and intervene with academic issues using counseling theory such as solution-focused therapy to deliver a program.

THE EFFICACY OF SMALL-GROUP COUNSELING IN THE SCHOOLS

The school setting is a microcosm of group work. Formal and informal groups already exist for the purpose of furthering the educational process. Groups include task-oriented groups to complete projects; cooperative learning groups; groups to organize and plan social events; groups to learn new athletic skills; extracurricular groups such as debate, drama, newspaper, and yearbook; groups to socialize; assessment groups to scrutinize curricula; and groups undertaking community projects with civic organizations, to name a few.

Small-group counseling should be an integral component of the professional school counseling program, because most professional school counselors may not see a counselee on an individual basis more than three times during the calendar year. Assistance provided is usually brief, with the presenting problem resolved contingent upon counselor expertise, the counselee's willingness to change, and the resources available. Critical concerns in a school and community setting predominantly focus upon academic, career, or personal and social concerns. The following components are necessary for the group process to work effectively:

- *Belonging.* Young people need to feel that they are sincerely welcomed, that no one objects to their presence, and that they are valued for who they are, rather than for what they have or where they have been.
- *Planning.* Young people need to be involved in planning the ground rules and goals of the group.
- *Expectations.* Young people need to know in some detail what is expected of them. Their role in the group, their level of involvement, and issues of confidentiality are important. This

information should routinely be made available to parents, teachers, and administrators to garner support for the program.

- *Goals.* Young people need to feel that their goals are within reach, that goals can be broken down into more manageable increments, and that they can effect change.
- *Responsibility.* Young people need to have responsibilities that are both challenging and within the range of their abilities. They need to stretch for improvement and growth. This can easily be accomplished in the school, because students are surrounded for the most part by caring adults such as teachers, club sponsors, coaches, and other support personnel. Sometimes the school is the only haven of safety for students, especially if they come from unstable families, chaotic, violent communities, or attachment disorder.
- *Progress.* Young people need to experience some successes and see some progress toward what they want to achieve. Milestones should be celebrated and shared with family and peers.

Group counseling helps group members learn new and more effective ways of dealing with their problematic issues and behavior and teaches and encourages them to practice and utilize these new behaviors with current and future problems of a similar nature (Association for Specialists in Group Work, 1998). The efficacy of small-group counseling for helping people change attitudes, perspectives, values, and behavior is well documented (Dyer & Vriend, 1977; Egan, 1982; Ohlsen, 1977; Yalom & Leszez, 2005; Berg, Landreth, & Fall, 2006; Brigman & Goodman, 2008). Young people, however, need to gain a sense of trust, confidence, and ownership in the group in order to feel secure and to remain loyal to the group process.

Many helping professionals want to be able to identify group skills and activities to provide for structure and accountability of service delivery to all students. Gill and Barry (1982) provide one of the most comprehensive classifications of counseling skills for the group process. Such a classification system can assist the professional school counselor by delineating an organized, operational definition of group-focused facilitation skills.

A classification of specific, group-focused facilitation skills has a number of significant benefits: clear objectives, visible procedures, competency-based accountability, and measurable outcomes. Evidence-based programs are critical to promote positive outcomes and accountability. This information is an important component of the group process that needs to be shared with administrators, teachers, support staff, and parents. Gill and Barry (1982) suggest the following selection criteria for building a system of group-focused counseling skills:

- *Appropriateness.* The behavior can reasonably be attributed to the role and function of a group counselor;
- *Definability.* The behavior can be described in terms of human performances and outcomes;
- *Observability.* Experienced as well as inexperienced observers can identify the behavior when it occurs. Different people in different settings can repeat the behavior;
- *Measurability.* Objective recording of both the frequency and quality of the behavior can occur with a high degree of agreement among observers;
- *Developmental appropriateness.* The behavior can be placed within the context of a progressive relationship with other skills, all contributing to movement of the group toward its goals. The effectiveness of the behaviors at one stage in the counseling process is dependent on the effectiveness of the skills used at earlier stages; and
- *Group focus.* The target of the behavior is the group, or more than one participant. The behavior is often related to an interaction between two or more participants. The purpose of the group is to facilitate multiple interactions among participants to encourage shared responsibility for helping to promote participation or to invite cooperative problem solving and decision making. (Gill & Barry 1982, pp. 24–29).

Furthermore, the group setting is a very pragmatic approach to use with adjustment concerns of children and adolescents. It allows them to share anxieties in a secure environment and to enhance their self-sufficiency, resiliency, and mastery over their environment. In addition, accountable group counseling programs have several key components that must be addressed concerning the use of data, program delivery, intervention, and evaluation:

1. Professional school counseling programs should be developed according to assessed needs at each individual school. Essentially, "one size fits all" no longer fits in today's diverse society (Johnson & Johnson, 2003).
2. Professional school counselors in this age of accountability are mandated to use and select interventions that are evidence based, that is, demonstrate empirically that they make a difference in student behavior (Carey & Dimmitt, 2006).
3. Professional school counselors are required by their knowledge of human growth and development to use valid and reliable assessment procedures to evaluate their activities and interventions (Steen & Kaffenberger, 2007; Studer, Oberman, & Womack, 2006).
4. Professional school counselors must not only collect and report data for demonstrating program improvement, but must also report their findings to important stakeholders such as teachers, administrators, and school board members. Professional school counselors are notorious for working hard to meet the needs of all students, but unfortunately fail to share their success and outcomes with others (Rowell, 2006).

TYPES OF COUNSELING GROUPS

The lack of a required sequentially developmental program in self-understanding and human behavior testifies to an educational paradox; we have taught children almost everything in school except to understand and accept themselves and to function more effectively in human relationships.

Don Dinkmeyer

Counseling groups can be categorized into three types:

1. Developmental/primary prevention groups
2. Problem-centered/structured intervention groups
3. Psychoeducational groups

Developmental groups are *primary prevention counseling*. Problem-centered groups are *structured intervention counseling*. Psychoeducational groups provide education and skill building in social, emotional, and cognitive domains.

Primary Prevention Groups

Developmental/primary prevention counseling is a more proactive approach to averting dysfunctional or debilitating behavior by providing critical social, emotional, and cognitive skills that promote healthy functioning. "Preventive counseling exists along a continuum with remedial and developmental counseling" (Conyne, 1994, p. 2). Multiple strategies can be organized to reduce risk factors and promote protective factors (Werner, 1982). Proponents contend that prevention strategies address behaviors such as self-esteem, social support, conflict resolution, problem solving, decision making, communication, and peer-pressure resistance training to reduce social pathogens (Albee, 1982, 1986; Albee & Ryan-Finn, 1993; Benard & Marshall, 1997; Benard, 1996a, 1996b, 1996c; Botvin & Tortu, 1988; Garland & Zigler, 1993).

Acquiring the desired competencies, according to Conyne (1994; Englander-Golden et al., 1996), will prevent potential problems in the future. As an example, a goal for date rape prevention might be how to negotiate clearly one's wants and needs with a date. A goal for substance abuse prevention might be how to say no without losing your friends. Preventive counseling offers a promising approach for professional school counselors in helping to stop or reduce the alarming swell of human dysfunction in contemporary society. It is employed before the fact with nondisturbed persons to promote healthy functioning and prevent the manifestations of dysfunctions. "Preventive counseling is directed by an intentional process of program development and implementation" (Conyne, 1994, p. 9).

The purpose of developmental/primary prevention groups is to provide information and skills for more accurate decision making and to prevent developmental issues from becoming a counseling concern. Descriptions of developmental/primary prevention groups gleaned from the literature include the following:

- Listening skills (Merritt & Walley, 1977; Rogers, 1980)
- Dealing with feelings (Omizo, Hershberger et al., 1988; Vernon, 1989)
- Social skills and interpersonal relationships (Barrow & Hayashi, 1990; Brown & Brown, 1982; Cantor & Wilkinson, 1982; Johnson, 1995; Keat, Metzgar, Raykovitz, & McDonald, 1985; Morganett, 1990; Rose, 1987; Vernon, 1989; Thompson, 1998, 2000, 2006; DeRosier, 2002, 2004, 2007)
- Academic achievement, motivation, and school success (Ames & Archer, 1988; Blum & Jones, 1993; Campbell & Myrick, 1990; Morganett, 1990; Chilcoat, 1988; Gage, 1990; Gerler, Kinney, & Anderson, 1985; Thompson, E. C., 1987; Thompson, 2006)
- Self-concept/personal identity/self-esteem (Canfield & Wells, 1976; Morganett, 1990; Omizo & Omizo, 1987, 1988a, 1988b; Tessier, 1982; Vernon, 1989; Thompson, 1998, 2000, 2006).
- Career awareness, exploration, and planning (McKinlay & Bloch, 1989; Rogala, Lambert, & Verhage, 1991; Super, 1990)
- Problem solving and decision making (Bergin, 1991; Vernon, 1989; Thompson, 1998, 2000, 2006).
- Communication and assertiveness (Alberti & Emmons, 1974; Donald, Carlisle, & Woods, 1979; Huey, 1983; Morganett, 1990; Myrick, 2003b; Thompson, 1998, 2000, 2006).
- Positive behavior support (Sugai & Homer, 2006; Frey, Lingo, & Nelson, 2008; Hendley & Lock, 2007; Thompson, 1998, 2000, 2006).

The developmental tasks of children and adolescents are to achieve a sense of identity, autonomy, and differentiation from family of origin. For youths to accomplish this life transition, they need to acquire skills, knowledge, and attitudes that may be classified into two broad categories: those involving self-development and those involving relating to other people. Inherent to this process are the critical need to belong, the need to communicate and be understood, the need to be respected, the need to be held in high esteem, the need to be assertive, the need to communicate effectively, and the need to resolve conflicts. Preventive counseling with primary prevention, such as developmental groups, help youths actualize their full potential.

The developmental task may serve as a catalyst or bridge between an individual's needs and environmental demands, and the total framework of such tasks provides a comprehensive network of important psychosocial learnings essential for living and well-being. Table 12.4 provides a hierarchy of developmental needs.

Problem-Centered, Structured Intervention Counseling

Problem-centered groups are initiated to meet the needs of counselees who are exhibiting dysfunctional or self-defeating behavior. The stressors from a student's particular circumstance may interfere with or hinder normal functioning. Professional school counselors must make a concerted effort to systematically examine the obstacles within their school environment that may be barriers to learning (Brigman,

TABLE 12.4 Hierarchy of Developmental Needs: Conditions of Deficiency and Fulfillment

NEED HIERARCHY	CONDITIONS OF DEFICIENCY	CONDITIONS OF FULFILLMENT	ILLUSTRATION
Self-actualization	• Alienation • Defenses • Absence of meaning in life • Boredom • Routine living • Limited activities	• Healthy curiosity • Understanding • Realization of potentials • Work that is pleasurable and embodies values • Creative living	Realizing what friendship really is or feeling awe at the wonder of nature
Esteem	• Feeling incompetence • Negativism • Feeling of inferiority	• Confidence • Sense of mastery • Positive self-regard • Self-respect • Self-extension	Receiving an award for an outstanding performance on some subject
Love	• Self-consciousness • Feeling of being unwanted • Feeling of worthlessness • Emptiness • Loneliness • Isolation • Incompleteness	• Free expression of emotions • Sense of wholeness • Sense of warmth • Renewed sense of life • Strength • Sense of growing together	Experiencing total acceptance in a love relationship
Safety	• Insecurity • Yearning • Sense of loss • Fear • Worry • Rigidity	• Security • Comfort • Balance • Poise • Calm • Tranquility	Being secure in a full-time job
Physiological	• Hunger, thirst • Tension • Fatigue • Illness • Lack of proper shelter	• Relaxation • Release from tension • Experiences of pleasure from senses • Physical well-being • Comfort	Feeling satisfied after a good meal

Webb, & Campbell, 2007; Brunner & Lewis, 2007; Kaffenberger & Young, 2007). For example, victims of bullying behaviors often exhibit psychological distress, including poor social adjustment and isolation, which can impair their ability to learn because of preoccupation with fears about their own safety (Bauman & Del Rio, 2006; Jacobsen & Bauman, 2007). The group experience allows counselees to handle more serious concerns rather than resolving typical developmental problems. Group members share anxieties in a secure environment and attempt to empower individuals to take action on their decisions by providing support, feedback, and unconditional acceptance.

With the assistance of the group, members try out new behaviors and develop and implement strategies to resolve their problems. Young people invariably turn to their peers for needed support, understanding, and advice. A problem-centered intervention group provides young people with experiences that enhance self-awareness and increase problem-solving and decision-making skills, so they can better cope with real-life situations. Themes for intervention groups range from dealing with physical or sexual abuse to coping with loss or adjustment concerns, such as parental divorce. Problem-centered intervention topics include the following:

- Obesity, bulimia, and anorexia nervosa (Williamson & Davis, 1990; DaCosta & Halmi, 1992; Favaro & Santonastraso, 2000; Gowers & Bryant-Waugh, 2004; Haines & Neumark-Sztainer, 2006; Thompson & Smolak, 2001)
- Physical or sexual abuse (Tahiroglu, Avci, & Cekin, 2008; Andrews, 2004; Birke, & Mayer, 2004; Davis, 2002; Lehman, 2005; Vermilyea, 2000; Chaffin & Friedrich, 2004; Halverstadt, 2000; National Center on Child Abuse and Neglect, 2003)
- Grief and loss (McCormack, Burgess, & Hartman, 1988; Petersen & Straub, 1992; Thompson, 1993; Archer, 2001; Davis & Nolen-Hoeksema, 2001; Ellis, 1998; Goodkin, Baldewicz, Blaney, Asthana, & Kumar, 2001; Schut, Stroebe, van den Bout, & Terheggen, 2001; Doka & Tucci, 2008; Noppe & Noppe, 2004, 2009; Worden, 2009)
- Aggressive behavior (Huey, 1987; Clayton, Ballif-Spanvill, & Hunsaker, 2001; DeVoe et al., 2004; DeVoe, Peter, Noonan, Snyder, & Baum, 2005; Lösel & Beelmann, 2003; Nangle, Erdley, Carpenter, & Newman, 2002)
- Divorce, loss, and separation (Omizo & Omizo, 1987; Amato & Cheadle, 2005; Bond, 2007; van Krieken, 2005; Yodanis, 2005; Paxton, Valois, & Drane, 2007; Day-Sclater, 2007)
- Drug abuse prevention (Berkowitz & Persins, 1988; Daroff, Masks, & Friedman, 1986; Sarvela, Newcomb, & Littlefield, 1988; Tweed & Ryff, 1991; Adalbjarnardottir & Rafnsson, 2002; Allgood, Mathiesen, & Delva, 2005; Anand, 2003; Bachman, Johnston, & O'Malley, 2001; Battjes, Gordon, O'Grady, & Kinlock, 2004; Battjes et al., 2004; Botvin et al., 2000; Cavanaugh & Doucette, 2004; Ciarrochi, Wilson, Deane, & Rickwood, 2003; Thompson, 2006; Deuschle, 2004; Godley & White, 2006; Kaminer, 2006; Nash, McQueen, & Bray, 2005; Valente, 2003)
- Teen pregnancy (Thompson, 1987; R. A. Thompson, 2006; Sadler, Swartz, & Ryan-Krause 2003; Suner, Nakamura, & Caulfield, 2003; Annie E. Casey Foundation, 2003; Card & Benner, 2008; Child Trends & National Campaign to Prevent Teen Pregnancy, 2004; Costello & Henry, 2003; Ehrlich & Vega-Matos, 2002; Healthy Teen Network, 2005; Kirby, 2007; Kirby, Lezin, Afriye, & Gallucci, 2003)

Group membership is targeted to students who are currently having difficulty with a specific problem. Problem-focused groups frequently use media and structured activities to stimulate discussion of issues and present relevant information to group members (Bergin, 1993). Role-playing, homework, contracts, and journal writing enhance problem-solving and coping skills for the type of group.

The group setting provides a secure arena for children and adolescents to share anxieties, express feelings, and identify coping strategies. They learn that their feelings are normal and that their peers share similar experiences. Bergin (1993) stresses the concept of involvement and how the interactive process of the group affects members in a number of positive ways:

1. The group offers acceptance and support for each member and encourages mutual trust and the sharing of individual concerns.
2. The group's orientation to reality and emphasis on conscious thoughts leads individuals to examine their current thoughts, feelings, and actions and to express them in a genuine manner.
3. The group's overt attempt to convey understanding to each member encourages tolerance and an accepting of individual differences in personal values and goals.
4. The group's focus on personal concerns and behavior encourages the individual to consider alternative ways of behaving; and to practice them within the context of a supportive environment. (p. 2)

Similarly, Yalom and Leszcz (2005) and Hansen, Warner, and Smith (1980) have stressed the "curative" and "therapeutic" factors responsible for producing change in productive groups.

The 11 primary factors highly visible in groups with children and adolescents are:

1. *Instilling hope.* Group members develop the belief that their problems can be overcome or managed. By learning new skills such as listening, paraphrasing, and expressing empathy, the child or adolescent develops a stronger sense of self, as well as a belief in the efficacy of the helping

process (i.e., that they have meaning and relatedness to their school, their community, and their families).

2. *Universality.* Group members overcome the debilitating, preconceived notion that their problem is unique only to them. Through mutual sharing of problems in a secure environment, the child or adolescent discovers a commonality of fears, fantasies, hopes, needs, and problems. Their problems are no longer unique; they are universal and shared with others.

3. *Imparting information.* Group members learn new information, as well as advice, suggestions, or direct guidance about developmental concerns. Advice-giving and advice-seeking behavior is central to the school counselor's role. By providing specific information such as establishing a group community, developing communication skills, and sharing concrete information, children and adolescents feel more self-sufficient and in control of their own behavior. Vicarious learning also occurs in the group setting as children and adolescents observe the coping strategies of others.

4. *Altruism.* Group members offer support and reassurance and are helpful to one another. The child or adolescent becomes Other-centered rather than self-centered. The participants often rediscover their self-importance by learning that they are of value to others. They feel a sense of purpose and that others value their expertise. Altruism can extend from the group to the community to more global concerns, such as service learning projects to protect the environment, help the homeless, or assist the elderly.

5. *The corrective recapitulation of the primary family group.* The group environment promotes a mirror of experiences typical of one's primary family group. During the group experience, the focus is on the vitality of work in the here and now. Outside of the group experience, the adolescent may internalize behavior change and enhance more interpersonal skills.

6. *Development of socializing skills.* The development and rehearsal of basic social skills are a therapeutic factor that is universal to all counseling groups. Adolescents learn such skills as establishing a relationship, refraining from critical judgment, listening attentively, communicating with empathy, and expressing warmth and genuineness. Once assimilated, these skills create an opportunity for personal growth and more rewarding interpersonal interactions that are transferred to daily functioning at home, in school, or on the job.

7. *Imitative behavior.* Group members learn new behaviors by observing the behavior of the leader and other members. In training, the process of modeling serves to create positive behavior that the adolescent can assimilate (e.g., body language, tone of voice, eye contact, and other important communication skills). The learner not only sees the behavior in action but also experiences the effects of it.

8. *Interpersonal learning.* Group members develop relationships typical of their life outside the group within the social microcosm of the group. Group training facilitates self-awareness and interpersonal growth. Adolescents often come to a group with distortions of their self-perceptions. These distortions are what Kottler (1983) identifies as self-defeating behaviors such as procrastination, unrealistic expectations, self-pity, anxiety, guilt, rigid thinking, ethnocentricity, psychological dependence, or an external locus of control. The nature and scope of the group process encourages self-assessment, risk taking, confrontation, feedback, goal setting, and decision making.

9. *Group cohesiveness.* Group membership offers participants an arena to receive unconditional positive regard, acceptance, and belonging, which enables members to fully accept themselves and be congruent in their relationships with others. The group community creates cohesiveness, that is, a "we"-ness or common vision. Once a group attains cohesiveness with established norms, members are more receptive to feedback, self-disclosure, confrontation, and appreciation, making themselves more open to one another. An effective training process facilitates this component.

10. *Emotional expression.* Learning how to express emotion reduces the use of debilitating defense mechanisms. Sharing emotions and feelings diminishes destructive fantasy-building as well as repressed anger and sets the stage for exploring alternatives to self-defeating behavior.

TABLE 12.5   Classification System for Group-Focused Counseling Skills

STAGE I	STAGE II	STAGE III
Group Formation: Facilitating cooperation toward common goals through development of group identity 1. *Norming* Stating explicitly the expected group behavior 2. *Eliciting Group Responses* Inquiries or invitations to members that encourage comments 3. *Eliciting Sympathetic Reactions* Inquiries or invitations to members that encourage disclosure of experiences or feelings similar to those being expressed 4. *Identifying Commonalities and Differences* Describing comparative characteristics of participants 5. *Eliciting Empathic Reactions* Inquiries or invitations to members that encourage reflection of one member's expressed content or feeling 6. *Task Focusing* Redirecting conversation to immediate objectives; restating themes being expressed by more than one member	*Group Awareness:* Facilitating a shared understanding of the group's behavior 1. *Labeling Group Behavior* Identifying and describing group feelings and performance. 2. *Implicit Norming* Describing behavior that has become typical of the group through common practice 3. *Eliciting Group Observations* Inquiries or invitations to members that encourage observations about group process 4. *Eliciting Mutual Feedback* Inquiries or invitations to members that encourage sharing of perceptions about each other's behavior 5. *Identifying Conflict* Labeling discordant elements of communication between members 6. *Identifying Nonverbal Behavior* Labeling unspoken communications between members (facial expression, posture, hand gestures, voice tone and intensity, etc.) 7. *Validating* Requesting group confirmation of the accuracy of the leader's or members' perceptions 8. *Transitioning* Changing the group's focus on content or feelings being expressed 9. *Connecting* Relating material from group events at a particular time or session to what is happening currently 10. *Extinguishing* Ignoring, cutting off, or diverting inappropriate talk or actions of members	*Group Action:* Facilitating cooperative decision making and problem solving 1. *Identifying Group Needs* Asking questions and making statements that clarify the wants and needs of the group 2. *Identifying Group Goals* Asking questions and making statements that clarify group objectives 3. *Attributing Meaning* Providing concepts for understanding group thoughts, feelings, and behavior 4. *Eliciting Alternatives* Providing descriptions of possible courses of action and inviting members to contribute alternatives 5. *Exploring Consequences* Inquiries or invitations to the group that evaluate actions and potential outcomes 6. *Consensus Testing* Requesting group agreement on a decision or course of action

Source: Gill, J., & Barry, R. A., *Personnel and Guidance Journal, 60*(5), 24–29, 1982. Reprinted with permission.

11. *Responsibility.* As group members face the fundamental issues of their lives, counselees learn that they are ultimately responsible for the way they live, no matter how much support the student receives from others. Contributions of the adolescent are validated, stressing issues of personal responsibility and consequences in life and urging choice and the development of one's potential.

When observing the group process with children and adolescents, many of these therapeutic factors appear. The curative factors that emerge more consistently in child and adolescent groups are universality, instilling of hope, and interpersonal learning. For example, adolescents are relieved when they realize that others share similar pain, such as feelings of abandonment or guilt regarding parents' divorce or posttraumatic stress disorders from a recent traumatic loss or a history of abuse. All too often, students feel that no one else has a problem as devastating as theirs and that their issues are unique. From the realization that this isn't true, children and adolescents gain a more hopeful perspective, believing that they, like their peers, can effect change, improve their conditions, or increase their coping skills. This fosters personal empowerment, resiliency, and self-sufficiency—a hallmark of professional school counselor effectiveness. Rather than relying on the collective adolescent angst of blaming others or blaming the system, children and adolescents gain the skills needed to enhance relationships and effect change in themselves and others.

Waldo (1985) further differentiates the curative factor framework when planning activities in structured groups. In a six-session structured group, activities can be arranged in relation to the group's development so that group dynamics can foster curative factors. The group can be structured as follows:

- *Session 1:* Establishing goals and ground rules (instilling of hope) and sharing perceptions about relationships (universality)
- *Session 2:* Identification of feelings about past, present, and future relationships (catharsis)
- *Session 3:* Demonstrating understanding of other group members' feelings (cohesion)
- *Session 4:* Feedback between group members (altruism)
- *Session 5:* Confrontation and conflict resolution between group members (interpersonal learning)
- *Session 6:* Planning ways group members can continue to improve relations with others, and closure (existential factors)

As Waldo (1985) explains: "Each session involves lectures and reading materials (imparting information), demonstrations by the leader (interpersonal learning), and within- and between-meeting exercises (social skills and own work techniques)" (p. 58–59). This model provides a conceptual map that can be utilized in school counseling for structured groups on conflict resolution, decision making, interpersonal relations, or any intervention that needs to be structured in order to learn important life skills.

Once children and adolescents recognize that their problems are not unique but are in fact universal, they begin to feel obligations to other people. The "I" becomes strongly submerged in the "we." When students reach this stage of interpersonal identity, they are able to enhance their own problem solving. By observing the way in which a student discusses his or her needs or reliance on others, the counselor can help the student realize that it is possible to change behavior and to ask for support.

Establishing primary prevention/developmental groups or problem-solving structured intervention groups can effectively meet the needs of youth if they are conducted with these parameters in mind:

1. Six to eight children or adolescents should meet for a maximum of 45 minutes.
2. The chronological age difference should not exceed two years.
3. The intellectual age should be controlled to prevent extremes (e.g., a gifted student and a special education student with severe handicapping conditions may not benefit from the group experience together).

The counseling intention is to build a caring program designed to support and assist students who are experiencing problems and to provide a secure environment in which to share experiences, to express and experience conflicting feelings, and to share personal struggles and develop support systems. Teachers also can be utilized to facilitate support groups. After preparation and training, teachers can devote one planning period per week to working with designated groups of students on enhancing cognitive skills (e.g., graphic organizers, learning-style assessments, time management, study skills, and cooperative learning groups).

Conducting Psychoeducational Groups to Enhance the Social, Emotional, and Cognitive Skills of All Students

Contemporary youths are indiscriminately confronted with critical developmental issues and decisions without the understanding or the experience of using critical social, emotional, and cognitive skills. Intervention and prevention strategies must focus on these social, emotional, and cognitive skill deficits that seem to permeate all dysfunctional manifestations of child and adolescent high-risk behavior. For example, incarcerated youths often have social skill deficits in anger management and conflict resolution skills; the adolescent facing an unintended pregnancy often lacks social and cognitive skills such as assertiveness and abstract reasoning (i.e., the ability to see the long-range consequences of high-risk behaviors); and the potential school dropout often manifests cognitive skill deficits in problem solving, decision making, and self-management.

Stellas (1992) has found that violent adolescents, similar to adult offenders, were missing one or more of the following six skills or characteristics:

1. *Assertiveness:* The ability to speak up appropriately for oneself (offenders often swing between passivity and aggression)
2. *Decision-making skills:* The ability to anticipate consequences
3. *Social support:* The ability to use community systems
4. *Empathy:* The ability to identify with the felt experiences of someone else
5. *Impulse control/problem-solving skills:* The ability to maintain self-control followed by the ability to explore and use alternative solutions
6. *Anger management:* The ability to deal with frustration without violating the rights of others

Criminologists, too, are finding a common psychological fault line in perpetrators of violence: They are incapable of empathy, one of the fundamentals of emotional intelligence (Goleman, 1994, 2006). This inability to feel their victim's pain provokes a proclivity toward violent or aggressive acts, and a lack of remorse perpetuates criminal recidivism. For example, an adolescent gang member may show little remorse for killing another gang member over a dispute about drug turf, or an elementary student may be insensitive to another child's feelings about his possessions as he destroys them. It is becoming increasingly apparent that both youths and adults need such critical skills as how to recognize and talk about feelings or how to understand that a problem involves at least two points of view (Levin & Carlsson-Paige, 1995).

Youths need an entire repertoire of nonviolent ways to deal with the problems they face in their social world to help them counteract the lessons they learn from exposure to violence. Some proponents advocate teaching *choice-response thinking* (Marshall, 1998), a counseling approach in which youths acknowledge inappropriate behavior, self-evaluate, take ownership of the problem, and develop a plan of action. It also is important to recognize that life-skill development is a lifetime-learning experience that includes the need to master many skills: communication skills, leadership skills, protocol skills, religious ritual skills, self-help skills, athletic skills, employer/employee skills, and relationship skills, to name just a few. Further, programs that promote social, emotional, and cognitive skills seem to have the greatest impact on attitudes about violent behavior. Such skills include descriptors such as *perspective taking, alternative solution generation, self-esteem enhancement, peer negotiation, problem-solving training,* and *anger management* (American Psychological Association, 1993, 2005a).

The Prevalence of Youth Violence and Self-Defeating Behavior

Indicators of troubled youth are all too familiar: school dropouts, gang involvement, alcohol and other drug abuse, unintended pregnancy, crime, violence, homicide, bullying, self-mutilation, suicide, and reactive attachment disorder. The threats to the physical, social, and emotional well-being of today's youth are unparalleled in human history. The United States has the highest murder rate for 12- to 24-year-olds of any industrialized nation (Viadero, 2002). As Marian Wright Edelman, the president of the Children's Defense Fund, wrote as early as 1994: "Our worst nightmares are coming true, after years of family disintegration, the crisis of children having children has been eclipsed by the greater crisis of children killing children" (Edelman, 1994, p. 7). Finkelhor, Ormrod, Turner, and Hamby (2005) concur:

> Violence is perhaps one of the most pervasive and serious threats to the mental health and well-being of youth in the United States. Young people are disproportionately represented as both victims and perpetrators of violence. National school-based data indicate that violence, especially bullying behavior, is prevalent in many schools. The 2003 Youth Risk Behavior Surveillance Survey indicated that 42% of adolescents were in a physical fight during the 12 months preceding the survey and 22% carried a weapon during the 30 days preceding the survey. (p. 6)

Serious violent crime involving juvenile victims and offenders went up between 2002 and 2003. In 2003, 18 juveniles out of 1,000 were victims of serious violent crimes—homicide, rape, aggravated assault, or robbery—and 15 per 1,000 were reported by victims to have committed such crimes. These rates were up dramatically from those of 2002, when 10 youths per 1,000 were victims of serious crimes and 11 per 1,000 were identified as offenders. However, rates had still declined markedly from their peaks in 1993 of 44 victims per 1,000 youths and 52 offending youths per 1,000 juveniles (America's Children: Key National Indicators of Well-Being, 2011).

These pervasive conditions will have long-range implications for schools and communities, business and industry, children and families, and youth and service agencies. The litany of statistics on child and adolescent well-being reflects family breakdown, poverty, violence, and abuse. The growing list of responsibilities American schools have undertaken in the last decade—violence (such as bullying) prevention programs, delinquency and dropout prevention, AIDS/HIV education, English-language learners, growing diversity, family life education, character education, crisis intervention, safe schools initiatives, and on and on—reflect the changing demographics that strain economic resources in providing critical services in the schools.

The concern over adolescent suicide rates, alcohol abuse, sexual irresponsibility, gang behavior, HIV and AIDS, dropout rates, and violence demonstrates the critical need for responsible adults to establish close helping relationships with our young people. Yet, important relationships between youth and adults and among youth themselves are seriously strained. Adolescents themselves are polarized, wearing the uniforms and insignia of their various tribes: the Crips, the Bloods, the Latin Kings, Mara Salvatrucha (MS-13), the home boys, the leather-clad death metal heads, the skinheads, the insane clown posse, the stoners, the surfers, the skaters, the preppies, the multipierced gypsies, the born-again hippies, and so on (Thompson, 2006).

Youth Gang Problems

Respondents to the National Youth Gang Survey provided information regarding the presence or absence of active youth gangs in their jurisdictions. The results showed that:

- Twenty-nine percent of the jurisdictions that city (populations of 2,500 or more) and county law enforcement agencies serve experienced youth gang problems in 2004.
- Gang problems are highly prevalent in larger cities; specifically, 99% of law enforcement agencies serving cities with populations of 100,000 or more have reported multiple years of gang problems.
- Gang problem prevalence rates in suburban and rural counties and smaller cities declined yearly from the mid-1990s through the early 2000s.
- Approximately half as many rural counties reported gang problems in 2005 compared with 1996. (National Youth Gang Center, 2007)

More American children of the current generation have been raised in day care than ever before or have spent long hours alone as "latchkey children" while two-parent families forge dual careers or a single parent juggles two jobs to make ends meet. Many older children have become parentified to take care of younger siblings. Children and adolescents have grown up with fast food, remote-control entertainment, and quick-response conveniences, all of which fulfill the need for immediate gratification and an attitude of entitlement. They have been labeled the "screen generation" (i.e., constantly using computers and iPhones, posting indiscriminately on social networks, and relying on the Internet to connect to a global network). In an era of rapid change, our youths have learned to accept the impermanence of even the most intimate relationship (Hersch, 1990). Those with reactive attachment disorder issues may have learned to become desensitized to the horror of violence, to gradually accept violence as a way to solve problems, to imitate the violence they observe on television, and to identify with certain characters or victimizers. Personality attributes may include impulsiveness, inability to delay gratification, little tolerance for individual differences, inability to empathize, and excessive anger.

Today the nation's schools are being driven by a psychometric high-stakes testing and instructional mentality, which is pressing for higher academic standards and creating barrier tests, thereby making school less palatable to those who are already struggling against insurmountable odds such as poverty, mental illness, and the language and cultural issues of immigrants. Relegated to lower-level skills classes, these students are often placed in the most boring classroom settings in the public schools, devoting most of their day to "drill and skill" instructional activities and worksheets under the auspices of teacher pacing guides to keep students accountable to standards of learning. Low-income students and students of color are not treated equitably in the schools (Gollnick & Chinn, 2006), and DeCastro-Ambrosetti and Cho (2005) have revealed that a significant number of teachers believe that education is not important to these students' parents and subsequently they dismiss their unique needs.

This is all emerging within the context of family dysfunction, changing family structure, increased ethnic diversity, and lack of respect for authority where the social, emotional, and cognitive potential of youth are threatened by alcohol and other drugs, gangs, suicide, violence, and other dysfunctional behavior, as well as influences in the media on youth norms. Student bullying is one of the most frequently reported discipline problems at school: 21% of elementary schools, 43% of middle schools, and 22% of high schools reported problems with bullying in 2005–2006 (Dinkes et al., 2007; NCES, 2006).

Children in this country are increasingly immersed in a culture of violence that comes in many forms: interpersonal violence in families, violence in the community and in the schools, and violence in the news and entertainment media. Our popular culture is saturated with gratuitous violence showing children inappropriate images, actions, and models for how people can treat each other.

THE IMPORTANCE OF PEER RELATIONSHIPS

Peer relations contribute substantially to social, emotional, and cognitive development and to the effectiveness with which children later function as adults. Schools and communities need to identify sources of friction and ways in which children and adolescents are encouraged to express their emotions. The single best childhood predictor of adult adaptation is not school grades or classroom behavior, but rather the adequacy with which the child gets along with his or her peers and significant adults.

Children who are aggressive and disruptive, who are unable to sustain close relationships with other children, and who cannot establish a place for themselves in the peer culture become emotionally disabled because of the lack of *affiliative relations* or friendship skills. Affiliative relations include having the emotional resources for both having fun and adapting to stress, mastering cognitive resources for problem solving and knowledge acquisition, and having contexts in which basic social skills are acquired. Research further corroborates the impression that a child's relationship with his or her friends supports cooperation, reciprocity, and effective conflict management. A child's initial friendships are thought to be the templates for subsequent relationships. They may also buffer the child from the adverse effects of negative events such as divorce, family conflict, terminal illness, parent unemployment, and school failure.

Children who show signs of poor peer relationships need to be targeted for early intervention to ensure that their aggressive tendencies do not interfere with their potential for educational achievement and result in diminished social and emotional learning. Nurturing social and emotional skills gives youths advantages in their cognitive abilities, interpersonal adjustment, and resiliency during stressful events. Systematic, ongoing education to enhance the social and emotional skills of youth can provide a stable foundation for successful cognitive and behavioral development.

Youths need critical skills such as how to recognize and talk about feelings or how to understand that a problem involves at least two points of view. Youths as well as adults need an entire repertoire of nonviolent ways to deal with problems they face in their social world to help them counteract the lessons they learn from exposure to violence directly or vicariously through the media and the community. Social, emotional, and cognitive skills seem to have the greatest impact on attitudes about violent or self-defeating behavior.

SOCIAL SKILLS TO HELP YOUTHS RELATE TO OTHERS BETTER INTERPERSONALLY

Social literacy skills (see Table 12.6) are interpersonal skills essential for meaningful interaction with others. One definition of *social skills* has been termed the "social validity definition" by Gresham (1981):

> Social skills are situational specific behaviors that predict important social outcomes for youth. In school settings, important social outcomes include, but are not limited to: (a) peer acceptance, (b) peer judgments of social skill, (c) academic achievement, (d) self-concept, and (e) school adjustment. (p. 398–399)

Another definition by Rinn and Markle (1979) focuses on a repertoire of verbal and nonverbal behaviors:

> The phrase *social skills* are defined as a repertoire of verbal and nonverbal behaviors by which children affect the responses of other individuals (e.g., peers, parents, siblings, and teachers) in the interpersonal context. This repertoire acts as a mechanism through which children influence their environment by obtaining, removing, or avoiding desirable and undesirable outcomes in the social sphere; i.e., the extent to which they are successful in obtaining desirable outcomes and avoiding or escaping undesirable ones without inflicting pain on others is the extent to which they are considered socially skilled. (p. 108)

Social skills promote successful interactions with peers and adults. When these skills are absent, there is an increase in the likelihood that a child's behavior may be labeled disabling, deviant, or antisocial. *Cooperation, assertion, responsibility,* and *self-control* represent major clusters of social skills. They include possessing the vocabulary and other language skills that allow for easy expression of ideas. Social skills include the following:

- *Social behavior skills:* Making and keeping friends
- *Social and general problem-solving skills:* Pausing to think before working on a problem, or thinking and doing in a step-by-step systematic manner
- *Following rules:* Adhering to formal rules and codes of behavior
- *Self-esteem:* Evaluating oneself positively as a result of acquiring skills and experiencing positive feedback and interactions with others
- *Verbal social skills:* Making clear requests, responding effectively to criticism, resisting negative influences, listening to others, helping others, participating in positive peer groups and relationships

TABLE 12.6   Social Literacy Skills

• DESCA inspirations	• Listening more effectively	• How to apologize
• Perception checking	• Responding to another	• Coping with anger in public
• Mediation process	person's anger	• Peer-pressure refusal skills
• Documenting a generalization about something	• Handling conflict among team members	• Responding with praise
• Giving constructive criticism	• Indexing a generalization about something	• Giving and accepting compliments
• Starting a conversation	• Being socially responsible	• Becoming more outgoing
• Asking someone out	• Keeping a conversation going	• Conventional arbitration
• Your assertive rights	• Steps in negotiating a conflict of interest	• Assertiveness and conflict
• Becoming more assertive and less aggressive	• Components of assertiveness	• Changing someone's undesirable behavior
• Problem solving	• Assertiveness	• Problem-solving acronym
• Anger management	• Dealing with conflict fairly and without violence	• Negotiation
• Defusing anger	• How to say no and still keep your friends	• Rules for conflict resolution
• Formula for active listening	• Social skills homework form	• Using elements of the "I" message to change behavior
• Self-awareness through feedback from others	• Sending an effective communication message	• Peer mediation process
• Giving constructive feedback	• "Carefrontation"	• Assertiveness and negotiating
• Assertive one-liners	• Negotiating	• Momentary delay
• Poor and good listening characteristics	• Enhancing friendship skills	• Asking for social support
• Persuading others to accept your ideas	• Using "I" messages, "you" messages, and "we" messages	• How to win the cooperation of others
• Interpersonal relationship skills	• Confirming your interpersonal hunches about others	• Active listening
	• Clarification and reflection	

Source: Copyright © 2006. From *Nurturing Future Generations: Promoting Resilience in Children and Adolescents through Social, Emotional, and Cognitive Skills,* (2nd ed.), by Rosemary A. Thomas. Reproduced by permission of Taylor and Francis Group, LLC, a division of Informa plc.

- *Nonverbal social skills:* Communicating through eye contact, facial expressiveness, tone of voice, gestures, and openness

Social skills fall into categories such as:

- Being kind, cooperative, and compliant to reduce problems associated with defiance, aggression, out-of-control conduct, and antisocial behavior
- Showing interest in people and socializing frequently and successfully to reduce behavior problems associated with withdrawal, depression, and fearfulness
- Possessing the vocabulary and other language skills that allow for easy expression of ideas to increase expressive vocabulary and syntax and allow for interesting conversation with peers and adults
- Coping with peer and media pressure to take dangerous risks
- Establishing and articulating realistic goals for health, education, leisure, and career pursuits

Social skills are interpersonal skills—those behaviors that, within a given situation, predict important social outcomes such as peer acceptance, popularity, self-efficacy, competence, and high self-esteem. Social skills include problem solving, assertiveness, impulse control, resolving conflict, managing anger in public, and utilizing peer-pressure refusal skills. Social skills ensure positive and effective interpersonal relationships. They reduce the number of negative experiences youths may encounter in their relationships in school, at home, and in the community.

EMOTIONAL SKILLS TO HELP YOUTH
FEEL BETTER INTRAPERSONALLY

Schools and communities across the nation are experiencing a new kind of deficit in behavior that is in many ways more alarming than the lack of social skills: *emotional skill deficits*. In the 21st century, the signs of this deficit can be seen in the increasing incidence of violence in the schools and the litany of statistics showing sharp rises in the number of teenage suicides, substance abuse (including the abuse of prescription drugs), homicides, and acts of violence. As Goleman (1994) poignantly observed:

> We pay the price for emotional deficits in failed marriages and troubled families, in stunted social and work lives, in deteriorating physical health and mental anguish, and in tragedies such as increasing violence and killings in our communities and in our schools. Our social nets for the emotionally illiterate are prisons safe systems, houses for abused wives and families, shelters for the homeless, mental hospitals, and the psychotherapist's office. (p. 2)

Emotional deficits observed in youth include short attention span, impulsive behavior, slowed language development, and poor sequential memory. Many youths manifest difficulty recognizing the relationship between feelings and behavior. This often-unrecognized inability intensifies the sensation of being out of control. For example, in the classroom, abused children often direct their attention toward interpreting their teacher's mood as a learned survival technique to anticipate an abusive parent's unpredictable behavior, which may range from benign indifference and neglect to explosive aggression and physical abuse.

Children living with violence in abusive home environments exhibit social, emotional, and cognitive dysfunction. The long-term effects of violence influence how children *encode material to be learned* and *how they interpret and act on new information*. Abusive family environments can influence a child's problem-solving behavior and relationships with peers and adults. These behaviors in turn can affect both social competence and school achievement, with grave implications for adult competence.

Emotional literacy skills (see Table 12.7) include such intrapersonal skills and abilities as identifying and labeling feelings, knowing one's emotions by recognizing a feeling as it happens; managing emotions (i.e., being able to shake off anxiety, gloom, irritability, and the consequences of failure); assessing the intensity of feelings; increasing one's feeling vocabulary; expressing feelings; motivating oneself to attain goals; delaying gratification; stifling impulsiveness; maintaining self-control; recognizing emotions in others with empathy and perspective taking; and handling interpersonal relationships effectively. Emotional skills fall into categories such as knowing the relationships among thoughts, feelings, and actions; establishing a sense of identity and acceptance of self; learning to value teamwork, collaboration, and cooperation; emotional processing and centering practices; regulating one's mood; engaging in silent reflection; and maintaining hope. The most visible emotional skills are the ability to express empathy, sensitivity, and tolerance of perceived differences.

Emotions drive our attention, health, learning, meaning, memory, and survival (Jensen, 1998). Excessive emotions can impair rational thinking, change attention, and influence memory levels in response to trauma. But the absence of emotion and feeling can also interfere with reasoning. Goleman (1994, 2006) maintains that a single course will not cover the full range of emotional skills that a proactive mental health program should provide.

Emotional literacy initiatives should include the following:

- *Self-awareness:* Building a vocabulary for feelings; knowing the relationships among thoughts, feelings, and reactions; knowing if thought or feeling is ruling an action
- *Decision making:* Examining actions and knowing their consequences; a self-reflective view of what goes into decisions; applying this to issues such as sex, alcohol, and other drugs

TABLE 12.7   Emotional Literacy Skills

- Inner processing of how you feel
- Dealing with fear and anxiety
- Enhancing relationship skills
- Positive affirmations
- Dealing with rumors and false accusations
- Describing feelings and empathizing
- How to let someone know they're bothering you
- Making intention statements
- How to handle a verbal "attack"
- 3-R strategy
- Preparing for a potential conflict
- Coping with agitation
- Using "I want" statements
- Estimating logical consequences
- Reframing a conflict
- The XYZ formula for a complaint
- Fair fighting rules
- Strategies to manage anger appropriately
- Maintaining your personal power
- Working through disappointment when you make a mistake
- Aggression control methods
- Psychological forces that block intelligent decision making
- Solutions to the big seven cognitive distortions
- The anxiety formula: knowness versus importance
- Daily activities to reduce irrational thinking
- Rational self-analysis
- Turning "you" statements into "I" statements

- Inner processing how another person might feel
- Dealing with deadline disorder
- Steps to overcome your fear of speaking in public
- Changing inner beliefs
- Supporting
- Self-disclosure
- Listening with empathy
- Making action statements
- Increasing your frustration tolerance
- Coping thoughts for anger reactions
- Confronting a conflict
- Seven skills to handle conflict and anger
- Empathic assertion
- Stop the action/accept the feelings
- Dealing with teasing
- Mirroring
- Communicating feelings in a nonblaming manner
- Interpretive confrontation
- Don't take it personal
- Using self-control techniques
- Writing a learning history of angry reactions
- Twelve distressing emotional myths
- Specific steps to resolve anxiety
- The ACT formula: Accept, Choose, Take action
- Disputing irrational beliefs (DIBS)
- Paraphrasing responses to others

- Handling peer pressure
- Toning down heated remarks
- Coping self-talk for stressful situations
- Nine ways to handle stress effectively
- Preparing for a difficult conversation
- Confronting self-defeating behavior
- Paraphrasing what someone has said
- Confrontation guidelines
- Rules of fair fighting
- Positive self statements
- Coping with the feeling of being overwhelmed
- Using the "I" language assertion
- Confrontive assertion
- Avoiding conflict by paraphrasing
- What to do when you are angry
- The art of the critique
- Setting boundaries with others and taking responsibility for yourself
- Self-talk to maintain composure and deal with situations more effectively
- Getting out of the middle of dueling relationships
- Aggression control methods
- Three quick questions to suppress or express anger
- Confronting irrational thoughts
- Changing thinking patterns and "internal conversations"
- The ABCs of stopping unhappy thoughts
- Disputing irrational beliefs (A FROG)
- Different ways to refuse a request

- *Managing feelings:* Monitoring "self-talk" to catch negative messages such as internal put-downs; realizing what is behind a feeling (e.g., the hurt that underlies anger)
- *Self-concept:* Establishing a firm sense of identity and feeling esteem for and acceptance of oneself

- *Handling stress:* Learning the value of exercise, calming techniques, guided imagery, and progressive relaxation
- *Communications:* Sending "I" messages instead of blame; being a good listener
- *Group dynamics:* Demonstrating cooperation; knowing when and how to lead and to follow
- *Conflict resolution:* How to fight fairly with peers, parents, and teachers; the win–win model for negotiating compromise and conflict

Social and emotional competence is the ability to understand, manage, and express the social and emotional aspects of one's life in ways that enable the successful management of developmental tasks, such as learning and forming relationships, solving everyday problems, and adapting to the complex demands of growth and development. It includes self-awareness, control of impulsivity, working cooperatively, and caring about oneself and others. Social and emotional learning is the process through which youths and adults develop the skills, attitudes, and values necessary to acquire social and emotional competence. The discovery of these and other correlates reveals that through education, we could begin to address these deficits and possibly reduce self-destructive and self-defeating behavior.

Many school and community initiatives assume that social, emotional, and cognitive skills will develop as a natural consequence of exposure to various parts of the school curriculum. Yet, it has become increasingly apparent that this may be an erroneous assumption.

COGNITIVE SKILLS TO HELP YOUTHS THINK BETTER

Cognitive deficits place individuals at a disadvantage academically and vocationally, making students more vulnerable to criminal influences and self-destructive and/or self-defeating behavior. It has become increasingly apparent that the further a child moves away from competing with his peers academically, the more he or she is inclined to compete in less constructive ways such as joining a gang, getting involved in drugs, or embracing violence. For example, Ross and Ross (1989) found that:

- Many delinquents are externally oriented. They believe what happens to them depends on fate, chance, or luck. They believe that they are powerless and are controlled by people and circumstances. External locus of control also is prevalent in the behavior manifestations of underachievers and teenage mothers.
- Many delinquents are very concrete in their thinking, and their lack of abstract reasoning makes it difficult for them to understand their world and the reason for rules and laws.
- Many antisocial individuals have deficits in interpersonal problem-solving and thinking skills that are required for solving problems and interacting with people.
- Many delinquents lack awareness or sensitivity to other people's thoughts or feelings, which severely impairs their ability to form acceptable relationships with people. (p. 35–39)

Policy makers, educators, and helping professionals can no longer conceptualize the process of learning as the result of rote memory and mnemonic strategies that merely link meaningless bits of information to each other. Much of the contemporary research on thinking and learning challenges the way teachers teach and students learn. Regrettably, high-stakes testing promotes rote learning, not higher-order thinking skills like critical reasoning. There is a need for new teaching and learning strategies promoted by cognitive scientists, such as cooperative learning, learning in context, brain-based learning, and real world application of knowledge. Proponents advocate authentic learning, which requires the learner to communicate an in-depth understanding of a problem or issue rather than memorizing sets of isolated facts as unconnected information. In addition, the rapid emergence of electronic media has catapulted us into a new communication age. The new demands of the information/digital age require patterning abilities (i.e., patterned thinking). The new learners (the screen generation) are "surfers and scanners" of information, rather than readers and viewers.

The productive workers of the new millennium must be able to think for a living. Our global society has shifted from an industrial economy based on capital goods to an information economy based on services. Information literacy is the ability to access, evaluate, and use information from a variety of sources. As we adjust to the digital age, traditional instruction in reading, writing, and mathematics needs to be coupled with practice in communication, conducting research, critical thinking, public speaking, working in teams, and problem-solving skills (Costa, 1991; Heinström, 2000). An information-literate person is one who:

- Recognizes that accurate and complete information is the basis for intelligent decision making
- Recognizes the need for information
- Formulates questions based on information needs
- Identifies potential sources of information
- Develops successful research strategies
- Accesses sources of information including computer-based and other technologies
- Evaluates information
- Organizes information for practical application
- Integrates new information into an existing body of knowledge

Critical-thinking and problem-solving skills for the knowledge and information age include:

- Communication skills, such as writing, public speaking, listening, reading, and researching
- Interpersonal skills, such as leadership, managing, negotiating, reflection, and arbitrating
- Personal skills, such as self-management, self-direction, time management, and the assessment of skills and abilities of others
- Information skills, such as organizing, researching, and problem solving

Unfortunately, these skills are not promoted in an era of high-stakes testing.

Character traits essential to success in the workplace include team cooperation, assessing alternative strategies, problem solving, informed judgment, and flexible thinking. Employees will be expected to have the basic knowledge necessary to manage the task at hand, learn quickly and routinely on the job, adapt to changing demands and venues, and cooperate and collaborate with a variety of people with different levels of skill development.

Cognitive psychologists advocate teaching youths a repertoire of cognitive and metacognitive strategies, such as using graphic organizers, understanding organizational patterns, self-monitoring, self-questioning, self-regulating, enhancing study skills, deciphering codes, understanding abstract formulas, seeing analogies, and making metacognitions. Cognitive skills also include higher-order thinking skills, such as knowing how to problem-solve, describe, associate, conceptualize, classify, analyze, evaluate, make inferences, and think critically. Analytical thinking involves researching, organizing, speaking, writing, and understanding technology. Quantitative and scientific reasoning also includes ethical applications (i.e., the ability to apply moral standards and appreciate values).

Cognitive skills include the following (see also Table 12.8):

- *Positive self-talk:* Conducting an inner dialogue as a way to cope with a topic or challenge or reinforce one's own behavior.
- *Reading and interpreting social cues:* Recognizing social influences on behavior and seeing oneself in the perspective of the larger community.
- *Using steps for problem solving and decision making:* Controlling impulses, setting goals, identifying alternative actions, and anticipating consequences.
- *Understanding the perspective of others.*
- *Understanding behavioral norms* of acceptable and unacceptable behavior.
- *Maintaining a positive attitude on life.*
- *Having self-awareness* of strengths and abilities and developing realistic expectations about oneself.

TABLE 12.8 Cognitive Literacy Skills

• Graphic organizers	• Agree/Disagree strategy	• Analyzing for bias: EOIOC
• ASSUME acronym	• Attribute web	• BET acronym
• Brainstorming	• Summarizing	• CLUES acronym
• Clustering	• DOVE acronym	• DRAW acronym
• Fact/opinion chart	• Flow chart	• IMAGES acronym
• INFER acronym	• The newspaper model	• People search
• Pencil ranking	• Problem solving	• RULE acronym
• SCAMPER acronym	• Scientific method	• Sequential thinking model
• Targeting	• Thought tree	• Venn diagram
• Reducing test anxiety	• Turning negative thoughts about studying into positive thoughts	• Cornell University note-taking method
• Rules for taking tests and exams		• S2ROS instructional strategy
• A blueprint for taking notes	• Mnemonic devices	• Higher-order thinking skill using analysis
• Higher-order thinking skill using synthesis	• Taking quality notes	• Higher-order thinking skill using application
• Higher-order thinking skill using critical skills	• Higher-order thinking skill using evaluation	• Analyzing for assumptions
• Drawing conclusions from evidence	• Higher-order thinking skill: analysis for bias	• Teaching for thinking
• Creative problem solving	• Analyzing for personification	• Strategies and attitudes in problem solving
• Helpful acronyms for thinking	• Academic growth group and mentoring	• Taking multiple-choice tests
• Tips for specific tests	• Personal abbreviation system	

Source: Copyright © 2006. From *Nurturing Future Generations: Promoting Resilience in Children and Adolescents through Social, Emotional, and Cognitive Skills*, (2nd ed.), by Rosemary A. Thomas. Reproduced by permission of Taylor and Francis Group, LLC, a division of Informa plc.

SOCIAL, EMOTIONAL, AND COGNITIVE SKILLS ARE INEXTRICABLY LINKED

Inherently, social, emotional, and cognitive skills can be systematically taught and cultivated to give youths and adults advantages with both their interpersonal and intrapersonal adjustment, as well as academic success. The goal is to maximize their resiliency and self-sufficiency through life's ultimate challenges.

There is a growing body of research linking intellectual, social, and emotional processes and inter-actions. Emerging theories of cognitive development (neuropsychology, in particular) acknowledge the role played by social context and interpersonal relationships to ensure success. Many elements of learning are relational, that is, are based on relationships. Social and emotional skills are essential for the successful development of thinking and for learning approaches that are routinely considered cognitive skills (Brendtro, Brokenleg, & Van Bockern, 1990). It is also important to recognize that learning is enhanced or hampered by emotions, that emotions drive learning and memory, and that depressed mood states are often correlated with decreased motivation in the classroom and represent barriers to learning (Goleman, 1994).

For example, Van der Kolk (1987) maintains that childhood trauma is particularly significant because uncontrollable terrifying experiences may have their most profound effects when the central nervous system and cognitive functions have not yet fully matured. "Long-range implications may lead to a significant impairment that may manifest in adulthood as psychopathology" (p. 11). In addition, many children experience posttraumatic stress as either victims of or witnesses to violence in the home, school, and community. They manifest such behaviors as intrusive imagery, emotional constriction or avoidance, fears of recurrence, sleep difficulties, disinterest in significant activities, and attention difficulties (American Psychological Association, 1993, 2005a).

Collectively, childhood trauma interferes with normal development, with learning in school, and with a fundamental sense of safety, security, and well-being. Relentless poverty, inequitable educational opportunity, latchkey homes, child abuse, domestic violence, family dysfunction, and a barrage of media generating antisocial behavior (e.g., premature sexual activity and relational aggression) promote unrealistic and destructive social expectations. Further, according to the American Psychological Association (1993, 2005a), the causes of violence are many and complex, ranging from biological factors, child-rearing conditions, ineffective parenting, and emotional and cognitive development to gender differences, sex role socialization, and poor peer relations.

THE PSYCHOEDUCTIONAL LIFE-SKILLS INSTRUCTIONAL MODEL TO ENHANCE SOCIAL, EMOTIONAL, AND COGNITIVE SKILLS: A PLAN OF ACTION TO NURTURE ALL STUDENTS

The life-skills repertoire of youth can be enhanced using a psychoeducational life skills instructional model. Teaching a life skill session or lesson follows a six-step learning model:

1. Instruction (teach)
2. Modeling (show)
3. Discussion (barriers to success of the skill)
4. Role-play (practice)
5. Feedback (reinforce)
6. Ownwork (apply)

Modeling, feedback, role-playing, instruction, situation logs, and homework assignments are used to reinforce desired behavior. The psychoeducational life-skills model is the most comprehensive approach to the remediation and enhancement of interpersonal effectiveness.

Life skills are practiced in a group setting and involve a combination of cognitive, social, emotional, and experiential components. An innovative skills delivery system emphasizes a psychoeducational model in which

- Help is provided by a counselor, teacher, or therapist.
- A person's difficulties are seen as gaps in knowledge or deficits rather than maladaptive behavior patterns.
- The person is active in the design of his or her individualized program.

Interactive rather than didactic approaches are often the most successful ways to diminish high-risk behavior.

The instructional techniques are derived from social learning theory. Social skills are acquired primarily through learning (e.g., observation, modeling, rehearsal, and feedback) and are maximized through social reinforcement (e.g., positive responses from one's social environment). Deficits and excesses in social performance can be remedied through direct instruction and modeling. Behavioral rehearsal and coaching reinforce learning. Youths need these prerequisite skills to defeat dysfunctional behaviors and enhance their resiliency during stressful events.

The Psychoeducational Life-Skills Process

The psychoeducational group leader as professional school counselor assumes the role of director, teacher, model, evaluator, encourager, motivator, facilitator, and protector. Role-playing within the psychoeducational life-skills model provides opportunities to:

- Rehearse and practice new learning in a safe setting;
- Discover how comfortable new behaviors can become;
- Assess which alternative actions work best; and
- Practice new learning by reality testing.

Essentially, intellectual insight alone is not sufficient to change self-defeating behavior, nor can it facilitate the integration of new social, emotional, or cognitive skills. Role-playing is a fundamental force of self-development and interpersonal learning.

Steps are outlined according to what the group leader should say and do to help youths integrate social, emotional, and cognitive skills into their behavioral repertoires. Training sessions are a series of action–reaction sequences in which effective skill behaviors are first rehearsed (role-play) and then critiqued (feedback). Groups should be small (10–12 members, with genders and races mixed) and should cover one skill in one or two sessions. Every member of the group role-plays the given skill correctly at least once. Role-playing is intended to serve as a behavioral rehearsal or practice for future use of the skill. A hypothetical future situation, rather than a reenactment of the past event, should be selected for role-playing. The sample life-skills model is provided below using the social skill of assertiveness.

Sample Psychoeducational Life-Skills Model

The role of group leader as director of the psychoeducational life skill process:
   STEP 1: Present an overview of the social, emotional, or cognitive skill. This is considered didactic instruction. In a minilecture (5–10 minutes) teach the social, emotional, or cognitive skill. Introduce the benefits of the skill in enhancing relationships, as well as the pitfalls for not learning the skill. A sample psychoeducational session plan follows:
   Social Skill: Being More Assertive

- Ask a question to help the members define the skill in their own. Use language, such as: "Who can define assertiveness?" "What does being assertive mean to you?" "How is assertiveness different from aggressiveness?"
- Make a statement about what will follow the modeling of the skill: "After we see the examples of the skill, we will talk about how you can use the skill."
- Distribute skill cards and asks a member to read the behavioral steps aloud
- Ask members to follow each step as the skill is modeled

   The role of the group leader as director of the process:
   STEP 2: Model the behavior following the steps listed on a flipchart, chalkboard, or whiteboard. This is moving into the experiential component. The leader models for the group members what he or she considers to be appropriate mastery of the skill. This enables group members to visualize the process. The model can be live or a media simulation. Identify and discuss the steps.
   STEP 3: Invite discussion of the skill that is modeled.

- "Did any of the situations you observed remind you of times that you had to use the skill?"
- Encourage a dialogue about skill usage and barriers to implementation among group members.

The role of the group leader as director of the process:
STEP 4: Organize a role-play between two group members.

- Designate one member as the *behavior-rehearsing member,* i.e., the individual who will be working on integrating a specific social, emotional, or cognitive skill such as assertiveness, impulse control, or problem solving. Go over guidelines for role-playing.
- Ask the behavior-rehearsing member to choose a partner—someone in the group that is reminiscent of a person with whom they would be likely to use the skill. Ask, for example, "Which member of the group reminds you of that person in some way?" If no one is identified, ask someone to volunteer to rehearse the skill with the member.
- Set the stage for the role-play, including setting, props, and furniture, if necessary. Ask questions such as, "Where will you be talking?" "What will be the time of day?" "What will you be doing?"
- Review with the behavior-rehearsing member what should be said and done during the role-play. Ask such questions as: "What will be the first step of the skill?" or "What will you do if your partner does such-and-such?"
- Provide final instructions to the behavior-rehearsing member and the partner:
  - To the behavior-rehearsing member: "Try to follow the steps as best you can."
  - To the partner: "Try to play the part the best that you can by concentrating on what you think you would do when the practicing member follows the steps."
- Direct the remaining members of the group to be observers of the process. Their role is to provide feedback to the behavior-rehearsing member and the partner after the exercise.

The role-play begins. One group member can stand at chalkboard or flip chart to point out each step for the role-playing team.
The role of the group leader as director of the process:

- Coach and prompt role-players when needed.

The role of the group leader as director of the process:
STEP 5: Elicit feedback from group members after the exercise is completed. Generous praise should be mixed with constructive suggestions. Avoid blame and criticism. The focus should be on how to improve. Suggestions should be achievable with practice. Important considerations:

- The behavior-rehearsing member is instructed to wait until everyone's comments have been heard.
- The partner describes his or her role, feelings, and reactions to the behavior-rehearsing member. Observers are asked to report on how well the behavioral steps were followed and their specific likes and dislikes and to comment on the role of the behavior-rehearsing member and the partner.
- Discuss group comments with the behavior-rehearsing member. The practicing member is asked to respond to how well he or she did in following the behavioral steps of the skill. For example, "On a scale from 1 to 10, how satisfied were you about following the steps?"

The role of the group leader as director of the process:
STEP 6: Assign "ownwork." This is work to be practiced outside of the group setting. It is actually homework, but calling it "ownwork" puts the responsibility on the learner to make further success in changing his or her behavior. This is a critical component that encourages follow-through and the transfer of training to other social, emotional, or cognitive settings. Participants need to transfer newly developed life skills to personally relevant life situations.

The behavior-rehearsing member is assigned ownwork to practice and apply the skill in real life. Group members are assigned to look for situations relevant to the skill they might role-play during the next group meeting.

- Ask the behavior-rehearsing member how, when, and with whom he or she might attempt the behavioral steps prior to the next group meeting.
- Assign an ownwork report to get a written commitment from the practicing member to try out the new skill and report back to the group the next group meeting. Discuss how and where the skill will be used. Set a specific goal to use the skill outside the group.

Ownwork is assigned to enhance the work of the session and to keep the behavior-rehearsing member aware of the life skill he or she wishes to enhance. The ultimate goal is to practice new behaviors in a variety of natural settings. Ownwork puts the onus of responsibility for change on the behavior-rehearsing member. The following examples are appropriate ownwork assignments:

- *Experiential/behavioral assignments:* Assign specific actions between session. For example, a behavioral assignment for lack of assertiveness may be to instruct the behavior-rehearsing member to say no to unreasonable requests from others.
- *Interpersonal assignments:* Assign these to enhance perceived communication difficulties by writing down unpleasant dialogues with others, which can be reviewed during the next session to show how someone inadvertently triggers rejection, criticism, and hostilities in others.
- *Thinking assignments:* These include making a list of things that are helpful to think about and practicing thinking these new thoughts throughout the day. For example, a person with low self-esteem can be instructed to spend time thinking about his or her proudest accomplishments.
- *Writing assignments:* These include writing in a journal or diary, which can help participants develop an outlet for their feelings while away from the sessions. For example, keep a diary that lists for each day the frequency of new behaviors that are practiced.
- *Solution-focused assignments:* In these assignments, the person actively seeks solutions to problems identified in the sessions, for example, seeking a resolution to an interpersonal problem by negotiating or resolving a conflict with another person.

Ownwork assignments (see Figure 12.1) serve to strengthen behavior rehearsal of skills between sessions. Students who experience maladjustment and difficulties in their peer relationships often exhibit coexisting behavioral, social, emotional, psychological, and academic problems are more vulnerable for further maladjustment later in life (Parker, Rubin, Erath, Wojslawowicz, & Buskirk, 2006; Rubin, Bukowski, & Parker, 2006).

STUDENT SUCCESS SKILLS: A CALL TO ACTION TO CLOSE THE GROWING ACHIEVEMENT GAP

In 2005, the U.S. Department of Education reviewed academic outcomes and revealed significant and alarming differences in academic achievement related to ethnicity: 39% of white students were proficient in reading at the end of eighth grade, while only 12% of African American students and 15% of Latino students were. In mathematics, 39% of African Americans, but only 13% of Latinos, were proficient at the end of the eighth grade (U.S. Department of Education, 2005a).

- *Skill to be practiced...*
- *"I will use this skill with..."*
- *"I will use it when...........................and where........................."*
- *The steps are as follows:*

1.
2.
3.
4.
5.

- *On a scale from 1-to-10 (1 = lowest; 10 = highest) rate yourself on how well you did.*

FIGURE 12.1   Ownwork assignment. *Source:* Copyright © 2006. From *Nurturing Future Generations: Promoting Resilience in Children and Adolescents through Social, Emotional, and Cognitive Skills,* (2nd ed.), by Rosemary A. Thomas. Reproduced by permission of Taylor and Francis Group, LLC, a division of Informa plc.

It is well known that if a student—regardless of race or ethnicity—falls behind his or her peers by two grade levels and does not pass ninth grade, the chances of graduating from high school with a standard diploma decrease markedly. High-stakes testing is another significant barrier for students behind grade level. Once a student drops off the school roll, he or she becomes more vulnerable to unemployment; welfare dependency; and the lure of gangs with their underground economy of selling stolen goods, drug trafficking, and illegal weapons distribution.

Successful Interventions: Student Success Skills (SSS)

One promising intervention to reverse the above trends is Student Success Skills (SSS; Miranda, Webb, Brigman, & Peluso, 2007). The National Study Group for the Affirmative Development of Academic Ability (Bennett et al., 2004) determined that the most effective approaches to successfully reverse the academic achievement gap may be those interventions that represent a comprehensive and multifaceted systematic strategy. The SSS program has been identified as an effective intervention to close the academic achievement gap for low-achieving students, a disproportionate number of whom are African American and Latino students. The original authors of the SSS program (Brigman & Campbell, 2003; Brigman et al., 2004; Brigman et al., 2007; Campbell & Brigman, 2005; Webb et al., 2005) designed their research on a strong theoretical basis with regard to content, delivery, and research design considered to be the "gold standard" of research design and evaluation by the U.S. Department of Education (2003). The program is effective in improving academic performance and closing the achievement gap for low-to mid-range-achieving students.

The SSS program is based on three skills sets consistently identified in extensive reviews of research as being contributors to improving academic and social outcomes (Hattie, Biggs, & Purdie, 1996; Masten & Coatsworth, 1998; Wang, Haertel, & Walberg, 1994):

- Cognitive and metacognitive skills such as goal setting, progress monitoring, and memory skills
- Social skills such as interpersonal skills, social problem solving, listening, and teamwork skills
- Self-management skills such as managing attention, motivation, and anger.

Further support for these skill sets has been reported by researchers who have empirically linked social and emotional competence to achievement outcomes, including that of students at risk for academic failure (Elias et al., 2003; Marzano et al., 2001; Zins, Weissberg, Wang, & Walberg, 2004).

Implications for Professional School Counselors

Trained professional school counselors are integral participants in SSS and the program's classroom and group interventions using a structured format and including them as a vital part of school improvement planning and intervention. Integrated into the classroom and group intervention are tools and strategies aimed at helping student succeed; these are represented in Table 12.9

The beginning of each session focuses on goal setting, progress monitoring, and success sharing based on five life skills: nutrition, rest, exercise, fun, and social support. The end of each session focuses on goal setting, progress monitoring, and success sharing as it pertains to cognitive, social, and emotional and self-management skills tied to academic success. Students share successes with peers, monitor individual progress toward previously set goals, and develop plans for new goals aimed at continued improvement. The middle of the classroom and group sessions is used to introduce new concepts, skills, and strategies aimed at the improvement of cognitive, social, and emotional functioning. Midgroup sessions focus on a social problem-solving model framed to reflect students' needs, interests, and goals. Students explore their own experiences related to managing anger and problem solving, while peers help conceptualize and try out potential solutions. Culturally relevant contexts are used to validate the background and values of students from diverse backgrounds. Social integration that further supports academic achievement is also embraced (Rang & Brown, 2002).

CONCLUSION

Before children and adolescents can change self-defeating or self-destructive behaviors, they need a secure environment in which to share their anxieties and developmental concerns. Small-group counseling

TABLE 12.9 Student Success Skills: Skills, Tools, Concepts, and Strategies Delivered by the Professional School Counselor

Creating a caring, supportive, and encouraging classroom	Students learn: Skills for listening and attending; ways to frame positive self-talk; acknowledging small improvements toward goals; and ways to encourage peers. Skills are practiced, encouraged, supported, and reinforced throughout the program to enhance academic, social, and emotional outcomes.
Goal setting, progress monitoring, and sharing success stories	Students learn: The "Seven Keys to Course Mastery," the "Looking Good/Feeling Good Life" skills and tools; grade-monitoring strategies; tools to identify success, patterns, and areas in need of improvement; how to develop plans for improvement.
Cognitive and memory skills	Students learn: Professional school counselors work collaboratively with teachers to introduce study-related tasks such as how to pick out important information, how to organize/chunk information to improve recall of information, and story structure to use as academic, social, and emotional skills.
Performing under pressure: Managing test anxiety	Students learn: How to create their own safe place; how to use breathing and positive self-talk to improve test performance; mental practice to improve performance; and test-taking strategies, positive self-talk, and music to enhance academic performance.
Building healthy optimism	Students learn: Healthy optimism through positive student storytelling; sharing success stories centered around chosen goals; and the language of optimism.

Source: Adapted from Miranda, A., Webb, L., Brigman, G., & Peluso, P., *Professional School Counseling, 10*(5), pp. 490–497, 2007. Reprinted with permission.

provides this opportunity. A psychoeducational life skills instructional model enhances social, emotional, and cognitive skills, and Student Success Skills serves as a schoolwide collaborative intervention to close the growing achievement gap. Schools already assume the role of providing information and opportunities for discussion, whether it is in the social studies classroom or the gym locker room. Small-group counseling provides the safety, security, and confidentiality that students need. The group process fosters positive peer pressure that encourages students to learn from each other, which has proven to be very effective.

Furthermore, teachers, administrators, and support staff can benefit from this group experience. One or two counselors in a school with a caseload that often exceeds 350 students on the high school level or 600 students on the elementary level can barely make a dent in the problems that children and adolescents face today. Support groups bring a manageable solution to the dilemma of overwhelming numbers and devastating problems. In a support group, a group leader can assist 6 to 10 students in the same amount of time normally devoted to one student.

Finally, very few instructional programs based on social, emotional, and cognitive skills have been developed. Children and adolescents are not provided with problem-focused coping skills to learn effective ways of mastering aspects of interpersonal relationships. Teachers, administrators, coaches, and community volunteers from a variety of backgrounds can become excellent group leaders of psychoeducational groups because of the emphasis on modeling and instruction (behaviors that they model every day). With the appropriate training in life skills, all those who interact within the school community can be involved in delivering effective services in a genuinely caring and empathic school environment. Such collective involvement can provide enduring interventions.

Crisis Intervention and Crisis Management Strategies for School-Based Response Teams

13

Schools are no longer the "islands of safety" that they once were believed to present, as street crime, random violence, and large-scale accidents pervade schools in all parts of the country and affect children of all ages on a regular basis.

David Schonfeld and Marsha Kline (1994, p. 155)

As violence, suicide rates, substance abuse, and depression continue to increase in our society, professional school counselors will be increasingly called upon to help students and their families, teachers, and support staff cope with the emotional and psychological stress that is a response to a sudden loss of a colleague or a student due to suicide, homicide, anticipated loss, or sudden unexpected death. Students, parents, teachers, administrators, and support staff experience the direct effects of a sudden death and the residual long-term effects of a significant loss.

Crisis management, crisis intervention, emergency response, disaster preparedness, catastrophic events, tragedy, traumatic events, and *critical incidents* are common vocabulary in schools today, and most schools have a crisis management plan, at least on paper. In addition to natural and manmade disasters such as earthquakes, hurricanes, and fires, students experience violence and death related to the suicide or sudden death of friends and significant adults, gang activity, bullying, harassment, rape, murder, and threats of terrorism. Unfortunately, the schools are a microcosm of society at large, which is becoming increasingly violent. Violent behavior in schoolchildren has more than doubled in the last two decades, and violent acts are becoming significantly more dangerous and insidious (McAdams, 2002; McAdams & Lambe, 2003).

Regrettably, within this context, some students react with severe emotional responses such as fear, grief, blame, anger, guilt, depression, anxiety, acute stress disorder, posttraumatic stress disorder (PTSD), and isolation. In some instances, such experiences can threaten a child's or adolescent's sense of worth and well-being, inducing the type of intense personal turmoil that leads students to think about hurting themselves or hurting others. Today, this is demonstrated by increased incidents of gang violence, relational aggression, self-injury, cyberbullying, suicide ideation, and other self-destructive or self-defeating behaviors. Concurrently, all traumatic experiences and violent behaviors are barriers to learning that inhibit healthy development at critical stages in a child's or adolescent's life. This chapter will provide first-response procedures and various debriefing strategies after traumatic incidents to restore the health and well-being of students, as well as of the adults who care for them.

Suicide and sudden death as the result of violence or terminal illness have become a recurring crisis for today's schools, requiring families, schools, and communities to help youths, even very young children, confront death, grief, and loss on an almost routine basis. This reality has intensified since the terrorist attacks of September 11, 2001, and the looming threat of terrorism in the future. The sudden or unexpected loss resulting from such occurrences at a school affects everyone involved and requires an immediate, effective, and efficient response by school personnel. An appropriate response is critical in order to prevent further harm and stress and to return the school and community to the precrisis equilibrium.

Crises or critical incidents can occur suddenly and in such a way as to have a ripple effect that permeates the entire interpersonal system of a school and a community. Suicide or sudden loss among student populations has become a major concern for professional school counselors, teachers, administrators, and support personnel, as well as all who interact with the system—both school and community. Within the context of the school and community, sudden loss due to suicide, homicide, or other acts of violence can create a crisis of ambiguous proportions because grief and loss are processed from different perspectives and from different levels of understanding and life experience. For example, in a society that is becoming increasingly diverse, sensitivity must be recognized and respected regarding rites, rituals, and mourning traditions.

CRISIS INTERVENTION AND CRISIS MANAGEMENT: A THEORETICAL PERSPECTIVE

The development of a crisis theory and practice has evolved out of an eclectic collection of processes and procedures from the social sciences and health and human services. Helping people in crisis is a complex, interdisciplinary team process. Since human beings encompass physical, emotional, social, religious, and spiritual belief systems, no one theory is adequate to explain the crisis experience or the most effective approach to helping people. What holds true, however, is that all who are affected can come through a crisis enriched and stronger—or can become paralyzed and feel helpless and hopeless about the future. Individuals can gain new insights and coping skills or lose emotional and physical well-being and possibly life itself.

Crisis is usually defined as a variant of stress so severe that the individual becomes disorganized and unable to function effectively (Kalafat, 1990). Crisis intervention differs from traditional counseling interventions in a number of ways. Petersen and Straub (1992) define *crisis intervention* as a

> helping process to assist an individual or group to survive an unsettling event so that the probability of debilitating effects (e.g., emotional trauma, social isolation, post-traumatic stress, or physical harm) is minimized, and the probability of growth (e.g., new coping skills, new perspectives on life, or more options in living) is identified and maximized. (p. 5)

Crisis intervention and counseling are considered much more directive, with the professional school counselor taking an active role in giving information, educating people about typical posttraumatic stress reactions, and offering strategies for coping with the crisis situation. A temporary dependency on the counselor (which is discouraged in traditional counseling) is often required to restore the school and community to equilibrium. The therapeutic relationship has curative powers for most counselees, and in many cases, the therapeutic relationship itself permeates all current solution-focused or brief therapy approaches.

Crises often fall into two major categories:

1. *Developmental crises* that are universal and are often experienced while negotiating developmental tasks
2. *Situational crises* such as injury, disaster, random acts of violence, homicide, suicide, death, divorce, or terminal illness

In an extensive study, Thompson (1993) found that loss events (e.g., death of a parent, sibling, or friend; divorce or separation) were the main precursors of crisis reactions in children and adolescents, followed by family troubles (e.g., abuse, neglect, or parent's loss of job). Lower on the scale were primary environmental changes (e.g., moving, attending a new school, or mother reentering a full-time career); sibling difficulties, physical harm (e.g., illness, accidents, and violence); and disasters (e.g., fire, floods, hurricanes, earthquakes, and tornadoes).

PSYCHOLOGICAL DISEQUILIBRIUM

A stressful event alone does not constitute a crisis; rather, crisis is determined by the individual's view of the event and his or her response to it. People in general have different thresholds of stress tolerance. If an individual sees an event as significant and threatening, has exhausted all of his or her usual coping strategies without effecting change, and is unaware of or unable to pursue alternatives, then the precipitating event may push the individual toward psychological disequilibrium—a state of crisis (Smead, 1988).

Psychological disequilibrium may be characterized by feelings of anxiety, helplessness, fear, inadequacy, confusion, agitation, and disorganization (Smead, 1988). At this point, the individual experiencing this disequilibrium may be most receptive to outside assistance to provide an opportunity for behavioral change and a return to balance. A crisis inherently results from a person's negative perception of a situation. A crisis is also often affected by culture, previous experience, and religious belief. For example, a fervently devoted Christian may view a significant loss as God's will.

Professional school counselors are often called upon to provide the first line of intervention for children and adolescents in psychological and emotional distress and have the training and resources for specialized intervention and access to mental health support networks (Thompson, 2006). Professional school counselors' primary goals in a crisis are to identify, assess, and intervene; to return the individual to his or her prior level of functioning as quickly as possible; and to lessen any negative impact on future mental health and well-being. It is important to focus on the event's significance in the child's or adolescent's present environment and on his or her current functioning and coping skills, while assessing the degree to which the person's functioning is impaired. Physical signs include changes in overall health, energy levels, and eating or sleeping patterns. Emotional signs include increased tension or fatigue and changes in temperament such as angry outbursts, withdrawal, or depression. Behavioral signs include such symptoms as the inability to concentrate, intrusive dreams, sleeplessness, or obsessive thoughts (Thompson, 2006).

The goal of crisis counseling is to restore the counselee to his or her precrisis equilibrium, with the number of counseling sessions ranging from one to eight (Thompson, 1990, 1993, 1995, 2006). A secondary therapeutic role involves "taking action rather than listening and allowing the client to take responsibility and control over his/her decision making and understanding" (p. 260). For individuals, crisis reactions often become cycles of mounting tension, anxiety, and ineffective coping. Often, the ability to think clearly, to plan decisively, and to act responsibly becomes impaired. This then becomes a barrier to learning that can have long-term implications such as school underachievement or failure. For example, it is not unusual to see a substance-abusing youth who is self-medicating because of depression experience a drop in grades and academic work along with attendance problems.

As a primary prevention and early intervention initiative, professional school counselors need to provide children and adolescents with coping skills before and when a crisis occurs. Such skills include an understanding of what constitutes a crisis event; an awareness of feelings, thoughts, or unfinished or unresolved issues in the past that can be reactivated by a crisis; changes in feelings and thoughts that occur over time; and coping strategies and behaviors that are useful in a time of crisis (Thompson, 1990, 1993, 1995, 2006).

MEETING THE EMOTIONAL NEEDS OF SURVIVORS

The death of a peer affects his or her family and members of the school, including administrators, teachers, and support personnel, as well as members of the greater community. The ramifications of loss and the causes of death among children and youth are multifaceted:

- The most frequent cause of death among the 15- to 24-year-old age group is motor vehicle accidents. These may be auto-related, recreational (hunting, boating, skiing), or other unintended fatal injury. Frequently, such accidents are unacknowledged or undetected suicide attempts; that is, in some incidences, a single-car accident may have been in reality a suicide attempt.
- Illness is another leading cause of death among young people. It seems "unfair" to see a strong young body waste away from cancer or other terminal illnesses, and for this reason, survivors often need help coping with an untimely death and the lack of concrete answers.
- Catastrophic events such as homicide, fire, and natural disasters also claim young victims. Teenagers are in the highest risk group to become victims of violent crimes. Youth gangs are on the rise, and drive-by shootings are frequent gang crimes. In this circumstance, grief is coupled with a volatile combination of anger and revenge when crime claims a young life and turf issues for rival gang activities occur.
- Suicide is an increasing cause of death among children and adolescents. The willful taking of one's own life is often the ultimate expression of despair. Survivors are left with intense feelings of loss and guilt. This is the reason that some school divisions have instituted depression screenings for adolescents as a prevention/intervention initiative to decrease teenage suicide rates. One caution regarding such schoolwide measures is to ensure the availability of mental health services for students and families who lack health care and to assess whether the community has adequate mental health services and providers.

Balk (1983a, 1983b) studied the acute emotional responses of students after the death of a peer. He revealed that, although peer support and chances to talk with friends about the death at such a time of loss are important aids in coping with death, many peers feel uncomfortable talking about death. They frequently avoid the survivors to decrease their own discomfort of not knowing what to say, or how to say it. Young people sometimes hide their feelings of grief because such feelings are not considered acceptable in public. As a result, youths are often confused about the source of their recurring grief reactions.

Young people often take cues on how to react from the adults around them more than from the event itself. It is critical, therefore, that professional school counselors, teachers, administrators, and support personnel process the emotional needs of survivors, especially children and adolescents. A structured opportunity to talk about the loss enhances the future coping skills of children and adolescents. Validation of feelings as a perceptual check is particularly important to youths. Talking about the death and related anxieties in a secure environment that fosters trust provides a means to "work through" the loss experience. It also serves to prevent "destructive fantasy building," which often occurs when young people cannot test their unprecedented perceptions and feelings against present reality.

Hawton (1986; see also Perrone, 1987; Thompson 2006) found that peers of adolescents who attempted suicide are vulnerable because suicide is higher in the following situations:

- Among persons with unstable social relationships,
- When a population is self-contained,
- When imitative behavior is common,
- When the element of bravado exists, and
- When the act is sure to be noticed.

Teachers, administrators, and support staff also need help in understanding and handling young people's normal, yet often inappropriate, reactions to death or loss. A paramount need is for professional school counselors, teachers, and other support personnel to process the emotional needs of survivors, especially those who were particularly close to the victim. Students often key into the behavioral clues provided by adults who are around them and allow these clues to direct their own reactions.

With adequate preparation, professional school counselors, teachers, administrators, and other helping professionals can provide the curative environment that fosters a responsive healing and therapeutic process. Collective efforts to provide structured programs and secure environments in which to work through significant losses are critical. Furthermore, all schools should have a detailed *crisis communication contingency plan* that includes steps to be taken to prevent further harm and a referral network for students and their families in need of long-term mental health counseling (Sheeley & Herily, 1989).

Without an available plan of action at the time of need, normal coping mechanisms for many students (and staff) will break down and disorganization will occur, fostering a negative climate of assigning inappropriate blame, instilling guilt, and lowering morale among school personnel. Later on, if survivors are not led to discover a balanced resolution to the traumatic event, they will become vulnerable to developmental crises or overidentification with the deceased, which can promote copycat suicides. Therefore, it is of paramount importance to process the emotional needs of survivors in a systematic caring manner.

THE NEED FOR SYSTEMATIC SCHOOL-BASED PROCEDURES AND INTERVENTIONS

If no effort is made by helping professionals in leadership positions to intervene with students who have experienced a crisis or critical incident, emotional reactions may interfere with a student's school achievement; worse, they can be imminently life threatening or may be the start of long-term social, emotional, and mental health problems such as depression, anxiety, or school phobia. In addition, when a significant portion of the student body is affected, major facets of the school and community are likely to be compromised (e.g., morale dissipates among faculty and staff, teacher retention declines, and overall school climate suffers, which carries over to the community with parent dissatisfaction with the leadership and responsiveness of the school).

In our current school climate, parents are more concerned about school safety than test scores. School-based crisis intervention procedures and debriefing strategies comprise a range of empirical-based approaches schools can plan and implement in response to crisis events and situations from suicide to terrorism. All school-based and school-linked staff can play an important role in crisis intervention and debriefing to restore the school and community to its precrisis equilibrium.

THE CRISIS MANAGEMENT RESPONSE TEAM: ROLES AND RESPONSIBILITIES

Each school should organize a *crisis response team,* preferably in-house because students do not respond well to strangers, especially mental health professionals, who do not know the ins and outs of the school and the dynamics of peer interaction. Team members should include school administrators, professional school counselors, a cadre of teachers, the school psychologist, the school social worker, the school nurse, and other significant adults based on skills, resources, and limitations. All local teams should be collectively assembled for training in crisis intervention and crisis management skills on an annual basis. The school crisis team's primary responsibility would be to mobilize school and community resources and to follow specific procedures in the event of a crisis.

Crisis team members can also include clergy or representatives of community agencies such as the health department or community services board. However, it is important that community agencies have *preexisting* collaborative training and close working relationships with current school personnel; without prior cooperation, they will be strangers to the school building and will hinder more than enhance the working relationships in a time of crisis, and their presence will have a tendency to alienate students as well as faculty.

As a group combination, crisis response team members should have strong individual and group facilitation skills, knowledge of how the school and community function, and experience with crisis intervention and crisis management procedures. Members need to be able to imagine multiple scenarios with their possible consequences and to think clearly under stress. They also need to be familiar with the uniqueness of the school and the specific needs of the community.

Over a two- to three-day period, a crisis management strategy might require maintaining the building's regular schedule and establishing, in addition to the school counseling office, a "care center" away from the central office to help small groups cope with the crisis. Students who need help and support, or who are too upset to be in class, would be permitted to spend debriefing time in the care center.

Crisis response team members should do the following:

- Address concerns individually with faculty members or with the entire faculty at early morning staff meetings.
- Set up a care center for both students and support staff who are trying to handle their classes during the crisis.
- Be prepared to cover classes for those teachers who seem especially upset or who need time to recover from the shock of the stressful news, especially if harm came to a student in their class.
- Help teachers review debriefing strategies for dealing with issues of death and dying in the classroom.
- Talk with individuals who have unresolved grief issues from the past.
- Help the building administrator develop a press release and a strategy for dealing with the media (when necessary).
- Recognize the importance of knowing how, when, and where to appropriately refer students whose concerns fall beyond the counselor's or helping professional's area of knowledge or skills (e.g., deep-seated mental health issues).
- Maintain a network of mental health professionals to confer with and consult.
- Undergo training or reeducation for crisis prevention and intervention skills. If every school has a designated crisis intervention and crisis management team, they should meet regionally to network, retrain, and renew their skills and resources on an annual basis. Counselors should obtain adequate supervision and develop a crisis team approach to facilitate intervention and prevention efforts.

Assisting, interviewing, and counseling a suicidal youth ultimately involves mobilizing the School Counselor Documented Action Plan (see the Appendix). Merely giving students a crisis hotline number and sending them on their way is inappropriate. Nondirective approaches to intervention should be avoided during the initial stages of intervention; they lack the control that school personnel will need to navigate the youth through the crisis situation.

A high degree of perceptiveness on the part of the interviewer is necessary to confirm the emotional state of the student's crisis and to intervene adequately. The interviewer's approach should focus on resolution of the immediate problem with the mobilization of personal, educational, social, and environmental resources, as well as the student's support network. The primary outcome is to help the student reestablish a feeling of control over his or her life by exploring more concrete and positive alternatives.

If the student is thought to be potentially suicidal, six crucial steps should guide the interview process:

1. Establish a therapeutic, student-centered relationship; strive to convey an atmosphere of acceptance, support, and a calm confidence about the future.
2. Obtain necessary information such as the *frequency, intensity,* and *duration* (FID) of suicidal ideation or self-destructive behavior. Directly question the student's perception of the crisis, the frequency and sequence of events, his or her feelings, and any history of attempts to deal with the stressful situation. While supporting and empathizing with the student, avoid using the phrase "I understand." This can cut off the full and open expression of feelings and emotions from the student, because one cannot truly understand the child's or adolescent's current world.
3. Clarify the nature of the stress and the presenting problem. Also, clarify the incident and acknowledge any social and cultural factors that may relate to the crisis to develop an awareness of the significance of the crisis from the student's point of view.
4. Evaluate suicidal or self-destructive potential and assess the student's present strengths and resources.
5. Document information and initiate the School Counselor Documented Action Plan (see the Appendix).
6. Inform the administration, notify the parent or guardian, and identify referral resources such as members of the regional crisis response team.

RESTORING EQUILIBRIUM: CRISIS TEAM ROLES AND RESPONSIBILITIES

When managing a crisis, helping professionals need to know what to do and how to restore stability in the school and community. It generally takes a period of up to three to four weeks to fully process the crisis or critical incident. After a suicide or sudden loss, however, some students (based on prior experience, coping skills, and support networks) may experience difficulties for months after the crisis has occurred. Every school needs a plan, which includes steps to be taken to prevent panic and a referral network for students and their families in need of services.

The ultimate goal of the crisis team should be to create a *crisis management plan* before a crisis occurs. A specific plan should outline all the agreed-upon steps for resolving the crisis situation. During the initial phases of the crisis, it is too difficult to clearly think through all details necessary to manage and contain the crisis. Therefore, a *first response procedures file* should be housed in both the counseling and administrative offices, updated regularly, and made available to the crisis response team.

In combination, members of the crisis response team should have strong individual and group facilitation skills, knowledge of how the school community functions, and experience with crisis intervention and crisis management procedures. Finally, all the interventions used should be guided by the principle of focusing on strengths and constructive behaviors rather than focusing on deficits or assigning blame to individuals or institutions.

CRISIS PROCEDURES

The lead professional school counselor and administrator should work collaboratively in the event of a traumatic situation involving the school. Some of the key procedures and considerations are described below, using a death of a student at the school as an example.

First Actions to Take

- Verify the death. This is critical and can become a liability issue. For example, a parent might insist, "This was an accidental hanging, not a suicide." Since the child or adolescent is a minor (under the age of 18), the parent's wishes must be honored and confidentiality must be upheld, even if it may not be the truth.
- Activate the phone tree to inform faculty and staff and arrange for an early morning faculty meeting to activate the crisis management plan.
- Contain information and prevent rumors. Notify the superintendent's office or the district information officer whose responsibility is to deal with the media.
- Convene the school crisis response team.
- Meet with faculty to provide accurate information and to review the crisis management plan.
- Designate a lead school counselor to serve as a case manager (e.g., someone who has been in ongoing training).
- Call on local crisis response teams or support services, if needed.
- Identify crisis response member(s) who will follow the deceased student's class schedule to meet with teachers and classmates and to work the hallways following the crisis.
- Contact resources in the community.
- Respond to the concerns of parents.
- Minimize the possibility that other students may imitate the behavior and take their own lives or seek revenge for the victim.
- Make all professional school counselors and support staff available to students and faculty.
- Identify students about whom faculty and staff have concerns.
- Provide care centers, rooms where students can meet in small groups.
- Set up information and evening education programs for parents and the community.

Critical Questions to Consider

- How and when should the students be informed?
- What specific information will be shared about the tragedy with the teachers and staff?
- How will the school protect the family's privacy?
- Who is the spokesperson for the school, and what information will be released to the media? What will staff members be told to say if contacted by the media?
- How should the personal possessions of the student be handled?
- If feeder schools are affected by the crisis, how should they be included in the overall response efforts? Usually, feeder school personnel are most helpful because they know the students and are willing to help in crisis management.
- Will there be a care center for those students who are upset? Where will it be located? Who will supervise it? How will students be identified to come to the care center? How many days will the care center be in existence?
- What available staff will be utilized from the regional crisis response team?
- How will teachers who are emotionally upset be assisted?
- Who will be the designated professional school counselor who will focus on and process the loss with those students in the victim's classes?
- Who will be assigned the responsibility of being the "floater" (i.e., the person who moves through the halls and facilitates communication among the care center, counseling office, crisis communication center, administration, and classrooms)?
- Who will be assigned the responsibility of being the "logger" (i.e., the person who documents activities and contacts with parents, students, and related personnel)?

- Don't release high-risk students during the school day until the parent or guardian has been contacted to pick them up to provide full supervision.
- Institute sign-in sheets to help monitor students who need attention.
- Designate "security personnel" to control access to crisis areas and keep order within them.
- How will the school handle releasing students for the funeral or a memorial service? Will the school itself have a memorial service? How will the service be handled?

Other Important Considerations

- After school (possibly between the hours of 5:00 p.m. and 7:00 p.m.), it may be helpful to leave the school open for students, parents, or other community members who need assistance in responding to the crisis. Professional school counselors, school psychologists, school social workers, and other direct service providers can be available for consultation.
- The crisis response team should follow up specifically on the faculty or school staff directly involved in the crisis. Custodians, cafeteria personnel, secretaries, bus drivers, teachers, professional school counselor staff, and administrators may all need to be involved in a relatively intense "debriefing session" if they were directly involved in the crisis.
- It is important not to glamorize the death, especially if it was a suicide. Doing something in memoriam for the deceased can be appropriate for allowing students to express their feelings. A one-time event is frequently used, such as writing a song or poem, planting a tree, or putting together a memory book of collected photos. However, there should *not* be a memorial in the event of a suicide. Such a memorial sends a message that there is "fame in death."
- The need for continued efforts exists beyond the days immediately following a crisis, particularly in the event of a suicide. Even though a critical period of up to three or four weeks generally exists for the school and community, death by suicide may create difficulties for some students for months.

Responsibilities of the School Administrator

- Verify the facts. Attempt to define the type and extent of the crisis as soon as possible.
- If the crisis involves a death, consult with the family of the deceased student or staff member before making any statement. Explain school system policy and assure them that confidential information will be protected.
- Delay releasing information until facts are verified and the school's position about the crisis is clear.
- Activate the phone tree to alert the school crisis response team and regional response teams, as well as others (e.g., police, rescue, fire department), if necessary.
- Activate the phone tree to alert faculty of the debriefing meeting before or after school, depending on the time of the incident, to be held by the crisis response team members.
- Cancel special scheduled activities, if necessary.
- Set the tone and direction for crisis management procedures (i.e., an expedient and positive resolution).
- Contact the superintendent's staff at the school administration building and inform them of the crisis. Apprise the appropriate administrator or designee of the current situation and emerging developments, and clarify information for all parties.
- Prepare a written statement for the faculty to give to students, if appropriate.
- Prepare a general announcement for students. A straightforward, sympathetic announcement of a loss with a simple statement of condolence is recommended. Also, a statement that more

information, when verified, will be forthcoming can be reassuring to the students, teachers, and support staff.

- Maintain a unified position and message when communicating with the media. Keep messages concise, clear, and consistent. Frame the message to each target group with accuracy and sensitivity.
- Prepare a written statement for the media. Designate a spokesperson, if applicable, or notify the public information officer of the school system. Remind employees that only designated spokespersons are authorized to talk with news media.
- Advise school staff of media procedures, and advise students of the media policy. Let them know that they do not have to talk to the media and that they can say no.
- If necessary, designate a central area as a crisis communications center and designate one person to manage and disseminate information. There will be many inquiries from many sources (e.g., the media, parents, feeder schools, community leaders, school board members, and concerned citizens). The center could be located in the main office, the attendance office, or a designated office in the counseling suite. One person should be responsible to manage the center to ensure consistency and accuracy of information and to provide a timely response to prevent destructive rumors. Employees should be instructed to refer all information and questions to the crisis communication center and the designated person. Sufficient staff should be assigned to handle phones and to seek additional information, and a log should be kept of all incoming and outgoing calls and personal contacts.
- Designate the lead school counselor as case manager.
- Designate security personnel to control access to crisis areas and to monitor parking lots and access to the building.
- Identify faculty and staff in need of counseling.
- Identify procedures for excused absences for students attending funeral services off campus.
- Keep staff updated with debriefings at the end of every day.
- Follow up specifically with the faculty or school staff directly involved in the crisis. They need to be involved in a relatively intense debriefing session.
- Remain highly visible and accessible to others.
- Relieve key people from their normal duties so they may focus on the crisis.
- Express appreciation to all persons who helped bring the crisis to an expedient and positive resolution.

School Counselor/Case Manager Responsibilities

- Announce the event to students. Clarify facts to eliminate rumors.
- Lead class discussions and generate activities to reduce the impact of the trauma (*not* discussing a loss with students can send a very powerful message—that someone's life is meaningless and expendable).
- Identify students in need of counseling and refer them to the counseling suite or care center. Notify the counseling office of the students needing counseling.
- Postpone testing. Restructure or shorten assignments.
- Keep the administration, counselors, and members of the crisis response team informed of concerns or problems.
- If appropriate, ask the class what they wish to do with the deceased's desk.
- In the event of a teacher's death, members of the department should rotate by planning bell to cover the class for the first week following the loss. On the elementary school level, assign a staff member whom the students know, not a stranger, to cover the class. This sends a message of caring and shared loss and avoids embedding the message to students that one's life and contributions do not matter.

- Prepare both students and teachers for funeral attendance, especially if they are asked to make a brief statement or deliver a eulogy. They may also need assistance with the religious customs or rituals of the deceased. Respect the traditional ethnic and cultural mores of students from different cultural or ethnic backgrounds. (The cultural diversity in school settings cannot be ignored.) Education on and responsiveness to different roles and rituals of mourning and loss will help soften rigidity and the expectations of other ethnic groups. This can be a powerful learning experience.
- Identify a crisis team member who will follow the deceased student's class schedule and make contact with classmates to discuss their concerns.
- Identify a floater who will be available throughout the building to roam the halls and facilitate communication between the care center, counseling office, administrative offices, and communication center. The floater should check parking lots and restrooms for group mourners.
- Identify a logger to record activities, school–community contacts, parent–teacher contacts, and other interactions.
- Seek additional community services and helping professional support, if necessary.
- Plan the logistics of the crisis counseling: Who will meet with individual students? With groups of students? With the faculty and staff? With parents? With school/community support services (i.e., school psychologists, community mental health counselors)? (It is important that the lead professional school counselor delegate tasks to others for personal well-being and shared responsibility.)
- Designate a care center away from the office for students who need additional time to cope with the situation or to meet with peers.
- Provide sign-in sheets to help monitor students who need further attention and follow-through.
- Debrief the counseling staff at the beginning and the end of each day. This is an area that is often neglected, but there needs to be time set aside for daily closure of traumatic events among the staff.
- Contact feeder or receiver schools so that they can provide support for students affected in their schools.
- Call parents of students counseled to provide continued support for the students who are very distressed. Provide information to parents. Setting up a hotline number is very helpful, as is posting information on the school website. Many schools also have parents' email addresses and cell phone numbers and use this as a form of communication in case of an emergency.
- Focus on the needs of survivors. Initiate groups for the victim's friends and conduct posttraumatic loss debriefings.
- Provide support personnel to be available for emergency counseling with students or faculty after hours.
- Communicate with faculty and enlist the help of teacher advisors, sponsors, and coaches to nurture and support their particular population of students, such as athletic teams, student government, and clubs.
- Identify students who attended the funeral and may need additional support for dealing with their grief and loss experience.
- Provide information and seek assistance from students who are peer helpers; they are frequently the "first finders" of students in distress.
- Plan for the transition and return of a student who attempted suicide or who was hospitalized due to illness or violence.
- Stop notifications on student activities (e.g., scholarship information, testing, placement, failure and attendance notices) from being sent to the home of a family whose child has died. Stopping routine notifications is often overlooked, and it retraumatizes the family and creates a negative relationship with school personnel.
- Remove personal items from desk(s) and locker(s) and save them for parents or guardians.

- Prepare students who are chosen to participate in the memorial service.
- Plan some debriefing time toward the end of the day or week to take care of one another and to share experiences.

Faculty and Support Staff Responsibilities

- Announce the event to students. Clarify facts to eliminate rumors.
- Lead a class discussion and generate activities to reduce the impact of the trauma (*not* discussing a loss with students can send a very powerful message—that someone's life is expendable).
- Identify students in need of counseling and refer them to the counseling suite or care center.
- Notify the counseling office of the students wanting counseling.
- Postpone testing. Restructure or shorten assignments, if necessary.
- Keep the administration, professional school counselors, and members of the crisis response team informed of concerns or problems.
- If appropriate, ask the class what they wish to do with the deceased's desk.
- Prepare both students and teachers for funeral attendance, especially if they are asked to make a brief statement or deliver a eulogy, and if they are unfamiliar with religious customs or rituals of the deceased. Respect the traditional ethnic and cultural mores of students from different cultural or ethnic backgrounds. (The cultural diversity in school settings cannot be ignored.) Education on and responsiveness to different roles and rituals of mourning and loss will help soften rigidity and the expectations of other ethnic groups. This can be a powerful learning experience.

DEBRIEFING STRATEGIES

It very important to differentiate between schoolwide, small-group, community, and individual crises and to follow the appropriate debriefing procedures for each incident. Crises or critical incidents can range from very minimal involvement between the school and the affected parties to large-scale school/community involvement, depending on the type of incident, the popularity of the individual involved, and the level of involvement of parents within the school community. It is also critical to debrief the crisis responders to prevent the insidious, often debilitating symptoms of secondary traumatic stress or compassion fatigue that can result in caregivers working with people in crisis.

Major Schoolwide Crises

A major schoolwide crisis could stem from a major earthquake, hurricane, or tornado; a fire in the building; a sniper on campus; a lethal chemical spill or biological threat; or a hostage situation. In such cases, the administration directs and coordinates emergency procedures such as a schoolwide lockdown or evacuation; contacts emergency personnel such as police, the fire department, or the local hospital; and communicates with parents via email, a preestablished hotline number, the school website, or a systematic voice/text message system. The preestablished crisis management team converges at a designated place and sets into motion procedures to:

- Gather and disperse accurate information to the district information officer (to handle the media and other outside inquiries); students; faculty and support staff; and parents (the goal is to control rumors, prevent school/community panic, provide support, and begin debriefing)

- Assess the need for possible psychological first aid (discussed later in this chapter), and identify a means to put psychological first aid in place (the goal is to establish and maintain a special drop-in counseling care center and seek out district resources, if needed)
- Direct students, faculty, and support staff, as well as parents and the greater community, to the central arena for psychological first aid and maintain communication with the administration to support its initiatives to restore equilibrium

Major Schoolwide Crisis Management Briefings: Large-Group Crisis Intervention

Large-group crisis intervention in response to terrorism, disasters, and violence are becoming paramount in our society in the wake of such tragedies as the 9/11 terrorist attacks, natural disasters such as Hurricane Katrina, and the massacre at Virginia Tech, one of the worst school massacres in U.S. history. It is helpful to note that DeWolfe (2000) describes four phases of a disaster, which were easily recognized with the victims of Katrina:

1. The *Heroic Phase* begins immediately upon the onset of the disaster or even in anticipation of the event itself. Efforts to protect lives and property become paramount. There is an outpouring of caring for one's fellow man and the well-being of others. Community members may collaboratively work together to protect property and rescue residents. Efforts become a collective altruistic initiative among survivors generating feelings of hope, euphoria, and survival.
2. The *Honeymoon Phase* is characterized by optimism, thanksgiving, and gratitude for the lives and property saved. There is a sigh of relief as the realization of survival is appreciated. Congratulatory behavior is commonly acknowledged. People who have performed heroic feats or unusual rescue efforts are recognized in the media.
3. The *Disillusionment Phase* may begin as early as three or four weeks after the disaster, with the realization and recognition that something disastrous has really taken place. There is a great deal of discussion about blame and lack of responsibility or the responsiveness of emergency services. Anger, frustration, and hopelessness begin to set in. The question "Why did this have to happen?" is often raised, and optimism and energy about the future become increasingly depleted. Religious beliefs may be questioned. Here the mourning process actually begins. The growth and development of individuals and communities is stagnated. This phase may last weeks, months, or even years. For some individuals in the poorest or most devastated communities, this phase may never end. It is the goal of crisis intervention to facilitate the transition from this disillusionment phase to the final phase of reconstruction.
4. In the *Reconstruction Phase,* the final phase, restoration of "normal" routine functioning finally evolves. "Memories of the disaster are not forgotten, but life begins to return to a normal rhythm, and people begin to move on with their lives, although perhaps less than ideal" (Everly, 2000, p. 2). Zunin and Myers (2000) provide a visual depiction of the phases of a disaster in Figure 13.1.

Crisis Management Briefings: Bringing Together Individuals Who Experienced a Common Crisis

The crisis management briefing (CMB) is a systematic, practical, four-phase, group crisis intervention process. It is designed to be highly efficient, because it may be used with "large" groups—from 10 to 300 individuals—and requires just 45–75 minutes to conduct. This is one component within the comprehensive Critical Incident Stress Management (CISM) system as described by Everly and Mitchell (1999;

Phases of disaster

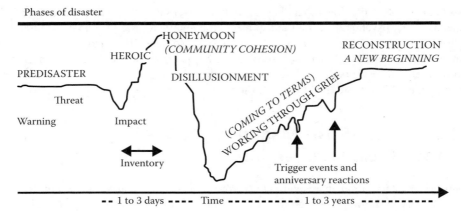

FIGURE 13.1   Phases of a disaster.
Source: Zunin, L. M., & Myers, D., *Training Manual for Human Service Workers in Major Disasters,* (2nd Ed.), DHHS
    Publication No. ADM 90-538, Department of Health and Human Services, Substance Abuse and Mental Health
    Services Administration, Center for Mental Health Services, Washington, DC, 2000.

Mitchell & Everly, 1996). The CMB is designed to be used within a comprehensive CISM model and
should not be used as a stand-alone intervention. The reader will see various formats for CISM, depending
upon the crisis event. There will be a need for CISM and CMB, as well as posttraumatic loss debriefing,
adaptive family debriefing, psychological first aid, and the family safety watch. The four phases of the
CMB are:

- *Phase One:* The first phase of the CMB consists of bringing together groups of individuals
  who have experienced a common crisis event such as a natural disaster, a major accident, or
  violence such as workplace or school shootings or terrorism. In response to a school crisis, for
  example, an assembly could be held in the auditorium. Depending upon the number of students,
  one grade or class (i.e., freshmen, sophomores, juniors, seniors) could be assembled as a group
  and addressed. In response to mass disasters, large-scale violence, or terrorism, local school
  auditoriums could be used to address the school and community populations that would correspond to the respective school districts' policies. An announcement to that effect could be made
  via email, newscasts, or local and district school websites. The CMB would be repeated until
  all constituents have been addressed within the given population at the school. This would also
  include feeder schools and local communities. "This act of collective assembly is the first step
  in reestablishing the sense of community and shared collective information that is so imperative to the recovery and rebuilding process" (Ayalon, 1993, p. 860).
- *Phase Two:* Once the group has been assembled, the next intervention component is to have
  the most appropriate and credible authority (the principal, lead professional school counselor,
  or district information officer) explain the *facts* of the crisis event. The choice of a respected
  and highly credible spokesperson assists in the development of the perceived credibility of the
  message and the belief that the actions and support will be effective. Objective and credible
  information should serve to (1) control destructive rumors; (2) reduce anticipatory anxiety, fear,
  and sense of hopelessness; and (3) return a sense of control to victims and to the community.
  Without breaching issues of confidentiality (e.g., regarding perpetrators or victims), the assembled group should receive factual information concerning that which is known and that which
  is not known regarding the crisis event. Rumors should be discredited. The ultimate goal is to
  restore the precrisis equilibrium within the school and the community.
- *Phase Three:* The third step is to have credible counselors and related health care professionals
  within the school and community discuss the most common *reactions* (signs, symptoms, and
  psychological themes) that are relevant to the particular crisis event. For example, in the case of

a suicide, the psychological theme of suicide should be addressed. In the case of terrorism, the dynamics of terrorism should be discussed. In the event of a natural disaster, common signs and symptoms of grief, anger, stress, survivor guilt, and even responsibility guilt among survivors, friends, and others should also be addressed.

- *Phase Four:* The final component of the CMB addresses personal coping and self-care strategies that may be of value in mitigating and alleviating the distressing reactions to the crisis event. Simple and practical stress management strategies should be provided and discussed. School and community resources should be made available to facilitate recovery. Lingering questions should be answered as appropriate. Each group participant should leave the CMB with a reference sheet that briefly describes common signs and symptoms, common stress management techniques, and local professional resources (with contact names and telephone numbers). Timing for the CMB is highly situation specific and flexible. The CMB can be repeated as long as it proves to be useful.

Posttraumatic Loss Debriefing: Debriefing Survivors Who Were Very Close to the

Victim

Posttraumatic loss debriefing provides immediate support for survivors of violence, suicide, homicide, or other sudden loss. Professional school counselors, administrators, and mental health professionals need to develop systematic strategies to intervene with survivors. Diminished responsiveness to one's immediate environment with "psychic numbing" or "emotional anesthesia" usually begins soon after the traumatic event. Sometimes the stress reactions appear immediately after the traumatic event; for other people, a delayed reaction may occur weeks or months later.

A sudden, unexpected death by suicide or a sudden loss from an accidental death often produces a characteristic set of psychological and physiological responses among survivors. Persons exposed to such traumatic events often manifest the following stress reactions: irritability, sleep disturbance, anxiety, startle reaction, nausea, headache, difficulty concentrating, confusion, fear, guilt, withdrawal, anger, and reactive depression. The particular pattern of these emotional reactions and the type of response will differ with each survivor, depending on the relationship the survivor had with the deceased, circumstances surrounding the death, and coping mechanisms of the survivors. The ultimate contribution that suicide or sudden loss intervention makes to survivor groups is the creation of an appropriate and meaningful opportunity to respond to suicide or sudden death. The seven stages of posttraumatic loss debriefing are:

1. *Introductory Stage:* The counselor introduces survivors to the debriefing process and defines the nature, limits, roles, and goals of the debriefing process. The counselor clarifies time limits, number of sessions, and confidentiality and creates a secure environment for sharing anxieties and concerns.
2. *Fact Stage:* Information is gathered to re-create the event from what is known about it. During the fact stage, participants are asked to re-create the event for the counselor. The focus of this stage is on facts, not feelings.

   Group members are asked to make a brief statement regarding their relationship with the deceased, how they heard about the death, and circumstances surrounding the event. It is important that the group shares the same story concerning the death and that secrets or rumors not be permitted to divide peers from each other. Group processing of the death also provides the counselor with an opportunity to listen to any attributions of guilt, extreme emotional responses, or posttraumatic stress reactions. Survivors are encouraged to engage in a moderate level of self-disclosure with counselor-facilitated statements such as: "I didn't know.... Could you tell me what that was like for you?"

It is important for the counselor to try to achieve an accurate sense of the survivors' world, be aware of the survivors' choice of topics regarding the death, gain insight into their priorities for the moment, and help survivors see the many factors that contributed to the death, in order to curtail self-blame. The low initial interaction is a nonthreatening warmup and naturally leads into a discussion of feelings in the next stage. It also provides a climate for sharing the details of the death and intervening to prevent secrets or rumors that may escalate conflict and divide survivors.

3. *Life Review Stage:* A life review of the deceased can be the next focus, if appropriate. A life review provides an opportunity for the group members to recount personal anecdotes about the deceased. The opportunity to share "Remember when..." stories lessens tension and anxiety within the survivor group. This also serves to ease the acceptance of the helping professional by the group.

4. *Feeling Stage:* Feelings are identified and integrated into the process. At this stage, survivors should have the opportunity to share the burden of the feelings they are experiencing in a non-judgmental, supportive, and understanding manner. Survivors must be permitted to identify their own behavioral reactions and to relate to the immediate present (i.e., the here and now).

   The counselor begins by asking feeling-oriented questions, such as: "How did you feel when that happened?" and "How are you feeling now?" This is a critical component where survivors acknowledge that things do get better with time.

   Each person in the group is offered an opportunity to answer these and a variety of other questions regarding his or her feelings. It is important that survivors express thoughts of responsibility regarding the event and process the accompanying feelings of sadness. At this stage, as in others, it is critical that no one gets left out of the discussion and that no one dominates the discussion at the expense of others. All feelings, positive or negative, big or small, are important and need to be listened to and expressed. More importantly, however, this particular stage allows survivors to see that subtle changes are occurring between what happened then and what is happening now.

5. *Reaction Stage:* This stage explores the physical, social, emotional, and cognitive stress reactions to the traumatic event. Acute reactions can last from a few days to a few weeks. Selected posttraumatic stress reactions include nausea, distressing dreams, difficulty concentrating, depression, feeling isolated, grief, anxiety, and fear of losing control. The counselor asks such questions as: "What reactions did you experience at the time of the incident?" and "What are you experiencing now?" The counselor encourages survivors to discuss what is going on in their school and/or work lives and in their relationships with parents, peers, and teachers.

6. *Learning Stage:* This stage is designed to assist survivors in learning new coping skills to deal with grief reactions. It is also therapeutic for survivors to realize that others are having similar feelings and experiences. The counselor assumes the responsibility of teaching the group something about their typical stress response reactions. The emphasis is on describing how typical and natural it is for people to experience a wide variety of feelings, emotions, and physical reactions to any traumatic event. Adolescents, in particular, need to know that their reactions are not unique, but are universally shared reactions. It is critical at this stage to be alert to danger signals in order to prevent destructive outcomes and to help survivors return to their precrisis equilibrium and interpersonal stability. This stage also serves as a primary prevention component for future self-defeating or self-destructive behavior by identifying the normal responses to a traumatic event in a secure, therapeutic environment with a caring, trusted adult.

7. *Closure Stage:* This final stage seeks to wrap up loose ends, answer outstanding questions, and provide final assurances. Survivor groups often need a direction or specific shared activity after a debriefing to bring closure to the process. Discussions surrounding memorials are often suggested and need appropriate direction. Survivors should be aware that closure is taking

place; therefore, no new issues should be introduced or discussed at this stage of the debriefing process. The professional school counselor should examine whether initial stress symptoms have been reduced or eliminated, assess the coping abilities of the survivors, and determine if increased levels of relating to others and the environment have occurred (i.e., Are the survivors genuinely hopeful regarding their immediate future? Are they managing their lives more effectively?) The group may also close by planning a group activity or "living task," such as attending a movie, concert, or similar activity to promote a sense of purpose and unity.

Ultimately, professional school counselors are in a unique position to guide intervention and closure efforts when a suicide or sudden loss occurs. The debriefing procedure described here provides the critical component for restoring the school community's equilibrium.

Critical Incident Stress Management: Debriefing Survivors Who Knew the Victim

Critical Incident Stress Management is an integrative, multicomponent crisis intervention system developed by Everly and Mitchell (1999; see also Everly, Flannery, & Eyler, 2000) and empirically validated through quantitative analysis and controlled investigations. A *critical incident* is a sudden powerful event that is outside the realm of ordinary experience and has the potential to overwhelm the coping skills of the individual or the group. Critical incidents in a school/community setting can include the death of a student, faculty member, administrator, or other popular figure; an accident or injury on or off campus such as a car crash or highly unusual accident; or random acts of violence such as a shooting, stabbing, gang violence, or a terrorist act.

CISM is the use of deliberate and structured interventions with students, faculty, and support staff who have witnessed a traumatic or extremely stressful event with the intent to lessen the critical incident and accelerate the recovery process. CISM is one strategy that the crisis response team could use with affected students. The debriefing usually takes an hour and a half to three hours to accelerate the recovery process and contains seven phases (see Figure 13.1):

1. *Introduction:* This phase clarifies the process and sets the ground rules and expectations for the debriefing. Confidentiality is a key component to this introductory phase and must be clarified. In the school setting, it important for professional school counselors to remember that students are minors and that parents or guardians have the right to any information regarding their child, especially if it concerns their health or well-being.

2. *Fact Phase:* Provide facts and offer general information about the incident. This is to control rumors and stop destructive fantasy-building, especially in adolescents. Each participant shares the nature of their experience. "What happened?" "What did you see, touch, hear?" "What is the last thing you remember?" The purpose is to regain memory and put things back into sequence.

3. *Thought Phase:* Review the thoughts each person had at the time of the incident and in the time since the incident. "What were your thoughts after the incident?" "What stands out in your mind?"

4. *Reaction Phase:* Review the reactions each person had at the time of the incident and since the incident. "What was the worst thing about the event?" "If you could erase or change just one thing, what would it be?"

5. *Symptom Phase:* The purpose of this phase is to identify personal symptoms of distress and examine the physical and psychological after-effects of the incidents in the areas of cognitive (concentration and thinking), physical (fatigue and headache), emotional (panic and anxiety), behavioral (withdrawal from family and friends), and spiritual (questioning faith). These are

TABLE 13.1   Some Common Symptoms of Psychological Trauma and PTSD

Intrusive symptoms	• Persistent reexperiencing of the event in images, thoughts, recollections, daydreams, and nightmares • Acting and feeling as if reliving the event • Distress in the presence of symbolic reminders
Avoidance symptoms	• Avoiding places and thoughts symbolic of the trauma • Problems recalling the event • Loss of interest in important activities • Restricted emotions • Sense of foreshortened future
Arousal symptoms	• Hypervigilance • Exaggerated startle response • Sleep disturbance • Difficulty concentrating • Irritability or angry outbursts

Source: Flannery, R. B., *International Journal of Emergency Mental Health, 2,* 135–140, 1999.

similar to PTSD symptoms but do not last as long (see Table 13.1). Students need to know that these are normal reactions to an abnormal event.

6. *Teaching Phase:* Educate the attendees about normal reactions and adaptive coping mechanisms, such as encouraging stress management. Provide information and handouts regarding the specific incident, as well as resources for counseling and treatment.

7. *Reentry Phase:* Clarify any ambiguous information or issues not raised or addressed. Ask if anything has been left out. Provide a summary statement and prepare for termination. Students may begin some planning, such as memorial activities. However, be aware planning memorial activities too soon may signal that the grieving process is over, and some students may not be ready to move on. In such cases, memorials may be premature. Figure 13.2 provides an example of a pocket card that can be given to professional school counselors as a quick guide to the debriefing process.

CISM or posttraumatic loss debriefing is best used in small groups of students directly affected by the critical incident or loss. It is effective with the sudden loss of a peer, a teacher, or a significant member of the school community. It is also appropriate with the increase in gang violence that many students experience in their neighborhoods, with the violent residue sometimes spilling over into the school. All these incidents are barriers to student learning and need to be addressed in a structured timely manner. It is not therapy, but simply a structured debriefing procedure to assist the recovery process and to restore normalcy within the school community and to all those who interact within the system of the school.

---

(1) **Introductions:** Clarify time limits; confidentiality.

(2) **Facts:** Everyone makes a brief statement regarding their relationship to the deceased and what they heard; to share the same story.

(3) **Thoughts:** How they head about it and circumstances surrounding the event.

(4) **Feelings:** Ask "How were you feeling then, how are you feeling now?" to show that things are getting better.

(5) **Symptoms:** Explore physical and emotional reactions to the traumatic event (difficulty sleeping, intrusive dreams, inability to concentrate, etc.).

(6) **Teaching:** Teach that symptoms are "normal reactions to abnormal events."

(7) **Reentry:** Closure: some activity like notes or cards to the family; memorials, etc. (Assess those that need parent contact or referral resources).

FIGURE 13.2   Pocket card: Seven phases of CISM.

Adapted Family Debriefing Model: Debriefing Young Children and Their Parents

The Adapted Family Debriefing Model (AFDM) was developed specifically as an assessment and intervention method for student populations exposed to violence, especially terrorism (Juhnke & Shoffner, 1999). Evolved from CISM's single-group experience, the AFDM for students requires two separate debriefings. The first is with students' parents only, and the second is a joint debriefing experience with both students and parents. Additionally, unlike the CISM process which utilizes nonprofessional, adult peer facilitators, the AFDM requires the use of trained professionals who have specific knowledge regarding children's developmental needs and reactions to traumatic events.

There are three primary team members within the AFDM for school students: a leader, a coleader, and a doorkeeper. The leader explains the debriefing process, creates a supportive environment, identifies those experiencing excessive levels of emotional discomfort, and directs team members to intervene with distraught students or parents. In addition, the leader discusses with parents and students common symptoms experienced by children who:

- Have personally experienced terrorist acts or have suffered loss as a result of such acts (e.g., the death of a grandparent, parent, sibling, or other relative resulting from terrorism, etc.);
- Have witnessed terrorist acts via the media (e.g., experiencing vicarious traumatization);
- Understand the potential for continued terrorist acts; or
- Experience the cumulative effects of multiple terrorist acts.

The leader attempts to normalize manifested symptoms (i.e., these are normal reactions to abnormal events) and encourages parents to watch their children for more severe symptomatology that may require additional counseling (e.g., recurrent encopresis, persistent outbursts of anger, chronic hypervigilance or regressive behaviors). Coleaders add relevant comments and supportive information during the session and give immediate assistance to students and parents who become emotionally distraught. The doorkeeper prevents nonparticipants, such as self-serving news journalists, politicians, or other individuals who want to further sensationalize the event, from entering the session and redirects them to another meeting time. Doorkeepers also prevent severely distraught students or parents from leaving the sessions prematurely.

Parent and student have different needs and want different kinds of information, so the first session is conducted with parents only. It is important to keep the number of parents small (fewer than 12). Parents often express frustration and anger regarding their inability to adequately protect their children from acts of terrorism or other forms of violence. Many will perceive the situation as "hopeless" and "out of their control." These feelings of powerlessness undermine a parent's innate need to protect and adequately care for their children. Thus, it is imperative that the team keeps parents focused on attending to the immediate needs of their children. Parents need to be reminded that the goals of this session are to:

- Learn about possible symptoms their children may exhibit,
- Obtain available referral sources if needed, and
- Learn to validate and normalize their children's concerns.

During the joint student–parent debriefing, two concentric circles are formed. No more than five or six students of similar ages should sit in the inner circle, with friends or familiar peers presenting with similar concerns or fears. Parents should sit behind their children, promoting a perception of stability, unity, and support. The AFDM process follows seven steps that are similar to those outlined for CISM. As described by Juhnke and Shoffer (1999), these are:

1. *Introduction step.* During the introduction step, the leader introduces team members and establishes rules for the debriefing experience. Confidentiality is explained in terms that are

developmentally understandable to the students. Participants are encouraged not to discuss what is said within the session outside the debriefing room when the session is over. The leader states that the purpose of the session is to help students better understand their feelings about the specific terrorist act and increase their coping skills related to the potential of future terrorist or violent threats.

2. *Fact-gathering step.* The second step of the process is fact gathering. The leader will ask the children to report what the experience of the terrorist act was like for them. Each student is encourage to speak. Should the debriefing be related to terrorist acts which the students indirectly observed via media coverage, the leader may begin by asking about what the students observed on television or other media outlets. Those speaking are encouraged to state what they did when they first saw or heard about the terrorism. Emphasis is placed upon telling the facts of what each student encountered, in an effort to observe discrepancies is what was observed and to share the same story. Parents should be advised to limit media viewing for their child.

3. *Thought step.* This transitional step helps participants move from the cognitive to the affective domain. The leader asks questions related to what students thoughts were when the terrorism or violence erupted. During this step it is crucial to continue to validate and normalize each student's reported thoughts and perceptions.

4. *Reaction step.* The thought step can quickly move into the more emotionally charged reaction step. Here, the focus should be kept upon participants' reactions to the terrorism. Typically, the leader will start with a question like, "What has been the most difficult part of the school catching on fire?"

5. *Symptom step.* During this step, the leader helps direct the group from the affective domain back to the cognitive domain. The leader uses age appropriate language to ask students about any physical, cognitive, or affective symptoms experienced since the violent episode. Symptoms such as nausea, sleep difficulties, inability to concentrate, or feelings of anxiety should be explained and those who have encountered such experiences should raise their hands. A show of hands helps normalize the described symptoms and often helps survivors experience relief in knowing that they have shared the same experiences and feelings.

6. *Teaching step.* Symptoms experienced by group members are reported in age appropriate ways as being both normal and expected. Possible future symptoms can be briefly described (e.g., reoccurring dreams of being attacked, nightmares, or difficulty falling asleep). This helps both parents and students better understand symptoms that they may encounter and gives permission to discuss such symptoms. During this step the group leader may ask, 'What have you done or noticed your friends, teachers, and parents doing that have helped you handle this situation?' This question helps them begin to look for signs of returning to normal. Sometimes older students will express feelings of support from peers, teachers, or parents. Younger students may use active fantasy, such as pretending to be a hero, to help them better cope with their fears or concerns.

7. *Reentry step.* The re-entry step attempts to place some closure on the experience and allows participants to discuss further concerns. The leader may ask students and parents to revisit pressing issues, which might help the debriefing process come to a more successful end. After addressing any issues, the debriefing team makes a few closing comments related to group progress or support. A hand-out for students and another written for adults discussing common reaction symptoms can be helpful. Younger children may prefer drawing faces which depict how they currently feel (e.g., anxious, sad, frightened). Later parents can use these pictures as conversation starters with their children at home. Hand-outs should list a 24-hour helpline number and include the telephone number for the student's professional school counselor and other support personnel. The promotion of peer support (both parent and student) is important. Students and parents should be encouraged to telephone one another over the next few days to aid in the recovery process (pp. 342–348).

The Adapted Family Debriefing Model for students described above demonstrates a structured debriefing opportunity for helping both student survivors of terrorism and their parents cope with negative psychological and social effects by formally educating them about what to expect and that these social, emotional, and physical reactions are normal reactions to abnormal events. The model has distinct differences from traditional CISM because it deals with parents separately and then together with their children. This is a very therapeutic intervention. AFDM is relatively easy to implement and can be modified to meet the needs of both students and parents collectively.

PSYCHOLOGICAL FIRST AID: RESPONDING TO AN INDIVIDUAL STUDENT IN CRISIS

Pynoos and Nader (1988) discuss psychological first aid for use during and in the immediate aftermath of a crisis (providing a detailed outline of steps according to age). Their work helps all of us consider some general points about responding to a student who is emotionally upset. Psychological first aid for students can be as important as medical aid. The immediate objective is to help individuals deal with the troubling psychological reactions.

The first step of the process is *managing the situation*. A student who is upset can produce a form of emotional contagion. To counter this, staff must:

- Present a calm, reassuring demeanor
- Clarify for classmates and others that the student is upset
- If possible indicate why the student is upset (correct rumors and distorted information)
- State what can and will be done to help the student

The next step is *mobilizing support*. The student needs support and guidance. Ways in which staff can help are to:

- Try to engage the student in a problem-solving dialogue
- Normalize the reaction as much as feasible
- Facilitate emotional expression (e.g., through use of empathy, warmth, and genuineness)
- Facilitate cognitive understanding by providing information
- Facilitate personal action by the student (e.g., help the individual do something to reduce the emotional upset and minimize threats to competence, self-determination, and relatedness)
- Encourage the student's support network of friends to provide social support
- Contact the student's home to discuss concerns with parent or guardian
- Refer the student to a specific counseling resource

The last step is *following up*. Over the following days (or sometimes longer), it is important to check on how things are progressing. Figures 13.3 through 13.7 provide important resources for the professional school counselor in a time of crisis. Figure 13.3 is a documented action plan for liability issues for a potential suicidal student; Figure 13.4 provide first response procedures in the time of a crisis as a guide of what needs to be done first, along with necessary resources. This information should be updated yearly. Figure 13.5 and Figure 13.6 provide guidelines for information for faculty or a schoolwide communication about a suicide and sudden loss. With media, parent concerns, and teacher and support staff inquires, it is difficult to have the time to compose a meaningful announcement with continuous interruptions. Finally Figure 13.7 provides an assessment of procedures that need to be in place before a crisis occurs.

- Has the student gotten the necessary support and services?
- Does the student need help in connecting with a referral resource?
- Is the student feeling better? If not, what additional support is needed and how can you help make certain that the student receives it?

TABLE 13.2   Symptoms and Psychological First Aid: Preschool Through Second Grade

SYMPTOM	PSYCHOLOGICAL FIRST AID
• Preoccupation with their own actions during the event; issues of responsibility and guilt	• Help to express their secretive imaginings about the event.
• Specific fears, triggered by traumatic reminders	• Help to identify and articulate traumatic reminders and anxieties; encourage them not to generalize.
• Retelling and replaying of the event through traumatic play	• Permit them to talk and act it out; address distortions, and acknowledge the normality of feelings and reactions.
• Impaired concentration and learning	• Encourage the child to let teachers know when thoughts and feeling interfere with learning.
• Sleep disturbances (bad dreams, fear of sleeping alone)	• Support them in reporting dreams; provide information about why we have bad dreams.
• Concerns about their own and other's safety	• Help to share worries; reassure with realistic information.
• Altered and inconsistent behavior (e.g., unusually aggressive or reckless behavior, inhibitions)	• Help to cope with the challenge to their own impulse control (e.g., acknowledge "it must be hard to feel so angry").

Adapted from Pynoos, R. S., & Nader, K., *Journal of Traumatic Stress 1*, 445–473, 1988.

Specific symptoms that may be exhibited by students are listed by age group in Tables 13.2 through 13.4, along with the appropriate psychological first aid.

Another form of "first aid" involves helping needy students and families connect with emergency services. This includes connecting them with agencies that can provide emergency food, clothing, housing, transportation, and so forth. Such basic needs constitute major crises for too many students and are fundamental barriers to learning, performing, and attending school (Pynoos & Nader, 1988, pp. 445–473).

TABLE 13.3   Symptoms and Psychological First Aid: Third Through Fifth Grades

SYMPTOM	PSYCHOLOGICAL FIRST AID
• Preoccupation with their own actions during the event; issues of responsibility and guilt	• Help to express their secretive imaginings about the event.
• Specific fears, triggered by traumatic reminders	• Help to identify and articulate traumatic reminders and anxieties; encourage them not to generalize.
• Retelling and replaying of the event (traumatic play)	• Permit them to talk and act it out; address distortions, and acknowledge the normality of feelings and reactions.
• Fear of being overwhelmed by their feelings (of crying, of being angry)	• Encourage expression of fear, anger, or sadness in your supportive presence.
• Hesitation to disturb parent with own anxieties	• Offer to meet with children and parent(s) to help children let parents know how they are feeling.
• Concern for other victims and their families	• Encourage constructive activities on behalf of the injured or deceased.
• Feeling disturbed, confused, and frightened by their grief responses; fear of ghosts	• Help them to retain positive memories as they work through the more intrusive traumatic memories.

Adapted from Pynoos, R. S., & Nader, K., *Journal of Traumatic Stress 1*, 445–473, 1988.

TABLE 13.4   Symptoms and Psychological First Aid: Sixth Grade and Up

SYMPTOM	PSYCHOLOGICAL FIRST AID
• Detachment, shame, and guilt (similar to adult response)	• Encourage discussion of the event, feelings about it, and realistic expectations of what could have been done.
• Self-consciousness about their fears, sense of vulnerability, and other emotional responses; fear of being labeled abnormal	• Help them understand the adult nature of these feelings; encourage peer understanding and support.
• Posttraumatic acting-out behavior (e.g., drug use, delinquent behavior, sexual acting out)	• Help them to understand that the acting-out behavior as an effort to numb their responses to, or to voice their anger over, the event.
• Life-threatening reenactment; self-destructive or accident-prone behavior	• Address the impulse toward reckless behavior in the acute aftermath; link it to the challenge to impulse control associated with violence.
• Abrupt shifts in interpersonal relationships	• Discuss the expectable strain on relationships with family and peers.
• Desires and plans to take revenge	• Elicit their actual plans of revenge; address the realistic consequences of these actions; encourage constructive alternatives that lessen the traumatic sense of helplessness.
• Radical changes in life attitudes, which influence identity formations	• Link attitude changes to the event's impact.
• Premature entrance into adulthood (e.g., leaving school or getting married) or reluctance to leave home	• Encourage postponing radical decisions in order to allow time to work through their responses to the event and to grieve.

Adapted from Pynoos, R. S., & Nader, K., *Journal of Traumatic Stress 1*, 445–473, 1988.

THE FAMILY SAFETY WATCH: HELPING FAMILIES CARE FOR THEIR OWN

The Family Safety Watch is an intensive intervention strategy to prevent self-destructive behavior on the part of a family member (e.g., a suicidal adolescent or self-injury). The safety watch also can apply to such problems as depression, self-mutilation, eating disorders, and drug or alcohol abuse. The procedure is as follows:

- Family members conduct the watch. They select people to be involved in the watch from among their nuclear family, extended family, and network of family friends.
- An around-the-clock shift schedule is established to determine how the youth is to spend his or her time over a 24-hour period, that is, when to sleep, eat, attend class, do homework, play games, view a movie, and so on.
- The case manager consults with the family to determine what the family's resources and support systems are and to figure out ways to involve these support systems in the effort (e.g., "How much time do you think Uncle Harry can give to watching your son?"). The case manager also designs a detailed plan for the safety watch, including devising schedules and shifts so that someone is with the at-risk child 24 hours a day.
- A backup system also is established so that the person on watch can obtain support from others if needed. A cardinal rule is that the child be within view of someone at all times, even while in the bathroom or when sleeping.

- The family is warned that the at-risk youth may try to manipulate situations to be alone, for example, pretending to be fine, and that the first days will be the hardest.
- A contractual agreement is established that if the watch is inadvertently slackened or compromised and the at-risk youth makes a suicide attempt or tries to challenge the program in some way, the regime will consequently be tightened. This is a therapeutic move that reduces the family's feeling of failure should a relapse occur.

The primary goal of the watch is to mobilize the family to "take care of their own" and to feel competent in doing so. The family, youth, and helping professionals collaborate in determining what tasks the adolescent must complete before the watch will be relaxed and ultimately terminated. Task issues should focus on personal responsibility, age-appropriate behavior, and handling of family and social relationships, such as:

- Arising in the morning without prompting
- Completing chores on time
- Substituting courteous and friendly behavior for grumbling and sulking
- Talking to parents and siblings more openly
- Watching less TV and spending more time with friends and significant others

The decision to terminate the watch is made conjointly by the family and the therapeutic team. It is contingent upon the absence of self-destructive behavior, as well as the achievement of an acceptable level of improvement in the other behavioral tasks assigned to the adolescent. If any member of the therapeutic team feels there is still a risk, the full safety watch is continued.

This approach appeals to families because it makes them feel empowered and useful and reduces the expense of an extended hospital program. It also reestablishes the intergenerational boundary, opens up communication within the family, reconnects the nuclear and extended families, and keeps the youth cared for and safe. In addition, it functions as a "compression" move, which pushes the youth and family members closer together and holds them there, while awaiting the rebound or disengagement that almost inevitably follows. This rebound is often a necessary step in bringing about appropriate distance within enmeshed subsystems and in opening the way for a more viable family structure—one that does not require a member to exhibit suicidal or self-destructive behavior to get someone's attention.

SPECIFIC COPING SKILLS FOR PROFESSIONAL SCHOOL COUNSELORS

With the increased incidence of violence in our society, professional school counselors and helping professionals will continue to be called upon to process emotionally stressful events. Holaday and Smith (1995) have concluded that "to protect their emotional well-being, helping professionals would benefit from five categories of coping strategies: social support, task-focused behaviors, emotional distancing, cognitive self-talk, and altruism" (p. 360). Some ways of engaging these strategies are described below.

To increase social support:

- Work in pairs or always be within speaking distance of another helping professional to ask for assistance or for additional emotional support.
- Smile and make eye contact with peers.
- Talk to peers about the situation, especially in terms of how they are handling the stress.
- Use humor to relieve tension and anxiety.

- Give comfort through physical contact (e.g., touch, hold, or hug people who are distraught).
- Take breaks with peers; share food if available to revitalize.

To maintain task-focused behaviors:

- Use problem-solving skills (i.e., think about and plan what needs to be done and take an active approach to helping).
- Generate solutions and quickly think of ways to resolve problems.
- Evaluate potential solutions. What is the most efficient thing you can do? Does it minimize harm?
- Identify and establish task-related priorities.
- Take action and request help if needed.
- Focus on the task at hand. Do not be distracted by what is happening around you.
- Avoid thinking about the consequences or long-term implications of the stressful event; focus on what has to be done now.

To increase emotional distancing:

- Think of the experience as a temporary event that will be over soon.
- Protect yourself from being overwhelmed by blocking emotions during the event and utilizing relaxation techniques.
- Pretend the event is not really happening, that it is merely a dream.
- Think about other things that are more pleasant.
- Talk about other things with other helping professionals, or talk to the person who is being helped about everyday, mundane things to avoid thinking about pain, loss, and other issues.
- In extreme situations, such as devastation from terrorist attacks, try not to think of victims as people, as having children or families whom will be affected. Do not look at their faces during intense rescue efforts.
- Distance yourself from the experience by singing or whistling; keep moving; look off into the distance and imagine being somewhere else.

To manage emotions through cognitive self-talk:

- Be mentally prepared; think about what will happen at the scene. Focus on the positive aspects of your work. Acknowledge that bad things happen to good people.
- Prepare physically. Take a deep breath, stand straight, and focus on staying in control.
- Use positive self-talk by focusing on self-competence, resourcefulness, and unique training experiences. Focus on strengths, maintain an "optimistic perseverance," and become aware of self-defeating thoughts.
- Reframe interpersonal language to reduce negative impact. Change statements such as "This is horrible" to "This is challenging."
- Translate arduous tasks into meaningful ones; find a deeper meaning in the tasks at hand. Do not just revive someone; "help someone get well." Celebrate with the survivors.

To feel better using altruism:

- Spare others by doing more work.
- Work for those who may not be as "strong" or who "cannot take it as well."
- Remember that it is a good thing to sacrifice for others; it feels good to help others. Be thankful for the opportunity to help.
- Put the needs of others paramount. Persevere and draw strength from adversity.

Inherently, the above coping skills reduce the negative effects of a stressful event. Helping professionals must be able to cope with their own posttraumatic stress. Daily crisis response team debriefings should be held to review and modify plans and communication to promote accountability.

DEBRIEFING THOSE WHO DEBRIEF: AN OFTEN-NEGLECTED FOLLOW-THROUGH PROCESS

In the aftermath of a major schoolwide crisis—violence, suicide, homicide, disaster, terrorist attack—professional school counselors as well as mental health professionals have themselves articulated feelings of guilt, sadness, anger, self-doubt, and concern about potential risk of counselees as well as awareness of impending doom or uncertainty about the future. These feelings can become intrusive and debilitating for years after the event if they are not processed in a structured manner in an accepting environment (LaFayette & Stern, 2004; McAdams & Foster, 2000, 2002). The potential for psychological, social, emotional, and professional impairment is especially great for new or novice counselors, especially if counselor preparation programs have failed to address crisis intervention and crisis management in the schools (McAdams & Foster, 2002; Trimble, Jackson, & Harvey, 2000). Therefore, it is critical that those who intervene with the crisis process the experience and debrief, too.

The debriefing process described below for those who debrief others is a variation of the International Critical Institute Stress Foundation (ICISF) model. It consists of three phases—Review, Response, and Remind—and is essential for debriefing caregivers (Myer, 1994).

The *review* phase is essentially a combination of the Introduction/Fact/Thought phase of the regular debriefing. It utilizes questions designed to have members think about and discuss the debriefing and their participation in it. Processing, sharing, and self-disclosing can be an effective mediation between exposure and prevention of secondary traumatic stress as well as the prevention of compassion fatigue. The following questions are examples of this phase:

- "How did it go?"
- "How do you think you did?"
- "What thing(s) did you do that think went well?"
- "What thing(s) did you feel did not go so well?"
- "What themes emerged?"
- "Is there anything you are worried about?"

During this phase, the leader focuses the discussion on what made the debriefings go well. Most participants will have a more vivid idea of what went wrong (that is human nature). So, it is important to be prepared to give examples of other ways to have handled some of the problems experienced. The intent, however, is to provide constant positive feedback on the work that was done. It is critical to validate their reactions to the experience and provide guidance on handling personal and interpersonal reactions after the event.

The *response* phase is a condensation of the Reaction/Symptom phase of the ICISF model and works to elicit comments on the self-perception of the team members and any reactions they may have. The following types of questions seem to work well:

- "What did you say that you wish you hadn't?"
- "What didn't you say that you wish you had?"
- "How has this experience affected you?"
- "What is the hardest part of this experience for you?"
- "In what areas did you feel the most useful?"
- "On a scale of 1 to 10, how well do you feel the students, faculty, and staff are adjusting?"
- "Are there any needs of the school/community that you feel need further attention or follow-up?"
- "Are there any special referral needs of students, faculty, or staff?"

During this phase, the leader guides some group discussion of the members' self-impressions. If someone is blaming herself for something or is worried that she did something really wrong, it usually comes out during this phase. What then usually follows is reassurance by the other team members that no major errors occurred and that, as in every event, some mistakes will inevitably occur. This is also an opportunity for the team leader and team members to reassure each other that each individual contributed to the process and to offer alternative methods for handling problem issues. This is the prime time to teach new techniques or reinforce what the team actually did.

The *remind* phase correlates to the Teaching/Reentry phase of the Everly & Mitchell (1999) model. Questions in this phase serve to help the team remember to do the same sort of things that debriefees are encouraged to do.

- "Is there any follow-up to be done?"
- "What are you going to do to take care of yourself in the next 24 to 48 hours?"
- "What will it take for you to eventually 'let go' of this experience?"
- "How are you going to manage your stress?"
- "Is there anyone you know who could give you some additional assistance?"

CONCLUSION

A workable referral system, using resources within the school (professional school counselors, social workers, school psychologists) and within the community (mental health counselors, agency personnel), becomes very important in achieving a positive resolution of the crisis that can be expected to develop when a sudden death or trauma occurs. When managing a crisis, professional school counselors and helping professionals need to know what to do and need to have the mechanisms to restore the school community to its precrisis equilibrium. This chapter has provided a general overview of such crisis situations and specific information pertinent to developing an effective crisis intervention and management plan. Schools need plans that will prevent panic and assist school personnel in dealing with shock, grief, and the healing process that follows an untimely death, suicide, or homicide.

APPENDIX

TABLE 13.5 Suicide Warning Signs

Feelings	• Hopelessness: "It will never get any better"; "There's nothing anyone can do"; "I'll always feel this way"
	• Fear of losing control, going crazy, and harming self or others
	• Helplessness, worthlessness: "Nobody cares"; "Everyone would be better off without me"
	• Overwhelming guilt, shame, or self-hatred
	• Pervasive sadness
	• Persistent anxiety or anger
Actions or events	• Drug or alcohol abuse
	• Themes of death or destruction in talk or written materials
	• Nightmares

continued

TABLE 13.5   Suicide Warning Signs (continued)

	• Recent loss through death, divorce, separation, broken relationships, or loss of job, money, status, or self-esteem • Loss of religious faith • Agitation, restlessness • Aggression, recklessness
Change	• In personality: More withdrawn, tired, apathetic, and indecisive, or more boisterous, talkative, and outgoing • In behavior: Can't concentrate on school, work, and routine tasks • In sleep pattern: Oversleeping or insomnia, sometimes with early waking • In eating habits: Loss of appetite and weight, or overeating • Loss of interest in friends, hobbies, personal grooming, sex, or other activities previously enjoyed • *Sudden* improvement after a period of being down or withdrawn
Threats	• Leading questions (e.g., "How long does it take to bleed to death?") • Threats (e.g., "I won't be around much longer") • Plans (e.g., putting affairs in order, giving away favorite things, studying drug effects, obtaining a weapon) • Gestures or attempts (e.g., overdosing, wrist cutting)

Warning signs can be organized around the word *FACT.*
Source: Kalafat, J., *School Counselor, 37*(5), 1990. Reprinted with permission.

Support resources identified by student	Support resources identified by counselor		
Lethality of Method	_____High	_____Medium	_____Low
Availability of Means (pills, gun, etc.)	_____High	_____Medium	_____Low
Specificity of Plan	_____High	_____Medium	_____Low

ACTION TO BE TAKEN

Date:_____ Time:_____ Crisis Team_____ Consultation_____

Action	Yes	No	N/A	Person Responsible	Date Completed
Notify administration					
Contact parents					
Consult with school/community mental health					
Is it safe to let student go home alone?					
Is the student in need of 24-hour supervision?					
Is the student provided with a contact person and phone number?					
Should child protective services be notified?					
Should the youth services officer (police liaison) be contacted?					
Other (specify)					

FIGURE 13.3   School Counselor Documented Action Plan. *Source:* Copyright © 1988. From *Preventing Adolescent Suicide* by David Capuzzi and Larry Golden (Eds.). Reproduced by permission of Taylor and Francis Group, LLC, a division of Informa plc.

In the time of crisis, it is difficult to clearly think through all the details necessary to manage and contain the crisis. A *first response procedures file* should be housed in the school counselor's and school administrator's offices and made available to the crisis response team. Included in the file should be the following items:

- Phone tree with emergency numbers for all faculty and crisis response team members (as well as regional social workers and school psychologists) who have been identified and assigned to the building.
- School map with the location of school phones and designated meeting rooms or care centers.
- Keys to all doors in the school facility and access to security personnel. (Security personnel should be included on the crisis response team when possible.)
- Bell schedule. (It may be necessary to adjust the bell schedule.)
- Bus schedule and bus numbers.
- Updated master schedule and a list of students enrolled in the school.
- In-house crisis management procedures (i.e., who is responsible for what?).
- Sign-in sheets for crisis team and school/community resource people.
- Name badges for crisis team members.
- Sample statement to the media.
- Sample letter from the principal informing parents of crisis and/or procedures.
- Sample statement informing the faculty of crisis and/or procedures (see Figure 13.5).
- Sample announcements for classroom or schoolwide communication (see Figure 13.6).
- Resource telephone numbers of community resources.
- Home or work telephone numbers of parent networks, school volunteers, clergy, and other resource people previously identified.
- Walkie-talkies.

FIGURE 13.4   First response procedures file.

CONFIDENTIAL

We need your help discussing the suicide of one of our students with your class during homeroom. Some students will already be aware of his suicide from the news on television or from this morning's paper. Others will be learning about the death from you.

It would be beneficial to give your class the opportunity to hear the necessary facts from you, to ask questions, to dispel rumors, and to discuss feelings and reactions. You can expect some students to be sad and upset as well as angry.

The crisis team will be available throughout the day, this evening, and over the weekend. If you need some assistance in discussing this death with your class, a team member will be available to come to your classroom. A crisis team member will be in the teachers' lounge if you wish to talk further about this tragedy. Please identify any student you think needs further help dealing with this loss and send him or her to the counseling office or to the care center which is set up adjacent to the cafeteria.

Students may be excused from classes to attend the student's funeral if they bring a written excuse from home. Funeral arrangements are still pending. We will give you that information when we receive it.

FIGURE 13.5   Sample memo informing faculty and staff.

Classroom Loss: We have something very tragic and very sad to tell you today. Melissa, our cocaptain, was driving home after basketball practice last night in the rain. The streets were slick and it was foggy. There was a car accident, and she was killed as a result. This is a tragic loss for all of us.

We will be around to talk with you all day. We will keep you updated about the funeral arrangements. We will also be open to any suggestions of activities that you might want to do in her memory.

Schoolwide Loss: Our school has had a tragic loss. As many of you know, Mrs. Smith, the school nurse, has been ill for many months. We just received word that she died this morning. We will be commemorating Mrs. Smith's contributions to our school. I would also like each class to discuss ways they would like to commemorate the life and work of Mrs. Smith.

FIGURE 13.6   Sample announcements for classroom or schoolwide communication.

TABLE 13.6   Posttraumatic Stress Reactions

PHYSICAL	COGNITIVE	EMOTIONAL
• Nausea • Upset stomach • Tremors (lips, hands) • Feeling uncoordinated • Profuse sweating • Chills • Diarrhea • Dizziness • Chest pain (should be checked at hospital) • Rapid heartbeat • Rapid breathing • Increased blood pressure • Headaches • Muscle aches • Sleep disturbance	• Slowed thinking • Difficulty making decisions • Difficulty problem-solving • Confusion • Difficulty calculating • Difficulty concentrating • Memory problems • Distressing dreams • Poor attention span • Seeing the event over and over • Disorientation (especially to place and time) • Difficulty naming common objects	• Anxiety • Fear • Guilt • Grief • Depression • Sadness • Feeling hurt • Feeling abandoned • Feeling isolated • Worry about others • Wanting to hide • Wanting to limit contact with others • Anger • Irritability • Feeling numb • Startling easily • Shock

Indicate all items that apply	Yes	Yes, but more of this is needed	No	If no, is this something you want?
I. Ensuring Immediate Assistance in Emergencies/Crises:				
A. Is there a plan that details a coordinating response				
1. For all at the school site?	___	___	___	___
2. With other schools in the complex?	___	___	___	___
3. With community agencies?	___	___	___	___
B. Are emergency/crisis plans updated appropriately with regard to:				
1. Crisis management guidelines (e.g., flow charts, check list)?	___	___	___	___
2. Plans for communicating with homes/community?	___	___	___	___
3. Media?	___	___	___	___
C. Are stakeholders regularly provided with information about emergency response plans?	___	___	___	___
D. Is medical first aid provided when crises occur?	___	___	___	___
E. Is psychological first aid provided when crises occur?	___	___	___	___
F. Other? (specify) _____	___	___	___	___
II. Providing Follow-up Assistance as Necessary:				
A. Are there programs for *short-term* follow-up assistance?	___	___	___	___
B. Are there programs for *longer-term* follow-up assistance?	___	___	___	___
C. Other? (specify) _____	___	___	___	___
III. Crisis Team to Formulate Response and Prevention Plans				
A. Is there an active Crisis Team?	___	___	___	___
B. Is the Crisis Team appropriately trained?	___	___	___	___
C. Does the team focus on prevention of school and personal crises?	___	___	___	___

FIGURE 13.7   Crisis assistance and prevention.

Indicate all items that apply	Yes	Yes, but more of this is needed	No	If no, is this something you want?
IV. Mobilizing Staff, Students, and Families to Anticipate Response Plans and Recovery Efforts With respect to planning and training for crisis response and recovery, are the following stakeholders? Are there programs to involved and integrate:				
A. Learning support staff?	—	—	—	—
B. Teachers?	—	—	—	—
C. Other school staff?	—	—	—	—
D. Students?	—	—	—	—
E. Families?	—	—	—	—
F. Other schools in the vicinity?	—	—	—	—
G. Other concerned parties in the community?	—	—	—	—
V. Creating a Caring and Safe Environment through Programs to Enhance Healthy Development and Prevent Problems	—	—	—	—
A. Are there programs for:				
1. Promoting healthy development?	—	—	—	—
2. Bullying and harassment abatement?	—	—	—	—
3. School community safety/violence reduction?	—	—	—	—
4. Suicide prevention?	—	—	—	—
5. Child abuse prevention?	—	—	—	—
6. Sexual abuse prevention?	—	—	—	—
7. Substance abuse prevention?	—	—	—	—
8. Other? (specify) _____	—	—	—	–
B. Is there an ongoing emphasis on enhancing a caring and safe learning environment:	—	—	—	—
1. Schoolwide?				
2. In classrooms?				
VI. Capacity-Building to Enhance Crisis Response and Prevention				
A. Is there an ongoing emphasis on enhancing a caring and safe learning environment through programs to enhance the capacity of:	—	—	—	—
	—	—	—	—
1. Learning support staff?	—	—	—	—
2. Teachers?	—	—	—	—
3. Other school staff?	—	—	—	—
4. Students?	—	—	—	—
5. Families?	—	—	—	—
6. Other schools in the feeder pattern?	—	—	—	—
7. Other concerned parties in the community?	—			
B. Is there ongoing training for learning support staffs with respect to the area of crisis assistance and prevention?	—			
C. Is there ongoing training for others involved in crisis response and prevention (e.g., teachers, office staff, administrators)?	—			
D. Which of the following topics are covered in educating stakeholders?	—	—	—	—
1. Anticipating emergencies	—	—	—	—
2. How to respond when an emergency arises	—	—	—	—
3. How to access assistance after an emergency (including watching for posttraumatic psychological reactions)	—	—	—	—
4. Indicators of abuse and potential suicide and what to do	—	—	—	—
5. How to respond to concerns related to death, dying, and grief	—	—	—	—
6. How to mediate conflicts and minimize violent reactions	—	—	—	—
7. Other (specify) _____	—	—	—	—
E. Indicate below other things you want the school to do in responding to and preventing crises.	—	—	—	—

FIGURE 13.7 Continued.

Ethical and Legal Issues for Professional School Counselors

14

Professional school counselors today are faced with a myriad of issues that are barriers to learning on a daily basis: suicidal ideation, custody issues, self-injury, dropouts, unintended pregnancies, violence, relational aggression, bullying, sexual harassment, educational malpractice, mandatory reporting in child abuse cases, gang violence, diversity, and special education accommodations, to name just a few. Essentially, professional school counselors serve five distinct entities:

1. Students
2. Teachers
3. Administrators
4. Parents/guardians
5. The school system at large, including the school board or central administration

From this perspective, Remley and Herlihy (2001) maintain that school counselors look to moral principles or "shared beliefs or agreed-upon assumptions upon which codes of ethics are based" (p. 3). The moral principles most often cited in relation to ethical practices for professional school counselors include the following:

- *Veracity:* Telling the truth, but only to necessary parties with a vested interest in the counselee (e.g., no gossiping about student or parental issues to other school personnel)
- *Justice:* Fairness, especially as it pertains to today's increasingly diverse populations within the school (e.g., making all advanced academic opportunities available to all students, not just those with high academic aspirations)
- *Nonmalfeasance:* Doing no harm (e.g., confidential information should not be shared, and conversations about others' private lives or about events inside or outside of the school should not be tolerated)
- *Beneficence:* Doing good (e.g., helping counselees and families gain something positive from the counseling experience; knowing appropriate referral sources in the community; communicating information on a consistent basis using all forms of media, including emails and school websites)
- *Autonomy:* Respecting freedom of choice (e.g., understanding that students will not necessarily accept their counselors' suggested assistance regarding personal, social, academic, or career options and that they sometimes overestimate or underestimate their potential or abilities as well as not having the knowledge to seek out the appropriate resources)
- *Fidelity:* Keeping promises; always following through on agreed-upon actions and contractual agreements (e.g., following through on documentation from local community agencies, colleges, and universities; student eligibility for extracurricular activities; or college or employment recommendations)

ETHICAL AND LEGAL CHALLENGES

Currently, little empirical evidence is available on the ethical dilemmas faced by school counselors. However, professional school counselors face a variety of issues that can have an impact on their professional identity and ethical responsibilities. This is particularly true when they are responsible to the five different entities mentioned above: students, teachers, parents, administrators, and the greater community, including the school board and central administration.

In an era of increasing litigation, professional school counselors should annually review the ethical standards for their profession and consult them when ethical dilemmas arise with students, parents, administrators, and the community (Remley & Herlihy, 2001). Professional school counselors should know the code of ethics of the American School Counselor Association (ASCA, 2010) and school board policy, as well as changing state legislative mandates, to avoid ethical pitfalls and to maintain the integrity in their role as a professional school counselor.

The literature in the last decade has documented the many challenges that professional school counselors encounter. Essentially, professional school counselors have no power—merely influence—to affect systemic change in schools, families, and communities. Yet, they have access to critical resources to resolve such critical issues as the following:

1. Providing confidentiality to minor students (Isaacs & Stone, 1999; Jackson & White, 2000).
2. Understanding issues regarding minors and abortion or adoption counseling and sexual matters (Fischer & Sorenson, 1996; Isaacs & Stone, 2001; Zirkel, 1991, 2001).
3. Assessing students who are self-mutilating or potentially suicidal, are engaging in self-harm, or have the potential to harm others (Beautrais, Joyce, & Mulder, 1999; Capuzzi & Gross, 2000).
4. Supervising any negligence in academic advising. Professional school counselors must keep constantly up to date on changing criteria and eligibility for the SAT, ACT, and National Collegiate Athletic Association (NCAA), as well as changes in legislation pertaining to children with disabilities, among other issues (Parrott, 2001; Reid, 2001; Zirkel, 2001).
5. Preventing the actions of and intervening with students who may be violent, engaged in relational aggression or cyberbullying, or involved in gang activity (Bailey, 2001; Hermann & Remley, 2000; Kass, 2001; Riley & McDaniel, 2000; Vossekuil, Reddy, Fein, Borum, & Modzeleski, 2000).
6. Assessing, evaluating, and conveying testing information includes the National Assessment of Educational Progress (NAEP), high-stakes testing, and making adequate yearly progress (AYP) aptitude tests, achievement tests, and online career assessments (American Counseling Association, 1997; Steinburg & Henriques, 2001; Wenglinsky, 2002; Wheelock, 2003).
7. Closing the achievement gap for students of poverty, minority students, and English-language learners (Education Trust, 1997, 2000; Education Watch, 1998; ASCA, 2005b).
8. Mandatory reporting in the case of child abuse or child maltreatment, including documentation and following reporting protocols (Berry, Cash, & Mathiesen, 2003; Berry, Charlson, & Dawson, 2003; Bloom, Fischer, & Orme, 2005; Chadwick Center for Children and Families, 2004; English, Shrikant, Bangdiwala, & Runyan, 2005; Freisthler, Merritt, & LaScala, 2006).
9. Intervention with sexual minority youth (i.e., gay, lesbian, and transgender youth). Sexual minority youth are entitled to a free and appropriate education that is safe and a school environment that has zero tolerance for harassment (Bernstein & Silberman, 1996; Bingham, 2001; D'Augelli, Hershberger, & Pilkington, 2001; Garofalo, Wolf, Wissow, Woods, & Goodman, 1999; Human Rights Watch, 2001).
10. Bullying behavior and relational aggression. Lack of intervention can escalate and have long-term implications in terms of later criminal activities and potential incarceration for the bully and psychological and emotional implications for the victim (Conway, 2005; Olweus &

Limber, 1999; Ortega & Lera, 2000; Stevens, Van Oost, & De Bourdeaudhuij, 2000; Smith & Brain, 2000).

11. Understanding special education regulations and 504 plans of specialized instructional services. For example, anything that denies a child the appropriate accommodations or a free and appropriate education can escalate to litigation against a negligent school (Fruchter, Berne, & Marcus, 1995; Fuchs, & Fuchs, 1995; Martin, 1991).

It is clearly evident from just these 11 selected issues that the professional school counselor is encountering many legal issues or dilemmas (Corey, Corey, & Callanan, 1998), and the school counselors' legal vulnerability is a concern. The professional school counselor is not afforded the same protection regarding confidentiality or privileged communication as those in the medical or legal professions. Lawrence and Kurpius (2000), Remley and Herlihy (2001), and White and Flynt (2000) explain that failing to follow mandatory reporting of reported suspected child abuse can result in civil and criminal liability. In particular, Lawrence and Kurpius (2000) note that confidentiality can be a difficult legal issue in the school setting, especially when counseling minors, because parents and those who share custody have the right to any information shared between counselor and counselee. Remley and Herlihy also point out that counselors can be subpoenaed to produce records and to appear at court proceedings. Neglecting to effectively manage a counselee's suicidal threats or failure to protect one from harming others can result in malpractice lawsuits, as well (Ahia & Martin, 1993; Corey et al., 1998; Glosoff, Herlihy, & Spence, 2000; Remley & Herlihy, 2001; Remley & Sparkman, 1993). Therefore, the roles and responsibilities are seemingly blurred—especially when it comes to confidentiality issues and counselees who, as minors, are ultimately under the supervision of their parent or guardian.

Confidentiality was the most frequent focus of concerns among professional school counselors, because of the legal status of minors and because of issues of parents' and teacher's rights to information about a student. For example, Isaacs and Stone (2001) present a study in which they surveyed 627 professional school counselors regarding the likelihood of breaking confidentiality in a variety of situations. Their study indicated that in many situations described, elementary school professional school counselors were more likely to break confidentiality than middle school professional school counselors, who were more likely to break confidentiality than high school professional school counselors. Studies also have indicated that elementary school counselors have more contact and consultation with both families and teachers than middle and high school counselors do (Isaacs & Stone, 1999) and that perceived school–family–community partnerships were more important on the elementary and middle school level than on the high school level (Bryan & Holcomb-McCoy, 2004).

Parental rights complicate this issue. Legally, confidentiality for minors is an ill-defined area. Ethically, confidentiality is needed within the counseling relationship, but so are the support, goodwill, and cooperation of student support networks, which frequently include families (ASCA, 2004a). Confidentiality for minors can be very ambiguous. It remains a debated issue that understandably causes many professional school counselors concern as to how to resolve situations when parents want more information than the counselor believes should be shared (Glosoff & Pate, 2002; Isaacs & Stone, 1999; Mitchell, Disque, & Robertson, 2002).

In the end, however, it is best to err on the side of the well-being of the child or adolescent. For example, Froeschle and Moyer (2004) outline the challenges of working with students who self-mutilate, including the challenge of disclosing information to parents and determining the level of potential harm to students when weighing the decision to breach confidentiality. There is also some dissension about whether self-injurious behavior is an effort at affect modulation (emotional regulation) or a precursor to a suicide attempt. Nevertheless, Capuzzi (2002) reminds professional school counselors that "suicidal ideation is a form of self-harm, thereby mandating the counselor to break confidentiality and inform parents or guardians" (p. 38).

Stone (2000) points out that sexual harassment presents a legal responsibility to inform school authorities who are in a position to take corrective action to stop the harassment. Additional studies have pointed out the ethical responsibility of protecting students from both harm and violent threats

(Hermann & Finn, 2002) and of practicing competently by receiving ongoing supervision (Herlihy, Gray, & McCollum, 2002).

In practice, confidentiality is the area that seems to cause most ethical concerns among professional school counselors, especially counselors who are caught between the dilemma of student confidentiality and the parental right to know. This is further complicated by professional school counselors' accountability to teachers, administrators, and the community, along with school board policies and central administration mandates. Perhaps that is why some professional school counselors retreat when they feel they are receiving too much information and don't feel they have the power to change the circumstances or the situation. Yet, it is their moral obligation and professional responsibility to break confidentiality when a child is a danger to self or others.

Davis and Mickelson (1994), Herndon (1990), and Rawls (1997) have found that professional school counselors face legal dilemmas in the areas of student privacy, reporting suspected child abuse, counseling students who pose a danger to others, and ensuring the safety of students. Remley and Herlihy (2001) note that malpractice lawsuits against mental health practitioners have increased dramatically in the recent years, although it is highly unusual for a professional school counselor to be sued (Parrott, 2001; Remley & Herlihy, 2001; Stone, 2001).

ETHICAL SCENARIOS AS CASE EXAMPLES

According to the American School Counselor Association's ethical standards:

- Each person has the right to be respected, be treated with dignity and have access to a comprehensive school counseling program that advocates for and affirms all students from diverse populations including: ethnic/racial identity, age, economic status, abilities/disabilities, language, immigration status, sexual orientation, gender, gender identity/expression, family type, religious/spiritual identity and appearance.
- Each person has the right to receive the information and support needed to move toward self-direction and self-development and affirmation within one's group identities, with special care being given to students who have historically not received adequate educational services, e.g., students of color, students living at a low socioeconomic status, students with disabilities and students from non-dominant language backgrounds.
- Each person has the right to understand the full magnitude and meaning of his/her educational choices and how those choices will affect future opportunities.
- Each person has the right to privacy and thereby the right to expect the school-counselor/student relationship to comply with all laws, policies and ethical standards pertaining to confidentiality in the school setting. (ASCA, 2010, p. 1)

The following scenarios or case examples are provided to test your knowledge of the ASCA ethical standards. Review each scenario and decide whether the professional school counselor's response was the correct action (CA) or incorrect action (IA) or if the situation is unclear (UC).

1. A high school professional school counselor meets with a student who confides in her that she maybe pregnant. The district policy states that if a student confides in another adult in the school setting, school personnel must inform the parent. Therefore, the professional school counselor tells the student that she (the counselor) must call her parents, but the student responds that, if she does, she will commit suicide. The professional school counselor says that now she must also tell her parents because she is a threat to herself and is in danger of harming herself. After a long discussion, the professional school counselor and the student agree that the student will

buy a pregnancy test and take it in the nurse's office the next day, and if it is positive, the professional school counselor and the student will tell her parent or guardian together. It turns out to be a false alarm; the student was not pregnant.

2. A male professional school counselor meets a male student who is struggling with sexual identity issues. The student feels more and more that he is attracted to males. He has recently been attending some gay clubs with older males and likes the attention and the unconditional acceptance of his sexual identity at the club. The professional school counselor, who believes in conversion therapy (a controversial therapy that is intended to convert a person back to their given sexual identity), tells the student that he knows someone who can help change his thinking about his identity and gives him a name of a free unlicensed counselor that the student can talk to at his church.

3. A female high school student confides in a male professional school counselor that she is being sexually abused by her father. The male professional school counselor hesitates to call child protective services because he thinks she may be doing it to get attention. He brings a female professional school counselor in, and the student tells the same story. The male professional school counselor calls child protective services and they come to the school and interview the student that afternoon.

4. An eight-year-old male student has been experimenting with marijuana. He comes to school in gang colors and is failing his schoolwork. There has been a lot of recent gang activity in the city around the school. The counselor suspects the student may be a "mule" (i.e., someone who is used by the gang to transport drugs). The professional school counselor informs the principal and the youth service officer about his or her concerns.

5. The director of counseling services at a high school just received the most recent grade-point averages of the two highest rated students in the senior class, and they have the potential of eliminating the current valedictorian from first place. The director regularly eats lunch with the senior class sponsor and other teachers who have the student in their classes. The director shares this news of the potential controversy with them at lunch.

6. An eighth-grade male student is being cyberbullied by a group of mean eighth-grade girls. They leave messages on his cell phone and computer, saying things like: "I heard you are going to kill yourself. I hope you succeed this time." The student's friend brings this to the professional school counselor's attention. Following the school's Internet harassment policy, the counselor brings it to the principal's attention. The professional school counselor and principal call in the parents/guardians and the local police for a conference, presenting samples of the messages from the girls. They document that if it happens again, they will press charges. In the meantime, the professional school counselor meets with the bullied student to offer assurance and support, while another professional school counselor meets with the girls who are doing the cyberbullying. In some cases, a parental meeting may also be necessary to explain the ramifications of cyberbullying.

7. A young female professional school counselor at a high school also coaches the girls' and boys' varsity track team. She has both track teams over for cookouts and sleepovers at her house. She doesn't mind if they drink alcoholic beverages, as long as they stay at her house and don't drive. Her boyfriend, who lives with her, is also at her house. The coach and her boyfriend retire around midnight but promise to be up to cook breakfast for the teams in the morning.

8. A nine-year-old male student's parents are going through a contentious divorce. He has been withdrawn in his interactions at school, has had angry outbursts with his peers, and has been failing his schoolwork. He is an only child and is struggling with the arguments and fights between his parents that he has to endure at home alone. He often cries himself to sleep. The professional school counselor is concerned, so she calls a meeting with his grade-level team to fill them in on his changed behavior and to encourage their support for his current circumstances.

9. Early in the school year, an elementary professional school counselor receives a subpoena to testify in court regarding a custody case. The mother's lawyer is very aggressive and asks the counselor for her notes regarding the case. The counselor says she does not keep any notes and only worked with the student during an academic classroom lesson with his teacher. She knows nothing about the parents or their relationship and has met them only briefly at a crowded open house during the introduction of faculty and staff at the beginning of the school year.

10. A middle school professional school counselor has recently become a licensed professional counselor (LPC) and licensed marriage and family therapist (LMFT). She feels very confident in her abilities to teach parenting skills and to counsel families. She thinks there is a real need for such programs in her school district. The counselor has an office established in a local church and has advertised her services to all the professional school counselors and parents in her school district. She uses the school database to get the names and addresses of students and their families.

11. A middle school counselor is meeting with an eighth-grade student who has had two previous suicide attempts and has been hospitalized twice. The student seems distraught and doesn't want to go home. The counselor views it as another effort to get attention, so the counselor gives the student a suicide hotline number and tells her to hurry so she does not miss her school bus ride home.

12. A male high school counselor is the supervisor of a female counseling intern from a local university. He is about five years older than she is, and he finds her attractive. They have some after-school meetings, and then begin to attend the school's sporting events, which escalates into dinner and a movie and attending some professional conferences together. The director of counseling services at the school is unable to supervise their relationship because she is on maternity leave. The intern feels conflicted, because she is already in a committed relationship. She turns him down at his next request, and he remarks, "Well, maybe then I shouldn't pass you for your internship this semester."

13. A fifth-grade female student with a special education disability was prostituted out to older men by her mother at a trailer park in a neighboring city. The student became pregnant, was put into foster care, and was placed at a new intermediate school. Students at the school constantly harass her because she was pregnant at such a young age, yet she is unaware of what really happened to her. The professional school counselor tries to reassure her, give her support, and deal with the students who harass her on an individual basis.

14. A single male high school counselor feels concerned about a student in his class load who is a foster child. The student is very intelligent and seems well adjusted, but lost both his parents very suddenly. The counselor decides to go to court to adopt this student. The student has adjusted well, graduated with honors, and is attending a prestigious college. Should the professional school counselor have the right to adopt this child?

15. One of the missions of your high school is to close the achievement gap and get more minorities and children of poverty into Advanced Placement (AP) courses and honors classes. The achievement gap between African American students and Caucasian students is as high as 10%. However, the AP and honors faculty at the school is somewhat of an elitist group and goes by hard test scores; they refuse to interview interested students or use any other kind of measure such as grades or rank in class for assignment to advanced classes. During the summer, the director of school counseling services manipulates the schedule to let interested students into the upper-level classes.

16. A well-known football coach from a university is interested in one of the school's student-athletes. He convinces the professional school counselor to allow him to look at the student's academic record informally, along with test scores and grades, to make sure that the potential athlete meets NCAA eligibility criteria, without a release form.

17. A student (at any grade level) is entering your public school from a private school. The private school refuses to release the student's records because the parents owe money to the private

school. What recourse does the professional school counselor have to obtain the records and enroll the student?

18. Parents who are trying to enroll a student in school (at any grade level) do not provide the proper documentation for immunization. What should the professional school counselor do?

19. A professional school counselor is working at a school with a growing diverse student population whose parents do not speak English, but their children do. The professional school counselor conducts a parent–teacher conference with an immigrant student and his parents regarding the student's academic performance. The professional school counselor allows the student to be the interpreter between teacher and parent.

20. A new professional school counselor is eager to facilitate a group on self-injury, since that has become a problem in the school. The professional school counselor has gone to one workshop at a regional conference and has decided to start a group at her school. She did not get informed consent. Three students in her group are self-mutilating and are already seeing a therapist.

CASE SCENARIO ANSWERS AND DISCUSSION

This section provides answers to the scenarios posed above. For each case example, the propriety of the professional school counselor's actions are assessed (key: UC = unclear; IA = incorrect action; CA = correct action) and the specific relevant passage from the ASCA (2010) Code of Ethics is cited.[1] A discussion of the situation follows.

Scenario 1: Potentially Pregnant Student
Answer: **UC**

> **A.7. Danger to Self or Others**
> **Professional school counselors:**
> **a. Inform parents/guardians and/or appropriate authorities when a student poses a danger to self or others. This is to be done after careful deliberation and consultation with other counseling professionals. (ASCA, 2010)**

In this case, it would depend on the level of rapport with the counselor and the level of trust between the counselor and counselee. The professional school counselor conferred with the director of counseling services within the school. In this particular case, the trust was high and the student followed through with the pregnancy test. She did not have to alarm her parents or consider thoughts of suicide. The crisis passed. Ethical decisions are usually not clear-cut; they tend to be in gray areas rather than in black and white. Furthermore, the right answer in one situation is not necessarily the right answer in a similar case at another time.

Scenario 2: Conversion Therapy
Answer: **IA**

> **A.1. Responsibilities to Students**
> **Professional school counselors:**
> **c. Respect students' values, beliefs and cultural background and do not impose the school counselor's personal values on students or their families. (ASCA, 2010)**

This is a clear violation. The professional school counselor did not respect the student's values and beliefs, and the counselor tried to impose his own personal values on the student regarding a

---

[1] See http://www.schoolcounselor.org/files/EthicalStandards2010.pdf for the specific language of each principle of ethical behavior cited.

controversial method to change the student's sexual orientation. The failure of many professional school counselors to adequately counsel sexual minority youth often stems from lack of education and training, which is circumvented in many school districts because of potential controversy, much like the controversy with the U.S. military and its "Don't ask, don't tell" policy regarding sexual minorities in the military.

When school counselors independently choose to disclose a student's sexual orientation to a parent or guardian, they violate professional standards and potentially place the youth at risk of rejection, abandonment, or violence by parents/guardians, peers, and the school community.

Scenario 3: Student claiming sexual abuse by her father
Answer: **CA**

> **A.2. Confidentiality**
> **Professional school counselors:**
> **c. Recognize the complicated nature of confidentiality in schools and consider each case in context. Keep information confidential unless legal requirements demand that confidential information be revealed or a breach is required to prevent serious and foreseeable harm to the student. Serious and foreseeable harm is different for each minor in schools and is defined by students' developmental and chronological age, the setting, parental rights and the nature of harm. School counselors consult with appropriate professionals when in doubt as to the validity of the exception. (ASCA, 2010)**

In this case, the counselor followed mandatory reporting procedures and contacted child protective services. He checked with his supervisors, the director of counseling services and the principal, for confirmation of his perceptions. Professional school counselors are considered mandatory reporters and are required by law to report abuse.

Scenario 4: Possible drug mule for gang
Answer: **CA**

> **D.1. Responsibility to the School**
> **Professional school counselors:**
> **b. Inform appropriate officials, in accordance with school policy, of conditions that may be potentially disruptive or damaging to the school's mission, personnel and property while honoring the confidentiality between the student and the school counselor. (ASCA, 2010)**

Even though the professional school counselor may know the dynamics of gang involvement, it is best to give the information to the principal and the youth service officer, who deal with these kinds of situations on a daily basis. If professional school counselors puts themselves in the middle of a potential gang involvement and activity, they may lose the confidence of students in general and specifically of students who may want to come forward with additional or future information or leave the gang altogether. It is best that the professional school counselor be knowledgeable and aware, but also pass the information on to the administration as well as not get involved in a legal matter. First and foremost, it is important to protect the safety and security of the entire school and those who work there.

Scenario 5: Valedictorian controversy
Answer: **IA**

> **A.2. Confidentiality**
> **Professional school counselors:**
> **h. Protect the confidentiality of students' records and release personal data in accordance with prescribed federal and state laws and school policies including the laws with the Family Education Rights and Privacy Act (FERPA). (ASCA, 2010)**

Even though the director of counseling services may have been disappointed or surprised by the information she received, she had no valid reason to share it with other colleagues, especially since the sharing was unsolicited and was gossiping. If she chose to share the information as an "interesting lunch topic" for the day, this is a clear breach of confidentiality and an abuse of knowledge and power.

Scenario 6: Cyberbullying
Answer: **CA**

> **A.10. Technology**
> **Professional school counselors:**
> **e. Consider the extent to which cyberbullying is interfering with students' educational process and base guidance curriculum and intervention programming for this pervasive and potentially danger-ous problem on research-based and best practices. (ASCA, 2010)**

Cyberbullying using the Internet, social networks, and text messaging (including sexting) has become a serious problem in schools and communities across the nation. In some states, laws have already been enacted to provide consequences for such abusive and harassing actions. States that now have laws against cyberbullying include Arkansas, Idaho, Iowa, New Jersey, Oregon, Missouri, New York, Rhode Island, and Vermont. This is a type of bullying that should be handled by the school administration, since it could lead to litigation between the victim and the bullies. The professional school counselor's responsibility is essentially to support the student and the ongoing bullying prevention initiatives within the school.

Scenario 7: Track team sleepover at counselor's house
Answer: **IA**

> **A.4. Dual Relationships**
> **Professional school counselors:**
> **a. Avoid dual relationships that might impair their objectivity and increase the risk of harm to stu-dents. . . .**
> **b. Maintain appropriate professional distance with students at all times. (ASCA, 2010)**

This risky behavior between teacher and student has crossed professional and student boundaries and represents a dual relationship. It is also reckless behavior, represents a "disorderly house" (lack of super-vision and underage drinking among minors) because there is not total adult supervision, and demon-strates contributing to the delinquency of a minor by allowing them to consume alcoholic beverages as underage minors.

Scenario 8: Student whose parents are going through a contentious divorce
Answer: **CA**

> **C.2. Sharing Information with Other Professionals**
> **Professional school counselors:**
> **e. Recognize the powerful role of ally that faculty and administration who function high in personal/ social development skills can play in supporting students in stress, and carefully filter confiden-tial information to give these allies what they "need to know" in order to advantage the student. Consultation with other members of the school counseling profession is helpful in determining need-to-know information. The primary focus and obligation is always on the student when it comes to sharing confidential information. (ASCA, 2010)**

The student was not performing well academically and not adjusting, so it was in his best interest for the professional school counselor to call a meeting with his grade-level team to share the difficult time that the student is going through, without divulging a lot of details. The counselor was advocating for the child to ensure that everyone understood the student's current emotional status, so they could offer support and wouldn't interpret his behavior incorrectly (e.g., as rebellion, defiance, or ambivalence toward his academic responsibilities).

Scenario 9: Subpoena to testify in court in a custody case
Answer: **CA**

> **B.2. Parents/Guardians and Confidentiality**
> **Professional school counselors:**
> **e. Make reasonable efforts to honor the wishes of parents/guardians concerning information regarding the student unless a court order expressly forbids the involvement of a parent(s). In cases of divorce or separation, school counselors exercise a good-faith effort to keep both parents informed, maintaining focus on the student and avoiding supporting one parent over another in divorce proceedings. (ASCA, 2010)**

In this case, the professional school counselor does not know the student or the parents well and could not testify in good faith regarding the relationship of the student to either parent. The school year had just begun, and the student was a new to the school.

Scenario 10: LPC/LMFT advertising her services
Answer: **IA**

> **F.1. Professionalism**
> **Professional school counselors:**
> **g. Do not use their professional position to recruit or gain clients, consultees for their private practice or seek and receive unjustified personal gains, unfair advantage, inappropriate relationships or unearned goods or services. (ASCA, 2010)**

Although the professional school counselor's intentions were to serve her general population in a more comprehensive way, she was using the current database of students and their families to build a client base for her own professional practice. This represents both a dual relationship and a conflict of interest by using the school district as opportunity to gain additional remuneration. It would be better judgment to align with a private practice elsewhere and to not recruit from within a school system, particularly her own. Professional school counselors should avoid confusing a license to work in school with a license to practice outside of school settings in a private venue.

Scenario 11: Distraught student who doesn't want to go home
Answer: **IA**

> **A.7. Danger to Self or Others**
> **Professional school counselors:**
> **c. Understand the legal and ethical liability for releasing a student who is in danger to self or others without proper and necessary support for that student. (ASCA, 2010)**

A middle-school counselor is meeting with an eighth grade student who has had two previous suicide attempts and has been hospitalized twice. The student seems distraught and doesn't want to go home. The counselor views it as another attempt to get attention so gives the student a suicide hotline number and tells her to hurry so she doesn't miss her bus ride home. This is a totally irresponsible action on the part of the professional school counselor, and she could be professionally liable if the student commits suicide. There is a definite history, with previous attempts. The student should not be left alone, the parents should be contacted immediately, and the student delivered into their safe hands before being released from school.

Scenario 12: Male counselor attracted to a female counseling intern
Answer: **IA**

> **A.4. Dual Relationships**
> **Professional school counselors:**
> **d. Avoid dual relationships with school personnel that might infringe on the integrity of the school counselor/student relationship. (ASCA, 2010)**

In this situation, the relationship was between a professional school counselor and a counseling intern from a local university he was supervising. The supervisor was crossing the boundaries of professional mentor and attempting to engage in a more interpersonal relationship with the intern. The intern felt conflicted and threatened, especially with the comment, "Then maybe I shouldn't pass you." This is bordering on sexual harassment as well as promoting a dual relationship in the workplace.

Scenario 13: Student-mother with a special education disability being harassed
Answer: **CA**

> **A.5. Appropriate Referrals**
> **Professional school counselors:**
> **b. Help educate about and prevent personal and social concerns for all students within the school counselor's scope of education and competence and make necessary referrals when the counseling needs are beyond the individual school counselor's education and training. Every attempt is made to find appropriate specialized resources for clinical therapeutic topics that are difficult or inappropriate to address in a school setting such as eating disorders, sexual trauma, chemical dependency and other addictions needing sustained clinical duration or assistance. (ASCA, 2010)**

This case is not unique. Young students are increasingly being exploited by predators on a routine basis. It is the professional school counselor's responsibility to protect the child, to network with community agencies, and to find her the necessary support and services so she can succeed academically, socially, and emotionally. In this case, the immediate concerns are adjustment to the school academically and avoiding harassment by peers. The student's long-term concerns may be preparing her to give the baby up for adoption or seeking out other support sources because she does not have the maturity or social support to care for the child.

Scenario 14: Counselor wanting to adopt a current student
Answer: **CA**

> **D.1. Responsibilities to the School**
> **Professional school counselors:**
> **a. Support and protect students' best interest against any infringement of their educational program. . . .**
> **d. Delineate and promote the school counselor's role and function as a student advocate in meeting the needs of those served. School counselors will notify appropriate officials of systemic conditions that may limit or curtail their effectiveness in providing programs and services. (ASCA, 2010)**

A single adult male obtaining custody of a high school student seems suspect. However, the foster student was well adjusted and goal-directed, and as a ward of the state, his college tuition was paid for at a prestigious university. He had grown into a very successful adult and was most grateful for his counselor's generosity and concern. Most older youths in foster care, especially high school students, are not this fortunate.

Scenario 15: Director of counseling manipulating the schedule to get students into AP classes
Answer: **UC**

> **E.2. Multicultural and Social Justice Advocacy and Leadership**
> **Professional school counselors:**
> **g. Work as advocates and leaders in the school to create equity-based school counseling programs that help close any achievement, opportunity and attainment gaps that deny all students the chance to pursue their educational goals. (ASCA, 2010)**

This is a conundrum many school counselors face: balancing between engrained academic dogma and pedagogy among faculty, on the one hand, and the need to close the achievement gap of minority children and children of poverty, on the other. The decision to discretely assign interested students into advanced courses is a real dilemma. Is it the ethical thing to do, or is it a moral obligation to meet the needs of all students?

Scenario 16: Counselor giving a university football coach access to student records
Answer: **IA**

> **C.2. Sharing Information with Other Professionals**
> **Professional school counselors:**
> **d. Understand about the "release of information" process and parental rights in sharing information and attempt to establish a cooperative and collaborative relationship with other professionals to benefit students. (ASCA, 2010)**

As in the earlier scenario of the valedictorian controversy, this is a FERPA violation. No one should have access to a student's record without first obtaining a release of information form with the parent or guardian's signature. The NCAA, the governing body for most college sports, has strict guidelines for required grade-point averages in core courses, so sometimes others try to get access to this information without a release form for potential recruiting purposes.

Scenario 17: Private school refusing to release records
Answer: **CA**

> **A.8. Student Records**
> **Professional school counselors:**
> **a. Maintain and secure records necessary for rendering professional services to the student as required by laws, regulations, institutional procedures and confidentiality guidelines. (ASCA, 2010)**

FERPA requires schools to release student records within a reasonable time—usually 14 working days. Ideally, the private school should forward the records of the student and then file with a collection agency to receive the tuition they feel they are entitled to receive. There are usually laws governing this situation; for example, Section 22.1-6 of the Code of Virginia states that no student's scholastic record, report card, or diploma shall be withheld because of nonpayment of any fee or charge.

Scenario 18: Student lacking proper documentation for immunization
Answer: **CA**

> **A.8. Student Records**
> **Professional school counselors:**
> **a. Maintain and secure records necessary for rendering professional services to the student as required by laws, regulations, institutional procedures and confidentiality guidelines. (ASCA, 2010)**

All students must be immunized in accordance with state law before entering public schools. For example, students in kindergarten through grade 12 need:

- Diphtheria, Tetanus Toxoid, and Pertussis Vaccine (DTP, DTap, DT, Td)—Five doses of any combination DTap/DTP, unless the fourth dose was given on or after the fourth birthday
- Polio (IPV)—Four doses, unless the third dose was on or after the fourth birthday
- Measles, Mumps, Rubella (MMR)—Two doses of a measles-containing vaccine with the first dose on or after the first birthday; second dose by age 5 or entry into kindergarten
- Hepatitis-B—Three doses
- Varicella—One dose; two doses strongly recommended. If the first dose was received after age 13, two doses are required. Parent validated history of previous chicken pox illness may substitute for vaccination.

Students age 7 or older need:

- Three doses of any combination DTP/DTap/DT/Td vaccine (pertussis vaccine is not required)

- One dose of Td required 10 years after last dose of DTP/DTap/DT. This requirement should be met prior to the start of the fall semester. One dose of Tdap is strongly recommended for age 11 and older.
- Polio (IPV)—Four doses, unless the third dose was on or after the fourth birthday
- Measles, Mumps, Rubella (MMR)—Two doses of a measles-containing vaccine with the first dose on or after the first birthday; second dose by age 5 or entry into kindergarten
- Hepatitis-B—Three doses
- Varicella—One dose; two doses strongly recommended. If the first dose was received after age 13, two doses are required. Parent validated history of previous chicken pox illness may substitute for vaccination.

Additional vaccines recommended by state health officials (i.e., yearly flu shot, meningitis, HPV).

For children who need medical exemptions, a written statement by the physician should be submitted to the school annually. Parents/guardians may also choose the exemption for reasons of conscience, including a religious belief. This is law in many states, but it represents an ethical dilemma for parents who do not believe in immunizations of their child on religious grounds or because of controversial issues like the hypothesized link between immunization and the early onset of autism.

Scenario 19: Counselor allowing a student to interpret between teacher and parent
Answer: **IA**

E.2. Multicultural and Social Justice Advocacy and Leadership
Professional school counselors:
d. Affirm the multiple cultural and linguistic identities of every student and all stakeholders. Advocate for equitable school and school counseling program policies and practices for every student and all stakeholders including use of translators and bilingual/multilingual school counseling program materials that represent all languages used by families in the school community and advocate for appropriate accommodations and accessibility for students with disabilities. (ASCA, 2010)

The professional school counselor should evaluate the situation and the resources and not rely exclusively on the child for interpretation of the parent–teacher conference. Resources such as local interpreters should be secured for better understanding of the academic, career, and social or emotional needs of the child. To the extent practicable, a counselor should never rely on a child as interpreter between parent or teacher regarding the child's progress and adjustment.

Scenario 20: New counselor facilitating a group on self-injury without informed consent
Answer: **IA**

E. Responsibilities to Self; E.1: Professional Competence
Professional school counselors:
a. Function within the boundaries of individual professional competence and accept responsibility for the consequences of their actions. . . .
c. Monitor personal responsibility and recognize the high standard of care a professional in this critical position of trust must maintain on and off the job and are cognizant of and refrain from activity that may lead to inadequate professional services or diminish their effectiveness with school community members. Professional and personal growth are ongoing throughout the counselor's career. (ASCA, 2010)

Professional school counselors need to be reminded that one workshop does not make them experts. When there are life-threatening behaviors going on in the lives of students and outside therapists are involved, the professional school counselor needs to step aside and allow the therapeutic process to occur outside the school setting. Maintaining a consulting relationship to assure the well-being of the child should be encouraged, but discussing a student's past relating to self-injury should be discouraged. Essentially, the professional school counselor must function within the boundaries of individual professional competence, based on their education, training, and experience, and accept responsibility for the consequences of his or her actions.

One of the primary roles of professional school counselors is to facilitate the personal and social development of all students (Schmidt, 1999). Professional school counselors cannot be competent in all areas or all student-presented personal/emotional issues. In this respect, school counselors have an ethical responsibility to assess whether they have the knowledge and skills to help the student explore concerns, examine alternatives, make appropriate decisions, and act accordingly (Schmidt, 1999).

Another recommendation in this scenario would be to have a specified person knowledgeable about self-injurious behavior who can be consulted when student self-injury issues arise. Also, since professional school counselors are charged with education of school faculty on the topic of self-injury, it is an important responsibility for professional school counselors to invite knowledgeable guest speakers to talk to the school community about this topic, rather than taking it on exclusively by themselves (Kress, Gibson, & Reynolds, 2004).

ETHICAL DECISION MAKING

Both the American Counseling Association (ACA) and the American School Counselor Association (ASCA) have developed guides to ethical decision making that can be used when a professional school counselor is concerned with a particular circumstance and needs to ascertain if an ethical dilemma exists. The ACA (2005) and ASCA (2010) models involve seven steps:

1. Identify the problem.
2. Apply the ACA or ASCA Code of Ethics.
3. Determine the nature and dimensions of the dilemma.
4. Generate potential courses of action.
5. Consider potential consequences of all options and choose a course of action.
6. Evaluate the course of action.
7. Implement the course of action.

Stone (2001) has taken the ACA (2005) model, which is similar to the ASCA model, and applied it to the school setting by providing a nine-step model called the STEPS model for school settings. The steps are:

1. Define the problem emotionally and intellectually.
2. Apply the ACA and ASCA ethical codes and the law (also be sure to consider school policy).
3. Consider the students' chronological and developmental levels.
4. Consider the setting, parental rights, and minors' rights.
5. Apply the moral principles.
6. Determine your potential courses of action and the consequences.
7. Evaluate the selected action.
8. Consult with other professionals.
9. Implement the course of action (Stone, 2001, pp. 17–19).

A more comprehensive Ethical Decision-Making Model is provided by the Josephson Institute of Ethics (1999):

1. Clarify
   a. Determine precisely what must be decided.
   b. Formulate and devise the full range of alternatives.

   c. Eliminate impractical, illegal, and improper alternatives.

   d. Force yourself to develop at least three ethically justifiable options.

   e. Examine each option to determine which ethical principles and values are involved.

2. Evaluate

   a. If any of the options requires the sacrifice of any ethical principle, evaluate the facts and assumptions carefully.

   b. Distinguish solid facts from beliefs, desires, theories, suppositions, unsupported conclusions, opinions, and rationalizations.

   c. Consider the credibility of sources, especially when they are for self-interest, ideological, or biased.

   d. With regard to each alternative, carefully consider the benefits, burdens, and risks to each stakeholder.

3. Decide

   a. Make a judgment about what is not true and what consequences are most likely to occur.

   b. Evaluate the viable alternatives according to personal conscience.

   c. Prioritize the values so that you can choose which values to advance and which to subordinate.

   d. Determine who will be helped the most and harmed the least.

   e. Consider the worst-case scenario.

   f. Consider whether ethically questionable conduct can be avoided by changing goals or methods, or by getting consent.

   g. Apply three "ethics guides":

      i. Are you treating others as you would want to be treated?

      ii. Would you be comfortable if your reasoning and decision were to be publicized?

      iii. Would you be comfortable if your children were observing you?

4. Implement

   a. Develop a plan of how to implement the decision.

   b. Maximize the benefits and minimize the costs and risks.

5. Monitor and modify

   a. Monitor the effects of decisions.

   b. Be prepared and willing to revise a plan, or take a different course of action.

   c. Adjust to new information.

Table 14.1 outlines a more comprehensive evidenced-based example of decision-making models published by the ACA (1997).

ETHICAL GUIDELINES FOR SCHOOLS COUNSELORS

As noted at the beginning of the chapter, professional school counselors are accountable to five distinct entities: (1) students as minors; (2) teachers and their right to know pertinent information; (3) administrators and their right to know if an issue will disrupt the school and affect students, faculty, staff, or parents; (4) parents/guardians and their right to know information about their child; and (5) the school system at large and its right to know if an issue or incident would reflect negatively on programs, policies, or procedures. Consequently, it is imperative to maintain the following in professional relationships:

• Act in good faith and in the absence of malice.
• Always used informed consent.
• Be aware of personal values, attitudes, and beliefs.
• Maintain a sense of cultural sensitivity and understanding of diversity.

TABLE 14.1 Summary of Steps or Stages of Practice-Based Ethical Decision-Making Models

COREY, COREY, & CALLANAN (1998)	FORESTER-MILLER & DAVIS (1996)	KEITH-SPIEGEL & KOOCHER (1985)	RAE, FOURNIER, & ROBERTS (2001)	STADLER (1986)	STEINMAN, RICHARDSON, & MCENROE (1998)	TARVYDAS (1998)	TYMCHUK (1986)	WELFEL (1998)
1. Identify the problem	1. Identify the problem	1. Describe the parameters	1. Gather information	1. Identify competing principles	1. Identify the problem	1. Interpret situation	1. Determine stakeholders	1. Develop ethical sensitivity
2. Identify potential issues involved	2. Apply the ACA Code of Ethics	2. Define the potential issues	2. Consult legal and ethical guidelines	2. Secure additional information	2. Identify the relevant ethical standard	2. Review problem or dilemma	2. Consider all possible alternatives	2. Define the dilemma and options
3. Review relevant ethical guidelines	3. Determine nature of dilemma	3. Consult legal and ethical guidelines	3. Generate possible decisions	3. Consult with colleagues	3. Determine possible ethical traps	3. Determine standards that apply to dilemma	3. Consider consequences for each alternative	3. Refer to professional standards
4. Obtain consultation	4. Generate potential courses of action	4. Evaluate the rights, responsibilities, and welfare of all	4. Examine possible outcomes in the given context	4. Identify hoped-for outcomes	4. Frame preliminary response	4. Generate possible and probable courses of action	4. Balance risks and benefits to make the decision	4. Search out ethics scholarship
5. Consider possible and probable courses of action	5. Consider potential consequences and determine course of action	5. Generate alternate decisions	5. Implement best choice and evaluate	5. Brainstorm actions to achieve outcomes	5. Consider consequences of that response	5. Consider consequences for each course of action	5. Decide on level of review	5. Apply ethical principles to situation
6. Enumerate consequences of various decisions	6. Evaluate selected course of action	6. Enumerate the consequences of each decision	6. Modify practices to avoid future problems	6. Evaluate effects of actions	6. Prepare an ethical resolution	6. Consult with supervisor and peers	6. Implement the decision	6. Consult with supervisor and peers
7. Decide on best course of action	7. Implement course of action	7. Estimate probability for outcomes of each decision		7. Identify competing nonmoral values	7. Get feedback from peers and supervisor	7. Select an action by weighing competing values in the given context	7. Monitor the action and outcome	7. Deliberate and decide
		8. Make the decision		8. Choose a course of action	8. Take action	8. Plan and execute the selected action		8. Inform supervisor and take action
				9. Test the course of action		9. Evaluate course of action		9. Reflect on the experience
				10. Identify steps, taken				

Source: American Counseling Association, *Code of Ethics and Standards of Practice*, Alexandria, VA, 1997. Reprinted with permission.

- Recognize limitations and boundaries in counseling and relationships.
- Know the ethical standards of ACA and ASCA.
- Network with other professional colleagues for knowledge and support.
- Join professional organizations.
- Always keep your immediate supervisor informed of issues in question.

These ethical guidelines are more defined more extensively below.

1. When working with students, parents, teachers, administrators, school board members, and the greater community, always keep their best interests at the forefront. Always act in good faith and in the absence of malice.
2. Always get informed consent when working with students. Make sure to outline the limitations of confidentiality and the counseling relationship prior to the beginning of individual or group counseling sessions. Some school systems require counselors to notify the parents if the counselor meets with a counselee for more than three sessions.
3. Be cognizant of personal values, attitudes, and beliefs. Defer to another colleague when there is a conflict of interest or when personal attributes or transference issues may hinder effectiveness in the counseling relationship.
4. Maintain cultural sensitivity when working with students and families from diverse cultural backgrounds. Recognize the manner in which personal perspectives of cultural, ethnic, or racial identity may affect beliefs about the counseling process. Seek ongoing professional development on cultural diversity, since that will affect the school counseling profession tremendously over the next decades.
5. Recognize the limitations and boundaries of personal counseling competence and accept your personal skill levels and areas of weakness. It is okay to say, "I don't know enough about this particular subject or situation, but I will be happy to find an expert in the field to talk to us about this."
6. Advocate for your professional role and personal identity. Know your own theoretical rationale that is the impetus for professional school counselor initiatives.
7. Understand that students are minors and that parents and guardians who have sole or joint custody are entitled to know sensitive or controversial information about their child. Also, be knowledgeable about local school policy, as well as state mandates and federal initiatives. Parental rights are more complicated when a minor child or adolescent is in the school.
8. Be aware of and follow written job descriptions for professional school counselors, especially the clause that states "and other duties deemed reasonable by the principal." Make sure appropriate functions are followed in the workplace and that the roles and responsibilities of the professional school counselor are not compromised for clerical duties or other noncounseling administrative tasks.
9. Secure a copy of the *Ethical Standards for School Counselors* from the ASCA website (http://www.schoolcounselor.org). Review the standards routinely, and act according to these guidelines.
10. Network and consult with other counseling professionals (i.e., colleagues, supervisors, counselor educators, and professional organizations). An accessible support network of professionals gives the counseling profession a vision and a voice. Use National School Counseling Week as an opportunity to showcase what professional school counselors do. Try to get legislative support and legislative representation in your particular district to enhance visibility and professional identity.
11. Join professional associations such as the ACA and ASCA and state and local organizations. Read their publications, and participate in ongoing professional development and professional conference events. Information is growing exponentially, and professional school counselors need to be consistently up to date in trends and expectations of changing roles and responsibilities, especially in light of the national initiative to close the achievement gap.

12. When one encounters an ethical dilemma, consult with the administration (principal) or district supervisor, as well as school board attorney, if necessary. Always seek legal advice before taking action. Also, professional liability insurance should be kept up to date.
13. Stay current with school board policy and with state and federal mandates such as FERPA, Health Insurance Portability and Accountability Act (HIPAA) compliance, and the Protection of Pupil Rights Amendment (PPRA), particularly with regard to confidentiality and counseling with minors.

CONCLUSION

Ethical decision making is a daily, ongoing practice for professional school counselors, and it involves constant good judgment, vigilance, and commitment to serving the best interests of multiple entities—students, parents, teachers, administrators, school boards, and the community at large. Professional school counselors will undoubtedly continue to be presented with dilemmas involving confidentiality, parental rights, information of danger to self and others, and dual relationships. These dilemmas are inherent in the work that professional school counselors perform on a daily basis. Schools are also a microcosm of society, and therefore professional school counselors are increasingly being faced with issues of child abuse, gender identity, depression and suicide ideation, self-injury, teen pregnancy, substance abuse, school violence, bullying, and relational aggression, within the context of parental rights and the limitations of confidentiality. Professional school counselors are advised to continue their ethical practices by continually updating their knowledge of ASCA ethical codes, school policy, and federal mandates such as FERPA, HIPAA, and PPRA and to use an ethical decision-making model in their practice.

APPENDIX: LEGAL TERMS FOR PROFESSIONAL SCHOOL COUNSELORS

The following legal terms are provided for professional school counselors as a reference point and as a resource guide to legal terminology. They have been gathered from various sources, such as the U.S. Department of Health and Human Services (2005), and professional experience.

Abandonment

Abandonment can occur when a husband and wife or a parent and child have severed ties in their relationship to the point that the family ceases to exist legally. It can lead to annulment of the marriage, divorce, adoption, or emancipation of an adolescent under the age of 18 to live independently on their own.

Abduction

Abduction is the crime of taking a person away by persuasion, grooming, fraud, or violence. It may occur when a parent involved in a domestic relations case removes a child from the jurisdiction of a court. Abductions by others may prompt an "Amber Alert," a system increasingly used to promote public awareness and aid in the return of missing children. Children and adolescents are also lured into potential abduction through the Internet and social networking sites.

Absent Parent

An absent parent is a noncustodial parent who has been obligated to pay partial child support and who is physically absent from the child's home. It also refers to a parent who has abandoned his or her child and has failed to maintain contact with the child.

Alternative Dispute Resolution (ADR)

Alternative dispute resolution refers to several different methods of resolving disputes, such as divorce cases, outside traditional legal and administrative forums. These philosophically similar methodologies, which include various types of arbitration and mediation, have emerged in recent years because the courts have become overwhelmed with the expense, time, and emotional toll involved in resolving disputes through the usual legal avenues.

Amber Alert

An Amber Alert is an urgent announcement of a child missing. "Amber" is technically an acronym for "America's Missing: Broadcasting Emergency Response," but the name was chosen in memory of nine-year-old Amber Hagerman, who was abducted and murdered in Arlington, Texas, in 1996. Parents of a missing or abducted child can contact their local police or sheriff's department to file a missing person report. If a child is missing and believed to be in danger, there is no longer a 24-hour waiting period. The law enforcement agency will immediately enter information about the child into the missing persons database and the National Crime Information Center's Missing Person File. Immediacy is the key to finding missing children.

Americans with Disabilities Act (ADA)

The Americans with Disabilities Act of 1990 and its follow-on, the ADA Amendments Act of 2008 (P.L. 110-325), which became effective on January 1, 2009, is designed to protect the civil rights of people who have physical and mental disabilities. The act requires the removal of physical and systemic barriers that deny individuals with disabilities equal opportunity and access to jobs, public accommodations, government services, public transportation, and telecommunications.

Beneficence

This is a fundamental ethical benchmark that maintains, above all, the responsibility and duty to do good, and to do no harm to others, in all situations.

Detailed Case Notes and a Caveat Regarding Sole-Possession Records

Case notes and personal notes (sole-possession records) can be a liability for professional school counelors, who are not entitled to confidentiality as are medical doctors, psychiatrists, and priests. School counselors must constantly remind themselves that what is written down about a student can be read in a court of law and that parents can request the records, especially in custody hearings, issues of abuse, or hearings on accommodations for children with disabilities. Anything written about a student can be read by others. Even when school counselors manage to meet the criteria of sole-possession records, in most states these records can be subpoenaed.

So when it doubt, leave it out. This also includes observations about special education students. Also, anecdotal information can be entered into the Individual Educational Plan (IEP) minutes if the meeting has started.

Children's Online Privacy Protection Act (COPPA)

The Children's Online Privacy Protection Act requires websites to explain their privacy policies on the site and to get parents' consent before collecting or using a child's personal information, such as a name, address, phone number, or Social Security number. The law also prohibits a site from requiring a child to provide more personal information than necessary to play a game or contest.

Class Action Lawsuit

A lawsuit brought by one person on behalf of himself and all other parties in the same situation because they have experienced the same wrongdoing. Class action lawsuits in the schools have occurred for such situations as wrongful termination, breach of contract, children denied services for disabilities, harassment due to sexual orientation, or charging parents/guardians fees for textbooks or computer access at school.

Code of Ethics

A set of principles of conduct within an organization whose purpose is to guide decision making and behavior and to aid in making responsible ethical choices. Members of an organization adopt a code of ethics to share a dedication to ethical behavior and to declare the organization's uniform principles and acceptable standards of practice. The American School Counselor Association code of ethics, in brief, declare that a professional school counselor maintains responsibilities to students; assures confidentiality; develops appropriate counseling plans; avoids dual relationships; makes appropriate referrals to outside agencies; implements group work and the importance of screening prospective group members; informs parents/guardians or appropriate authorities if a student is a danger to himself or others; manages students according to such laws as FERPA and confidentiality guidelines; follows professional standards regarding selecting, administering, and interpreting assessments; promotes the benefits and limitations of various technology applications, such Internet safety; collaborates with parents and respects their rights; maintains professional relationships with faculty, staff, and administration to promote an optimum counseling program; honors the school's mission and protects it against potential disruptive situations; collaborates with agencies, organizations, and individuals in the community; respects and affirms the diversity of staff, students, and their families; contributes to the development of the profession; maintains ethical standards; and reports violations (ASCA, 2010).

Compulsory School Attendance

Compulsory school attendance means that school is mandatory, rather than optional, in a public, private, or home-school setting. For example, a compulsory school attendance law may state that all children who are six years of age, or who will be six years old by a certain date, must attend school regularly during the entire school term and remain in school until the age of 16–18, depending on the state. For example, in North Carolina, compulsory education ends at age 16, while in the neighboring state of Virginia, the age is 18.

Confidentiality

A professional school counselor's promise of confidentiality, or contract to respect a student's right to privacy by not disclosing anything revealed during counseling, must not be breached by the counselor except when there is clear and present danger to the student or to another person (see "Duty to Warn/ Duty to Protect"). A student has the right to privacy and confidentiality. However, personal or emotional counseling for minors in schools brings immediate tension between student's right to privacy and their parents' right to be the guiding force in the child's social and emotional development (Isaacs & Stone, 1999; Remley & Herlihy, 2001). In particular, the parent has the right to know about anything discussed between a minor (under age 18) and the professional school counselor.

Conflict of Interest

A conflict of interest exists when someone, such as a professional school counselor or educational official, has competing professional or personal obligations or personal or financial interests that would make it difficult to fulfill his or her duties fairly. For example, if a professional school counselor were coaching a team at his school and also had a business on the side that sold athletic team T-shirts, selling his business's shirts to his team would constitute a conflict of interest. Essentially, the counselor would be receiving remuneration twice, as both coach and owner of the T-shirt business that sold shirts to the team. A school employee may not receive two paychecks at the same place of employment, even if it is after school hours. This is also true for professional school counselors who are licensed in private practice; it would be unethical for them to solicit students and their families as potential private practice clients.

Copyright Law

The owner of a copyright has the right to exclude any other person from reproducing, preparing derivative works of, distributing, performing, displaying, or using the copyrighted work for a specific period of time. Copyright can be extended to a literary work, musical work, dramatic work, choreographic work, pictorial work, graphic work, sculptural work, motion picture, audiovisual work, sound recording, or computer program. A copyright gives the owner the exclusive right to reproduce, distribute, perform, display, or license his or her own work or derivatives thereof. Limited exceptions to this exclusivity exist for types of "fair use," such as book reviews.

Once the term of a copyright (or a patent) expires, it is said to become a part of the "public domain," that is, it becomes community property, and anyone may use it. Photographs, magazine articles, and books are among the most common public domain materials used today. Professional school counselors must be careful to make sure material (e.g., materials that they take off the Internet) are not copyrighted.

Corporal Punishment

Corporal punishment is the intentional infliction of physical pain as a method of changing behavior. It may include such methods as hitting; slapping; punching; kicking; pinching; shaking; use of various objects (paddles, belts, sticks, and so on); or placing someone in painful body posture or isolated, dark room. Historically, corporal punishment was a common method of disciplining children and youths in the school setting (often publicly as a form of humiliation to control unwanted behavior). Many states have now enacted legislation prohibiting corporal punishment. As of this writing, 27 states consider corporal punishment in schools to be illegal (American Academy of Pediatrics, 2011).

Curfew

A curfew is an official local, state, or federal mandate to return to one's home before a stated time, often imposed to maintain public order. Some jurisdictions impose curfews on minors under the age of 18 to keep them off the streets and away from gangs, drugs, crime, and other self-defeating activities that may be harmful or destructive. Curfews, which normally apply to nighttime hours, are there to keep the adolescents from being hurt or becoming victims of crime.

Custody of Children

Custody of a child is the legal right and responsibility to care for that child. Custody battles most often arise in a divorce or separation, requiring a court's determination of which parent, relative, or other adult should have physical or legal control and responsibility for a minor under the age of 18. The *custodial parent* is the parent who is given physical or legal custody of a child by court order. *Joint custody* occurs when both parents share custody of a child after a divorce. *Physical custody* designates where the child will actually live, whereas *legal custody* gives the custodial parent the right to make decisions for the child's welfare.

Child custody can be decided by a local court in a divorce, if one or both parents are deceased, or if a child, relative, close friend, or state agency has reason to believe that one or both parents are unfit, absent, or dangerous to the child's well-being. In such cases, custody can be awarded to a grandparent or other relative, to a foster parent, or to an orphanage or other organization or institution. In the case of joint custody by both parents, professional school counselors are obligated to provide information like grades, progress reports, academic opportunities, and newsletters to both parents in a timely manner; in such cases, email addresses should be linked together. If only one parent has custody, the other parent is not entitled to this information. This is critical to know when parents sign students out of school—only a custodial parent has this right. Students have been abducted from school by the noncustodial parent in the past.

Due Process Hearing

A due process hearing (or impartial due process hearing) is a procedure to resolve disputes between parents and schools—an administrative hearing before an impartial hearing officer or administrative law judge to gain resolution of a problem, accommodation, or placement in a program for a child with a disability.

Duty to Warn and Duty to Protect

Duty to warn others about potential harm and duty to protect from potential harm is the responsibility of the professional school counselor to inform third parties or authorities if a client poses a threat to himself or herself or to another identifiable individual. The legal duty to warn was established in the case of *Tarasoff* v. *Regents of the University of California* (1976), in which a family sued a counselor after the therapist failed to inform a young woman and her parents of specific death threats made by a client and the young woman was subsequently killed. The duty to warn provides the professional school counselor the right to breach confidentiality if a client poses a risk to himself or herself or another person, for example, in cases of suicide ideation, substance abuse, self-injury, and unintended teenage pregnancy.

Educational Neglect

Educational neglect occurs when parents fail to ensure that their children are provided an education consistent with standards adopted by the state. Some examples include failure to enroll or register the child in school, requiring the student to stay home to care for younger siblings, inattention to special education needs, and allowing chronic truancy.

Emancipation

Emancipation occurs when minors have achieved independence from their parents before the age of 18, for example, by getting married, joining military service, or by court order. It may be possible for a child to petition a court for emancipation to free himself or herself from the control of parents and to be allowed to live on their own or under the control of others. It usually applies to adolescents who leave the parents' household by agreement or demand.

Extracurricular Activities

Extracurricular activities are those activities that are not part of the standard academic curriculum. They typically are scheduled outside of the regular school day. These activities afford students an opportunity to practice social, interpersonal, and team-building skills and to gain experience in fields that may represent a career interest. Extracurricular activities are not graded and do not earn credits. Eligibility, requirements, and costs are established by educational boards and independent organizations, which vary by local districts and nationally agencies like the National Collegiate Athletic Association (NCAA), which sets core course requirements, grade-point averages, and SAT/ACT score minimums to participate in college or university sports. The NCAA was established so talented athletes would not be exploited in colleges or universities if they did not meet academic requirements.

Family Educational Rights and Privacy Act (FERPA)

FERPA is a federal statute that addresses issues about confidentiality and access to education records. Student records are confidential, although directory information (name, address, birth date, etc.) can be released to third parties unless parents request that it be withheld. Parents have the right to review and amend the student's record if they find discrepancies or inaccurate information contained in the file.

Foster Care

Foster care is a social system enabling a child without parental support and protection to be placed with a person or family to be cared for, usually by local welfare services or by court order. Foster parents do not have custody or proceed with adoption of the child, but they are expected to treat the foster child as they would their own in providing food, housing, clothing, and education. Most foster parents are paid by a local or state governmental agency. The child's parents may retain their parental rights, and the child may ultimately return home. Under permanent foster care, however, the agency has guardianship; the child may then be available for adoption by the foster parents or others. Foster care can also provide a supervised setting for adults with mental or emotional disabilities who cannot care adequately for themselves.

Group Home

A group home is an alternative to traditional in-home foster care in which unrelated children are housed in a more intimate or homelike setting, with a single set of house parents or a rotating staff of trained caregivers. More specialized therapeutic or treatment group homes have specially trained staff to assist children with emotional or behavioral difficulties or intellectual disabilities. The makeup and staffing of the group home varies according to the needs of its residents. There are also group homes for other types of residents, such as troubled teens. The group home's mission is generally aimed at providing residents with skills needed to become a productive member of society and to integrate them into successful independent living in society.

Health Insurance Portability and Accountability Act (HIPAA)

HIPAA provides national standards to protect the privacy of personal health information and ensure it is not shared with a third party without permission. For example, if a student has HIV/AIDS, this information is protected and not shared among faculty or staff unless it interferes with academic performance and his or her success. Sometimes delicate information needs to be shared on a case-by-case basis.

Informed Consent and Confidentiality in the Schools

Informed consent is both a legal and ethical principle requiring professional school counselors to disclose adequately in writing to students and their parents the potential risks, benefits, and alternatives to proposed counseling interventions. Minors cannot legally give informed consent—only their parents or guardians can give informed consent because they are under the age of 18. It is critical that professional school counselors engage in effective informed consent practices with their counselees and significant adults.

As an ethical standard, informed consent rests primarily on the moral principles of autonomy and fidelity. *Autonomy* is the principle requiring professional school counselors to respect their clients as capable individuals who have the right to make choices regarding entering into counseling and being actively involved in the counseling process. *Fidelity* means that professional school counselors create "a trusting and therapeutic climate in which people can search for their own solutions, and assure that they do not deceive or exploit clients" (Herlihy & Corey, 1996, pp. 4–5).

Informed consent in the school setting should be viewed as an ongoing process tailored to the developmental levels of the client. For example, a simple statement such as the following may be appropriate for a seven-year-old client. "Whatever you tell me will be just between us unless I am worried about your health and safety. Do you have any questions about that?" However, when counseling a 16-year-old, it is wise to expand on examples of conditions under which the counselor may need to disclose confidential information to the counselee's parents or to school personnel: "I might have to disclose information that you tell me if you are about to harm yourself or someone else. Do you understand my professional obligation to you and others?"

In Loco Parentis

In loco parentis is a Latin term for "in place of a parent" and is used when a person or institution assumes parental rights and duties for a minor. During school hours and extended extracurricular activities, schools serve in loco parentis.

Malpractice

Malpractice is failure to render professional service. The test for failure is determined by what is known as the *standard of care*—the expected performance level of the profession designated by state and national standards (Cottone & Tarvydas, 1998). Professional school counselors should acquire professional liability insurance for protection against any accusations of negligence or malpractice. Issues of releasing information to appropriate agencies, supervising interns, the duty to warn and protect, and confidentiality can all become targets for malpractice allegations and potential litigation.

Megan's Law

Megan's Law, which was signed on May 17, 1996, by President Bill Clinton, has two components: The first, sex offender registration, involves the 1994 Jacob Wetterling Act, which requires states to register individuals convicted of sex crimes against children. Sex offender registration laws are justified on the basis that (1) sex offenders have a high rate of reoffending after release from custody, and (2) public agencies and the general public need information available to help protect the public safety of youth. The second component of the statute is community notification. States have discretion to establish criteria for disclosure, but are required to make private and personal information on registered sex offenders available to the public (Proctor, Badzinski, & Johnson, 2002, p. 358).

Negligence

Negligence is a civil wrong—in legal terms, a tort—in which one person breaches a duty to another (Remley & Herlihy, 2001). Fortunately, negligence has been judicially rejected in most cases against professional school counselors and other educators in the area of educational advising and personal counseling (Gladding, Remley, & Huber, 2001). However, today professional school counselors are expected to be current in their knowledge about college admissions, financial aid and scholarships, NCAA eligibility requirements, FERPA, PPRA, the Individual with Disabilities Education Act (IDEA), local policy, and state and federal mandates. In addition, professional school counselors' clients extend beyond the students to include parents, guardians, teachers, local- and district-level administrators, school board members, and the community at large. This multiplicity of responsibilities makes the legal and ethical realm of professional school counseling a complex one to negotiate. Information should be verified and nothing should be put in writing that the school would hesitate to see published in the media.

Noncustodial Parent

A noncustodial parent is the parent who does not have physical or legal custody of a child in the case of divorce or separation and with whom the child does not live with the majority of the time.

Prayer in the Schools

As of September 1, 2002, school districts must now allow religious speech on the same terms as they allow other speech. Therefore, students have the same right to engage in individual or group prayer and religious discussion during the school day as they do to in other comparable activities, and prayer is constitutionally protected in public elementary schools and secondary schools. Section 9524 of the Elementary and Secondary Education Act (ESEA) of 1965, as amended by the No Child Left Behind Act of 2001, outlines constitutionally protected prayer in public elementary and secondary schools. Section 9524 requires that, as a condition of receiving ESEA funds, a local educational agency (LEA) must certify in writing to its state educational agency (SEA) that it has no policy that prevents, or otherwise denies participation in, constitutionally protected prayer in public schools (Lim, 2003).

Privileged Communication

A privileged communication is a statement made by a person within a relationship the law protects from forced disclosure in a court proceeding. Privilege belongs to the counselee, and the counselor acts for the counselee in asserting privilege. Unless privilege exists or is granted, professional school counselors can be compelled to disclose counseling notes and information given to them by counselees or face contempt of court or court penalties.

This is an even more complex issue when considering who has the privilege. Parents of minors, rather than the minors themselves, are assumed to control the privilege if one exists, so professional school counselors have limits to their ability to protect counselee confidences in the school setting. Furthermore, FERPA establishes clearly that parents control the privacy rights of students under the age of 18. Professional school counselors are sometimes confused by the FERPA provision allowing confidential notes or memory aids to be protected from the law's requirement that official school records be disclosed to parents or guardians. In most cases, any material, including counselors' "confidential" case notes, can be subpoenaed in court. Therefore, professional school counselors need to err on the side of caution with personal information that they keep on students.

Protection of Pupil Rights Amendment (PPRA)

PPRA is a federal law that affords certain rights to parents of minor students with regard to surveys that ask personal questions. Briefly, the law requires that schools obtain written consent from parents before minor students are required to participate in any U.S. Department of Education–funded survey, analysis, or evaluation that reveals information concerning the following areas:

- Political affiliations
- Mental and psychological problems potentially embarrassing to the student and his or her family
- Sex behavior and attitudes
- Illegal, antisocial, self-incriminating, and demeaning behavior
- Critical appraisals of other individuals with whom respondents have close family relationships
- Legally recognized privileged or analogous relationships, such as those of lawyers, physicians, and ministers
- Religious practices, affiliations, or beliefs of the student or student's parent
- Income (other than that required by law to determine eligibility for participation in a program or for receiving financial assistance under such a program, e.g. free and reduced lunch)

The No Child Left Behind Act of 2001 contains a major amendment to PPRA. PPRA now requires that schools and contractors make instructional materials available for review by parents of participating students if those materials will be used in an Department of Education–funded survey, analysis, or evaluation if information in any of the aforementioned eight areas is revealed (U.S. Department of Education, 2005b).

Reasonable Suspicion

Reasonable suspicion pertains to school searches of students and their personal possessions in their lockers, desks, or cars on school property. An on-campus school search is lawful if the school has a reasonable suspicion that a school rule has been violated (e.g., having drugs, guns, or other illegal contraband on the premises). This means the search must be justified when made and reasonably related to the circumstances being investigated. It is not unusual for schools to enlist the assistance of police officers and drug dogs to sweep the school campus for potential drugs in the building.

Restraining Order

A restraining order is a temporary order by a court to preserve current conditions as they are until a hearing can be held, for example, to protect a student from an adult or another student. The order is designed to prohibit harassment and potential physical harm. A restraining order may be issued in a divorce matter to prevent taking a child out of the country or to prohibit one of the parties from selling marital property.

It may also be issued when there has been a violent relationship or threatening behavior between two students. As another example, a person who is a victim of harassment, or the parent or guardian of a harassed minor, may seek a restraining order from the court against an individual who has engaged in harassment or against organizations that have sponsored or promoted harassment. The restraining order frequently specifies a minimum distance the restrained party is required to maintain.

Rotating Custody Agreement

A rotating custody agreement is a form of shared parental responsibility for a child, in which no primary custodial parent is designated and the parents alternate custody of the child. For instance, the mother may have the child at her home from Sunday through Wednesday and the father may have the child from Thursday through Saturday. Rotating custody is governed by state laws, which vary. For example, in Florida, there is a presumption that rotating custody is not in the best interests of the child. Some of the factors that a court may consider in deciding whether to grant rotating custody include whether the child's parents live in the same school district, the disruptive effect on the child, the child's preferences, and the level of hostility between the parents. In such cases, it is a good idea for the child to possess two sets of textbooks, one set per house, to prevent forgetting materials and requirements for class.

Split Custody

Split custody is when siblings are separated in a divorce or separation, with each parent having sole custody of one or more of their children.

Subpoena

A subpoena is a court order demanding that an individual appear in court on a certain day to testify or produce documents in a pending lawsuit. The power to subpoena a person is given to officers of the court, such as clerks of courts, attorneys, and judges. A person may be subpoenaed to appear in court or at another designated location to provide testimony for trial or a deposition or to produce documents or other evidence. If subpoenaed, professional school counselors should seek consultation with their local school board attorney or administration for support and guidance, especially in complicated child custody cases.

Supervised Visitation

Supervised visitation accompanies some divorce proceedings and may be ordered by a court to minimize visitation-related conflict between custodial and noncustodial parents, to support the development of parenting skills, to assist in rebuilding a healthy parent–child relationship, and to prevent further child abuse or neglect. Supervised visitation often takes place in a neutral location under the supervision of paid staff from the supporting agency.

Unfit Parent

An unfit parent is a parent deemed unworthy of that role due to a history of being abusive or neglectful or failing to provide proper care for a child. A parent with a mental disturbance or addiction to drugs or alcohol may also be found to be an unfit parent. Failure to visit or provide support and being incarcerated are other examples of grounds for being found unfit.

Youthful Offender

A youthful offender is a minor convicted of a crime. The age requirements vary by state, but a youthful offender generally is between 8 and 18. Many states have special youth offender programs, which may offer such services as secure detention, home detention, observation and assessment, secure facilities, work camps, diversion services, community programs, and case management to remediate the youth back into society.

Professional Development and Personal Renewal

15

That which is to give light must endure burning.

Viktor E. Frankl (1963, p. 129)

As counselors we have all volunteered to be givers of light. In making this effort, we are all going to burn. It hurts to work with the population of clients with whom we provide care. It is not a pleasant thing to see track marks in the arm of a 17-year-old prostitute nor bear witness to the stories of rape and torture that occur millions of times daily to children in the "war zones" of middle-class American homes. It challenges our views of an ordered world, a benevolent God and makes our heart hurt.

J. Eric Gentry (2002, p. 37)

Administering a professional school counseling program and counseling children are demanding and often physically and emotionally exhausting. The pressures on time are continuous and relentless. Yet, through the development of carefully negotiated habits, time can be a resource instead of a threatened commodity. Professional school counselors do not have to succumb to the "Pareto Principle" or the 80:20 rule, which, simply stated, says that 80% of unfocused effort generates only 20% of results, and the remaining 80% of results are achieved with only 20% of the effort. Time management strategies are critical if school counselors are to avoid spending the bulk of their time doing clerical, trivial, or mundane tasks with only a small portion of their time spent on significant activities that contribute to their role as a professional school counselor.

Concurrently, professional school counselors are expected to be involved in a greater variety of guidance and counseling activities than their predecessors ever envisioned. Their roles and functions include work in the curriculum; conducting placement and follow-up activities; remediation; consultation; specialized testing; observation; and interfacing with business and industry to secure student mentors, crisis counseling, teacher and parent consultation, and mental health referrals. In addition, they are expected to perform routine noncounseling administrative services, which often are delegated by uninformed administrators or support personnel who do not understand the role of the professional school counselor. Professional school counselors are trying to extricate themselves from clerical and administrative minutia, but since the currency of a bureaucracy is paper, professional school counselors have often become the "designated tellers."

Professional school counselors can play a pivotal role in shaping the nature of their work and the future of their profession. To do so, they must articulate the new standards of the American School Counselor Association's National Model (ASCA, 2005a) and engage important stakeholders such as administrators, central office personnel, and school board members.

Professional school counselors often lament that they are "all things to all people"; they are said to have type-E personalities, "E" standing for "everything to everybody." For any helping professional, meeting insurmountable needs with few resources often seems like an exercise in futility. As colleagues remark, "You can't save them all."

Fundamental to implementing time management techniques is understanding the stress that creates impositions to professional functioning. Stressful activities or responsibilities include:

- Trying to resolve conflicts among parents, the school, teachers, and students
- Having to abide by administrative decisions or school policies that disengage or alienate students (e.g., discipline policies, attendance or eligibility requirements to participate in extracurricular activities)
- Complying with state, federal, and district rules, policies, and mandates that are often incompatible
- Imposing excessively high expectations on self or others
- Not setting healthy limits on personal and professional obligations and commitments
- Trying to gain public or peer approval and/or financial support for professional school counseling programs or activities
- Always feeling overextended with a heavy caseload or workload that never seems to achieve fruition
- Feeling that meetings, committees, and conferences take up too much time
- Trying to complete reports and other paperwork—sometimes unplanned—on time
- Being interrupted frequently by phone calls, emails, and walk-ins of colleagues, students, parents, and others.

ANALYZING TIME CONSUMERS

To the noble art of getting things done, we must add the noble art of leaving things undone.

Ancient Oriental saying

In addition to understanding a professional school counselor's stressors (also called "pinch points" or "time crunches"), it is important to understand which activities consume large blocks of your time (see also Figure 15.1 in Appendix A). These may include:

- Telephone interruptions
- Email inquiries from teachers, staff, parents, and the greater public
- Drop-in visitors
- Meetings, scheduled as well as unscheduled
- Crisis situations for which planning ahead was not possible
- Lack of objectives, priorities, and deadlines
- A cluttered desk and personal disorganization
- Involvement in routines and details that should be delegated to other support personnel
- Attempting too much at one time and underestimating the time it takes to do it
- Failure to set up clear lines of responsibility, boundaries, and authority
- Inadequate, inaccurate, or delayed information from others
- Indecision and procrastination
- Lack of clear communication and instruction
- Inability to say no and/or failure to understand what saying yes entails in terms of your time and resources
- Lack of standards, conflicting information, and professional reports that need a quick turn-around time
- Compassion fatigue and burnout

- Family demands
- Mail, both "snail" and electronic
- Incompetent or unreliable colleagues

Adding the following situations to the foregoing list, one can easily understand why professional school counselors begin to feel burnout:

- Being all things to all people (i.e. type "E, Everything to Everyone)
- Commuting time to confer with teachers, principals, and families
- Changing accreditation standards and new programs that need to be implemented
- More diverse student populations
- Changing demographics (the needs of students of poverty, minorities, and immigrants)
- Conferring with business and industry, service organizations, central office personnel, satellite offices, and others

This workload is also affected by federal mandates and local policy, for example, regarding the flow of communication among support personnel, home-school instructional staff, and parents. This can be aptly understood by viewing the number of people who must sign off, review, interview, assess, or peruse a child's individual educational plan in order to comply with the Individuals with Disabilities Education Act.

Nearly all support personnel will have to interface with the professional school counseling program or staff to obtain the necessary information on a child enrolled in the school. Support personnel include nurses, special education coordinators, school psychologists, educational diagnosticians, school community workers, resource teachers, school counselors, regular education teachers, administrators, social workers, probation officers, vocational program liaisons, community mental health liaisons, parents, foster parents, speech therapists, court liaisons, and program administrators.

Try keeping a log for several days of how your time is spent. The more frequent the entries, the better the database for analysis and understanding. Analyze the log to see on what the bulk of time is spent. The bottom line: Is time spent with students or with paper?

MANAGING YOUR PAPER CHASE

Professional school counselors often suffer from a condition known as the *battered mind syndrome*, which means that they have many thoughts competing in their heads at one time. They worry about what remains to be done and lose focus as new concerns divert them from the task at hand. They expect to be interrupted and, as a result, don't become deeply involved in their work. The devastating outcome of this syndrome is a belief that one has little or no control over one's time and is destined to be battered by other people's priorities.

Professional school counselors also often suffer from another condition: *compassion fatigue*, which involves caring very deeply about helping children and adolescents and realizing there is not enough time in the day to meet all the demands. It often results in stress, depression, and potential burnout.

The following suggestions may provide some structure and management to your present modus operandi and free up extra time in the day to accomplish more:

- Follow the OHIO principle—"Only Handle It Once"—when managing papers; use it, lose it, or file it away.
- Have incoming mail screened or sorted by a secretary, if possible. If that's not possible, move the trash can under your mailbox and deposit the junk mail there. Why let unnecessary mail clutter your workspace?

- If a brief reply to a letter is needed, write it on the incoming letter or memo, make a copy for your file, and return to sender.
- Avoid making unnecessary paper copies. They waste your own and others' time to make, distribute, file, trash, or read. Do not become a disciple of the "fat paper philosophy," induced by "memoitis" and spread by copy machines. Go green! Almost everything can be sent electronically: newsletters, reports, other important information, and more.
- Set aside a regular time each day to do paperwork—but no more than an hour a day. Examine how much of your clerical work can be given to a secretary or clerical worker.
- Implement a "time truce" or quiet hour to frame a large block of uninterrupted time for your most important tasks or deadlines. Set aside other blocks of time for more detailed concentration. Have the secretary screen your calls and guard against interruptions. Make sure that the first hour of the day, or the last, is a productive one. This requires discipline, but also provides peace of mind.
- Read flyers, catalogs, and routine memos at a designated time once a week. Follow the technique of "rip and read"—rip out useful article that can be read and used later and throw other irrelevant materials away). Better yet, have a designated reader on the staff who will "rip and read" or "clip and save" for you and others.

Although we learn quickly in Foundations of Counseling 101 not to label individuals or limit our understanding by convenient descriptions, much is to be gained from the value of minimalism. We also know that we continue to seek a life balance between expectation and effort where getting the "maximum from the minimum" is the typical contemporary consumer perspective. Ahrens (1988) provides a number of salient strategies to incorporate minimalism into school counseling:

- Decide which information to carry around in your head and which to leave on the bookshelf or in the computer.
- Decide what paper to keep and what to recycle.
- Know when to do paperwork and when to have someone else do it if it needs to be done.
- Resist the urge to have more than one four-drawer filing cabinet. Organize the one you have. Better yet, give the filing cabinet away and keep all your information organized in computer files or in one-inch binders.
- If you are responsible for a flexible system, be sure it is maximally organized. If you have a tightly controlled system, ensure that it is creatively flexible.
- Return all phone calls as soon as possible (setting aside a block of time each day for phone calls is also helpful), and gently but quickly refer those that can be made by others.
- Control your appointment schedule. If you don't, it will control you.
- Know when to say yes and when to say no. Be assertive by expressing your needs and wants.
- Don't do anything for those you counsel that they can do for themselves (p. 86).

STRESS MANAGEMENT

It has been estimated that the average American will spend three years sitting in meetings, five years waiting in lines, more than 17,000 hours playing telephone tag, 4,000 hours stopped at red lights—and a lifetime trying to wind down. It's true that life without a little stress would be incredibly dull and boring, but life with too much stimulus can become unpleasant and tiring, ultimately damaging your health and well-being. Too much stress can seriously interfere with your ability to perform effectively. The art of stress management is to keep a level of stimulation that is healthy, productive, and enjoyable.

Stress for the professional school counselor evolves from an imbalance between the demands made from administrators, teachers, students and their families, special populations, and supervisors, on the one hand, and one's own expectations of what should be accomplished (realistic or not) in the course of a day, week, month, or year, on the other. Most stressors to which professional school counselors strive to adapt are subtle and symbolic. Situations that can trigger a stress reaction include the threat of rejection, a heated argument with a colleague, the passing of an important milepost, or the pressures of an approaching project deadline. Chronic and accumulated stress can have devastating physical and emotional consequences. Researchers suggest that stress lowers our resistance to illness and can play a contributory role in diseases of the kidney, heart, and blood vessels; migraine and tension headaches; gastrointestinal problems; and asthma, allergies, or respiratory disease.

The way we feel and behave under these multiple stressors is determined in part by what we think (self-statements such as the "shoulds" and "oughts") in a given situation. The stress reaction involves two major elements: 1) heightened physical arousal (increased heart rate, rapid breathing, muscular tension); anxious thoughts (e.g., a sense of helplessness); and 2) panic from being overwhelmed or a desire to escape. Since behavior and emotions are learned and controlled by inner thoughts or expectations, the best way to exert control over them is by assimilating the appropriate skills (such as progressive relaxation or cognitive restructuring) to change both the uncomfortable sensation and the relentless thoughts.

Of course, stress in small amounts can be a very positive life force. It is the impetus for growth, change, and adaptation. The key is to alleviate *negative* stress on a routine basis.

- If you feel socially isolated, try to share your concerns, experiences, or situations with a peer network or with other professionals you can trust. Capitalize on existing professional and personal networks to form support groups. Sometimes it is very helpful to use a peer network or support group to share ideas, diffuse stress, or access opportunities for personal growth.
- If you feel unrecognized or unappreciated, inventory what you have accomplished in the past year. Identify your strengths and successes. Share these with a confidant for feedback and validation.
- If you feel emotionally overextended, isolated, or overloaded, make an effort to do more non-work-related activities for yourself.
- When everything seems to be out of control, make a list of what is going *right* in your life. Include those things to be thankful for. Dwell on the positive things to regain a proper perspective on your life.
- If you are intellectually stagnant or understimulated, attend workshops, seminars, or cross-disciplinary courses. Take a course in, say, business management or horticulture.
- If worries and concerns are keeping you awake at night, try writing down what you're worrying about before going to bed, telling yourself you'll address these concerns the next day. Your mind will be encouraged to let go of the thoughts, knowing they are written down and won't be forgotten.
- If you have influence but very little power to change things, identify the formal and informal networks and influence that you actually have, and note positive change.
- If you are alienated administratively, discuss with one or two professional friends in whom you can confide ways to make positive contributions.
- Stress triggers cravings for fats, salts, and simple carbohydrates, that is, nervous food—the kind that is found in vending machines. Don't bring change or dollar bills to work. Substitute fruit and vegetables instead.
- Learn to say no to obligation overload. If you're feeling drained or overwhelmed by your commitments, start taking steps to unload as many things as needed to invest in your own well-being and regain some peace of mind.
- Try being a little more type-A—that is, *alter* what you can, *avoid* what you can, and *adjust* yourself to the rest.

Some Strategies to Incorporate into Everyday Living to Reduce Stress

- Plan "down time" or "debriefing time" every day.
- Grab a folder (preferably empty) and get out of the office periodically. People will not interrupt you because with folder in hand you look like you are on an important mission.
- Avoid irritating and overly competitive people prior to lunch or near the end of the day.
- At least three days a week, have lunch conversations that are not school or work related.
- Design your daily schedule so you have a chance to perform at least one activity each day that makes you feel successful or that completes a goal.
- Form a support group based on the willingness and ability to listen, share problems, give assistance, admit mistakes, and develop trusting relationships.
- Interact at least once each day with someone in your school who makes you laugh.
- Try to avoid, or at least spend less time with, people who are constantly angry, pessimistic, intimidating, or critical. Work on setting boundaries to reduce the number and frequency of stressful interactions.
- Plan a free weekend to "kick back" at least once a month.
- Do a small, but in-depth, one-to-one activity with each of your family members during the course of each month. This helps to renew close interpersonal relationships.
- Develop a "vacation attitude" after work; treat your home as a vacation home.
- Get involved with a friend, spouse, or child in an activity that will teach you a new concept, skill, or process—an opportunity to learn an unrelated work skill in itself is refreshing.
- Make a date for self-preservation. Periodically plan ahead and mark your calendar scheduling time to be alone with yourself. Perceive these planned occasions as genuine "meetings." Make yourself unavailable to the needs and manipulations of other people. Practice saying "I have a date" or "I'm sorry, I have other plans" as a way of saying no without feeling guilty.
- Use positive affirmations to reduce negative thinking. Examples:
    - I can do this.
    - I can achieve my goals.
    - I am completely myself and people will like me.
    - I am completely in control of my life.
    - I learn from my mistakes. They increase the experience on which I can draw.
    - I am a good, valued person in my own right.

Being at the constant mercy of other people's needs (teachers, administrators, coordinators, social services personnel, the courts, parents, students, volunteers, etc.) creates frustration, fragmentation, and overextension. Using some of the healthy techniques listed above will make you feel focused and back in control over time. Ultimately, you are more likely to face a challenge with equanimity when you plan some rewarding time for yourself.

Have a holistic approach to physical and mental well-being. Physical exercise makes us feel better and gives us energy, especially if it occurs at the beginning or end of a stressful day. Treat your brain as if it were a muscle and exercise it routinely, as well.

Taking Your Own Advice: Using Guided Imagery to Reduce Stress

Use imagery to track down the reasons behind anxiety and to help you say no to unreasonable or unwanted requests for your time. Lazarus (1981) suggests that you concentrate on any unwanted or unreasonable request from a person to whom you generally say yes even though you want to refuse. Be specific as to the task. Then picture yourself tactfully but firmly declining. As you picture yourself saying no, you may become aware of some tense feelings. Concentrate on these tensions and see what other images emerge. To counter the tension, imagine your family and the relaxed relations you would have with them if you were not overextended.

Strategies for Leaving Stress at the Office

Finish each day and be done with it. You have done what you could. Some blunders and absurdities no doubt crept in; forget them as soon as you can.

Tomorrow is a new day; begin it well and serenely and with not too high a spirit to be cumbered with old nonsense.

The day is all that is good and fair. It is too dear with its hopes and invitations to waste a moment on yesterday.

Ralph Waldo Emerson

End the day as calmly and smoothly as possible. Make it a habit to wind down for a half hour before you leave. Leave unfinished business at your desk. Bringing work home (into your family space) on a daily basis is a bad habit. Ask yourself, "Is this project an emergency?" "Can it wait until tomorrow?" "Can this be delegated?" If you feel you'll spend the evening worrying about the unfinished business from the end of the day, try the following exercise: Make a list of all outstanding tasks; imagine your feeling of accomplishment when every item is completed to your satisfaction; then forget about it until the morning.

How many days have you lost trying to control what is beyond your control? Making a list relieves the stress of worrying about forgetting something and helps you feel more in control. The satisfaction of being able to notice progress as you begin crossing items off the list is intrinsically rewarding. If you are a more compulsive type, you might try securing three folders (preferably high-tech plastic) in green, red, and yellow. Red is for "hot" projects that need your attention now, green for ongoing projects that need your daily attention, and yellow for "cautionary" items that will need your attention soon. On the outside of each folder, stick a Post-It note of prioritized items that must be accomplished. Smaller lists on three tracks (red, green, and yellow) will give you a better feeling of having things under control. You also will be able to "put your hands on things" when you need them.

Use your commute home as decompression time. As professional school counselors, we are overwhelmed by emotion and information overload. Don't listen to the news or rock 'n' roll on the radio because they both tend to overstimulate. Instead, make this a quiet time to let the thoughts of the day filter out of your head. And, since you can't utilize guided imagery on the road, pop one of those new age music or self-help audiobook CDs in the player.

At home, take a few minutes to be alone, change clothes, or rinse your troubles down the drain with a quick shower. Don't make dinner (or children's homework) into an ordeal. Turn off the television and turn on the answering machine. Learn to maintain a healthy perspective. Despite the day's worst disasters—you arrived late because the bridge was up, spilled coffee on the computerized answer sheets, worried about how well you did in an important presentation, and spent an hour trapped in a meeting with someone you despise—it really could have been worse. You could have come to work with two different colored shoes, which your burned-out colleagues wouldn't notice until midday.

Finally, encourage humor within and without. "Humor is serious business." It can serve as a powerful tool for people at all levels to prevent the buildup of stress, improve communication, enhance motivation and morale, build relationships, encourage creative problem solving, smooth the way for organizational change, and make workshops fun.

The use of humor decreases problems of discipline, increases listening and attention on the part of participants, decreases the pressure on people to be perfect, increases retention, and increases the comfort level of others. The resulting positive attitude can greatly contribute to achievement and productivity. Humor, according to Goodman (1982), makes it easier to hear feedback and new information. Humor helps us to step back from a problem situation and see the situation and possible solutions in perspective. This is a very important skill for counselors to have.

Strategies for Reducing Stress at the Office

Is there a neon "Do Drop In" sign above your office door? Being a professionally inviting counselor, many former students and their families will want to share their experiences and successes with you. Drop-in visitors also include salespersons, administrators, colleagues, school psychologists, special education coordinators, probation officers, police, and a multitude of other well-meaning but time-consuming people. The following strategies could redirect the flow of traffic and help you manage interruptions less stressfully.

- Locate your counseling department secretary's desk physically so that he or she can act as a buffer to anyone who may want to interrupt you. Your secretary can easily screen visitors, handle many information-seeking questions, or direct inquiries to those who could adequately respond.
- Your secretary could schedule an appointment for a drop-in visitor after you assure the caller "I am so glad to see you, but I'm scheduled to meet within someone in five minutes!" or "We really need to spend some time on this issue—let me see if I can clear my calendar for Thursday!"
- Avoid the "Rolls-Royce syndrome"—a malady suffered by professional school counselors who always feel they must do better than required. Although the Rolls-Royce is iconic as the finest automobile in the world, most people can get by with a less.
- Use secretarial assistance efficiently. Secretaries are an unlimited resource if used efficiently. Weekly schedules and monthly calendars (part of the ASCA 2005b model) are essential. They can also manage the flow of information and activities. A secretary should know your program goals, routine deadlines (data processing, testing, etc.), priorities, and general time-management procedures. Often, they can suggest creative ways to streamline or completely eliminate ineffective or redundant procedures. The checklist of secretary's responsibilities given in Figure 15.2 in Appendix A can help you manage your time better and reduce stress.

How to Say No and Help Others Assume Responsibility

Professional school counselors often assume the legacy of "being all things to all people" and ultimately lose sight of their own priorities. Too often, we assume responsibility for tasks that others should perform. For example, if a coach comes in to check on a player's eligibility, we are inclined to say, "I don't know," and follow it up with, "but I'll check it out for you." Or a teacher may come in during his planning period and remark, "Johnny has been absent for four days, and I don't have time to check on this today. Would you please call his family and find out if everything's all right?" Assuming responsibility for the coach or the teacher should not supersede your own priorities. After all, who has the largest caseload, the coach, the teacher, or the counselor? (Answer: Counselors average 540, teachers 150, and coaches under 50.) Help them assume their share of responsibility.

Shipman, Martin, McKay, and Anastiasi (1983) list 10 suggestions that can help school counselors say no to time-consuming activities that do not move them toward completion of their major priorities:

1. Realize what is being asked of you.
2. Think about the consequences of saying yes.
3. Determine why others are asking you rather than someone else or doing it themselves.
4. Think about whether or not you are a soft touch.
5. Ask, "Why me?" when you are asked to do something.
6. Estimate the amount of time you will need to respond to the request if you say yes.
7. Say no, but give an alternate suggestion.

8. Reroute the request to someone else—that is, delegate.
9. Never promise what you cannot deliver.
10. Simply say, "No."

Do not let others hold you responsible for things over which you have little control or influence. Help others assume responsibility for their own priorities.

- Help others do their jobs, but be sure they take responsibility for handling their own problems.
- Help students, teachers, and parents—all those with whom you work—know that they have responsibilities, too.
- Define the boundaries of your influence and the responsibilities that others have.
- Do not accept blame for problems caused by others.
- Clarify roles among parties involved in conflicts; that is, what each can do to help solve the problem.

Effective Communication with Administrators, Faculty, Parents, Students, and Staff

Avoid barriers to communication by using and modeling basic counseling skills and communicating positively. For example, maintain eye contact with the other person, tilt your head slightly to show you are listening, adopt the other person's pose to garner acceptance, and be nonjudgmental when reflecting concerns back to the person. Test your understanding by rephrasing statements and repeating them to the speaker. Be alert to nonverbal warning signs such as evasive eye contact and verbal ones such as hesitation or contradiction in statements; these may provide clues to the truthfulness of the issue being discussed.

Be sensitive to cultural differences (e.g., Asians may feel it is more respectful to be silent). Being cognizant of personal space is also critical. When standing with most people, leave a personal space of about one yard. Intruding into another's personal territory can make the other person defensive and foster hostility.

When listening, *emphasize* by drawing out the speaker and information in a supportive, helpful way; *analyze* by seeking concrete information about the situation and trying to separate fact from emotion; and *synthesize* by proactively guiding the verbal exchange toward a manageable objective or goal. Misunderstandings between people are often caused by "wishful listening," that is, hearing only what you want to hear. Attending to constant interruptions such as email alerts, phone calls, and intercom messages can make the person you are talking to feel that their concerns are being dismissed or are unimportant.

Voice Mail, Email, and Away Messages

With voice mail, always deal with incoming messages that are waiting for you as soon as you can, and always within 24 hours. When leaving a message for someone else, start with your name, phone number, and the time of your call. Speak slowly and clearly, so information will not be confusing or lost.

If you leave an "away message" on your email, state that the person's message is important to you, when you will return, and either another way you can be reached (e.g., perhaps personal cell phone) or a name and contact information of someone who can help them in your absence. An example is: "Your message is very important to me. However, I will be out of the office until Monday, November 7. If you need help before then, you may reach me on my cell phone at [phone number] or you can contact Doreen, the student services coordinator, at [phone number] or [email address]. Thank you, and I am looking forward to talking with you soon."

Electronic media such as email, text messaging, Twitter, and social networking websites have transformed communication. They can be both an asset and a liability. Communicating with someone else far away has never been easier. But once you send something out in cyberspace, it cannot be taken back or erased; it remains forever in cyberspace and may be accessed by others. The following rules of "netiquette" should be followed:

- Use meaningful subject titles.
- Be as brief as possible.
- Proofread your message before you send it because you cannot count on the spell-check function.
- Differentiate between school-related and nonschool-related information. It is not a good idea to advertise a personal garage sale during school business hours. This also applies to things of a political nature or using school email as a forum to promote special interests.
- Be selective about the recipients of your emails, and know the difference between reply and reply to all. If you say something unflattering about someone in the email string and hit "Reply All," that person will receive this information.
- Avoid attaching unnecessary files or overly large files to your email, especially if you are mailing to a lot of people. Some people may not have enough server space or mailbox space to receive a large amount of information.
- Don't email in all capital letters. That is called "flaming" and is the equivalent of yelling at the person.
- Avoid emoticons such as :-) as well as common texting abbreviations like BTW ("by the way") or U ("you"). These can be misinterpreted and do not look very professional.
- Never give confidential information about a student, family situation, teacher, or administrator in an email. This can come back to haunt you, especially if you received misinformation.
- For your own protection, have a confidentiality statement in the footer of your email such as this: "This email and any attachments may contain information which is confidential, proprietary, privileged or otherwise protected by law. The information is solely intended for the named addressee (or a person responsible for delivering it to the addressee). If you are not the intended recipient of this message, you are not authorized to read, print, retain, copy, or disseminate this message or any part of it. If you have received this email in error, please notify the sender immediately by return email and delete it from your computer."
- Let your computer work for you. Set up files for documentation purposes such as "Parent Conferences," "Teacher Conferences," "Important Meeting Contents," or "Policy Changes."
- Never use obscene language or insults, and let the administration know if you receive any racist or sexist mail from anyone else.
- Be careful about social networking sites such as Facebook and Myspace. Information and pictures are in the public domain, and your information and pictures can be cut and pasted anywhere in cyberspace.

CHAIRING A SUCCESSFUL MEETING

A well-run meeting is a productive way to communicate and serves as a means to get things done and to move schoolwide and region-wide initiatives forward. When chairing a meeting, maintain control of proceedings and never let arguments or dissent get out of hand because this produces ill will and a reluctance for members to commit their time and energy to a hostile venue. The following are important tips for running meetings:

- Have a copy of the agenda printed for or emailed to all participants.
- Make any necessary introductions of special guests or attendees.
- Remind members of the meeting's purpose and desired outcomes.

- Go over any ground rules.
- If there was a previous meeting, minutes may need to be approved.
- Go to the first agenda item and perhaps ask a member to initiate a discussion.
- Allow everyone to state their opinion.
- Set time limits to discussions in order to end the meeting on time.
- To close the meeting, summarize the discussion and confirm that others concur with your summation.
- If there is any unfinished business, designate someone to follow up on it.
- Go over any actions that will result from the meeting. Assign each action to a person and attach a target time that it should be completed.
- Meetings can also be held via videoconferencing or on Skype via computer camera and microphone. This is very helpful for regional or state meetings to save travel time and meeting expenses.

MANAGING YOUR TIME

Professional school counselors are often in a precarious situation because everyone wants a piece of their time during the day. For example, the football coach needs to check on his team's grade-point average for eligibility to participate in sports; a student needs three transcripts sent to college for early decision; someone from Children with Disabilities Services needs a classroom observation of a student; divorced parents who have joint custody of their daughter each want separate progress reports for their child; and the principal needs a count of the number of minorities taking AP courses for the central office, while you have planned two groups that you routinely run in the morning, and all these tasks must be completed by noon.

The following are some time management suggestions:

- Think through your day on your way to work.
- Set aside some time before students and teachers arrive to review and prioritize demands on your time.
- Update your daily calendar on your computer, print it out, and post it on your door. That way everyone knows where you are and what you are doing throughout the day. In a subtle way, it demonstrates accountability. Also, having your activities planned out enables you to be in command of your time by managing situations before they get out of control.
- When dealing with paperwork, identify a small chunk of a difficult task and deal with it right away to give you a sense of accomplishment.
- Whenever possible, delegate tasks that are not time-efficient for you to do yourself. Delegate to clerical staff, support staff, or parent volunteers as long as the information is not confidential.
- To keep discussion short with parents and teachers, avoid open-ended questions.
- As a workplace, the school setting is often noisy and chaotic, so schedule some quiet time to collect your thoughts, assess priorities, and make a task list.
- Don't commit to a punishing and overambitious schedule that you cannot realistically maintain. This will set you up for failure and jeopardize your credibility with parents, students, faculty, and staff.
- Make sure that you do at least one thing every day that you enjoy.
- Keep your desk clear of everything but the current job at hand.
- Clean up daily and never leave a mess to confront in the morning. That way, you will start your day with feelings of being in control.
- When processing important documents, glance at them when they first come in. If they are urgent, take immediate action or delegate immediately. If they are less urgent and require additional input before they can be processed, like data from another department, place them into a "Pending" tray. Put all other nonurgent papers into your inbox to be processed routinely during the day.

- Highlight key points on paperwork in order to speed up rereading.
- Position a clock in your office so it is visible to both you and visitors.

Avoiding and Managing Interruptions

To make your day as productive as possible, you may need to create your own feng shui by reorganizing your office so you are less visible. To discourage unnecessary interruptions—a teacher who wants to discuss her wonderful weekend with someone she found on eHarmony.com, or the principal coming in to chat because he has a conference call in 15 minutes and wants to have a cup of coffee and kill some time at your expense—there may be the need to set boundaries. Boundaries are important; otherwise, you become "everything to everyone," the type "E" professional school counselor.

To discourage interruptions, use negative body language to fend off unwanted intrusions. Turn your head, but not your whole body, toward the visitor. Use subtle signals such as glancing at your watch. Holding a pen signals an unwillingness to be interrupted. Other tips include the following:

- Pick up the phone to indicate the end of a meeting or conversation.
- Ask your secretary or a colleague to screen incoming phone calls for you.
- Do not sit down if you are followed into your office.
- Place your chair out of view if your door is open.
- Position your desk so you can see who is approaching the door.
- Keep your office door closed when you don't want to interrupted. (Teachers get daily planning bells; professional school counselors do not.)
- Keep all chance meetings short by standing; that way, it will be easier to excuse yourself.
- Don't become a pack rat. Throw away information you think you do not need. You can't be a clearinghouse for every cause, concern, or school community initiative.
- Stop subscriptions to journals you no longer read. File interesting articles from journals you do read and throw the rest away. If journals are online, keep an electronic file of interesting articles.
- Keep only essential reading on your desk.
- Prepare yourself for a phone conversation as you would for a meeting. Have an agenda and stay focused on the facts.
- When returning calls, bunch calls together. If a number is busy, try it again later after completing other calls.
- Use the speakerphone option so that you can multitask while waiting for answers from phone calls. Have another project to work on in the event you are kept waiting. For example, if you hear, "Please wait for the next operator," pull up your Outlook calendar and update it as needed.
- Signaling the end of a phone conversation is also helpful. The following phrases might work:
  - "I have a call on my other line. Is it okay if I call you back at a later time?"
  - "Perhaps we can revisit this topic further the next time we speak?"
  - "I have to go. My principal is signaling me to join her at the end of the suite."
  - "Is there anything else we need to discuss before I go?"

Delegating Effectively

Delegating is not a sign of weakness or laziness, it is working smart. Assuming responsibility for everything and everyone enables others to *not* take responsibility for their own personal job requirements. Here are some guidelines:

- Make sure you define goals and objectives clearly when you delegate a task to a member of your department.

- Set precise and realistic deadlines for tasks that have been delegated.
- Keep a checklist to assist in monitoring the progress of tasks delegated to others.
- When delegating, you delegate the right to perform the action and the responsibility to make informed decisions. But make sure that you are informed if significant changes are made in a procedure.
- Be flexible about new ideas. The person tasked with the job may have a better and more efficient way of completing the assignment. Be open to efficient ideas.
- Provide constructive feedback on performance that needs to be improved by colleagues, and work out a timeline.
- Try not to allow colleagues to distract you with unimportant topics or personal domestic issues such as a colleague's separation or divorce. You are a counselor for students and their families, not for faculty or staff.
- Hold meetings in colleagues' offices so you can easily leave when necessary and focus on the needs at hand.

Finally, establish a culture that recognizes success and avoids blame for missteps. When things have gone wrong, look for solutions rather than for a scapegoat. This can promote an open rather than a punitive environment. Use feedback sessions to analyze what has gone wrong to ensure that lessons are learned about how similar mistakes can be avoided in the future. Always take time to recognize the effort that was put into the task and reward it. Use handwritten notes rather than typed letters to praise colleagues, although it may be more appropriate to provide a typed letter for a big project that was undertaken by a colleague that affected a large group of people (such as a college or career fair) and send a copy to the colleague's supervisor (i.e., their principal and district supervisor).

COMPASSION FATIGUE: THE PROFESSIONAL LIABILITY FOR ABSORBING THE PAIN OF OTHERS

Professional school counselors who listen to the stories of fear, pain, and suffering of others may feel similar fear, pain, and suffering because, by their calling, they care. According to the American Psychological Association, professionals who absorb another person's pain and carry it with them are experiencing compassion fatigue. Helping professionals in all therapeutic and institutional settings—emergency health care workers, professional school counselors, teachers, school administrators, mental health professionals, clergy, advocate volunteers, human service workers, among others—are especially vulnerable to compassion fatigue.

Compassion fatigue is a condition that develops over time, taking weeks or sometimes years to surface. Essentially, it is a low-level, chronic clouding of caring and concern for others. Over time, the ability to feel and care for others becomes eroded through the overuse of skills expressing compassion. Compassion fatigue occurs when caregivers become emotionally drained from being exposed to the pain and trauma of the people they are helping. Compassion fatigue can affect seven domains:

1. Cognitive
2. Emotional
3. Behavioral
4. Spiritual
5. Personal relations
6. Somatic
7. Work performance

Common symptoms of compassion fatigue include low morale, reduced ability to concentrate, guilt, appetite changes, intolerance, depleted energy, insomnia, immune system impairment, apathy, depression, negativity, isolation, perfectionism, rigidity, regression, a feeling of pervasive hopelessness, a loss of purpose, questioning the meaning of life, shock, decreased interest in intimacy and sex, anger, and mood swings.

Burnout or *cumulative stress* is the state of physical, emotional, and mental exhaustion caused by a depletion of the ability to cope with one's environment (e.g., school demands and community demands). It results from human responses to the ongoing stressors of our daily lives (Maslach, 1982). Symptoms such as exhaustion, frustration, anger, and depression are typical of burnout.

Secondary traumatic stress is exposure to extreme events directly experienced by another and being overwhelmed by this secondhand exposure to trauma. For example, if you are exposed to others' traumatic events as a result of your work—such as in an emergency room, working with child protective services, or being the student assistance counselor for a school—this is secondary exposure. Symptoms are usually of rapid onset and are associated with the particular event; they may include being anxious or afraid, having difficulty sleeping, visualizing reoccurring images of the event, or avoiding things that remind you of the event.

STRATEGIES FOR TAKING CARE OF SELF AND OTHERS

Self-Awareness and Self-Care

1. Know your own emotional or psychological "triggers" and areas of vulnerability. Learn how to defuse or divert them in constructive ways.
2. Recognize and resolve your own personal or interpersonal issues with others and become aware of your own reactions to other people's pain and suffering.
3. Develop realistic expectations about the rewards as well as the limitations of being a helping professional. You cannot be all things to all people. Challenge your irrational thoughts and beliefs. Set boundaries for yourself and others.
4. Balance your work with other professional activities that provide opportunities for positive growth and personal renewal.

Don't Hesitate to Accept Help from Other Professional Colleagues

1. Seek out opportunities to acknowledge, express, and work through difficult experiences in a supportive environment with colleagues you trust. Debrief on a routine basis, and build healthy support groups.
2. Delegate responsibilities and get help from others for routine work, when appropriate.
3. Develop a healthy support system to protect yourself from further fatigue and emotional exhaustion.

Emphasize Healthy Living and a Balanced Life

1. Eat nutritious food, exercise on a regular basis, rest, meditate, pray, and take care of yourself as a whole being.
2. Set and keep healthy boundaries at work. Ask yourself, "Would the school fall apart if I stepped away from my work for a day?"
3. Think about the notion that if you never say no to a request, your "yes" isn't really worth much, especially if you have already overextended yourself.

4. Find avenues to provide yourself with emotional and spiritual renewal for strength for the future.
5. Develop and reward a sense of humor. Expose yourself to humorous situations like comedy shows or videos.
6. Learn to laugh at mistakes, see solutions rather than problems, enjoy life, and maintain healthy personal relationships.

Strategies for Taking Care of Yourself to Prevent Compassion Fatigue

1. Spend quality time alone. Learning mindfulness meditation is an excellent way to ground yourself in the moment and keep your thoughts from pulling you in different directions. The ability to reconnect with a spiritual source will also help you achieve inner balance.
2. Recharge your batteries daily. A regular exercise regimen can reduce stress, help you achieve outer balance, and reenergize you for time with friends and family.
3. Hold one focused, connected, and meaningful conversation with someone you care about each day. Time with family or close friends renews depleted batteries, but unfortunately, it often becomes the first thing we cut out of our life in times of stress.

Compassion Fatigue Also Comes with Some Important "Don'ts"

1. Don't make important, life-changing decisions immediately. Caregivers who are suffering from compassion fatigue should not try to make any major life decisions until they have recovered physically, emotionally, cognitively, and spiritually. Ill-considered actions like quitting a job, getting a divorce, having an extramarital affair, or spending money you don't have only complicates issues in the long term.
2. Don't try to find blame in others. Blaming the administration, faculty, staff, or "the system" is not productive. Being adversarial will only create further exhaustion and hinder the healing and moving on that needs to take place.
3. Don't spend energy complaining. Similarly, avoid commiserating with discontented or disgruntled colleagues. It's easy to succumb to the tendency to complain when experiencing compassion fatigue, but it will only make things feel worse. There are other more constructive environments to share and express feelings. The universality of knowing that everyone is experiencing the same emotions or feelings can be a catharsis in itself.
4. Don't try a quick fix. Compassion fatigue often makes one vulnerable to addictive behaviors. Many helping professionals with compassion fatigue try to deal with clients by working longer and harder. Others self-medicate with food, alcohol, or prescription drugs. Don't fall prey to a quick fix, because it always ends up complicating an already overburdened life, escalating the downward spiral to burnout and depression.

Compassion Fatigue and Burnout Websites

The following websites may be helpful:

- Green Cross Academy of Traumatology, http://www.greencross.org (initiated by Charles Figley; see Appendix C)
- Professional Quality of Life: Compassion Satisfaction and Fatigue (ProQOL), http://www.proqol.org or http://www.isu.edu/~bhstamm (by Beth Hudnall Stamm et al.; see Appendix B)

CONCLUSION

Professional school counselors are a resourceful, creative, and highly motivated contingency of helping professionals who use these same qualities to help the children, adolescents, and families they serve. Yet, the emotional, physical, and cognitive demands of being a professional school counselor can be overwhelming. Excessive demands experienced on a daily basis can produce burnout in distinct stages:

1. *Enthusiasm*, which is a tendency to be overly available to students and their families and to teachers and other support personnel
2. *Stagnation*, in which expectations shrink to normal proportions and personal discontent begins to surface
3. *Frustration*, in which difficulties seem to multiply and the counselor becomes less tolerant and less sympathetic and compensates by avoiding or withdrawing from relationships
4. *Apathy*, which is characterized by depression and listlessness

It's important to establish boundaries of what can and cannot be accomplished, to delegate responsibilities among members of the school community, and to maintain the true focus on the role of the professional counselor to enable and empower youth to make the transition to successful adulthood.

APPENDIX A

FIGURE 15.1   Time robbers for professional school counselors.

IMPOSED UPON US	SELF-IMPOSED
⊕ Interruptions	⊕ Failure to delegate
⊕ Needed answers slow to arrive	⊕ Poor attitude
⊕ Unclear job description	⊕ Personal disorganization
⊕ Unnecessary meetings	⊕ Absentmindedness
⊕ Too much work	⊕ Failure to listen
⊕ Poor communication	⊕ Indecision
⊕ Shifting priorities	⊕ Socializing (random)
⊕ Failure to delegate	⊕ Fatigue
⊕ Poor attitude	⊕ Lack of self-discipline
⊕ Personal disorganization	⊕ Leaving tasks unfinished
⊕ Absentmindedness	⊕ Paper shuffling
⊕ Indecision	⊕ Procrastination
⊕ Socializing (scheduled)	⊕ Outside activities
⊕ Computer failure	⊕ Cluttered workspace
⊕ Disorganized administrator	⊕ Unclear personal goals
⊕ Red tape	⊕ Perfectionism
⊕ Conflicting priorities	⊕ Poor planning
⊕ Low morale; untrained colleagues	⊕ Preoccupation
⊕ Teacher, parent, school support staff	⊕ Attempting too much
⊕ Lack of authority	⊕ Failure to listen
⊕ Mistakes of others; revised deadlines	

FIGURE 15.2 Checklist of secretary's responsibilities.

Does your secretary:

Telephone
- Place outgoing calls for you?
- Handle parental inquiries?
- Deal with requests for information from other schools or organizations?
- Make decisions as to which calls are important and which can be handled by someone else in the school (such as the nurse or attendance clerk)?
- Answer the phone in a pleasant voice?
- Use good human relations skills when dealing with a complaint or an irate parent?

Correspondence
- Screen all notes leaving the counseling office?
- Respond to some requests using your signature?
- Compose most letters from notes?
- Keep departmental notes on a standardized template and email it to others?
- Anticipate a response and initiate a letter?
- Make corrections on language usage, spelling, organization, and so on?
- Accurately proofread your correspondence?
- Read all incoming mail so that you are informed?
- Handle confidential information appropriately?
- Route incoming mail to the proper person on the counseling staff?
- Screen all junk mail?
- Place incoming mail in the "In" basket, in accordance with the schedule for handling it?
- Remove correspondence from the "Out" basket on a regular schedule?
- Summarize or highlight information in lengthy reports or letters?

Files
- Have a filing system that is designed for easy retrieval and that your staff can use in your absence?
- Keep up to date on your filing?
- Maintain a checkout system for information, materials, and videos from the counseling department?
- Maintain a tickler file for future action items?
- Maintain a monthly schedule of routines that happen at the same time annually?
- File in cumulative folders the results of aptitude and achievement tests and interest inventories?
- File student data forms, health screenings, physical education records, student activity and student profile sheets, and so on?
- Refill records according to promotions, retentions, withdrawals, graduations, and GED results?

Meetings
- Notify those involved in meetings in advance?
- Help gather materials and prepare visuals, handouts, or summaries?
- Make sure space is available?
- Make sure all necessary equipment is in place?
- Keep minutes of all meetings and forward information to participants?
- Prepare the meeting agenda and distribute it to participants before the meeting? (See Figure 15.3)

Scheduling Appointments
- Keep a calendar of your schedule?
- Update the calendar daily (reconciling the desk calendar with the personal pocket calendar)?
- Make appointments with the appropriate time allocations?
- Avoid scheduling an appointment with a person if that person should be seeing someone else?
- Interrupt visitors (tactfully) when the allotted time has expired?

Visitors
- Make visitors feel welcome and comfortable?
- Give new students and families a warm, receptive feeling about the school?
- Help visitors and staff when possible without bothering you?
- Act as a "buffer" to intercept drop-in visitors?

FIGURE 15.2　(Continued)

Miscellaneous
- Keep a folder of all pertinent information for substitutes?
- Help in training new staff members about procedures?
- Demonstrate punctuality, loyalty, and conscientiousness?
- Know where you are and when you are expected back?
- Meet with you each day to have questions answered and set priorities for the day?
- Keep aware of deadlines and inform you of the status in relation to deadlines?
- Maintain confidentiality?

FIGURE 15.3　Professional school counseling department minutes template

Date_____

TYPE OF MEETING	
FACILITATOR & NOTETAKER	Meeting facilitator:_____Notetaker:_____
ATTENDEES	

Agenda topics

AGENDA ITEM 1

DISCUSSION	
CONCLUSIONS	

ACTION ITEMS	PERSON RESPONSIBLE	DEADLINE

AGENDA ITEM 2

DISCUSSION	
CONCLUSIONS	

ACTION ITEMS	PERSON RESPONSIBLE	DEADLINE

AGENDA ITEM 3

DISCUSSION	
CONCLUSIONS	

FIGURE 15.3   (Continued)

ACTION ITEMS	PERSON RESPONSIBLE	DEADLINE

AGENDA ITEM 4

DISCUSSION	

CONCLUSIONS	

ACTION ITEMS	PERSON RESPONSIBLE	DEADLINE

AGENDA ITEM 5

DISCUSSION	

CONCLUSIONS	

ACTION ITEMS	PERSON RESPONSIBLE	DEADLINE

AGENDA ITEM 6

DISCUSSION	

CONCLUSIONS	

ACTION ITEMS	PERSON RESPONSIBLE	DEADLINE

AGENDA ITEM 7

DISCUSSION	.

CONCLUSIONS	

ACTION ITEMS	PERSON RESPONSIBLE	DEADLINE
SPECIAL NOTES		

APPENDIX B: PROFESSIONAL QUALITY OF LIFE SCALE (PROQOL)

Compassion Satisfaction and Fatigue
(ProQOL) Version 5 (2009)

When you *[help]* people you have direct contact with their lives. As you may have found, your compassion for those you *[help]* can affect you in positive and negative ways. Below are some questions about your experiences, both positive and negative, as a *[helper]*. Consider each of the following questions about you and your current work situation. Select the number that honestly reflects how frequently you experienced these things in the *last 30 days*.

1 = NEVER	*2 = RARELY*	*3 = SOMETIMES*	*4 = OFTEN*	*5 = VERY OFTEN*

_____	1. I am happy.
_____	2. I am preoccupied with more than one person I *[help]*.
_____	3. I get satisfaction from being able to *[help]* people.
_____	4. I feel connected to others.
_____	5. I jump or am startled by unexpected sounds.
_____	6. I feel invigorated after working with those I *[help]*.
_____	7. I find it difficult to separate my personal life from my life as a *[helper]*.
_____	8. I am not as productive at work because I am losing sleep over traumatic experiences of a person I *[help]*.
_____	9. I think that I might have been affected by the traumatic stress of those I *[help]*.
_____	10. I feel trapped by my job as a *[helper]*.
_____	11. Because of my *[helping]*, I have felt "on edge" about various things.
_____	12. I like my work as a *[helper]*.
_____	13. I feel depressed because of the traumatic experiences of the people I *[help]*.
_____	14. I feel as though I am experiencing the trauma of someone I have *[helped]*.
_____	15. I have beliefs that sustain me.
_____	16. I am pleased with how I am able to keep up with *[helping]* techniques and protocols.
_____	17. I am the person I always wanted to be.
_____	18. My work makes me feel satisfied.
_____	19. I feel worn out because of my work as a *[helper]*.
_____	20. I have happy thoughts and feelings about those I *[help]* and how I could help them.
_____	21. I feel overwhelmed because my case [work] load seems endless.
_____	22. I believe I can make a difference through my work.
_____	23. I avoid certain activities or situations because they remind me of frightening experiences of the people I *[help]*.
_____	24. I am proud of what I can do to *[help]*.
_____	25. As a result of my *[helping]*, I have intrusive, frightening thoughts.
_____	26. I feel "bogged down" by the system.
_____	27. I have thoughts that I am a "success" as a *[helper]*.
_____	28. I can't recall important parts of my work with trauma victims.
_____	29. I am a very caring person.
_____	30. I am happy that I chose to do this work.

What is my score and what does it mean?

In this section, you will score your test and then you can compare your score to the interpretation below.

Scoring

1. Be certain to respond to all items.
2. Go to items 1, 4, 15, 17, and 29 and reverse your score. For example, if you scored the item 1, write a 5 beside it. We ask you to reverse these scores because we have learned that the test works better if you reverse these scores.

YOU WROTE	CHANGE TO
1	5
2	4
3	3
4	2
5	1

To find your score on **Compassion Satisfaction**, add your scores on questions 3, 6, 12, 16, 18, 20, 22, 24, 27, 30.

THE SUM OF MY COMPASSION SATISFACTION QUESTIONS WAS	SO MY SCORE EQUALS	MY LEVEL OF COMPASSION SATISFACTION
22 or less	43 or less	Low
Between 23 and 41	Around 50	Average
42 or more	57 or more	High

To find your score on **Burnout**, add your scores on questions 1, 4, 8, 10, 15, 17, 19, 21, 26, and 29. Find your score in the table below.

THE SUM OF MY BURNOUT QUESTIONS	SO MY SCORE EQUALS	MY LEVEL OF COMPASSION SATISFACTION
22 or less	43 or less	Low
Between 23 and 41	Around 50	Average
42 or more	57 or more	High

To find your score on **Secondary Traumatic Stress**, add your scores on questions 2, 5, 7, 9, 11, 13, 14, 23, 25, 28. Find your score in the table below.

THE SUM OF MY SECONDARY TRAUMATIC STRESS QUESTIONS	SO MY SCORE EQUALS	MY LEVEL OF COMPASSION SATISFACTION
22 or less	43 or less	Low
Between 23 and 41	Around 50	Average
42 or more	57 or more	High

© B. Hudnall Stamm, 2009. *Professional Quality of Life: Compassion Satisfaction and Fatigue Version 5 (ProQOL)*. Reprinted with permission.

Your Scores on the ProQOL: Professional Quality of Life Screening

Based on your responses, your personal scores are below. If you have any concerns, you should discuss them with a physical or mental health care professional.

Compassion Satisfaction _____

Compassion satisfaction is about the pleasure you derive from being able to do your work well. For example, you may feel like it is a pleasure to help others through your work. You may feel positively about your colleagues or your ability to contribute to the work setting, or even the greater good of society. Higher scores on this scale represent a greater satisfaction related to your ability to be an effective caregiver in your job.

The average score is 50 (SD 10; alpha scale reliability .88). About 25% of people score higher than 57, and about 25% of people score below 43. If you are in the higher range, you probably derive a good deal of professional satisfaction from your position. If your scores are below 40, you may either find problems with your job, or there may be some other reason – for example, you might derive you satisfaction from activities other than your job.

Burnout _____

Most people have an intuitive idea of what burnout is. From the research perspective, burnout is one of the elements of compassion fatigue. It is associated with feelings of hopelessness and difficulties in dealing with work or in doing your job effectively. These negative feelings usually have a gradual onset. They can reflect the feeling that your efforts make no difference, or they can be associated with a very high workload or a non-supportive work environment. Higher scores on this scale mean that you are at higher risk for burnout.

The average score on the burnout scale is 50 (SD 10; alpha scale reliability .75). About 25% of people score above 57, and about 25% of people score below 53. If your score is below 18, this probably reflects positive feelings about your ability to be effective in your work. If you score above 57, you may wish to think about what at work makes you feel like you are not effective in your position. Your score may reflect your mood: perhaps you were having a "bad day" or are in need of some time off. If the high score persists, or if it is reflective of other worries, it may be a cause for concern.

Secondary Traumatic Stress _____

The second component of Compassion Fatigue (CF) is secondary traumatic stress (STS). It is about your work-related, secondary exposure to extremely or traumatically stressful events. Developing problems due to exposure to other's trauma is somewhat rare, but does happen to many people who care for those who have experienced extremely or traumatically stressful events. For example, you may repeatedly hear stories about the traumatic things that happen to other people, commonly called Vicarious Traumatization. You may see or provide treatment to people who have experienced horrific events. If your work puts you directly in the path of danger, due to your work as a soldier or civilian working in military medicine personnel, this is not secondary exposure; your exposure is primary. However, if you are exposed to others' traumatic events as a result of your work, such as providing care to casualties or for those in a military medical rehabilitation facility, this is secondary exposure. The symptoms of STS are usually rapid in onset and associated with a particular event. They may include being afraid, having difficulty sleeping, having images of the upsetting event into your mind, or avoiding things that remind you of the event.

The average score on this scale is 50 (SD 10; alpha scale reliability .81). About 25% of people score below 43 and about 25% of people score above 57. If your score is above 57, you may want to take some time to think about what at work may be frightening to you or if there is some other reason for the elevated score. While higher scores do not mean that you do have a problem, they are an indication that you may want to examine how you feel about your work and your work environment. You may wish to discuss this with your supervisor, a colleague, or a health care professional.

APPENDIX C: GREEN CROSS ACADEMY OF TRAUMATOLOGY STANDARDS OF SELF-CARE GUIDELINES

I. Purpose of the Guidelines

As with the standards of practice in any field, the practitioner is required to abide by standards of self care. These guidelines are utilized by all members of the Green Cross. The purpose of the guidelines is twofold: First, *do no harm to yourself* in the line of duty when helping/treating others. Second, attend to your physical, social, emotional, and spiritual needs as a way of ensuring high-quality services that look to you for support as a human being.

II. Ethical Principles of Self-Care in Practice

These principles declare that it is unethical *not* to attend to your self-care as a practitioner because sufficient self-care prevents harming those we serve.

1. *Respect for the dignity and worth of self:* A violation lowers your integrity and trust.
2. *Responsibility of self-care:* Ultimately it is your responsibility to take care of yourself and no situation or person can justify neglecting it.
3. *Self-care and duty to perform:* There must be a recognition that the duty to perform as a helper can not be fulfilled if there is not, at the same time, a duty to self-care.

III. Standards of Humane Practice of Self-Care

1. *Universal right to wellness:* Every helper, regardless of her or his role or employer, has a right to wellness associated with self-care.
2. *Physical rest and nourishment:* Every helper deserves restful sleep and physical separation from work that sustains them in their work role.
3. *Emotional rest and nourishment:* Every helper deserves emotional and spiritual renewal both in and outside the work context.
4. *Sustenance modulation:* Every helper must utilize self restraint with regard to what and how much they consume (e.g., food, drink, drugs, stimulation) since it can compromise their competence as a helper.

IV. Standards for Expecting Appreciation and Compensation

1. *Seek, find, and remember appreciation from supervisors and clients:* These and other activities increase worker satisfactions that sustain them emotionally and spiritually in their helping.
2. *Make it known that you wish to be recognized for your service:* Recognition also increases worker satisfactions that sustain them.
3. *Select one or more advocates:* They are colleagues who know you as a person and as a helper and are committed to monitoring your efforts at self-care.

V. Standards for Establishing and Maintaining Wellness

Section A. Commitment to Self-Care

1. *Make a formal, tangible commitment:* Written, public, specific, and measurable promises of self-care.
2. *Set deadlines and goals:* The self-care plan should set deadlines and goals connected to specific activities of self-care.
3. *Generate strategies that work and follow them:* Such a plan must be attainable and followed with great commitment and monitored by advocates of your self-care.

Section B: Strategies for Letting Go of Work

1. *Make a formal, tangible commitment:* Written, public, specific, and measurable promise of letting go of work in off-hours and embracing rejuvenation activities that are fun, stimulating, inspiriting, and generate joy of life.
2. *Set deadlines and goals:* The letting-go-of-work plan should set deadlines and goals connected to specific activities of self-care.
3. *Generate strategies that work and follow them:* Such a plan must be attainable and followed with great commitment and monitored by advocates of your self-care.

Section C. Strategies for Gaining a Sense of Self-Care Achievement

1. *Strategies for acquiring adequate rest and relaxation:* The strategies are tailored to your own interest and abilities which result in rest and relaxation most of the time.
2. *Strategies for practicing effective daily stress reductions method(s):* The strategies are tailored to your own interest and abilities in effectively managing your stress during working hours and off-hours with the recognition that they will probably be different strategies.

VI. Inventory of Self-Care Practice—Personal

Section A: Physical

1. *Body work:* Effectively monitoring all parts of your body for tension and utilizing techniques that reduce or eliminate such tensions.
2. *Effective sleep induction and maintenance:* An array of healthy methods that induce sleep and a return to sleep under a wide variety of circumstances including stimulation of noise, smells, and light.
3. *Effective methods for assuring proper nutrition:* Effectively monitoring all food and drink intake and lack of intake with the awareness of their implications for health and functioning.

Section B: Psychological

1. Effective behaviors and practices to sustain balance between work and play
2. Effective relaxation time and methods
3. Frequent contact with nature or other calming stimuli
4. Effective methods of creative expression
5. Effective skills for ongoing self-care
   a. Assertiveness
   b. Stress reduction

    c. Interpersonal communication
    d. Cognitive restructuring
    e. Time management
  6. Effective skill and competence in meditation or spiritual practice that is calming
  7. Effective methods of self-assessment and self-awareness

Section C: Social/Interpersonal

  1. *Social supports:* At least five people, including at least two at work, who will be highly supportive when called upon
  2. *Getting help:* Knowing when and how to secure help—both informal and professional—and the help will be delivered quickly and effectively
  3. *Social activism:* Being involved in addressing or preventing social injustice that results in a better world and a sense of satisfaction for trying to make it so

VII. Inventory of Self-Care Practice—Professional

  1. *Balance between work and home:* Devoting sufficient time and attention to both without compromising either.
  2. *Boundaries/limit setting:* Making a commitment and sticking to regarding
    a. Time boundaries/overworking
    b. Therapeutic/professional boundaries
    c. Personal boundaries
    d. Dealing with multiple roles (both social and professional)
    e. Realism in differentiating between things one can change and accepting the others
  3. Getting support/help at work through
    a. Peer support
    b. Supervision/consultation/therapy
    c. Role models/mentors
  4. *Generating work satisfaction:* By noticing and remembering the joys and achievements of the work

VIII. Prevention Plan development

  1. Review current self-care and prevention functioning
  2. Select one goal from each category
  3. Analyze the resources for and resistances to achieving goal
  4. Discuss goal and implementation plan with support person
  5. Activate plan
  6. Evaluate plan weekly, monthly, yearly with support person
  7. Notice and appreciate the changes

Source: Charles Figley, Tulane University Traumatology Institute, New Orleans, LA, http://www.green cross.org. Reprinted with permission.

References

About Our Kids Mental Health. (1999). Attention deficit disorder. Retrieved from http://www.aboutourkids.org.

Abt Associates. (1994). *Conditions of confinement: Juvenile detention and correction facilities.* Washington, DC: Office of Juvenile Justice and Delinquency Prevention.

Abu El-Haj, T. R. (2002). Contesting the politics of culture, rewriting the boundaries of inclusion: Working for social justice with Muslim and Arab communities. *Anthropology and Education Quarterly, 33,* 308–316.

Abu El-Haj, T. R. (2006). Race, politics and Arab American youth. *Educational Policy, 20*(1), 13–34.

Abudabbeh, N. (1996). Arab families. In M. McGoldrick, J. Giordano, & J. K. Pearce (Eds.), *Ethnicity and Family Therapy* (2nd ed.). New York: London, 333–346.

Achatz, M., & MacAllum, C. A. (1994). Young unwed fathers: Report from the field. Philadelphia: Public/Private Ventures.

Acredolo, C., Adams, A., & Schmid, J. (1984). On the understanding of the relationships between speed, duration, and distance. *Child Development, 55,* 2151–2159.

Adalbjarnardottir, S., & Rafnsson, F. D. (2002). Adolescent antisocial behavior and substance use longitudinal analyses. *Addictive Behaviors, 27,* 227–240.

Adelman, H. S., & Taylor, L. (1993). School-based mental health: Toward a comprehensive model. *Journal of Mental Health Administration, 20,* 32–45.

Adelman, H. S., & Taylor, L. (1997). Addressing barriers to learning: Beyond school-linked services and full service schools. *American Journal of Orthopsychiatry, 67,* 408–421.

Adelman, H. S., & Taylor, L. (1998). Reframing mental health in school and expanding school reform. *Educational Psychologist, 33,* 135–152.

Adelman, H. S., & Taylor, L. (1999). Mental health in schools and system restructuring. *Clinical Psychology Review, 19,* 137–163.

Adelman, H. S., & Taylor, L. (2000). Promoting mental health in schools in the midst of school reform. *Journal of School Health, 70,* 171–178.

Adelman, H. S., & Taylor, L. (2002). School counselors and school reform: New directions. *Professional School Counseling, 5,* 235–248.

Adelman, H. S., & Taylor, L. (2005). *The school leaders guide to student learning supports*: New directions for addressing barriers to learning. Thousand Oaks, CA: Corwin Press.

Adelson, J., & Doehrman, M. J. (1980). The psycho-dynamic approach to adolescence. In J. Adelson (Ed.), *Handbook of adolescent psychology* (pp. 99–116). New York: Wiley.

Adger, C. T. (2000*). School/community partnerships to support language minority student success.* Research Brief No. 5. Santa Cruz, CA: Center for Research on Education, Diversity and Excellence. Retrieved from http://www.cal.org/crede/pubs/ResBrief5.htm.

After-School Corporation. (2006). *Increasing family and parent engagement in after-school.* New York: Author.

Ahia, C. E., & Martin, D. (1993). *The danger-to-self-or-others exception to confidentiality.* Alexandria, VA: American Counseling Association.

Ahrens, R. (1988). Minimalism in school counseling. *School Counselor, 36*(2), 85–87.

Ainsworth, M. D. S. (1989). Attachments beyond infancy. *American Psychologist, 44,* 709–716.

Ainsworth, U. W. (2002). Why does it take a village? The mediation of neighborhood effects on educational achievement. *Social Forces, 81,* 117–152.

Ainsworth-Darnell, J. W., & Downey, D. B. (1998). Assessing the oppositional culture explanations for racial/ethnic differences in school performance. *American Sociological Review, 63,* 554–570.

Akiskal, H. S. (1983). Dysthymic disorder: Psychopathology of proposed chronic depressive subtypes. *American Journal of Psychiatry, 140,* 11–20.

Albee, G. W. (1982). Preventing psychopathology and promoting human potential. *American Psychologist, 37,* 1043–1050.

Albee, G. W. (1986). Advocates and adversaries of prevention. In M. Kessler & S. E. Goldston (Eds.), *A decade of progress in primary prevention* (pp. 309–332). Hanover, NH: University Press of New England.

Albee, G. W., & Ryan-Finn, K. D. (1993). An overview of primary prevention. *Journal of Counseling and Development, 7*(2), 115–123.

Alberti, R., & Emmons, M. (1974). *Your perfect right.* San Luis Obispo, CA: Impact.

Alexander, K. L., & Entwisle, D. R. (1988). Achievement in the first two years of school: Patterns and processes. *Monographs of the Society for Research in Child Development, 53*(2), serial no. 218, 1–4.

Alexander, K. L., Entwisle, D. R., & Olson, L. S. (2001). Schools, achievement, and inequality: A seasonal perspective. *Educational Evaluation and Policy Analysis, 23*(2), 171–191.

Allbritten, D., Mainzer, R., & Ziegler, D. (2004). Will students with disabilities be scapegoats for school failure? *Educational Horizons, 82*, 153–160.

Allen, J. P., Weissberg, R. P., & Hawkins, J. A. (1989). The relation between values and social competence in early adolescence. *Developmental Psychology, 25*, 458–464.

Allensworth, E., & Easton, J. (2005). *The Ontrack indicator as predictor of high school graduation.* Chicago: Consortium on Chicago School Research.

Allgood, J. G., Mathiesen, S., & Delva, J. (2005). Adolescent marijuana abusers and access to family-based services. *Journal of Child and Adolescent Substance Abuse, 15*(1), 51–62.

Allsopp, A., & Prosen, S. (1988). Teacher reactions to a child sexual abuse training program. *Elementary School Guidance and Counseling, 22*(4), 299–305.

Altarriba, J., & Bauer, L. M. (1998). Counseling the Hispanic client: Cuban Americans, Mexican Americans, and Puerto Ricans. *Journal of Counseling and Development, 76*, 389–396.

Alva, S. A., & de los Reyes, R. (1999). Psychosocial stress, internalized symptoms, and academic underachievement of Hispanic adolescents. *Journal of Adolescent Research, 14*, 343–358.

Amato, P. R. (2001). The concensus of divorce for adults and children. In R. M. Milardo (Ed.), *Understanding families in the new millennium: A decade in review* (pp. 488–506). Lawrence, KS: National Council on Family Relations.

Amato, P. R., & Cheadle, J. (2005). The long reach of divorce: Divorce and child well-being across three generations. *Journal of Marriage and Family, 67*(1), 191–206.

American Academy of Child and Adolescent Psychiatry. (1991). Practice parameters for the assessment and treatment of attention deficit/hyperactivity disorders. *Journal of the American Academy of Child and Adolescent Psychiatry, 30*, 1–3.

American Academy of Child and Adolescent Psychiatry. (1998). Practice parameters for the assessment and treatment of children and adolescents with posttraumatic disorder. *Journal of the American Academy of Child and Adolescent Psychiatry, 37*(10), 4–26.

American Academy of Pediatrics. (2000). Policy statement: Corporal punishment in schools (RE9754). *Pediatrics, 106*(2), 343.

American Academy of Pediatrics. (2001). Committee on Psychosocial Aspects of Child and Family Health and Committee on Adolescence. Sexuality education for children and adolescents. *Pediatrics, 108*, 498–502.

American Academy of Pediatrics. (2004). Policy statement: School-based mental health services. *Pediatrics, 113*(6), 1839–1849.

American-Arab Anti-Discrimination Committee. (2003). Report on hate crimes and discrimination against Arab Americans. Retrieved from http://www.adc.org/hate_crimes.html.

American Counseling Association. (1997). *Code of ethics and standards of practice.* Alexandria, VA: Author.

American Counseling Association. (2000). ACA briefing paper: Discrimination based on sexual orientation. Alexandria, VA: Author.

American Counseling Association. (2011). Retrieved from http://www.counseling.org/aboutus/tp/home/ct2.aspx 9/11/11.

American Medical Association. (2005). GLBT policy compendium. Retrieved from http://www.ama-assn.org/ama1/pub/upload/mm/42/glbt_policy0905.pdf.

American Psychiatric Association. (1994). *Diagnostic and statistical manual of mental disorders* (4th ed.). Washington, DC: Author.

American Psychiatric Association. (1999). 1998 position statement on psychiatric treatment and sexual orientation. *American Journal of Psychiatry, 156*, 1131. Retrieved from http://www.psych.org/psych_pract/copptherapyaddendum83100.cfm.

American Psychiatric Association. (2000a). *Diagnostic and statistical manual of mental disorders.* (4th ed., text revision). Washington, DC: Author.

American Psychiatric Association. (2000b). Therapies focused on attempts to change sexual orientation: Position statement on homosexuality. Arlington, VA: Author.

American Psychiatric Association. (2002). Position statement on adoption and coparenting of children by same-sex couples. Washington, DC: Author. Retrieved from http://www.psych.org/edu/other_res/lib_archives/archives/200214.pdf.

American Psychiatric Association. (2004). Position statement on same-sex civil unions (revised). Washington, DC: Author. Retrieved from http://www.psych.org/edu/other_res/lib_archives/archives/200502.pdf.

American Psychological Association. (1993). *Violence and youth: Psychology's response.* Vol. 1: *Summary report of the American Psychological Association Commission on Violence and Youth.* Washington, DC: Author.

American Psychological Association. (1997). Appropriate therapeutic responses to sexual orientation. Retrieved from http://www.apa.org/pi/lgbc/policy/appropriate.html.

American Psychological Association. (2001). Policy statement on evidence-based practice in psychology. Retrieved from http://www2.apa.org/practice/ebpstatement.pdf.

American Psychological Association. (2005a). Is youth violence just another fact of life? Retrieved from http://www.apa.org/ppo/issues/pbviolence.html.

American Psychological Association. (2005b). Policy statements on lesbian, gay, and bisexual concerns, 1975–2005. Retrieved from http://www.apa.org/pi/lgbc/policy/pshome.html.

American School Counselor Association. (1980). ASCA role statement: The practice of guidance and counseling by school counselors. *The School Counselor, 29*(6), 7–15.

American School Counselor Association. (1990). Role statement: The school counselor. Alexandria, VA: Author.

American School Counselor Association. (1997). The professional school counselor and comprehensive school counseling programs [position statement]. Retrieved from http://www.school counselor.org/content.cfm?L1=1000&L2-9.

American School Counselor Association. (1999a). The national standards for school counseling. Alexandria, VA: Author.

American School Counselor Association. (1999b). The professional school counselor and counselor supportive staff [position statement]. Alexandria, VA: Author.

American School Counselor Association. (1999c). The professional school counselor and cross/multicultural counseling [position statement]. Retrieved from http://www.schoolcounselor.org/content.cfm?L1=1000& L2=26.

American School Counselor Association. (1999d). The professional school counselor and the special needs student. Retrieved from http://www.schoolcounselor.org/content.cfm?L1=1000&L2=32.

American School Counselor Association. (1999e). The role of the professional school counselor [position statement]. Retrieved from http://www.schoolcounselor.org/content.cfm?L1=1000&L2=69.

American School Counselor Association. (2000a). ASCA position statement: Sexual orientation (revised). Alexandria, VA: Author.

American School Counselor Association. (2000b). The professional school counselor and attention deficit/hyperactivity disorder (ADHD). Retrieved from http://www.schoolcounselor.org/content.cfm?L1=1000&L2=4.

American School Counselor Association. (2003a). *The ASCA National Model: A framework for school counseling programs.* Alexandria, VA: Author.

American School Counselor Association. (2003b). Child abuse/neglect prevention: The professional school counselor and child abuse and neglect prevention. Retrieved from http://www.schoolcounselor.org/content.asp?contentid=194.

American School Counselor Association. (2003c). The professional school counselor and child abuse and neglect prevention. Retrieved from http://www.schoolcounselor.org/content.cfm?L1=1000&L2=B.

American School Counselor Association. (2004a). Ethical standards for school counselors. Retrieved from http://www.schoolcounselor.org/content.asp?contentid=173.

American School Counselor Association (2004b). The professional school counselor and the special needs student [position statement]. Retrieved from http://www.schoolcounselor.org/content.asp?contentid=218.

American School Counselor Association. (2004c). The role of the professional school counselor. Retrieved from http://www.schoolcounselor.org/content.asp?contentid=240.

American School Counselor Association. (2005a). *The ASCA National Model: A framework for school counseling programs* (2nd ed.). Alexandria, VA: Author.

American School Counselor Association. (2005b). Why middle school counselors. Retrieved from http://www.school counselor.org/content.asp?contentid=231.

American School Counselor Association. (2009). The role of the professional school counselor. Retrieved from http://www.schoolcounselor.org/content.asp?contentid=240.

American School Counselor Association. (2010). Ethical standards for school counselors. Retrieved from http://www.schoolcounselor.org/content.asp?contentid=173.

American School Counselor Association. (2011). Learn About Ramp. Retrieved from http://ascamodel.timberlake publishing.com/content.asp?pl=11&contentid=11.

American School Counselor Association. (2011). About ASCA. Retrieved from http://www.schoolcounselor.org/content.asp?pl=328&contentict.328.

Ames, C., & Archer, J. (1988). Achievement goals in the classroom: Students' learning strategies and motivational processes. *Journal of Educational Psychology, 80,* 260–267.

Ames, L., Ilg, F., & Baker, S. (1988). *Your ten- to fourteen-year-old.* New York: Delacorte Press.

Amos, J. (2008). *Dropouts, diplomas, and dollars: U.S. high schools and the nation's economy.* Washington, DC: Alliance for Excellent Education.

Anand, K. J. S. (2003). Early exposure to marijuana and the risk of later drug use. *Journal of the American Medical Association, 290*(3), 330.

Ancess, J., & Ort, S. W. (1999). *How the coalition campus schools have re-imagined high school: Seven years later.* New York: Teachers College, National Center for Restructuring Education, Schools and Teaching.

Anderson, J. C., & McGee, R. (1994). Comorbidity of depression in children and adolescents. In W. M. Reynolds & H. F. Johnson (Eds.), *Handbook of depression in children and adolescents* (pp. 581–601). New York: Plenum.

Anderson K. G., Frissell, K. C., & Brown, S. A. (2007). Relapse contexts for substance abusing adolescents with comorbid psychopathology. *Journal of Child & Adolescent Substance Abuse, 17*(1), 65–82.

Andrews, P. (2004). *Survivor: The long journey back from abuse.* Peterborough, UK: Inspire.

Anfara, V. A., Jr. (2006). *Research summary: Advisory programs.* Retrieved from http://www.nmsa.org/Research/ ResearchSummaries/AdvisoryPrograms/tabid/812/Default.aspx.

Angold, A., & Costello, E. J. (1993). Depressive comorbidity in children and adolescents: Empirical, theoretical, and methodological issues. *American Journal of Psychiatry, 150*, 1779–1791.

Annie E. Casey Foundation. (2003). *Walking the plain talk: A guide for trainers.* Baltimore: Author.

Antunez, B., DiCerbo, P. A., & Menken, K. (2000). *Framing effective practice: Topics and issues in educating English language learners, a technical assistance synthesis.* Washington, DC: George Washington University, National Clearinghouse for Bilingual Education, Center for the Study of Language and Education.

Arab American Institute Foundation. (2002a). *Healing the nation: The Arab American experience after September 11.* Washington, DC: Author.

Arab American Institute Foundation. (2002b). *Profiling and pride: Arab American attitudes and behavior since September 11.* Washington, DC: Author.

Arango, V., Huang, Y. Y., Underwood, M. D., & Mann, J. J. (2003). Genetics of the serotonergic system in suicidal behavior. *Psychiatric Research, 5*, 375–386.

Arbona, C. (2000).The development of academic achievement in school aged children: Precursors to career development. In S. D. Brown & R. W. Lent (Eds.), *Handbook of counseling psychology* (3rd ed., pp. 270–309). New York: John Wiley & Sons.

Archer, V. (2001). Adult daughters and mother loss: The impact of bereavement groups. *Dissertation Abstracts International Section A: Humanities and Social Sciences, 62*(2), A:770.

Arredondo, P., Toporek, R., Brown, S. P., Jones, J., Locke, D. C., Sanchez, J., & Stadler, H. (1996). Operationalization of the multicultural counseling competencies. *Journal of Multicultural Counseling and Development, 70*, 477–486.

Arthur, M. W., Hawkins, J. D., Pollard, J. A., Catalano, R. F., & Baglioni, A. J., Jr. (2002). Measuring risk and protective factors for substance use, delinquency, and other adolescent problem behaviors: The Communities That Care Youth Survey. *Evaluation Review, 26*(6), 575–601.

Asarnow, J. R., & Callan, J. W. (1985). Boys with social adjustment problems: Social cognitive processes. *Journal of Consulting and Clinical Psychology, 53*, 80–87.

Asher, S. R., Hymel, S., & Renshaw, P. D. (1984). Loneliness in children. *Child Development, 55*, 1456–1464.

Ashton, P. T., & Webb, R. B. (1986). *Making a difference: Teacher's sense of efficacy and student achievement.* New York: Longman.

Aspy, C. B., Oman, R. F., Vesely, S. K., McLeroy, K., Rodine, S., & Marshall, L. (2004). Adolescent violence: The protective effects of youth assets. *Journal of Counseling and Development, 82*, 269–277.

Associated Press. (2006, May 21). U.S. report: 2.2. million now in prison, jails. Retrieved from http://www.msnbc. msn.com/id/12901873/.

Association for Specialists in Group Work (1990). Professional Standards for the Training of Group Workers. Alexandria, VA.

Association for Treatment and Training in the Attachment of Children. (2006). *Standards of practice.* Retrieved from http://www.attach.org.

Atkins, M. S., Frazier, S. L., Adil, J. A., & Talbott, E. (2003) School-based mental health services in urban communities. In M. Weist, S. Evans, & N. Tashman (Eds.), *Handbook of school mental health: Advancing practice and research* (pp. 165–178). New York: Kluwer Academic.

Atkinson, D. R., & Juntunen, C. L. (1994). School counselors and school psychologists as school–home–community liaisons in ethnically diverse schools. In P. B. Pedersen & J. C. Carey (Eds.), *Multicultural counseling in the schools: A practical handbook* (pp. 103–119). Boston: Allyn & Bacon.

Atkinson, J. W., & Birch, D. (1978). *Introduction to motivation* (2nd ed.). New York: Van Nostrand.

Aubrey, R. F. (1983). A house divided: Guidance and counseling in 20th-century America. *Personnel and Guidance Journal, 61*(4), 6–10.

August, G. J., Winters, K. C., Realmuto, G. M., Fahnhorst, T., Botzet, A., & Lee, S. (2006). Prospective study of adolescent drug use among community samples of ADHD and non-ADHD participants. *Journal of the American Academy of Child and Adolescent Psychiatry, 45*(7), 824–832.

AVID Center. (2005). Retrieved from http://www.avidonline.org/info/?tabid=4&ID=513#AVID_High_School.

Ayalon, O. (1993). Posttraumatic stress recovery of terrorist survivors. In J. Wilson & B. Raphael (Eds.), *International handbook of traumatic stress syndromes* (pp. 855–866). New York: Plenum.

Babcock, R. J., & Kaufman, M. A. (1976). Effectiveness of a career course. *Vocational Guidance Quarterly, 24*, 241–266.

Bachman, J. G., Johnston, L. D., & O'Malley, P. M. (2001). *Monitoring the future: Questionnaire responses from the nation's high school seniors, 1996*. Ann Arbor, MI: Institute for Social Research.

Baer, J. S., Ginzler, J. A., & Peterson, P. L. (2003). *DSM-IV* alcohol and substance abuse and dependence in homeless youth. *Journal of Studies on Alcohol, 64*(1), 5–14.

Bailey, A., Le Couteur, A., Gottesman, I., Bolton, P., Simonoff, E., Yuzda, E., & Rutter, M. (1995). Autism as a strongly genetic disorder: Evidence from a British twin study. *Psychological Medicine, 25*, 63–77.

Bailey, J. M., & Guskey, T. R. (2002). *Implementing student-led conferences*. Thousand Oaks, CA: Corwin Press.

Bailey, K. A. (2001). Legal implications of profiling students for violence. *Psychology in the Schools, 38*, 141–155.

Baker, S. B. (2000). *School counseling for the twenty-first century* (3rd ed.). Upper Saddle River, NJ: Merrill.

Baker, S. B. (2001). Reflections on forty years in the school counseling profession: Is the glass half full or half empty? *Professional School Counseling, 5*(2), 75.

Baker, S. B., Swisher, J. D., Nadenichek, P. E., & Popowicz, C. L. (1984). Measured effects of primary prevention strategies. *Personnel and Guidance Journal, 62*, 459–464.

Balk, D. (1983a). Adolescents' grief reactions and self-concept perceptions following sibling death: A study of 33 teenagers. *Journal of Youth and Adolescence, 12*(2), 137–161.

Balk, D. (1983b). How teenagers cope with sibling death: Some implications for school counselors. *School Counselor, 31*(2), 150–158.

Ballon, B., & Chaim, G. (2006). HELP!!! An interactive experiential simulation of youth with concurrent disorders accessing help from "the system." *Addiction Research & Theory, 14*(6), 603–617.

Bamburg, J. D. (1994). *Raising expectations to improve student learning*. Monograph, North Central Regional Educational Laboratory. Seattle: University of Washington, Center for Effective Schools. Retrieved from http://www.ncrel.org/sdrs/areas/issues/educatrs/leadrshp/le0bam.htm.

Bandura, A. (1982). Self-efficacy mechanism in human agency. *American Psychologist, 37*, 122–147.

Bandura, A., & Schunck, D. H. (1981). Cultivating competence, self-efficacy, and intrinsic interest through proximal self-motivation. *Journal of Personality and Social Psychology, 41*, 586–598.

Bank Street College of Education. (2006). *Welcoming the stranger: Essays on teaching and learning in a diverse society*. New York: Author.

Banks, J. (1993). Multicultural education for young children: Racial and ethnic attitudes and their modifications. In B. Spodek (Ed.), *Handbook of research on the education of young children* (pp. 246–258). New York: Macmillan.

Banks, J. (2003). *Teaching strategies for ethnic studies* (7th ed.). Needham Heights, MA: Allyn & Bacon.

Banks, J. A. (2004a). *Handbook of research on multicultural education*. San Francisco: Jossey-Bass.

Banks, J. A. (2004b). Multicultural education: Historical development, dimensions, and practice. In J. A. Banks & C. A. M. Banks (Eds.), *Handbook of multicultural education*, San Francisco: John Wiley & Sons.

Banks, J. A. (2005). *Multicultural education: Issues and perspectives*. Hoboken, NJ: John Wiley & Sons.

Banks, J. A., Cookson, P., Gay, G., Hawley, W. D., Irvine, J. J., Nieto, S., Schofield, J. W., & Stephan, W. G. (2001). Diversity within unity: Essential principles for teaching and learning in a multicultural society. Seattle: University of Washington, Center for Multicultural Education. Retrieved from http://education.washington.edu/cme/DiversityUnity.pdf.

Barkley, R. A. (1997). *Defiant children: A clinician's manual for assessment and parent training*. New York: Guilford Press.

Barkley, R. A., Fischer, M., Smalish, L., & Fletcher, K. (2004). Young adult follow-up of hyperactive children's antisocial activities and drug use. *Journal of Child Psychology and Psychiatry, 45*(2), 195–211.

Barkley, R. A., Fischer, M., Smalish, L., & Fletcher, K. (2006). Young adult outcome of hyperactive children: Adaptive functioning in major life activities. *Journal of the American Academy of Child and Adolescent Psychiatry, 45*(2), 192–202.

Barkley, R. A., & Murphy, K. R. (2006). *Attention deficit hyperactivity disorder: A clinical workbook*. New York: Guilford Press.

Barrera, I. (2003). *Skilled dialogue: Strategies for responding to cultural diversity in early childhood*. Baltimore: P. H. Brookes.

Barret, B., & Logan, C. (2001). *Counseling gay men and lesbians: A practice primer*. Belmont, CA: Brooks/Cole.

Barrow, J., & Hayashi, J. (1990). Shyness clinic: A social development program for adolescents. *Personnel and Guidance Journal, 59*, 58–61.

Bart, M. (1998, September). Creating a safer school for gay students. *Counseling Today*, 36–39.

Barth, P. (2003). A common core curriculum for the new century. *Thinking K–16, 7*(1), 3–31.

Baruth, L. G., & Burggrat, M. Z. (1983). Helping single-parent families. Counseling and Human Development, 1–15.

Battjes, R. J., Gordon, M. S., O'Grady, K. E., & Kinlock, T. W. (2004). Predicting retention of adolescents in substance abuse treatment. *Addictive Behaviors, 29*, 1021–1027.

Battjes, R. J., Gordon, M. S., O'Grady, K. E., Kinlock, T. W., Katz, E. C., & Sears, E. A. (2004). Evaluation of a group-based substance abuse treatment program for adolescents. *Journal of Substance Abuse Treatment, 27*(2), 123–134.

Battle, J., Cohen, C., Warren, D., Fergerson, G., & Audam, S. (2000). Say it loud, I'm Black and I'm proud: Black pride survey. National Gay and Lesbian Task Force.

Baum, K. (2005, August). *Juvenile victimization and offending, 1993–2003.* Washington, DC: U.S. Department of Justice, Bureau of Justice Statistics.

Baum, S., & Ma, J. (2007). *Education pays: The benefits of higher education for individuals and society.* Princeton, NJ: College Board.

Bauman, S., & Del Rio, A. (2006). Pre-service teachers' responses to bullying scenarios: Comparing physical, verbal, and relational bullying. *Journal of Educational Psychology, 98*, 219–231.

Baumberger, J. P., & Harper, R. E. (1999). *Assisting students with disabilities: What school counselors can and must do.* Thousand Oaks, CA: Corwin Press.

Baumrind, D. (1982). Are androgynous individuals more effective persons and parents? *Child Development, 53*, 44–75.

Beautrais, A. L., Joyce, P. R., & Mulder, R. T. (1999). Personality traits and cognitive styles as risk factors for serious suicide attempts among young people. *Suicide and Life-Threatening Behavior, 29*, 37–47.

Beauvais, F., Chavez, E., Oetting, E., Deffenbacher, J., & Cornell, G. (1996). Drug use, violence, and victimization among white American, Mexican American, and American Indian dropouts, students with academic problems, and students in good academic standing. *Journal of Counseling Psychology, 43*, 292–299.

Beck, A., Rush, A., Shaw, B., & Emery, G. (1979). *Cognitive therapy of depression.* New York: Guilford.

Becker, A. E., Grinspoon, S. K., Klibanski, A., & Herzog, D. B. (1999). Eating disorders. *New England Journal of Medicine, 340*, 1092–1098.

Beers, C. W. (1908). *A mind that found itself.* Garden City, NY: Doubleday, Doran.

Bemak, R. (1998). Interdisciplinary collaboration for social change: Redefining the counseling profession. In C. C. Lee & G. R. Walz (eds.), *Social action: A mandate for counselors,* Alexandria, VA. American Counseling Association & ERIC/CASS, 279–292.

Beesley, D. (2004). Teachers' perceptions of school counselor effectiveness: Collaborating for student success. *Education, 125*, 259–270.

Bemak, F. (2000). Transforming the role of the counselor to provide leadership in educational reform through collaboration. *Professional School Counseling, 3*, 323–331.

Benard, B. (1990). *The case for peers: The corner on research.* Portland, OR: Far West Laboratory for Educational Research and Development.

Benard, B. (1996a). Creating resiliency-enhancing schools: Relationships, motivating beliefs, and schoolwide reform. *Resiliency in Action, 4*(13), 9–14.

Benard, B. (1996b). *From research to practice: The foundations of the resiliency paradigm: Resiliency in action.* Rio Rancho, NM.

Benard, B. (1996c). *Musing II: Rethinking how we do prevention.* Western Center News. Milwaukee, WI.

Benard, B., & Marshall, K. (1997). *A framework for practice: Tapping innate resilience: Research and practice.* Minneapolis: University of Minnesota, Center for Applied Research and Educational Improvement.

Bennett, A., Bridglall, B. L., Cauce, A. M., Everson, H. T., Gordon, E. W., & Lee, C. D. (2004). *All students reaching the top: Strategies for closing academic achievement gaps.* Report of the National Study Group for the Affirmative Development of Academic Ability. Naperville, IL: Learning Point Associates.

Bennett, E. C. (1975). *Operation C.O.D.: A program designed to improve pupil self-esteem thereby reducing future school dropouts.* Chicago: Nova University.

Benson, P. L., Scales, P. C., Hamilton, S. F., & Sesma, A. (2006). Positive youth development so far: Core hypotheses and their implications for policy and practice. *Insights & Evidence, 3*(1), 1–13.

Benvenuti, A. C. (1986, November). *Assessing and addressing the special challenge of gay and lesbian students for high school counseling programs.* Paper presented at the annual meeting of the California Educational Research Association, San Jose, CA. ERIC Document Reproduction Service No. ED279958.

Berg, I. K., & Miller, S. D. (1992). *Working with the problem drinker: A solution focused approach.* New York: Norton.

Berg, R. C., Landreth, G. L., & Fall, K. (2006). Group counseling: Concepts and procedures (4th ed.). New York: Routledge/Taylor & Francis.

Bergin, J. J. (1991). *Escape from Pirate Island*. Doyleston, PA: MarCo.

Bergin, J. J. (1993). Group counseling with children and adolescents. *Counseling and Human Development, 25*(9), 1–20.

Berkner, L., & Choy, S. (2008). *Descriptive summary of 2003–04 beginning postsecondary students: Three years later.* NCES 2008-174. Washington, DC: National Center for Education Statistics, Institute of Education Sciences, U.S. Department of Education.

Berkowitz, A., & Persins, H. W. (1988). Personality characteristics of children of alcoholics. *Journal of Consulting and Clinical Psychology, 56*(2), 16–21.

Bern, S. L. (1981). Gender schema theory: A cognitive account of sex-typing. *Psychological Bulletin, 88*, 354–364.

Bern, S. L. (1989). Genital knowledge and gender constancy in preschool children. *Child Development, 60*, 649–662.

Berndt, T. J. (1981). Relations between social cognition, nonsocial cognition, and social behavior: The case of friendship. In J. H. Flavell & L. D. Ross (Eds.), *Social cognitive development* (pp. 249–256). Cambridge: Cambridge University Press.

Berndt, T. J. (1982). The features and effects of friendship in early adolescence. *Child Development, 53*, 1447–1460.

Bernstein, R., & Silberman, S. C. (Eds.). (1996). *Generation Q.* Los Angeles: Alyson.

Berry, J. O. (1987). A program for training teachers as counselors of parents of children with disabilities. *Journal of Counseling and Development, 65*(9), 508–509.

Berry, M., Cash, S. J., & Mathiesen, S. G. (2003). Validation of the strengths and stressors tracking device with a child welfare population. *Child Welfare, 82*, 293–319.

Berry, M., Charlson, R., & Dawson, K. (2003). Promising practices in understanding and treating child neglect. *Child and Family Social Work, 8*, 13–24.

Bertoldi, A. R. (1975). *Remediation for auxiliary services students evaluation period, school year 1974–75*. Brooklyn: New York City Board of Education, Office of Educational Evaluation.

BEST Foundation for a Drug Free Tomorrow. (2005). *Project ALERT*. Retrieved from http://www.projectalert.best.org/Default.asp?bhcp=1.

Biederman, J. (2005). Attention deficit/hyperactivity disorder: A selective overview. *Biological Psychiatry, 57*(11), 1215–1220.

Billstedt, F., Gillberg, C., & Gillberg, C. (2005). Autism after adolescence: Population-based 13- to 22-year follow-up study of 120 individuals with autism diagnosed in childhood. *Journal of Developmental Disorders, 35*, 351–360.

Bingham, C. W. (2001). *Schools of recognition: Identity politics and classroom procedures*. Lanham, MD: Rowman & Littlefield.

Birk, J. M., & Blimline, C. A. (1984). Parents as career development facilitators: An untapped resource for the counselor. *School Counselor, 31*(4), 310–317.

Birke, S., & Mayer, K. (2004). *Together we heal* (2nd ed.). West Conshohocken, PA: Infinity.

Birmaher, B., Arbelaez, C., & Brent, D. (2002). Course and outcome of child and adolescent major depressive disorder. *Child and Adolescent Psychiatric Clinics of North America, 11*, 619–638.

Birmaher, B., Axelson, D., Strober, M., Gill, M. K., Valeri, S. Chiappetta, L., & Keller, M. (2006). Clinical course of children and adolescents with bipolar spectrum disorders. *Archives of General Psychiatry, 63*, 175–183.

Birmaher, B., Ryan, N. D., Williamson, D. E., Brent, D. A., & Kaufman, J. (1996). Childhood and adolescent depression: A review of the past 10 years: Part 2. *Journal of the American Academy of Child and Adolescent Psychiatry, 35*, 1575–1583.

Bishop, J. H., Bishop, M., Bishop, M., Gelbwasser, L., Green, S., & Peterson, E. (2004). Why we harass nerds and freaks: A formal theory of student culture and norms. *Journal of School Health, 74*, 235–251.

Bjoerkqvist, K., Lagerspetz, K. M., & Kankianen, A. (1992). Do girls manipulate and boys fight? Developmental trends in regard to direct and indirect aggression. *Aggressive Behavior, 18*, 117–127.

Blank, R. (2001). An overview of trends in social and economic well-being, by race. In N. J. Smelser, W. J. Wilson, & F. Mitchell (Eds.), *America becoming: Racial trends and their consequences* (Vol. 1). Washington, DC: National Academies Press. Retrieved from http://www.nap.edu/catalog/9599.html.

Bloom, B. L. (1992). Planned short-term psychotherapy: Current status and future challenges. *Applied and Preventive Psychology, 1*, 157–164.

Bloom, B. L. (1997). *Planned short-term psychotherapy: A clinical handbook* (2nd ed.). Boston: Allyn & Bacon.

Bloom, M., Fischer, J., & Orme, J. G. (2005). *Evaluating practice: Guidelines for the Blueprints for Violence Prevention*. Denver: C&M Press.

Blum, D. J., & Jones, L. A. (1993). Academic growth group and mentoring program for potential dropouts. *School Counselor, 40*(3), 25–29.

Blyth, D. A., Bulcroft, R., & Simmons, R. G. (1981). *The impact of puberty on adolescents: A longitudinal study*. Paper presented at the annual convention of the American Psychological Association, Los Angeles, August 1981.

Bolognini, M., Plancherel, B., Laget, J., & Halfon, O. (2003). Adolescent's suicide attempts: Populations at risk, vulnerability and substance use. *Substance Use and Misuse, 38*(11–13), 1651–1669.

Bond, Richard. (2007). The lingering debate over the Parental Alienation Syndrome phenomenon. *Journal of Child Custody, 4*(1/2), 37–54.

Bonner, B., Walker, C. E., & Berliner, L. (1999a). *Treatment manual for cognitive behavioral group therapy for children with sexual behavior problems.* Washington, DC: National Clearinghouse on Child Abuse and Neglect.

Bonner, B., Walker, C. E., & Berliner, L. (1999b). *Treatment manual for cognitive behavioral group treatment for parents/caregivers of children with sexual behavior problems.* Washington, DC: National Clearinghouse on Child Abuse and Neglect.

Bonner, B., Walker, C. E., & Berliner, L. (1999c). *Treatment manual for dynamic group play therapy for children with sexual behavior problems and their parents/caregivers.* Washington, DC: National Clearinghouse on Child Abuse and Neglect.

Bonner, B., Walker, C. E., & Berliner, L. (2000). *Children with sexual behavior problems: Assessment and treatment: Final report.* Grant No. 90-CA-1469. Washington, DC: National Clearinghouse on Child Abuse and Neglect.

Bontempo, D. E., & D'Augelli, A. R. (2002). Effects of at-school victimization and sexual orientation on lesbian, gay, or bisexual youths' health risk behavior. *Journal of Adolescent Health, 30*, 364–374.

Borders, L. D., & Drury, S. M. (1992a). Comprehensive school counseling programs: A review for policymakers and practitioners. *Journal of Counseling and Development, 70*, 487–501.

Borders, L. D., & Drury, S. M. (1992b). *Counseling programs: A guide to evaluation.* Newbury Park, CA: Corwin Press.

Borg, M. G. (1998). The emotional reactions of school bullies and their victims. *Educational Psychology, 18*, 433–444.

Borman, G., Stringfield, S., & Rachuba, L. (2000). *Advancing minority high achievement: National trends and promising programs and practices.* New York: College Board.

Borowsky, I., Ireland, M., & Resnick, M. (2001). Adolescent suicide attempts: Risks and protectors. *Pediatrics, 107*, 485–93.

Borowsky, I. W., Resnick, M. D., Ireland, M., & Blum, R. W. (1999). Suicide attempts among American Indian and Alaska Native youth: Risk and protective factors. *Archives of Pediatrics and Adolescent Medicine, 153*(6), 573–580.

Borr, J. (1988, October 21). Use of hyperactivity drug rises in Baltimore County schools. *Baltimore Sun,* 1.

Boswell, J. (1980). *Christianity, social tolerance, and homosexuality.* Chicago: University of Chicago Press.

Bottoms, G., & Mikos, P. (1995). *Seven most improved high schools that work: Sites raise achievement in reading, mathematics, and science: School and classroom practices that advance the performance of career-bound high school students: A report on improving student learning.* Atlanta: Southern Regional Education Board.

Botvin, G. J., Baker, E., Dusenbury, L., Botvin, E. M., & Diaz, T. (1995). Long-term follow-up results of randomized drug abuse prevention trial in a white middle-class population. *Journal of the American Medical Association, 273*, 1106–1112.

Botvin, G. J., Griffin, K. W., Diaz, T., Scheier, L. M., Williams, C., & Epstein, J. A. (2000). Preventing illicit drug use in adolescents: Long-term follow-up data from a randomized control trial of a school population. *Addictive Behaviors, 5*, 769–774.

Botvin, G. J., & Tortu, S. (1988). Preventing adolescent substance abuse through life skills training. In R. H. Price, E. L. Cowen, R. P. Lorion, & J. Ramos-McKay (Eds.), *14 ounces of prevention: A casebook for practitioners* (pp. 34–46). Washington, DC: American Psychological Association.

Bowen, M. (1978). *Family practice in clinical practice.* New York: Jason Aronson.

Bowers, J. L., & Hatch, P. A. (2002). The national model for school counseling programs. Alexandria, VA: American School Counselor Association.

Bowlby, J. (1969). *Attachment and loss.* Vol. 1: *Attachment.* London: Hogarth Press.

Boyer, E. L. (1983). *High school: A report on secondary education in America.* New York: Carnegie Foundation for the Advancement of Teaching and Harper Colophon Books.

Brack, G., Jones, E. S., Smith, R. M., White, J., & Brack, C. J. (1993). A primer on consultation theory: Building a flexible worldview. *Journal of Counseling and Development, 71*, 619–628.

Bradley, R. H., Whiteside, L., Mundfrom, D., Casey, P., Kelleher, K., & Pope, S. (1994). Early indications of resilience and their relations to experiences in the home environments of low birthweight premature children living in poverty. *Child Development, 65*(2), 346–360.

Bragg, D. D., Puckett, P. A., Reger, W., IV, Thomas, H. S., Ortman, J., & Dornsife, C. (1997). *Tech prep/school-to-work partnerships: More trends and challenges.* Berkeley: University of California, Berkeley, Graduate School of Education, National Center for Research in Vocational Education. Retrieved from http://vocserve.berkeley.edu/Summaries/1078s um.html.

Brake, K. J., & Gerler, E. R. (1994). Discovery: A program for fourth and fifth graders identified as discipline problems. *Elementary School Guidance and Counseling, 28*, 170–181.

Brandeis University. (2000). Center for Human Resources. *Expanding college access, strengthening schools: Evaluation of the GE Fund College Bound Program*. Waltham, MA: Prepared for the GE Fund. Retrieved from www.ge.com/foundation/GEFund_CollegeBound.pdf.

Bransford, J. D., Brown, A. L., & Cocking, R. R. (Eds.). (2000). *How People Learn: Brain, Mind, Experience, and School* (expanded ed.). Washington, DC: National Academies Press.

Braucht, S., & Weime, B. (1992). The school counselor as consultant on self-esteem: An example. *Elementary School Guidance and Counseling, 26*(3), 229–236.

Brendtro, L. K., Brokenleg, M., & Van Bockern, S. (1990). *Reclaiming youth at risk: Our hope for the future*. Bloomington, IN: National Education Service.

Brent, D., Johnson, B., & Perper, J. (1994). Personality Disorder, personality traits, impulsive violence and completed suicide in adolescents. *Journal of the American Academy of Child and Adolescent Psychiatry, 33*, 1080–1086.

Brestan, E. V., & Eyberg, S. M. (1998). Effective psychosocial treatments of conduct-disordered children and adolescents: 29 years, 82 studies, and 5,272 kids. *Journal of Clinical Child Psychology, 27*, 180–189.

Brewer, J. (1932). *Education as guidance*. New York: Macmillan.

Briere, J., & Spinazzola, J. (2005). Phenomenology and psychological assessment of complex postraumatic stress. *Journal of Traumatic Stress, 18*(5), 401–412.

Brigman, G., & Campbell, C. (2003). Helping students improve academic achievement and school success behavior. *Professional School Counseling, 7*, 91–98.

Brigman, G., Campbell, C., & Webb, L. (2004). *Student Success Skills: Helping students develop the academic, social and self-management skills they need to succeed*. Group counseling manual. Boca Raton, FL: Atlantic Education Consultants.

Brigman, G., & Goodman, B. E. (2003). Academic and social support: Student success skills. In G. Brigman & B. E. Goodman (Eds.), *Group counseling for school counselors: A practical guide* (pp. 106–131). Portland, ME: J. Weston Walch.

Brigman, G., & Goodman, B. E. (2008). *Group counseling for school counselors: A practical guide* (3rd ed.). Portland, ME: J. Weston Walch.

Brigman, G., & Webb, L. (2004). *Student Success Skills: Helping students develop the academic, social and self-management skills they need to succeed*. Classroom guidance manual. Boca Raton, FL: Atlantic Education Consultants.

Brigman, G., Webb, L., & Campbell, C. (2007). Building skills for school success: Improving the academic and social competence of students. *Professional School Counseling, 10*, 279–288.

Bronfenbrenner, E. (1979). *The ecology of human development*. Cambridge, MA: Harvard University Press.

Brooks-Gunn, J., & Furstenberg, F. F., Jr. (1989). Adolescent sexual behavior. *American Psychologist, 44*, 249–257.

Brott, P. E. (2001). The storied approach: A postmodern approach to career counseling. *Career Development Quarterly, 49*, 304–313.

Brott, P. E. (2005). Making it count: Accountability for school counselors. In T. Davis, *Exploring school counseling: Professional practices and perspectives* (pp. 279–297). Boston: Lahaska Press.

Brott, P. E. (2006). Counselor eduction accountability: Training the effective professional school counselor. *Professional School Counseling, 10*, 179–188.

Brott, P. E. (2008). Get a GRIP! In *Virginia professional school counseling program manual* (pp. 86–93). Yorktown, VA: Virginia School Counselor Association.

Brown, B. (1999). *Organization and management of a guidance and counseling program*. Retrieved from http://www.cceanet.org/Research/Brown/Brown.htm.

Brown, C., & Brown, J. (1982). *Counseling children for social competence: A manual for teachers and counselors*. Springfield, IL: Charles C. Thomas.

Brown, D., & Trusty, J. (2005). School counselors, comprehensive school counseling programs, and academic achievement: Are school counselors promising more than they can deliver? *Professional School Counseling, 9*, 1–8.

Brown, I., Jr., & Inouye, D. K. (1978). Learned helplessness through modeling: The role of perceived similarity in competence. *Journal of Personality and Social Psychology, 36*, 900–908.

Brown, K. M., Anfara, V. A., Jr., & Roney, K. (2004). Student achievement in high performing, suburban middle schools and low performing, urban middle schools: Plausible explanations for the differences. *Education and Urban Society, 36*(4), 428–456.

Brown, L. (2003). *Girlfighting: Betrayal and rejection among girls*. New York: New York University Press.

Brown, S. (1991). *Counseling victims of violence*. Alexandria, VA: American Counseling Association.

Bruce, M. A. (1995). Brief counseling: An effective model for change. *School Counselor, 42*, 353–363.

Brunner, J., & Lewis, D. (2007). Ten strategies to address bullying. *Principal Leadership, 7*(9), 73–75.

Brustad, R. J. (1988). Affective outcomes in competitive youth sport: The influence of intrapersonal and socialization factors. *Journal of Sport and Exercise Psychology, 10*, 307–321.

Bry, B. H. (1982). Reducing the incidence of adolescent problems through preventive interventions: One- and five-year follow-up. *American Journal of Community Psychology, 10*, 265–276.

Bryan, J. A. (2005). Fostering educational resilience and achievement in urban schools through school–family–community partnerships: School counselors' roles. *Professional School Counseling, 8*, 219–227.

Bryan, J. A., & Holcomb-McCoy, C. H. (2004). School counselors' perceptions of their involvement in school–family–community partnerships. *Professional School Counseling, 7*, 162–171.

Bryan, J. A., & Holcomb-McCoy, C. H. (2006). School counselors' training and involvement in school–family–community partnership roles: An exploratory study. *Journal of School Counseling, 4*(13), 45–52.

Bryan, J. A., & Holcomb-McCoy, C. H. (2007). An examination of school counselor involvement in school–family–community partnerships. *Professional School Counseling, 7*, 91–98.

Bryson, S. E., & Smith, I. M. (1998). Epidemiology of autism: Prevalence, associated characteristics, and service delivery. *Mental Retardation and Developmental Disabilities Research Reviews, 4*, 97–103.

Bumpass, L., & Lu, H. (2000). Trends in cohabitation and implications for children's family context in the United States. *Population Studies, 54*, 29–41.

Bundy, M. L., & Poppen, W. A. (1986). School counselors' effectiveness as consultants: A research review. *Elementary School Guidance and Counseling, 21*, 215–222.

Bureau of Indian Affairs. (2008). Department of Interior Open Government Plan. Retrieved from http://www.doi.gov/bia/index.html.

Bureau of Justice Assistance. (1997). *Urban street gang enforcement.* Washington, DC: Author.

Bureau of Legislative Research, Arkansas Legislative Council. (2006). *Best practices in child maltreatment prevention and intervention.* Little Rock, AR: Author.

Burnham, J., Dahir, C., Stone, C., & Hooper, L. (2009). An examination of the psychometric properties of the assessment of school counselor needs for professional development. *Research in the Schools, 15*, 51–63.

Burnham, J. J., & Jackson, C. M. (2000). School counselor roles: Discrepancies between actual practice and existing models. *Professional School Counseling, 4*(1), 41–49.

Burns, P. (1981). *Feeling good: A new mood therapy.* New York: Signet Books.

Bushaw, W. J., & McNee, J. A. (2009). The 41st Annual Phi Delta Kappa/Gallup Poll of the public's attitudes toward the public schools: Americans speak out: Are educators and policy makers listening? *Phi Delta Kappan, 91*(1), 8–23.

Butler, R. (1989). Mastery versus ability appraisal: A developmental study of children's observations of peers' work. *Child Development, 60*, 1350–1361.

Butler, R. (1990). The effects of mastery and competitive conditions on self-assessment at different ages. *Child Development, 61*, 201–210.

Butler, S. K. (2003). Helping urban African American high school students excel academically: The roles of school counselors. *High School Journal, 87*, 51–57.

Butterfield, E. C., Nelson, T. O., & Peck, V. (1988). Developmental aspects of the feeling of knowing. *Developmental Psychology, 24*, 654–663.

Cabrera, A. F., & La Nasa, S. M. (2000a). *On the path to college: Three critical tasks facing America's disadvantaged.* University Park: Pennsylvania State University, Center for the Study of Higher Education.

Cabrera, A. F., & La Nasa, S. M. (2000b). Understanding the college choice process. In A. F. Cabrera & S. M. La Nasa (Eds.), *Understanding the college choice of disadvantaged students* (pp. 5–22). New Directions for Institutional Research, No. 107. San Francisco: Jossey-Bass.

Cabrera, A. F., La Nasa, S. M., & Burkum, K. R. (2001). *Pathways to a four-year degree: The higher education story of one generation.* University Park: Pennsylvania State University, Center for the Study of Higher Education.

CACREP (Council for Accreditation of Counseling and Related Educational Programs). (2009). *2009 Standards.* Retrieved from http://www.cacrep.org/doc/2009%20Standards%20with%20cover.pdf.

Caldera, Y. M., Huston, A. C., & O'Brien, M. (1989). Social interactions and play patterns of parents and toddlers with feminine, masculine, and neutral toys. *Child Development, 60*, 70–76.

Calhoun, G., Jr., & Morse, W. C. (1977). Self-concept and self-esteem: Another perspective. *Psychology in the Schools, 14*, 318–322.

Calhoun, K. S., & Resick, P. A. (1993). Treatment of PTSD in rape victims. In D. H. Barlow (Ed.), *Clinical handbook of psychological disorders* (pp. 48–98). New York: Guilford Press.

Camara, W. (2003). *College persistence, graduation and remediation.* College Board Research Notes RN-19. New York: College Board.

Camarota, S. A. (2007). Immigrants in the United States, 2007: A profile of America's foreign-born population. Washington, D.C.: Center for Immigration Studies.

Cambron-McCabe, N. H., McCarthy, M. M., & Thomas, S. B. (2004). *Public school law: Teacher's and student's rights* (5th ed.). Boston: Pearson Education.

Camp, W. G. (1990). Participation in student activities and achievement: A covariance structural analysis. *Journal of Educational Research, 83*(5), 272–278.

Campbell, C. A. (1992). The school counselor as consultant: Assessing your aptitude. *Elementary School Guidance and Counseling, 26*(3), 237–250.

Campbell, C. A., & Brigman, G. (2005). Closing the achievement gap: A structured approach to group counseling. *Journal for Specialists in Group Work, 30*, 67–82.

Campbell, C. A., & Dahir, C. A. (1997). *Sharing the vision: The national standards for school counseling programs.* Alexandria, VA: American School Counselor Association.

Campbell, C. A., & Myrick, R. (1990). Motivational group counseling for low-performing students. *Journal of Specialist in Group Work, 15*(10), 43–50.

Campbell, D. P. (1965). *The result of counseling: Twenty-five years later.* Philadelphia: Saunders.

Campbell, P. R. (1994). *Population projections for states, by age, race, sex, 1993–2000: Current population reports.* Washington, DC: U.S. Census Bureau.

Campos, J. J., Bertenthal, B., & Kermoian, R. (1992). Early experience and emotional development: The emergence of wariness of heights. *Psychological Science, 3*, 61–64.

Cams, A. W., & Cams, M. R. (1991). Teaching study skills, cognitive strategies, and metacognitive skills through self-diagnosed learning styles. *School Counselor, 38*, 341–346.

Canfield, J., & Wells, H. C. (1976). *100 ways to enhance self-concept in the classroom.* Englewood Cliffs, NJ: Pergamon Press.

Cantor, W., & Winkinson, J. (1982). *Social skills manual.* Somerset, NJ: Wiley.

Caplan, M., Weissberg, R. P., Grober, J. S., Sivo, P. J., & Jacoby, C. (1992). Social competence promotion with inner-city and suburban young adolescents: Effects on social adjustment and alcohol use. *Journal of Consulting and Clinical Psychology, 60*, 56–63.

Capuzzi, D. (2002). Legal and ethical challenges in counseling suicidal students. *Professional School Counseling, 6*, 36–45.

Capuzzi, D., & Golden, L. (1988). *Preventing adolescent suicide.* Muncie, IN: Accelerated Development.

Capuzzi, D., & Gross, D. (2000). "I don't want to live": The adolescent at risk for suicidal behavior. In D. Capuzzi & D. Gross (Eds.), *Youth at risk: A prevention resource for counselors, teachers and parents* (3rd ed., pp. 319–352). Alexandria, VA: American Counseling Association.

Card, J. J., & Benner, T. (2008). *Model programs for adolescent sexual health: Evidence-based HIV, STI, and pregnancy prevention interventions.* New York: Springer.

Carey, J. C. (2004). *Does implementing a research-based school counseling curriculum enhance student achievement?* School Counseling Research Brief 2.3. Amherst, MA: Center for School Counseling Outcome Research.

Carey, J. C. (2006). *Evaluation is not a four letter word: How to know whether or not what you are doing is working.* Paper presented at the Colorado School Counselors Association, Denver: CO

Carey, J. C., & Dimmitt, C. (Eds.). (2004, June). *Evidence-based school counseling interventions: Rules of evidence, outcomes and outcome measures.* Symposium papers presented at the annual meeting of the American School Counselor Association, Reno, NV.

Carey, J. C., & Dimmitt, C. (2006). Resources for school counselors and counselor educators: The Center for School Counseling Outcome Research. *Professional School Counseling, 9*, 416–420.

Carkhuff, R. R., & Berenson, B. G. (1976). *Teaching as treatment.* Amherst, MA: Human Resource Development Press.

Carlson, C. (1996). Changing the school culture toward integrated services. In R. Illback & C. Nelson (Eds.), *Emerging school-based approaches for children with emotional and behavioral problems* (pp. 225–249). New York: Haworth Press.

Carmona, M., & Stewart, K. (1996). *A review of alternative activities and alternatives programs in youth-oriented prevention.* National Center for the Advancement of Prevention, for the Substance Abuse and Mental Health Services Administration (SAMHSA), Center for Substance Abuse Prevention.

Carnevale, A. P., & Desrochers, D. M. (2003). *Standards for what? The economic roots of K-12 reform.* Princeton, N.J.: Educational Testing Service.

Carns, A. W., & Carns, M. R. (1991). Teaching study skills, cognitive strategies, and metacognitive skills through self-diagnosed learning styles. *School Counselor, 38*, 341–346.

Carr, M., Kurtz, B. E., Schneider, W., Turner, L. A., & Borkowski, J. G. (1989). Strategy acquisition and transfer among American and German children: Environmental influences on metacognitive development. *Developmental Psychology, 25*, 765–771.

Carroll, J. L., & Rest, J. R. (1982). Moral development. In B. B. Wolman (Ed.), *Handbook of developmental psychology* (pp. 434–451). Englewood Cliffs, NJ: Prentice-Hall.

Casas, M., & Furlong, M. J. (1994). School counselors as advocates for increased Hispanic parent participation in schools. In P. B. Pedersen & J. C. Carey (Eds.), *Multicultural counseling in schools: A practical handbook* (pp. 121–155). Boston: Allyn & Bacon.

Casas, J. M., Furlong, M. J., & Ruiz de Esparza, C. (2003). Increasing Hispanic parent participation in schools: The role of the counselor. In P. B. Pedersen & J. C. Carey (Eds.), *Multicultural counseling in schools: A practical handbook* (pp. 105–130). Boston: Allyn & Bacon.

Casas, J. M., & Vasquez, M. J. T. (1996). Counseling the Hispanic: A guiding framework for a diverse population. In P. B. Pedersen, J. G. Draguns, & W. J. Lonner (Eds.), *Counseling across cultures* (4th ed., pp. 146–176). Thousand Oaks, CA: Sage.

Castelló, A., & Doménech, R. (2002). Human capital inequality and economic growth: Some new evidence. *Economic Journal, 112*(478), 187–200.

Catalano, R. F., Haggerty, K. P., Oesterle, S., Fleming, C. B., & Hawkins, J. D. (2004). The importance of bonding to school for health development: Findings from the Social Development Research Group. *Journal of School Health, 74*, 252–261.

Cataldi, E. F., Laird, J., & KewalRamani, A. (2009). *High school dropout and completion rates in the United States, 2007.* NCES 2009-064. Washington, DC: National Center for Education Statistics, Institute of Education Sciences, U.S. Department of Education. Retrieved from http://nces.ed.gov/pubsearch/pubsinfo.asp?pubid=2009064.

Catsambis, S., & Beveridge, A. A. (2001). Does neighborhood matter? Family, neighborhood, and school influences on eighth-grade mathematics achievement. *Social Focus, 34*, 435–457.

Cavanaugh, D. A., & Doucette, A. (2004). Using administrative data to access the process of treatment services for adolescents with substance use disorders. *Journal of Psychoactive Drugs, 36*(4), 473–482.

Cecil, J. H., & Cobia, D. C. (1990). Educational challenge and change. In H. Hackney (Ed.), *Changing contexts for counselor preparation in the 1990s* (pp. 21–36). Alexandria, VA: Association for Counselor Education and Supervision.

Cedar, B., & Levant, R. F. (1990). A meta-analysis of the effects of parent effectiveness training. *Journal of Consulting and Clinical Psychology, 60*, 56–63.

Center for Community Solutions. (2008). *School-based mental health tool kit for Cuyahoga County school districts.* Cleveland, OH: Author.

Center for Mental Health in the Schools. (1999). *School–community partnerships: A guide.* Los Angeles: Author.

Center for Mental Health in the Schools. (2006). *The current status of mental health in schools: A policy and practical analysis.* Los Angeles: Author. Retrieved from http://smhp.psych.ucla.edu/currentstatusmh.htm.

Center on Addiction and Substance Abuse. (1999). *No safe haven: Children of substance abusing parents.* New York: Columbia University.

Centers for Disease Control and Prevention. (1999). Suicide deaths and rates per 100,000, United States, 1999. *Morbidity and Mortality Weekly Report, 47*(SS-3).

Centers for Disease Control and Prevention. (2003). Injury mortality among American Indian and Alaska Native children and youth, United States, 1989–1998. *Morbidity and Mortality Weekly Report, 52*, 697–701.

Centers for Disease Control and Prevention. (2007, September 8). Teen suicide rate: Highest increase in 15 years. *Science Daily.*

Chadwick Center for Children and Families (2004). *Closing the quality chasm in child abuse treatment: Identifying and disseminating best practices: The findings of the Kauffman Best Practices Project to help children heal from child abuse.* San Diego: Kauffman Foundation.

Chaffin, M., & Friedrich, B. (2004). Evidence-based treatments in child abuse and neglect. *Children and Youth Services Review, 26*(11), 1097–1113.

Chalmers, J. B., & Townsend, M. A. R. (1990). The effects of training in social perspective taking on socially maladjusted girls. *Child Development, 61*, 178–190.

Chamberlain, P., Reid, J. B., Ray, J., Capaldi, D. M., & Fisher, P. (1997). Parent inadequate discipline (PID). In T. A. Widiger, A. J. Francis, H. A. Pincus, R. Ross, M. B. First, & W. Davis (Eds.), *DSM-IV sourcebook* (Vol. 3, pp. 569–629). Washington, DC: American Psychiatric Association.

Chambers, J. C., Shkolnik, J., & Perez, M. (2003). *Total expenditures for students with disabilities, 1999–2000: Spending variations by disability.* Washington, DC: American Institutes for Research.

Chan, C. (1989). Issues of identity development among Asian-American lesbians and gay men. *Journal of Counseling and Development, 68*, 16–20.

Chandler, J. W. (2006). School counseling in Alabama: Comparisons of counseling and non-counseling duties. (Unpublished doctoral dissertation). University of Alabama, Tuscaloosa.

Chang, D. F. (2002). Understanding the rates and distribution of mental disorders. In K. S. Kurasaki, S. Okazaki, & S. Sue (Eds.), *Asian mental health: Assessment theories and methods* (pp. 9–27). New York: Kluwer Academic/Plenum Press.

Chapa, J., & De la Rosa, B. (2004). Latino population growth, socioeconomic and demographic characteristics, and implications for educational attainment. *Educational and Urban Society, 36*(2), 130–149.

Chapman, D., O'Brien, C. H., & DeMasi, M. F. (1987). The effectiveness of the public school counselor in college advising. *Journal of College Admissions, 1159*, 11–18.

Chapman, M. (1988). *Constructive evolution: Origin and development of Piaget's thought.* New York: Cambridge University Press.

Chase, A. (2002). Violent reactions: What do teen killers have in common? *In These Times, 25*(16).

Cheng, S., & Starks, B. (2002). Racial differences in the effects of significant others on students' educational expectations. *Sociology of Education, 75*, 306–327.

Chen-Hayes, S. F. (2007). The ACCESS questionnaire: Assessing school counseling programs and interventions to ensure equity and success for every student. *Counseling and Human Development, 6*, 1–11.

Chilcoat, G. W. (1988). Developing student achievement with verbal feedback. *NASSP Bulletin, 72*(507), 6–10.

Child Trends. (2002). Charting parenthood: A statistical portrait of fathers and mothers in America. Washington, DC: Author. Retrieved from http://www.childtrends.org/files/ParenthoodRPT2002.pdf.

Child Trends. (2003). Retrieved from http://www.childtrendsdatabank.org/indicators/34SuicidalTeens.cfm.

Child Trends. (2009). *Child trends databank: Racial and ethnic composition of the child population.* Retrieved from http://www.childtrendsdatabank.org/indicators/60RaceandEthnicComposition.cfm.

Child Trends & National Campaign to Prevent Teen Pregnancy. (2004). *Science says: Early childhood programs.* Washington, DC: National Campaign to Prevent Teen Pregnancy.

Children's Defense Fund. (2010). *The State of America's Children.* Washington, DC: Author.

Choi, H. (2002). Understanding adolescent depression in ethnocultural context. *Advancing in Nursing Science, 25*, 71–85.

Chomsky, N. (1986). Middle East terrorism and the American ideological system. *Race and Class, 18*, 2–28.

Christenson, S. L., Sinclair, M. F., Lehr, C. A., & Godber, Y. (2001). Promoting successful school completion: Critical conceptual and methodological guidelines. *School Psychology Quarterly, 16*(4), 468–484.

Christoffel, K. K., Scheidt, P. C., Agran, P. F., Kraus, J. F., McLoughlin, E., & Paulson, J. A. (1992). Standard definitions for childhood injury research: Excerpts of a conference report. *Pediatrics, 89*, 1027–1034.

Christy, E. B., Stewart, F. J., & Rosecrance, F. C. (1930). Guidance in the senior high school. *Vocational Guidance, 9*, 51–57.

Chung, Y. B., & Katayama, M. (1998). Ethnic and sexual identity development of Asian-American lesbian and gay adolescents. *Professional School Counseling, 1*(3), 21–25.

Ciarrochi, J., Wilson, C. J., Deane, F. P., & Rickwood, D. (2003). Do difficulties with emotions inhibit help-seeking in adolescence? The role of age and emotional competence in predicting help-seeking intentions. *Counselling Psychology Quarterly, 16*(2), 103–120.

Cicchetti, D. (1989). How research on child maltreatment has informed the study of child development: Perspectives from developmental psychopathology. In D. Cicchetti & V. Carlson (Eds.), *Child maltreatment: Theory and research on the causes and consequences of child abuse and neglect* (pp. 377–431). New York: Cambridge University Press.

Cicero, G., & Barton, P. (2003). Parental involvement, outreach, and the emerging role of the professional school counselor. In B. T. Erford (Ed.), *Transforming the school counseling profession* (pp. 191–207). Upper Saddle River, NJ: Merrill Prentice Hall.

Ciechalski, J. C., & Schmidt, M. W. (1995). The effects of social skills training on students with exceptionalities. *Elementary School Guidance and Counseling, 29*, 217–222.

Clark, D. B., & Miller, T. W. (1998). Stress adaptation in children: Theoretical models. In T. W. Miller (Ed.), *Stressful life events: Children and trauma* (pp. 3–27). Madison, CT: International Universities Press.

Clark, G. N., Hops, H., Lewinsohn, P. M., Andrews, J., Seeley, J. R., & Williams, J. (1992). Cognitive-behavioral group treatment of adolescent depression: Prediction of outcome. *Behavior Therapy, 13*, 341–354.

Clark, M. A., & Stone, C. (2000).The developmental school counselor as educational leader. In J. Wittmer (Ed.), *Managing your school counseling programs: K–12 developmental strategies* (2nd ed., pp. 85–81). Minneapolis, MN: Educational Media.

Clark, M. L., & Ayers, M. (1988). The role of reciprocity and proximity in junior high school friendships. *Journal of Youth and Adolescence, 17*, 403–411.

Clark, R. W. (2001). *Dual credit: A report of programs and policies that offer high school students college credits.* Washington, DC: Pew Charitable Trust.

Clausen, J. A. (1975). The social meaning of differential physical and sexual maturation. In S. E. Dragastin & G. H. Elder (Eds.), *Adolescence in the life cycle: Psychological change and social context.* Washington, DC: Hemisphere.

Clayton, C. J., Ballif-Spanvill, B., & Hunsaker, M. D. (2001). Preventing violence and teaching peace: A review of promising and effective antiviolence, conflict-resolution, and peace programs for elementary school children. *Applied and Preventive Psychology, 10*, 1–35.

Clemente, R., & Collison, B. B. (2000). The relationship among counselors, ESL teachers, and students. *Professional School Counseling, 3*, 339–349.

Cleveland, M. J., Gibbons, F. X., Gerrard, M., Pomery, E. A., & Brody, G. H. (2005). The impact of parenting on risk cognitions and risk behavior: A study of mediation and moderation in a panel of African American adolescents. *Child Development, 76*(4), 800–916.

Cloitre, M., Stovall-McClough, K. C., Miranda, R., & Chemtob, C. M. (2004). Therapeutic alliance, negative mood regulation, and treatment outcome in child abuse related post-traumatic stress disorder. *Journal of Consulting and Clinical Psychology, 72*(3), 411–416.

Coalition of Essential Schools. (2001). *Principles at work.* Oakland, CA: CES National.

Coeyman, M. (2003, April 22). Twenty years after "A nation at risk." *Christian Science Monitor.*

Cohen, J. A., & Mannarino, A. P. (1993). A treatment model for preschoolers. *Journal of Interpersonal Violence, 8*, 115–131.

Cohen, J. A., Mannarino, A. P., Murray, L. K., & Igelman, R. (2006). Psychosocial interventions for maltreatment and violence-exposed children. *Journal of Social Issues, 62*, 737–766.

Cole, C. V. (1995). Sexual abuse of middle school students. *The School Counselor, 42*(3), 239–245.

Coleman, E., & Remafedi, G. (1989). Gay, lesbian, and bisexual adolescents: A critical challenge to counselors. *Journal of Counseling and Development, 68*, 36–40.

Coleman, H. L. K. (1995). Cultural factors and the counseling process: Implications for school counselors. *School Counselor, 42*, 180–185.

College Board. (2000). *Equity 2000: A systemic education reform model: Summary report, 1990–2000.* Retrieved from http://www.collegeboard.com/prod_downloads/about/association/equity/EquityHistorical Report.pdf.

College Board. (2001). *Advanced Placement course descriptions.* Retrieved from http://cbweb2s.collegeboard.org/ap/pdf/history_00-01.pdf.

Comer, J. P. (2001). Schools that develop children. *American Prospect, 12*(7), 36–47.

Comer, J. P. (2005). The rewards of parent participation. *Educational Leadership, 62*(6), 38–42.

Commission on Adolescent Eating Disorders. (2005). Defining eating disorders. In D. L. Evans, E. B. Foa, R. E. Gur, H. Hendin, C. P. O'Brien, M. E. P. Seligman, & Walsh, B. T. (Eds), *Treating and preventing adolescent mental health disorders: What we know and what we don't know* (pp. 257–332). New York: Oxford University Press.

Committee for Children. (1987). *Committee for Children: Second step violence prevention curriculum.* Seattle: Author.

Conderman, G., Ikan, P. A., & Hatcher, R. E. (2000). Student led conferences in inclusive settings. *Intervention in School and Clinical Settings, 36*(1), 22–26.

Conference Board, Partnership for 21st Century Skills, Corporate Voices for Working Families, & Society for Human Resource Management. (2006). *Are they really ready to work? Employers' perspectives on the basic knowledge and applied skills of new entrants to the 21st-century U.S. workforce.* Retrieved from http://www.21stcenturyskills.org/index.php?option=com_content&task=view&id=250&Itemid=64.

Conner, J. D. (1983). Admissions policies and practices: Selected findings of the AACRAD CEEB Survey. *NASSP Bulletin, 67*(460), 8–12.

Conoley, J. C., & Conoley, C. W. (1982). *School consultation: A guide to practice and training.* New York: Pergamon Press.

Conway, A. (2005) Girls, aggression, and emotion regulation. *American Journal of Orthopsychiatry, 75*(2), 334–339.

Conyne, R. K. (1994). Preventive counseling. *Counseling & Human Development, 27*(1), 345–346.

Cook, D. W. (1989). Systematic need assessment: A primer. *Journal of Counseling and Development, 67*, 462–464.

Cook, J. B., & Kaffenberger, C. J. (2003). Solution Shop: A solution-focused counseling and study skills program for middle school. *Professional School Counseling, 7*, 116–123.

Cooley, J. J. (1998). Gay and lesbian adolescents: Presenting problems and the counselor's role. *Professional School Counseling, 1*(3), 30–34.

Cooley, L. (2009). *The power of groups: Solution-focused group counseling in schools.* Thousand Oaks, CA: Corwin Press.

Corey, G., Corey, M., & Callanan, P. (1998). *Issues and ethics in the helping professions* (5th ed.). Pacific Grove, CA: Brooks/Cole.

The Corsini Encyclopedia of Psychology, 4th ed., 2010, 4 vols. New York: Wiley.

Costa, A. (Ed.). (1991). *Developing minds: A resource book for teaching thinking.* Alexandria, VA: Association of Supervision and Curriculum.

Costello, C., & Henry, J. (Ed.) (2003*). Across America: Preventing teen pregnancy in California, Georgia, and Michigan.* Washington, DC: National Campaign to Prevent Teen Pregnancy.

Costello, E. J. (1990). Child psychiatric epidemiology: Implications for clinical research and practice. In B. B. Lahey & A. E. Kazdin (Eds.), *Advances in clinical child psychology* (Vol. 13, pp. 53–90). New York: Plenum.

Cottle, W. C. (1957). The evaluation of guidance services. *Review of Educational Research, 37*, 229–235.

Cottone, R. R., & Tarvydas, V. M. (Eds.). (1998). *Ethical and professional issues in counseling*. Upper Saddle River, NJ: Prentice-Hall.

Council on Islamic Education (2002). *Teaching about Islam and Muslims in the public school classroom* (3rd ed.). Fountain Valley, CA: Author.

Cowen, E. L., Hightower, A. D., Pedro-Carroll, J. L., Work, W. C., Wyman, P. A., & Haffey, W. G. (1996). *School-based prevention for children at risk: The primary mental health project*. Washington, DC: American Psychological Association.

Cox, J. E. (1994). Self-care in the classroom for children with chronic illness: A case study of a student with cystic fibrosis. *Elementary School Guidance and Counseling, 29*, 121–128.

Crick, N. R. (1996). The role of overt aggression, relational aggression, and prosocial behavior in the prediction of children's future social adjustment. *Child Development, 67*, 2317–2327.

Crick, N. R., & Bigbee, M. A. (1998). Relational and overt forms of peer victimization: A multi-informant approach. *Journal of Consulting and Clinical Psychology, 66*, 337–347.

Crick, N. R., Casas, J. F., & Nelson, D. A. (2002). Toward a more comprehensive understanding of peer maltreatment: Studies of relational victimization. *Current Directions in Psychological Science, 11*, 98–101.

Crick, N. R., & Grotpeter, J. K. (1995). Relational aggression, gender, and social-psychological adjustment. *Child Development, 66*, 710–722.

Crick, N. R., & Grotpeter, J. K. (1996). Children's treatment by peers: Victims of relational and overt aggression. *Development and Psychopathology, 8*, 367–380.

Crick, N. R., & Nelson, D. A. (2002). Relational and physical victimization within friendships: Nobody told me there'd be friends like these. *Journal of Abnormal Child Psychology, 30*, 599–607.

Croninger, R., & Lee, V. E. (2001). Social capital and dropping out of high school: Benefits to at-risk students of teachers' support and guidance. *Teachers College Record, 103*(4), 548–581.

Crooks, T. J. (1988). The impact of classroom evaluation practices on students. *Review of Educational Research, 58*, 438–481.

Cross, D. R., & Paris, S. G. (1988). Developmental and instructional analyses of children's metacognition and reading comprehension. *Journal of Educational Psychology, 80*, 131–142.

Cross, T. L., Bazron, B. J., Dennis, K. W., & Isaacs, M. R. (1989). *Toward a culturally competent system of care*. Vol. 1: *A monograph on effective services for minority children who are severely emotionally disturbed*. Washington, DC: Georgetown University, Child Development Center, Child and Adolescent Service System Program, Technical Assistance Center.

Crosson-Tower, C. (2002). *When children are abused: An educator's guide to intervention*. Boston: Allyn & Bacon.

Crouse, T., & Trusheim, D. (1988). *The case against the SAT*. Chicago: Chicago University Press.

Cruz, G. P., & Brittingham, A. (2003). *The Arab population, 2000*. Census 2000 Brief C2KBR-23. Washington, DC: U.S. Census Bureau, U.S. Department of Commerce.

Cuban, L. (1990). Reforming again, again, and again. *Educational Researcher, 19*(1).

Curtner-Smith, M. E., Middlemiss, W., Green, K., Murray, A. D., Barone, M., Stolzer, J., Parker, L., & Nicholson, B. (2006). An elaboration on the distinction between controversial parenting and therapeutic practices versus developmentally appropriate attachment parenting: A comment on the APSAC Task Force Report. *Child Maltreatment, 11*, 373–374.

DaCosta, M., & Halmi, K. A. (1992). Classification of anorexia nervosa: Question of subtypes. *International Journal of Eating Disorders, 11*(4), 305–313.

Dahir, C. (1997). National standards for school counseling programs: A pathway to excellence. *ASCA Counselor, 35*(2), 11.

Dahir, C. (2001). The national standards for school counseling programs: Development and implementation. *Professional School Counseling, 4*, 320–327.

Dahir, C. (2004). Supporting a nation of learners: The role of school counseling in education reform. *Journal of Counseling and Development, 82*, 344–353.

Dahir, C., Burnham, J. L., & Stone, C. (2009). Listen to the voices: School counselors and comprehensive school counseling programs. *Professional School Counseling, 12*(3), 182–192.

Dahir, C., Sheldon, C., & Valiga, M. (1998). *Vision into action: Implementing the national standards for school counseling programs*. Alexandria, VA: American School Counselor Association.

Dahir, C., & Stone, C. (2003a). Accountability: A M.E.A.S.U.R.E. of the impact school counselors have on student achievement. *Professional School Counseling, 6*, 214–221.

Dahir, C., & Stone, C. (2003b). Assessment of School Counselor Needs for Professional Development Survey (ASCNPD). Unpublished survey.

Dahir, C., & Stone, C. (2007). School counseling at the crossroads of change. ACA Professional Counseling Digests (ACAPCD-05). Alexandria, VA: American Counseling Association.

Dahlkemper, L. (2002). School board leadership: Using data for school improvement. *National School Board Association Research Policy Brief, 2*(1).

Daly, E. J., III, Duhon, G. J., & Witt, J. C. (2002). Proactive approaches for identifying and treating children at risk for academic failure. In K. L. Lane, F. M. Gresham, & T. E. O'Shaughnessy (Eds.), *Interventions for children with or at risk for emotional and behavioral disorders* (pp. 18–32). Boston: Allyn & Bacon.

Damon, W. (1980). Patterns of change in children's social reasoning: A two-year longitudinal study. *Child Development, 51*, 1010–1017.

Dana, R. H. (1998). *Understanding cultural identity in intervention and assessment.* Thousand Oaks, CA: Sage.

Dana, R. H. (2000). The cultural self as a locus for assessment and intervention with American Indian/Alaska Natives. *Journal of Multicultural Counseling and Development, 28*, 66–82.

D'Andrea, M., & Daniels, J. (1995). Helping students learn to get along: Assessing the effectiveness of a multicultural development guidance project. *Elementary School Guidance and Counseling, 30*, 143–154.

Daniels, M. H., Karmos, J. S., & Presely, C. A. (1983). *Parents and peers: Their importance in the career decision-making process.* Carbondale: Southern Illinois University.

Danielsson, S., Gillberg, I. C., Billstedt, E., Gillberg, C., & Olsson, I. (2005). Epilepsy in young adults with autism: A perspective population-based follow-up study of 120 individuals diagnosed in childhood. *Epilepsia, 46*, 918–923.

Darling-Hammond, L. (1996). The right to learn and the advancement of teaching: Research, policy and practice for democratic education. *Educational Researcher, 25*, 5–17.

Darling-Hammond, L. (1997). *Right to learn: A blueprint for creating schools that work.* San Francisco: Jossey-Bass.

Darling-Hammond, L. (1999). *Teacher quality and student achievement: A review of state policy evidence.* Seattle: University of Washington, Center for the Study of Teaching and Policy.

Darling-Hammond, L., Ancess, J., & Wichterle-Ort, S. (2002). Reinventing high school: Outcomes of the Coalition Campus Schools Project. *American Educational Research Journal, 39*(3), 639–673.

Daroff, L. H., Masks, S. J., & Friedman, A. S. (1986). Adolescent drug abuse: The parent's predicament. *Counseling and Human Development, 24*(13), 36–42.

D'Augelli, A. R., Hershberger, S. L., & Pilkington, N. W. (2001). Suicidality patterns and sexual orientation-related factors among lesbian, gay, and bisexual youths. *Suicide and Life-Threatening Behavior, 31*(3), 250–264.

D'Augelli, A. R., Pilkington, N. W., & Hershberger, S. L. (2002). Incidence and mental health impact of sexual orientation victimization of lesbian, gay, and bisexual youths in high school. *School Psychology Quarterly, 17*, 148–167.

David-Ferdon, C., & Kaslow, N. J. (2008). Evidence-based psychosocial treatments for child and adolescent depression. *Journal of Clinical Child and Adolescent Psychology, 37*, 62–104.

Davila, R. R., Williams, M. L., & MacDonalt, J. T. (1991, September 16). Clarification of policy to address the needs of children with attention deficit disorders within general and/or special education. Washington, DC: U.S. Department of Education, Office of Special Education and Rehabilitation Services.

Davis, C. G., & S. Nolen-Hoeksema (2001). Loss and meaning: How do people make sense of loss? *American Behavioral Scientist, 44*, 726–741.

Davis, J. L., & Mickelson, D. J. (1994). School counselors: Are you aware of ethical and legal aspects of counseling. *School Counselor, 42*, 5–13.

Davis, L. (2002) *"I thought we'd never speak again": The road from estrangement to reconciliation.* New York: HarperCollins.

Davis, T. E., & Osborn, C. J. (2000). *The solution-focused school counselor: Shaping professional practice.* Philadelphia: Accelerated Development.

Day-Sclater, S. (2007). Understanding the divorce cycle: The children of divorce in their own marriages. *Journal of Social Policy, 36*(3), 511–512.

de Shazer, S. (1985). *Keys to solution in brief therapy.* New York: Norton.

de Shazer, S. (1991). *Putting difference to work.* New York: Norton.

de Shazer, S. (1994). *Words were originally magic.* New York: Norton.

de Shazer, S., & Berg, I. K. (1997). What works? Remarks on research aspects of solution-focused brief therapy. *Journal of Family Therapy, 19*, 121–124.

de Shazer, S., Berg, I. K., Lipchik, E., Nunnally, E., Molnar, A., Gingerich, W., & Weiner-Davis, M. (1986). Brief therapy: Focused solution development. *Family Process, 25*, 207–221.

Deblinger, E., & Heflin, A. H. (1996). *Treatment for sexually abused children and their non-offending parents: A cognitive-behavioral approach.* Thousand Oaks, CA: Sage.

Debold, E. (1995). Helping girls survive the middle grades. *Principal, 74*(3), 22–24.

DeCastro-Ambrosetti, D., & Cho, G. (2005). Do parents value education? Teachers' perceptions of minority parents. *Multicultural Education, 13*(2), 44–46.

DeLeon, P. H. (1998). Proceedings of the American Psychological Association, Inc., for the legislative year 1997: Minutes of the annual meeting of the Council of Representatives, August 14 and 17, Chicago, Illinois; and June, August, and December 1997 meetings of the Board of Directors. *American Psychologist, 53,* 882–939. Retrieved from http://www.apa.org/pi/lgbc/policy/appropriate.html.

Delicath, T. (1999, October). The Influence of dual credit programs on college students' integration and goal attainment. *Journal of College Student Retention,* 377–398.

Delpit, L. (1995). *Other people's children: Cultural conflict in the classroom.* New York: New Press.

Demetriou, A., & Efklides, A. (1985). Structure and sequence of formal and postformal thought: General patterns and individual differences. *Child Development, 56,* 1062–1091.

Dennis, M., Babor, T. F., Roebuck, M. C., & Donaldson, J. (2002). Changing the focus: The case for recognizing and treating cannabis use disorders. *Addictions, 97*(1), 4–15.

Derman-Sparks, L. (2006). *What if all the kids are white? Anti-bias multicultural education with young children and families.* New York: Teachers College Press.

DeRosier, M. E. (2002). *Group interventions and exercises for enhancing children's communication, cooperation, and confidence.* Sarasota, NY: Professional Resource Press.

DeRosier, M. E. (2004). Building relationships and combating bullying: Effectiveness of a school-based social skills group intervention. *Journal of Clinical Child and Adolescent Psychology, 33*(1), 196–201.

DeRosier, M. E. (2007). *Social Skills Group Intervention (S.S.GRIN): Group interventions and exercises for enhancing children's communication, cooperation, and confidence* (4th ed.). Cary, NC: 3-C Institute for Social Development.

Detroit Free Press (2001). 100 questions and answers about Arabic Americans in America: A journalist's guide. Detroit: Author.

Deuschle, C. (2004). Talking with kids about alcohol and other drugs. *Student Assistance Journal, 16*(2), 24–27.

Devlin, M. J. (1996). Assessment and treatment of binge eating disorder. *Psychiatric Clinics of Norih America, 19,* 761–772.

DeVoe, J. F., Peter, K., Kaufman, P., Miller, A., Noonan, M., Snyder, T. D., & Baum, K. (2004). Indicators of school crime and safety, 2004. NCES 2005-002/NCJ205290. Washington, DC: U.S. Department of Education and U.S. Department of Justice.

DeVoe, J. F., Peter, K., Noonan, M., Snyder, T. D., & Baum, K. (2005). Indicators of school crime and safety, 2005. NCES 2006-001/NCJ 210697. Washington, DC: U.S. Department of Education and U.S. Department of Justice.

DeWolfe, D. J. (2000). *Training manual for mental health and human service workers in major disasters* (2nd ed.). DHHS Publication No. ADM 90-538. Rockville, MD: Substance Abuse and Mental Health Services Administration.

Deyhle, D., & Swisher, K. (1999). Research in American and Indian and Alaska Native education: From assimilation to self-determination. *Review of Research in Education, 22,* 113–194.

Diller, J. V. (2007). Cultural diversity: A primer for the human services. Belmont, CA: Thomson Higher Education.

Dimmitt, C., Carey, J. C., & Hatch, T. (2007). Evidence-based school counseling: Making a difference with data-driven practices. Thousand Oaks, CA: Corwin Press.

Dinkes, R., Cataldi, E. F., & Lin-Kelly, W. (2007). *Indicators of school crime and safety, 2007.* NCES 2008-021/NCJ 219553. Washington, DC: National Center for Education Statistics, Institute of Education Sciences, U.S. Department of Education; and Bureau of Justice Statistics, Office of Justice Programs, U.S. Department of Justice.

Dinkmeyer, D., & Caldwell, E. (1970). *Developmental counseling and guidance: A comprehensive school approach.* New York: McGraw-Hill.

Diver-Stamnes, A. C. (1991). Assessing the effectiveness of an inner-city high school peer counseling program. *Urban Education, 26,* 269–284.

Doan, J., Roggenbaum, S., & Lazear, K. (2003). *Youth suicide prevention school-based guide—Issue brief 3b: Risk Factors: How can a school identify a student at risk?* FMHI Series Publication #218-3b. Tampa, FL: Department of Child and Family Studies, Division of State and Local Support, Louis de la Parte Florida Mental Health Institute, University of South Florida.

Dodge, K. A. (1983). Behavior antecedents of peer social status. *Child Development, 54,* 1386–1399.

Dodge, K. A., Murphy, R. R., & Buchsbaum, K. (1984). The assessment of intention-cue detection skills in children: Implications for developmental psychopathology. *Child Development, 55,* 163–173.

Dodge, K. A., & Pettit, G. S. (2003). A biopsychosocial model of the development of chronic conduct problems in adolescence. *Developmental Psychology, 39,* 349–371.

Dodge, K. A., Pettit, G. S., McClaskey, C. L., & Brown, M. M. (1986). *Social competence in children.* Monographs of the Society for Research in Child Development, 51 (2, serial no. 213).

Doka, K. J., & Tucci, A. S. (Eds.). (2008). *Living with grief: Children and adolescents*. Washington, DC: Hospice Foundation of America.

Dollarhide, C. T., & Lemberger, M. E. (2006). No Child Left Behind: Implication for school counselors. *Professional School Counseling, 9*, 295–304.

Dollarhide, C. T., & Saginak, K. A. (2008). *Comprehensive school counseling programs: K–12 delivery systems in action*. Boston: Allyn & Bacon.

Donald, K., Carlisle, J. S., & Woods, E. (1979). *Before assertiveness: A group approach for building self-confidence*. Santa Barbara: University of California.

Downey, D. B., & Ainsworth-Darnell, J. W. 2002. The search for oppositional culture among black students. *American Sociological Review, 67*, 156–164.

Downey, G., & Walker, E. (1989). Social cognition and adjustment in children at risk for psychopathology. *Developmental Psychology, 25*, 835–845.

Downs, W. R. (1993). Developmental considerations for the effects of childhood sexual abuse. *Journal of Interpersonal Violence, 8*(3), 331–345.

Dryfoos, J. G. (1990). *Adolescents at risk: Prevalence and prevention*. New York: Oxford University Press.

Dryfoos, J. G. (1994). *Full-service schools: A revolution in health and social services for children, youth, and families*. San Francisco: Jossey-Bass.

Dryfoos, J. G., & Maguire, S. (2002). *Inside full-service community schools*. Thousand Oaks, CA: Corwin Press.

Dube, E. M., & Savin-Williams, R. C. (1999). Sexual identity development among ethnic sexual-minority male youths. *Developmental Psychology, 35*, 1389–1398.

Dudley-Grant, G. B. (2001). Eastern Caribbean family psychology with conduct-disordered adolescents from the Virgin Islands. *American Psychologist, 56*, 47–57.

Dukes, R. L., & Stein, J. A. (2001). Effects of assets and deficits on the social control of at-risk behavior among youth: A structural equation approach. *Youth Society, 32*, 337–359.

Dumais, S. A. (2002). Cultural capital, gender, and school success: The role of habitus. *Sociology of Education, 75*, 44–68.

Dumont, M., & Provost, M. C. (1999). Resilience in adolescents: Protective role of social support, coping strategies, self-esteem, and social activities on experience of stress and depression. *Journal of Youth and Adolescence, 28*, 343–363.

Duncan, G., Brooks-Gunn, J., & Klebanov, P. (1994). Economic deprivation and early childhood development. *Child Development, 65*(2), 296–318.

Dunham, C., & Frome, P. (2003). Guidance and advisement: Influence on students' motivation and course-taking choices. Atlanta, GA: Research Triangle Foundation and Southern Regional Education Board.

Dunn, C. W., & Veltman, G. C. (1989). Addressing the restrictive career maturity patterns of minority youth: A program evaluation. *Journal of Multicultural Counseling and Development, 17*, 156–164.

Dunn, J. A. (1972). *The guidance program in the plan system of individualized education*. Palo Alto, CA: American Institutes of Research.

Dunst, C., & Trivette, C. M. (1994). Aims and principles of family support programs. In C. Dunst, C. M. Trivette, & A. G. Deal (Eds.), *Supporting and strengthening families,* Vol. 1: *Methods, strategies and practices* (pp. 30–48). Cambridge, MA: Brookline Books.

Dunst, C. J., & Trivette, C. M. (2005). *Measuring and evaluating family support program quality*. Asheville, NC: Winterberry Press.

Durodoye, B. A. (1998). Fostering multicultural awareness among teachers: A tripartite model. *Professional School Counseling, 1*(5), 9–13.

Dustin, D., & Ehly, S. (1992). School consultation in the 1990s. Special issue: Consultation. *Elementary School Guidance and Counseling, 26*(3), 165–175.

Dweck, C. S., & Elliot, E. S. (1983). Achievement motivation. In P. H. Mussen (Ed.), *Handbook of child psychology* (4th ed., Vol. 4). New York: Wiley.

Dworkin, A. G., & Dworkin, R. J. (1999). *The minority report: An introduction to racial, ethnic, and gender relations* (3rd ed.). Fort Worth, TX: Harcourt Brace.

Dyer, W. W., & Vriend, J. (1977). *Counseling techniques that work*. New York: Funk & Wagnalls.

East, P. L., Hess, L. E., & Lerner, R. M. (1987). Peer social support and adjustment of early adolescent peer groups. *Journal of Early Adolescence, 7*, 153–163.

Eaton, D. K., Kann, L., Kinchen, S., Ross, J., Hawkins, J., Harris, W. A., Lowry, R., McManus, T., Chyen, D., Shanklin, S., Lim, C., Grunbaum, J. A., & Wechsler, H. (2006). Youth risk behavior surveillance—United States, 2005. *Morbidity and Mortality Weekly Report Surveillance Summaries, 55*(SS-5). Retrieved from http://www.cdc.gov/mmwr/PDF/SS/SS5505.pdf.

Eck, D. L. (2001). *A new religious America: How a "Christian country" has become the world's most religiously diverse nation*. New York: Harper San Francisco.

Edelman, M. W. (1994). *State of America's children yearbook 1994*. Washington, DC: Children's Defense Fund.

Edmondson, J. H., & White, J. (1998). A tutorial and counseling program: Helping students at risk of dropping out. *Professional School Counseling, 1*, 43–47.

Education Trust. (1997). *The National Guidance and Counseling Reform Program*. Washington, DC: Author.

Education Trust. (2000). *National Initiative for Transforming School Counseling Summer Academy for Counselor Educators proceedings*. Washington, DC: Author.

Educaton Trust. (2004). *EdWatch state reports*. Retrieved from http://www.edtrust.org/dc/resources/edwatch-state-reports.

Education Trust. (2005). *EdWatch Online: 2005 State Summary Reports,* retrieved from http://www.edtrust.org.

Education Trust (2005a). *Achievement in America: 2005*[computer diskette]. Washigton, DC:Author.

Education Trust (2005b). *The Education Trust's National Center for Transforming School Counseling Inititiative Web site*. Retrieved from http://www2.edtrust,org/EdTrust/Transforming+School +Counseling.

Education Trust (2005c). *Mission statement*. Retrieved August from www2.edtrust,org/EdTrust/Transforming+School +Counseling/main.

Education Trust. (2007). National Center for Transforming School Counseling. Retrieved from http://www2.edtrust. org/EdTrust/Transforming+School+Counseling/main.

Education Trust. (2010). *Close the Hidden Funding Gaps in Americas Public Schools*. Washington, DC: Author.

Education Watch (1998). *The Education Trust state and national data book* (Vol. 2). Washington, D.C.: Education Trust.

Egan, G. (1982). *The skilled helper: A model for systematic helping*. Monterey, CA: Brooks/Cole.

Egan, G., & Cowan, M. A. (1979). *People in systems: A model for development in the human-service professions and education*. Monterey, CA: Brooks/Cole.

Egley, A., Jr., & O'Donnell, C. E. (2009). Highlights of the 2007 National Youth Gang Survey. Washington, DC: Office of Juvenile Justice and Delinquency Prevention, Office of Justice Programs, U.S. Department of Justice.

Ehrlich, G., & Vega-Matos, C. A. (2002). *The impact of adolescent pregnancy and parenthood on educational achievement: A blueprint for education policymakers' involvement in prevention efforts*. Alexandria, VA: National Association of State Boards of Education.

Elias, M. J. (1989). Schools—a source of stress to children: An analysis of causal and ameliorative influences. *Journal of School Psychology, 27*, 393–407.

Elias, M. J., Beier, J. J., & Gara, M. A. (1989). Children's responses to interpersonal obstacles as a predictor of social competence. *Journal of Youth and Adolescence, 18*, 451–465.

Elias, M. J., Lantieri, L., Patti, J., Walberg, H. J., & Zins, J. E. (1999). Violence is preventable. *Education Week, 18*(36), 49.

Elias, M., Fredricks, L., Greenberg, M., O'Brian, M., Resnick, H., Weissberg, R., Zins, J. E. (2003). Enhancing school-based prevention and youth development through coordinated social, emotional, and academic learning. *American Psychologist, 58*, 466–474.

Elliot, M. N., Hanser, L. N., & Gilroy, C. L. (2001). *Evidence of positive student outcomes in JROTC career academies*. Prepared for the Office of the Secretary of Defense. Santa Monica, CA: RAND, National Defense Research Institute.

Elliott, D. S., Hamburg, B. A., & Williams, K. R. (1998). Violence in American schools: An overview. In D. S. Elliott, B. A. Hamburg, & K. R. Williams (Eds.), *Violence in American schools* (pp. 1–18). New York: Cambridge University Press.

Ellis, R. R. (1998). Multicultural grief counseling. In K. J. Doka & J. D. Davidson (Eds.), *Living with grief: Who we are; how we grieve* (pp. 248–260). Washington, DC: Hospice Foundation of America.

Elmore, R. (1996). Getting to scale with good educational practice. *Educational Review, 66*, 1–26.

Elster, A. B., & Marcell, A. V. (2003). Health care of adolescent males: Overview, rationale, and recommendations. *Adolescent Medicine, 14*(3), 525–540.

Embry, D. D., & Flannery, D. J. (1999). Two sides of the coin: Multilevel prevention and intervention to reduce youth violent behavior. In D. J. Flannery & C. R. Huff (Eds.), *Youth violence: Prevention, intervention, and social policy* (pp. 47–72). Washington, DC: American Psychiatric Press.

Englander-Golden, P., Golden, D., Brookshire, W., Snot, C., Haag, M., & Chang, A. (1996). Communication skills program for prevention of risky behaviors. *Journal of Substance Misuse, 1*, 38–46.

Engle, J., & Lynch, M. (2009). Charting a necessary path: A baseline report of the access to success initiative. Washington, DC: Education Trust.

English, D. J., Shrikant, I., Bangdiwala, B., & Runyan, D. K. (2005). The dimensions of maltreatment: Introduction. *Child Abuse & Neglect, 29*, 441–460.

Entwisle, D. R., Alexander, K. L., Pallas, A. M., & Cadigan, D. (1987). The emergent academic self-image of first-graders: Its response to social structure. *Child Development, 58*, 1190–1206.

Epstein, J. L. (1983). Selection of friends in differently organized schools and classrooms (pp. 79–92). In J. Epstein & N. Karweit (Eds.), *Friends in school: Patterns of selection and influence in secondary schools*. New York: Academic Press.

Epstein, J. L. (1987). Toward a theory of family–school connections: Teacher practicees and parent involvement. In K. Hurrelman, F. X. Kaufman, & F. Lösel (Eds.), *Social intervention: Potential and constraints* (pp. 121–136). Berlin: de Gruyter.

Epstein, J. L. (1995). School/family/community partnerships: Caring for the children we share. *Phi Delta Kappan, 76*(9), 701–712.

Epstein, J. L. (2001). *School, family, and community partnerships: Preparing educators and improving schools*. Boulder, CO: Westview Press.

Epstein, J. L., Coates, L., Salinas, K. C., Sanders, M. G., & Simon, B. S. (1997). *School, family, and community partnerships: Your handbook for action*. Thousand Oaks, CA: Corwin Press.

Epstein, J. L., Salinas, K. C., & Jackson, V. E. (1995). *Manual for teachers and prototype activities: Teachers Involve Parents in Schoolwork (TIPS) language arts, science/health, and mathematics interactive homework in the middle grades* (Rev. ed.). Baltimore: Johns Hopkins University Center on School, Family, and Community Partnerships.

Epstein, J. L., & Sanders, M. G. (2002). Family, school, and community partnerships. In M. H. Bornstein (Ed.), *Handbook of parenting,* Vol. 5: *Practical issues in parenting* (pp. 507–437). Mahwah, NJ: Erlbaum.

Epstein, J. L., Sanders, M. G., Sheldon, S. B., Simon, B. S., Salinas, K. C., Jansorn, Van Voorhis, F. L., Martin, C. S., Thomas, B. G., Greenfeld, M. D., Hutchinson, D. J., & Williams, K. J. (2009). *School, family, and community partnerships: Your handbook for action* (3rd ed.). Thousand Oaks, CA: Corwin Press.

Erchul, W. P., & Conoley, C. W. (1991). Helpful theories to guide counselors' practice of school-based consultation. *Elementary School Guidance and Counseling, 25*(3), 204–211.

Erickson, M. R., Egeland, B., & Pianta, R. (1989). The effects of maltreatment on the development of young children. In D. Cicchetti & V. Carlson (Eds.), *Child maltreatment theory and research on the causes and consequences of child abuse and neglect*. Cambridge, MA: Harvard University Press.

Erikson, E. H. (1963). *Childhood and society* (2nd ed.). New York: Norton.

Espin, O. (1993). Issues of identity in the psychology of Latina lesbians. In L. Garnets & D. Kimmel (Eds.), *Psychological perspectives on lesbian and gay male experiences* (pp. 405–414. New York: Columbia University Press.

Esser, G., Schmidt, M. H., & Woerner, W. (1990). Epidemiology and course of psychiatric disorders in school-age children: Results of a longitudinal study. *Journal of Child Psychology and Psychiatry, 31*, 243–263.

Ettinger, J. M. (1991). *Improved career decision making in a changing world: Integrating occupational information and guidance*. Washington, DC: National Occupational Information.

Everly, G. S., Jr. (2000). Five principles of crisis intervention: Reducing the risk of premature crisis intervention. *International Journal of Emergency Mental Health, 2000, 2*(1), 1–4.

Everly, G. S., Jr., Flannery, R. B., Jr., & Eyler, V. (2000, April). Effectiveness of a crisis intervention: A meta-analysis. Paper presented to the Third International Conference on Psychological and Social Services in a Changing Society, Kuwait City, Kuwait.

Everly, G. S., Jr., & Mitchell, J. T. (1999). *Critical Incident Stress Management (CISM): A new era and standard of care in crisis intervention* (2nd ed.). Ellicott City, MD: Chevron.

Eyberg, S. M. (1988). Parent–child interaction therapy: Integration of traditional and behavioral concerns. *Child and Family Behavior Therapy, 10*, 33–46.

Eyberg, S. M., & Calzada, E. J. (1998). *Parent–Child Interaction Therapy: Procedures manual.* (Unpublished manuscript). University of Florida.

Fabes, R. A., Eisenberg, N., McCormick, S. E., & Wilson, M. S. (1988). Preschoolers' attributions of the situational determinants of others' naturally occurring emotions. *Developmental Psychology, 24*, 376–385.

Fairburn, C. G., & Harrison, P. J. (2003). Eating disorders. *Lancet, 361*, 407–416.

Fairburn, C. G., Jones, R., Peveler, R. C., Hope, R. A., & O'Connor, M. (1993). Psychotherapy and bulimia nervosa: Long-term effects of interpersonal psychotherapy, behavior therapy, and cognitive behavior therapy. *Archives of General Psychiatry, 50*, 419–428.

Fairchild, T. N., & Seeley, T. J. (1995). Accountability strategies for school counselors: A baker's dozen. *School Counselor, 42*, 377–392.

Family Services Research Center. (1995). *Multisystemic therapy using home-based services: A clinically effective and cost-effective strategy for treating serious clinical problems in youth*. Charleston, SC: Author.

Fantuzzo, J., Sutton-Smith, B., Atkins, M., & Meyers, R. (1996). Community-based resilient peer treatment of withdrawn maltreated preschool children. *Journal of Clinical and Consulting Psychology, 64*, 1377–1368.

Fantuzzo, J., Weiss, A., & Coolahan, K. (1998). Community-based partnership-directed research: Actualizing community strengths to treat victims of physical abuse and neglect. In R. J. Lutzker (Ed.), *Child abuse: A handbook of theory, research, and treatment* (pp. 213–238). New York: Pergamon Press.

Faragallah, M. H., Schumm, W. R., & Webb, F. J. (1997). Acculturation of Arab-American immigrants: An exploratory study. *Journal of Comparative Family Studies, 28*, 182–203.

Farkas, G., Lieras, C., & Maczuga, S. (2002). Does oppositional culture exist in minority and poverty peer groups? *American Sociological Review, 67*, 148–155.

Farquharson, M. (1988, March). Ideas for teaching Arab students in a multicultural setting. Paper presented at the Annual Meeting of the Teachers of English to Speakers of Other Languages, Chicago. (ERIC Abstract).

Favaro, A., Ferrara, S., & Santonastaso, P. (2003). The spectrum of eating disorders in young women: A prevalence study in a general population. *Psychosomatic Medicine, 65*, 701–708.

Favaro, A., & Santonastraso, P. (2000). Self-injurious behavior in anorexia nervosa. *Journal of Nervous and Mental Disease, 188*(8), 537–542.

Federal Bureau of Investigation. (1995). *Crime in the United States.* Washington, DC: U.S. Department of Justice.

Feller, R., & Whichard, J. (2005). *Knowledge nomads and the nervously employed.* Austin, TX: ProEd.

Feng, J. (1994). *Asian-American children: What teachers should know.* ERIC Digest ED369577. Retrieved from http://www.ed.gov/databases?ERIC_Digests/ed369577.html.

Fennimore, B. S. (2000). *Talk matters: Refocusing the language of public schooling.* New York: Teachers College Press.

Fenske, R. H., Geranios, C. A., Keller, J. E., & Moore, D. E. (1997). *Early intervention programs: Opening the door to higher education.* ASHE-ERIC Higher Education Report, 25, No. 6. Retrieved from OCLC First Search database. http://www.oclc.org/support/documentation/firstsearch/managing/fsdja/.

Ferguson, R. F. (1998). Can schools narrow the black–white test score gap? In C. Jencks & M. Phillips (Eds.), *The black-white test score gap* (pp. 318–374). Washington, DC: Brookings Institution.

Ferguson, R. F. (2003). Teachers' perceptions and expectations and the black-white test score gap. *Urban Education, 38*(4), 460–507.

Ferguson, S. (2003). Whatever happened to partnerships? *Gaining Ground, 5*, 1–2. Retrieved from http://www.ccsso.org/content/PDFs/GGSummer03.pdf.

Fergusson, D. M., Swain, N. R., & Horwood, L. J. (2002). Deviant peer affiliations, crime and substance use: A fixed effects regression analysis. *Journal of Abnormal Child Psychology, 30*, 419–430.

Fielding, M. (2000). Community, philosophy and education policy: Against effectiveness ideology and the immiseration of contemporary schooling. *Journal of Educational Policy, 15*(4), 397–415.

Fieldman, S., Backman, J., & Bayer, J. (2002). Mental health parity: A review of research and bibliography. *Administration and Policy in Mental Health and Mental Health Services Research, 29*(3), 215–228.

Finkelhor, D., & Jones, L. (2006). Why have child maltreatment and child victimization declined? *Journal of Social Issues, 62*, 685–716.

Finkelhor, D., Ormrod, R., Turner, H., & Hamby, S. (2005). The victimization of children and youth: A comprehensive, national survey. *Child Maltreatment, 10*, 5–25.

Fisch, R., Weakland, J., & Segal, L. (1982). *The tactics of change.* San Francisco: Jossey–Bass.

Fischer, L., & Sorenson, G. P. (1996). *School law for counselors, psychologists, and social workers* (3rd ed.). New York: Longman.

Fischer, L., Schimmel, D., & Stellman, L. R. (2003). *Teachers and the law* (6th ed.). Boston: Allyn & Bacon.

Fischer, M., Barkley, R.A., Smallish, L., & Fletcher, K. (2005). Executive functioning in hyperactive children as young adults: Attention, inhibition, response perseveration, and impact of comorbidity. *Developmental Neuropsychology, 27*(1), 107–133.

Fitch, T. J., & Marshall, J. L. (2004). What counselors do in high achieving schools: A study on the role of the school counselor. *Professional School Counseling, 7*, 172–177.

Flaherty, L. T., Garrison, E. G., Waxman, R., Uris, P. F., Keys, S. G., Glass-Siegel, M., & Weist, M. D. (1998). Optimizing the roles of school mental health professionals. *Journal of School Health, 68*, 420–424.

Flaherty, L. T., & Osher, D. (2003). History of school-based mental health services. In M. D. Weist, S. W. Evans, & N. A. Lever (Eds.), *Handbook of school mental health: Advancing practice and research* (pp. 11–22). New York: Kluwer Academic.

Flake, M. H., Roach, A. J., & Stenning, W. F. (1975). Effects of short-term counseling on career maturity of tenth grade students. *Journal of Vocational Behavior, 6*, 73–80.

Flannery, R. B. (1999). Psychological trauma and posttraumatic stress disorder: A review. *International Journal of Emergency Mental Health, 78*(2), 135–140.

Flavell, J. H. (1963). *The developmental psychology of Jean Piaget.* Princeton, NJ: Van Nostrand.

Fleming, C. B., Haggerty, K. P., Catalano, R. F., Harachi, T. W., Mazza, J. J. & Gruman, D. H. (2005). Do social and behavioral characteristics targeted by preventive interventions predict standardized test scores and grades? *Journal of School Health, 75*(9), 342.

Fletcher, K. E. (2003). Childhood posttraumatic stress disorder. In E. J. Mash & R. A. Barkley (Eds.), *Child Psychopathology*, 2nd Edition. New York, NY: Guilford Press.

Fletcher, T. V., & Cardona-Morales, C. (1990). Implementing effective instructional interventions for minority students. In A. Barona & E. E. García (Eds.), Children at risk: Poverty, minority status, and other issues in educational equity (pp. 151–70). Washington, DC: National Association of School Psychologists.

Floyd, C. (1996). Achieving despite the odds: A study of resilience among a group of African American high school seniors. *Journal of Negro Education, 65*, 181–189.

Fombonne, E., & Chakrabarti, S. (2001). No evidence for a new variant of measles-mumps-rubella-induced autism. *Pediatrics, 108*, 1–8.

Fonagy, P., Steele, M., Steele, H., Higgitt, A., & Target, M. (1994). The Emmanuel Miller Memorial Lecture, 1992: The theory and practice of resilience. *Journal of Child Psychology and Psychiatry, 34*(2), 231–257.

Fontaine, J. H. (1998). Evidencing a need: School counselors' experiences with gay and lesbian students. *Professional School Counseling, 1*(3), 8–14.

Ford, D. Y. (1997). Counseling middle-class African Americans. In C. C. Lee (Ed.), *Multicultural issues in counseling* (2nd ed., pp. 81–108). Alexandria, VA: American Counseling Association.

Forester-Miller, H., & Davis, T. E. (1996). *A practitioner's guide to ethical decision making.* Alexandria, VA: American Counseling Association.

Forum on Child and Family Statistics. (2009). *America's children: Key national indicators of well-being, 2009.* Retrieved from http://childstats.gov/americaschildren/index3.asp.

Foster, S., Rollefson, M., Doksum, T., Noonan, D., Robinson, G., & Teich, J. (2005). *School mental health services in the United States, 2002–2003.* DHHS Pub. No. SMA 05-4068. Rockville, MD: Center for Mental Health Services, Substance Abuse and Mental Health Services Administration. Retrieved from http://download.ncadi.samhsa.gov/ken/pdf/SMA05-4068/SMA05-4068.pdf.

Fouad, N. A. (1995). Career linking: An intervention to promote math and science career awareness. *Journal of Counseling and Development, 73*, 527–534.

Fracasso, M. P., & Busch-Rossnagel, N. A. (1992). Parents and children of Hispanic origin. In M. E. Procidano & C. B. Fisher (Eds.), *Contemporary families: A handbook for school professionals* (pp. 83–98). New York: Teachers College Press.

Frank, J. W., Moore, R. S., & Ames, G. M. (2000). Historical and cultural roots of drinking problems among American Indians. *American Journal of Public Health, 90*, 344–351.

Frankl, V. E. (1963). *Man's search for meaning.* New York: Washington Square Press, Simon & Schuster.

Frankowski, B. L., & American Academy of Pediatrics Committee on Adolescence. (2004). Clinical report: Sexual orientation and adolescents. *Pediatrics 113*(6), 1827–1832.

Frazier, J. A., Doyle, R., Chiu, S., & Coyle, J. T. (2002). Treating children with Asperger's disorder and comorbid bipolar disorder. *American Journal of Psychiatry, 159*, 13–21.

Freisthler, B., Merritt, D. H., & LaScala, E. A. (2006). Understanding the ecology of child maltreatment: A review of the literature and directions for future research. *Child Maltreatment, 11*, 263–280.

Frey, A. J., Lingo, A., & Nelson, C. M. (2008). Positive behavior support: A call for leadership. *Children and Schools, 30*, 5–14.

Frey, K. S., & Ruble, D. N. (1987). What children say about classroom performance: Sex and grade differences in perceived competence. *Child Development, 58*, 1066–1078.

Frick, P. J., & Silverthorn, P. (2001). Psychopathology in children. In P. B. Sutker & H. E. Adams (Eds.), *Comprehensive handbook of psychopathology* (3rd ed., pp. 881–920). New York: Kluwe Academic/Plenum Press.

Friedman, R. C., & Downey, J. I. (1994). Homosexuality. *New England Journal of Medicine, 331*, 923–930.

Friedman, T. (2006). *The world is flat.* New York: Farrar, Straus & Giroux.

Friedrich, W. N. (1995). *Psychotherapy with sexually abused boys.* Thousand Oaks, CA: Sage.

Friedrich, W. N. (1998). *Treating sexual behavior problems in children: A treatment manual.* Rochester, MN: Mayo Clinic, Department of Psychiatry and Psychology.

Froehlich, C. P. (1949). *Evaluating guidance procedures: A review of the literature.* Washington, DC: Federal Security Agency, Office of Education.

Froeschle, J., & Moyer, M. (2004). Just cut it out: Legal and ethical challenges in counseling students who self-mutilate. *Professional School Counseling, 7*, 321–356.

Fruchter, N., Berne, R., & Marcus, A. (1995). *Focus on learning: A report on reorganizing special education in New York City.* New York: New York University Institute for Education and Social Policy.

Fry, R. (2002). *Latinos in higher education: Many enroll but few graduate.* Washington, DC: Pew Hispanic Center.

Fry, R. (2003). *Hispanic youth dropping out of U.S. schools: Measuring the challenge.* Washington, DC: Pew Hispanic Center.

Fuchs, D., & Fuchs, L. S. (1995). Special education can work. In *Issues in educational placement: Students with emotional and behavioral disorders.* Hillsdale, NJ: Erlbaum.

Fuligni, A. J., & Hardway, C. (2004). Preparing diverse adolescents for the transfer to adulthood. *Future of Children, 14*(2), 99–116.

Fuqua, D. R., & Kurpius, D. J. (1993). Conceptual models in organizational consultation. *Journal of Counseling and Development, 71*, 607–618.

Gage, N. L. (1990). Dealing with the dropout problem. *Phi Delta Kappan, 72*(4), 280–285.

Galassi, J. P., & Akos, P. (2004). Developmental advocacy: Twenty-first-century school counseling. *Journal of Counseling and Development, 82*(2), 146–157.

Gallagher, N. (2003). Effects of parent–child interaction therapy on young children with disruptive behavior disorders. *Bridges, 1*, 1–17.

Garbarino, J., & deLara, E. (2002). *And words can hurt forever.* New York: Simon & Schuster.

Garcia, D. C., & Hasson, D. J. (2004). Implementing family literacy programs for linguistically and culturally diverse populations: Key elements to consider. *School Community Journal, 14*(1), 113–137.

Garcia, J. G. (2003). Latinos in the United States in 2000. *Hispanic Journal of Behavioral Sciences, 25*(11), 13–34.

Garcia, J. G., & Marotta, S. (1997). Characterization of the Latino population, in J. G. Garcia & M. C. Zea (Eds.), *Psychological interventions and research with Latino populations* (pp. 1–14). Needham Heights, MA: Allyn & Bacon.

Gargiulo, R. M. (2006). Special education in contemporary society: An introduction to exceptionality (2nd ed). Belmont, CA: Thomson/Wadsworth.

Garland, A. E., & Zigler, E. (1993). Adolescent suicide prevention: Current research and social policy implications. *American Psychologist, 48*, 169–182.

Garmezy, N. (1985). Stress-resistant children: The search for protective factors. In J. E. Stevenson (Ed.), *Recent research in developmental psychopathology* (pp. 213–233). New York: Pergamon Press.

Garofalo, R., Wolf, R. C., Kessel, S., & Palfrey, J. (1998). Sexual orientation and risk of suicide attempts among a representative sample of youth. *Pediatrics, 101*(5), 895–902.

Garofalo, R., Wolf, R. C., Wissow, L. S., Woods, E. R., & Goodman, E. (1999). Sexual orientation and risk of suicide attempts among a representative example of youth. *Archives of Pediatric and Adolescent Medicine, 153*, 487–493.

Garrison, C. Z., Schuchter, M. D., Schoenback, V. J., & Kaplan, B. K. (1989). Epidemiology of depressive symptoms in young adolescents. *Journal of American Academy of Child and Adolescent Psychiatry, 28*, 343–351.

Garrison, C. Z., Waller, J. L., Cuffee, S. P., McKeown, R. E., Addy, C. L., & Jackson, K. L. (1997). Incidence of major depressive disorder and dysthymia in young adolescents. *Journal of the American Academy of Child and Adolescent Psychiatry, 36*, 458–465.

Garrity, C., Jens, K., Porter, W., Sager, N., & Short-Camilli, C. (2004). *Bully-proofing your school: Teacher's manual and lesson plans for elementary schools* (3rd ed.). Longmont, CO: Sopris West.

Gavin, L. A., & Furman, W. (1989). Age differences in adolescents' perceptions of their peer groups. *Developmental Psychology, 25*, 827–834.

Gay, G. (2000). *Culturally Responsive Teaching: Theory, Research, and Practice.* New York: Teachers College Press.

Gay, Lesbian and Straight Education Network. (2004). *2003 National school climate survey: The school related experiences of our nations's lesbian, gay, bisexual and trangendered youth.* New York: Author.

Gehring, J. (2001). The International Baccalaureate: "Cadillac" of college-prep programs. *Education Week, 20*(2), 19.

Gelles, R. (1989). Child abuse and violence in single parent families: Parent absences and economic deprivation. *American Journal of Orthopsychiatry, 59*, 492–502.

Gentry, D. B., & Benenson, W. A. (1992). School-age peer mediation transfer knowledge and skills to home settings. *Mediation Quarterly, 10*, 101–109.

Gentry, J. E. (2002). Compassion fatigue: The crucible of transformation. *Journal of Trauma Practice, 1*(3/4), 37–61.

George, P., & McEwin, K. (1999). High schools for a new century: Why is the high school changing? *NASSP Bulletin, 83*, 10–24.

Gerler, E. R., Kinney, J., & Anderson, R. (1985). The effects of counseling on classroom performance. *Journal of Humanistic Education and Development, 24*(4), 155–165.

Gerler, E. R., & Herndon, E. Y. (1993). Learning how to succeed academically in middle school. *Elementary School Guidance & Counseling, 27*, 186–198.

Gibbs, J. C. (1979). Kohlberg's moral stage theory: A Piagetian revision. *Human Development, 22*, 89–112.

Gibson, M. A., & Bejines, L. F. (2002). Dropout prevention: How migrant education supports Mexican youth. *Journal of Latinos and Education, 1*, 155–175.

Gibson, P. (1989). Gay male and lesbian youth suicide. In M. R. Feinleib (Ed.), *Report of the Secretary's task force on youth suicide,* Vol. 3: *Preventions and interventions in youth suicide* (pp. 110–142). U.S. Department of Health and Human Services Pub. No. ADM 89-1623. Washington, DC: Government Printing Office.

Gil, E. (1991). *The healing power of play.* New York: Guilford Press.

Gil, E. (1996). *Treating abused adolescents.* New York: Guilford Press.

Gil, E. (1998). *Essentials of play therapy with abused children.* New York: Guilford Press.

Gill, S. J., & Barry, R. A. (1982). Group focused counseling: Classifying the essential skills. *Personnel and Guidance Journal, 60*(5), 24–29.

Gillberg, C., & Coleman, M. (2000). *The biology of autistic syndromes* (3rd ed.). London: MacKeith.

Gilligan, C., Rogers, A. G., & Tolman, D. L. (Eds.). (1991). *Women, girls and psychotherapy: Reframing resistance.* New York: Haworth Press.

Gladding, S. T. (2004). *Counseling: A comprehensive profession* (5th ed.). Upper Saddle River, NJ: Prentice-Hall.

Gladding, S. T., Remley, T. P., Jr., & Huber, C. (2001). *Ethical, legal, and professional issues in the practice of marriage and family therapy* (3rd ed.). Upper Saddle River, NJ: Merrill Prentice Hall.

Glosoff, H. L., Herlihy, B., & Spence, E. B. (2000). Privileged communication in the counselor–client relationship. *Journal of Counseling and Development, 78*, 454–462.

Glosoff, H. L., & Pate, R. H. (2002). Privacy and confidentiality in school counseling. *Professional School Counseling, 6*, 20–28.

Godley, S. H., & White, W. (2006). Student assistance programs: A valuable resource for substance-involved adolescents. *Counselor, 7*(2), 66–70.

Gold, M., & Yanof, D. S. (1985). Mothers, daughters, and girlfriends. *Journal of Personality and Social Psychology, 49*, 654–659.

Goldston, D. (2004). Conceptual issues in understanding the relationship between suicidal behavior and substance abuse during adolescence. *Drug and Alcohol Dependence, 76*, 79–91.

Goldston, D., Reboussin, B., & Daniel, S. (2006). Predictors of suicide attempts: State and trait components. *Journal of Abnormal Psychology, 115*, 842–849.

Goleman, D. (1994). *Emotional literacy: A field report*, Kalamazoo, MI: Fetzer Institute.

Goleman, D. (2006). *Emotional intelligence: Why it can matter more than I.Q.* (10th anniversary ed.) New York: Bantam Dell.

Gollnick, D. M., & Chinn, P. C. (2006). *Multicultural education in a pluralistic society* (7th ed.). Upper Saddle River, NJ: Pearson.

Good, T. L., & Brophy, J. E. (2000). *Looking in classrooms.* New York: Harper & Row.

Goodenow, C. (2003). *Violence-related experiences of sexual minority youth: Looking at data from the Massachusetts youth risk behavior survey, 1995–2001.* Springfield: Massachusetts Department of Education.

Goodkin, K., Baldewicz, T. T., Blaney, N. T., Asthana, D., & Kumar, M. (2001). Physiological effects of bereavement and bereavement support group interventions. In M. S. Stroebe, R. O. Hansson, W. Stroebe, & H. Schut (Eds.), *Handbook of bereavement research: Consequences, coping and care.* Washington, DC: American Psychological Association.

Goodlad, J. I. (1984). *A place called school: Prospects for the future.* New York: McGraw Hill.

Goodman, J. (1982). *Using humor in workshops: The 1983 Annual Conference for Facilitators, Trainers and Consultants.* San Diego: University Associates.

Goodwin, A. L. (2003) Growing up Asian in America: A search for self. In C. Park, A. L. Goodwin, & S. Lee (Eds.), *Asian American identities, families, and schooling.* Greenwich, CT: Information Age.

Goodwin, B. (May 2000). Raising the achievement of low-performing students. Aurora, CO: Mid-continent Research for Education and Learning. Retrieved from http://www.mcrel.org/products/learning/raising.html.

Goodyear, R. K. (1984). On our journal's evolution: Historical developments, transitions, and future directions. *Journal of Counseling and Development, 63*, 3–9.

Gopaul-McNicol, S., & Thomas-Presswood, T. (1998). *Working with linguistically and culturally different children: Innovative clinical and educational practices.* Boston: Allyn & Bacon.

Gordon, E. W., Brownell, C., & Brittell, J. (1972). *Desegregation.* New York: Columbia University Press.

Gottfredson, D. C. (1997). School-based crime prevention. In L. W. Sherman, D. Gottfredson, D. MacKenzie, J. Eck, P. Reuter, & S. Bushway (Eds.), *Preventing crime: What works, what doesn't, what's promising: A report to the United States Congress* (pp. 224–249). Washington, DC: National Institute of Justice.

Gould, M., Greenberg, T., Velting, D. M., & Shaffer, D. (2003). Youth suicide risk and preventive interventions: A review of the past 10 years. *Journal of the American Academy of Child and Adolescent Psychiatry, 42*, 386–405.

Gould, M., Marrocco, F., Kleinman, M., Thomas, J., Mostkoff, K., & Cote, J. (2005). Evaluating introgenic risk of youth suicide screening programs: A randomized controlled trial. *Journal of the American Medical Association, 293*, 1635–1643.

Gould, S. J. (1981). *The mismeasure of man.* New York: Norton.

Governing. (2004, February). *Promises unfilfilled,* Retrieved from http//governing.com/gpp/2004/mental.htm.

Gowers, S., & Bryant-Waugh, R. (2004). The management of children and adolescents with eating disorders. *Journal of Child Psychology and Psychiatry, 45*, 63–83.

Grand Council of American Indians. http://furtradetomahawks.tripod.com/id15.html.

Granello, D. H., & Granello, P. F. (2007). *Suicide: An essential guide for helping professionals and educators*. Boston: Allyn & Bacon.

Grant, C. (2007). *Turning on learning: Five approaches for multicultural teaching plans for race, class, gender, and disability*. Hoboken, NJ: John Wiley.

Gray, N. A., & Ahmed, I. (1988). *The Arab-American family: A resource manual for human service providers*. Dearborn, MI: Arab Community Center for Economic and Social Services.

Greenberg, M. T., Kusche, C. A., Cook, E. T., & Quamma, J. P. (1995). Promoting emotional competence in school-aged children: The effects of the PATHS curriculum. *Development and Psychopathology, 7*, 117–136.

Greenberg, M. T., Kusche, C., & Mihalic, S. F. (1998). *Blueprints for violence prevention: Promoting alternative thinking strategies*, Boulder: University of Colorado, Institute of Behavioral Science, Center for the Study and Prevention of Violence.

Greenberg, M. T., Weissberg, R. P., O'Brien, M. U., Zins, J. E., Fredericks, L., Resnik, H., & Elias, M. (2003). Enhancing school-based prevention and youth development through coordinated social, emotional, and academic learning. *American Psychologist, 58*, 466–474.

Greenblatt, J. C. (2000). Patterns of alcohol use among adolescents and associations with emotional and behavioral problems. Washington, DC: U.S. Department of Justice.

Greene, B. (1997). Ethnic minority lesbians and gay men: Mental health and treatment issues. In B. Greene (Ed)., *Ethnic and cultural diverstiy among lesbian and gay men*. Thousand Oaks, CA: Sage.

Greene, J. P., & Winters, M. A. (2005). *Public high school graduation and college readiness rates, 1991–2002*. New York: Manhattan Institute for Policy Research. Retrieved from http://www.manhattaninstitute.org/html/ewp_08.htm.

Greenfield, P. M., Raeff, C., & Quiroz, B. (1996). Cultural values in learning and education. In B. Williams (Ed.), *Closing the achievement gap: A vision for changing beliefs and practices*. Alexandria, VA: ASCD.

Greenstone, J. L., & Leviton, S. C. (1993). *Elements of crisis intervention: Crises and how to respond to them*. Pacific Grove, CA: Brooks/Cole.

Greenwood, P. W., Model, K. E., Rydell, C. P., & Chiesa, J. R. (1998). *Diverting children from a life of crimes: Measuring costs and benefits*. Document No. MR-699-1-UCB/RC/IF. Santa Monica, CA: U.S. Department of Justice.

Gregg, S. (1996). *Preventing antisocial behavior in disabled and at-risk students*. Charleston, WV: Appalachia Educational Laboratory.

Greenya, J. (2005). Bullying: Are schools doing enough to stop the problem? CQ Press, A division of Congressional Quarterly, Inc., Vol. 15, No. 5, p.101–124.

Grella, C., Hser, Y. I., Joshi, V., & Rounds-Bryant, J. (2001). Drug treatment outcomes for adolescents with comorbid mental and substance use disorders. *Journal of Nervous and Mental Disease, 189*, 384–392.

Gresham, F. M. (1981). Validity of social skills measures for assessing the social competence in low-status children: A multivariate investigation. *Developmental Psychology, 17*, 398–399.

Grieco, E. M., & Cassidy, R. C. (2001). *Overview of race and hispanic origin*. Census 2000 Brief, C2KBR/01-1. Retrieved from http://www.census.gov/prod/2001pubs/c2kbr01-1.pdf.

Griffin, D., & Steen, S. (2010). School–family–community partnerships: Applying Epstein's theory of the six types of involvement to school counselor practice. *Professional School Counseling, 13*(4), 218.

Griggs, S. A. (1983). Counseling high school students for their individual learning styles. *Clearing House, 56*, 293–296.

Grobe, T., Niles, J., & Weisstein, E. (2001). *Helping all youth succeed: Building youth development systems in our communities*. Boston: Commonwealth Corp.

Gross, B., & Gross, R. (1969). *Radical school reform*. New York: Simon & Schuster.

Grossman, J. B., & Garry, E. M. (1997). Mentoring a proven delinquency strategy. *OJJDP Bulletin*; U.S. Department of Justice.

Grossman, D. C., Neckerman, H. J., Koepsell, T. D., Liu, P., Asher, K. N., Beland, K., Frey, K., & Rivara, F. P. (1997). Effectiveness of a violence prevention curriculum among children in elementary school. *Journal of the American Medical Association, 227*(20), 1605–1611.

Grotberg, E. H. (1995). *A guide to promoting resilience in children: Strengthening the human spirit*. The Hague, Netherlands: Bernard van Leer Foundation.

Grotberg, E. H. (1998, Spring). I am, I have, I can: What families worldwide taught us about resilience. *Reaching Today's Youth*, 36–39.

Grunbaum, J. A., Kann, L., Kinchen, S., Ross, J., Hawkins, J., Lowry, R., & Harris, L. (2004). Youth Risk Behavior Survey surveillance–United

Gustavsson, N. S., & MacEachron, A. E. (1998). Violence and lesbian and gay youth. In L. M. Sloan & N. S. Gustavsson (Eds.), *Violence and social injustice against lesbian, gay and bisexual people* (pp. 41–50). New York: Harrington Park Press.

Gutman, L. M., & McLoyd, V. C. (2000). Parents' management of their children's education within the home, at school, and in the community: An examination of African-American families living in poverty. *Urban Review, 32*, 1–24.

Guttmacher Institute. (2006a). *In brief: Facts on sex education in the United States.* New York: Author.

Guttmacher Institute. (2006b). *U.S. teenage pregnancy statistics: National and state trends and trends by race and ethnicity.* New York: Author.

Guyton, J. M., & Fielstein, L. L. (1989). Student-led parent conferences: A model for teaching responsibility. *Elementary School Guidance and Counseling, 24*, 169–172.

Gysbers, N. C. (1990). *Comprehensive guidance programs that work.* Ann Arbor, MI: ERIC Counseling and Personnel Services Clearinghouse.

Gysbers, N. C. (2001). School guidance and counseling in the 21st century: Remember the past into the future. *Professional School Counseling, 5*, 96–104.

Gysbers, N. C. (2003). The center of education [preface]. In *The ASCA National Model: A framework for school counseling programs* (pp. 4–5). Alexandria, VA: American School Counselor Association.

Gysbers, N. C. (2004). Comprehensive guidance and counseling programs: The evolution of accountability. *Professional School Counseling, 8*, 1–14.

Gysbers, N. C., Bragg Stanley, J., Kosteck-Bunch, L., Magnuson, C. S., & Starr, M. F. (2008). *Missouri Comprehensive Guidance Program: A manual for program development, implementation, evaluation and enhancement.* Warrensburg: Missouri Center for Career Education, University of Central Missouri.

Gysbers, N. C., & Henderson, P. (2000). *Developing and managing your school guidance program* (3rd ed.). Alexandria, VA: American Counseling Association.

Gysbers, N. C., & Henderson, P. (2001). Comprehensive guidance and counseling programs: A rich history and a bright future. *Professional School Counseling, 4*, 246–256.

Gysbers, N. C., & Henderson, P. (2006). *Developing and managing your school guidance program* (4th ed.). Alexandria, VA: American Counseling Association.

Gysbers, N. C., & Moore, E. J. (1974). *Career guidance, counseling and placement: Elements of an illustrative program guide.* Columbia: Career Guidance, Counseling and Placement Project, University of Missouri–Columbia.

Haberman, M. (1991). The pedagogy of poverty versus good teaching. *Phi Delta Kappan, 73*, 290–294.

Hacker, D. J. (1994). The existential view of adolescence. *Journal of Early Adolescence, 14*, 300–327.

Hadley, H. R. (1988). Improving reading scores through a self-esteem intervention program. *Elementary School Guidance and Counseling, 22*, 248–252.

Haines, A. A. (1994). The effectiveness of a school-based, cognitive-behavioral stress management program with adolescents reporting high and low levels of emotional arousal. *Journal of Child & Family Studies, 5*(4), 399–414.

Haines, J., & Neumark-Sztainer, D. (2006). Prevention of obesity and eating disorder: A consideration of shared risk factors. *Health Education Research, 21*(6), 770–782.

Hall, A. S., & Lin, M.-J. (1994). An integrative consultation framework: A practical tool for elementary school counselors. *Elementary School Guidance and Counseling, 19*(1), 16–27.

Hall, D. (2007). *Graduation matters: Improving accountability for high school graduation.* Washington, DC: Education Trust.

Hall, D., Wiener, R., & Carey, K. (2003). *What new AYP information tells us about schools, states and public education.* Washington, DC: Education Trust.

Hallfors, D. D., Waller, M. W., Bauer, D., Ford, C. A., & Halpern, C. T. (2005). Which comes first in adolescence— Sex and drugs or depression? *American Journal of Preventive Medicine, 29*, 163–170.

Hallinan, M. (1979). Structural effects on children's friendships and cliques. *Social Psychological Quarterly, 42*, 43–54.

Halmi, K. A. (1983). Anorexia nervosa and bulimia. *Psychosomatics, 24*, 111–129.

Halverstadt, J. (2000). Strategies for teaching abused or traumatized students. Seattle, Washington: Pacific University Press.

Hamann, E. T., Wortham, S., & Murillo, E. G. (2002). Education and policy in the new Latino diaspora. In S. Wortham, E. G. Murillo, & E. T. Hamann (Eds.), *Education in the new Latino diaspora* (pp. 1–16). Westport, CT: Ablex.

Hamburg, D. A. (1992). *Today's children: Creating a future for a generation in crisis.* New York: Times Books.

Hamilton, B. E, Martin, J. A., & Ventura, S. J. (2009). Births: Preliminary data for 2007. *National Vital Statistics Reports, 57*(12). Hyattsville, MD: National Center for Health Statistics.

Hammond, R. (1991). *Dealing with anger: Givin' it, takin' it, Workin' it out,* Champaign, IL: Research Press.

Hammond, R., & Young, B. (1993). *Evaluation and activity report: Positive adolescent choices training.* (Unpublished grant report). Washington, DC: U.S. Maternal and Child Health Bureau.

Handy, C. (1989). *The age of unreason.* Boston: Harvard Business School Press.

Hankin, B. L., Fraley, R. C., Lahey, B. B., & Waldman, I. D. (2005). Is depression best viewed as a continum of discrete category? A taxometric analysis of childhood and adolescent depression in a population-based sample. *Journal of Abnormal Psychology, 114*, 96–110.

Hansen, J. C., Warner, R. W., & Smith, E. J. (1980). *Group counseling: Theory and practice* (2nd ed.). Chicago: Rand McNally.

Hanson, R. F., & Spratt, E. G. (2000). Reactive Attachment Disorder: What we know about the disorder and implications for treatment. *Child Maltreatment, 5*, 137–145.

Hanson, S. L., Myers, D. R., & Ginsburg, A. L. (1987). The role of responsibility and knowledge in reducing teenage out-of-wedlock childbearing. *Journal of Marriage and the Family, 49*, 241–256.

Hargreaves, A., & Fuller, A. (Eds.). (1992). *Understanding teacher development.* New York: Teachers College Press.

Harlow, C. W. (2003). *Education and correctional populations.* NCH 195670. Washington, DC: U.S. Department of Justice, Bureau of Justice Statistics.

Harris, E., & Wimer, C. (2004). *Out-of-school time evaluation snapshot: Engaging with families in out-of-school time learning.* Cambridge, MA: Harvard Family Research Project, Harvard Graduate School of Education.

Harris, M. J., & Rosenthal, R. (1985). Mediation of interpersonal expectancy effects: 31 meta-analyses. *Psychological Bulletin, 97*, 363–386.

Harter, S. (1982). The perceived competence scale for children. *Child Development, 53*, 87–97.

Hartup, W. W. (1983). Peer relations. In P. H. Mussen (Ed.), *Handbook of child psychology* (4th ed., Vol. 4). New York: John Wiley.

Hartup, W. W. (1989). Social relationships and their developmental significance. *American Psychologist, 44*, 120–126.

Harvey, W. B. (2003). *Minorities in higher education, 2002–2003: Twentieth annual status report.* Washington, DC: American Council on Education.

Hatch, T. (2002). National standards for school counseling programs: A source of legitimacy or of reform? *Dissertation Abstracts International, 63*(8), 2798–2800.

Hatch, T. (2008). Professional challenges in school counseling: Organizational, institutional, and political. *Journal of School Counseling, 39*(5), 12–17.

Hatch, T., & Bowers, J. (2002). The block to build on. *ASCA School Counselor, 39*(5), 12–17.

Hattie, J., Biggs, J., & Purdie, N. (1996). Effects of learning skills interventions on student learning: A meta-analysis. *Review of Educational Research, 66*, 99–130.

Hawes, D. J. (1989). Communication between teachers and children: A counselor consultant/trainer model. *Elementary School Guidance and Counseling, 24*(1), 58–67.

Hawkins, J. D., & Catalano, R. F. (1992). Communities that care: Action for drug abuse prevention. San Francisco: Jossey-Bass.

Hawkins, J. D., Catalano, R. F., & Arthur, M. (2002). Promoting science-based prevention in communities. *Addictive Behaviors 90*(5), 1–26.

Hawkins, J. D., Van Horn, M. L., & Arthur, M. W. (2004). Community variation in risk and protective factors and substance use outcomes. *Prevention Science 5*(4), 213–220.

Hawton, K. (1986). *Suicide and attempted suicide among children and adolescents.* Beverly Hills, CA: Sage.

Haycock, K. (2001). Closing the achievement gap. *Educational Leadership, 58*(6). Retrieved from http://www.ascd.org/readingroom/edlead/0103/haycock.html.

Hayes, R. L., Nelson, J., Tabin, M., Pearson, G., & Worthy, C. (2002). Using school-wide data to advocate for student success. *Professional School Counseling, 6*, 86–95.

Hayslip, J. B., & VanZandt, Z. (2000). Using national standards and models of excellence as a framework for accountability. *Journal of Career Development, 27*(2), 81–87.

Healthy Teen Network. (2005). *Replicating success: One program at a time.* Washington, DC: Healthy Teen Network.

Heinström, J. (2000). The impact of personality and approaches to learning on information behaviour. *Information Research, 5*(3). Retrieved from http://informationr.net/ir/5-3/paper78.html.

Helms, N. E., & Katsiyannis, A. (1992). Counselors in elementary schools: Making it work for students with disabilities. *School Counselor, 39*, 232–237.

Hembree-Kigin, T., & McNeil, C. B. (1995). *Parent–child interaction therapy.* New York: Plenum.

Henderson, A. T., & Mapp, K. L. (2002). *A new wave of evidence: The impact of school family and community connections on student achievement.* Austin, TX: Southwest Educational Development Laboratory. Retrieved from http://www.sedl.org/connections/resources/evidence.pdf.

Henderson, N., & Milstein, M. (1996). *Resiliency in schools: Making it happen for students and educators.* Thousand Oaks, CA: Corwin Press.

Hendley, S. L., & Lock, R. H. (2007). Use positive behavior support for inclusion in the general education classroom. *Intervention in School and Clinic, 42*, 225–228.

Hendren, R., & Mullen, D. (1997). Conduct disorder in childhood. In J. M. Weiner (Ed.), *Textbook of child and adolescent psychiatry* (2nd ed., pp. 427–440). Washington, DC: American Academy of Child and Adolescent Psychiatry and American Psychiatric Press.

Henggeler, S. W. (1991). *Treating conduct problems in children and adolescents.* (Treatment manual). Columbia: South Carolina Department of Mental Health.

Henggeler, S. W., & Borduin, C. M. (1990). *Family therapy and beyond: A multisystemic approach to treating behavior problems of children and adolescents.* Pacific Grove, CA: Brooks/Cole.

Henggeler, S. W., Schoenwald, S. K., Borduin, C. M., Rowland, M. D., & Cunningham, P. B. (1998). *Multisystematic treatment of antisocial behavior in children and adolescents.* New York: Guilford Press.

Herek, G. M. (2004). Beyond "homophobia": Thinking about sexual stigma and prejudice in the twenty-first century. *Sexuality Research and Social Policy, 1*(2), 6–24.

Herlihy, B., & Corey, G. (1996). *ACA ethical standards casebook* (5th ed.). Alexandria, VA: American Counseling Association.

Herlihy, B., Gray, N., & McCollum, V. (2002). Legal and ethical issues in school counselor supervision. *Professional School Counseling, 6*, 55–60.

Hermann, M. A., & Finn, A. (2002). An ethical and legal perspective on the role of school counselors in preventing violence in schools. *Professional School Counseling, 6*, 46–54.

Hermann, M. A., & Remley, T. P., Jr. (2000). Guns, violence, and schools: The results of school violence—litigation against educators and students shedding more constitutional rights at the school house gate. *Loyola Law Review, 46*, 389–439.

Herndon, E. H. (1990). Legal aspects of the role of the public school counselor in North Carolina. *Dissertation Abstracts International, 51-09A*, 2985.

Herr, E. L. (1976, April). *Does counseling work?* Paper presented at the Seventh International Round Table for the Advancement of Counseling. University of Würzburg, Germany.

Herr, E. L. (2001). The impact of national policies, economics, and school reform on comprehensive guidance programs. *Professional School Counselor, 4*, 236–245.

Herr, E. L. (2002). School reform and perspectives on the role of school counselors: A century of proposals for change. *Professional School Counselor, 5*(4), 220–234.

Herr, E. L., & Cramer, S. H. (1984). *Career guidance and counseling through the life span* (2nd ed.). Boston: Little, Brown.

Herr, K. (1999). Institutional violence in the everyday practice of school: The narrative of a young lesbian. *Journal for a Just and Caring Education, 5*(3), 242–255.

Herring, R. (1990). Suicide in the middle school: Who said kids will not? *Elementary School Guidance and Counseling, 25*, 129–137.

Herring, R. (1998). *Career counseling in schools: Multicultural and developmental perspectives.* ERIC Document Reproduction Service No. ED431994. Alexandria, VA: American Counseling Association.

Herschell, A. D., Calzada, E. J., Eyberg, S. M., & McNeil, C. B. (2002). Parent–Child Interaction Therapy: New directions in research. *Cognitive and Behavioral Practice, 9*, 9–20.

Hershberger, S., & D'Augelli, A. (1995). The impact of victimization on the mental health and suicidality of lesbian, gay, and bisexual youths. *Developmental Psychology, 31*, 65–74.

Herzog, D. B., Dorer, D. J., Keel, P. K., Selwyn, S. E., Ekeblad, E. R., Flores, A. T., Greenwood, S. N., Burwell, R. A., & Keller, M. B. (1999). Recovery and relapse in anorexia and bulimia nervosa: A 7.5-year follow-up study. *Journal of the American Academy of Child and Adolescent Psychiatry, 38*, 829–837.

Herzog, D. B., Greenwood, D. N., Dorer, D. J., Flores, A. T., Ekebald, E. R., & Richards, A. (2000). Mortality in eating disorders: A descriptive study. *International Journal of Eating Disorders, 28*, 20–26.

Hess, R. D. (1981). Approaches to the measurement and interpretation of parent–child interaction. In R. W. Henderson (Ed.), *Parent–child interaction.* New York: Academic Press.

Hetherington, E. M. (1967). The effects of familial variables on sex typing, on parent–child similarity, and on imitation in children. In J. P. Hill (Ed.), *Minnesota Symposium on Child Psychology* (Vol. 1, pp. 82–107). Minneapolis: University of Minnesota Press.

Hetherington, E. M., Cox, M., & Cox, R. (1979). Play and social interaction in children following divorce. *Journal of Social Issues, 35*, 26–49.

Heward, W. L. (2006). *Exceptional children: An introduction to special education* (8th ed.). Upper Saddle River, NJ: Pearson Education.

Hiatt-Michael, D. (Ed.). (2001). Promising practices for family involvement in schools: A volume in family–school–community partnership. Greenwich, CT: Information Age.

Higgins, P. S. (1976). *The desegregation counselor aid program of the 1974–75 Minneapolis Emergency School Aid Act Project.* Minneapolis: Minneapolis Public Schools.

Hill, J. P. (1988). Adapting to menarche: Familial control and conflict. In M. R. Gunnar & W. A. Collins (Eds.), *Minnesota Symposium on Child Psychology,* Vol. 21: *Development during the transition to adolescence,* pp. 43–77). Hillsdale, NJ: Erlbaum.

Hill, N. E., & Taylor, L. C. (2004). Parent school involvement and children's academic achievement: Pragmatics and issues. *Current Directions in Psychological Science, 13*, 161–164.

Hill, N. E., Tyson, D. F., & Bromell, I. (2009). Parental involvement in middle school: Developmentally appropriate strategies across SES and ethnicity. In N. E. Hill & R. K. Chao (Eds.), *Families, schools, and the adolescent: Connecting research, policy, and practice* (pp. 53–72). New York: Teachers College Press.

Hinderman, R. A. (1930). Evaluating and improving guidance services. *Nation's Schools, 5*, 47–52.

Hinshaw, S. P., & Erhardt, D. (1991). Attention-deficit hyperactivity disorder. In P. Kendall (Ed.), *Child and adolescent therapy: Cognitive-behavioral procedures* (pp. 98–128). New York: Guilford Press.

Hinshaw, S. P., & Lee, S. S. (2003). Conduct and oppositional defiant disorders. In E. J. Mash & R. A. Barkley (Eds.), *Child psychopathology* (2nd ed., pp. 144–198). New York: Guilford Press.

Hoagwood, K. E., Radigan, M., Rodriguez, J., Levitt, J. M., Fernandez, D., & Foster, J., (2006). Final report on the Child and Adolescent Trauma Treatment Consortium (CATS) Project for the Substance Abuse and Mental Health Services Administration. Washington, DC: U.S. Department of Health and Human Services.

Hobbs, B. B., & Collison, B. B. (1995). School–community collaboration: Implications for the school counselor. *School Counselor, 43*(3), 58–65.

Hobson, S. M., & Kanitz, H. M. (1996). Multicultural counseling: An ethical issue for school counselors. *School Counselor, 43*(4), 45–55.

Hoffman, L., Sable, J., Naum, J., & Gray, D. (2005). *Public elementary and secondary students, staff, schools, and school districts: School year 2002–2003*. Washington, DC: U.S. Department of Education.

Hoffner, C., & Badzinski, D. M. (1989). Children's integration of facial and situational cues to emotion. *Child Development, 60*, 411–422.

Hohenshil, T. H. (1993). Teaching the *DSM-III-R* in counselor education. *Counselor Education and Supervision, 32*, 267–275.

Holaday, M., & Smith, A. (1995). Coping skills training: Evaluating a training model. *Journal of Mental Health Counseling, 17*(3), 360–367.

Holcomb-McCoy, C. (2004). Assessing the multicultural competencies of school counselors: A checklist. *Professional School Counseling, 7*(3), 178.

Holcomb-McCoy, C. (2007). School counseling to close the achievement gap: A social justice framework for success. Thousand Oaks, CA: Corwin Press.

Holland, A., & Andre, T. (1987). Participation in extracurricular activities in secondary school: What is known, what needs to be known? *Review of Educational Research, 57*, 437–466.

Holloway, J. H. (2002). Research link/extracurricular activities and student motivation. *Educational Leadership, 60*(1). Retrieved from http://www.ascd.org/readingroom/edlead/0209/holloway.html.

Holmes, D. R., Dalton, H. F., Erdmann, D. G., Hayden, T. C., & Roberts, A. O. (1986). *Frontiers of possibility: Report of the National College Counseling Project, National Association of College Admissions Counselors.* Burlington: Instructional Development Center, University of Vermont.

Holmes, S. A., & Morin, R. (2006, June 3). Black men torn between promise and doubt. *MSNBC.com.* Retrieved from http://www.msnbc.msn.com/id/print/1/displaymode/1098.

Holt, J. (1967). *How children fail.* New York: New American Library.

Hong, E., Whiston, S. C., & Milgram, R. M. (1993). Leisure activities in career guidance for gifted and talented adolescents: A validation of the Tel-Aviv Activities Inventory. *Gifted Child Quarterly, 37*, 65–68.

Horn, L., & Kojaku, L. K. (2001). *High school academic curriculum and the persistence path through college: Persistence and transfer behavior of undergraduates 3 years after entering 4-year institutions.* NCES 2001163. Washington, DC: National Center for Education Statistics. Retrieved from http://nces.ed.gov/pubs2001/2001163.pdf.

House, R. M., & Hayes, R. L. (2002). School counselors becoming key players in school reform. *Professional School Counseling, 5*, 249–256.

House, R. M., & Martin, P. J. (1998). Advocating for better futures for all students: A new vision for school counselors. *Education, 119*, 284–291.

Howard, G. R. (2006). *We can't teach what we don't know: White teachers, multiracial schools.* New York: Teachers College Press.

Howard, J. (1995). You can't get there from here: The need for a new logic in education reform [Electronic version]. *Daedelus, 124*(4), 85–92.

Hoyert, D. L., Kochanek, K. D., & Murphy, S. L. (1999). Deaths: Final data for 1997. *National Vital Statistics Reports, 47*(9), 2–4.

Hser, Y. I., Grella, C. E., Hubbard, R. L., Hsieh, S. C., Fletcher, B. W., & Brown, B. S. (2001). An evaluaton of drug treatment for adolescents in four U.S. cities. *Archives of General Psychiatry, 58*(7), 689–695.

Hsieh, S., & Hollister, C. D. (2004). Examining gender differences in adolescent substance abuse behavior: Comparison and implications for treatment. *Journal of Child and Adolescent Substance Abuse, 13*, 53–70.

Huang, G., Reiser, M., Parker, A., Muniec, J., & Salvucci, S. (2003). *Institute of Education Sciences findings from interviews with education policymakers.* Arlington, VA: Synectics. Retrieved from http://www.ed.gov/rschstat/research/pubs/findingsreport.pdf.

Huey, W. (1983). Reducing adolescent aggression through group assertiveness training. *School Counselor, 30*(3), 193–203.

Huff, C. R. (1999). Source, recency, and degree of stress in adolescence and suicide ideation. *Adolescence, 34*(133), 81–89.

Hughes, K. L., & Karp, M. H. (2004). School-based career development: A synthesis of the literature. New York: Columbia University, Institute on Education and the Economy.

Hughes, J. N., & Hasbrouck, J. E. (1996). Television violence: Implications for violence prevention. *School Psychology Review, 25*, 134–142.

Hughey, K. F., Lapan, R. T., & Gysbers, N. C. (1993). Evaluating a high school guidance-language arts career unit: A qualitative approach. *School Counselor, 41*, 96–101.

Human Rights Campaign Foundation. (2004). National Coming Out Project. *Resource guide to coming out for gay, lesbian, bisexual and transgendered Americans.* Washington, DC: Author.

Human Rights Watch. (2001). *Hatred in the hallways: Violence and discrimination against lesbian, gay, bisexual, and transgender students in U.S. schools.* New York: Author. Retrieved from http://www.hrw.org/reports/2001/uslgbt/Final-02.htm#P341_27673.

Hunter, F. T. (1985). Adolescents' perception of discussions with parents and friends. *Developmental Psychology, 21*, 433–440.

Hunter, F. T., & Youniss, J. (1982). Changes in functions of three relations during adolescence. *Developmental Psychology, 18*, 806–811.

Hurtado, S., Carter, D. F., & Spuler, A. (1996). Latino student transition to college: Assessing difficulties and factors in successful college adjustment. *Research in Higher Education 37*, 135–157.

Hutchins, D. E., & Cole, C. G. (1986). *Helping relationships and strategies*, Monterey, CA: Brooks/Cole.

Hutson, P. W. (1935). Testing the guidance program. *Nation's Schools, 15*, 21–23.

Ialongo, N., Poduska, J., Werthamer, L., & Kellam, S. (2001). The distal impact of two first-grade preventive interventions on conduct problems and disorder in early adolescence. *Journal of Emotional and Behavioral Disorders 9*, 146–160.

Individuals with Disabilities Education Improvement Act of 2004 (Pub. L. No. 108-446), 20 U.S.C. §1400 et seq. Available at http://idea.ed.gov/download/statute.html.

Inhelder, B., & Piaget, J. (1958). *The growth of logical thinking from childhood to adolescence.* New York: Basic Books.

Institute of Medicine. (2001). Committee on Quality of Health Care in America. *Crossing the quality chasm: A new health system for the 21st century.* Washington, DC: National Academies Press.

Isaacs, M. L. (2003). Data-driven decision-making: The engine of accountability. *Professional School Counseling, 6*, 288–295.

Isaacs, M. L., & Duffus, L. R. (1995). Scholars' Club: A culture of achievement among minority students. *School Counselor, 42*, 204–210.

Isaacs, M. L., & Stone, C. (1999). School counselors and confidentiality: Factors affecting professional choices. *Professional School Counseling, 2*, 258–266.

Isaacs, M. L., & Stone, C. (2001). Confidentiality with minors: How mental health counselors manage dangerous behaviors. *Journal of Mental Health Counseling, 23*, 342–356.

Ishitani, T. T. (2006). Studying attrition and degree completion behavior among first generation college students in the United States. *The Journal of Higher Education 77*, 861–885.

Izzo, R. L., & Ross, R. R. (1990). Meta-analysis of rehabilitation programs for juvenile delinquents. *Criminal Justice and Behavior, 17*, 134–142.

Jackson, M. L. (1995). Counseling youth of Arab ancestry. In C. C. Lee (Ed.), *Counseling for diversity: A guide for school counselors and related professionals* (pp. 41–60). Boston: Allyn & Bacon.

Jackson, S. A., & White. J. (2000). Referrals to the school counselor: A qualitative study. *Professional School Counseling, 3*, 277–286.

Jacobs, E. E., Masson, R. L., & Harvill, R. L. (2008). Group counseling: Strategies and skills. Belmont, CA: Thomson Brooks/Cole.

Jacobsen, K. E., & Bauman, S. (2007). Bullying in schools: School counselors' responses to three types of bullying incidents. *Professional School Counseling, 11*, 1–9.

Jainchill, N., Yagelka, J., Hawke, J., & De Leon, C. (1999). Adolescent admissions to residential drug treatment: HIV risk behaviors pre- and post-treatment. *Psychology of Addictive Behaviors, 13*(3), 163–173.

James, M., & Spradling, N. (2001). *From advisory to advocacy: Meeting every student's needs.* Westerville, OH: National Middle School Association.

Jenny, C., Roesler, T., & Poyer, K. (1994). Are children at risk for sexual abuse by homosexuals? *Pediatrics, 94*(1), 41–44.

Jensen, R. W. (1998). *White privilege shapes the U.S.* Austin: University of Texas, Department of Journalism.

Johnson, C. D., & Johnson, S. K. (2001). *Results-based student support programs: Leadership academy workbook.* San Juan Capistrano, CA: Professional Update.

Johnson, C. D., & Johnson, S. K. (2002). *Building stronger school counseling programs: Bringing futuristic approaches into the present.* Greensboro, NC: CAPS.

Johnson, C. D., Johnson, S. K., & Downs, L. (2006). *Building a results-based student support program.* New York: Lahaska Press.

Johnson, C. J., & Kritsonis, W. (2006). A national dilemma: African American students underrepresented in advanced mathematics courses. *Doctoral Forum National Journal for Publishing and Mentoring Doctoral Student Research, 3*(1), 1–160.

Johnson, D. L., & Breckenridge, J. N. (1982). The Houston Parent–Child Development Center and the primary prevention of behavior problems in young children. *American Journal of Community Psychology, 10,* 305–316.

Johnson, D. W. (1990). *Reaching out: Interpersonal effectiveness and self-actualization* (4th ed.). Englewood Cliffs, NJ: Prentice-Hall.

Johnson, D. W., & Johnson, R. T. (1995a). *Teaching students to be peacemakers* (3rd ed.). Edina, MN: Interaction Book.

Johnson, D. W., & Johnson, R. T. (1995b). Teaching students to be peacemakers: Results of five years of research. *Peace and Conflict, 4,* 417–438.

Johnson, D. W., Johnson, R., Dudley, B., Ward, M., & Magnuson, D. (1995). The impact of peer mediation training on the management of school and home conflicts. *American Educational Research Journal, 32,* 829–844.

Johnson Institute. (1996). *The No-Bullying Program: Preventing bully/victim violence at school.* Minneapolis, MN: Author.

Johnson, J. G., Cohen, P., Kasen, S., & Brook, J. S. (2002). Eating disorders during adolescence and the risk for physical and mental disorders during early adulthood. *Archives of General Psychiatry, 59,* 545–552.

Johnson, K. W., Anderson, N. B., Bastida, E., Kramer, B. J., Williams, D., & Wong, M. (1995). Macrosocial and environmental influences on minority health. *Health Psychology, 14,* 601–612.

Johnson, L. S. (1995). Enhancing multicultural relations: Intervention strategies for the school counselor. *School Counselor, 43*(2), 103–113.

Johnson, M. (1984). Blacks in mathematics: A status report. *Journal of Research in Mathematics Education, 15*(2), 145–153.

Johnson, S. K., & Johnson, C. D. (2003). Results-based guidance: A systems approach to student support programs. *Professional School Counseling, 6,* 180–184.

Johnson, S. K., & Whitfield, E. A. (Eds.). (1991). *Evaluating guidance programs: A practitioner's guide.* Iowa City, IA: American College Testing Program and National Consortium of State Career Guidance Supervisors.

Johnson, V. R. (2001). Family centers in schools: Expanding possibilities for partnership. In D. B. Hiatt-Michael (Ed.), *Promising practices for family involvement in schools: A volume in family–school–community partnership* (pp. 85–107). Greenwich, CT: Information Age.

Johnston, L. D., Bachman, J. G., & O'Malley, C. T. (1982). *Student drug use attitudes and beliefs: National trends, 1975–1982.* Washington, DC: Government Printing Office.

Johnston, L. D., O'Malley, P. M., Bachman, J. G., & Schulenberg, J. E. (2005). *Monitoring the Future national survey results on drug use, 1975–2004.* Vol. 1: *Secondary school students.* NIH Publication No. 05-5727. Bethesda, MD: National Institute on Drug Abuse.

Johnston, L. D., O'Malley, P. M., Bachman, J. G., & Schulenberg, J. E. (2006). *Monitoring the Future national survey results on drug use, 1975–2005.* Vol. 1, *Secondary school students.* NIH Publication No. 06-5883. Bethesda, MD: National Institute on Drug Abuse.

Johnston, L. D., O'Malley, P. M., Bachman, J. G., & Schulenberg, J. E. (2009). *Monitoring the Future national results on adolescent drug use: Overview of key findings, 2008* NIH Publication No. 09-7401. Bethesda, MD: National Institute on Drug Abuse. Retrieved from http://monitoringthefuture.org/pubs/monographs/overview2008.pdf.

Johnston, L. D., O'Malley, P. M., Bachman, J. G., & Schulenberg, J. E. (2010). *Monitoring the Future national results on adolescent drug use: Overview of key findings, 2009.* NIH Publication No. 10-7583. Bethesda, MD: National Institute on Drug Abuse.

Jones, A. J. (1951). *Principles of guidance* (4th ed.). New York: McGraw-Hill.

Jones, G. B., Helliwell, C. B., & Ganschow, L. H. (1975). A planning model for career guidance. *Vocational Guidance Quarterly, 23,* 220–226.

Jones, L. V., Burton, N. W., & Davenport, E. C., Jr. (1984). Monitoring the mathematics achievement of black students. *Journal of Research for Mathematics Education, 15*(2), 154–164.

Jones, M. B., & Offord, D. R. (1989). Reduction of anti-social behavior in poor children by nonschool skill development. *Journal of Child Psychology and Psychiatry and Allied Disciplines, 30,* 737–750.

Jones, V. H. (1980). *Adolescents with behavior problems: Strategies for teaching counseling and parenting.* Boston: Allyn & Bacon.

Jordan, J., & McMenamy, J. (2004). Interventions for suicide survivors: A review of the literature. *Suicide and Life Threatening Behavior, 34,* 337–349.

Jordan, K. M., Vaughan, J. S., & Woodworth, K. J. (1997). "I will survive": Lesbian, gay, and bisexual youths' experience of high school. In M. B. Harris (Ed.), *School experiences of gay and lesbian youth* (pp. 17–34). New York: Harrington Park Press.

Josephson Institute of Ethics. (1999). Five steps of principled reasoning. Retrieved from http://josephsoninstitute.org/MED/med5steps.htm.

Juhnke, G. A., & Shoffner, M. F. (1999). The Family Debriefing Model: An adapted critical incident stress debriefing for parents and older sibling suicide survivors. *Family Journal, 7,* 342–348.

Juvonen, J., Le, V., Kaganoff, T., Augustine, C., & Louay, C. (2004). *Focus on the Wonder Years: Challenges facing American middle school.* RAND Education, Rand, CA.

Kaffenberger, C., & Young, A. (2007). *Making data work.* Alexandria, VA: American School Counselors Association.

Kalafat, J. (1990). Adolescent suicide and the implications for school response programs. *School Counselor, 37*(5), 21–27.

Kaminer, Y. (2006). Group counseling for adolescents: Is it harmful or effective? *Counselor, 7*(2), 38–42.

Kamps, D., & Kay, P. (2001). Preventing problems through social skills instruction. In B. Algozzine & P. Kay (Eds.), *Preventing problem behaviors: A handbook of successful prevention strategies* (pp. 57–84). Thousand Oaks, CA: Corwin Press.

Kandel, E. R. (1998). A new intellectual framework for psychiatry. *American Journal of Psychiatry, 155,* 457–469.

Kaplan, S., Pelcovitz, D., Salzinger, S., Mandel, F., & Weiner, M. (1997). Adolescent physical abuse and suicide attempts. *Journal of the American Academy of Child and Adolescent Psychiatry, 36*(6), 799–808.

Karcher, M. (2002). The cycle of violence and disconnection among rural middle school students: Teacher disconnection as a consequence of violence. *Journal of School Violence, 1,* 35–51.

Kaslow, N. J., & Thompson, M. P. (1998). Applying the criteria for empirically supported treatments to studies of psychosocial interventions for child and adolescent depression. *Journal for Clinical Child Psychology, 27,* 146–155.

Kass, J. (2001, November 29). Columbine seeks closure—out of court. *Christian Science Monitor,* p. 2.

Katz, E. R., Rubinstein, C. L., Hubert, N. C., & Blew, A. (1988). School and social reintegration of children with cancer. *Journal of Psychosocial Oncology, 6,* 123–140.

Katz, P. A., & Zalk, S. R. (1978). Modification of children's racial attitudes. *Developmental Psychology, 14,* 447–461.

Kaye, W., Strober, M., Stein, D., & Gendall, K. (1999). New directions in treatment research of anorexia and bulimia nervosa. *Biological Psychiatry, 45,* 1285–1292.

Kazdin, A. E. (1996). Cognitive behavioral approaches. In M. Lewis (Ed.), *Child and adolescent psychiatry: A comprehensive textbook* (2nd ed., pp. 115–126). Baltimore: Williams & Wilkins.

Kazdin, A. E. (1997). Behavior modification. In J. M. Weiner (Ed.), *Textbook of child and adolescent psychiatry* (2nd ed., pp. 821–842). Washington, DC: American Academy of Child and Adolescent Psychiatry.

Keat, D. B., Metzgar, K. L., Raykovitz, D., & McDonald, J. (1985). Multimodal counseling: Motivating children to attend school through friendship groups. *Journal of Humanistic Education and Development, 23,* 166–175.

Keel, P. K., Dorer, D. J., Eddy, K. T., Franko, D., Charatan, D. L., & Herzog, D. B. (2003). Predictors of mortality in eating disorders. *Archives of General Psychiatry, 60,* 179–193.

Keith, P. B., & Lichtman, M. V. (1994). Does parental involvement influence the academic achievement of Mexican-American eighth graders? Results from the National Educational Longitudinal Study. *School Psychology Quarterly, 9,* 256–273.

Keith-Spiegel, P., & Koocher, G. P. (1985). *Ethics in psychology.* New York: Random House.

Kelly, B. T., Thornberry, T. P., & Smith, C. A. (1997, August). In the wake of childhood maltreatment. OJJDP Juvenile Justice Bulletin. Washington, DC: U.S. Department of Justice.

Kelly, J. F., Myers, M. G., & Brown, S. A. (2000). A multivariate process model of adolescent 12-step attendance and substance use outcome following inpatient treatment. *Psychology of Addictive Behaviors, 4,* 376–389.

Kelly, P. (2005). *As America becomes more diverse: The impact of state higher education inequality.* Retrieved from http://www.nchems.org/pubs/detail.php?id=86.

Kemple, J. J., & Snipes, J. C. (2000). *Career academies: Impacts on students' engagement and performance in high school.* New York: Manpower Demonstration Research.

Kendall, P. C. (1994). Treating anxiety disorders in children: Results of a randomized clinical trial. *Journal of Consulting and Clinical Psychology, 62,* 100–110.

Kendall, P. C., Chansky, T. E., Kane, M. T., Kim, R. S., Kortlander, E., Ronan, K. R., Sessa, F. M., & Siqueland, L. (1992). *Anxiety disorders in youth: Cognitive-behavioral interventions,* Needham Heights, MA: Allyn & Bacon.

Kendall, P. C., Hudson, J. L., Gosch, E., Flannery-Schroeder, E., & Suveg, C. (2008). Cognitive-behavioral therapy for anxiety disordered youth: A randomized clinical trial evaluating child and family modalities. *Journal of Consulting and Clinical Psychology, 76,* 282–297.

Kennedy, D. M., Piehl, A. M., & Braga, A. A. (1996). *Youth gun violence in Boston: Gun markets, serious youth offenders, and a use reduction strategy.* Cambridge, MA: Harvard University.

Kern, R. M., & Mullis, F. (1993). An Adlerian consultation model. *Individual Psychology, 49*(2), 242–247.

Kerr, B. A., & Ghrist-Priebe, S. L. (1988). Intervention for multipotentiality: Effects of a career counseling laboratory for gifted high school students. *Journal of Counseling and Development, 66,* 366–369.

Kessler, R. C., Berglund, P., Demler, O., Jin, R., Merikangas, K. R., & Walters, E. E. (2005). Lifetime prevalence and age-of-onset distributions of *DSM–IV* disorders in the National Comorbidity Survey Replication. *Archives of General Psychiatry, 62,* 593–602.

Keys, S., & Bemak, F. (1997). School–family–community linked services: A school counseling role for changing times. *School Counselor, 44*(3), 255–263.

Keys, S., Bemak, F., Carpenter, S., & King-Sears, M. (1998). Collaborative consultant: A new role for counselors serving at-risk youths. *Journal of Counseling and Development, 76,* 123–133.

Keys, S., Bemak, F., & Lockhart, E. S. (1998). Transforming school counseling to serve the mental health needs of at-risk youth. *Journal of Counseling and Development, 76*(4), 16–19.

Kilpatrick, D., Acierno, R., Saunders, B., Resnick, H., Best, C., & Schnurr, P. (2000). Risk factors for adolescent substance abuse and dependence: Data from a national sample. *Journal of Consulting and Clinical Psychology, 68,* 19–30.

Kilpatrick, D. G., Ruggiero, K. J., Acierno, R. E., Saunders, B. E., Resnick, H. S., & Best, C. L. (2003). Violence and risk of PTSD, major depression, substance abuse/dependence, and comorbidity: Results from the National Survey of Adolescents. *Journal of Consulting and Clinical Psychology, 71,* 692–700.

Kim, A., & Yeh, C. J. (2002). *Stereotypes of Asian American Students.* New York: Teachers College Press.

Kim, J. A., Szatmari, P., Bryson, S. E., Streiner, D. L., & Wilson, F. J. (2000). The prevalence of anxiety and mood problems among children with autism and Asperger syndrome. *Autism, 4,* 117–132.

Kim, J. J., Crasco, L. M., Smith, R. B., Johnson, G., Karantonis, A., & Leavitt, D. J. (2001). *Academic excellence for all urban students: Their accomplishments in science and mathematics.* Norwood, MA: Systemic Research. Retrieved from http://www.systemic.com/pdfs/Booklet.pdf.

King, J. (1996). *The decision to go to college: Attitudes and experiences associated with college attendance among low-income students.* Washington, DC: College Board.

King, R. D., Gaines, L. S., Lambert, E. W., Summerfelt, W. T., & Bickman, L. (2000). The co-occurrence of psychiatric substance use diagnosis in adolescents in different service systems: Frequency, recognition, cost, and outcomes. *Journal of Behavioral Health Services and Research, 27*(4), 417–430.

King, N. J., Muris, P., & Ollendick, T. H. (2004). Specific phobia. In T. L. Morris & J. S. March (Eds.), *Anxiety disorders in children and adolescents* (2nd ed., pp. 263–279). New York: Guilford Press.

Kinney, J. M., Haapala, D., & Booth, C. L. (1991). *Keeping families together: The Homebuilders Model.* New York: Aldine de Gruyter.

Kirby, D. (2007). *Emerging answers, 2007: Research findings on programs to reduce teen pregnancy and sexually transmitted diseases.* Washington, DC: National Campaign to Prevent Teen Pregnancy.

Kirby, D., Lepore, G., & Ryan, J. (2005). Factors affecting teen sexual behavior, pregnancy, childbearing and sexually transmitted disease: Which are important? Which can you change? Washington, DC: National Campaign to Prevent Teen Pregnancy.

Kirby, D., Lezin, N., Afriye, R. A., & Gallucci, G. (2003). *Preventing teen pregnancy: Youth development and after-school programs.* Scotts Valley, CA: ETR.

Kirst, M. W. (1991). Improving children's services: Overcoming barriers, creating new opportunities. *Phi Delta Kappan, 72,* 615–618.

Kirst, M. W. (2001). *Overcoming the high school senior slump: New education policies.* Washington, DC: Institute for Educational Leadership and National Center for Public Policy and Higher Education.

Kiselica, M. S., & Robinson, M. (2001). Bringing advocacy counseling to life: The history, issues, and human dramas of social justice working in counseling. *Journal of Counseling and Development, 79*(4), 387–397.

Kiselica, M. S., Stroud, J., Stroud, J., & Rotzien, A. (1992). Counseling the forgotten client: The teen father. *Journal of Mental Health Counseling, 14*(3), 271–277.

Kitmitto, S., & Bandeira de Mello, V. (2008). *Measuring the status and change of NAEP state inclusion rates for students with disabilities.* NCES 2009-453. Washington, DC: National Center for Education Statistics, Institute of Education Sciences, U.S. Department of Education.

Klein, D. N., Lewinsohn, P. M., & Seeley, J. R. (1997). Psychosocial characteristics of adolescents with a past history of dysthymic disorder: Comparison with adolescents with past histories of major depressive and non-affective disorders, and never mentally ill controls. *Journal of Affective Disorders, 42,* 127–135.

Klein, J. A., Wiley, H. I., & Thurlow, M. L. (2006). *Uneven transparency: NCLB tests take precedence in public assessment reporting for students with disabilities.* Technical Report 43. Minneapolis: University of Minnesota, National Center on Educational Outcomes. Retrieved from http://education.umn.edu/nceo/OnlinePubs/Technical43.html.

Klern, A. M., & Connell, J. P. (2004). Relationships matter: Linking teacher support to student engagement and achievement. *Journal of School Health, 74*, 262–273.

Klingman, A. (1990). Action research notes on developing school staff suicide-awareness training. *School Psychology International, 11*(2), 133–142.

Klint, K. A., & Weiss, M. R. (1987). Perceived competence and motives for participating in youth sports: A test of Harter's competence motivation theory. *Journal of Sport Psychology, 9*, 55–65.

Knapp, L. G., Kelly-Reid, J. E., & Ginder, S. A. (2009). *Enrollment in postsecondary institutions, Fall 2007; graduation rates, 2001 and 2004 cohorts; and financial statistics, fiscal year 2007.* NCES 2009-155. Washington, DC: National Center for Educational Statistics, Institute of Education Sciences, U.S. Department of Education. Retrieved from http://nces.ed.gov/pubs 2009/2009155.pdf.

Knapp, M. S., Shields, P. M., & Turnbull, B. J. (1995). Academic challenge in high-poverty classrooms. *Phi Delta Kappan, 76*(10), 770–776.

Knoff, H. (1986). *The assessment of child and adolescent personality,* New York: Guilford.

Knoff, H. M. (2004). Inside Project Achieve: A comprehensive, research-proven whole school improvement process focused on student academic and behavioral outcomes. In K. Robinson (Ed.), *Advances in school-based mental health: Best practices and program models.* Kingston, NJ: Civic Research Institute.

Kohlberg, L. (1976). Moral stages and moralization: The cognitive-developmental approach. In T. Lickona (Ed.), *Moral development and behavior.* New York: Holt, Rinehart & Winston.

Kokotailo, P. (1995). Physical health problems associated with adolescent substance abuse. In E. Rahdert & D. Czechowicz (Eds.), *Adolescent drug abuse: Clinical assessment and therapeutic interventions* (pp. 112–129). Rockville, MD: National Institute on Drug Abuse.

Kolko, D. J. (1996a). Clinical monitoring of treatment course in child physical abuse: Child and parent reports. *Child Abuse & Neglect, 20*, 23–43.

Kolko, D. J. (1996b). Individual cognitive behavioral therapy and family therapy for physically abused children and their offending parents: A comparison of clinical outcomes. *Child Maltreatment, 1*, 322–342.

Kolko, D. J., & Swenson, C. C. (2002). *Assessing and treating physically abused children and their families: A cognitive-behavioral approach.* Thousands Oaks, CA: Sage.

Kolvin, I., Barrett, M. L., Bhate, S. R., Berney, T. P., Famuyiwa, O. O., Fundudis, T., & Tyler, S. (1991). The Newcastle child depression project: Diagnosis and classification of depression. *British Journal of Psychiatry Supplement, 11*, 9–21.

Kosciw, J. G. (2004). *The 2003 National School Climate Survey: The school-related experiences of our nation's lesbian, gay. bisexual and transgender youth.* New York: GLSEN.

Kosciw, J. G., & Diaz, E. M. (2006). The 2005 National School Climate Survey. Retrieved from http://www.glsen. org.

Koss, M. P., & Shiang, J. (1994). Research on brief psychotherapy. In S. L. Garfield & A. E. Bergin (Eds.), *Handbook of psychotherapy and behavior change* (4th ed., pp. 627–700). New York: Wiley.

Koss-Chioino, J. D., & Vargas, L. A. (1999). *Working with Latino youth: Culture, development, and context.* San Francisco: Jossey-Bass.

Kotter, J. P. (1995). *The new rules: How to succeed in today's post-corporate world.* New York: Free Press.

Kottler, J. (1983). *Pragmatic group leadership.* Monterey, CA: Brooks/Cole.

Kovacs, M., Akiskal, H. S., Gatsonis, C., & Parrone, P. L. (1994). Childhood-onset dysthymic disorder. Clinical features and prospective naturalistic outcome. *Archives of General Psychiatry, 51*, 365–374.

Kovacs, M., Devlin, B., Pollock, M., Richards, C., & Mukerji P. A. (1997). Controlled family history study of childhood-onset depressive disorder. *Archives of General Psychiatry. 54*, 613–623.

Kovacs, M., Obrosky, D. S., Gastonis, C., & Richards, C. (1997). First episode major depression and dysthymic disorder in childhood: Clinical and sociodemographic factors in recovery. *Journal of the American Academy of Child and Adolescent Psychiatry, 36*, 777–784.

Kress, V. E., Gibson, D., & Reynolds, C. (2004). Adolescents who self-injure: Implications and strategies for school counselors. *Professional School Counseling, 7*, 195–201.

Kretzmann, J., & McKnight, J. (1993). *Building communities from the inside out: A path toward finding and mobilizing a community's assets.* Chicago: ACTA.

Krumboltz, J. D., & Thoresen, D. F. (1964). The effects of behavior counseling in groups and individual settings on information-seeking behavior. *Journal of Counseling Psychology, 11*, 324–332.

Kuhn, D., Amsel, E., & O'Loughlin, M. (1988). *The development of scientific thinking skills.* New York: Academic Press.

Kush, K., & Cochran, L. (1993). Enhancing a sense of agency through career planning. *Journal of Counseling Psychology, 40*, 434–439.

LaFayette, J. M., & Stern, T. A. (2004). The impact of a patient's suicide on psychiatric trainees: A case study and review of the literature. *Harvard Review of Psychiatry, 12*, 49–55.

LaFontaine, L. (1994). Quality school and gay and lesbian youth: Lifting the cloak of silence. *Journal of Reality Therapy, 14*(1), 26–28.

LaFromboise, T. D. (2006). American Indian youth suicide prevention. *Prevention Researcher, 13,* 16–18.

Laird, J., Cataldi, E. F., KewalRamani, A., & Chapman, C. (2008). *Dropout and completion rates in the United States, 2006.* NCES 2008-053. Washington, DC: National Center for Education Statistics, Institute of Education Sciences, U.S. Department of Education. Retrieved from http://nces.ed.gov/pubsearch/pubsinfo.asp?pubid=2008053.

Lambie, G. W. (2005). Child abuse and neglect: A practical guide for professional school counselors. *Professional School Counseling, 8*(3), 249–258.

Land, D., & Legters, N. (2001). The extent and consequences of risk in U. S. education. In *Educating at-risk students: 101st yearbook of the National Society for the Study of Education* (Part 2). Chicago: University of Chicago Press.

Langley, A. K., Bergman, R. L., McCracken, J., & Piacentini, J. C. (2004). Impairment in childhood anxiety disorders: Preliminary examination of the Child Anxiety Impact Scale—Parent Version. *Journal of Child and Adolescent Psychopharmacology, 14*(1), 105–114.

Lapan, R. T. (2001). Results-based comprehensive guidance and counseling programs: A framework for planning and evaluation. *Professional School Counseling, 4,* 289–299.

Lapan, R. T. (2005). Evaluating school counseling programs. In C. A. Sink (Ed.), *Contemporary school counseling: Theory, research, and practice* (pp. 257–295). Boston: Houghton Mifflin.

Lapan, R. T., Gysbers, N., Hughey, K., & Ami, T. J. (1993). Evaluating a guidance and language arts unit for high school juniors. *Journal of Counseling and Development, 71,* 444–451.

Lapan, R. T., Gysbers, N. C., & Kayson, K. (2007). How implementing comprehensive guidance programs improves academic achievement for all Missouri students. Jefferson City: Missouri Department of Elementary and Secondary Education, Division of Career Education.

Lapan, R. T., Gysbers, N. C., & Petroski, G. F. (2001). Helping seventh graders be safe and successful: A state-wide study of the impact of comprehensive guidance and counseling programs. *Journal of Counseling and Development, 79,* 320–330. Reprinted in *Professional School Counseling, 6*(3), 186–197.

Lapan, R. T., Gysbers, N. C., & Sun, Y. (1997). The impact of more fully implemented guidance programs on the school experiences of high school students: A statewide evaluation study. *Journal of Counseling and Development, 75,* 292–302.

Lapan, R. T., Kardash, C. M., & Turner, S. (2002). Empowering students to be self-regulated learners. *Professional School Counseling, 5,* 257–265.

Lapan, R. T., Osana, H. P., Tucker, B., & Kosciulek, J. F. (2002). Challenges for creating community career partnerships: Perspectives from practitioners. *Career Development Quarterly, 51,* 172–190.

Laport, R., & Noth, R. (1976). Roles of performance goals in prose learning. *Journal of Educational Psychology, 3,* 260–264.

Larson, R., & Lampman-Petraitis, C. (1989). Daily emotional states as reported by children and adolescents. *Child Development, 60,* 1250–1260.

Laub, J. H., & Lauritsen, J. L. (1998). The interdependence of school violence with neighborhood and family conditions. In D. S. Elliott, B. A. Hamburg, & K. R. Williams (Eds.), *Violence in American schools* (pp. 127–155). New York: Cambridge University Press.

Lavigne, J., Arend, I., Rosenbaum, D., Binns, H., Christoffel, K., Burn, A., & Smith, A. (1998). Mental health service use among young children receiving pediatric primary care. *Journal of the American Academy of Child and Adolescent Psychiatry, 37,* 1175–1183.

Lavoritano, J., & Segal, P. B. (1992). Evaluating the efficacy of a school counseling program. *Psychology in the Schools, 29,* 6–70.

Lawrence, G., & Kurpius, S. E. (2000). Legal and ethical issues involved when counseling minors in nonschool settings. *Journal of Counseling and Development, 78,* 130–136.

Laye-Gindhu, A., & Schonert-Reichl, K. (2005). Non-suicidal self-harm among community adolescents: Understanding the "whats" and "whys" of self-harm. *Journal of Youth and Adolescents, 34,* 447–457.

Lazarus, A. A. (1978). What is multimodal therapy? A brief overview. *Elementary School Guidance and Counseling, 17*(3), 24–29.

Lazarus, A. A. (1981). *The practice of multimodal therapy.* New York: McGraw-Hill.

Le, C. N. (2006). *Population statistics and demographics.* From Asian-Nation: The Landscape of Asian America. Retrieved from http://www.asiannation.org/population.shtml.

Leaf, P. J., Schultz, D., Kiser, L. J., & Pruitt, D. B. (2003) School mental health in systems of care. In M. D. Weist, S. W. Evans, & N. A. Lever (Eds.), *Handbook of school mental health programs: Advancing practice and research* (pp. 239–256). New York: Kluwer Academic.

Lerner, R. M. (1995). *America's youth in crisis: Challenges and options for programs and policies.* Thousand Oaks, CA: Sage.

Lee, C. C. (1995). *Counseling for diversity: A guide for school counselors and related professionals.* Alexandria, VA: American Counseling Association.

Lee, C. C. (2001). Culturally responsive school counselors and programs: Addressing the needs of all students. *Professional School Counseling, 4,* 257–261.

Lee, C. C., & Workman, D. J. (1992). School counselors and research: Current status and future direction. *School Counselor, 40,* 15–19.

Lee, R. S. (1993). Effects of classroom guidance on student achievement. *Elementary School Guidance and Counseling, 27,* 163–171.

Lee, S. (2005). *Up against whiteness: Race, school and immigrant youth.* New York: Teachers College Press.

Lee, V. E., & Bryk, A. S. (1988). Curriculum tracking as mediating the social organization of high school achievement. *Sociology of Education, 61,* 78–94.

Lee, V. E., & Burkham, D. T. (2003). Dropping out of high school: The role of school organization and structure. *American Educational Research Journal, 40,* 353–393.

Lee, V. E., & Ekstrom, R. B. (1987, Summer). Student access to guidance counseling in high school. *American Educational Research Journal 24,* 287–309.

Lehman, C. (2005). *Strong at the heart: How it feels to heal from sexual abuse.* New York: Farrar, Straus & Giroux.

Lehr, C. A., Johnson, D. R., Bremer, C. D., Cosio, A., & Thompson, M. (2004) *Essential tools: Increasing rates of school completion: Moving from policy and research to practice.* Minneapolis, MN: Institute on Community Integration, National Center on Secondary Education.

Lemke, J. M. et al. (Summer 1995). New directions for corporate careers. *Career Planning and Adult Development Journal, 11*(2), 3–27.

Leone, P. E., & Cutting, C. A. (2004). Appropriate education, juvenile corrections, and No Child Left Behind. *Behavioral Disorders, 29,* 260–265.

Leong, F. T. L., & Brown, M. T. (1995). Theoretical issues in cross-cultural career development: Cultural validity and cultural specificity. In W. B. Walsh & S. H. Osipow (Eds.), *Handbook of vocational psychology: Theory, research, and practice* (2nd ed., pp. 143–180). Mahwah, NJ: Erlbaum.

Levin, D. L., & Carlsson-Paige, N. (1995). The mighty morphin power rangers: Teachers voice concern. *Young Children, 50,* 67–72.

Levy, E. (1992). Strengthening the coping resources of lesbian families. *Families in Society, 73,* 23–31.

Levy, T. M., & Orlans, M. (1999). Kids who kill: Attachment disorder, antisocial personality, and violence. *Forensic Examiner, 8*(3/4), 10–15.

Lewinsohn, P. M., Clark, G. N., Rohde, P., Hops, H., & Seeley, J. (1996). A course in coping: A cognitive behavioral approach to the treatment of adolescent depression. In D. Hibbs & P. S. Jensen (Eds.), *Psychosocial treatments for child and adolescent disorders: Empirically based strategies for clinical practice* (pp. 109–135). Washington, DC: American Psychological Association.

Lewinsohn, P. M., & Essau, C. A. (2002). Depression in adolescents. In I. H. Gotlib & C. L. Hammen (Eds.), *Handbook of depression* (pp. 541–559). New York: Guilford Press.

Lewinsohn, P. M., Hops, H., Roberts, R. E., Seeley, J. R., & Andrews, J. A. (1993). Adolescent psychopathology: Prevalence and incidence of depression and other *DSM II-R* disorders in high school students. *Journal of Abnormal Psychology, 102,* 133–144.

Lewinsohn, P. M., Rohde, P., Seeley, J., & Baldwin, C. (2001). Gender differences in suicide attempts from adolescence to young adulthood. *Journal of the American Academy of Child and Adolescent Psychiatry, 40,* 427–434.

Lewis, A., & Palk, S. (2001). *Add it up: Using research to improve education for low-income and minority students.* Washington, DC: Poverty and Race Research Action Council. Retrieved from http://www.prrac.org/additup.pdf.

Lewis, A. C., & Hayes, S. (1991). Multiculturalism and the school counseling curriculum. *Journal of Counseling and Development, 70,* 119–125.

Lewis, A. C., & Henderson, A. T. (1998). *Urgent message: Families crucial to school reform.* Washington, D.C.: Center for Law and Education.

Lewis, J. A., & Arnold, M. S. (1998). From multiculturalism to social action. In C. Lee & G. R. Waltz (Eds.), *Social action: A mandate for counselors* (pp. 263–278). Alexandria, VA: American Counseling Association.

Lewis, J. A., & Schaffner, M. (1970). Draft counseling in the secondary school. *School Counselor, 18,* 89–90.

Lewis, J. D. (1983). Guidance program evaluation: How to do it. *School Counselor, 31,* 111–119.

Lewis, J. P., & Boyle, R. (1976). *Evaluation of the 1975–76 vocational and basic educational programs in the eight Pennsylvania state correctional institutes.* Harrisburg: Pennsylvania Department of Education.

Lewis, M., & Lewis, J. (1970). Relevant training for relevant roles: A model for educating inner-city counselors. *Counselor Education & Supervision, 10,* 31–38.

Leyendecker, B., & Lamb, M. E. (1999). Latino families. In M. E. Lamb (Ed.), *Parenting and child development in "nontraditional" families* (pp. 247–262). Mahwah, NJ: Erlbaum.

Libbey, H. P. (2004). Measuring student relationships to school: Attachment, bonding, connectedness, and engagement. *Journal of School Health, 74*, 274–283.

Lim, J. (2003, February 7). Guidance on constitutionally protected prayer in public elementary and secondary schools. Washington, DC: U.S. Department of Education, Office of Elementary and Secondary Education.

Linehan, M. M., Heard, H. L., & Armstrong, H. E. (1993). Naturalistic follow-up of a behavioral treatment for chronically parasuicidal borderline patients. *Archives of General Psychiatry, 50*, 971–974.

Linn, M. C., Clement, C., Pulos, S., & Sullivan, P. (1989). Scientific reasoning during adolescence: The influence of instruction in science knowledge and reasoning strategies. *Journal of Research in Science Teaching, 26*, 171–187.

Lipman, P. (1998). *Race, class and power in school restructuring.* New York: State University of New York Press.

Lipovsky, J., Swenson, C. C., Ralston, M. E., & Saunders, B. E. (1998). The abuse clarification process in the treatment of intra-familial child abuse. *Child Abuse & Neglect, 22*, 729–741.

Little, A. W., & Allen, J. (1989). Student-led parent–teacher conferences. *Elementary School Guidance and Counseling, 23*, 210–218.

Littrell, J. M., Malia, J. A., & Vanderwood, M. (1995). Single-session brief counseling in high school. *Journal of Counseling and Development, 73*, 451–458.

Lochman, J. E. (1992). Cognitive-behavior intervention with aggressive boys: Three-year follow-up and prevention effects. *Journal of Consulting and Clinical Psychology, 60*, 426–432.

Lock, D. (1995). Counseling interventions with African American youth. In C. C. Lee (Ed.), *Counseling for diversity: A guide for school counselors and related professionals* (pp. 61–80). Boston: Allyn & Bacon.

Locke, D. (1990). Fostering the self-esteem of African-American children. In E. R. Gerler, J. C. Ciechalski, & L. D. Parker (Eds.), *Elementary school counseling in a changing world* (pp. 12–18). Alexandria, VA: American School Counselor Association.

Lockwood, A. T., & Secada, W. G. (1999). *Transforming education for Hispanic youth: Exemplary practices, programs, and schools.* Washington DC: George Washington University, National Clearinghouse for Bilingual Education, Center for the Study of Language and Education.

Loeber, R., & Stouthamer-Loeber, M. (1986). Family factors as correlates and predictors of juvenile conduct problems and delinquency. In M. Tonry & N. Morris (Eds.), *Crime and justice* (Vol. 7). Chicago: University of Chicago.

Logan, D. C., & Kritzell, B. (1997). *Reinventing your career: Following the five new paths to career fulfillment.* New York: McGraw-Hill.

Lombana, J. H. (1985). Guidance accountability: A new look at an old problem. *School Counselor, 32*(5), 340–346.

Lösel, F., & Beelmann, A. (2003). Effects of child skills training in preventing antisocial behavior: A systematic review of randomized evaluations. *Annals of the American Academy of Political and Social Science, 587*, 84–109.

Losen, D. J., & Orfield, G. (Eds). (2002). *Racial inequity in special education.* Cambridge, MA: Civil Rights Project at Harvard University and Harvard Education Press.

Love, N. (2004). Bridging the data gap. (Online presentation). Retrieved from http://hub.mspnet.org/index.cfm/oe_bdg.

Luthar, S. S. (1991). Vulnerability and resilience: A study of high-risk adolescents. *Child Development, 62*, 600–616.

Luthar, S. S., & Zigler, E. (1991). Vulnerability and competence: A review of research on resilience in childhood. *American Journal of Orthopsychiatry, 61*, 6–22.

Maag, J. W., & Katsiyannis, A. (1996). Counseling as a related service for students with emotional and behavioral disorders: Issues and recommendations. *Behavioral Disorders, 221*, 293–305.

Maag, J. W., Rutherford, R. B., Jr., & Parks, B. T. (1988). Secondary school professionals' ability to identify depression in adolescents. *Adolescence, 23*, 73–82.

Maccoby, E. E. (1988). Gender as a social category. *Developmental Psychology, 24*, 755–765.

Maccoby, E. E., & Jacklin, C. N. (1987). Gender segregation in childhood. In E. H. Reese (Ed.), *Advances in child development and behavior* (Vol. 20, pp. 239–287). New York: Academic Press.

Maccoby, E. E., & Martin, J. A. (1983). Socialization in the context of the family: Parent–child interaction. In P. E. Mussen (Ed.), *Handbook of child psychology* (4th ed., Vol. 4, pp. 38–42). New York: Wiley.

Mace-Matluck, B., Alexander-Kasparik, R., & Queen, R. (1998). *Through the golden door: Educational approaches for immigrant adolescents with limited schooling.* Washington, DC: Center for Applied Linguistics.

MacLaury, S. (2002). *Student advisories in grades 5–12: A facilitator's guide.* Norwood, MA: Christopher-Gordon.

Mahoney, H. J. (1950). 10 years of evaluating guidance services. *Occupations, 29*, 194–197.

Maisto, S. A., Pollock, N. K., Lynch, K. G., Martin, C. S., & Ammerman, R. (2001). Course of function in adolescents 1 year after alcohol and other drug treatment. *Psychology of Addictive Behaviors, 15*, 68–76.

Malinosky-Rummell, R., & Hansen, D. J. (1993). Long-term consequences of childhood physical abuse. *Psychological Bulletin, 114*(1), 68–79.

Malloy, P., & Killoran, J. (2007). Children who are deaf blind: Practice perspectives: Highlighting information on deaf-blindness. Monmouth, OR: National Consortium on Deaf-Blindness (NCDB), 2, 1–4. Teaching Research Institute, Western Oregon University. Retrieved from http://nationaldb.org/documents/products/population.pdf.

Mamchak, P., & Mamchak, S. (1980). *101 pupil/parent/teacher situations and how to handle them.* West Nyack, NY: Parker.

Mandell, D. S., Novak, M. M., & Zubritsky, C. D. (2005). Factors associated with age of diagnosis among children with autism spectrum disorders. *Pediatrics, 11,* 1480–1486.

Maples, M. F. (1992). Teachers need self-esteem too: A counseling workshop for elementary school teachers. *Elementary School Guidance and Counseling, 27*(1), 33–38.

March, J. S., Franklin, M. E., Leonard, H., Garcia, A., Moore, P., Freeman, J., & Foa, E. (2007). Tics moderate treatment outcome with sertraline but not cognitive-behavior therapy in pediatric obsessive-compulsive disorder. *Biological Psychiatry, 61,* 344–347.

Marino, T., Sams, W., & Guerra, P. (1999). ACA wins introduction of 100,000 new counselors and other counselor-friendly legislation in U.S. Senate. Alexandria, VA: American Counseling Association. Retrieved from http://www.counseling.org/enews/volume_2/0210.htm.

Marotta, S. A., & Garcia, J. G. (2003). Latinos in the United States in 2000. *Hispanic Journal of Behavioral Science, 15,* 13–34.

Marshall, M. (1998). Rethinking our thinking on discipline ourpower—rather than overpower. Education Week, XVII, No. 37. pp. 32, 36.

Martin, C. L. (1989). Children's use of gender-related information in making social judgements. *Developmental Psychology, 25,* 80–88.

Martin, D., & Stone, G. L. (1977). Psychological education: A skill oriented approach. *Journal of Counseling Psychology, 24,* 153–157.

Martin, E. W., Martin, R., & Terman, D. L. (1996). The legislative and litigation history of special education. *Future of Children, 6*(1), 25–39.

Martin, P. J. (2002). Transforming school counseling: A national initiative. *Theory into Practice, 41*(3), 148–153.

Martin, R. (1991). *Extraordinary children, ordinary lives: Stories behind special education case law.* Champaign, IL: Research Press.

Martinez, M., & Bray, J. (2002). *All over the map: State policies to improve the high school.* Washington, DC: HS Alliance. Retrieved from http://www.hsalliance.org/resources/docs/Allfinal.pdf.

Martinez, M., & Klopott, S. (2003). Improving college access for low-income, minority, and first-generation students. Boston, MA: Pathways to College Network white paper.

Martinez, M., & Klopott, S. (2005). *Link between high school reform and college access and success for low-income and minority youth.* Washington, DC: American Youth Policy Forum and Pathways to College Network.

Martinussen, R., Hayden, J., Hogg-Johnson, S., & Tannock, R. (2005). A meta-analysis of working memory impairments in children with Attention-Deficit/Hyperactivity Disorder. *Journal of the American Academy of Child and Adolescent Psychiatry, 44* (4), 377–384.

Marzano, R., Pickering, D., & Pollock, J. (2001). *Classroom instruction that works: Research-based strategies for increasing student achievement.* Alexandria, VA: Association for Supervision and Curriculum Development.

Maslach, C. (1982). *Burnout: The cost of caring.* New York: Prentice-Hall.

Maslow, A. H. (1954). *Toward a psychology of being.* New York: Van Nostrand Reinholt.

Massachusetts 2020 (2004). *The Transition to Success Pilot Project.* Boston: Author.

Masten, A. S., & Coatsworth, J. D. (1998). The development of competence in favorable and unfavorable environments: Lessons from research on successful children. *American Psychologist, 53,* 205–220.

Masten, A. S., Garmezy, N., Tellegen, A., Pellegrini, D. S., Larkin, K., & Larsen, A. (1988). Competence and stress in school children: The moderating effects of individual and family qualities. *Journal of Child Psychology and Psychiatry, 29*(6), 745–764.

Mathias, C. E. (1992). Touching the lives of children: Consultative interventions that work. *Elementary School Guidance and Counseling, 26,* 190–201.

Mathis, W. J. (2004). NCLB and high-stakes accountability: A cure? Or a symptom of the disease? *Educational Horizons, 82,* 143–152.

Matthay, E. R. (1989). A critical study of the college selection process. *School Counselor, 36*(5), 359–370.

Matthay, E. R., & Nieuwenhuis, M. (1995). Planning extracurricular activities. In E. R. Matthay (Ed.), *Counseling for college: A professional's guide to motivating, advising, and preparing students for higher education* (2nd ed., pp. 50–56). Princeton, NJ: Peterson's.

Mattingly, R. (2004). Listening is the key. In S. D. Klein & J. D. Kemp (Eds.), *Reflections from a different journey: What adults with disabilities wish all parents knew* (pp. 175–178). New York: McGraw-Hill.

Mau, W. C. (1995). Educational planning and academic achievement of middle school students: A racial and cultural comparison. *Journal of Counseling & Development, 73*, 518–526.

May, H., Supovitz, J., & Perda, D. (2004). *A longitudinal study of the impact of America's Choice on student performance in Rochester, New York, 1998–2003*. Philadelphia: University of Pennsylvania.

McAdams, C. R. (2002). Trends in the occurrence of reactive and proactive aggression among children and adolescents: Implications for preparation and practice in child and youth care. *Child and Youth Care Forum, 31*, 89–109.

McAdams, C. R., & Foster, V. A. (2000). Client suicide: Its frequency and impact on counselors. *Journal of Mental Health Counseling, 22*, 107–121.

McAdams, C. R., & Foster, V. A. (2002). An assessment of resources for counselor coping and recovery in the aftermath of client suicide. *Journal of Humanistic Counseling, Education, and Development, 41*, 232–241.

McAdams, C. R., & Lambe, G. (2003). The changing face of youth aggression in schools: Its impact and implications for school counselors. *Preventing School Failure, 47*, 122–130.

McAuley, E., Duncan, T. E., & McElroy, M. (1989). Self-efficacy cognitions and causal attributions for children's motor performance: An exploratory investigation. *Journal of Genetic Psychology, 150*, 65–73.

McCormack, A., Burgess, A. W., & Hartman, C. (1988). Familial abuse and post-traumatic stress disorder. *Journal of Traumatic Stress, 1*(2), 231–242.

McDaniel, H. B. (1970). *Youth guidance systems*. Palo Alto, CA: College Entrance Examination Board.

McDaniel, J. S., Purcell, D., & D'Augelli, A. R. (2001). The relationship between sexual orientation and risk for suicide: Research findings and future directions for research and prevention. *Suicide & Life-Threatening Behavior, 31*(1, Suppl.), 84–105.

McDonough, P. M. (1997). *Choosing colleges: How social class and schools structure opportunity*. Albany: State University of New York Press.

McDonough, P. M. (2005). *Counseling and college counseling in America's high schools*. Alexandria, VA: National Association for College Admission Counseling.

McEvoy, A., & Welker, R. (2000). Antisocial behavior, academic failure, and school climate: A critical review. *Journal of Emotional Behavior Disorders, 8*, 130–140.

McFarland, W. P., & Dupuis, M. (2001). The legal duty to protect gay and lesbian students from violence in school. *Professional School Counseling, 4*, 171–179.

McGannon, W., Carey, J., & Dimmitt, C. (2005). *The current status of school counseling outcome research*. Amherst: University of Massachusetts, Center for School Counseling Outcome Research.

McGee, R., Feehan, M., Williams, S., Partridge, F., Silva, P. A., & Kelly, J. (1990). *DSM-III* disorders in a large sample of adolescents. *Journal of the American Academy of Child and Adolescent Psychiatry, 29*, 611–619.

McGoldrick, M., Giordano, J., & Pearce, J. K. (Eds.). (1996). *Ethnicity and family therapy* (2nd ed.). New York: Guilford Press.

McGuiness, D. (1985). *When children don't learn*. New York: Basic Books.

McIntosh, P. (1990). *White privilege: Unpacking the invisible knapsack*. Wellesley, MA: Wellesley Centers for Women's Publications.

McKinlay, B., & Bloch, D. P. (1989). Career information motivates at risk youth. *Oregon School Study Council, 31*(5), 111–116.

McLaughlin, M. W. (2000). Community counts: How youth organizations matter for youth development. Washington, DC: Public Education Network.

McLeod, J., & Yates, L. (2006). *Making modern lives: Schooling, subjectivity and social change*. Albany: State University of New York Press.

McNeely, C., & Falci, C. (2004). School connectedness and the transition into and out of health-risk behavior among adolescents: A comparison of social belonging and teacher support. *Journal of School Health, 74*, 284–292.

McPartland, J., Balfanz, R., Jordan, W., & Legters, N. (1998). Improving climate and achievement in a troubled urban high school through the Talent Development Model. *Journal of Education for Students Placed at Risk, 3*, 337–361.

Mead, M. A. (1994). Counselors' use and opinions of the *Diagnostic and Statistical Manual of Mental Disorders* (3rd ed., Revised) (*DSM–III–R*). (Unpublished doctoral dissertation). Virginia Polytechnic University, Blacksburg, VA.

Mead, S. (2008). Open the preschool door, close the preparation gap. Washington, DC: Progressive Policy Institute. Retrieved from http://www.dlc.org/documents/PreK_0904.pdf.

Medway, F. J. (1989). Further considerations on a cognitive problem-solving perspective on school consultation. *Professional School Psychology, 4*(1), 21–27.

Meier, D. (2000). Educating a democracy. In J. Cohen & J. Rogers (Eds.), *Will standards save public education?* (pp. 3–31). Boston: Beacon Press.

Melaville, A., & Blank, M. J. (1998). *Learning together: The developing field of school-community initiatives.* Flint, MI: Mott Foundation.

Merritt, R., & Walley, F. (1977). *The group leader's handbook: Resources, techniques, and survival skills.* Champaign, IL: Research Press.

Metcalf, L. (2008). *Counseling toward solutions: A practical solution-focused program for working with students, teachers, and parents.* San Francisco: Jossey-Bass.

Meyer, I. H. (2003). Prejudice, social stress, and mental health in lesbian, gay, and bisexual populations: Conceptual issues and research evidence. *Psychological Bulletin, 129*(5), 674–697.

Meyer, J. B., Strowig, W., & Hosford, R. E. (1970). Behavioral reinforcement counseling with rural youth. *Journal of Counseling Psychology, 17*(1), 117–120.

Meyers, K., & Pawlas, G. (1989). Simple steps assure parent–teacher conference success. *Instructor, 99*(2), 66–67.

Miller, D., Azreal, L., Hepburn, L., Hemenway, D., & Lippmann, S. J. (2006). Guns in the home and the risk of violent death in the home: Findings from a national study. *American Journal of Public Health, 96*(10), 1752–1755.

Minuchin, S., Nichols, M. P., & Lee, W. (2007). *Assessing families and couples: From symptom to system.* Boston: Allyn & Bacon.

Miranda, A., Webb, L., Brigman, G., & Peluso, P. (2007). Student success skills: A promising program to close the achievement gap for African American and Latino students. *Professional School Counseling, 10*(5), 490–497.

Mischel, W., Shoda, Y., & Rodriguez, M. L. (1989). Delay of gratification in children. *Science, 244,* 933–938.

Mitchell, C. W., Disque, J. G., & Robertson, P. (2002). When parents want to know: Responding to parental demands for confidential information. *Professional School Counseling, 6,* 156–161.

Mitchell, J. T., & Everly, G. S., Jr. (1996a). CISM and CISD: Evolution, effects, and outcomes. In B. Raphael & J. Wilson (Eds.), *Psychological Debriefing.* Cambridge: Cambridge University Press.

Mitchell, J. T., & Everly, G. S., Jr. (1996b). *Critical Incident Stress Debriefing: An operations manual for the prevention of traumatic stress among emergency services and disaster personnel* (2nd ed.). Ellicott City, MD: Chevron.

Molnar, B., Berkman, L., & Buka, S. (2001). Psychopathology, childhood sexual abuse, and other childhood adversities: Relative links to subsequent suicidal behavior in the U.S. *Psychological Medicine, 31,* 965–977.

Mondimore, F. M. (1996). *A natural history of homosexuality.* Baltimore: Johns Hopkins University Press.

Monroe, C. R. (2005). Why are "bad boys" always black? Causes of disproportionality in school discipline and recommendations for change. *Clearing House, 79,* 45–50.

Morey, R. E., Miller, C. D., Fulton, R., Rosen, L. A., & Daly, J. L. (1989). Peer counseling: Students served, problems discussed, overall satisfaction and perceived helpfulness. *School Counselor, 37,* 137–143.

Morey, R. E., Miller, C. D., Rosen, L. A., & Fulton, R. (1993). High school peer counseling: The relationship between student satisfaction and peer counselor's style of helping. *School Counselor, 40,* 293–300.

Morganett, R. (1990). *Skills for living: Group counseling activities for young adolescents.* Champaign, IL: Research Press.

Morris, T. L., & March, J. S. (2004). Anxiety disorders in children and adolescents. New York: Guilford Press.

Morrison, J. A., Olivos, K., Dominguez, G., Gomez, D., & Lena, D. (1993). The application of family systems approaches to school behavior problems on a school-level discipline board: An outcome study. *Elementary School Guidance and Counseling, 27,* 199–205.

Moscicki, E. K. (1999). Epidemiology of suicide. In D. J. Jacobs (Ed.), *The Harvard Medical School guide to suicide assessment and intervention.* Hoboken, NJ: Jossey-Bass.

Moscicki, E. K. (2001). Epidemiology of completed and attempted suicide: Toward a framework for prevention. *Clinical Neuroscience Research, 1,* 310–23.

Muijs, D. (2007). Leadership in full-service extended schools: Communicating across cultures. *School Leadership and Management, 27*(4), 347–362.

Murdock, T. B., & Bolch, M. B. (2005). Risk and protective factors for poor school adjustment in lesbian, gay, and bisexual (LGB) high school youth: Variable and person-centered analysis. *Psychology in the Schools, 42*(2), 159–172.

Murphy, J. J. (1997). *Solution-focused counseling in middle and high schools.* Alexandria, VA: American Counseling Association.

Musheno, S., & Talbert, M. (2002). The transformed school counselor in action. *Theory into Practice, 41*(3), 186–191.

Myers, C. E. (1926). *Some tentative standards for judging a comprehensive guidance plan.* Pittsburgh, PA: Department of Vocational Guidance, Pittsburgh Public Schools.

Myers, D. (1994). *Disaster response and recovery: A handbook for mental health professionals.* Rockville, MD: Center for Mental Health Services.

Myers, H. F., Kagawa-Singer, M., Kumanyika, S. K., Lex, B. W., & Markides, K. S. (1995). Panel III: Behavioral risk factors related to chronic diseases in ethnic minorities. *Health Psychology, 14,* 613–621.

Myers, J. E., Shoffner, M. F., & Briggs, M. A. (2002). Developmental counseling and therapy: An effecive approach to understanding and counseling children. *Professional School Counseling, 5*, 194–202.

Myrick, R. D. (1993). *Developmental guidance and counseling: A practical approach* (2nd ed.). Minneapolis: Educational Media.

Myrick, R. D. (2003a). Accountability: Counselors count. *Professional School Counseling, 6*, 174–179.

Myrick, R. D. (2003b). *Developmental guidance and counseling: A practical approach* (4th ed.). Minneapolis, MN: Educational Media.

Nangle, D. W., Erdley, C. A., Carpenter, E. M., & Newman, J. E. (2002). Social skills training as a treatment for aggressive children and adolescents: A developmental clinical integration. *Aggression and Violent Behavior, 7*, 169–199.

Nansel, T. R., Overpeck, M. D., Haynie, D. L., Ruan, W. J., & Scheidt, P. C. (2003). Relationships between bullying and violence among U.S. youth. *Archives of Pediatric and Adolescent Medicine, 157*(4), 348–353.

Nansel, T. R., Overpeck, M., Pilla, R. S., Ruan,W. J., Simons-Morton, B., & Scheidt, P. (2001). Bullying behaviors among US youth: Prevalence and association with psychosocial adjustment. *Journal of the American Medical Association, 285*(16), 2094–2100.

Nasaw, D. (1979). *Schooled to order: A social history of public schooling in the United States.* New York: Oxford University Press.

Nash, S. G., McQueen, A., & Bray, J. H. (2005). Pathways to adolescent alcohol use: Family environment, peer influence, and parental expectations. *Journal of Adolescent Health, 37*(1), 19–28.

Nathan, J., & Febey, K. (2001). *Smaller, safer, saner, successful schools.* Washington, DC: National Clearinghouse for Educational Facilities; Minneapolis: Center for School Change, Humphrey Institute of the University of Minnesota.

National Advisory Mental Health Council. (1990). *National plan for research on child and adolescent mental disorders.* Report No. NIMH 90-163. Rockville, MD: National Institute of Mental Health.

National Alliance of Business. (1996). The contingent workforce: Temporary phenomenon or permanent fixture? *Workforce Economics, 2*(2), 7–10.

National Association of Social Workers. (1997). Lesbian, gay and bisexual issues. In *Social work speaks: NASW policy statements* (4th ed.). Washington, DC: NASW Press. Retrieved from http://www.socialworkers.org/resources/abstracts/abstracts/lesbian.asp.

National Career Development Association. (2011). NCDA Mission Statement. Retrieved from http://associationdatabase.com/aws/NCDA/pt/sp/about.

National Career Development Guidelines. (2004). *National Career Development Association*, Broken Arrow, OK: Author.

National Center for Cultural Competence (NCCC). (2006). *Conceptual Frameworks/Models, Guiding Values and Principles.* Washington, DC: Georgetown University Child Development Center.

National Center for Education Statistics. (1999). Digest of education statistics, 1998. Washington, DC: U.S. Department of Education.

National Center for Education Statistics. (2002). *Dropout rates in the United States, 2000.* Retrieved from http://nces.ed.gov/pubs2002/droppub_2001/.

National Center for Education Statistics. (2003a). *The condition of education, 2003.* NCES 2003-067. Washington, DC: U.S. Department of Education.

National Center for Education Statistics. (2003b). *National Center for Educational Statistics (2001 data year): United States student-to-counselor ratio.* Washington, DC: U.S. Department of Education.

National Center for Education Statistics. (2005a). *Dual credit and exam-based courses in U.S. public high schools, 2002–03.* NCES 2005-009, by T. Waits, J. C. Setzer, & L. Lewis. Washington, DC: U.S. Department of Education.

National Center for Education Statistics. (2005b). *Digest of educational statistics.* NCES 2006-030. Washington, DC: U.S. Department of Education.

National Center for Education Statistics. (2006). *2005–06 School Survey on Crime and Safety (SSOCS).* Washington, DC: U.S. Department of Education.

National Center for Education Statistics. (2007). *Teacher attrition and mobility: Results for the 2004–2005 Teacher Follow-up Survey.* NCES 2007-307. Washington, DC: U.S. Department of Education.

National Center for Health Statistics. (2007). *Multiple cause-of-death public-use data files, 1990 through 2004.* Hyattsville, MD: U.S. Department of Health and Human Services, Centers for Disease Control and Prevention. Retrieved from http://www.cdc.gov/mmwr/preview/mmwrhtml/mm5635a2.htm.

National Center on Child Abuse and Neglect. (2003). *The role of educators in preventing and responding to child abuse and neglect.* Retrieved from http://childwelfare.gov/pubs/usermanuals/educator/educatora.cfm.

National Center on Education and the Economy. (1990). *America's choice: High skills or low wages! The report of the Commission on the Skills of the American Workforce.* ED 323 297. Rochester, NY: Author.

National Clearinghouse for Comprehensive School Reform & Northwest Regional Educational Laboratory. (2001). *Catalog of school reform models.* Retrieved from http://www.nwrel.org/scpd/catalog/index.shtml.

National Commission on Excellence in Education. (1983). *A nation at risk: The full account.* Portland, OR: USA Research.

National Consortium of State Career Guidance Supervisors. (1999). The seven *C*'s of career planning. Columbus, OH: Author.

National Consortium on Deaf-Blindness (2008). *2007 national child count of children and youth who are deaf-blind.* Monmouth, OR: Teaching Research Institute.

National Dissemination Center for Children with Disabilities. (2004). Blindness/visual impairment. Retrieved from http://nichcy.org/disability/specific/visualimpairment.

National Education Association. (1989, September). A million kids take Ritalin: Is that bad? N.EA. Today, Washington DC: Author.

National Gang Center. *National Youth Gang Survey Analysis.* Retrieved from http://www.nationalgangcenter.gov/Survey-Analysis.

National Federation of State High School Associations (2002). The case for high school activities. Retrieved from http://www.nfhs.org/case.htm.

National Institute for Healthcare Management Research and Education Foundation. (2005, February). *Children's mental health: An overview and key considerations for health system stakeholders.* NIHCM Foundation Issue Paper.

National Institute for Drug Abuse. (n.d.). Retrieved from http://www.nida.nih.gov/scienceofaddiction/citations.html.

National Institute of Mental Health. (2011). Alphabetical list of medications. Retrieved from http://www.nimh.nih.gov/health/publications/mental-health-medications/alphabetical-list-of-medications.shtml.

National Institute on Drug Abuse. (2011). *High School and Youth Trends.* National Institute of Health-U.S. Department of Health and Human Services. Author.

National Middle School Association Research Committee. (2003). Research and resources in support of "This We Believe." Westerville, OH: NMSA.

National Youth Gang Center. (2007). Best practices to address community gang problems, OJJDP's Comprehensive Gang Model. Office of Juvenile Justice and National Youth Gang Center. Delinquency Prevention. Washington, DC: U.S. Department of Justice, Office of Justice Programs.

Nauert, C. (2002). A view from the front line: Enabling legislators—Public Law 94–142, the Education of the Handicapped Act. *Premier Outlook, 3*(3), 19–29.

Nearpass, G. L. (1990). Counseling and guidance effectiveness in North American high schools: A meta-analysis of the research findings. *Dissertation Abstracts, 49*, 1948-A.

Neidt, C. O. (1965). *Relation of guidance practice to student behavioral outcomes.* OE-5-99-222. Washington, DC: U.S. Department of Health, Education, and Welfare.

Neimark, E. D. (1975). Longitudinal development of formal operations thought. *Genetic Psychology Monographs, 91*, 171–225.

Neimark, E. D. (1982). Adolescent thought: Transition to formal operations. In B. B. Wolman (Ed.), *Handbook of developmental psychology* (pp. 486–499). Englewood Cliffs, NJ: Prentice-Hall.

Nelson, R., & Crawford, B. (1990). Suicide among elementary school-aged children. *Elementary School Guidance and Counseling, 25*, 123–128.

Nettles, M. T. (2002, June). *Gaps in achievement: What standardized tests measure.* Presentation at the CCSSO National Conference on Large-Scale Assessment, Orlando, FL.

Neugebauer, B. (Ed.). (1992). *Alike and different: Exploring our humanity with young children,* Washington, DC: National Association for the Education of Young Children.

New York State Archives. (2007). Overview of mental health in New York and the nation. Retrieved from http//www.archieves.nysed.gov/a/researchroom/rr_health_mh_timeline.shtml.

Newcomer, S., & Udry, J. R. (1987). Parental marital status effects on adolescent sexual behavior. *Journal of Marriage and the Family, 49*, 235–240.

Newman, B. S., & Muzzonigro, P. G. (1993). The effects of traditional family values on the coming out process of gay male adolescents. *Adolescence, 28*, 213–226.

Newmann, F. R., & Associates. (1996). *Authentic achievement: Restructuring schools for intellectual quality.* San Francisco: Jossey-Bass.

Nichols, S. L. (1999). Gay, lesbian, and bisexual youth: Understanding diversity and promoting tolerance in schools. *Elementary School Journal, 99*, 505–519.

Nicolosi, J. (1991). *Reparative therapy of male homosexuals.* Northvale, NJ: Aronson.

Nixon, M., Cloutier, P., & Aggarwal, S. (2002). Affect regulation and addictive aspects of repetitive self-injury in hospitalized adolescents. *Journal of the American Academy of Child and Adolescent Psychiatry, 4*, 1333–1341.

No Child Left Behind Act of 2001, Pub. L. No. 107-110, 115 Stat. 1425 (2002).

Nock, M. K., & Prinstein, M. (2004). A functional approach to the assessment of self-mutiliative behavior. *Journal of Consulting and Clinical Psychology, 72*, 885–890.

Noddings, N. (1992). *The challenge to care in schools: An alternate approach to education.* New York: Teachers College Press.

Noeth, R. J., Engen, H. B., & Noeth, P. E. (1984). Making career decisions: A self-report of factors that help high school students. *Vocational Guidance Quarterly, 32*(4), 240–248.

Noguera, P. A. (1999, April 10). Confronting the challenge of diversity in education. *In Motion.* Retrieved from http://www.inmotionmagazine.com/pndivers.html.

Noguera, P. A. (2001). Transforming urban schools through investments in the social capital of parents. In S. Saegert, J. P. Thompson, & M. R. Warren (Eds.), *Social capital and poor communities* (pp. 189–214). New York: Russell Sage Foundation.

Noppe, I. C., & Noppe, L. D. (2004). Adolescent experience with death: Letting go of immortality. *Journal of Mental Health Counseling, 2*, 146–167.

Noppe, I. C., & Noppe, L. D. (2009). Adolescents, accidents and homicide. In Balk, D. E., & Corr, C. A. (Eds.), *Adolescent encounters with death, bereavement and coping* (pp. 61–80). New York: Springer.

Norton, T. L., & Vare, J. W. (2002, June). Understanding gay and lesbian youth: Sticks, stones, and silence. Albany, NY: Lexis Nexis.

Nugent, F. A., & Jones, K. D. (2005). *Introduction to the profession of counseling* (4th ed.). Upper Saddle River, NJ: Pearson/Merrill.

Nuttall, E. V., Romero, I., & Kalesnik, J. (1992). *Assessing and screening preschoolers: Psychological and educational dimensions.* Needham, MA: Allyn & Bacon.

Nydell, M. (1987). *Understanding Arabs: A guide for Westerners.* Yarmouth, ME: Intercultural Press.

Oakes, J. (1985). *Keeping track: How schools structure inequality.* New Haven, CT: Yale University Press.

Obed, N., Charles, R., Jr., & Bentz, B. (2001). The black-white "achievement gap" as a perennial challenge of urban science education: A sociocultural and historical overview with implications for research and practice. *Journal of Research in Science Teaching, 38*, 1101–1114.

Oden, S. (1987). Alternative perspectives in children's peer relationships. In T. D. Yawkey & J. E. Johnson (Eds.), *Integrative processes and socialization: Early to middle childhood.* Elmsford, NJ: Erlbaum.

OECD (Organization for Economic Cooperation and Development). (2000). *Education at a glance: OECD indicators.* Paris: Author.

Oetting, E., Edwards, R., Kelly, K., & Beauvais, F. (1997). Risk and protective factors for drug use among rural American youth. In: E. B. Robertson, Z. Sloboda, G. M. Boyd, L. Beatty, & N. J. Kozel, (Eds.), *Rural Substance Abuse: State of Knowledge and Issues.* NIDA Research Monograph No. 168. Washington, DC: U.S. Government Printing Office, pp. 90–130.

Office of the Surgeon General. (1997). *The first Surgeon General's report on mental health.* Washington, DC: U.S. Public Health Service. Retrieved from http://www.surgeongeneral.gov/library/mentalhealth/.

Office of the Surgeon General. (1999a). *Mental health: A report of the Surgeon General.* Washington, DC: U.S. Public Health Service. Retrieved from http://www.surgeongeneral.gov/Library/MentalHealth/chapter3/sec1.html.

Office of the Surgeon General. (1999b). *The Surgeon General's call to action to prevent suicide.* Washington, DC: U.S. Public Health Service. Retrieved from http://www.surgeongeneral.gov/osg/calltoaction/fact3.htm.

Office of the Surgeon General. (2000). *Report of the Surgeon General's Conference on Children's Mental Health: A national action agenda.* Washington, DC: U.S. Public Health Service. Retrieved from http://www.surgeongeneral.gov/topics/cmh/childreport.htm.

Ohlsen, M. M. (1977). *Group counseling.* New York: Holt, Rinehart & Winston.

Ohlsen, M. M. (1983). *Introduction to counseling.* Itasca, IL: F. E. Peacock.

Ollendick, T. H., & King, N. J. (1998). Empirically supported treatments for children with phobic and anxiety disorders: Current status. *Journal of Clinical Child Psychology, 27*, 156–167.

Ollendick, T. H., & March, J. (2004). Integrated psychosocial and pharmacological treatment. In T. H. Ollendick and J. S. March (Eds.), *Phobic and anxiety disorders in children and adolescents.* New York: Oxford University Press.

O'Loughlin, M. (2006). *Embodiment and education: Exploring creatural existence.* New York: Springer.

Olsen, L., Bhattacharya, J., & Scharf, A. (2006). *Cultural competency, What it is and why it matters.* Palo Alto, CA: California Tomorrow, Lucile Packard Foundation for Children's Health.

Olweus, D., & Limber, S. (1999). *Bullying Prevention Program.* Blueprints for Violence Prevention, Book 9. Boulder: Center for the Study and Prevention of Violence, Institute of Behavioral Science, University of Colorado.

Omizo, M. M., Hershberger, J. M., & Omizo, S. A. (1988). Teaching children to cope with anger. *Elementary School Guidance and Counseling, 22*, 241–245.

Omizo, M. M., & Omizo, S. A. (1987). The effects of group counseling on classroom behavior and self-concept among elementary school learning disabled children. *Exceptional Child, 34*(1), 57–64.

Omizo, M. M., & Omizo, S. A. (1988a). The effects of participation in group counseling sessions on self-esteem and locus of control among adolescents from divorced families. *School Counselor, 36*, 54–60.

Omizo, M. M., & Omizo, S. A. (1988b). Group counseling's effects on self-concept and social behavior among children with learning disabilities. *Journal of Humanistic Education and Development, 26*, 109–117.

Omizo, M. M., Omizo, S. A., & D'Andrea, M. J. (1992). Promoting wellness among elementary school children. *Journal of Counseling and Development, 71*, 194–198.

Omizo, M. M., Omizo, S. A., & Okamoto, C. M. (1998). Gay and lesbian adolescents: A phenomenological study. *Professional School Counseling, 1*(3), 35–37.

Ortega, R., & Lera, M. (2000). The Seville Anti-Bullying in School Project. *Aggressive Behavior, 26*, 113–123.

Osher, D., Woodruff, D., & Sims, A. (2001). *Exploring relationships between inappropriate and ineffective special education services for African American children and youth and their overrepresentation in the juvenile justice system.* Cambridge, MA: Harvard University Civil Rights Project. Retrieved from http://www.law.harvard.edu/civilrights/conferences/SpecEd/osherpaper2.html.

Osipow, S. H., & Fitzgerald, L. F. (1996). *Theories of career development* (4th ed.). Needham Heights, MA: Allyn & Bacon.

Ostrov, E., Offer, D., & Howard, K. I. (1989). Gender differences in adolescent symptomatology: A normative study. *Journal of the American Academy of Child and Adolescent Psychiatry, 28*, 394–398.

Otto, L. B., & Call, V. R. A. (1985). Parental influences on young people's career development. *Journal of Career Development, 12*(1), 65–69.

Otto, R., Greenstein, T., Johnson, M., & Friedman, R. (1992). Prevalence of mental disorders among youth in the juvenile justice system. In J. Cocozza (Ed.), *Responding to the mental health needs of youth in the juvenile justice system* (pp. 7–48). Seattle: National Coalition for the Mentally Ill in the Criminal Justice System.

Otwell, P. S., & Mullis, F. (1997). Counselor-led staff development: An efficient approach to teacher consultation. *Professional School Counseling, 1*(1), 25–30.

Ozonoff, S., Goodlin-Jones, B., & Solomon, M. (2005). Evidence-based assessment of autism spectrum disorders in children and adolescents. *Journal of Clinical Child and Adolescent Psychology, 34*(3), 523–540.

Ozonoff, S., Williams, B. J., & Landa, R. (2005). Parental report of the early development of children with regressive autism. *Autism, 9*, 461–486.

Padron, Y. N., Waxman, H. C., & Rivera, H. H. (2002). *Educating Hispanic students: Effective instructional practices.* Practitioner Brief #5. Retrieved from http://www.cal.org/crede/Pubs/PracBrief5.htm.

Paige, R. (2003, September 24). Back-to-school address. National Press Club, Washington, DC.

Paisley, P. O. (2001). Maintaining and enhancing developmental focus in school counseling programs. Professional School Counseling, 4(4), 271–277.

Paisley, P. O., & Borders, L. D. (1995). School counseling: An evolving specialty. *Journal of Counseling and Development, 74*, 150–153.

Paisley, P. O., & Hayes, R. L. (2003). School counseling and the academic domain: Transformations in preparation and practice. *Professional School Counseling, 6*, 198–204.

Paisley, P. O., & Hubbard, G. T. (1994). *Developmental school counseling programs: From theory to practice.* Alexandria, VA: American Counseling Association.

Paisley, P. O., & McMahon, H. G. (2001). School counseling for the 21st century: Challenges and opportunities. *Professional School Counseling, 5*, 106–115.

Paisley, P. O., & Peace, S. D. (1995). Developmental principles: A framework for school counseling programs. *Elementary School Guidance and Counseling, 30*, 85–93.

Palmer, S., & Cochran, L. (1988). Parents as agents of career development. *Journal of Counseling Psychology, 35*, 71–76.

Pang, V. O., & Cheng, L-R. L. (1998). *Struggling to be heard: The unmet needs of Asian Pacific American children.* New York: State University of New York Press.

Paniagua, F. A. (1994). *Assessing and treating culturally diverse clients: A practical guide.* Thousand Oaks, CA: Sage.

Parker, J. G., Rubin, K. H., Erath, S. A., Wojslawowicz, J. C., & Buskirk, A. A. (2006). Peer relationships, child development, and adjustment: A developmental psychopathology perspective. In D. Cicchetti & D. J. Cohen (Eds.), *Developmental psychopathology*, Vol. 1: *Theory and methods* (2nd ed., pp. 96–161). New York: Wiley.

Parks, C. W. (2001). African-American same-gender-loving youths and families in urban schools. *Journal of Gay & Lesbian Social Services, 13*(3), 41–56.

Parrott, J. (2001, July 9). Are advisors risking lawsuits for misadvising students? *Mentor.* Retrieved from http://www.psu.edu/dus/mentor/.

Parsad, B., & Lewis, L. (2003). Remedial education at degree-granting postsecondary institutions in Fall 2000. *NCES Quarterly, 5*(4), 1–166.

Parsons, F. (*1909*). *Choosing a vocation.* Boston: Houghton Mifflin.

Parsons, J. E., Adler, T. F., & Kaczala, C. M. (1982). Socialization of achievement attitudes and beliefs: Parental influences. *Child Development, 53*, 310–321.

Paternite, C. E., & Johnston, T. C. (2005). Rationale and strategies for central involvement of educators in effective school-based mental health programs. *Journal of Youth and Adolescence, 34*, 41–49.

Patterson, G. R. (1982). *Coercive family processes.* Eugene, OR: Castalia.

Patterson, G. R., Reid, J. B., & Dishion, T. J. (1992). *Antisocial boys: A social interactional approach.* Eugene, OR: Castalia.

Patterson, J. M., McCubbin, H., & Neede, R. H. (1983). *A-COPE: Adolescent-Coping Orientation for Problem Experiences.* Madison: Family Stress Coping and Health Program, University of Wisconsin.

Paxton, R., Valois, R., & Drane, J. (2007). Is there a relationship between family structure and substance use among public middle school students? *Journal of Child & Family Studies, 16*(5), 593–605.

Payne, A. F. (1924). Problems in vocational guidance. *National Vocational Guidance Association Bulletin, 2*, 61–63.

Peeks, B. (1993). Revolutions in counseling and education: A systems perspective in the schools. *Elementary School Guidance and Counseling, 27*, 245–251.

Pelham, W. E., Fabiano, G. A., & Massetti, G. M. (2005). Evidence-based assessment of attention deficit hyperactivity disorder in children and adolescents. *Journal of Clinical Child and Adolescent Psychology, 34*, 449–476.

Pelham, W. E., & Fabiano, G. A. (2008). Evidenced-based psychological treatment for attention deficit/hyperactivity disorder. *Journal of Clinical Child and Adolescent Psychology, 37*(1), 184–214.

Pelham, W. E., Gnagy, E. M., Greenslade, K. E., & Milich, R. (1992). Teacher ratings of *DSM-III-R* symptoms for the disruptive behavior disorders. *Journal of the American Academy of Child and Adolescent Psychiatry, 31*, 210–218.

Pellegrini, D. S. (1985). Social cognition and competence in middle childhood. *Child Development, 56*, 253–264.

Pellegrini, D. S., Masten, A. S., Garmezy, N., & Ferrarese, M. J. (1987). Correlates of social and academic competence in middle childhood. *Journal of Child Psychology and Psychiatry and Allied Disciplines, 23*(5), 699–714.

Pepitone, E. A., Loeb, H. W., & Murdock, E. M. (1977). *Social comparison and similarity of children's performance in competitive situations.* Paper presented at the annual convention of the American Psychological Association, May 2–6, Toronto, Canada.

Perkins Collaborative Network. (2010). The National Career Development Guidelines (NCDG) Framework. Retrieved from http://cte.ed.gov/acrn/ncdg/ncdg.

Perrin, E. C., & American Academy of Pediatrics Committee on Psychosocial Aspects of Child and Family Health. (2002). Coparent or second-parent adoption by same-sex parents. *Pediatrics, 109*(2), 341–344. Retrieved from http://aappolicy.aappublications.org/cgi/reprint/pediatrics;109/2/339.pdf.

Perrone, P. A. (1987). Counselor response to adolescent suicide. *School Counselor, 35*(1), 24–29.

Perry, N. S. (1993). School counseling. In G. R. Walz & J. C. Bleuer (Eds.), *Counselor efficacy: Assessing and using counseling outcome research* (pp. 37–49). Ann Arbor, MI: ERIC.

Perry, N. S. (1995). The school counselor's role in educational reform. *NASSP Bulletin, 79*, 224–229.

Perusse, R., & Goodnough, G. E. (Eds.). (2004). *Leadership, advocacy, and direct service strategies for professional school counselors.* Belmont, CA: Thomson Learning/Brooks/Cole.

Perusse, R., Goodnough, G. E., Donegan, J., & Jones, C. (2004). Perceptions of school counselors and school principals on the national standards for school counseling programs and the Education Trust initiative: A national study. *Professional School Counseling, 7*, 161.

Perusse, R., Goodnough, G. E., & Noel, C. J. (2001). Use of the national standards for school counseling programs in preparing school counselors. *Professional School Counseling, 5*, 49–56.

Peters, H. J., & Farwell, G. (1959). *Guidance: A developmental approach.* Chicago: Rand McNally.

Petersen, A. C., Schulenberg, J. E., Abramowitz, R. H., Offer, D., & Jarcho, H. D. (1984). A self-image questionnaire for young adolescents (SEQYA): Reliability and validity studies. *Journal of Youth and Adolescence, 13*, 93–111.

Petersen, S., & Straub, R. (1992). *School crisis survival guide.* West Nyack, NY: Center for Applied Research.

Peterson, G. W., Long, K. L., & Billups, A. (1999). The effect of three career interventions on educational choices of eighth grade students. *Professional School Counseling, 3*, 34–42.

Pew Hispanic Center. (2005). *Hispanics: A people in motion.* Washington, DC: Pew Research Center.

Phelps, J. D. (2002). *The No Child Left Behind Act of 2001: Opportunities for career technical education.* Washington, DC: National Association of State Directors of Career Technical Education Consortium. Retrieved from http://www.nasdvtec.org/NCLB.doc.

Piacentini, J., & Langley, A. K. (2004) Cognitive-behavioral therapy for children who have obsessive-compulsive disorder. *Journal of Clinical Psychology, 60*, 1181–1194.

Piaget, J. (1948). *The moral judgment of the child.* (1st American ed.) Glencoe, IL: Free Press.

Piaget, J. (1970). Piaget's theory. In P. H. Mussen (Ed.), *Carmichael's manual of child psychology* (3rd ed., Vol. 1, pp. 345–365). New York: Wiley.

Piaget, J. (1972). Intellectual evolution from adolescence to adulthood. *Human Development, 15*, 1–12.

Piaget, J., & Inhelder, B. (1969). *The psychology of the child.* New York: Basic Books.

Picciotto, L. P. (1996). *Student-led parent conferences.* Jefferson City, MO: Scholastic Professional Books.

Pike, G. R., & Kuh, G. D. (2005). First- and second-generation college students: A comparison of their engagement and intellectual development. *Journal of Higher Education, 76*, 276–300.

Pikes, T., Burrell, B., & Holliday, C. (1998). Using academic strategies to build resilience. *Reaching Today's Youth, 4*(2), 44–47.

Pine, G. J. (1975). Evaluating school counseling programs: Retrospect and prospect. *Measurement and Evaluation in Guidance, 8*, 136–144.

Pine, G. J. (1981). Collaborative action research in school counseling: The integration of research and practice. *Personnel and Guidance Journal, 59*, 495–501.

Pleis, J. R., & Lethbridge-Çejku, M. (2006). Summary health statistics for U.S. adults: National Health Interview Survey, 2005. *Vital Health Statistics, 10*(232). Hyattsville, MD: National Center for Health Statistics.

Plymouth Educational Center. Student support services. Retrieved from http://www.plymouthed.org/studentServices.htm.

Policy Leadership Cadre for Mental Health in Schools. (2001). Mental health in schools: Guidelines, models, resources and policy considerations. Los Angeles: Center for Mental Health at UCLA.

Pope, M. (1995). The "salad bowl" is big enough for us all: An argument for the inclusion of lesbians and gays in any definition of multiculturalism. *Journal of Counseling and Development, 73*, 301–304.

Pope, M. (2000). Preventing school violence aimed at gay, lesbian, bisexual, and transgender youth. In D. S. Sandhu & C. B. Aspy (Eds.), *Violence in American schools: A practical guide for counselors* (pp. 285–304). Alexandria, VA: American Counseling Association.

Pope, M., Bunch, L. K., Szymanski, D. M., & Rankins, M. (2003). Counseling sexual minority students in the schools. In B. Erford (Ed.), *Handbook for professional school counseling* (pp. 221–245). Greensboro, NC: CAPS Press.

Powell, A. G., Farrar, E., & Cohen, D. K. (1985). *The shopping mall high school.* Boston: Houghton-Mifflin.

Poynton, T. A., & Carey, J. C. (2006). An integrative model and data-based decision making for school counseling. *Professional School Counseling, 10*, 121–130.

Poynton, T. A., Carlson, M. W., Hopper, J. A., & Carey, J. C. (2006). Evaluation of an innovative approach to improving middle school students' academic achievement. *Professional School Counseling, 9*(3), 190. Retrieved February 2, 2009, from EBSCOHOST.

Pratt, R. (2000). *The condition of education.* National Center for Educational Statistics, U.S. Department of Education, Office of Educational Research and Improvement.

Preciado, J., & Henry, M. (1997). Linguistic barriers in health education services. In J. G. Garcia & M. C. Zea (Eds.), *Psychological interventions and research with Latino populations* (pp. 235–254). Needham Heights, MA: Allyn & Bacon.

Prediger, D. J., Roth, J. D., & Noeth, R. J. (1973). *Nationwide study of student career development: Summary of results.* Iowa City, IA: American College Testing Program.

Prediger, D. J., & Sawyer, R. L. (1985). Ten years of student career development: A nationwide study. Paper presented at the convention of the American Association for Counseling and Development.

President's Advisory Commission on Educational Excellence for Hispanic Americans. (1996). *Our nation on the fault line: Hispanic American education.* Washington, DC: Author.

Prevent Child Abuse America (2003). *What everyone can do to prevent child abuse: 2003 child abuse prevention community resource packet.* Chicago: Author.

Price, R., & Smith, S. (1985). *A guide to evaluating prevention programs in mental health.* DHHS Pub. No. ADM 85-1365. Rockville, MD: National Institute of Mental Health.

Prinstein, M. J., Boergers, J., & Vernberg, E. M. (2001). Overt and relational aggression in adolescents: Social-psychological adjustment of aggressors and victims. *Journal of Clinical Child Psychology, 30*, 479–491.

Proctor, C. D., & Groze, V. K. (1994). Risk factors for suicide among gay, lesbian, and bisexual youths. *Social Work, 39*, 504–513.

Proctor, J. L., Badzinski, D. M., & Johnson, M. (2002). Impact of media on knowledge and perception of Megan's Law. *Criminal Justice Policy Review, 13*(4), 356–379.

Proctor, W. M. (1930). Evaluating guidance activities in high schools. *Vocational Guidance, 9*, 58–66.

Prodente, C. A., Sander, M. A., & Weist, M. D. (2002). Furthering support for expanded school mental health programs. *Children's Services, 5*, 172–188.

Project GRAD. (2003). Graduation Really Achieves Dreams. Retrieved July 6, 2009, from http://www.projectgradusa.org/managedcontent/downloadFiles/download6/Files/file/OriginalSlides.ppt.

Protheroe, N. (2001). Improving teaching and learning with data-based decisions: Asking the right questions and acting on the answers. *ERS Spectrum, 19*(3), 4–9.

Prout, H. T., & DeMartino, R. A. (1986). A meta-analysis of school-based studies of psychotherapy. *Journal of School Psychology, 24*, 285–292.

Pynoos, R. S., & Nader, K. (1988) Psychological first aid and treatment approach to children exposed to community violence: Research implications. *Journal of Traumatic Stress, 1*, 445–473.

QEV Analytics. (2008). *National survey of American attitudes on substance abuse XIII: Teens and parents.* New York: National Center on Addiction and Substance Abuse at Columbia University.

Quint, J. (2001). *Scaling up First Things First: Site selection and the planning year.* New York: Manpower Demonstration Research.

Quint, J., Bloom, H., Black, A., & LaFleur, S. (2005). *The challenge of scaling up education reform: Findings from First Things First.* New York: Manpower Demonstration Research.

Rabinowitz, M. (1988). On teaching cognitive strategies: The influence of accessibility of conceptual knowledge. *Contemporary Educational Psychology, 13*, 229–235.

Rae-Grant, N., Thomas, H., Offord, D., & Boyle, J. (1989). Risk, protective factors, and the prevalence of behavioral and emotional disorders in children and adolescents. *Journal of the American Academy of Child and Adolescent Psychiatry, 28*, 262–268.

Raffaelli, M., & Duckett, E. (1989). "We were just talking …": Conversations in early adolescence. *Journal of Youth and Adolescence, 18*, 567–582.

Raine, A. (2002). Biosocial studies of antisocial and violent behavior in children and adults: A review. *Journal of Abnormal Child Psychology, 30*, 311–326.

Raine, A., Brennan, R., & Mednick, S. A. (1997). Interaction between birth complications and early maternal rejection in predisposing individuals to adult violence: Specificity to serious, early-onset violence. *American Journal of Psychiatry, 154*, 1265–1271.

Ralston, M. E. (1982). *Intrafamilial sexual abuse: A community system response to a family system problem.* Charleston, SC: Author.

Ralston, M. E. (1998). A community system of care for abused children and their families. *Family Futures, 2*, 11–15.

Ralston, M. E., & Swenson, C. C. (1996). *The Charleston Collaborative Project: Intervention manual.* Charleston, SC: Author.

Ramirez, A. Y. F. (2003). Dismay and disappointment: Parental involvement of Latino immigrant parents. *Urban Review, 35*(2), 93–110.

Ramsey, P., & Derman-Sparks, L. (1992). Multicultural education reaffirmed. *Young Children, 47*(2), 10–11.

Rang, X., & Brown, F. (2002). Immigrant and urban education in the new millennium: The diversity and the challenges. *Education and Urban Society, 34*, 123–133.

Rawls, R. K. (1997). Virginia high school counselors and school law. *Dissertation Abstracts International, 58-08A*, 3024.

Raywid, M. A. (1993). Community: An alternative school achievement. In G. A. Smith (Ed.), *Public schools that work* (pp. 23–44). New York: Routledge.

Raywid, M. A. (1994). A school that really works: Urban Academy. *Journal of Negro Education, 63*, 93–110.

Raywid, M. A., Schmerler, G., Phillips, S. E., & Smith, G. A. (2003). *Not so easy going: The policy environments of small urban schools and schools within schools.* Charleston, WV: AEL.

Reid, K. (2001, May 2). Iowa's high court holds counselors liable. *Education Week.* Retrieved from http://www.edweek.org/ew/ewstory.cfm?slug=33guide.h20.

Reis, B. (2004). Glossary of terms. Safe Schools Coalition. Retrieved from http://www.safeschoolscoalition.org/Elevenaspectsofsexuality.pdf.

Remafedi, G. J., Resnick, M., Blum, R., & Harris, L. (1992). Demography of sexual orientation in adolescents. *Pediatrics, 89*, 714–721.

Remley, T. P., Jr., & Herlihy, B. (2001). *Ethical, legal, and professional issues in counseling.* Upper Saddle River, NJ: Prentice Hall.

Remley, T. P., Jr., & Sparkman, L. B. (1993). Student suicides: The counselor's limited legal liability. *School Counselor, 40*(3), 164–169.

Renshaw, E. D., & Asher, S. R. (1982). Social competence and peer status: The distinction between goals and strategies. In K. H. Rubin & H. S. Ross (Eds.), *Peer relationships and social skills in childhood* (pp. 348–358). New York: Springer-Verlag.

Resick, P. A., & Schnicke, M. K. (1993). *Cognitive processing therapy for rape victims: A treatment manual.* Newbury Park, CA: Sage.

Rest, J. R. (1983). Morality. In J. H. Flavell & E. M. Markman (Eds.), *Handbook of child psychology: Cognitive development* (Vol. 3). New York: Wiley.

Reyhner, J. (2002). *American Indian/Alaska Native education: An overview.* Retrieved from http://www.jan.ucc.nau.edu/~jar?AIE/Ind_Ed.html.

Rice, G. E., & Smith, W. (1993). Linking effective counseling and teaching skills. *School Counselor, 40*(3), 201–206.

Richburg, M. L., & Cobia, D. C. (1994). Using behavioral techniques to treat elective mutism: A case study. *Elementary School Guidance and Counseling, 28*, 214–220.

Rifkin, J. (1995). *The end of work.* New York: Putnam.

Riley, P. L., & McDaniel, J. (2000). School violence prevention, intervention, and crisis response. *Professional School Counseling, 4*, 120–125.

Ringwalt, C. L., Ennett, S., & Johnson, R. (2003). Factors associated with fidelity to substance use prevention curriculum guides in the nation's middle schools. *Health Education & Behavior, 30*, 375–391.

Rinn, R. C., & Markle, A. (1979). Modification of social skill deficits in children (556–629). In A. S. Bellack & M. Hersen (Eds.), *Research and practice in social skills training.* New York: Plenum.

Ripley, V., Erford, B. T., Dahir, C., & Eschbach, L. (2003). Planning and implementing a 21st-century comprehensive developmental school counseling program. In B. T. Erford (Ed.), *Transforming the school counseling profession* (pp. 63–119). Upper Saddle River, NJ: Merrill Prentice Hall.

Roberts, R. N., & Wasik, B. H. (1990). Home visiting program for families with children birth to three: Results of a national survey. *Journal of Early Intervention, 14*(3), 274–284.

Robertson, J. F., & Simons, R. L. (1989). Family factors, self-esteem and adolescent depression. *Journal of Marriage and the Family, 51*, 125–138.

Robinson, S. E., Morrow, S., Kigin, T., & Lindeman, M. (1991). Peer counselors in a high school setting: Evaluation of training and impact on students. *School Counselor, 39*, 35–40.

Roderick, M., Nagaoka, J., Coca, V., Moeller, E., Roddie, K., Gilliam, J., & Patton (2008). *From high school to the future: Potholes on the road to college.* Chicago: University of Chicago, Consortium on Chicago School Research.

Roffman, J. G., Suarez-Orozco, C., & Rhodes, J. E. (2003). Facilitating positive development in immigrant youth: The role of mentors and community organizations. In F. Villarruel, D. Perkins, L. Borden, & J. Keith (Eds.), *Community youth development: Programs, policies, and practices* (pp. 90–118). Thousand Oaks, CA: Sage.

Rogala, J., Lambert, R., & Verhage, K. (1991). *Developmental guidance classroom activities for use with the national career development guidelines.* Madison: University of Wisconsin Vocational Studies Center.

Rogers, C. R. (1942). *Counseling and psychotherapy.* Boston: Houghton-Mifflin.

Rogers, C. R. (1969). *Freedom to learn: A view of what education might become.* Columbus, OH: Charles E. Merrill.

Rogers, C. R. (1980). *A way of being.* Boston: Houghton-Mifflin.

Rohde, P., Lewinsohn, P. M., Klein, P. M., & Seeley, D. N. (2005). Association of parental depression with psychiatric course from adolescence to young adulthood among formerly depressed individuals. *Journal of Abnormal Psychology, 111*(3), 409–420.

Rones, M., & Hoagwood, K. (2000). School-based mental health services: A research review. *Clinical Child and Family Psychology Review, 3*, 223–240.

Roscigno, V. J. (2000). Family/school inequality and African American/Hispanic achievement. *Social Problems, 47*, 266–290.

Rose, L., Gallup, A., & Elam, S. (1997). The 29th annual Phi Delta Kappa Gallup poll of the public's attitudes toward the public schools. *Phi Delta Kappan, 79*(1), 49.

Rose, S. (1987). Social skills training in middle school. *Journal for Specialists in Group Work, 12*(4), 144–149.

Rosecrance, F. C. (1930). Organizing guidance for the larger school system. *Vocational Guidance, 9*, 243–249.

Rosenberg, M. (1979). *Conceiving the self.* New York: Basic Books.

Rosenblatt, A. (1998). Assessing the child and family outcomes of systems of care for youth with serious emotional disturbance. In M. H. Epstein & K. Kutash (Eds.), *Outcomes for children and youth with emotional and behavioral disorders and their families:Programs and evaluation best practices* (pp. 329–362). Austin, TX: PRO-ED, Inc.

Rosenheim, M. K., & Testa, M. E. (1992). *Early parenthood and coming of age in the 1990s.* New Brunswick, NJ: Rutgers University Press.

Rosenholtz, S. (1989). *Teachers' workplace: The social organization of schools.* New York: Longmans.

Ross, R. R., & Ross, B. (1989). Delinquency prevention through cognitive training. *Educational Horizons, 15*(2), 35–39.

Ross, S., & Heath, N. (2002). A study of the frequency of self-mutilation in a community sample of adolescents. *Journal of Youth and Adolescence, 31*(1), 67–77.

Rossi, R. J., & Stringfield, S. C. (1995). What we must do for students placed at risk. *Phi Delta Kappan, 77*(1), 73–76.

Rotheram, M. J. (1982). Social skills training with underachievers, disruptive, and exceptional children. *Psychology in the Schools, 19*, 532–539.

Rothman, R. (2002). Closing the achievement gap: How schools are making it happen. *Journal of the Annenberg Challenge, 5*(2), 1–11.

Rothstein, R. (2004). *Class and schools: Using social, economic, and educational reform to close the black–white achievement gap.* Washington, DC: Economic Policy Institute; New York: Teachers College, Columbia University.

Rotter, J. C., & Robinson, E. H. (1982). Parent–teacher conferencing. Washington, DC: National Education Association.

Rowell, L. L. (2006). Action research and school counseling: Closing the gap between research and practice. Professional School Counseling, 9, 376–384.

Royal, M. A., & Rossi, R. J. (1996). Individual-level correlates of sense of community: Findings from workplace and school. *Journal of Community Psychology, 24*(4), 395–416.

Rubin, K. H., Bukowski, W., & Parker, J. (2006). Peer interactions, relationships, and groups. In N. Eisenberg (Ed.), *Handbook of child psychology: Social, emotional, and personality development* (6th ed., pp. 571–645). New York: Wiley.

Rudolph, K. D., Lambert, S. F., Clark, A. G., & Kurlakowsky, K. D. (2001). Negotiating the transition to middle school: The role of self-regulatory processes. *Child Development, 72*, 929–949.

Rutter, M. (1981). Stress, coping, and development: Some issues and some questions. *Journal of Child Psychology and Psychiatry, 22*(4), 323–356.

Rutter, M. (1984). Resilient children. *Psychology Today, 43*(5), 57–65.

Rutter, M. (1987). Psychosocial resilience and protective mechanisms. *American Journal of Orthopsychiatry, 57*(3), 246–257.

Rutter, M., & Giller, H. (1984). *Juvenile delinquency: Trends and perspectives.* New York: Penguin.

Sadler, L. S., Swartz, M. K., & Ryan-Krause, P. (2003). Supporting mothers and their children through a high school–based child care center and parent support program. *Journal of Pediatric Health Care, 17*(3), 109–117.

Saigh P. A., Yasik, A. E., Sack, W., & Koplewicz, H. (1999). Child-adolescent post-traumatic disorder: Prevalence, comorbidity and risk factors. In P. A. Saigh & J. D. Bremmel (Eds.), Posttraumatic stress disorder: A comprehensive text (pp. 19–43). Neeedham Heights, MA: Allen and Bacon.

St. Pierre, T. (1998). Involving parents of high-risk youth in drug prevention. In K. Bogenschneider & J. Olson (Eds.), *Building resiliency and reducing risk: What youth need from families and communities to succeed.* Wisconsin Family Impact Seminar Briefing Report No. 10. Madison: University of Wisconsin Center for Excellence in Family Studies. Retrieved from http://familyimpactseminars.org/reports/fis10two.pdf.

St. Pierre, T. L., Mark, M. M., Kaltreider, D. L., & Aikin, K. J. (1997). Involving parents of high-risk youth in drug prevention: A three-year longitudinal study in Boys and Girls Clubs. *Journal of Early Adolescence, 17*, 21–50.

Samhan, H. H. (1999). Not quite white: Race classification and the Arab American experience. In M. Suleiman (Ed.), *Arabs in America: Building a new future* (pp. 209–226). Philadelphia: Temple University Press.

SAMHSA. *See* Substance Abuse and Mental Health Services Administration

Sampson, R. J., & Laub, J. H. (1993). *Crime in the making: Pathways and turning points through life.* Cambridge, MA: Harvard University Press.

Sanchez, W. (1995). *Working with diverse learners and school staff in a multicultural society.* ERIC Document No. ED390018. Greensboro, NC: ERIC Clearinghouse on Counseling and Student Services.

Sandhu, D. S. (1997). Psychocultural profiles of Asian and Pacific Islander Americans: Implications for counseling and psychotherapy. *Journal of Multicultural Counseling and Development, 25*, 7–22.

Sandhu, D. S. (2000). Alienated students: Counseling strategies to curb school violence. Professional School Counseling, 4, 81–85.

Sandhu, D. S., & Aspy, C. B. (Eds.). (2000). Violence in American schools: A practical guide for counselors (pp. 285–304). Alexandria, VA: American Counseling Association.

Santiago-Rivera, A. L. (1995). Developing a culturally sensitive treatment modality for bilingual Spanish-speaking clients: Incorporating language and culture in counseling. *Journal of Counseling and Development, 74*, 12–17.

Santrock, J. W. (2002). *Life-span development* (8th ed.). Boston: McGraw-Hill.

Sarvela, P. D., Newcomb, P. R., & Littlefield, E. R. (1988). Sources of drug and alcohol information among rural youth. *Health Education, 19*(3), 27–31.

Saunders, B. E., Berliner, L., & Hanson, R. F. (Eds.). (2004). *Child physical and sexual abuse: Guidelines for treatment (Revised report: April 26, 2004).* Charleston, SC: National Crime Victims Research and Treatment Center.

Saunders, B. E., & Meinig, M. B. (2000). Immediate issues affecting long-term family resolution in cases of parent–child sexual abuse. In R. M. Reece (Ed.), *Treatment of child abuse: Common ground for mental health, medical, and legal practitioners.* Baltimore: Johns Hopkins University Press.

Saunders, B. E., & Meinig, M. B. (2001). *Family resolution therapy in cases of child abuse.* Charleston, SC: Authors.

Savin-Williams, R. C. (1990). Gay and lesbian adolescents. In F. W. Bozett & M. B. Sussman (Eds.), *Homosexuality and family relations* (pp. 197–216). New York: Haworth Press.

Savin-Williams, R. C. (1994). Verbal and physical abuse as stressors in the lives of lesbian, gay male, and bisexual youths: Associations with school problems, running away, substance abuse, prostitution, and suicide. *Journal of Consulting and Clinical Psychology, 62*, 261–269.

Sawyer, R., Porter, J. D., Lehman, T., Anderson, C., Anderson, K., &. (2006). Education and training needs of school staff relevant to preventing risk behaviors and promoting health behavior among gay, lesbian, bisexual and questioning youth. *Journal of HIV/AIDS, 7*(1), 37–53.

Scheier, L., Botvin, G., Diaz, T., & Griffin, K. (1999). Social skills, competence, and drug refusal efficacy as predictors of adolescent alcohol use. *Journal of Drug Education 29*(3), 251–278.

Schinke, S. P., Orlandi, M. A., & Cole, K. C. (1992). Boys and Girls Clubs in public housing developments: Prevention services for youth at risk. *Journal of Community Psychology, 45*(8), 118–128.

Schlossberg, S. M., Morris, J. D., & Lieberman, M. G. (2001). The effects of a counselor-led guidance intervention on students' behaviors and attitudes. *Professional School Counseling, 4*, 156–164.

Schmidt, J. A. (1976). Career guidance in the elementary schools. *Elementary School Guidance and Counseling, 11*(7), 149–154.

Schmidt, J. J. (1999). *Counseling in schools: Essential services and comprehensive programs* (3rd ed.). Boston: Allyn & Bacon.

Schonfield, D., & Klein, M. (1994). A Resource aid: Responding to a crisis at a school. Center for Mental Health in Schools at UCLA, pp. 1–159.

School Mental Health Alliance. (2005). *Working together to promote learning, social-emotional competence and mental health for all children.* New York: Columbia University Center for the Advancement of Children's Mental Health.

Schorr, L. B. (1997). *Common purpose: Strengthening families and neighborhoods to rebuild America.* New York: Doubleday.

Schreiber, K. *The Arizona model: A framework for school counseling programs handbook, 2009–2020.* Phoenix: Arizona Department of Education, Development and Innovation Group.

Schunk, D. H. (1981). Modeling and attributional effects on children's achievement: A self-efficacy analysis. *Journal of Educational Psychology, 4*(73), 93–105.

Schut, H., Stroebe, M. S., van den Bout, J., & Terheggen, M. (2001). The efficacy of bereavement interventions: Determining who benefits. In M. S. Stroebe, R. O. Hansson, W. Stroebe, & H. Schut (Eds.), *Handbook of bereavement research* (pp. 705–737). Washington, DC: American Psychological Association.

Sciarra, D. T. (2004). *School counseling: Foundations and professional issues.* Belmont, CA: Thompson Brooks/Cole.

Scott, T. M., & Eber, L. (2003). Functional assessment and wraparound as systemic school processes: Primary, secondary and tertiary system examples. *Journal of Positive Behavior Interventions, 5*, 131–143.

Sears, S. J. (2005). Large group guidance: Curriculum development and instruction. In C. A. Sink (Ed.), *Contemporary school counseling: Theory, research, and practice* (pp. 189–213). Boston: Houghton Mifflin.

Sears, S. J., & Granello, D. H. (2002). School counseling now and in the future: A reaction. *Professional School Counseling, 5*, 164–171.

Secretary's Commission on Achieving Necessary Skills. (1992). *Learning and living: A blueprint for high performance: SCANS Report for America, 2000.* Washington, DC: Author.

Seitz, V., & Apfel, N. (1994). Parent-focused intervention: Diffusion effects on siblings. *Child Development, 65*(2), 677–683.

Seligman, L., & Moore, B. M. (1995). Diagnosis of mood disorders. *Journal of Counseling and Development, 74*, 65–69.

Seligman, M. (2000). *Conducting conferences with parents of children with disabilities.* New York: Guilford Press.

Sessions Stepp, L. (2001, June 19). A lesson in cruelty: Anti-gay slurs common at school. *Washington Post.*

Sexton, T. L. (1996). The relevance of counseling outcome research: Current trends and practical implications. *Journal of Counseling and Development, 74*, 590–600.

Sexton, T. L., & Whiston, S. C. (1996). Integrating counseling research and practice. *Journal of Counseling and Development, 74*, 588–589.

Sexuality Information and Education Council of the United States (SIECUS). (1995). *Facts about sexual health for America's adolescents.* New York: SIECUS.

Shaffer, D., & Craft, L. (1999). Methods of adolescent suicide prevention. *Journal of Clinical Psychiatry, 142*, 1061–1064.

Shaffer, D., Fisher, P., Dulcan, M. K., Davies, M., Piacentini, J., Schwab-Stone, M. E., Lahey, B., B., Bourdon, K., Jensen, P. S., Bird, H. R., Canino, G., & Regier, D. A. (1996). The NIMH Diagnostic Interview Schedule for Children, Version 2.3 (DISC-2.3): Descriptions, acceptability, prevalence rates, and performance in the MECA Study: Methods for the epidemiology of child and adolescent mental disorders study. *Journal of the American Academy of Child and Adolescent Psychiatry, 35*, 865–877.

Shaffer, D., Gould, M. S., Fisher, P., Trautment, P., Moreau, D., Kleinman, M., & Flory, M. (1996). Psychiatric diagnosis in child and adolescent suicide. *Archives of General Psychiatry, 53,* 339–348.

Shaffer, D., & Pfeffer, C. R. (2001). Practice parameter for the assessment and treatment of children and adolescents with suicidal behavior. *Journal of the American Academy of Child and Adolescent Psychiatry, 40*(1 Suppl.), 24–51.

Shanahan, T., Mulhern, M., & Rodriguez-Brown, F. (1995). Project FLAME: Lessons learned from a family literacy program for linguistic minority families. *Reading Teacher, 48*(7), 586–593.

Shaw, G., Ramirez, L., Trost, A., Randall, P., & Stice, F. (2004). Body image and eating disturbances across ethnic groups: More similariites than differences. *Psychology of Addictive Behaviors, 18,* 12–18.

Shechtman, Z. (2002). Child group psychotherapy in the school at the threshold of a new millennium. *Journal of Counseling and Development, 80,* 293–299.

Sheeley, V. L., & Herily, B. (1989). Counseling suicidal teens: A duty to warn and protect. *School Counselor, 37,* 89–101.

Sheppard, D. (1999). Strategies to reduce gun violence. OJJDP Fact Sheet No. 93. Washington, DC: U.S. Department of Justice, Office of Juvenile Justice and Delinquency Prevention.

Sherman, L. W., Gottfredson, D., Mackenzie, D., Eck, J., Reuter, P., & Bushway, S. (1997). *Preventing crime: What works, what doesn't, what's promising: A report to the United States Congress.* Washington, DC: National Institute of Justice.

Shields, M. K., & Behrman, R. E. (Eds.). (2004). Children of immigrant families: Analysis and recommendations. *Future of Children, 14*(2), 4–16.

Shipman, N. J., Martin, J. B., McKay, A. B., & Anastiasi, R. E. (1983). *Effective time management techniques for school administrators.* Englewood Cliffs, NJ: Prentice Hall.

Shneidman, E. (1996). *The suicidal mind.* New York: Oxford University Press.

Shonkoff, P. J., & Phillips, D. A. (2000). *From neurons to neighborhoods: The science of early childhood development.* Washington, DC: Institute of Medicine.

Shure, M. B. (1992). *I Can Problem Solve (ICPS): An interpersonal cognitive problem-solving program.* Champaign, IL: Research Press.

Shure, M. B. (1996). *Raising a thinking child: Help your young child to resolve everyday conflicts and get along with others.* New York: Pocket Books.

Shure, M. B. (1997). Interpersonal cognitive problem solving: Primary prevention of early high-risk behaviors in the preschool and primary years. In G. W. Albee & T. P. Gullota (Eds.), *Primary prevention works* (pp. 167–190). Thousand Oaks, CA: Sage.

Siegler, R. S., Liebert, D. E., & Liebert, R. M. (1973). Inhelder and Piaget's pendulum problem: Teaching pre-adolescents to be scientists. *Developmental Psychology, 9,* 97–101.

Silberg, J. L. (2000). Fifteen years of dissociation in maltreated children: Where do we go from here? *Child Maltreatment, 5*(2), 119–136.

Silberg, J. L. (2001). Treating maladaptive dissociation in a young teen-age girl. Retrieved from http://www.issd.org/indexpage/ChildGuidelinesFinal.pdf.

Silverman, W. K., & Hinshaw, S. P. (2008). The Second Special Issue on Evidence-Based Psychosocial Treatments for Children and Adolescents: A Ten-Year Update. *Journal of Clinical Child and Adolescent Psychology 37*(1).

Simmons, R. (2002). *Odd girl out: The hidden culture of aggression in girls.* New York: Harcourt.

Simon, B. S., & Epstein, J. L. (2001). School, family, and community partnerships: Linking theory to practice. In D. B. Hiatt-Michael (Ed.), *Promising practices for family involvement in schools: A volume in family–school–community partnership* (pp. 1–24). Greenwich, CT: Information Age.

Sink, C. A. (2005a). Comprehensive school counseling programs and academic achievement—A rejoinder to Brown and Trusty. *Professional School Counseling, 9,* 9–12.

Sink, C. A. (2005b). Fostering academic development and learning: Implications and recommendations for middle school counselors. *Professional School Counseling, 9*(2), 128–135.

Sink, C. A., & Stroh, H. R. (2003). Raising achievement test scores of early elementary school students through comprehensive school counseling programs. *Professional School Counseling, 6*(5), 350–365.

Siperstein, R., & Volkmar, F. (2004). Parental reporting of regression in children with pervasive developmental disorders. *Journal of Autism and Developmental Disorders, 34,* 731–734.

Sitlington, P. L., & Neubert, D. A. (2004). Preparing youths with emotional or behavioral disorders for transition to adult life: Can it be done within the standards-based reform movement? *Behavioral Disorders, 29,* 279–288.

Sizer, T. R. (1984). *Horace's compromise: The dilemma of the American high school.* Boston: Houghton Mifflin.

Skaalvik, E. M., & Hagtvet, K. A. (1990). Academic achievement and self-concept: An analysis of causal predominance in a developmental perspective. *Journal of Personality and Social Psychology, 58,* 292–307.

Skrtic, T., & Sailor, W. (1996). School-linked services integration: Crisis and opportunity in the transition to postmodern society. *Remedial and Special Education, 17,* 271–283.

Slaby, R. G., Roedell, W. C., Arezzo, D., & Kendrix, K. (1995). *Early violence prevention: Tools for teachers of young children.* ED 382 384. Washington, DC: National Association for the Education of Young Children.

Slade, E. P. (2004). Effects of school-based mental health programs on mental health services by adolescents at school and in the community. *Mental Health Services Research, 4,* 151–166.

Slavin, R. E., & Calderon, M. (2001). *Effective programs for Latino students.* Mahwah, NJ: Erlbaum.

Smead, V. S. (1988). Best practices in crisis intervention. In A. Thomas & J. Grimes (Eds.), *Best practices in school psychology* (pp. 674–693). Washington, DC: National Association of School Psychologists.

Smith, B. H., Barkley, R. A. & Shapiro, C. I. (2006). Attention-deficit/hyperactivity disorder. In E. J. Mash & R. A. Barkley (Eds.), *Treatment of childhood disorders* (3rd ed., pp. 65–136). New York: Guilford Press.

Smith, C. (1996). The link between childhood maltreatment and teenage pregnancy. *Social Work Research* 20(3), 131–141.

Smith, D. D. (2004). *Introduction to special education: Teaching in an age of opportunity* (5th ed.). New York: Pearson.

Smith, P., & Brain, P. (2000). Bullying in schools: Lessons from two decades of research. *Aggressive Behavior, 26,* 1–9.

Smith, S. C., & Scott, J. J. (1990). *The collaborative school: A work environment for effective instruction.* Eugene: University of Oregon, ERIC Clearinghouse on Educational Management.

Smith, S. E. (1994). Parent-initiated contracts: An intervention for school-related behaviors. *Elementary School Guidance and Counseling, 28,* 182–187.

Smolak, L., & Striegel-Moore, R. H. (2001). Challenging the myth of the golden girl: Ethnicity and eating disorders. In R. H. Striegel-Moore & L. Smolak (Eds.), *Eating disorders* (pp. 111–132). Washington, DC: American Psychological Association.

Snyder, C. R. (1995). Conceptualizing, measuring, and nurturing hope. *Journal of Counseling and Development, 73*(3), 130–157.

Snyder, H. N., & Sickmund, M. (2006). *Juvenile offenders and victims: 2006 national report.* Washington, DC: U.S. Department of Justice, Office of Justice Programs, Office of Juvenile Justice and Delinquency Prevention.

Snyder, T. D., Dillow, S. A., & Hoffman, C. M. (2009). *Digest of education statistics, 2008.* Washington, DC: U.S. Department of Education, National Center for Education Statistics, Institute of Education Sciences.

Spaccarelli, S., Coder, S., & Penman, D. (1992). Problem-solving skills training as a supplement to behavioral parent training. *Cognitive Therapy and Research, 27,* 171–186.

Spear, R. C. (2005). *Taking the lead in implementing and improving advisory.* Westerville, OH: National Middle School Association.

Spence, J. T. (1982). Comments on Baumrind's "Are androgynous individuals more effective persons and parents?" *Child Development, 53,* 76–80.

Spencer, M. B. (1982). Personal and group identity of black children: An alternative synthesis. *Genetic Psychology Monographs, 103,* 59–84.

Spencer, M. B. (1988). Self-concept development. In D. T. Slaughter (Ed.), *Black children in poverty: Developmental perspectives* (pp. 59–72). San Francisco: Jossey-Bass.

Spencer, R., Jordan, J. V., & Sazama, J. (2004) Growth-promoting relationships between youth and adults: A focus group study. *Families in Society, 85,* 354–362.

Splete, H., & Freeman-George, A. (1985). Family influences on career development of young adults. *Journal of Career Development, 12*(1), 55–64.

Sprinthall, N. A. (1981). A new model for research in the science of guidance and counseling. *Personnel and Guidance Journal, 59,* 487–493.

SRI International. (2000). *The National Longitudinal Transition Study-2 (NLTS2) conceptual framework and research outcomes.* Menlo Park, CA: Author.

Stice, E., Presnell, K., Shaw, H., & Rohde, P. (2005). Psychological and behavioral risk factors for onset of obesity in adolescent girls: A prospective study. *Journal of Consulting and Clinical Psychology, 73,* 195–202.

Stadler, H. A. (1986). Making hard choices: Clarifying controversial ethical issues. *Counseling and Human Development, 19,* 1–10.

Stamm, B. H. (2009). Professional Quality of Life: Compassion and Fatigue. Version 5 (ProQQL).

Stanford University News Service (1991). 100th Commencement, June 18, 1991.

Stapley, J. C., & Haviland, J. M. (1989). Beyond depression: Gender differences in normal adolescents' emotional experiences. *Sex Roles, 20,* 295–308.

Stark, K. D., Reynolds, W. M., & Kaslow, N. J. (1987). A comparison of the relative efficacy of self-control therapy and a behavioral problem-solving therapy for depression in children. *Journal of Abnormal Child Psychology, 15,* 91–113.

Stark, K. D., Rouse, L., & Livingston, R. (1991). Treatment of depression during childhood and adolescence: Cognitive-behavioral procedures for the individual and family. In P. Kenall (Ed.), *Child and adolescent therapy* (pp. 165–206). New York: Guilford.

Steen, S., & Kaffenberger, C. J. (2007). Integrating academic interventions into small group counseling in elementary school. *Professional School Counselor, 10,* 516–519.

Stein, A. H., & Bailey, M. M. (1973). The socialization of achievement orientation in females. *Psychological Bulletin, 80,* 345–365.

Stein, W., & French, J. L. (1984). Teacher consultation in the affective domain: A survey of expert opinion. *School Counselor, 31,* 339–345.

Steinberg, L. (1996a). *Beyond the classroom.* New York: Simon & Schuster.

Steinberg, L. (1996b). Ethnicity and adolescent achievement. *American Educator, 20*(2), 28–35.

Steinburg, J., & Henriques, D. (2001, May 21). When a test fails the schools, careers and reputations suffer. *New York Times.*

Steinman, S. O., Richardson, N. F., & McEnroe, T. (1998). *The ethical decision-making manual for helping professionals.* Pacific Grove, CA: Brooks/Cole.

Stellas, E. (1992). No more victims, no more victimizers violence prevention education: Social skills for risk reduction. In R. C. Morris (Ed.), *Solving the problems of youth at risk: Involving parents and community resources.* Lancaster, PA: Technomic.

Stevens, H., & Wilkerson, K. (2010). *Developmental assets and ASCA's national standards: A crosswalk review. Professional School Counseling, 13*(4), 231.

Stevens, V., Van Oost, P., & De Bourdeaudhuij, I. (2000). *The effects of an anti-bullying intervention programme on peers' attitudes and behavior. Journal of Adolescence, 23,* 21–34.

Stevenson, M. R. (2000). Public policy, homosexuality, and the sexual coercion of children. *Journal of Psychology & Human Sexuality, 12*(4), 1–19.

Stewart, N. R., & Thoreson, C. R. (1968). *Behavioral group counseling.* Boston: Houghton Mifflin.

Stice, E., Presnell, K., Shaw, H., & Rohde, P. (2005). Psychological and behavioral risk factors for onset of obesity in adolescent girls: A prospective study. *Journal of Counsulting and Clinical Psychology, 73,* 195–202.

Stiggins, R. J. (1994) *Student-centered classroom assessment.* New York: Macmillan.

Stigler, J. W., Smith, S., & Mao, L. (1985). The self-perception of competence by Chinese children. *Child Development, 56,* 1259–1270.

Stoltenberg, C. D. (1993). Supervising consultants in training: An application of a model of supervision. *Journal of Counseling and Development, 72,* 131–138.

Stone, C. (2000). Advocacy for sexual harassment victims: Legal support and ethical aspects. *Professional School Counseling, 4,* 23–31.

Stone, C. (2001). *Legal and ethical issues in working with minors in schools.* Alexandria, VA: American Counseling Association.

Stone, C. B., & Dahir, C. A. (2004). *School counselor accountability: A MEASURE of student success.* Upper Saddle River, NJ: Pearson Education.

Stone, C., & Dahir, C. (2006). *The transformed school counselor.* Boston: Houghton Mifflin/Lahaska Press.

Stone, C., & Dahir, C. (2007). *School counselor accountability: A MEASURE of student success* (2nd ed.). Upper Saddle River, NJ: Pearson Education.

Storch, E. A., Nock, M. K., Masia-Warner, C., & Barlas, M. E. (2003). Peer victimization and social-psychological adjustment in Hispanic and African-American children. *Journal of Child & Family Studies, 12,* 439–455.

Striegel-Moore, R. H., Seeley, J. R., & Lewinsohn, P. M. (2003). Psychosocial adjustment in young adulthood of women who experience and eating disorder during adolescence. *Journal of the American Academy of Child and Adolescent Psychiatry, 42,* 587–593.

Stronski Huwiler, S. M., & Remafedi, G. (1998). Adolescent homosexuality. *Advanced Pediatrics, 45,* 107–144.

Strother, J., & Jacobs, E. (1986). Parent consultation. *School Counselor, 33,* 24–26.

Studer, J. R., Oberman, A., & Womack, R. H. (2006). Producing evidence to show counseling effectiveness in the schools. *Professional School Counseling, 9,* 385–391.

Substance Abuse and Mental Health Services Administration. (2003). Achieving the Promise: Transforming Mental Health Care in America. *The President's New Freedom Commission on Mental Health.* Rockville, MD.

Substance Abuse and Mental Health Services Administration. (2004). Project Achieve. Retrieved from http://www.modelprograms.samhsa.gov/pdfs/model/ProjectACHIEVE.pdf.

Substance Abuse and Mental Health Services Administration. (2007). *Depression among adolescents: The HSDUH report.* Retrieved from http://oas.samhsa.gov/2k5/youthdepression/youthDepression.htm.

Substance Abuse and Mental Health Services Administration. (2010). National registry of evidence-based programs and practices. Washington, DC: U.S. Department of Health and Human Services. Retrieved from http://www.nrepp.samhsa.gov.

Sue, D. W. (1978). Counseling across cultures. *Personnel and Guidance Journal, 56,* 451–459.

Sue, D. W., & Sue, D. (1977). Barriers to cross-cultural counseling. *Journal of Counseling Psychology, 24,* 420–429.

Sue, D. W., & Sue, D. (2003). *Counseling the culturally diverse: Theory and practice* (4th ed.). New York: John Wiley & Sons.

Sugai, G., & Homer, R. R. (2006). A promising approach to expanding and sustaining school-wide positive behavior support. *School Psychology Review, 35*, 245–259.

Suleiman, M. W. (1999). *The Arab immigrant experience*. Philadelphia: Temple University Press.

Sullivan, H. S. (1953). *The interpersonal theory of psychiatry*. New York: Norton.

Sunderman, G. L. (Ed.) (2008). *Holding NCLB accountable: Achieving, accountablity, equity and school reform*. Thousand Oaks, CA: Corwin Press.

Suner, J., Nakamura, S., & Caulfield, R. (2003). Kids having kids: Models of intervention. *Early Childhood Education Journal, 31*(1), 71–74.

Supovitz, J. A., Poglinco, S. M., & Snyder, B. A. (2001). *Moving mountains: Successes and challenges of the America's Choice comprehensive school reform design*. Philadelphia: Consortium for Policy Research in Education, University of Pennsylvania.

Swail, S., Carbera, A., Lee, C., & Williams, A. (2005). *Latino students and the education pipeline: Part III of a three-part series*. Stafford, VA: Educational Policy Institute.

Swanson, C. B. (2008). *Special eduction in America: The state of students with disabilities in the nation's high schools*. Bethesda, MD: Educational Projects in Education Research Center.

Swick, K., & Graves, S. (1993). *Empowering at-risk families during the early childhood years*. Washington, DC: National Education Association.

Tahiroglu, A., Avci, A., & Cekin, N. (2008). Child abuse, mental health, mandatory reporting law. *Anatolian Journal of Psychiatry, 9*(1), 1–7.

Tamminen, A. W., & Miller, G. D. (1968). *Guidance programs and their impact on students*. Research Project No. OE 5-85-035. St. Paul: Minnesota Department of Education.

Tarasoff v. Regents of University of California, 529 P.2d 533,118 Cal. Rptr. (1974), vacated, 17 Cal. 3d. 425,551 P.2d 334, 131 Cal. Rptr. 14 (1976).

Tarter, R. E., Vanyukov, M., Kirisci, L., Reynolds, M., & Clark, D. B. (2006). Predictors of marijuana use in adolescents before and after licit drug use: Examination of the gateway hypothesis. *American Journal of Psychiatry, 63*(12), 2138.

Tarvydas, V. M. (1998). Ethical decision-making processes. In R. R. Cottone & V. M. Tarvydas (Eds.), *Ethical and professional issues in counseling* (pp. 144–155). Upper Saddle River, NJ: Prentice-Hall.

Tatem, K. B., Thornberry, T. P., & Smith, C. A. (1997). In the wake of childhood maltreatment. *Juvenile Justice Bulletin*. Washington, DC: U.S. Department of Justice.

Taylor, L. & Adelman, H. S. (2000). Connecting schools, families, and communities. *Professional School Counseling, 3*(5), 298–307.

Tedesco, L. A., & Gaier, E. L. (1988). Friendship bonds in adolescence. *Adolescence, 23*, 127–136.

Tessier, D. (1982). A group counseling program for gifted and talented students. *Pointer, 26*(3), 43–46.

Teyber, E., & McClure, F. (2000). Therapist variables. In C. R. Snyder & R. E. Ingram (Eds.), *Handbook of psychological change: Psychotherapy processes and practices for the 21st century* (pp. 62–87). New York: John Wiley & Sons.

Thomas, A. J., & Schwarzbaum, S. (2006). *Culture and identity: Life stories for counselors and therapists*. London: Sage.

Thomason, T. C. (1995). Counseling Native American students. In C. C. Lee (Ed.), *Counseling for diversity: A guide for school counselors and related professionals* (pp. 109–126). Boston: Allyn & Bacon.

Thompson, C. L., & O'Quinn, S. D., III. (2001). *Eliminating the black–white achievement gap: A summary of research*. Raleigh: North Carolina Education Research Council.

Thompson, C. L., & Poppen, W. (1979). *Guidance activities for counselors and teachers*. Monterey, CA: Brooks/Cole.

Thompson, E. C., III. (1987). The "yagottawanna" group: Improving students self-perceptions through motivational teaching of study skills. *School Counselor, 35*(2), 134–142.

Thompson, J. K., & Smolak, L. (2001). *Body image, eating disorders and obesity: Assessment, prevention and treatment*. Washington, DC: American Psychological Association.

Thompson, R. A. (1985). Expressed versus tested vocational interests of non-college-bound students. *Journal of Research and Development in Education, 18*(4), 62–67.

Thompson, R. A. (1987). Creating instructional partnerships to improve the academic performance of underachievers. *School Counselor, 3*(4), 62–66.

Thompson, R. A. (1990). Strategies for crisis management in the schools. *National Association of Secondary School Principals Bulletin, 74*(523), 54–58.

Thompson, R. A. (1993). Post-traumatic stress and post-traumatic loss debriefing: Brief strategic intervention for survivors of sudden loss. *School Counselor, 41*, 16–21.

Thompson, R. A. (1995). Being prepared for suicide or sudden death in schools: Tools to restore equilibrium. *Journal of Mental Health Counseling, 36*(4), 13–19.

Thompson, R. A. (1996). Teenage pregnancy. In D. Capuzzi & D. R. Gross (Eds.), *Youth at risk: A resource for counselors, teachers, and parents*. Alexandria, VA: American Association for Counseling and Development.

Thompson, R. A. (1998). *Nurturing an endangered generation: Empowering youth with critical social, emotional, and cognitive skills*. Bristol, PA: Accelerated Development.

Thompson, R. A. (1999). Empowering youth-at-risk with skills for school and life. In D. Rae & R. Warkentin (Eds.), *The need to empower youth with critical social, emotional and cognitive skills*. New York: McGraw-Hill.

Thompson, R. A. (2000). *Helping youth think better, feel better, and relate better: A skillbook to maximize human potential*. Norfolk, VA: Black Bird Press.

Thompson, R. A. (2002). *School counseling: Best practices for working in the schools* (2nd ed.). New York: Brunner-Routledge.

Thompson, R. A. (2006). *Nurturing future generations: Promoting resilience in children and adolescents through social, emotional and cognitive skills* (2nd ed.). New York: Routledge/Taylor & Francis.

Thornton, T. N., Craft, C. A., Dahlberg, L. L., Lynch, B. S., & Baer, K. (2002). *Best practices of youth violence prevention: A sourcebook for community action* (Rev. ed.). Atlanta: Centers for Disease Control and Prevention, National Center for Injury Prevention and Control.

Thurlow, M., Bremer, C., & Albus, D. (2008). *Good news and bad news in disaggregated subgroup reporting to the public on 2005–2006 assessment results*. Technical Report No. 52. Minneapolis: University of Minnesota, National Center on Educational Outcomes. Retrieved from http://cehd.umn.edu/nceo/OnlinePubs/Tech52/Technical52.pdf.

Thurlow, M. L., Moen, R. E., Liu, K. K., Scullin, S., Hausmann, K. E., & Shyyan, V. (2009). *Disabilities and reading: Understanding the effects of disabilities and their relationship to reading instruction and assessment*. Minneapolis: University of Minnesota, Partnership for Accessible Reading Assessment.

Tierney, J. P., & Grossman, J. B. (1995). *Making a difference: An impact study of Big Brothers/Big Sisters*. Philadelphia: Public/Private Ventures.

Tizard, J., Schofield, W., & Hewison, J. (1982). Collaboration between teachers and parents in assisting children's reading. *British Journal of Educational Psychology, 52*, 1–15.

Tobias, A. K., & Myrick, R. D. (1999). A peer facilitator-led intervention with middle school problem-behavior students. *Professional School Counseling, 3*, 27–33.

Tornatzky, L. G., Cutler, R., & Lee, J. (2002). *College knowledge: What Latino parents need to know and why they don't know it*. Claremont, CA: Tomas Rivera Policy Institute.

Toth, S. L., & Cicchetti, D. (2006). Promises and possibilities: The application of research in the area of child maltreatment to policies and practices. *Journal of Social Issues, 62*, 863–880.

Tremblay, R., & Craig, W. (1995). Developmental crime prevention. In M. Tonry & D. P. Farrington (Eds.), *Building a safer society: Strategic approaches to crime prevention*. Chicago: University of Chicago Press.

Trevisan, M. S., & Hubert, M. (2001). Implementing comprehensive guidance program evaluation support: Lessons learned. *Professional School Counseling, 4*, 225–228.

Trimble, J. E., Fleming, C. M., Beauvais, F., & Jumper-Thurman, P. (1996). Essential cultural and social strategies for counseling Native American Indians. In P. B. Pedersen, J. G. Draguns, W. J. Lonner, & J. E. Trimble (Eds.), *Counseling across cultures* (4th ed., pp. 177–209). Thousand Oaks, CA: Sage.

Trimble, L., Jackson, K., & Harvey, D. (2000). Client suicidal behavior: Impact, interventions, and implications for psychologists. *Australian Psychologist, 35*, 227–232.

Troiden, R. R. (1979). The formation of homosexual identities. *Journal of Homosexuality, 17*, 362–373.

Trusty, J. (2004). *Effects of students' middle school and high school experiences on completion of the bachelor's degree*. Research monograph published by Center for School Counseling Outcome Research, University of Massachusetts-Amherst.

Trusty, J., & Niles, S. G. (2003). High-school math courses and completion of the bachelor's degree. *Professional School Counseling, 7*, 99–107.

Tuma, J. M. (1989). Mental health services for children: The state of the art. *American Psychologist, 44*, 188–199.

Tweed, S. H., & Ryff, C. D. (1991). Adult children of alcoholics: Profiles of wellness amidst distress. *Journal of Studies on Alcohol, 52*(2), 37–46.

Tyack, D. B. (1974). *The one best system: A history of American urban education*. Cambridge, MA: Harvard University Press.

Tymchuk, A. J. (1986). Guidelines for ethical decision-making. *Canadian Psychology, 27*, 36–43.

Ulzen, T., & Hamilton, H. (1998). The nature and characteristics of psychiatric comorbidity in incarcerated adolescents. *Canadian Journal of Psychiatry, 43*, 57–63.

Urban, D., & Sammartano, R. (1989). Maximizing cognition. *Learning, 18*(3), 47–53.

Underwood, M. K. (2003). *Social aggression among girls*. New York: Guilford Press.

Underwood, M. K., Galen, B. R., & Paquette, J. A. (2001). Top ten challenges for understanding gender and aggression in children: Why can't we all just get along? *Social Development, 10*, 248–266.

Uribe, V. (1994). Project 10: A school-based outreach for gay and lesbian youth. *The High School Journal, 77*, 108–112.

U.S. Bureau of Indian Affairs, Division of Tribal Affairs, Division of Tribal Government Services. (2008). *Indian entities recognized and eligible to receive services from the United States.* Washington, DC: Author.

U.S. Census Bureau. (1997). America's children at risk. Census brief CENBR/97-2. Washington, DC: Government Printing Office.

U.S. Census Bureau. (2001). *Poverty in the United States, 2000.* Washington, DC: Government Printing Office. Retrieved from http://www.census.gov/prod/2001pubs/p60-214.pdf.

U.S. Census Bureau. (2003). *The Hispanic population in the United States, March 2002.* Washington, DC: Government Printing Office.

U.S. Census Bureau. (2004). *The foreign-born population in the United States, 2003.* Washington, DC: Government Printing Office.

U.S. Census Bureau. (2005a). *We the people: Blacks in the United States.* Washington, DC: Government Printing Office.

U.S. Census Bureau. (2005b). *We the people: Pacific Islanders in the United States.* Washington, DC: Government Printing Office.

U.S. Census Bureau. (2006a). *American Community Survey.* Washington, DC: Government Printing Office.

U.S. Census Bureau. (2006b). *Current Population Survey, October Supplement, 1972–2006.* Washington, DC: Government Printing Office. Retrieved from http://www.census.gov/cps.

U.S. Census Bureau. (2006c). *We the people: American Indians and Alaska Natives in the United States.* Washington, DC: Government Printing Office.

U.S. Census Bureau. (2008a). *Current Population Survey.* Washington, DC: Government Printing Office. Retrieved from http://www.census.gov/cps.

U.S. Census Bureau. (2008b, August 14). An older and more diverse nation by midcentury. (Press release). Washington, DC: Author. Retrieved from http://www.census.gov/newsroom/releases/archives/population/cb08-123.html.

U.S. Census Bureau. (2009, May 14). Census bureau estimates nearly half of children under age 5 are minorities: Estimates find nation's population growing older, more diverse. (Press release). Washington, DC: Author. Retrieved from http://www.census.gov/newsroom/releases/archives/population/cb09-75.html.

U.S. Citizenship and Immigration Services. (2006). *Immigration and Nationality Act.* Washington, DC: Government Printing Office.

U.S. Department of Education. (2000). Office of Special Education Programs. *History: Twenty-five years of progress in educating children with disabilities through IDEA.* Washington, DC: Government Printing Office.

U.S. Department of Education. (2002). Office of Elementary and Secondary Education. *No Child Left Behind: A desktop reference.* Washington, DC: Government Printing Office, 2002.

U.S. Department of Education. (2003). *Identifying and implementing educational practices supported by rigorous evidence: A user friendly guide.* Washington, DC: Government Printing Office.

U.S. Department of Education. (2005a). National household education survey, NHES Series. No. 4599. Ann Arbor, MI: Inter-university Consortium for Political and Social Research.

U.S. Department of Education. (2005b). *Protection of Pupil Rights Amendment (PPRA).* Washington, DC: Government Printing Office. Retrieved from http://www2.ed.gov/policy/gen/guid/fpco/ppra/index.html.

U.S. Department of Health and Human Services. (2005). *Administration on Children and Families. Child maltreatment.* Washington, DC: Government Printing Office.

U.S. Department of Education. (2007). National Center for Educational Statistics. *Public Elementary and Secondary Student Enrollment, High School Completions, and Staff from the Common Core of Data: School Year 2005–2006, NCES 2007, 352,* by Jennifer Stable, Anthony Garofano, & Lee McGraw Hoffman. Washington, D.C.:2007. Retrieved from http://nces.ed.gov/pubs 2009/2007352.pdf on July 22, 2010.

U.S. Department of Health and Human Services. (2008). Administration on Children, Youth and Families. *Child Maltreatment, 2006.* Washington, DC: Government Printing Office.

U.S. Department of Health and Human Services. (2009). Identifying and Selected Evidence-Based Interventions. SAMHSA, Substance Abuse and Mental Health Services Administration. Author.

U.S. Department of Justice. (2005). Bureau of Justice Statistics. *School Crime Supplement (SCS) to the National Crime Victimization Survey, various years, 2001–2005.* Washington, DC: Government Printing Office.

U.S. Public Health Service. (2000). Report of the Surgeon General's Conference on Children's Mental Health: A National Action Agenda. Washington, DC: Department of Health and Human Services, Author.

University of Arizona. (1999). *Community college and AP credit: An analysis of the impact on freshman grades.* Tucson: Author.

Upward Bound (2001). *Informational booklet.* Riverside: University of California.

Urban, D., & Sammartano, R. (1989). Maximizing cognition. *Learning, 18*(3), 47.

Urban Institute. (2006). *Parents and children facing a world of risk: Next steps towards a workir* Retrieved from http://www.urban.org/UploadedPDF/311288parentsandchildren.pdf

Uribe, V. (1990). Summer Update, 1990. Friends of Project 10.

Urquiza, A. J., & McNeil, C. B. (1996). Parent–child interaction therapy: An intensive dyadic intervention for physically abusive families. *Child Maltreatment, 1*(2), 132–141.

Valente, T. W. (2003). Social network influences on adolescent substance use: A introduction. *Connections, 25*(2), 11–16.

Van der Kolk, B. A., & Kadish, W. (1987). Amnesia, dissociation, and the return of the repressed. In B. A. van der Kolk (Ed.), Psychological Trauma. American Psychiatric Press, Inc., Washington, DC.

van Krieken, Robert. (2005). The "best interests of the child" and parental separation: On the "civilizing of parents." *Modern Law Review, 68*(1), 25–48.

Vazquez-Nuttall, E., DeLeon, B., & Valle, M. (1990). Best practices in considering cultural factors. In A. Thomas & J. Grimes (Eds.), *Best practices in school psychology II* (pp. 219–235). Washington, DC: National Association of School Psychologists.

Verduyn, C. M., Lord, W., & Forrest, G. C. (1990). Social skills training in schools: An evaluation study. *Journal of Adolescence, 13*, 3–16.

Vermilyea, E. G. (2000). *Growing beyond survival: A traumatic stress toolbox.* Lutherville, MD: Sidran Press.

Vernon, A. (1989). *Thinking, feeling, behaving: An emotional education curriculum for adolescents, grades 7–12.* Champaign, IL: Research Press.

Vieth, V. I., Bottoms, B. L., & Perona, A. R. (2005). *Ending child abuse: New efforts in prevemtion, investigation, and training.* Binghamton, NY: Haworth Press.

Virginia Department of Education. (2005, May). Division of Special Education and Student Services. *Guidance document on the implementation of IDEA 2004-Part B requirements.* Richmond: Author.

Vobejda, B. (1996, October 29). Research group confirms decrease in births to teens. *Washington Post.*

Vossekuil, B., Reddy, M., Fein, R., Borum, R., & Modzeleski, W. (2000). *U.S. Safe School Initiative: An interim report on the prevention of targeted violence in schools.* Washington, DC: U.S. Secret Service, National Threat Assessment Center.

Wadsworth, B. (1989). *Piaget's theory of cognitive and affective development.* New York: Longman.

Wakschlag, L. S., & Danis, B. (2004). Assessment of disruptive behaviors in young children: A clinical-developmental framework. In R. Del Carmen & A. Carter (Eds.), *Handbook of infant and toddler mental health assessment* (pp. 421–440). New York: Oxford University Press.

Waldfogel, J., Garfinkel, I., & Kelly, B. (2005). Public assistance programs: How much could be saved with improved education? Prepared for the Equity Symposium on "The Social Costs of Inadequate Education" at Teachers' College, Columbia University.

Waldo, M. (1985). A curative factor framework for conceptualizing group counseling. *Journal of Counseling and Development, 64*(1), 58–59.

Walker, J. D., Jurich, S., & Estes, S. (2001). *Raising minority academic achievement: A compendium of education programs and practices.* Washington, DC: American Youth Policy Forum.

Walsh, M. E., Barrett, J. G. & DePaul, J. (2007). Day-to-day activities of school counselors: Alignment with new directions in the field and the ASCA National Model. *Professional School Counseling, 10*, 370–378.

Walsh, M. E., Howard, K. A., & Buckley, M. A. (1999). School counselors in school–community partnerships: Opportunities and challenges. *Professional School Counseling, 2*, 349–356.

Walsh-Bowers, R. T. (1992). A creative drama prevention program for easing early adolescents' adjustment to school transition. *Journal of Primary Prevention, 13*, 131–147.

Walter, J. L., & Peller, J. E. (1992). *Becoming solution-focused in brief therapy.* New York: Brunner/Mazel.

Wang, C. T., & Holton, J. (2007). *Total estimated cost of child abuse and neglect in the United States.* Chicago: Prevent Child Abuse America.

Wang, M. C., Haertel, G. D., & Walberg, H. J. (1994). What helps students learn? *Educational Leadership, 51*, 74–79.

Wang, M. C., Haertel, G. D., & Walberg, H. J. (1995). The effectiveness of collaborative school-linked services. In L. C. Rigsby & C. Maynard (Eds.), *School–community connections: Exploring issues for research and practice* (pp. 283–309). Oxford, England: Elsevier.

Wang, M. C., Haertel, G. D., & Walberg, H. J. (1998). *Educational resilience.* Laboratory for Student Success Publication Series, No. 11. Philadelphia: Temple University Center for Research in Human Development and Education.

Wardenski, J. J. (2005). A minor exception?: The impact of Lawrence vs. Texas on LGBT Youth. *The Journal of Criminal Law & Criminology.* Northwestern University, School of Law.

ʌaschbusch, D. A. (2002). A meta-analysis examination of comorbid hyperactive-impulsive-attention problems and conduct problems. *Psychological Bulletin, 128*, 118–150.

Washington, K. R. (1977). Success counseling: A model workshop approach to self-concept building. *Adolescence, 12*(47), 405–409.

Wasley, P. A., Fine, M., Gladden, M., Holland, N. E., King, S., Mosak, E., & Powell, L. C. (2000). *Small schools: Great strides, a study of new small schools in Chicago.* New York: Bank Street College of Education.

Waslick, B., & Greenhill, L. (1997). Attention-deficit/hyperactivity disorder. In J. M. Weiner (Ed.), *Textbook of child and adolescent psychiatry* (2nd ed., pp. 389–410). Washington, DC: American Academy of Child and Adolescent Psychiatry and American Psychiatric Press.

Watt, K., Yanez, D., & Cossio, G. (2003). AVID: A comprehensive school reform model for Texas. *National Forum for Educational Administration and Supervisions Journal, 19*(3), 46–53.

Webb, L. D., Brigman, G. A., & Campbell, C. (2005). Linking school counselors and student success: A replication of the Student Success Skills approach targeting the academic and social competence of students. *Professional School Counseling, 8*, 407–413.

Webster-Stratton, C. (1982). The long-term effects of a videotape modeling parent-training program: Comparison of immediate and 1-year follow-up results. *Behavior Therapy, 13*, 702–714.

Webster-Stratton, C. (1992). Individually administered videotape parent training: Who benefits? *Cognitive Therapy and Research, 16*, 31–51.

Webster-Stratton, C. (1998). Preventing conduct problems in Head Start children: Strengthening parenting competencies. *Journal of Consulting and Clinical Psychology, 66*, 715–730.

Webster-Stratton, C., Reid, J., & Hammond, M. (2001). Preventing conduct problems, promoting social competence: A parent and teacher training partnership in Head Start. *Journal of Clinical Child Psychology 30*, 282–302.

Weiner, I. B. (1980). Psychopathology in adolescence. In J. Adelson (Ed.), *Handbook of adolescent psychology.* New York: Wiley.

Weiner, J. M. (1997). Oppositional defiant disorder. In J. M. Weiner (Ed.), *Textbook of child and adolescent psychiatry* (2nd ed., pp. 459–463). Washington, DC: American Academy of Child and Adolescent Psychiatry and American Psychiatric Press.

Weinstein, R. S., Marshall, H. H., Sharp, L., & Botkin, M. (1987). Pygmalion and the student: Age and classroom differences in children's awareness of teacher expectations. *Child Development, 58*, 1079–1093.

Weinstock, H., Berman, S., & Cotes, W. (2004) Sexually transmitted diseases among American youth: Incidence and prevalence estimates, 2000. *Perspectives on Sexual and Reproductive Health, 36*(1), 6–10.

Weissberg, R. P., Caplan, M., & Sivo, P. (1989). A new conceptual framework for establishing school-based social competence promotion programs. In L. Bond & B. Compass (Eds.), *Primary prevention and promotion in the schools* (pp. 255–296). Newbury Park, CA: Sage.

Weist, M. (1997). Expanded school mental health services: A national movement in progress. In T. H. Ollendick & R. J. Prinz (Eds.), *Advances in clinical child psychology* (pp. 319–352). New York: Plenum.

Weist, M. D., Evans, S. W., & Lever, N. A. (Eds.). (2003). *Handbook of school mental health: Advancing practice and research* (pp. 11–22). New York: Kluwer Academic.

Weist, M. D., Paternite, C. E., & Adelsheim, S. (2005). *School-based mental health services.* Washington, DC: Institute of Medicine, Board of Health Care Services, and Crossing the Quality Chasm: Adaptation to Mental Health and Addictive Disorders Committee.

Welfel, E. R. (1998). *Ethics in counseling and psychotherapy: Standards, research, and emerging issues.* Pacific Grove, CA: Brooks/Cole.

Wellman, F. E., & Twiford, D. D. (1961). *Guidance counseling and testing program evaluation suggestions for secondary schools Title V-A National Defense Education Act of 1958.* Washington, DC: Government Printing Office.

Wenglinsky, H. (2002). How schools matter: The link between teacher classroom practice and student academic performance. *Educational Policy Analysis Archives, 10*(12), 45–59.

Werner, E. E. (1982). Resilient children. *Young Children, 40*, 68–72.

Werner, E. E. (1987). Thriving despite hardship: Key childhood traits identified. *New York Times.*

Werner, E. E. (1996, Winter). How children become resilient: Observations and cautions. *Resilience in Action*, 18–28.

Werner, E. E., & Smith, R. S. (1982). *Vulnerable but invincible: A study of resilient children.* New York: McGraw-Hill.

Werner, E. E., & Smith, R. S. (1992). *Overcoming the odds: High-risk children from birth to adulthood.* Ithaca, NY: Cornell University Press.

Westheimer, J., & Kahne, J. (1993). Building school communities: An experience-based model. *Phi Delta Kappan, 75*(4), 324–328.

Wheelock, A. (2003). *School awards programs and accountability in Massachusetts: Misusing MCAS scores to assess school quality.* Cambridge, MA: Fair Test.

Whiston, S. C. (2002). Response to the past, present, and future of school counseling: Raising some issues. *Professional School Counseling, 5*, 148–155.

Whiston, S. C. (2003). Outcomes research and school counseling services. In B. T. Erford (Ed.), *Transforming the school counseling profession* (pp. 435–447). Upper Saddle River, NJ: Prentice Hall.

Whiston, S. C., & Sexton, T. L. (1998). A review of school counseling outcome research: Implications for practice. *Journal of Counseling and Development, 76*, 412–426.

Whitaker, T., & Fiore, D. (2001). *Dealing with difficult parents and parents in difficult situations.* Larchmont, NY: Eye on Education.

White, J., & Flynt, M. (2000). The school counselor's role in prevention and remediation of child abuse. In J. Wittmer (Ed.), *Managing your school counseling program: K–12 developmental strategies* (pp. 149–160). Minneapolis, MN: Educational Media.

Whittaker, J. K., Kinney, J. M., Tracy, E. M., & Booth, C. L. (Eds.) (1990). *Reaching high-risk families: Intensive family preservation in human services.* New York: Aldine de Gruyter.

Widom, C. S. (1994). Childhood victimization and risk for adolescent problem behavior. In M. E. Lamb & R. Ketterlinus (Eds.), *Adolescent problem behaviors.* New York: Erlbaum.

Wiggins, J. D., & Wiggins, M. M. (1992). Elementary students' self-esteem and behavioral ratings related to counselor time-task emphases. *School Counselor, 39*, 377–381.

Wiggins, J. L. (1977). Some counseling does help. *School Counselor, 25*, 196–202.

Wilds, D. J. (2000). *Minorities in higher education, 1999–2000: Seventeenth annual status report.* Washington, DC: American Council on Education.

Wilgus, E., & Shelley, V. (1988). The role of the elementary-school counselor: Teacher perceptions, expectations, and actual function. *School Counselor, 35*, 259–266.

William T. Grant Commission on Work, Family, and Citizenship. (1988). *The forgotten half: Pathways to success for America's youth and young families.* New York: William T. Grant Foundation.

Williams, B. (Ed.). (1996). *Closing the achievement gap: A vision for changing beliefs and practices.* Alexandria, VA: ASCD. Retrieved from http://www.ascd.org/readingroom/books/williams96book.html.

Williams, B. T., & Katsiyannis, A. (1998). The 1997 IDEA amendments: Implications for school principals. *NASSP Bulletin, 82*(594), 12–17.

Williamson, D. A., & Davis, C. J. (1990). *Assessment of eating disorders: Obesity, anorexia and bulimia.* New York: Pergamon Press.

Williamson, E. G. (1939). *How to counsel students: A manual of techniques for clinical counselors.* New York: McGraw-Hill.

Wilson, B. L., & Corbett, H. D. (2001). *Listening to urban kids: School reform and the teachers they want.* New York: State University of New York Press.

Wilson, D. (2004). The interface of school climate and school connectedness and relationships with aggression and victimization. *Journal of School Health, 74*, 293–299.

Wilson, G. T., Becker, C. B., & Heffernan, K. (2003). Eating disorders. In E. J. Mash & R. A. Barkley (Eds.), *Child psychopatholgy* (2nd ed., pp. 687–715). New York: Guilford Press.

Wilson, N. O. (1992). *Optimizing special education: How parents can make a difference.* New York: Insight Books.

Wilson-Brewer, R. (1995). Peer violence prevention programs in middle and high schools. *Adolescent Medicine: State of the Art Reviews, 6*(2), 233–250.

Wimberly, G. L., & Noeth, R. J. (2004). *Schools involving parents in postsecondary planning: ACT Policy Report.* Iowa City, IA: ACT.

Winters, K. C., Leitten, W., Wagner, E., & O'Leary Tevyaw, T. (2007). Use of brief interventions in a middle and high school setting. *Journal of School Health, 77*, 196–206.

Winters, K. C., Stinchfield, R. D., Opland, E., Weller, C., & Latimer, W. W. (2000). The effectiveness of the Minnesota Model for treating adolescent drug abusers. *Addictions, 95*, 601–612.

Wise, P. S., & Ginther, D. (1981). Parent conferences: A brief commentary and an annotated bibliography. *School Psychology Review, 10*, 100–103.

Wiske, S. (2004). Teaching for meaning. *Educational Leadership, 62*(1), 46–50.

Wittmer, J. (1993). *Managing your school counseling program: K–12 developmental strategies.* Minneapolis, MN: Educational Media.

Wittmer, J. (2000a). Developing school guidance and counseling: Its history and reconceptualization. In J. Wittmer (Ed.), *Managing your school counseling programs: K–12 developmental strategies* (2nd ed., pp. 2–13). Minneapolis, MN: Educational Media.

Wittmer, J. (2000b). Implementing a comprehensive developmental school counseling program. In J. Wittmer (Ed.), *Managing your school counseling programs: K–12 developmental strategies* (2nd ed., pp. 14–34). Minneapolis, MN: Educational Media.

Wolfe, D. A. (1991). *Preventing physical and emotional abuse of children.* New York: Guilford Press.

Wolfe, D. A., Edwards, B., Manion, I., & Koverola, C. (1988). Early intervention for parents at risk for child abuse and neglect: A preliminary investigation. *Journal of Consulting and Clinical Psychology, 56*, 40–47.

Wolraich, M. L., Hannah, J. N., Pinnock, T. Y., Baumgaertel, A., & Brown, J. (1996). Comparison of diagnostic criteria for attention-deficit hyperactivity disorder in a county-wide sample. *Journal of the American Academy of Child and Adolescent Psychiatry, 35*, 319–324.

Wong, K. S. (1996). The transformation of culture: Three Chinese views of America. *American Quarterly, 48*(2), 201–232.

Worden, J. W. (2009). *Grief counseling and grief therapy: A handbook for the mental health practitioner* (4th ed.). New York: Springer.

World Health Organization. (2000). Department of Mental Health. *Preventing suicide: A resource for teacher's and other school staff.* Geneva: Author.

Worrell, J., & Stilwell, W. E. (1981). *Psychology for teachers and students.* New York: McGraw-Hill.

Wright, D. & Pemberton, M. (2004). *Risk and protective factors for adolescent drug use: Findings from the 1999 National Household Survey on Drug Abuse.* DHHS Publication No. SMA 04-3874, Analytic Series A-19. Rockville, MD: Substance Abuse and Mental Health Services Administration, Office of Applied Studies.

Yagi, D. T., & Oh, M. Y. (1995). Counseling Asian American students. In C. C. Lee (Ed.), *Counseling for diversity: A guide for school counselors and related professionals* (pp. 85–108). Boston: Allyn & Bacon.

Yalom, I., & Leszcz, M. (2005). *The theory and practice of group psychotherapy* (5th ed.). New York: Basic Books.

Yate, M. (1995). *Beat the odds: Career buoyancy tactics for today's turbulent job market.* New York: Ballantine Books.

Yates, A. (1989). Current perspectives on the eating disorders: I. History, psychological, and biological aspects. *Journal of the American Academy of Child and Adolescent Psychiatry, 28*, 813–828.

Yeargin-Allsopp, M., Rice, C., Karapurkar, T., Doernberg, N., Boyle, C., & Murphy, C. (2003). Prevalence of autism in a US metropolitan area. *Journal of the American Medical Association, 289*(1), 49–55.

Yeh, T. (2002). Asian American college students who are educationally at risk. *New Directions for Student Services, 97*, 61–71.

Ying, Y., & Han, M. (2007). The longitudinal effect of intergenerational gap in acculturation on conflict and mental health in Southeast Asian American adolescents. *American Journal of Orthopsychiatry, 77*(1), 61–66.

Yodanis, Carrie. (2005). Divorce culture and marital gender equality: A cross-national study. *Gender & Society, 19*(5), 644–659.

Yoshikawa, H. (1994). Prevention as cumulative protection: Effects of early family support and education on chronic delinquency and its risks. *Psychological Bulletin, 115*, 28–54.

Yoshikawa, H. (1995). Long-term effects of early childhood programs on social outcomes and delinquency. *Future of children, 5*(3), 51–75.

Youniss, J. (1980). *Parents and peers in social development: A Sullivan-Piaget perspective.* Chicago: University of Chicago Press.

Young, N., Gardner, S., & Dennis, K. (1998). *Responding to alcohol and other drug problems in child welfare: Weaving together practice and policy.* Washington, DC: Child Welfare League of America Press.

Zapata, J. T. (1995). Counseling Hispanic children and youth. In C. C. Lee (Ed.), *Counseling for diversity: A guide for school counselors and related professionals* (pp. 85–108). Boston: Allyn & Bacon.

Zehler, A. M., Fleischman, H. L., Hopstock, P. J., Pendzick, M. L., & Stephenson, T. G. (2003). *Descriptive study of services to LEP students and LEP students with disabilities.* Arlington, VA: Development Associates.

Zehr, M. A. (1999, January 20). Guardians of the faith. *Education Week,* pp. 26–31.

Zera, D. (1992). Coming of age in a heterosexual world: The development of gay and lesbian adolescents. *Adolescence, 27*(108), 849–854.

Zill, N., & Schoenborn, C. A. (1990). *Developmental, learning, and emotional problems: Health of our nation's children, United States, 1988: Advance data from vital and health statistics.* Report No. 190. Hyattsville, MD: National Center for Health Statistics.

Zingraff, M. T., Leiter, J., Johnsen, M. C., & Myers, K. A. (1994). Mediating effect of good school performance on the maltreatment-delinquency relationship. *Journal of Research in Crime and Delinquency, 31*(1), 62–91.

Zins, J. E. (1993). Enhancing consultee problem-solving skills in consultative interactions. *Journal of Counseling and Development, 72*, 185–190.

Zins, J. E., Weissberg, R. P., Wang, M. C., & Walberg, H. J. (Eds.). (2004). *Building academic success on social and emotional learning: What does the research say?* New York: Teachers College Press.

Zirkel, P. (1991). End of story. *Phi Delta Kappan, 72*, 640–642.

Zirkel, P. (2001). A pregnant pause? *Phi Delta Kappan, 82*, 557–558.

Zogby, J. (1990). *Arab America today: A demographic profile of Arab Americans.* Washington, DC: Arab American Institute.

Zogby, J. (2001). Arab American attitudes and the September 11 attacks. Retrieved from http://www.aaiusa.org/PDF/attitudes.pdf.

Zunin, L. M., & Myers, D. (2000). *Training manual for human service workers in major disasters* (2nd ed.). DHHS Publication No. ADM 90-538. Washington, DC: Department of Health and Human Services, Substance Abuse and Mental Health Services Administration, Center for Mental Health Services. Retrieved from http://www.mentalhealth.org/publications/allpubs/ADM90-538/tmpreface.asp.

Index